CONTENTS

CW00369128

Cover Picture: Pennyhill Park, Bagshot, Surrey (page 73)

Key to symbols 2

Foreword 3

Johansens 1999 Awards for Excellence 4

How to use this guide 5

Introduction from Channings,
Winner of the Johansens 1999 Most Excellent City Hotel Award *(see page 429)* 6

Introduction from Summer Lodge,
Winner of the Johansens 1999 Most Excellent Country Hotel Award *(see page 169)*.......8

Introduction from Ynyshir Hall,
Winner of the Johansens 1999 Most Excellent Restaurant Award *(see page 401)* 10

Map of London 12

Johansens Recommended Hotels in London..13

Johansens Recommended Hotels in England 47

Johansens Recommended Hotels in Wales 377

Johansens Recommended Hotels in Scotland..409

Johansens Recommended Hotels in Ireland 473

Johansens Recommended Hotels in the Channel Islands..501

List of Johansens Recommended Traditional Inns, Hotels and Restaurants 2000 507

List of Johansens Recommended Country Houses and Small Hotels 2000 508

List of Johansens Recommended Hotels – Europe & The Mediterranean 2000 510

List of Johansens Recommended Hotels – North America, Bermuda & The Caribbean 2000 512

List of Johansens Recommended Hotels – Southern Africa, Mauritius & The Seychelles 2000....513

Maps of the British Isles (except London) showing all Johansens recommendations 514

Indexes 523

Johansens Guide Order Forms and Guest Survey Reports 531

KEY TO SYMBOLS

 Total number of rooms

MasterCard accepted

Visa accepted

American Express accepted

Diners Club accepted

Quiet location

Access for wheelchairs to at least one bedroom and public rooms

 Nombre de chambres

MasterCard accepté

Visa accepté

American Express accepté

Diners Club accepté

Un lieu tranquille

Accès handicapé

 Anzahl der Zimmer

MasterCard akzeptiert

Visa akzeptiert

American Express akzeptiert

Diners Club akzeptiert

Ruhige Lage

Zugang für Behinderte

(The 'Access for wheelchairs' symbol (♿) does not necessarily indicate that the property fulfils National Accessible Scheme grading)

Chef-patron

M 20 Meeting/conference facilities with maximum number of delegates

Children welcome, with minimum age where applicable

Dogs accommodated in rooms or kennels

At least one room has a four-poster bed

Cable/satellite TV in all bedrooms

Fax available in rooms

No-smoking rooms (at least one no-smoking bedroom)

Lift available for guests' use

Air Conditioning

 Indoor swimming pool

 Outdoor swimming pool

Tennis court at hotel

Croquet lawn at hotel

Fishing can be arranged

Golf course on site or nearby, which has an arrangement with the hotel allowing guests to play

Shooting can be arranged

Riding can be arranged

Hotel has a helicopter landing pad

Licensed for wedding ceremonies

Chef-patron

M 20 Salle de conférences – capacité maximale

Enfants bienvenus

Chiens autorisés

Lit à baldaquin

TV câblée/satellite dans les chambres

Fax dans votre chambre

Chambres non-fumeurs

Ascenseur

Climatisée

 Piscine couverte

 Piscine de plein air

Tennis à l'hôtel

Croquet à l'hôtel

Pêche

Golf

Chasse

Équitation

Piste pour hélicoptère

Cérémonies de noces

Chef-patron

M 20 Konferenzraum-Höchstkapazität

Kinder willkommen

Hunde erlaubt

Himmelbett

Satellit-und Kabelfernsehen in allen Zimmern

Fax in Schlafzimmern

Zimmer für Nichtraucher

Fahrstuhl

Klimatisiert

Hallenbad

Freibad

Hoteleigener Tennisplatz

Krocketrasen

Angeln

Golfplatz

Jagd

Reitpferd

Hubschrauberlandplatz

Konzession für Eheschliessungen

2

FOREWORD

We are pleased to welcome 60 new recommendations in the guide this year, including Mallory Court *(p223)*, Kinnaird *(p424)* and Claridge's *(p24)*.

Our inspectors annually visit every recommended establishment in addition to the many hotels, inns, country houses and business meeting venues which regularly apply for inclusion. Only those that match our standards of diversity and excellence can be recommended.

The new millennium editions of our guides include the launch of 'Recommended Hotels & Game Lodges – Southern Africa, Mauritius & The Seychelles'. You will find these exciting new recommendations together with those for North America and Europe in the index at the back of this guide.

A complete reference to our year 2000 recommendations representing 40 countries may be found together with a direct on line availability service (DOLAS) on our Internet site www.johansens.com The guides are also available on CD-ROM. We hope that you enjoy these recommendations and our thanks go to the many thousands of you who have sent us 'Guest Survey Reports' that are invaluable to maintaining our standards and are also available at the back of this guide.

Your experience has proved that to mention that you use Johansens when making a booking is a positive benefit to the enjoyment of your stay.

We wish you many more of them.

Andrew Warren
Managing Director

JOHANSENS AWARDS FOR EXCELLENCE
RECOMMENDED HOTELS IN GREAT BRITAIN & IRELAND

The 1999 Awards for Excellence winners at the Dorchester

The Johansens Awards for Excellence were presented at the Johansens Annual Dinner held at The Dorchester on November 2nd 1998. The Most Excellent London Hotel Award was presented to **The London Outpost of the Carnegie Club.**

The Most Excellent City Hotel was **Channings** in Edinburgh whose exceptional qualities were identified by scores of guests who sent in Johansens report forms after an enjoyable stay at the hotel.

Guests' reports are exclusively the means by which the winner of The Most Excellent Service Award is annually chosen. This award was deservedly won by **Burpham Country Hotel** in West Sussex.

A long-standing recommendation in Johansens Hotels guide with an infallible record for hospitality of the highest standard received the Country Hotel of the Year accolade: **Summer Lodge**, Dorset.

A special award for Outstanding Excellence and Innovation presented by Johansens Preferred Partner, Knight Frank, was made to Robin Hutson and Gerard Basset for their work at the **Hotel du Vin** group of hotels.

Congratulations to these five winners and thank you to everyone who sent in Guest Survey Report forms.

Each year we rely on the appraisals of Johansens guests, alongside the nominations of our team of inspectors, as a basis for making all our awards, not only to our Recommended Hotels but also to our Country Houses and Inns with Restaurants in Great Britain & Ireland, Recommended Hotels – Europe and the Mediterranean and Recommended Hotels & Inns – North America, Bermuda & The Caribbean. In these categories the award winners for 1999 were:

Johansens Most Excellent Country House Award:
Caragh Lodge, Co. Kerry, Ireland

Johansens Most Excellent Traditional Inn Award:
The New Inn at Coln, Gloucestershire

Johansens Most Excellent Value for Money Award:
Beechwood Hotel, North Walsham, Norfolk

Johansens Most Excellent Restaurant Award:
Ynyshir Hall, Machynlleth, Wales

Johansens – Europe: The Most Excellent Waterside Resort Hotel:
The Marbella Club, Marbella, Spain

Johansens – Europe: The Most Excellent Country Hotel:
Schlosshotel Igls, Igls, Austria

Johansens – Europe: The Most Excellent City Hotel:
La Tour Rose, Lyon, France

Johansens – North America: Special Award for Excellence:
The Lodge at Moosehead Lake, Greenville, Maine

Johansens – North America: Most Excellent Inn:
Carter House, Eureka, California

Johansens – North America: Most Excellent Hotel:
Monmouth Plantation, Natchez, Mississippi

Published by
Johansens Limited, Therese House, Glasshouse Yard, London EC1A 4JN
Tel: 020 7566 9700 Fax: 020 7490 2538
Find Johansens on the Internet at: **http://www.johansens.com**
E-Mail: admin@johansen.u–net.com

Publishing Director:	Peter Hancock
P.A. to Publishing Director:	Carol Sweeney
Editorial Manager:	Yasmin Razak
Regional Inspectors:	Christopher Bond
	Geraldine Bromley
	Robert Bromley
	Julie Dunkley
	Martin Greaves
	Joan Henderson
	Marie Iversen
	Pauline Mason
	John O'Neill
	Mary O'Neill
	Fiona Patrick
	Brian Sandell
Production Manager:	Daniel Barnett
Production Controller:	Kevin Bradbrook
Senior Designer:	Michael Tompsett
Designer:	Sue Dixon
Copywriters:	Simon Duke
	Norman Flack
Sales and Marketing Manager:	Laurent Martinez
Marketing Executive:	Stephen Hoskin
Sales Administrator:	Susan Butterworth
Webmaster:	John Lea
P.A. to Managing Director :	Glenda Walshaw
Managing Director:	Andrew Warren

Copyright © 1999 Johansens Limited

Johansens is a subsidiary of the Daily Mail & General Trust plc

ISBN 1 86017 7069

Printed in England by St Ives plc
Colour origination by Graphic Facilities

Distributed in the UK and Europe by Johnsons International Media Services Ltd, London (direct sales) & Biblios PDS Ltd, West Sussex (bookstores). In North America by Hunter Publishing, New Jersey. In Australia and New Zealand by Bookwise International, Findon, South Australia.

HOW TO USE THIS GUIDE

If you want to identify a Hotel whose name you already know, look for it in the Regional Indexes on pages 523–524.

If you want to find a Hotel in a particular area you can

• Turn to the Maps on page 12 and pages 514–520

• Search the Indexes on pages 523–528

• Look for the Town or Village where you wish to stay in the main body of the Guide. This is divided into Countries. Place names in each Country appear at the head of the pages in alphabetical order.

The Indexes list the Hotels by Countries and by Counties, they also show those with amenities such as wheelchair access, conference facilities, swimming, golf, etc. (Please note some recent Local Government Boundary changes).

The Maps cover all regions including London. Each Hotel symbol (a blue circle) relates to a Hotel in this guide situated in or near the location shown.

Red Triangles show the location of Johansens Recommended Traditional Inns, Hotels & Restaurants. Green Squares show the location of Johansens Recommended Country Houses & Small Hotels. If you cannot find a suitable hotel near where you wish to stay, you may decide to choose one of these smaller establishments as an alternative. They are all listed by place names on pages 507–510.

Properties which did not feature in our last (1999) edition are identified with a "NEW" symbol at the top of the page.

New telephone codes:
From April 2000 the following new area codes apply:
London – 0207 replaces 0171
London – 0208 replaces 0181
Coventry – 02476 replaces 01203
Southampton – 02380 replaces 01703
Belfast – 02890 replaces 01232
Cardiff – 02920 replaces 01222
Portsmouth – 02392 replaces 01705

Rates are correct at the time of going to press but always should be checked with the hotel before you make your reservation.

We occasionally receive letters from guests who have been charged for accommodation booked in advance but later cancelled. Readers should be aware that by making a reservation with a hotel, either by telephone, e-mail or in writing, they are entering into a legal contract. A hotelier under certain circumstances is entitled to make a charge for accommodation when guests fail to arrive, even if notice of the cancellation is given.

All guides are obtainable from bookshops or by Johansens Freephone 0800 269397 or by using the order coupons on pages 531–536.

INTRODUCTION

From Channings, Edinburgh
Winner of the 1999 Johansens Most Excellent City Hotel Award

Ten years ago, we at The Town House Company had a vision to create Channings, a peaceful and intimate country club hotel, suited to the ambience and splendour of Edinburgh's New Town. Through time, effort and conviction – the five town houses were refurbished and restored to their fullest Edwardian elegance.

Since those early years, Channings has become one of Edinburgh's most successful hotels in the hospitality industry. Our commitment to our people and our ability to work effectively as a team has been rewarded through the re-accreditation of Investors in People. Now the unique formula which has endeared so many to Channings; namely its combination of individually designed rooms and stylish Brasserie, has provided the impetus for our other flourishing, but equally unique town house hotels – The Bonham and The Howard.

We are delighted to be a part of this guide and honoured to have received our award. The Johansens Most Excellent City Hotel Award 1999, is for us, a major endorsement of the commitment, enthusiasm and professionalism of all our staff. It comes at an exciting time for Scotland and Edinburgh and proves that we are ready and willing to play a full part in the cultural renaissance.

Peter Taylor
Managing Director of The Town House Company

HILDON

AN ENGLISH
NATURAL MINERAL WATER
OF EXCEPTIONAL TASTE

DELIGHTFULLY STILL

WELL... DE GUSTIBUS
NON EST DISPUTANDUM

Composition in accordance with the results of the officially
recognized analysis 26 March 1992. ☎ (1794-301 747

Hildon Ltd., Broughton, Hampshire SO20 8DG.

750 ml e

"FOR BEST BEFORE DATE SEE CAP".
Bottled at source, Broughton, Hampshire

"FOR BEST BEFORE DATE SEE CAP".
Bottled at source, Broughton, Hampshire

Hildon Ltd., Broughton, Hampshire SO20 8DG, ☎ 01794 - 301 747

INTRODUCTION

From Summer Lodge, Dorset
Winner of the 1999 Johansens Most Excellent Country Hotel Award

It's hard to believe that it is only 20 years since we escaped from London with our daughters aged 9 and 10 who manned the bar each evening whilst Margaret cooked the set dinner and I did the front of house (a part-time chambermaid being the only staff we employed) to this, the Johansens Most Excellent Country Hotel 1999 with 43 full-time employees plus a few part-timers.

Little realising that Country House Hotels were about to enjoy a renaissance during the eighties, our intention was simply to look after those who found their way to our door as if they were personal guests and think of those who assisted us as family; though always keeping just enough distance from both to offer the promise of efficiency to the former and a sense of purpose to the latter!

I pay tribute to our staff who have over the years made a truly significant contribution to whatever others consider to be our achievements, to everyone who has given us invaluable assistance and not least of all to our guests without whose support, encouragement and loyalty none of this would have been possible.

An award such as this acts not only as a splendid boost to morale for today but also as a challenge for tomorrow, something we have been lucky enough to pass over to the next generation: I therefore thank the team at Johansens for the support they have given not only to us but to all sections of our exciting industry.

Nigel Corbett

INTRODUCTION

From Ynyshir Hall, Machynlleth
Winner of the 1999 Johansens Most Excellent Restaurant Award

We were all thrilled to win the Johansens Most Excellent Restaurant award this year, especially against such distinguished competition. "Wonderful food in wonderful surroundings" was the inspector's phrase! With the wealth of superb Welsh produce, coupled with exciting young chefs, it is no surprise that Wales is fast being put on the culinary map. In the ten years we have been at Ynyshir we have always put great emphasis on our food and see the whole dining experience as a very important part of a guest's stay.

We were very pleased, four years ago, to attract a chef of the calibre of Chris Colmer to Wales. He had just won the Roux Diner's Club Scholarship. He was amazed at the quality of the Welsh produce and was soon awarded Welsh Chef of the year. His style is Modern British, with a fusion of influences from around the world, but still letting the flavour of our wonderful Welsh ingredients sing through.

Chris' food is also very visual and our restaurant provides the ideal stage on which to show it, with both stunning views of the Welsh countryside from the windows and Rob's bold paintings on the walls. Our restaurant staff, headed by Catherine Jones, aim to create the perfect ambience in which to relax and enjoy the meal with unobtrusive, professional and friendly service.

The award comes on our tenth anniversary at Ynyshir Hall. We see it as a recognition of ten years of striving to improve and of our staff's dedication, attention to detail and hard work. We thank both of them and Johansens for this award and for all the guests they bring us!

Joan & Rob Reen

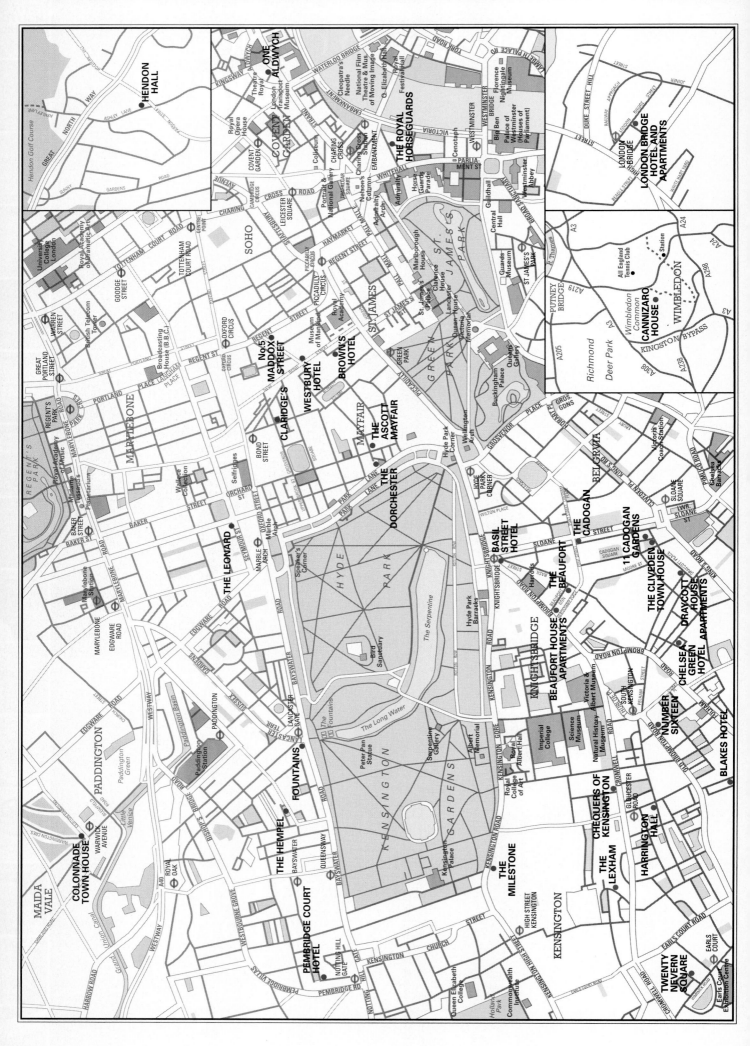

Johansens Recommended Hotels & Apartments

London

London recommendations represent a fine selection of full service, luxury hotels, town house hotels and apartments, from the grand to the bijou. Our choice is based on location, reputation, value for money and excellence, above all else. The Johansens guest can be comfortably accommodated within easy reach of the principal shopping areas, museums, galleries, restaurants, theatres and Wimbledon!

The Millennium Dome

What's new in the capital?

•The Millennium Dome is located beside the Thames on Greenwich peninsula. It is almost finished and opens on 1st January 2000.

•Take a look at the Millennium Countdown Clock at the Old Royal Observatory and take a glimpse of the Dome itself.

•The Millennium Bridge is currently being built across the Thames near St Paul's Cathedral along with the Millennium Wheel which will offer visitors an amazing 30-mile view over London. This should be completed by the autumn.

•The British Film Institute opened a 482 seat cinema on the South Bank on 1st May. The £20 million cinema boasts the UK's biggest cinema screen: 20 metres high by 26 metres wide with an IMAX projection system and digital surround sound. The cinema will be open seven days a week and tickets cost £6.50 for adults and £4.50 for children.

•London Zoo has created a £4.4 million conservation education centre promoting conservation in the natural world and endeavours to change our approach to zoos in the 21st century. Built in a new glass pavilion, the Web of Life Exhibition brings people closer to live animals in amazing settings.

•The FA Premier League Hall of Fame has been created in the old County Hall. This attraction offers visitors the chance to experience an entertaining and informative celebration of English football from past to present incorporating wax models and a wall of hand casts.

•Madame Tussaud's Rock Circus has now completed it's multi-million pound redevelopment and offers visitors a range of audiovisual and animatronic effects and wax portraits of some of the biggest stars in music.

For further information contact:

London Tourist Board
Glen House
Stag Place
London
SW1E 5LT

Tel: 0207 932 2000
Fax: 0207 932 0222
Website: www.LondonTown.com

THE ASCOTT MAYFAIR

49 HILL STREET, LONDON W1X 7FQ
TEL: 020 7499 6868 FAX: 020 7499 0705 E-MAIL: ascottmf@scotts.com.sg

This, the latest concept in city centre accommodation, offers all the benefits of a hotel and yet also privacy and space in what the brochure describes as "residences", with one, two or three bedrooms, in a spectacular art deco building. The apartments have a 24 hour concierge for security and assistance. A maid will be assigned to you for the full duration of your stay. A complimentary Continental breakfast is served in The Terrace, overlooking the private gardens. There is an Honour Bar in The Club where guests can mingle or entertain. The Hothouse offers a gym, sauna, steam room and solarium. The Business Service includes the use of a private boardroom. A marvellous kitchen is provided in each apartment with everything necessary for entertaining in the versatile lounge. The study area has fax and computer links. The sitting room is extremely comfortable and beautifully decorated. It has satellite television, a music system and video. The luxurious bedrooms have amazing en suite bathrooms, full of soft white towels. The Ascott is in the heart of London – Mayfair being close to all the major shopping centres and best restaurants, theatre-land and sightseeing. **Directions:** Hill Street is off Berkeley Square, near Green Park Underground Station. Price guide: 1 bed £185–£270 daily, £1,240–£1,800 weekly; 2 beds from £395 daily–£2,600 weekly. (All rates are subject to VAT).

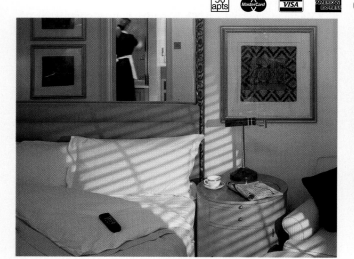

THE BEAUFORT

33 BEAUFORT GARDENS, KNIGHTSBRIDGE, LONDON SW3 1PP
TEL: 020 7584 5252 FAX: 020 7589 2834 E–MAIL: thebeaufort@nol.co.uk.

The Beaufort offers the sophisticated traveller all the style and comfort of home – combining warm contemporary colourings with the highest possible personal attention. The owner Diana Wallis (pictured below) believes that much of the success of the hotel is due to the charming, attentive staff. The Beaufort is situated in a quiet tree-lined square only 100 yards from Harrods and as guests arrive they are all greeted at the front door and given their own door key to come and go as they please. The closed front door gives added security and completes that feeling of home. All the bedrooms are individually decorated, with air conditioning, twice daily maid service and a great many extras such as shortbread, Swiss chocolates and brandy. The hotel owns a video and cassette library and is home to a magnificent collection of original English floral watercolours. Breakfast comprises hot rolls and croissants, freshly squeezed orange juice and home-made preserves, tea and coffee. Complimentary offerings include grand cru champagne and all drinks from the 24-hour bar, membership of a top London Health Club, a chauffeured limousine to and from the airport and English cream tea, not forgetting Beluga caviar and vodka in the evening. The hotel is proud of its no tipping policy and is open all year. **Directions:** From Harrods exit at Knightsbridge underground station take third left turn left. Price guide: Single from £170; double/twin from £200; junior suite £325 (rates excl. 17.5% VAT).

BEAUFORT HOUSE APARTMENTS

45 BEAUFORT GARDENS, KNIGHTSBRIDGE, LONDON SW3 1PN
TEL: 020 7584 2600 FAX: 020 7584 6532 US TOLL FREE: 1 800 23 5463 E-MAIL: info@beauforthouse.co.uk

Situated in Beaufort Gardens, a quiet tree-lined Regency cul-de-sac in the heart of Knightsbridge, 250 yards from Harrods, Beaufort House is an exclusive establishment comprising 22 self-contained fully serviced luxury apartments. All the comforts of a first-class hotel are combined with the privacy and discretion and the relaxed atmosphere of home. Accommodation ranges in size from an intimate one-bedroomed suite to a spacious, four-bedroomed apartment. Each apartment has been individually decorated in a traditional style to a standard which is rigorously maintained. All apartments have direct dial telephones, personal safes, satellite TV and video systems. Most bedrooms benefit from en suite bathrooms and several have west facing balconies. The fully fitted and equipped kitchens include washers/dryers; many have dishwashers. A daily maid service is included at no additional charge. Full laundry/dry cleaning services are available. For your added security, a concierge is on call 24 hours a day, through whom taxis, theatre tickets, restaurant reservations and other services are also available. Executive support services are provided with confidentiality assured at all times. Complimentary membership at Champneys Piccadilly Club is offered to all guests during their stay. Awarded 4 Keys Highly Commended by the English Tourist Board. **Directions:** Beaufort Gardens leads off Brompton road near Knightsbridge Tube. 24hr car park down the road. Price Guide: £160–£493 per night (excl. VAT).

BASIL STREET HOTEL

BASIL STREET, LONDON SW3 1AH

TEL: 020 7581 3311 FAX: 020 7581 3693 FROM USA TOLL FREE: UTELL 1 800 448 8355 E-MAIL: thebasil@aol.com

The Basil feels more like an English home than a hotel. Privately owned by the same family for three generations, this traditional Edwardian hotel is situated in a quiet corner of Knightsbridge, on the threshold of London's most exclusive residential and shopping area. Harrods, Harvey Nichols and other famous stores are only minutes away. It is close to museums and theatres. The spacious public rooms are furnished with antiques, paintings, mirrors and *objets d'art*. The lounge, bar and dining room are on the first floor, reached by the distinctive staircase that dominates the front hall. Bedrooms, all individually furnished, vary in size, style and décor. The Hotel's Dining Room is an ideal venue either for unhurried, civilised lunch or dinner by candlelight with piano music. The Parrot Club, a lounge for the exclusive use of ladies, is a haven of rest in delightful surroundings. The Basil combines tradition and caring individual service with the comfort of a modern, cosmopolitan hotel. There is a discount scheme for regular guests, for weekends and stays of five nights or more. Garage parking space available on request. **Directions:** Close to Pavilion Road car park. Basil Street runs off Sloane Street in the direction of Harrods. Near Knightsbridge underground and bus routes. Price guide: Single from £125; double/twin from £185; family room from £245. (excluding VAT).

BLAKES HOTEL

33 ROLAND GARDENS, LONDON SW7 3PF

TEL: 020 7370 6701 FAX: 020 7373 0442 FROM USA CALL FREE: 1 800 926 3173 E-MAIL: blakes@easynet.co.uk

Created by Anouska Hempel, designer, hotelier and couturière, Blakes is unique – a connoisseur's refuge. Each room has been individually designed, the colour schemes are daring, stunning and dramatic – black and mustard, rich cardinal reds, lavender, vanilla washes of tea rose and a room that is white on white on white offering style and elegance to the discerning traveller. "If ever dreams can become reality, then Blakes is where it will happen". The bedrooms and suites have been described as each being a fantasy. A full 24 hour room service is provided and if a guest is travelling on business the hotel will provide a room fax machine, full secretarial services and a courier service if required. Blakes intimate restaurant is recognised as one of the finest in the capital and is open until midnight. Breakfast, summer lunches and candlelit dinners can be enjoyed on the Garden Terrace which overlooks the private and secluded courtyard – an explosion of greenery all year round. Blakes Hotel is licensed for wedding ceremonies. The smart, fashionable shops of Brompton Cross are only a short stroll away through the leafy streets of South Kensington and Harrods can be reached by taxi in five minutes. **Directions:** Roland Gardens is a turning off Old Brompton Road. The nearest underground tube station is South Kensington. Price guide: Small twin £160; double £220–£310; suite £475–£695 (excluding VAT).

Brown's Hotel

ALBEMARLE STREET, LONDON W1X 4BP
TEL: 020 7493 6020 FAX: 020 7493 9381 E-MAIL: brownshotel@brownshotel.com

Quality of service and traditional English opulence are the essence of Brown's, a luxurious hotel located at the very centre of London's fashionable Mayfair. Recently renovated by owners Raffles International, the hotel is simply steeped in history. The first London hotel to have a lift and telephone, it has retained all its 19th century charm. On entering, visitors are immediately struck by antique furnishings and the oak-panelled interior. St. George's Bar, an elegant retreat from the hectic pace of London life, has a soothing air enhanced by its stained glass windows and a crackling log fire. The seven dining suites, each named after a historic event that took place there, are the epitome of sophistication. The hotel has also gained a formidable reputation for its food. The Chef is at the forefront of the contemporary classical cuisine movement, while the cellar can only be described as sensational. In keeping with Brown's magnificent interior, each of the 118 rooms is individually decorated, blending modern convenience with its historic origins. A short taxi ride from the City, the hotel is ideally located for the business and leisure traveller alike. Among the nearby attractions are the exclusive boutiques of Regent Street, Buckingham Palace and Sotheby's auctioneers. **Directions:** Nearest underground station is Green Park. Price guide: Single £260; double/twin £290–£355; suite £425–£705.

THE CADOGAN

SLOANE STREET, LONDON SW1X 9SG
TEL: 0207 235 7141 FAX: 0207 245 0994 E-MAIL: info@thecadogan.u-net.com
FROM USA FAX TOLL FREE ON: 800 260 8338 CALL TOLL FREE Prima Hotels: 800 447 7462

The Cadogan is an imposing late-Victorian building in warm terracotta brick situated in a most desirable location in Sloane Street, Knightsbridge. It is well-known for its association with Lillie Langtry, the 'Jersey Lily', actress and friend of King Edward VII and her house in Pont Street now forms part of the hotel. Playwright and wit Oscar Wilde was a regular guest at The Cadogan and was arrested in the hotel in 1895. The Cadogan's elegant drawing room is popular for afternoon tea and the meals served in the air-conditioned restaurant, which has 2 AA Rosettes, combine imaginatively prepared food with value for money. The hotel has 65 comfortable and air conditioned bedrooms and suites equipped to the highest standards. The Langtry Rooms on the ground floor, once the famous actress's drawing room, make a delightful setting for private parties, wedding receptions and small meetings. The hotel is an excellent base for shopping trips, being close to Harrods and Harvey Nichols. Business visitors will find its central position and easy access make it a fine place to stay when visiting London. **Directions:** The hotel is halfway along Sloane Street at junction with Pont Street. Close to Knightsbridge and Sloane Square tubes. Price guide: Single £180–£240; double/twin £246–£283; studio/suite £320–£410 (including continental breakfast and VAT).

CANNIZARO HOUSE

WEST SIDE, WIMBLEDON COMMON, LONDON SW19 4UE
TEL: 020 8879 1464 FAX: 020 8879 7338 E-MAIL: cannizaro.house@thistle.co.uk

Cannizaro House, an elegant Georgian country house, occupies a tranquil position on the edge of Wimbledon Common, yet is only 18 minutes by train from London Waterloo and the Eurostar terminal. Cannizaro House restored as a superb hotel has, throughout its history, welcomed Royalty and celebrities such as George III, Oscar Wilde and William Pitt. The 18th century is reflected in the ornate fireplaces and mouldings, gilded mirrors and many antiques. All the hotel's 45 bedrooms are individually designed, with many overlooking beautiful Cannizaro Park. Several intimate rooms are available for meetings and private dining, including the elegant Queen Elizabeth Room – a popular venue for wedding ceremonies. The Viscount Melville Suite offers air-conditioned comfort for up to 100 guests. There is a spacious south facing summer terrace as ideal for afternoon tea and receptions as it is for evening cocktails. The award-winning kitchen, under the leadership of Pascal Vallee, produces the finest modern and classical cuisine, complemented by an impressive list of wines. **Directions:** The nearest tube and British Rail station is Wimbledon. Price guide (room only): Double/twin from £175; suite from £290. Special weekend rates and celebratory packages available.

Chelsea Green Hotel

35 IXWORTH PLACE, CHELSEA, LONDON SW3 3QX
TEL: 020 7225 7500 FAX: 020 7225 7555 E-MAIL: CGHOTEL@dircon.co.uk

The Chelsea Green Hotel is a luxuriously peaceful haven of charm, warmth and elegance. Its 1920s facade cleverly conceals a London town house hotel of traditional spaciousness and comfort. The Chelsea Green offers 46 air-conditioned bedrooms and suites which have been pleasantly furnished to the highest standards and include an extensive array of quality fittings and facilities. There are mini-bars, modem points, personal safes and thick, soft robes in the bathrooms which have marble décor. One suite has a steam bath, Jacuzzi and fully-fitted kitchen. The hotel's main restaurant is in the delightful garden conservatory where the decoration, table accessories, plants and original paintings change with the seasons of the year. Imaginative breakfasts, luncheons, afternoon teas and seasonally adjusted excellent dinner menus are served here with grace and flair. Pre-dinner cocktails and late evening drinks can be enjoyed in the elegant drawing room against a background of restful soft music and in winter months, a glowing fireplace. London's most fashionable shopping areas, restaurants and West End theatres are within easy reach. **Directions:** Ixworth Place is the first road on the right after following Pelham Street into Sloane Avenue southeastward from South Kensington underground. Price guide: Single from £135; double/twin £180; suites £240–£300. (Exclusive of VAT).

NEW

CHEQUERS OF KENSINGTON

58–66 CROMWELL ROAD, LONDON SW7 5DA
TEL: 020 7969 3555 FAX: 020 7969 3501 E-MAIL: reservations@chequershotel.com

Chequers of Kensington is a contemporary apartment hotel offering the visitor style, ambience and comfort situated in the heart of London just a short stroll from some of the capital's most famous attractions and exclusive shopping areas. It has all home-from-home comforts and is fully equipped for the leisure and business visitor, including the availability of 24 satellite and cable television channels and full internet access. Opened in 1998, the apartments have been designed in attractive styles to provide the ideal surroundings for discerning visitors, combining space, privacy and security with a convenient location. Each apartment has a sitting area and kitchenette. There is a maid service six days per week and laundry and dry cleaning services are provided. Daily complimentary continental breakfast is served and there is a bar in which to relax in over a drink at the end of the day. Corporate visitors can take advantage of a business centre where secretarial services can be provided. Arrangements can also be made for guests to attend a local fitness club. The Natural History Museum, Victoria and Albert Museum and the Royal Albert Hall are close by. **Directions:** From Gloucester Road tube station, turn right along Cromwell Road. Chequers is on the left. Price guide: Studio (2–4 persons) £150–£165; duplex (4 pers) £175; 1 bedroom apartment (4 pers) £195; 2 bedroom apartment (6 pers) £235.

CLARIDGE'S

BROOK STREET, MAYFAIR, LONDON W1A 2JQ
TEL: 020 7629 8860 FAX: 020 7499 2210 E-MAIL: info@claridges.co.uk

From the moment visitors enter Claridge's marble front hall with its open fire, tall mirrors and fine art décor they know they are in a hotel of true grandeur. A few more steps past liveried footmen into the beautiful classical foyer and they realise they are in for a unique experience of luxury and service. Situated in the heart of Mayfair close to the fashion houses and jewellers of Bond Street with Regent Street, Berkeley Square, Grosvenor Square and Hyde Park within walking distance, Claridge's is excellence personified. When its doors opened in 1812 the hotel was named Mivart's. It changed to Claridge's in 1854 and has been host to the cream of society, the arts and political life ever since. The individual bedrooms and suites include two seventh floor penthouses with two bedrooms, two bathrooms, a sitting room with terrace and private butler service. Three opulent Royal Suites can be used in combination with up to 50 individual rooms for large entourages. The remainder of Claridge's traditional and art décor style suites and double rooms are spacious, comfortable and offer the latest in high-tech communication and entertainment facilities. Dining is a memorable occasion in the magnificent restaurant which has original mirrored murals and lighting. Award-winning chef John Williams creates delicious French and English cuisine. **Directions:** Nearest underground station is Bond Street. Price guide (excl. VAT): Single from £280; suite £465–£3,500.

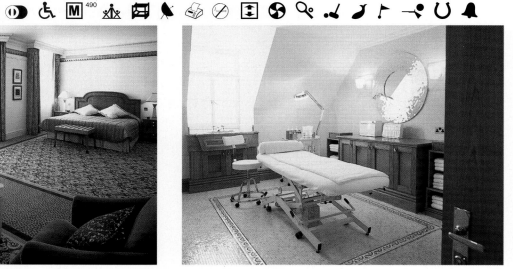

THE CLIVEDEN TOWN HOUSE

26 CADOGAN GARDENS, LONDON SW3 2RP

TEL: 020 7730 6466 FAX: 020 7730 0236 FROM USA TOLL FREE 1 800 747 4942 E-MAIL: reservations@clivedentownhouse.co.uk

The Cliveden Town House offers the perfect balance of luxury, service, privacy and location. Tucked discreetly away in a tranquil, tree-lined garden square between Harrods and Kings Road it is at the very centre of fashionable London and is the epitome of stylish good taste and elegance. Like its gracious country cousin at Cliveden, one of England's most famous stately homes, The Cliveden Town House combines the grandeur of the past with the luxuries and conveniences of today, offering the sophisticated traveller all the exclusive comforts and ambience of a grand private residence. The Town House has enhanced its charm with the addition of 9 opulent suites with a fully-equipped kitchen and/or a separate sitting room. Exclusive use of the 9 suites, boardroom and dining room can be arranged creating the atmosphere of a private home. The full-time services of the steward are included. The spacious rooms are splendidly decorated, reflecting the Edwardian period, and combine the highest 24-hour service with state-of-the-art technology. The fashionable shops and restaurants of Knightsbridge, Chelsea and Belgravia, West End theatres and the City are all within easy reach and the gym is accessible 24 hours a day. The chauffeur is available for airport transfers and personalised tours. Enjoy complimentary afternoon tea or a glass of Champagne each evening in the Drawing Room. **Directions:** Nearest tube station is Sloane Square. Price guide: Single from £105; double/twin £190–£235; suite £320–£990.

THE COLONNADE TOWN HOUSE

2 WARRINGTON CRESCENT, LONDON W9 1ER
TEL: 020 7286 1052 FAX: 020 7286 1057 E-MAIL: mette@etontownhouse.com

The publishers base their recommendation, in this case, on a visit carried out before the hotel was fully operational and not on a full inspection of the facilities which were completed whilst this guide was going to press. This tall, elegant Victorian town house is delightfully situated in the smart and sophisticated residential area of Little Venice which embodies the tranquil Regents Canal. It is a beautifully furnished residence offering all the comforts of a luxury hotel and is conveniently within reach of London's many sights, restaurants, theatres and business areas. The Colonnade was originally built as two private homes in 1865 and later converted into a girl's boarding school and a hospital for ladies until opening as a hotel in 1935. The House has recently been completely refurbished and has an innovative, boutique style interior. Sumptuous fabrics and lavish antiques have been carefully selected to create a unique style and ambience in each of the 43 guest rooms and suites, many of them with a terrace and four poster bed. All are individually decorated and feature every modern facility. Guests can enjoy afternoon tea or evening cocktails in the relaxing drawing room and be served breakfast and excellent dinners in the attractive conservatory. Car parking and airport transfers can be arranged. **Directions:** Warwick Avenue underground station and taxi rank are a short stroll from the Town House. Price guide: Single £110; suites £195 (excluding VAT).

THE DORCHESTER

PARK LANE, MAYFAIR, LONDON W1A 2HJ
TEL: 020 7629 8888 FAX: 020 7409 0114 E-MAIL: reservations@dorchesterhotel.com

The Dorchester first opened its doors in 1931, offering a unique experience which almost instantly became legendary. Its reopening in November 1990 after an extensive refurbishment marked the renaissance of one of the world's grand hotels. Its history has been consistently glamorous; from the early days a host of outstanding figures has been welcomed, including monarchs, statesmen and celebrities. The architectural features have been restored to their original splendour and remain at the heart of The Dorchester's heritage. The 195 bedrooms and 53 suites have been luxuriously designed in a variety of materials, furnishings and lay-outs. All bedrooms are fully air-conditioned and have spectacular Italian marble bathrooms. In addition to The Grill Room, there is The Oriental Restaurant where the accent is on Cantonese cuisine. Specialised health and beauty treatments are offered in The Dorchester Spa with its statues, Lalique-style glass and water fountain. The Bar, a classic, is the venue for some of the best live traditional jazz in London. A series of meeting rooms, with full supporting services, is available for business clientèle. As ever, personalised care is a pillar of The Dorchester's fine reputation. **Directions:** Toward the Hyde Park Corner/Piccadilly end of Park Lane. Price guide excluding VAT: Single £265–£285; double/twin £295–£325; suite £425–£1,925. Year round special packages are available.

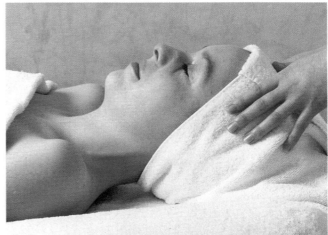

DRAYCOTT HOUSE APARTMENTS

10 DRAYCOTT AVENUE, CHELSEA, LONDON SW3 3AA
TEL: 020 7584 4659 FAX: 020 7225 3694 E-MAIL: sales@draycotthouse.co.uk

Draycott House stands in a quiet, tree-lined avenue in the heart of Chelsea. Housed in an attractive period building, the apartments have been designed in individual styles to provide the ideal surroundings for a private or business visit, combining comfort, privacy and security with a convenient location. All are spacious, luxury, serviced apartments, with three, two or one bedrooms. Some have private balconies, a roof terrace and overlook the private courtyard garden. Each apartment is fully equipped with all home comforts; cable television, video, radio/cassette, a private direct lines for telephone/fax/answer machine/data. Complimentary provisions on arrival, milk and

newspapers delivered daily. Maid service Monday to Friday. In-house laundry room and covered garage parking. Additional services, laundry and dry cleaning services. On request cars, airport transfers, catering, travel and theatre arrangements, child-minders etc and an introduction to an exclusive health club. The West End is within easy reach. Knightsbridge within walking distance. **Directions:** Draycott House is situated on the corner of Draycott Avenue and Draycott Place, close to Sloane Square. Price guide: from £1122–£2781 +VAT per week: £178–£437 +VAT per night. Long term reservations may attract preferential terms. Contact: Jane Renton, General Manager.

FOUNTAINS

1 LANCASTER TERRACE, HYDE PARK, LONDON W2 3PF
TEL: 020 7706 7070 FAX: 020 7706 7006 E-MAIL: sales@living–rooms.co.uk

The exterior is an art decor lover's delight, the interior a contemporary design connoisseur's dream. Overall, Fountains is an attractive and discreet London residence which offers guests the opportunity to live, work, eat, sleep and entertain in style and comfort. Mark Brazier, one of England's leading furniture designers and top interior designer Christopher Neville created and co-ordinated these recently upgraded apartments which overlook Hyde Park's magnificent Italian Water Gardens. The generous proportions of the apartments, along with the striking individuality of their furnishings and décor, creates a unique atmosphere and are a showcase for British design. The 16 one, two or three bedroom apartments accommodate up to seven guests in home style comfort. Many of them incorporate separate living and dining areas, kitchen, bedrooms and bathrooms. There is a Big Bar facility which offers a value for money entertaining option different from the normal hotel mini bar. A complimentary grocery pack is augmented by the Big Bar's options which include organic or more indulgent items payable on consumption. For guests wishing to entertain at home, chefs and butlers are available on request. London's leading restaurants and theatres are within easy reach. **Directions:** Paddington Heathrow Link railway station with Lancaster Gate underground railway stations are nearby. Price guide: Single £177; suites £450 (Excl. VAT).

HARRINGTON HALL

5-25 HARRINGTON GARDENS, LONDON SW7 4JW
TEL: 020 7396 9696 FAX: 020 7396 9090 E-MAIL: harringtonhall@compuserve.com

The original façade of late Victorian houses cleverly conceals a privately owned hotel of substantial proportions and contemporary comfort. Harrington Hall offers 200 air-conditioned spacious bedrooms which have all been most pleasantly furnished and equipped with an extensive array of facilities. 125 of the rooms feature king-size beds. A marble fireplace dominates the comfortable and relaxing Lounge Bar, where guests can enjoy a drink in pleasant surroundings. Serving a varied international menu, the restaurant is a delightful setting for all diners from large luncheon parties to those enjoying intimate evening meals. A choice of buffet or à la carte menu is available, both offering a tempting selection of dishes. Nine fully air-conditioned conference and banqueting suites, with walls panelled in rich lacewood and solid cherry, provide a sophisticated venue for conferences, exhibitions or corporate hospitality. Harrington Hall also has a Business Centre for the exclusive use of its guests, along with a private Fitness Centre with multigym, saunas and showers. **Directions:** Harrington Hall is situated in the Royal Borough of Kensington and Chelsea, in Harrington Gardens south of the Cromwell Road, close to Gloucester Road underground station, two stops from Knightsbridge and Harrods. Price guide: Single £180; double £180; suites £220 (including VAT & service).

THE HEMPEL

31-35 CRAVEN HILL GARDENS, LONDON W2 3EA
TEL: 020 7298 9000; FAX: 020 7402 4666 E-MAIL: the–hempel@easynet.co.uk

Designer Anouska Hempel has created The Hempel to be elegant and relaxing for the traveller. Situated within easy reach of London's many attractions, the hotel has an immaculately preserved Georgian façade with 50 individually designed rooms and suites. Influenced by the peace and simplicity of the Orient, with up-to-the-minute technology from the Western World, The Hempel is innovative and full of surprises – an open fireplace that appears to float, a mix of light and shadow that can keep guests guessing and pondering on just how this can all be real. The huge atrium within the lobby is astounding. A delicious mix of Italian-Thai and Japanese food, devised by Anouska Hempel, is presented with style and flair in the I-Thai restaurant. Guests enjoying a pre-dinner drink in The Shadow Bar are surrounded by illusion and fantasy as The Hempel aims to take them out of this world and make their dreams a reality. **Directions:** The Hempel is situated in Lancaster Gate with a short walk to Kensington Gardens and Hyde Park. Paddington Heathrow Link railway station with Lancaster Gate and Queensway underground railway stations nearby. Price guide: Room/suite/apartment: from £235–£1200 (excluding VAT).

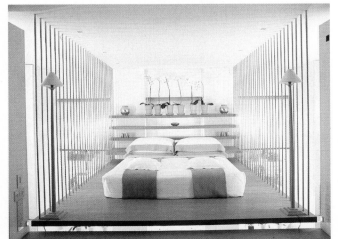

HENDON HALL

ASHLEY LANE, OFF PARSONS STREET, HENDON, LONDON NW4 1HF
TEL: 020 8203 3341 FAX: 020 8203 9709 E-MAIL: Hendon.Hall@Thistle.co.uk

Hendon Hall stands imposingly at the head of a sweeping drive encircling a manicured lawn. Its white entrance way is framed by four massive pillars soaring up to a rooftop encased with an attractive ornamental parapet. An elegant, Georgian building with award-winning gardens it is situated in a residential area seven miles from the heart of London and an eight minutes drive from the M1. Hendon Hall was originally known as Hendon Manor and dates back to the 16th century. King Henry's son, Edward, gave the manor to the Earl of Pembroke in return for 'good and faithful service' and he gave it to his son, Edward, as a wedding present in 1569. Over the succeeding years the Hall was home to a number of families, a girl's school and a RAF convalescent home. Behind its classical facade it has been refurbished to provide spacious and stylish accommodation with many original features retained. All bedrooms and suites are beautifully decorated and have every modern amenity. Visitors can sip apéritifs in an intimate cocktail bar before enjoying the tasty Pavillion Restaurant cuisine created by chef Jack Brabham, who previously worked at Cliveden and Tylney Hall. **Directions:** From M1, exit at junction 2 signposted North Circular East (A406) and The City A1. At the first set of traffic lights turn right into Parson Street. Hendon Hall is on the right in Ashley Lane. Nearest underground station is Hendon Central (Northern line). Price guide: Double/twin from £130; suite from £190.

THE LEONARD

15 SEYMOUR STREET, LONDON W1H 5AA
TEL: 020 7935 2010 FAX: 020 7935 6700 E-MAIL: the.leonard@dial.pipex.com

Four late 18th century Georgian town houses set the character of this exciting Johansens award winning property which opened in 1996 and has proved to be extremely popular with Johansens guests. Imaginative reconstruction has created 9 rooms and 20 suites decorated individually to a very high standard. Wall coverings present striking colours, complemented by exquisite French furnishing fabrics creating a warm luxurious atmosphere. All rooms are fully air-conditioned and include a private safe, mini-bar, hi-fi system and provision for a modem/fax. Bathrooms are finished in marble and some of the larger suites have a butler's pantry or fully-equipped kitchen. For physical fitness and stress reductions there is a compact exercise room. "Can do" staff ensure that guests can enjoy the highest level of attention and service. Breakfast is available in the café bar and light meals are served throughout the day. 24-hour room service is also available. The Leonard Residence opposite, also part of the hotel, offers five serviced appartments available for longer stay requirements. There are many good restaurants nearby, a Leonard restaurant guide is available in all suites and bedrooms. The Wallace Collection is just a short walk away and one of London's premier department stores, Selfridges, is round the corner in Oxford Street. **Directions:** The Leonard is north of Marble Arch and off Portman Square. Parking in Bryanston Street. Price guide (excl. VAT): Double from £190; suites £240– £480.

THE LEXHAM APARTMENTS

32-38 LEXHAM GARDENS, KENSINGTON, LONDON W8 5JE
TEL: 020 7559 4444 FAX: 020 7559 4400 E-MAIL: reservations@lexham.com

The Lexham has been created from two of the tall, elegant and gracious early Victorian houses surrounding a quiet, tree-lined garden square in the heart of one of the most fashionable areas of London. The Lexham's luxury one and two bedroom apartments have been stylishly furnished to provide the ideal surroundings for a family or business visit, combining comfort, flexibility, privacy and security with a convenient location. All are spacious, light and airy and are equipped with all home comforts, including cable television, safes, voice mail and private phone and fax lines. Each has a full-sized, well-appointed kitchen including a washing machine/tumble dryer and a dishwasher. Many feature extra comforts such as an additional sofa bed. There is a daily maid service on weekdays and 24 hour porterage. Reservations for a restaurant, theatre, car or nearby health club/swimming pool can be arranged. The Lexham has a spacious colourful, landscaped garden at the rear in which guests can relax on warmer days and evenings. The fashionable shops and restaurants of Kensington, Knightsbridge and Chelsea are close by and West End theatres and the capital's tourist attractions are within easy reach. Minimum stay at the Lexham is seven days. **Directions:** Nearest underground station are Gloucester Road and High Street Kensington. Price guide (excl VAT): One-bedroom apartments £1,175 per week; two-bedroom apartments £1,475 per week. Additional days pro rata.

LONDON BRIDGE HOTEL & APARTMENTS

8–18 LONDON BRIDGE STREET, LONDON SE1 9SG
TEL: 020 7855 2200 FAX: 020 7855 2233 E-MAIL: sales@london–bridge–hotel.co.uk

This new, modern four-star hotel is equally ideal for the leisure visitor seeking to enjoy the historic and cultural delights of the City of London as it is to the business executive. It stands on the edge of the City with easy access to Docklands, the Millennium Dome and the West End. The site has a heritage dating back to Roman times and significant archaeological finds unearthed during the hotel's £11million development are to be found in the Museum of London. All the en suite bedrooms and suites are air-conditioned and have a blend of modern and classic furnishings with up-to-date facilities. The two-bedroomed serviced apartments are extremely spacious and comfortable and available for short and long term lets. There are six rooms specially designed for the less mobile guest, two non-smoking floors and an executive floor where some rooms have a rooftop view over the capital. The hotel also provides five conference rooms complete with the latest audiovisual equipment. Hitchcock's city bar is a convenient venue for an informal chat over drinks or a snack. As well as their private dining facilities, London Bridge is home to one of the famed Simply Nico restaurants which provides a popular and sophisticated setting in which to enjoy excellent and imaginative cuisine with a modern French flavour. Guests have free use of a newly opened gymnasium. **Directions:** Opposite London Bridge tube/rail station. Price guide: Single £155; suites £375.

THE MILESTONE

1 KENSINGTON COURT, LONDON W8 5DL

TEL: 020 7917 1000 FAX: 020 7917 1010 FROM USA TOLL FREE: 1 800 323 7500 E-MAIL: reservations@milestone.redcarnationhotels.com

The beautifully appointed Milestone Hotel is situated opposite Kensington Palace with uninterrupted views over Kensington Gardens and the remarkable Royal parklands. A Victorian showpiece, this unique hotel has been carefully restored to its original splendour whilst incorporating every modern facility. The 57 bedrooms including 12 suites are all individually designed with antiques, elegant furnishings and some have private balconies. Guests may relax in the comfortable, panelled Park Lounge which, in company with all other rooms, provides a 24-hour service. The hotel's restaurant, Cheneston's, the early spelling of Kensington, has an elaborately carved ceiling, original fireplace and ornate windows. The newly created Windsor Suite is a versatile function room, perfect for private dining and corporate meetings. The health and fitness centre offers guests the use of a Jacuzzi, sauna and gymnasium. The traditional bar, Stables, on the ground floor is an ideal place for meeting and entertaining friends. The Milestone is within walking distance of some of the finest shopping in Kensington and in Knightsbridge and is a short taxi ride to the West End, the heart of London's Theatreland. The Royal Albert Hall and all the museums in Exhibition Road are nearby. **Directions:** At the end of Kensington High Street, at the junction with Princes Gate. Price guide: Single from £250; double/twin £270; suites from £430.

NO 5 MADDOX STREET

5, MADDOX STREET, MAYFAIR, LONDON W1R 9LE
TEL: 020 7647 0200 FAX: 020 7647 0300 E-MAIL: no5maddoxst@living–rooms.co.uk

No 5 Maddox Street is a haven of peace, tranquillity and bijou style centrally situated in a quiet West End street running between Bond Street and Regent Street, Soho and Mayfair. A sister property to Fountains, at Lancaster Gate, it combines, space and relaxed personal service with comfortable, understated interiors and all the comforts of home. All suites feature bamboo floors whilst the de luxe bedroom suites have open fireplaces and decked balconies. Those with two and three bedrooms offer private terraces with bamboo furniture. All the suites are beautifully decorated with sumptuous bathrooms and fully fitted kitchens which include a unique Big Bar offering 'good' and 'bad' options from Ben and Jerry's Chocolate Fudge Brownie ice cream to Yogi tea. A complimentary starter grocery pack awaits each new arrival, personal shopping is available if required and a chef can be arranged to cater for guests and their invitees. Each living room has wide screen satellite television, dual playback video, music system, personal safe and business facilities which include ISDN modem lines and fax machine, cordless telephones with voicemail and fax machine with photocopy facilities. Secretarial services and computer equipment hire can be arranged. For the energetic, a fleet of bicycles is available for use and temporary membership of a local private gymnasium can be obtained. **Directions:** Nearest underground station is Oxford Street. Price guide: Single from £195; suites from £495.

NUMBER ELEVEN CADOGAN GARDENS

11 CADOGAN GARDENS, SLOANE SQUARE, KNIGHTSBRIDGE, LONDON SW3 2RJ
TEL: 020 7730 7000 FAX: 020 7730 5217 E-MAIL: reservations@number–eleven.co.uk

In a quiet tree-lined square between Harrods and the Kings Road, Number Eleven Cadogan Gardens is an elegant town house hotel with a reputation for first class service. The hotel remains traditional yet stylish; no reception desk, no endless signing of bills, total privacy and security. The 60 bedrooms are well-appointed and furnished with antiques and oriental rugs. The Garden Suite, with its large double bedroom, has a particularly spacious drawing room overlooking the attractive gardens. Pre-dinner drinks and canapés are served in the Drawing Room or in the Library where small parties can be held. Room service is round the clock whilst laundry service is same day. Sauna and massage facilites are available and for a more strenuous work out, a personal trainer is on call in the in-house gymnasium. The fashionable shops and restaurants of Knightsbridge and Chelsea are within easy walking distance whilst the chauffeured Mercedes is available for airport and Eurostar connections. Theatre tickets, restaurant bookings and travel arrangements are all part of our unique personal service. **Directions:** Off Sloane Street. Nearest underground is Sloane Square. Price guide: Single from £135; double/twin from £170; suite from £250. (excluding VAT).

NUMBER SIXTEEN

16 SUMNER PLACE, LONDON SW7 3EG

TEL: 020 7589 5232 US TOLL FREE: 1 800 592 5387 FAX: 020 7584 8615 E-MAIL: reservations@numbersixteenhotel.co.uk

On entering Number Sixteen with its immaculate pillared façade visitors find themselves in an atmosphere of seclusion and comfort which has remained virtually unaltered in style since its early Victorian origins. The staff are friendly and attentive, regarding each visitor as a guest in a private home. The relaxed atmosphere of the library is the perfect place to pour a drink from the honour bar and meet friends or business associates. A fire blazing in the drawing room in cooler months creates an inviting warmth, whilst the conservatory opens on to a beautiful secluded walled garden which once again has won many accolades and awards for its floral displays. Each spacious bedroom is decorated with a discreet combination of antiques and traditional furnishings. The rooms are fully appointed with every facility that the discerning traveller would expect. A light breakfast is served in the privacy of guests' rooms and a tea and coffee service is available throughout the day. Although there is no dining room at Number Sixteen, some of London's finest restaurants are just round the corner. The hotel has membership of Aquilla Health and Fitness Club, 5 minutes walk away. The hotel is close to the West End, Knightsbridge and Hyde Park. **Directions:** Sumner Place is off Old Brompton Road near Onslow Square. South Kensington Tube Station is a 2 minute walk. Price guide: Single £95–£130; double/twin £165–£205; junior suite £215.

ONE ALDWYCH

ONE ALDWYCH, LONDON, WC2B 4BZ
TEL: 020 7300 1000 FAX: 020 7300 1001 E-MAIL: sales@onealdwych.co.uk

This contemporary hotel, created within one of the most renowned Edwardian properties in the city, opened in July 1998 in an enviable location just minutes from London's best theatres and shops. Understated elegance prevails in the interior with the spacious lobby and grand entrance furnished in a sleek contemporary style featuring bespoke furniture. The 105 guest rooms and suites are superbly equipped with ISDN lines, European and US sockets, CD players, touch control air conditioning, fibre optic reading lights and mini televisions in every bathroom. Thoughtful touches include fresh fruit and flowers every day. The choice of restaurants at One Aldwych is wonderfully diverse with Axis serving modern European cuisine in a sophisticated yet relaxed setting and Indigo, with a healthy and creative menu. The Cinnamon Bar serves great coffee and light food. Fitness facilities include an 18 metre lap swimming pool with an underwater sound system, a large fully-equipped gymnasium, a personal training centre, treatment rooms, massage and beauty therapies. The hotel is surrounded by theatres, museums and shops. Many of London's famous landmarks are nearby such as Westminster, Trafalgar Square and St Paul's Cathedral. **Directions:** The hotel is located at the point where the Strand meets Aldwych, opposite Waterloo Bridge on the edge of Covent Garden. Price guide (excl. VAT): Single £245–£300; double/twin £265–£320; suite £395. Weekend programmes available.

PEMBRIDGE COURT HOTEL

34 PEMBRIDGE GARDENS, LONDON W2 4DX
TEL: 020 7229 9977 FAX: 020 7727 4982 E-MAIL: reservations@pemct.co.uk

This gracious Victorian town house has been lovingly restored to its former glory whilst providing all the modern facilities demanded by today's discerning traveller. The 20 rooms all of which have air conditioning and are individually decorated with pretty fabrics and the walls adorned with an unusual collection of framed fans and Victoriana. The charming and tranquil sitting room is as ideal for a quiet drink as it is for a small informal meeting. The Pembridge Court is renowned for the devotion and humour with which it is run. Its long serving staff and its two famous cats "Spencer" and "Churchill" assure you of an immensely warm welcome and the very best in friendly, personal service. Over the years the hotel has built up a loyal following amongst its guests, many of whom regard it as their genuine 'home from home' in London. The Pembridge is situated in quiet tree-lined gardens just off Notting Hill Gate, an area described by Travel & Leisure magazine as 'one of the liveliest, most prosperous corners of the city'. "The Gate" as it is affectionately known, is certainly lively, colourful and full of life with lots of great pubs and restaurants and the biggest antiques market in the world at nearby Portobello Road. **Directions:** Pembridge Gardens is a small turning off Notting Hill Gate/Bayswater Road, just 2 minutes from Portobello Road Antiques Market. Price guide: Single £120–£160; double/twin £180–£195 (inclusive of both English breakfast & VAT).

THE ROYAL HORSEGUARDS

WHITEHALL COURT, LONDON, SW1A 2EJ
TEL: 020 7839 3400 FAX: 020 7925 2263 E-MAIL: royal.horseguards@thistle.co.uk

Overlooking the River Thames, this elegant hotel offers an excellent standard of service and fine accommodation making it an ideal choice for both the leisure and business traveller. The Reception Hall is spacious and airy with high ceilings and marble floors and forms a delightful contrast to the cosy and intimate lounge. The 280 air-conditioned bedrooms, many with splendid views across the river, offer pleasant fabrics and furnishings reminiscent of a country house hotel. Guests may dine in the exquisite One Twenty One Two Restaurant and Bar, serving modern European cuisine with Oriental influences. Hotel facilities include a business centre, fitness room and a delightful terrace linked to the Embankment Gardens. One

Whitehall Place, adjoining The Royal Horseguards, is a superb conference and meeting venue. Steeped in history, the centre offers a wide range of facilities for all events and provides state-of-the-art technology. Galleries including the prestigious National Gallery, theatres and boutiques abound. The many tourist attractions such as Buckingham Palace, Trafalgar Square and the Houses of Parliament all lie within easy reach. **Directions:** The hotel is just off Whitehall, near Downing Street. Nearest underground stations are Charing Cross and Embankment. Price guide (incl. VAT): Executive single/double from £185; deluxe single/double from £205. For special weekend and promotional rates, contact the reservations office.

TWENTY NEVERN SQUARE

LONDON SW5 9PD

TEL: 020 7565 9555 FAX: 020 7565 9444 E-MAIL: hotel@twentynevernsquare.co.uk

A unique experience in hospitality awaits guests at this newly-restored elegant town house overlooking a tranquil, leafy square. Originally built in the 1880s, Twenty Nevern Square is superbly furnished throughout with the 20 luxury bedrooms all having full-marbled, compact, en suite facilities and creatively decorated with beautiful hand crafted furniture echoing both Asian and European influences. Each bedroom is unique, from the delicate silks of the Chinese Room contrasting with the opulence of the Rococo Room through to the grandeur of the Pasha Suite with its balcony overlooking the garden square. All rooms have full modern facilities, including wide-screen digital television and fax and modem points.

Guests can also choose from specially carved de luxe four-poster beds, Egyptian Sleigh beds, doubles, twin rooms, or four-foot beds for sole use. Room service includes a late-night picnic tray. Excellent lunches and dinners are served in the intimate restaurant which adjoins a restful drawing room with open fire. Car parking is available. London's most fashionable shopping areas, restaurants, West End theatres, the Natural History and Science museums are all accessible. Visitors to Earls Court and Olympia exhibition centres would also find the hotel an ideal find. **Directions:** A short walk from Earls Court station. Price guide Single £130; double/twin £165–£195; suite £275. Weekend programmes available.

WESTBURY HOTEL

BOND STREET, MAYFAIR, LONDON W1A 4UH
TEL: 020 7629 7755 FAX: 020 7495 1163 E-MAIL: westburyhotel@compuserve.com

Situated grandly in the heart of Mayfair, the Westbury Hotel is surrounded by fashionable neighbours such as Versace, Tiffany's, Armani and Sotheby's and the attractions of the major stores of Knightsbridge, Oxford Street and Regent Street. Rising tall and imposingly it has an architecturally splendid exterior and a luxurious interior with an atmosphere that arriving guests find instantly calming. The spacious public rooms are light and airy with soft lighting, wood panelling, delicate fabrics and tasteful furnishings. Individually decorated, all Westbury's en suite guest rooms and 19 suites offer every comfort from air-conditioning and satellite television to a private bar and monogrammed, fluffy bathrobes. Guests

can enjoy breakfast or a chat over a drink on their private balcony while absorbing a rooftop view over the capital. The Polo Bar has been a favourite meeting place for four decades and is a delightful, soothing venue for cocktails prior to dining on modern British cuisine in a charming restaurant decorated with contemporary art and looking out onto a flower garden. Light meals and afternoon tea are also served in the Polo Lounge. Major tourist attractions and theatreland are within walking distance with St James' and Hyde Park just minutes away. **Directions:** Close to Green Park underground station. Price guide: Single £210; double/twin £275; suites £300–£650 (Excluding VAT).

SWAN HELLENIC MINERVA

77 NEW OXFORD STREET, LONDON WC1A 1PP
TEL: 020 7800 2200 FAX: 020 7800 2723

Swan Hellenic's Minerva cruises to some of the most interesting destinations in the world from the Mediterranean and the Baltics to the Far East and India. Each itinerary is a perfect blend of discovery and relaxation and each cruise is accompanied by expert guest speakers whose informal talks bring the destinations to life. Minerva is in some ways reminiscent of a fine English country house hotel. This small, modern cruise ship carrying just 300 passengers offers spacious, tastefully furnished rooms with all the welcoming touches expected in a well-regarded hotel. The potted palms and cane furniture in the Orpheus Room create a tropical air whilst the leather and suede in the club-style Smoking Room exude a more traditional ambience. Bronze fittings and more than 1,000 paintings, prints and lithographs decorate the cabins, corridors and public rooms. Accommodation ranges from suites with balconies to deluxe and superior cabins with en suite baths and standard cabins with showers. Guests can relax over a drink in the wood-panelled Wheeler Bar. Superb food and fine wines may be sampled in the sophisticated restaurant which, like the main lounge, stretches the width of the ship. Less formal meals are served in the Bridge Café which leads to the teak decks where loungers tempt those who wish to simply recline in the sunshine. Fitness enthusiasts can work out in the gym, relax in the sauna or pamper themselves with a massage or beauty treatment. All inclusive Price guide: Upon request.

As recommended

Johansens Recommended Hotels
England

England has so much to offer – castles, cathedrals, museums, magnificent country houses and the opportunity to stay in areas of great historical importance.

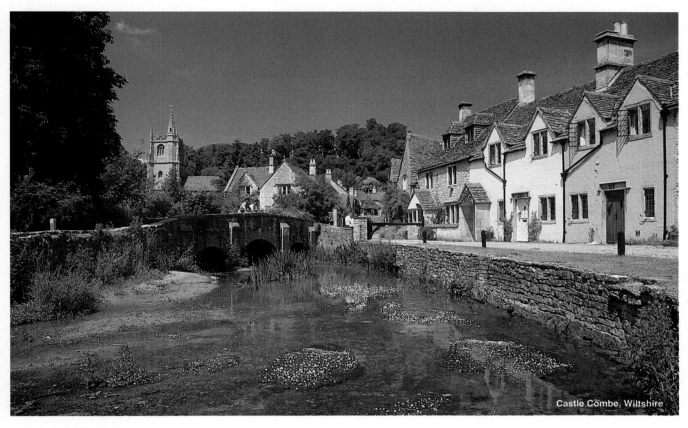
Castle Combe, Wiltshire

Regional Tourist Boards

Cumbria Tourist Board
Ashleigh, Holly Road, Windermere
Cumbria LA23 2AQ
Tel: 015394 44444
England's most beautiful lakes and tallest mountains reach out from the Lake District National Park to a landscape of spectacular coasts, hills and dales.

East of England Tourist Board
Toppesfield Hall, Hadleigh
Suffolk IP7 5DN
Tel: 01473 822922
Cambridgeshire, Essex, Hertfordshire, Bedfordshire, Norfolk, Suffolk and Lincolnshire.

Heart of England Tourist Board
Woodside, Larkhill Road.
Worcester WR5 2EZ
Tel: 01905 763436
Gloucestershire, Hereford & Worcester, Shropshire, Staffordshire, Warwickshire, West Midlands, Derbyshire, Leicestershire, Northamptonshire, Nottinghamshire & Rutland. Represents the districts of Cherwell & West Oxfordshire in the county of Oxfordshire.

London Tourist Board
Glen House, Stag Place
London SW1E 5LT
Tel: 0171 932 2000
The Greater London area (see page 13)

Northumbria Tourist Board
Aykley Heads
Durham DH1 5UX
Tel: 0191 375 3000
The Tees Valley, Durham, Northumberland, Tyne & Wear.

North West Tourist Board
Swan House, Swan Meadow Road, Wigan Pier
Lancashire WN3 5BB
Tel: 01942 821222
Cheshire, Greater Manchester, Lancashire, Merseyside & the High Peak District of Derbyshire.

South East England Tourist Board
The Old Brew House, Warwick Park, Tunbridge Wells, Kent TN2 5TU
Tel: 01892 540766
East & West Sussex, Kent & Surrey

Southern Tourist Board
40 Chamberlayne Road, Eastleigh
Hampshire SO50 5JH
Tel: 01703 620006
East & North Dorset, Hampshire, Isle of Wight, Berkshire, Buckinghamshire & Oxfordshire.

West Country Tourist Board
60 St David's Hill, Exeter
Devon EX4 4SY
Tel: 01392 425426
Bath & NE Somerset, Bristol, Cornwall and the Isles of Scilly, Devon, Dorset (Western), North Somerset & Wiltshire.

Yorkshire Tourist Board
312 Tadcaster Road
York YO2 2HF
Tel: 01904 707961
Yorkshire and North & North East Lincolnshire.

Further Information

English Heritage
23rd Floor, Portland HouseStag Place
London SW1E 5EE
Tel: 0171-973 3000
Offers an unrivalled choice of properties to visit.

Historic Houses Association
2 Chester Street
London SW1X 7BB
Tel: 0171-259 5688
Ensures the survival of historic houses and gardens in private ownership in Great Britain

The National Trust
36 Queen Anne's Gate
London SW1H 9AS
Tel: 0171-222 9251
Cares for more than 590,000 acres of countryside and over 400 historic buildings.

THE ELMS

ABBERLEY, WORCESTERSHIRE WR6 6AT
TEL: 01299 896666 FAX: 01299 896804

Built in 1710 by a pupil of Sir Christopher Wren and converted into a country house hotel in 1946, The Elms has achieved an international reputation for excellence spanning the past half century. Standing tall and impressively between Worcester and Tenbury Wells this fine Queen Anne mansion is surrounded by the beauties of the meadows, woodland, green hills, hop fields and orchards of cider apples and cherries of the Teme Valley whose river runs crimson when in flood from bank-side soil tinged with red sandstone. Each of the hotel's 16 bedrooms has its own character, furnished with period antiques and having splendid views across the landscaped gardens and beyond to the beauty of the valley. There is a panelled bar and the elegant restaurant offers fine imaginative cuisine. The surrounding countryside offers opportunities for walking, fishing, shooting, golf and horse-racing. Within easy reach are the attractions of the market town of Tenbury Wells, Witley Court, Bewdley and the ancient city of Worcester with its cathedral, county cricket ground and famous porcelain factory. **Directions:** From the M5, exit at junction 5 (Droitwich) or junction 6 (Worcester) then take the A443 towards Tenbury Wells. The Elms is two miles after Great Witley. Do not take the turning into Abberley village. Price guide: Single £90–£110; double/twin £140–£175.

THE MOAT HOUSE

ACTON TRUSSELL, STAFFORD, STAFFORDSHIRE ST17 0RJ
TEL: 01785 712217 FAX: 01785 715344 E-MAIL: info@moathouse.co.uk

This impressive, oak-beamed and moated manor house is excellent in every way. History, luxurious comfort, warmth, superb food, ultra modern amenities and a spectacular canal side setting all combine in a picturesque village in the heart of rural Staffordshire. Built in the 15th century, the Moat House is the perfect retreat for those seeking peace, tranquillity and leisurely enjoyment. There are 21 luxury en suite bedrooms, including two suites, with facilities to suit the most discerning guest. Most are air-conditioned. The bar retains the character and charm of the hotel's past with exposed beams and a magnificent inglenook fireplace. Dining is an experience, with chef Matthew Davies

producing sophisticated and imaginative dishes in the elegant, 2 AA Rosette restaurant. The Moat House is also a first-class business venue, offering seven meeting rooms including a suite. Local attractions include Alton Towers, The Potteries, Weston Hall, Shrugborough Hall, and Cannock Chase Country Park. Clay pigeon shooting, fishing, archery and off road driving facilities are close by. Uttoxeter racecourse is within easy reach. **Directions:** From the M6, exit at junction 13 and take the A449 towards Stafford. At the first island turn right, signposted Acton Trussell. The Moat House is at the far end of the village. Price guide: Single £65–£120; double/twin £80–£130; suite £140–£160.

WENTWORTH HOTEL

WENTWORTH ROAD, ALDEBURGH, SUFFOLK IP15 5BD
TEL: 01728 452312 FAX: 01728 454343 E-MAIL: wentworth.hotel@anglianet.co.uk

The Wentworth Hotel is ideally situated opposite the beach at Aldeburgh on Suffolk's unspoilt coast. Aldeburgh has maritime traditions dating back to the 15th century which are still maintained today by the longshore fishermen who launch their boats from the shore. It has also become a centre for music lovers: every June the Aldeburgh International Festival of Music, founded by the late Benjamin Britten, is held at Snape Maltings. Privately owned by the Pritt family since 1920, the Wentworth has established a reputation for comfort and service, good food and wine, for which many guests return year after year. Relax in front of an open fire in one of the hotel lounges, or sample a pint of the famous local Adnam's ales in the bar, which also serves meals. Many of the 38 elegantly furnished en suite bedrooms have sea views. The restaurant offers an extensive menu for both lunch and dinner and there is a comprehensive wine list. The garden terrace is the perfect venue for a light lunch *alfresco*. Nearby, the Minsmere Bird Sanctuary will be of interest to nature enthusiasts, while for the keen golfer, two of Britain's most challenging courses are within easy reach of the hotel at Aldeburgh and Thorpeness. Closed from December 27 to early new year. **Directions:** Aldeburgh is on A1094 just 7 miles from the A12 between Ipswich and Lowestoft. Price guide: Single £61; double/twin £105.

THE ALDERLEY EDGE HOTEL

MACCLESFIELD ROAD, ALDERLEY EDGE, CHESHIRE SK9 7BJ
TEL: 01625 583033 FAX: 01625 586343 E-MAIL: sales@alderley–edge–hotel–co.uk

This privately owned award-winning hotel has 31 executive bedrooms, 11 superior rooms and 4 suites including the Presidential and Bridal Suites offering a high standard of decor. The restaurant is in the sumptuous conservatory with exceptional views and attention is given to the highest standards of cooking; fresh produce, including fish delivered daily, is provided by local suppliers. Specialities include hot and cold seafood dishes, puddings served piping hot from the oven and a daily selection of unusual and delicious breads, baked each morning in the hotel bakery. The wine list features 100 champagnes and 600 wines. Special wine and champagne dinners are held quarterly. In addition to the main conference room there is a suite of meeting and private dining rooms. The famous Edge walks are nearby, as are Tatton and Lyme Parks, Quarry Bank Mill and Dunham Massey. Manchester's thriving city centre is 15 miles away and the airport is a 20 minute drive. **Directions:** Follow M6 to M56 Stockport. Exit junction 6, take A538 to Wilmslow. Follow signs 1½ miles through to Alderley Edge. Turn left at the end of main shopping area on to Macclesfield Road (B5087) and the hotel is situated 200 yards on the right. From the M6 take junction 18 and follow signs for Holmes Chapel and Alderley Edge. Price guide: Single £108; double £132.50–£152.50; suites from £175.

WHITE LODGE COUNTRY HOUSE HOTEL

SLOE LANE, ALFRISTON, EAST SUSSEX BN26 5UR
TEL: 01323 870265 FAX: 01323 870284

The White Lodge, an elegant Edwardian country house, has a perfect and peaceful position, looking down on Alfriston, one of the prettiest villages in the Sussex Downs. It stands in five acres of well tended grounds, surrounded by the verdant rolling countryside. Skillful modernisation has taken place, yet its old-world charm remains and a stylish ambience has been created with bold décor, all appropriate to the age of the house. The bedrooms are handsome, some have balconies, most have magnificent views over the Downs. Graceful furniture, soft colours and attention to detail, anticipating the needs of seasoned travellers, ensures that guests will have a comfortable stay. The residents' lounges are relaxing, with delightful furnishings, tall windows and a tranquil atmosphere. Guests can mingle in the convivial bar or lounges before dining in splendour in the Orchid Restaurant. Local fish is among the specialities on the menu. An additional pleasure is the extensive wine list. Glyndebourne is 20 minutes away. The area abounds with famous golf courses, castles and gardens. The joys of Eastbourne are nearby and France is 2 hours away via the new Fast Ferry from Newhaven. **Directions:** Alfriston is on the B2108 between the A27/A259. The hotel is accessed from the Market Cross via West Street. Price guide: Single from £50; double/twin £100–£130; suite £146.

LOVELADY SHIELD COUNTRY HOUSE HOTEL

NENTHEAD ROAD, ALSTON, CUMBRIA CA9 3LF
TEL: 01434 381203 FAX: 01434 381515 E-MAIL: enquiries@lovelady.co.uk

Two-and-a-half miles from Alston, England's highest market town, Lovelady Shield, nestles in three acres of secluded riverside gardens. Bright log fires in the library and drawing room enhance the hotel's welcoming atmosphere. Owners Peter and Marie Haynes take great care to create a peaceful and tranquil haven where guests can relax and unwind. The five-course dinners created by master chef Barrie Garton, rounded off by home-made puddings and a selection of English farmhouse cheeses, have won the hotel 2 AA Rosettes for food. Many guests first discover Lovelady Shield en route to Scotland. They then return to explore this beautiful and unspoiled part of England and experience the comforts of the hotel. Golf, fishing, shooting, pony-trekking and riding can be arranged locally. The Pennine Way, Hadrian's Wall and the Lake District are within easy reach. Facilities for small conferences and boardroom meetings are available. Closed 3rd January to 4th February. Special Christmas, New Year, and short breaks are offered with special rates for 2 and 3 day stays. **Directions:** The hotel's driveway is by the junction of the B6294 and the A689, $2^1/_4$ miles east of Alston. Price guide (including 5-course dinner): Single £80–£106; double/twin £160–£215.

WOODLAND PARK HOTEL

WELLINGTON ROAD, TIMPERLEY, NR ALTRINCHAM, CHESHIRE WA15 7RG
TEL: 0161 928 8631 FAX: 0161 941 2821

Woodland Park is an attractive family owned hotel conveniently situated off the beaten track in a secluded residential area four miles from Manchester international airport. Owners Brian and Shirley Walker offer guests the highest standards of comfort, service and friendliness. Whatever your requirements nothing is too much trouble for them or for their professional staff. The hotel's 46 bedrooms are individually designed and furnished with every facility from colour television to direct line telephone to make a guest's stay as comfortable and restful as possible. All are en suite with the executive rooms having the added luxury of an aero spa bath in which to pamper yourself. Chef Jeff Spencer serves an inspired choice of dishes to satisfy the most discriminating palate in the Terrace Restaurant where diners have the choice of a Brasserie style menu or table d'hôte. Cocktails and after dinner drinks can be enjoyed in the beautifully furnished and decorated lounge or the elegant, traditional conservatory which adjoins the restaurant. The hotel has extensive facilities for business meetings, conferences and weddings. For the sports enthusiast there is an 18-hole municipal golf course close by. A comprehensive leisure centre and Sale Water Park are within easy reach. Parking for 150 cars. **Directions:** Leave M56 at junction 3 and take A560 towards Altrincham. Turn right onto Wellington Road. Price guide: Single £56–£90; double/twin £62–£135.

AMBERLEY CASTLE

AMBERLEY, NR ARUNDEL, WEST SUSSEX BN18 9ND
TEL: 01798 831992 FAX: 01798 831998

Winner of the Johansens 1995 Country Hotel Award, Amberley Castle is over 900 years old and is set between the rolling South Downs and the peaceful expanse of the Amberley Wildbrooks. Its towering battlements give breathtaking views while its massive, 14th-century curtain walls and mighty portcullis bear silent testimony to its fascinating history. Resident proprietors, Joy and Martin Cummings, have transformed this medieval fortress into a unique country castle hotel. They offer a warm, personal welcome and their hotel provides the ultimate in contemporary luxury, while retaining an atmosphere of timelessness. Five distinctive new suites are added this year in the Bishopric by the main gateway. Each room is individually designed and has its own Jacuzzi bath. The exquisite 12th-century Queen's Room Restaurant is the perfect setting for the creative cuisine of head chef Billy Butcher and his team. Amberley Castle is a natural first choice for romantic or cultural weekends, sporting breaks or confidential executive meetings. Roman ruins, antiques, stately homes, castle gardens, horse racing and history 'everywhere' you look, all within a short distance. It is easily accessible from London and the major air and channel ports. **Directions:** Amberley Castle is on the B2139, off the A29 between Fontwell and Bury. Price guide Double/twin £145–£300.

HOLBECK GHYLL COUNTRY HOUSE HOTEL

HOLBECK LANE, WINDERMERE, CUMBRIA LA23 1LU
TEL: 015394 32375 FAX: 015394 34743 E-MAIL: accommodation@holbeck-ghyll.co.uk

The saying goes that all the best sites for building a house in England were taken long before the days of the motor car. Holbeck Ghyll has one such prime position. It was built in the early days of the 19th century and is superbly located overlooking Lake Windermere and the Langdale Fells. Today this luxury hotel has an outstanding reputation and is managed personally and expertly by its proprietors, David and Patricia Nicholson. As well as being awarded the RAC Blue Ribbon and 3 AA Red Stars they are among an élite who have won an AA Courtesy and Care Award, Holbeck Ghyll was 1998 Cumbria Tourist Board Hotel of the Year. The majority of bedrooms are large and have spectacular and breathtaking views. All are recently refurbished to a very high standard and include decanters of sherry, fresh flowers, fluffy bathrobes and much more. There are six new suites in the lodge. The oak-panelled restaurant, awarded 3 AA Rosettes, is a delightful setting for memorable dining and the meals are classically prepared, with the focus on flavours and presentation, while an extensive wine list reflects quality and variety. The hotel has an all-weather tennis court and a health spa with gym, sauna and treatment facilities. **Directions:** From Windermere, pass Brockhole Visitors Centre, then after $^1/_2$ mile turn right into Holbeck Lane (signed Troutbeck). Hotel is $^1/_2$ mile on left. Price guide (inc. dinner): Single from £95; double/twin £150–£300; suite £200–£300.

THE LANGDALE HOTEL & COUNTRY CLUB

GREAT LANGDALE, NR AMBLESIDE, CUMBRIA LA22 9JD
TEL: 015394 37302 FAX: 015394 37694 E-MAIL: itsgreat@langdale.co.uk

The Langdale Valley is in the heart of the Lake District National Park, an especially beautiful part of England, surrounded by the dramatic terrain that inspired the poet Wordsworth. The hotel is part of an imaginative complex, that is partly timeshare. Local stone has been used when renovating cottages, winning awards for its sensitivity to the environment. The pleasant bedrooms are both in the hotel and in cottages on the estate. They are comfortable and nearly all the bathrooms are de luxe with whirlpool baths and other amenities. All today's anticipated extras are provided. Families are particularly welcome. Next to the hotel is the Country Club, with its many facilities. Formal meals are in the sophisticated Purdey's Restaurant, while informality is the keynote in the Terrace Restaurant and Cocktail Bar, with barbecues on the patio. Children have their own menu. A stroll to Chapel Stile takes guests to Wainwright's Inn, authentically furnished, serving real ale and pub food. There is an indoor pool, squash, tennis and a nature trail to observe wildlife. Additionally visitors enjoy climbing, fishing, boat trips and exploring the fascinating countryside. **Directions:** M6/Jct36, take A591 through Windermere. At Ambleside left onto A593, then B5343 at Skelwith Bridge, signposted Langdale. Price guide: Single £95–£125; double/twin £170–£210.

NANNY BROW COUNTRY HOUSE HOTEL & RESTAURANT

CLAPPERSGATE, AMBLESIDE, CUMBRIA LA22 9NF
TEL: 015394 32036 FAX: 015394 32450 E-MAIL: reservations@nannybrowhotel.demon.co.uk

Away from the tourists visiting Ambleside at the northern end of Lake Windermere, a Victorian architect built Nanny Brow for himself on this magnificent site on Loughrigg Fell, which overlooks the dramatic Langdale Pikes and River Brathay. Set in five acres of landscaped gardens, the house has been converted into a comfortable elegant hotel whilst retaining its country house charm and has been awarded many accolades such as Hotel of the Year 1998 – Lancashire & Lake District Life, AA Romantic Hotel of the Year and holds two AA Red Rosettes. New arrivals appreciate the welcoming atmosphere of the lounge hall, filled with local antiques and find the drawing room with its graceful furniture and log fires very restful. The pretty bedrooms, individually decorated, have been thoughtfully equipped with many extras. The romantic Garden Suites have balconies or patios outside the sitting rooms. Guests mingle in the inviting Library Bar, before dining by candlelight in the RAC Merit Awards RHCC restaurant. The ever-changing five course menu features the chef's inspired rendition of traditional English dishes, complemented by the many fine wines. Fishing, putting and spa facilities, with membership of a private leisure club and a sailing cruiser on Lake Windermere are offered. **Directions:** From Ambleside A593 Coniston Road for 1m. Nanny Brow is on the right. Price guide: Single £55–£90; double/twin £110–£180; suite £150–£180. (Special Breaks available)

ROTHAY MANOR

ROTHAY BRIDGE, AMBLESIDE, CUMBRIA LA22 0EH
TEL: 015394 33605 FAX: 015394 33607 E-MAIL: hotel@rothaymanor.co.uk

Situated half a mile from Lake Windermere, this Georgian listed building stands in 1½ acres of grounds. The bedrooms include three beautifully furnished suites, two of which are in the lodge beside the manor and afford an unusual measure of space and privacy. One suite is equipped for five people and designed with particular attention to the comfort of guests with disabilities: it has a ramp leading to the garden and a spacious shower. Care and consideration are evident throughout. The menu is varied and meals are prepared with flair and imagination to high standards, complemented by an interesting wine list. For health and fitness residents have free use of the nearby Low Wood Leisure Club, with swimming pool, sauna, steam room, Jacuzzi, squash, sunbeds and a health and beauty salon. Permits are available for fishing, while locally guests can play golf, arrange to go riding, take a trip on a steam railway or visit Wordsworth's cottage. Small functions can be catered for with ease. Closed 3 January to 4 February. Represented in the USA by Josephine Barr: 800 323 5463. Each winter a full programme of special breaks with reduced rates is offered, as well as music, antiques, walking and painting holidays. **Directions:** ¾ mile from Ambleside on A593, the road to Coniston. Price guide: Single £79; double/twin £122–£137; suite £173.

ESSEBORNE MANOR

HURSTBOURNE TARRANT, ANDOVER, HAMPSHIRE SP11 0ER
TEL: 01264 736444 FAX: 01264 736725 E-MAIL: esseborne–manor@compuserve.com

Esseborne Manor is small and unpretentious, yet stylish. The present house was built at the end of the 19th century and carries the name used to record details of the local village in the *Domesday Book*. It is set in a pleasing garden amid the rich farmland of the North Wessex Downs in a designated area of outstanding natural beauty. Ian and Lucilla Hamilton, who manage the house, have established the restful atmosphere of a private country home where guests can unwind and relax. There are just 15 comfortable bedrooms, some reached via a courtyard. Two doubles and a delightful suite are in converted cottages with their own patio overlooking the main gardens. The pretty sitting room and cosy library are comfortable areas in which to relax. Ben Tunnicliffes' fine 2 Rosette cooking is set off to advantage in the new dining room and adjoining bar. There is now a spacious meeting and function facility. In the grounds there is a herb garden, an all-weather tennis court, a croquet lawn and plenty of good walking beyond. Nearby Newbury racecourse has a busy programme of steeple-chasing and flat racing. Places to visit include Highclere Castle, Stonehenge, Salisbury, Winchester and Oxford. **Directions:** Midway between Newbury and Andover on the A343, 1 1/2 miles north of Hurstbourne Tarrant. Price guide: Single £88–£130; double/twin £95–£160.

          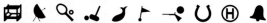

FIFEHEAD MANOR

MIDDLE WALLOP, STOCKBRIDGE. HAMPSHIRE SO20 8EG
TEL: 01264 781565 FAX: 01264 781400

The foundations of this lovely Manor House date from the 11th century when it was owned by the wife of the Saxon Earl of Godwin whose son, King Harold, was killed at the Battle of Hastings. Today, Fifehead Manor offers all the comfort of a country house hotel but, with its barns and stables surrounded by acres of gardens, the historic atmosphere lingers. The beamed dining room with its lead-paned windows and huge open fireplace has a unique atmosphere illuminated by the light of flickering candles and a warmth generated by centuries of hospitality. Substantial changes have brought about vast improvements to this fine hotel. The award-winning cuisine is outstanding and the restaurant is featured in major guides throughout Europe. All 17 en suite bedrooms are individually furnished and have every amenity, 9 are located in the garden wing. Fifehead Manor is ideally situated for visiting Salisbury, Winchester, Stonehenge, Romsey Abbey, Broadlands and Wilton House. Golf, fishing, riding and motor racing at Thruxton are nearby. **Directions:** From M3, exit at junction 8 onto A303 to Andover. Then take A343 south for 6 miles to Middle Wallop. Price guide: Single £75–£90; double/twin £120–£140.

APPLEBY MANOR COUNTRY HOUSE HOTEL

ROMAN ROAD, APPLEBY-IN-WESTMORLAND, CUMBRIA CA16 6JB
TEL: 017683 51571 FAX: 017683 52888 E-MAIL: reception@applebymanor.co.uk

Surrounded by half a million acres of some of the most beautiful landscapes in England, sheltered by the mountains and fells of the Lake District, by the North Pennine Hills and Yorkshire Dales, in an area aptly known as Eden stands Appleby Manor, a friendly and relaxing hotel owned and run by the Swinscoe family. The high quality, spotlessly clean, bedrooms induce peaceful, undisturbed sleep. (Dogs are welcome in The Coach House accommodation). The public areas are also restfully comfortable – the inviting lounges nicely warmed by log fires on cooler days, the cocktail bar and sunny conservatory luring guests with a choice of more than 70 malt whiskies and the restaurant offering an imaginative selection of tasty dishes and fine wines. The hotel pool, sauna, steam room, Jacuzzi, solarium and games room keep indoor athletes happy. Locally there are outdoor sports: fishing, golf, riding, squash and for the more venturesome, rambling on the fells. Appleby is an ideal base from which to visit the Lake District and an attractive stopover on journeys north-south. **Directions:** From the South take junction 38 of the M6 and then the B6260 to Appleby (13 miles). Drive through the town to a T-junction, turn left, first right and follow road for two-thirds of a mile. Price guide: Single £72–£88; double/twin £104–£144.

TUFTON ARMS HOTEL

MARKET SQUARE, APPLEBY-IN-WESTMORLAND, CUMBRIA CA16 6XA
TEL: 017683 51593 FAX: 017683 52761

This distinguished Victorian coaching inn, owned and run by the Milsom family, has been refurbished to provide a high standard of comfort. The bedrooms evoke the style of the 19th century, when the Tufton Arms became one of the premier hotels in Victorian England. The kitchen is run under the auspices of David Milsom, who spoils guests for choice with a gourmet dinner menu as well as a grill menu. The AA Rosette and RAC Merit awarded restaurant is renowned for its fish dishes. Complementing the cuisine is an extensive wine list. There are conference and meeting rooms including the air conditioned Hothfield Suite which can accommodate up to 100 people. RAC award for hospitality. Appleby, the historic county town of Westmorland, stands in splendid countryside and is ideal for touring the Lakes, Yorkshire Dales and Pennines. It is also a convenient stop-over en route to Scotland. Superb fishing for wild brown trout on a 24-mile stretch of the main River Eden, salmon fishing can be arranged on the lower reaches of the river. Shooting parties for grouse, duck and pheasant are a speciality. Appleby has an 18-hole moorland golf course. **Directions:** In centre of Appleby (bypassed by the A66), 38 miles west of Scotch Corner, 13 miles east of Penrith (M6 junction 40), 12 miles from M6 junction 38. Price guide: Single £60–£95; double/twin £90–£130; suite £145.

BAILIFFSCOURT

CLIMPING, WEST SUSSEX BN17 5RW
TEL: 01903 723511 FAX: 01903 723107 E-MAIL: bailiffscourt@hshotels.co.uk

Bailiffscourt is a perfectly preserved "medieval" house, built in the 1930s using authentic material salvaged from historic old buildings. Gnarled 15th century beams and gothic mullioned windows combine to recreate a home from the Middle Ages. Set in 30 acres of beautiful pastures and walled gardens, it provides guests with a wonderful sanctuary in which to relax or work. The bedrooms are all individually decorated and luxuriously furnished, with many offering four poster beds, open log fires and beautiful views over the surrounding countryside. The restaurant offers a varied menu and summer lunches can be taken alfresco in a rose-clad courtyard or the walled garden. A good list of well-priced wines accompanies meals. Private dining rooms are available for weddings, conferences and meetings and companies can hire the hotel as their 'country house' for 2 or 3 days. Bailiffscourt, which is AA two Rosettes and AA Courtesy & Care Award 1997 accredited, is surrounded by tranquil parkland with a golf practice area, heated outdoor pool and tennis courts. Climping Beach, 100 yards away, is ideal for windsurfing. Nearby are Arundel with its castle, Chichester and Goodwood. **Directions:** Three miles south of Arundel, off the A259. Price guide: Single from £125; double from £140.

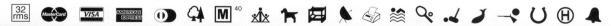

THE ROYAL BERKSHIRE

LONDON ROAD, SUNNINGHILL, ASCOT, BERKSHIRE SL5 0PP
TEL: 01344 623322 FAX: 01344 627100/01344 874240

For over 100 years The Royal Berkshire was the home of the Churchill family. Now it is an elegant hotel, ideally located between Ascot racecourse and the Guards Polo Club. This Queen Anne mansion, built in 1705 by the Duke of Marlborough for his daughter, is set in 15 acres of gardens and woodlands. The wide range of leisure facilities include a croquet lawn, putting green, 2 tennis courts, indoor heated pool, squash court, Jacuzzi and sauna. The spacious interiors are smartly decorated in keeping with the country house retreat. Afternoon tea or drinks can be enjoyed in the drawing rooms or on the terrace with views across the lawns. The Stateroom restaurant has been recognised and awarded two Red Rosettes. All dishes from the wonderful menu are carefully prepared with meticulous attention to presentation. A series of well-equipped function rooms, combined with easy accessibility from Heathrow and central London, makes The Royal Berkshire a popular venue for business events. For golfers, Sunningdale and Wentworth are all nearby. Royal Windsor and Eton are a short drive away. **Directions:** One mile from Ascot on the corner of A329 and B383. Nearest M25 exit is junction 13. Price guide: Midweek – Single £171; double/twin £196. Weekend – Single from £95; double/twin £160.

CALLOW HALL

MAPPLETON ROAD, ASHBOURNE, DERBYSHIRE DE6 2AA
TEL: 01335 343403 FAX: 01335 343624

The approach to Callow Hall is up a tree-lined drive through the 44-acre grounds. On arrival visitors can take in the splendid views from the hotel's elevated position, overlooking the valleys of Bentley Brook and the River Dove. The majestic building and Victorian gardens have been restored by resident proprietors, David, Dorothy and their son, Anthony Spencer, who represent the fifth and sixth generations of hoteliers in the Spencer family. The famous local Ashbourne mineral water and home-made biscuits greet guests in the spacious period bedrooms. Fresh local produce is selected daily for use in the kitchen, where the term 'home-made' comes into its own. Home-cured bacon, sausages, fresh bread, traditional English puddings and melt-in-the-mouth pastries are among the items prepared on the premises. Visiting anglers can enjoy a rare opportunity to fish for trout and grayling along a mile-long private stretch of the Bentley Brook, which is mentioned in Izaak Walton's *The Compleat Angler*. Callow Hall is ideally located for some of England's finest stately homes. Closed at Christmas. **Directions:** Take the A515 through Ashbourne towards Buxton. At the Bowling Green Inn on the brow of a steep hill, turn left, then take the first right, signposted Mappleton and the hotel is over the bridge on the right. Price guide: Single £73–£97.50; double/twin £110–£136.50; suite £170.

THE IZAAK WALTON HOTEL

DOVEDALE, NEAR ASHBOURNE, DERBYSHIRE DE6 2AY
TEL: 01335 350555 FAX: 01335 350539

This 17th century farmhouse hotel, named after the renowned author of 'The Compleat Angler', enjoys glorious views of the surrounding Derbyshire Peaks. The River Dove runs in the valley below. The Izaak Walton is ideal for guests wishing to indulge in a warm welcome and a relaxing ambience. The 30 en suite bedrooms are diverse in their designs; some have four-poster beds whilst others are located in the old farmhouse building and still retain their old oak beams and décor. All the bedrooms are beautifully furnished and offer television, radio, hairdryer, direct dial telephone and several other amenities. Paintings from the Duke of Rutland's Family collection adorn the walls of the lounges and bygones from his homes add their character to the comfortable rooms. The Haddon Restaurant has a diverse menu of creative yet traditional cuisine. Informal meals and light snacks may be enjoyed in the Farmhouse Kitchen, situated in the original farmhouse itself. Leisure pursuits include rambling, fishing, mountain biking, hand-gliding and pony-trekking. There are several attractions nearby including The Peak District, Alton Towers, the Staffordshire Potteries and fine properties such as Haddon Hall and Chatsworth. **Directions:** Dovedale is 2 miles northwest of Ashbourne between the A515 and the A52. Price guide: Single £81; double/twin £105–135.

HOLNE CHASE HOTEL AND RESTAURANT

NR ASHBURTON, DEVON TQ13 7NS
TEL: 01364 631471 FAX: 01364 631453 E-MAIL: info@holne.chase.co.uk

With sweeping lawns and an outstanding position in over 70 acres of park and woodland inside Dartmoor National Park, Holne Chase is dedicated to relaxation. Its previous role as a 11th century hunting lodge has become the hotel's theme for attracting visitors to traditional pursuits in a break from the bustle of everyday life. Fly-fishermen can enjoy the hotel's mile-long beat on the River Dart and driven shoots can be arranged in season. The hotel's stables have been converted to provide "Sporting Lodges" with sitting room and fire downstairs and bedroom suite upstairs. All the hotel's en suite bedrooms are individually furnished and many command spectacular views over the Dart Valley. A walled garden supplies the inviting restaurant, where a talented young brigade provides imaginative cuisine. Holne Chase is a good base for exploring Dartmoor's open moorland and wooded valleys. Picturesque villages and sandy beaches are within reach. Special interest breaks – gardens, painting and cookery. Canoeing, golf and riding can all be arranged. Good Hotel Guide César Award Winner 1999, AA 3 Star, 3 Rosettes. **Directions:** Take the Ashburton turning off the A38 and follow the signs for Two Bridges. Holne Chase is on the right after the road crosses the River Dart. Price guide: Single £85–£100; double/twin £120–£140; suite £160.

EASTWELL MANOR

BOUGHTON LEES, ASHFORD, KENT TN25 4HR
TEL: 01233 213000 FAX: 01233 635530 E-MAIL: eastwell@btinternet.com

Set in the 'Garden of England', Eastwell Manor has a past steeped in fine tradition and history which dates back to the 16th century when Richard Plantagenet, son of Richard III lived on the estate. The Manor is surrounded by impressive grounds encompassing a formal Italian garden, deliciously scented rose gardens and attractive lawns and parkland. The magnificence of the exterior is matched with the splendour of the interior. The public rooms are enhanced by exquisite plasterwork and carved oak panelling whilst throughout the Manor interesting antique pieces abound. The bedrooms and suites, some of which afford fine views across the gardens, have been individually furnished and feature every possible comfort. The recent development of 19 courtyard apartments has resulted in a further 39 bedrooms, all with en suite facilities. Guests recline on the leather sofas and enjoy the cosy ambience of the bar before indulging in the modern British cuisine served in the handsome dining room. Fitness facilities include the new outdoor heated pool and spa. Nearby attractions include the cathedral city of Canterbury, Leeds Castle and several charming market towns. Situated near to Ashford Eurostar station, Eastwell is a perfect departure point for trips to Paris and Brussels. **Directions:** M20 Jct 9. A28 towards Canterbury, then A251 signed Faversham. Hotel is 3 miles north of Ashford in Boughton Lees. Price guide: Single £150–£200; double/twin £180–£230; suites £250–£340.

RIVERSIDE HOUSE

ASHFORD-IN-THE-WATER, NR BAKEWELL, DERBYSHIRE DE45 1QF
TEL: 01629 814275 FAX: 01629 812873 E-MAIL: riversidehouse@enta.net

Nestling in one of the Peak District's most picturesque villages, the Riverside House is an intimate country hotel in the finest traditions of classic hospitality. The small ivy-clad Georgian mansion sits in secluded grounds with the tranquil river Wye flowing past landscaped gardens and lawns. The individually designed bedrooms with rich fabrics and antique pieces and the elegant yet cosy public rooms combine with a warmth of welcome and a sense of informality to create an atmosphere of complete relaxation. The 2 AA Rosetted restaurant, with its distinctive fusion of modern English, international and local cuisine, is enhanced by the use of fresh and seasonal ingredients. Conveniently situated for some of the national park's leading attractions such as Chatsworth and Haddon Hall, the hotel is also an ideal touring base for those wishing to explore the Derbyshire Dales, Lathkill and Dovedale. **Directions:** 1¹/₂ miles north of Bakewell on the A6 heading towards Buxton. Ashford-in-the-Water lies on the right side of the river. The hotel is at the end of the village main street next to the Sheepwash Bridge. Price guide: Single £85–£120; double/twin £115–£150.

HARTWELL HOUSE

OXFORD ROAD, NR AYLESBURY, BUCKINGHAMSHIRE HP17 8NL
TEL: 01296 747444 FAX: 01296 747450 FROM USA FAX FREE: 1 800 260 8338 E-MAIL: info@hartwell–house.com

Standing in 90 acres of gardens and parkland landscaped by a contemporary of 'Capability' Brown, Hartwell House has both Jacobean and Georgian façades. This beautiful house, brilliantly restored by Historic House Hotels, was the residence in exile of King Louis XVIII of France from 1809 to 1814. The large ground floor reception rooms, with oak panelling and decorated ceilings, have antique furniture and fine paintings which evoke the elegance of the 18th century. There are 46 individually designed bedrooms and suites, some in the house and some in Hartwell Court, the restored 18th-century stables. The dining room at Hartwell is the setting for excellent food awarded three Rosettes by the AA. (Gentlemen are requested to wear a jacket and tie for dinner). The Hartwell Spa adjacent to the hotel includes an indoor swimming pool, whirlpool spa bath, steam room, saunas, gymnasium and beauty salons. Situated in the Vale of Aylesbury, the hotel, which is a member of Relais & Chateaux, is only an hour from London and 20 miles from Oxford. Blenheim Palace, Waddesdon Manor and Woburn Abbey are nearby. Dogs are permitted only in the Hartwell Court bedrooms. **Directions:** On the A418 Oxford Road, 2 miles from Aylesbury. Price guide: Single £130–£165; double/twin £205–£345; suites £305–£600.

THE PRIORY HOTEL

HIGH STREET, WHITCHURCH, AYLESBURY, BUCKINGHAMSHIRE HP22 4JS
TEL: 01296 641239 FAX: 01296 641793

The Priory Hotel is a beautifully preserved, timber-framed house dating back to 1360. It is set in the picturesque conservation village of Whitchurch, which is about 5 miles north of Aylesbury. With its exposed timbers, leaded windows and open fires, it retains all its traditional character and charm – a refreshing alternative to the all-too-familiar chain hotels of today. All ten bedrooms are individually furnished and many of them have four-poster beds. At the heart of the hotel is La Boiserie Restaurant, where classical French cuisine is served in intimate surroundings. An imaginative à la carte fixed-price menu is offered, including a range of seasonal dishes. Start, for example, with a rich terrine of partridge, wild mushrooms and pistachios, then perhaps choose marinated saddle of venison in Cognac butter sauce and garnished with truffles. Specialities include fresh lobster and flambé dishes. The self-contained conference suite can be used for private lunches, dinners and receptions. Among the places to visit locally are Waddesdon Manor, Claydon House, Stowe, Silverstone motor circuit and Oxford. Closed between Christmas and New Year's Eve; the restaurant, not the hotel, also closes on Sunday evenings. **Directions:** Situated on the A413 4 miles north of Aylesbury. Price guide: Single £70–£85; double £110–£120; suite from £115.

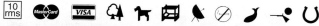

PENNYHILL PARK HOTEL AND COUNTRY CLUB

LONDON ROAD, BAGSHOT, SURREY GU19 5EU
TEL: 01276 471774 FAX: 01276 473217 E-MAIL: pennyhillpark@msn.com

Bagshot has been a centre of hospitality since the early Stuart sovereigns James I and Charles I had a hunting lodge there. Pennyhill Park Hotel continues to uphold that tradition. Built in 1849, this elegant mansion reflects its journey through Victorian and Edwardian times while providing every modern amenity. The bedrooms are outstanding: no two are identical, and infinite care has been invested in creating practical rooms with distinctive features. Impeccable service is to be expected, as staff are trained to classical, Edwardian standards. Haute cuisine and a listing of fine wines is offered in the wonderful oak panelled Latymer Room or less formal eating is available in the sparkling new Italian themed St James Restaurant. Recreational facilities are available within the grounds, which span 120 acres and include landscaped gardens, a 9-hole golf course, a swimming pool, a three acre lake, gym, rugby/football pitch, archery, jogging and walking path. Pennyhill Park is conveniently located only 27 miles from central London and not far from Heathrow, Windsor Castle, Ascot, Wentworth and Sunningdale. **Directions:** From the M3, exit 3, take A322 towards Bracknell. Turn left on to A30 signposted to Camberley. ³/₄ mile after Bagshot; turn right 50 yards past the Texaco garage. Price guide: Single from £150; double/twin £165–£275; suite from £300–£395.

HASSOP HALL

HASSOP, NR BAKEWELL, DERBYSHIRE DE45 1NS
TEL: 01629 640488 FAX: 01629 640577 E-MAIL: Hassophallhotel@BTInternet.com

The recorded history of Hassop Hall reaches back 900 years to the *Domesday Book*, to a time when the political scene in England was still dominated by the power struggle between the barons and the King, when the only sure access to that power was through possession of land. By 1643, when the Civil War was raging, the Hall was under the ownership of Rowland Eyre, who turned it into a Royalist garrison. It was the scene of several skirmishes before it was recaptured after the Parliamentary victory. Since purchasing Hassop Hall in 1975, Thomas Chapman has determinedly pursued the preservation of its outstanding heritage. Guests can enjoy the beautifully maintained gardens as well as the splendid countryside of the surrounding area. The bedrooms, some of which are particularly spacious, are well furnished and comfortable. A four-poster bedroom is available for romantic occasions. A comprehensive dinner menu offers a wide and varied selection of dishes, with catering for most tastes. As well as the glories of the Peak District, places to visit include Chatsworth House, Haddon Hall and Buxton Opera House. Christmas opening – details on application. **Directions:** From M1 exit 29 (Chesterfield), take A619 to Baslow, then A623 to Calver; left at lights to B6001. Hassop Hall is 2 miles on right. Price guide: (excluding breakfast) Single from £79; Double/twin £79–£139. Inclusive rates available on request.

WROXTON HOUSE HOTEL

WROXTON ST MARY, NR BANBURY, OXFORDSHIRE OX15 6QB
TEL: 01295 730777 FAX: 01295 730800 E-MAIL: wroxtonhse@aol.com

Built of honeyed local stone, Wroxton House has undergone a sensitive restoration linking three village houses, dating from the 17th century, with a delightful clock tower wing and conservatory lounge. The relaxing character of the hotel is created by the carefully selected staff, who combine attentive service with friendliness and informality. The spacious and bright lounges contain thoughtfully chosen furnishings, comfortable armchairs and a profusion of flowers and plants. The 32 en suite bedrooms have been individually decorated and the original timbers preserved in many of the older rooms. The classic English styles complement the deeply polished woods of the furniture.

Guests may dine by candlelight in the intimate restaurant, where a traditional Cotswold atmosphere is evoked by original beams, inglenooks, carved oak recesses, horse brasses and pewter. The expertly prepared menus display a personal interpretation of classic British dishes which make imaginative use of the freshest local produce. Wroxton House Hotel is a popular choice with businessmen, as it offers good meeting facilities in a quiet setting. Golf and riding can be arranged locally. **Directions:** Easily reached via M40, Wroxton is two miles outside Banbury on the A422 Stratford-upon-Avon road. Price guide: Single £98.95; double/twin £118.90.

TYLNEY HALL

ROTHERWICK, HOOK, HAMPSHIRE RG27 9AZ
TEL: 01256 764881 FAX: 01256 768141 E-MAIL: reservations@tylneyhall.com

Arriving at this hotel in the evening with its floodlit exterior and forecourt fountain, you can imagine that you are arriving for a party in a private stately home. Grade II listed and set in 66 acres of ornamental gardens and parkland, Tylney Hall typifies the great houses of the past. Apéritifs are taken in the wood-panelled library bar; haute cuisine is served in the glass-domed Oak Room restaurant, complemented by conscientious service. The hotel holds 2 AA Rosettes for food and also AA 4 Red Stars. Extensive leisure facilities include indoor and outdoor heated swimming pools, multi-gym, sauna, tennis, croquet and snooker, while hot-air ballooning, archery, clay pigeon shooting, golf and riding can be arranged. Surrounding the hotel are wooded trails ideal for rambling or jogging. Functions for up to 100 people are catered for in the Tylney Suite or Chestnut Suite, while more intimate gatherings are held in one of the other ten private banqueting rooms. Tylney Hall is licensed to hold wedding ceremonies on site. The cathedral city of Winchester and Stratfield Saye House are nearby. Legoland and Windsor Castle are only 40 minutes drive away. **Directions:** M4, junction 11, towards Hook and Rotherwick – follow signs to hotel. M3, junction 5, 3rd exit, A287 towards Newnham – over A30 into Old School Road. Left for Newnham and right onto Ridge Lane. Hotel is on the left after one mile. Price guide: Single £120–£299; double/twin £152–£330; suite £230–£330.

CAVENDISH HOTEL

BASLOW, DERBYSHIRE DE45 1SP
TEL: 01246 582311 FAX: 01246 582312 E-MAIL: info@cavendish–hotel.net

This enchanting hotel offers travellers an opportunity to stay on the famous Chatsworth Estate, close to one of England's greatest stately houses, the home of the Duke and Duchess of Devonshire. The hotel has a long history of its own – once known as the Peacock Inn on the turnpike road to Buxton Spa. When it became The Cavendish in 1975, the Duchess personally supervised the transformation, providing some of the furnishings from Chatsworth and her design talents are evident throughout. Guests have a warm welcome before they are conducted to the luxurious bedrooms, all of which overlook the Estate. Harmonious colours, gorgeous fabrics and immense comfort prevail. Every imaginable extra is provided, from library books to bathrobes. Breakfast is served until lunchtime – no rising at cockcrow – and informal meals are served from morning until bed-time in The Garden Room. Sit at the kitchen table and watch super food being prepared as you dine. At dusk you can sample cocktails and fine wines in the bar before dining in the handsome restaurant with its imaginative menu and list of over 100 carefully selected wines. Climbing The Peak, exploring The Dales, fishing, golf and Sheffield's Crucible Theatre are among the many leisure pursuits nearby. **Directions:** M1/J29, A617 to Chesterfield then A619 west to Baslow. Price guide (excluding breakfast): Single £95; double/twin £125.

FISCHER'S

BASLOW HALL, CALVER ROAD, BASLOW, DERBYSHIRE DE45 1RR
TEL: 01246 583259 FAX: 01246 583818

Situated on the edge of the magnificent Chatsworth Estate, Baslow Hall enjoys an enviable location surrounded by some of the country's finest stately homes and within easy reach of the Peak District's many cultural and historical attractions. Standing at the end of a winding chestnut tree-lined driveway, this fine Derbyshire manor house was tastefully converted by Max and Susan Fischer into an award winning country house hotel in 1989. Since opening, Fischer's has consistently maintained its position as one of the finest establishments in the Derbyshire/South Yorkshire regions earning the prestigious Egon Ronay 'Restaurant of the Year' award in 1995. Whether you are staying in the area for private or business reasons, it is a welcome change to find a place that feels less like a hotel and more like a home, combining comfort and character with an eating experience which is a delight to the palate. Max presides in the kitchen. His Michelin starred cuisine can be savoured either in the more formal main dining room or in 'Café Max' – where the emphasis is on more informal eating and modern tastes. Baslow Hall offers facilities for small conferences or private functions. **Directions:** Baslow is within 12 miles of the M1 motorway, Chesterfield and Sheffield. Fischer's is on the A623 in Baslow. Price guide: Single £80–£95; double/twin £95–£130; suite £130.

THE BATH PRIORY HOTEL AND RESTAURANT

WESTON ROAD, BATH, SOMERSET BA1 2XT
TEL: 01225 331922 FAX: 01225 448276 E-MAIL: 106076.1265@compuserve.com

Lying in the seclusion of landscaped grounds, The Bath Priory Hotel is close to some of England's most famous and finest architecture. Within walking distance of Bath city centre, this Gothic-style mellow stone building dates from 1835, when it formed part of a row of fashionable residences on the west side of the city. Visitors will sense the luxury as they enter the hotel: antique furniture, plush rugs and *objets d'art* add interest to the two spacious reception rooms and the elegant drawing room. Well-defined colour schemes lend an uplifting brightness throughout, particularly in the tastefully appointed bedrooms. Michelin – starred Head Chef, Robert Clayton's classical style is the primary inspiration for the cuisine,

served in three interconnecting dining rooms which overlook the garden. An especially good selection of wines can be recommended to accompany meals. Private functions can be accommodated both in the Drawing Room and the Orangery, with garden access an added bonus. The Roman Baths, Theatre Royal, Museum of Costume and a host of bijou shops offer plenty for visitors to see.
Directions: Leave M4 at junction 18 to Bath on A46. Enter city on A4 London road and follow signs for Bristol. Turn right into Park Lane which runs through Royal Victoria Park. Then turn left into Weston Road. The hotel is on the left. Price guide: Double/twin from £210 including full English breakfast.

COMBE GROVE MANOR HOTEL & COUNTRY CLUB

BRASSKNOCKER HILL, MONKTON COMBE, BATH, SOMERSET BA2 7HS
TEL: 01225 834644 FAX: 01225 834961

This is an exclusive 18th-century country house hotel situated two miles from the beautiful city of Bath. Built on the hillside site of a Roman settlement, Combe Grove Manor is set in 82 acres of private gardens and woodland, with magnificent views over the Limpley Stoke Valley. In addition to the Georgian Restaurant, which boasts an exciting varied menu, there is a private dining room, plus a bar and bistro restaurant with a terrace garden. After dinner guests may relax with drinks in the elegant drawing room or library. The bedrooms are lavishly furnished, all individually designed with en suite facilities, three of which have Jacuzzi baths. Within the grounds are some of the finest leisure facilities in the South West, including indoor and outdoor heated pools, hydrospa beds and steam room, four all-weather tennis courts, a 5-hole par 3 golf course and a two-tiered driving range. Guests may use the Nautilus gym, aerobics studio, saunas and solaria or relax in the Clarins beauty rooms where a full range of treatments are offered. Separate from the Manor House is the Garden Lodge which provides 31 rooms, with spectacular views and some have a private terrace. 2 Rosettes. **Directions:** Set south-east of Bath off the A36 near the University. Map can be supplied on request. Price guide: Single from £110; double/twin from £120; suite from £200.

HOMEWOOD PARK

HINTON CHARTERHOUSE, BATH, SOMERSET BA3 6BB
TEL: 01225 723731 FAX: 01225 723820 E-MAIL: res@homewoodpark.com

Standing amid 10 acres of beautiful grounds and woodland on the edge of Limpley Stoke Valley, a designated area of natural beauty is Homewood Park, one of Britain's finest privately-owned smaller country house hotels. This lovely 19th century building has an elegant interior, adorned with beautiful fabrics, antiques, oriental rugs and original oil paintings. Lavishly furnished bedrooms offer the best in comfort, style and privacy. Each of them has a charm and character of its own and all have good views over the Victorian garden. The outstanding cuisine overseen by chef Andrew Hamer has won the hotel an excellent reputation. The à la carte menu uses wherever possible produce both from local suppliers and from Homewood itself. A range of carefully selected wines, stored in the hotel's original medieval cellars, lies patiently waiting to augment lunch and dinner. Before or after a meal guests can enjoy a drink in the comfortable bar or drawing rooms, both of which have a log fire during the cooler months. The hotel is well placed for guests to enjoy the varied attractions of the wonderful city of Bath with its unique hot springs, Roman remains, superb Georgian architecture and American Museum. Further afield but within reach are Stonehenge and Cheddar caves. **Directions:** On the A36 six miles from Bath towards Warminster. Price guide: Single £109–£112; double/twin £139–£177; semi-suite £209; suite £249.

HUNSTRETE HOUSE

HUNSTRETE, PENSFORD, NR BRISTOL, SOMERSET BS39 4NS
TEL: 01761 490490 FAX: 01761 490732 E-MAIL: reservations@hunstretehouse.co.uk

In a classical English landscape on the edge of the Mendip Hills stands Hunstrete House. This unique hotel, surrounded by lovely gardens, is largely 18th century, although the history of the estate goes back to 963AD. Each of the bedrooms is individually decorated and furnished to a high standard, combining the benefits of a hotel room with the atmosphere of a charming private country house. Many offer uninterrupted views over undulating fields and woodlands. The reception areas exhibit warmth and elegance and are liberally furnished with beautiful antiques. Log fires burn in the hall, library and drawing room through the winter and on cooler summer evenings. The Terrace dining room looks out on to an Italianate, flower filled courtyard. A highly skilled head chef offers light, elegant dishes using produce from the extensive garden, along with the best of English meat and fish. The menu changes regularly and the hotel has an excellent reputation for the quality and interest of its wine list. In a sheltered corner of the walled garden there is a heated swimming pool for guests to enjoy. For the energetic, the all weather tennis court provides another diversion and there are riding stables in Hunstrete village, a five minute walk away. **Directions:** From Bath take the A4 towards Bristol and then the A368 to Wells. Price guide: Single from £126; double/twin from £136; suite from £265.

LUCKNAM PARK

COLERNE, NR BATH, WILTSHIRE SN14 8AZ
TEL: 01225 742777 FAX: 01225 743536 E-MAIL: reservations@lucknampark.co.uk

For over 250 years Lucknam Park has been a focus of fine society and aristocratic living, something guests will sense immediately upon their approach along the mile-long avenue lined with beech trees. Built in 1720, this magnificent Palladian mansion is situated just six miles from Bath on the southern edge of the Cotswolds. The delicate aura of historical context is reflected in fine art and antiques dating from the late Georgian and early Victorian periods. Award winning food can be savoured in the elegant restaurant, at tables laid with exquisite porcelain, silver and glassware, accompanied with wines from an extensive cellar. Set within the walled gardens of the hotel is the Leisure Spa, comprising an indoor pool, sauna, solarium, steam room, whirlpool spa, gymnasium, beauty salon and snooker room. Numerous activities can be arranged on request, including hot-air ballooning, golf and archery. The Lucknam Park Equestrian Centre, which is situated on the estate, welcomes complete beginners and experienced riders and takes liveries. Bowood House, Corsham Court and Castle Combe are all nearby. **Directions:** Fifteen minutes from M4, junctions 17 and 18, located between A420 and A4 near the village of Colerne. Price guide (room only): Single from £140; double/twin from £230; suite from £390.

THE QUEENSBERRY

RUSSEL STREET, BATH, SOMERSET BA1 2QF
TEL: 01225 447928 FAX: 01225 446065 E-MAIL: queensberry@dial.pipex.com

When the Marquis of Queensberry commissioned John Wood to build this house in Russel Street in 1772, little did he know that 200 years hence guests would still be being entertained in these elegant surroundings. An intimate town house hotel, The Queensberry is in a quiet residential street just a few minutes' walk from Wood's other splendours – the Royal Crescent, Circus and Assembly Rooms. Bath is one of England's most beautiful cities. Regency stucco ceilings, ornate cornices and panelling combined with enchanting interior décor complement the strong architectural style. However, the standards of hotel-keeping have far outpaced the traditional surroundings, with high quality en suite bedrooms, room service and up-to-date office support for executives. The Olive Tree Restaurant is one of the leading restaurants in the Bath area. Proprietors Stephen and Penny Ross are thoroughly versed in offering hospitality and a warm welcome. Represented in America by Josephine Barr. The hotel is closed for one week at Christmas. **Directions:** From junction 18 of M4, enter Bath along A4 London Road. Turn sharp right up Lansdown Road, left into Bennett Street, then right into Russel Street opposite the Assembly Rooms. Price guide: Single £90–£140; double/twin £120–£210.

THE ROYAL CRESCENT HOTEL

ROYAL CRESCENT, BATH, SOMERSET BA1 2LS
TEL: 01225 823333 FAX: 01225 339401 E-MAIL: reservations@royalcrescent.co.uk

The Royal Crescent Hotel is a Grade I listed building of the greatest historical and architectural importance, situated in the centre of one of Europe's finest masterpieces. A sweep of 30 houses with identical façades stretch in a 500ft curve, built in 1765. The Royal Crescent Hotel was completely refurbished in 1997 and the work undertaken has restored many of the classical Georgian features with all the additional modern comforts. Each of the 45 bedrooms is equipped with air conditioning, the Cliveden bed, video/compact disc player and personal facsimile machine. The hotel has two restaurants, the Brasserie & Bar offers a relaxed and informal dining atmosphere. Pimpernel's offers a menu of modern English cuisine with subtle flavours from the Far East. Comprehensively equipped, the two secure private boardrooms provide self-contained business meeting facilities. Exclusive use of the hotel can be arranged for a special occasion or corporate event. Magnificent views of Bath and the surrounding countryside may be enjoyed from the Royal Crescent vintage river launch and hot air balloon. In September 1998, the opening of the Bath House created a unique spa combining the essence of ancient spa traditions within a tranquil and relaxed environment. **Directions:** Detailed directions are available from the hotel on booking. Price guide: Single from £200 double/twin from £200; suites £395–£750.

STON EASTON PARK

STON EASTON, BATH, SOMERSET BA3 4DF
TEL: 01761 241631 FAX: 01761 241377 E-MAIL stoneastonpark@stoneaston.co.uk

The internationally renowned hotel at Ston Easton Park is a Grade I Palladian mansion of notable distinction. A showpiece for some exceptional architectural and decorative features of its period, it dates from 1739 and has recently undergone extensive restoration, offering a unique opportunity to enjoy the opulent splendour of the 18th century. A high priority is given to the provision of friendly and unobtrusive service. The hotel has won innumerable awards for its décor, service and food. Jean Monro, an acknowledged expert on 18th century decoration, supervised the design and furnishing of the interiors, complementing the original features with choice antiques, paintings and *objets d'art.*

Fresh, quality produce, delivered from all parts of Britain, is combined with herbs and vegetables from the Victorian kitchen garden to create English and French dishes. To accompany the meal, a wide selection of rare wines and old vintages is stocked in the house cellars. The grounds, landscaped by Humphry Repton in 1793, consist of romantic gardens and parkland. The 17th century Gardener's Cottage, close to the main house on the wooded banks of the River Norr, provides private suite accommodation. **Directions:** 11 miles south of Bath on the A37 between Bath and Wells. Price guide: Single £155; double/twin £185–£320; four-poster £320–£405.

NETHERFIELD PLACE HOTEL AND COUNTRY CLUB

NETHERFIELD HILL, BATTLE, EAST SUSSEX TN33 9PP
TEL: 01424 774455 FAX: 01424 774024 E-MAIL: reservations@netherfieldplace.co.uk

Guests coming to Netherfield Place follow in the footsteps of William the Conqueror who landed nearby in 1066, but today they will be able to stay in style in this splendid country house, surrounded by 30 acres of verdant parkland and elegant gardens. Netherfield is an intimate hotel, with just fourteen spacious bedrooms – each differing from the next and decorated with period furniture and delicate chintz. The bathrooms are charmingly decorated. The pleasant lounge, next to the cocktail bar, is peaceful and comfortable, perfect for afternoon tea. On fine days guests may prefer refreshments on the terrace, the air is fragrant from the colourful flowers and shrubs. Dining in the spacious restaurant is a pleasure with delicious dishes benefitting from the extensive kitchen garden with its many herbs, unusual fruits and vegetables. The wine list is reasonably priced. The famous Sissinghurst Gardens, the old towns of Rye, Winchelsea and Hastings and the superb Bodiam Castle are close by. Active guests appreciate tennis, croquet and putting at the hotel, with excellent golf courses and trout fishing nearby. Brighton is 30 miles along the coast. Battle is convenient for Glyndebourne and day crossings to France. **Directions:** Leave the M25 on the A21, then taking the A2100, finding the hotel signed just north of Battle. Price guide: Single £68–£80; double/twin £115–£160.

PowderMills Hotel

POWDERMILL LANE, BATTLE, EAST SUSSEX TN33 0SP
TEL: 01424 775511 FAX: 01424 774540 E-MAIL: powdc@aol.com

Situated outside the historic Sussex town famous for the 1066 battle, PowderMills is an 18th century listed country house which has been skilfully converted into an elegant hotel. Nestling in 150 acres of parks and woodland, the beautiful and tranquil grounds feature a 7-acre specimen fishing lake. Wild geese, swans, ducks, kingfishers and herons abound. Privately owned and run by Douglas and Julie Cowpland, the hotel has been carefully furnished with locally acquired antiques. On cooler days, log fires burn in the entrance hall and drawing room. The bedrooms – five with four-posters – are all individually furnished and decorated. The Orangery Restaurant offers fine classical cooking by chef Daniel Ayton. Guests may dine on the terrace in summer, looking out over the swimming pool and grounds. Light meals and snacks are available in the library. The location an is ideal base from which to explore the beautiful Sussex and Kent countryside and there are many villages and small towns in the area. **Directions:** From centre of Battle take the Hastings road south. After ¼ mile turn right into Powdermill Lane. After a sharp bend, the entrance is on the right; cross over the bridge and lakes to reach the hotel. Price guide: Single from £70; double/twin £95–£150.

BRIDGE HOUSE HOTEL

BEAMINSTER, DORSET DT8 3AY
TEL: 01308 862200 FAX: 01308 863700 E-MAIL: enquiries@bridge–house.co.uk

This country town hotel, built of mellow stone, was once a priest's house and dates back to the 13th century. It is set in the heart of Beaminster, an old market town. In this charming hotel, enclosed by a beautiful walled garden, emphasis is placed on creating a relaxing atmosphere for guests and providing them with the highest standards of comfort without sacrificing the character of the surroundings. The warm stone, beams and large fireplaces combine with every modern day amenity to provide a pleasant environment which visitors will remember. Attractively decorated and furnished bedrooms include a colour television and tea and coffee making facilities. Four of them are on the ground floor and

offer easy access. The pride of the house is its food, where attention to detail is evident. In the candlelit Georgian dining room an imaginative menu offers dishes that make use of fresh produce from the local farms and fishing ports. Beaminster is convenient for touring, walking and exploring the magnificent Dorset countryside. Places of interest nearby include many fine houses and gardens. Several golf courses, fresh and salt water fishing, riding, sailing and swimming in the sea are all within reach. **Directions:** From M3 take A303 Crewkerne exit then A356 through Crewkerne, then A3066 to Beaminster. Hotel is 100 yds from town centre car park, on the left. Price guide Single £63–£88; twin/double £70–£123.

THE MASTER BUILDER'S HOUSE

BUCKLER'S HARD, BEAULIEU, NEW FOREST, HAMPSHIRE SO42 7XB
TEL: 01590 616253 FAX: 01590 616297 E-MAIL: res@themasterbuilders.co.uk

A careful and extensive refurbishment of the hotel has transformed The Master Builder's House into a top quality 3 star property, set in a magnificent location with beautiful views across the Beaulieu river. The heart of the estate was originally home to the Master shipbuilder Henry Adams who built Nelson's favourite, the Agamemnon. The 25 en suite bedrooms are beautifully appointed, offering every modern facility and a range of thoughtful extras. The public rooms are charming with Inglenook fireplaces and comfortable furnishings. A hearty full English breakfast is served in the morning whilst the restaurant, awarded 2 AA Rosettes, specialises in traditional cuisine comprising classic recipes and local produce. The beaches at Barton-on-Sea and Milford-on-Sea, the National Motor Museum and the Georgian town of Lymington are all worth a visit. The more adventurous may wish to explore the New Forest with its wildlife and picturesque villages or enjoy the many nearby indoor swimming pools, five golf courses and sailing centres. Other sports such as fishing, salt-water angling, riding, trekking and wagon-riding may be practised close by. **Directions:** Leave the M27 at junction 1, then take the A337 to Lyndhurst and then the B3056 to Beaulieu. Follow signs to Buckler's Hard. Price guide: Single £95–£150; double/twin £135–£210.

THE MONTAGU ARMS HOTEL

BEAULIEU, NEW FOREST, HAMPSHIRE SO42 7ZL
TEL: 01590 612324 FAX: 01590 612188 E-MAIL: enquiries@montagu–arms.co.uk

Situated at the head of the River Beaulieu in the heart of the New Forest, The Montagu Arms Hotel carries on a tradition of hospitality started 700 years ago. As well as being a good place for a holiday, the hotel is an ideal venue for small conferences. Each of the 24 bedrooms has been individually styled and many are furnished with four-poster beds. Dine in the oak-panelled restaurant overlooking the garden, where you can enjoy cuisine prepared by award-winning chef Paul Sutcliffe. The menu is supported by an outstanding wine list. Alternatively dine less formally in Monty's Bar Brasserie now delightfully presented in keeping with the building. It offers homemade fare together with real ales and a good choice of wine.

The hotel offers complimentary membership of an exclusive health club 6 miles away. Facilities there include a supervised gymnasium, large indoor ozone pool, Jacuzzi, steam room, sauna and beauty therapist. With much to see and do around Beaulieu why not hire a mountain bike? Visit the National Motor Museum, Exbury Gardens or Bucklers Hard, or walk for miles through the beautiful New Forest. Special tariffs are available throughout the year. **Directions:** The village of Beaulieu is well-signposted and the hotel commands an impressive position at the foot of the main street. Price guide: Single from £72; double/twin £125–£135; suites £165–£205. Inclusive terms available.

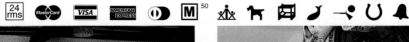

WOODLANDS MANOR

GREEN LANE, CLAPHAM, BEDFORD, BEDFORDSHIRE MK41 6EP
TEL: 01234 363281 FAX: 01234 272390 E-MAIL: woodlands.manor@pageant.co.uk

Woodlands Manor is a secluded period manor house, set in acres of wooded grounds and gardens, only two miles from the centre of Bedford. The hotel is privately owned and a personal welcome is assured. In the public rooms, stylish yet unpretentious furnishings preserve the feel of a country house, with open fires in winter. The en suite bedrooms are beautifully decorated and have extensive personal facilities. All have views of the gardens and surrounding countryside. The elegantly proportioned restaurant, once the house's main reception room, provides an agreeable venue for dining. The menus balance English tradition with the French flair for fresh, light flavours, complemented by wines from well-stocked cellars. The private library and conservatory are well suited to business meetings, launches and intimate dinner parties. Woodlands Manor is conveniently located for touring: the historic centres of Ely, Cambridge and Oxford, all within easy reach and stately homes such as Woburn Abbey and Warwick Castle are not far away. The hotel is two miles from the county town of Bedford, with its riverside park and the Bunyan Museum. Other places of interest nearby include the RSPB at Sandy and the Shuttleworth Collection of aircraft at Biggleswade. **Directions:** Clapham village is two miles north of the centre of Bedford. Price guide: Single £65–£85; double/twin £85–£97.50; suite £150.

MARSHALL MEADOWS COUNTRY HOUSE HOTEL

BERWICK-UPON-TWEED, NORTHUMBERLAND TD15 1UT
TEL: 01289 331133 FAX: 01289 331438

Marshall Meadows can truly boast that it is England's most northerly hotel, just a quarter of a mile from the Scottish border, an ideal base for those exploring the rugged beauty of Northumberland. A magnificent Georgian mansion standing in 15 acres of woodland and formal gardens, Marshall Meadows today is a luxurious retreat, with a country house ambience – welcoming and elegant. This is not a large hotel, there are just nineteen bedrooms, each individually designed. Restful harmonious colour schemes, comfortable beds and the tranquillity of its surroundings ensure a good night's sleep! The lounge is delightful, with traditional easy chairs and sofas, overlooking the patio. Ideal for summer afternoon tea. The congenial "Duck & Grouse Bar" stocks forty whiskies and real ale. Marshall Meadows has three restaurants, "The Borderers", a traditional dining room, the candlelit "Music Room" overlooking the sea and the intimate panelled "Gallery". Diners enjoy local game, fresh seafood and good wine. The manor has its own burn with a small waterfall, croquet and tennis. Excellent golf and historic Berwick-on-Tweed are nearby. **Directions:** A1 heading North, take Berwick by-pass and at Meadow House roundabout, head towards Edinburgh. After 300 yards, turn right, indicated by white sign – hotel is at end of small side road. Price guide: Single £75; double/twin £90.

TILLMOUTH PARK

CORNHILL-ON-TWEED, NEAR BERWICK-UPON-TWEED, NORTHUMBERLAND TD12 4UU
TEL: 01890 882255 FAX: 01890 882540 E-MAIL: reservations@tillmouthpark.force9.co.uk

Designed by Charles Barry, the son of the famous Victorian architect of the Houses of Parliament in Westminster, Tillmouth Park offers the same warm welcome today as it did when it was an exclusive private country house. It is situated in a rich countryside farmland of deciduous woodland and moor. The generously sized bedrooms have been recently refurbished in a distinctive old fashioned style with period furniture, although all offer modern day amenities. The kitchen prides itself on traditional country fare, with the chef using fresh local produce to create imaginative and well-presented dishes. The restaurant serves a fine table d'hôte menu, while the Bistro is less formal. Fresh salmon and game are always available with 24 hours' notice. A well chosen wine list and a vast selection of malt whiskies complement the cuisine. Tillmouth Park is an ideal centre for country pursuits including field sports, fishing, hill-walking, shooting, riding, bird-watching and golf. For the spectator there is rugby, curling and horse-racing during the season. Places of interest nearby include stately homes such as Floors, Manderston and Paxton. Flodden Field, Lindisfarne and Holy Island are all within easy reach and the coast is just 15 minutes away. **Directions:** Tillmouth Park is on the A698 Coldstream to Berwick-on-Tweed road. Price guide: Single £90–£120; twin/double £120–£175.

THE SWAN HOTEL AT BIBURY

BIBURY, GLOUCESTERSHIRE GL7 5NW
TEL: 01285 740695 FAX: 01285 740473 E-MAIL: swanhotl@swanhotel-cotswold.co.uk

The Swan Hotel at Bibury in the South Cotswolds, a 17th century coaching inn, is a perfect base for both leisurely and active holidays which will appeal especially to motorists, fishermen and walkers. The hotel has its own fishing rights and a moated ornamental garden encircled by its own crystalline stream. Bibury itself is a delightful village, with its honey-coloured stonework, picturesque ponds, the trout filled River Coln and its utter lack of modern eyesores. The beautiful Arlington Row and its cottages are a vision of old England. When Liz Rose acquired The Swan, she had the clear intention of creating a distinctive hotel in the English countryside which would acknowledge the needs of the sophisticated traveller of the 1990s and into the new millennium. A programme of refurbishment and upgrading of the hotel and its services began with the accent on unpretentious comfort. Oak-panelling, plush carpets and sumptuous fabrics create the background for the fine paintings and antiques that grace the interiors. The 18 bedrooms are superbly appointed with luxury bathrooms and comfortable furnishings. Guests may dine in either the restaurant or the brasserie which serves meals all day. **Directions:** Bibury is signposted off A40 Oxford–Cheltenham road, on the left-hand side. Midweek saver rates available. Price guide: Single £99–£119; double/twin £165–£250.

THE BURLINGTON HOTEL

BURLINGTON ARCADE, 126 NEW STREET, BIRMINGHAM, WEST MIDLANDS B2 4JQ
TEL: 0121 643 9191 FAX: 0121 643 5075 E-MAIL: mail@burlingtonhotel.com

The Burlington is a new hotel embodying the legendary old Midland Hotel which had played such an important role since its opening in 1871. The original handsome Victorian façade has not been destroyed, only embellished, while skilful restoration has retained much of the historic charm within. The new hotel is in Birmingham's pedestrianised City Centre, approached through an attractive arcade. It is focused on the commercial arena, with a strong emphasis on facilities for conferences and corporate activities. All bedrooms are pleasantly furnished, spacious, well-equipped and comfortable, with the extras expected by today's traveller, including fax and modem links, electronic voice mail box and satellite television. The bathrooms are well designed. On the first floor, guests will find the delightful lounge – a peaceful retreat – the traditional bar and the splendid Victorian restaurant with its swathed windows, chandeliers and moulded ceilings. The fifth floor houses the leisure centre. The main function area is self-contained, with its own entrance and foyer. Other rooms are ideal for seminars or board meetings. The Burlington is well placed for shopping, the Symphony Hall and just 15 minutes drive from the NEC. **Directions:** Close to New Street Station, 10 minutes from the airport, accessible from the M5, M6, M42. NCP parking. Price guide (room only): Single £135; double/twin £157; suite £310.

THE MILL HOUSE HOTEL AND LOMBARD ROOM RESTAURANT

180 LIFFORD LANE, KING'S NORTON, BIRMINGHAM B30 3NT
TEL: 0121 459 5800 FAX: 0121 459 8553

Situated just 15 minutes away from the city of Birmingham, the Mill House offers the latest up-to-date hospitality to both the leisure guest and business visitor. Owner Anthony Morgan prides himself on providing the highest standards of efficiency and service. Winner of the AA Courtesy and Care Award 1998. Standing in landscaped terraced gardens complete with a small indoor heated swimming pool, the hotel provides luxuriously appointed accommodation. Each of the nine superb, beautifully decorated bedrooms has en suite marble bathrooms, colour television, minibars, bathrobes, mineral water and fresh fruit. Chef Anthony Morgan serves a tempting selection of English and continental specialities in the elegantly refurbished Lombard Room restaurant which is re-establishing its reputation as one of Birmingham's finest dining areas. Alternatively, guests can enjoy a light lunch or host a pre-dinner reception in the relaxing atmosphere of the spacious Victorian conservatory. Mill House also has excellent conference facilities for up to 100 delegates. **Directions:** From M42, exit at junction 3 onto A435 until Maypole Island, left King's Norton until the Poacher's Pocket, 2nd left Broadmeadow Lane just over bridge on left. Price guide: Single £98–£110; double/twin £110–£120; suite £150-£175. Special weekend breaks available.

NEW HALL

WALMLEY ROAD, ROYAL SUTTON COLDFIELD, WEST MIDLANDS B76 1QX
TEL: 0121 378 2442 FAX: 0121 378 4637

Set in 26 acres of private gardens and surrounded by a lily-filled moat, New Hall dates from the 12th century and is reputedly the oldest fully moated manor house in England. This prestigious hotel offers a warm welcome to both the discriminating business visitor and leisure guest looking for a quiet tranquil retreat. Much acclaimed, New Hall proudly holds the coveted RAC Blue Ribbon Award, for eight years, and AA Inspectors' Hotel of the Year for England 1994. The cocktail bar and adjoining drawing room overlook the terrace from which a bridge leads to the yew topiary, orchards and sunlit glades. Individually furnished bedrooms and suites offer every modern comfort and amenity with lovely views. A 9-hole golf course and floodlight tennis court are available for guests' complimentary use. Surrounded by a rich cultural heritage, New Hall is convenient for Lichfield Cathedral, Warwick Castle, Stratford-upon-Avon, the NEC and the ICC in Birmingham (only seven miles away). The Belfry Golf Centre is also nearby. Details of champagne weekend breaks, opera, ballet and wine weekends are available on request. **Directions:** From exit 9 of M42, follow A4097 (ignoring signs to A38 Sutton Coldfield). At B4148 turn right at the traffic lights. New Hall is one mile on the left. Price guide: Single £135–£180; double/twin £160–£255; suite £210–£395.

THE SWALLOW HOTEL

12 HAGLEY ROAD, FIVEWAYS, BIRMINGHAM B16 8SJ
TEL: 0121 455 7073 FAX: 0121 456 3442

As soon as it opened, this very special hotel became the first in the Midlands to achieve five stars and since then it has won innumerable awards. These include the Caterer and Hotelkeeper's 'Hotel of the Year 1992', AA Courtesy and Care award and five AA Stars. Two of the most highly regarded other accolades have been received – English Tourist Board 'England for Excellence Award' 1993 (the Lanesborough in 1992 and the Chewton Glen in 1991) and more recently Johansens 'City Hotel of the Year' 1994. Awards, however, do not give the whole picture. The Swallow Hotel offers business and leisure travellers an oasis of calm and warm hospitality in a fascinating and culturally diverse city. Service and surroundings are quite outstanding. Ninety eight luxuriously comfortable bedrooms and suites offer all one would expect from a hotel of this calibre. Dining is memorable whether in the Sir Edward Elgar Restaurant or in Langtry's which has three AA Rosettes: traditional afternoon tea in the Drawing Room is a favourite indulgence with all guests. Nowhere is luxury more apparent than in the Swallow Leisure Club with its theme of Ancient Egypt – including hieroglyphics. **Directions:** Fiveways roundabout – junction 1 (M5) 5 miles, junction 6 (M6) $5\frac{1}{2}$ miles. Price guide from: Single £160; double/twin £190; suite from £325.

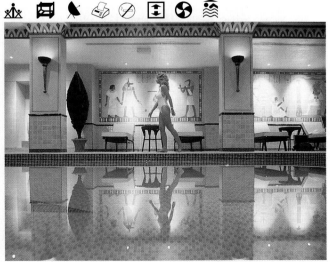

DOWN HALL COUNTRY HOUSE HOTEL

HATFIELD HEATH, NR BISHOP'S STORTFORD, HERTFORDSHIRE CM22 7AS
TEL: 01279 731441 FAX: 01279 730416 E-MAIL: sales@downhall.demon.co.uk

Down Hall is a magnificent Italian-style mansion set in 110 acres of woodland, park and landscaped gardens. The hotel is a splendid example of quality Victorian craftsmanship, with superb attention to detail throughout. The well-proportioned bedrooms have antique-style inlaid mahogany furniture and brass chandeliers. Italian granite is an opulent feature of the luxurious en suite bathrooms. The public rooms display fine furnishings, with high ceilings, crystal chandeliers and stunning views of the gardens. There are two restaurants, offering English and international cuisine, with a wide selection of superb dishes. For conferences, there are 26 meeting rooms, including 16 purpose-built syndicate rooms. Indoor and outdoor leisure facilities include a heated pool, whirlpool, sauna, croquet and putting lawns, giant chess, tennis courts and a fitness trail. Down Hall is within easy access of London and of Stansted Airport. For excursions, Cambridge, Constable country and the old timbered village of Thaxted are all within a few miles. **Directions:** Exit at junction 7 of M11. Follow the A414 towards Harlow. At the 4th roundabout follow the B183 to Hatfield Heath. Bear right towards Matching Green and the hotel is 1.3 miles on the right. Price guide: Single £109–£130; double/twin £145–£163; suite £186.

ASTLEY BANK HOTEL & CONFERENCE CENTRE

BOLTON ROAD, DARWEN, LANCASHIRE BB3 2QB
TEL: 01254 777700 FAX: 01254 777707 E-MAIL: sales@astleybank.co.uk

Astley Bank stands high and impressive overlooking six acres of magnificent grounds and flower-filled gardens adjacent to the peaceful West Pennine Moors midway between Blackburn and Bolton. Built in the early 19th century it was, over the years, home to some of Lancashire's leading dignitaries. Today it is a stylish, comfortable country retreat with a character and ambience reflecting its mansion house era combined with all modern facilities demanded by today's discerning visitor. The public rooms are spacious and elegant and the en suite bedrooms are decorated and furnished to the highest standard. Most of them enjoy superb views over the garden and the four-poster and executive bedrooms provide additional luxury. In the attractive garden restaurant chef James Andrew produces tasty à la carte and table d'hôte menus which are complemented by an extensive selection of wines. Being within easy reach of the motorway network and Manchester Airport, Astley Bank is a popular venue with meetings organisers. There are three conference rooms supported by six purpose built syndicate rooms. All have natural daylight and are fitted with a variety of audiovisual equipment. **Directions:** From Blackburn take the M65 east. Exit at junction 4 and take the A666 south towards Bolton. After approximately two miles pass through Darwen. The hotel is on the right. Price guide: Single £70–£95; double/twin £90–£120.

THE DEVONSHIRE ARMS COUNTRY HOUSE HOTEL

BOLTON ABBEY, SKIPTON, NORTH YORKSHIRE BD23 6AJ
TEL: 01756 710441 FAX: 01756 710564 E-MAIL: dev.arms@legend.co.uk

The Devonshire reflects its charming setting in the Yorkshire Dales: a welcome escape from a busy and crowded world, peace and quiet, beauty and the perfect place to relax. The hotel is owned by the Duke and Duchess of Devonshire and is set in 12 acres of parkland on their Bolton Abbey estate, in the Yorkshire Dales National Park. Many antiques and paintings from Chatsworth in the public rooms and bedrooms (several of which are themed) add to the country house atmosphere, which is complemented by excellent service and an award-winning restaurant. As well as a wide choice of outdoor activities and themed or activity breaks, The Devonshire Club is adjacent to the hotel and offers a full range of leisure, health and beauty therapy facilities including: heated indoor swimming pool, steam room, sauna, spa bath, cold water plunge pool, high-powered sunbed, fully equipped gymnasium, beauty therapy rooms – staffed by "Clarins" trained therapists – health and relaxation treatments. 5 Crowns De Luxe, three AA Red Stars and two Rosettes. **Directions:** Off the A59 Skipton–Harrogate road at junction with the B6160. Price guide: Single £110–£180; double/twin £155–£240; suite £325.

THE DORMY

NEW ROAD, FERNDOWN, NEAR BOURNEMOUTH, DORSET BH22 8ES
TEL: 01202 872121 FAX: 01202 895388 E-MAIL: devere.dormy@airtime.co.uk

Situated on the edge of the picturesque New Forest, The Dormy is the essence of comfort. The country style hotel, with its glowing log fires and oak panelled lounges, is surrounded by 12 acres of magnificent landscaped gardens. The 115 bedrooms are furnished in either a traditional or a more modern fashion and include all the latest amenities such as satellite television, radio, telephone and hospitality tray. A relaxing ambience may be found in the Dormy Bar and the golf themed Alliss Bar. At meal times you are spoilt for choice – the elegant new Hennessys offers the finest contemporary cuisine, the popular Garden Restaurant continues to build upon its reputation and a third, more relaxed, option is presented in the Pavillion Brasserie. The Leisure Club comprises of a large indoor pool and various other health facilities such as a sauna, spa bath and solaria. Fitness fanatics may exercise in the well-equipped gymnasium and aerobics studio or make use of the squash and tennis courts. The Dormy lies adjacent to the Ferndown Golf Club, renowned for its Championship 18-hole and 9-hole president's course. Other nearby sporting activities include quad biking, clay pigeon shooting and riding in the New Forest. **Directions:** Nearest motorway is M27 to Ringwood, then A31 to Ferndown, then left at the traffic lights onto A347. The hotel is just 1m on the left hand side of the road. Price guide: Single £110; double/twin £145–£200; suite £225–£255.

LANGTRY MANOR

DERBY ROAD, EAST CLIFF, BOURNEMOUTH, DORSET BH1 3QB
TEL: 01202 553887 FAX: 01202 290115 E-MAIL: lillie@langtrymanor.com

Known originally as The Red House, this fine house was built in 1877 by Edward VII (then Prince of Wales) as a love nest for his mistress. The concept of a themed small hotel was created by the present owners around the famous Lillie Langtry story exactly a hundred years later. The Edward VII suite is a fine spacious room which retains two original floral wall paintings and features a grand Jacobean four poster bed and of course benefits from an ensuite bathroom. Several other feature rooms have corner spa baths and are all designed to engender a romantic ambience. This was the first hotel in Dorset to be licensed for civil marriages; it is a popular wedding venue – and a natural for honeymoons, anniversaries and birthdays. Saturday night guests are invited to take part in a delicious 6 course Edwardian Banquet – which features an interlude of words and music based on the life of the 'Jersey Lily' – served in the quite splendid Dining Hall with its minstrels gallery and stained glass windows. Some of the bedrooms offered are close by in The Lodge – once the home of Lord Derby where Edward and Lillie stayed while the Red House was being built. Sandy beaches, Hardy country, the New Forest, art galleries, theatres and gardens. **Directions:** Take A338 Wessex Way to the station. First exit at roundabout, over next roundabout, first left into Knyveton Road, second right into Derby Road. Price guide: Single from £79.75; double/twin £119.50–£199.50.

NORFOLK ROYALE HOTEL

RICHMOND HILL, BOURNEMOUTH, DORSET BH2 6EN
TEL: 01202 551521 FAX: 01202 299729 E-MAIL: norfolkroyale@englishrosehotels.co.uk

Bournemouth has long been a popular seaside resort and has not lost its unique character – The Norfolk Royale is a fine example of the elegant buildings that grace the town. It is a splendid Edwardian house, once the holiday home of the Duke of Norfolk, after whom it is named. Extensive restoration work throughout the hotel, while enhancing its comfort, has not eliminated the echoes of the past and new arrivals are impressed by the elegant furnishings and courtesy of the staff. The designs of the spacious bedrooms reflect consideration for lady travellers, non-smokers and the disabled. The rich fabrics of the delightful colour schemes contribute to their luxurious ambience. Guests relax in the lounge or attractive club bar, in summer enjoying the gardens or patio – all with waiter service – and delicious breakfasts, lunches and candle-lit dinners are served in the Orangery Restaurant, which has an excellent wine list. The good life includes the pleasures of a pool and spa while Bournemouth offers golf courses, tennis, water sports, a casino and theatre. It has a large conference and exhibition centre. Poole Harbour, The New Forest, Thomas Hardy country and long sandy beaches are nearby. **Directions:** From the M27, A31 & A338 find the hotel on the right, halfway down Richmond Hill approaching the town centre. Price guide: Single £95–£115; double/twin £135–£175; suite £185–£330.

THE EDGEMOOR

HAYTOR ROAD, BOVEY TRACEY, SOUTH DEVON TQ13 9LE
TEL: 01626 832466 FAX: 01626 834760 E-MAIL: edgemoor@btinternet.com

Built in 1870, The Edgemoor Country House Hotel, owned and managed by Rod and Pat Day, stands in a peaceful location in two acres of grounds literally on the eastern boundary of the Dartmoor National Park. There are 12 charming bedrooms, two of which are on the ground floor. All have en suite bathrooms and some have four-poster beds. The public rooms look over the hotel grounds and provide comfortable and sophisticated surroundings in which guests enjoy their stay. In the restaurant, awarded 2 AA Rosettes, chef Edward Elliott prepares modern English and French cuisine using locally produced West Country specialities. The wine list offers an interesting and varied selection. Children are welcome and a special high-tea is provided for them. With the hotel's close proximity to Dartmoor, walkers and naturalists are well catered for. Shooting, fishing and riding can be arranged locally. The Edgemoor is also a good touring base for the West Country. Castle Drogo, Becky Falls and Haytor are worth a visit. **Directions:** On leaving the M5, join the A38 in the direction of Plymouth. At Drumbridges roundabout, take A382 towards Bovey Tracey. At the second roundabout turn left and after approximately ½ mile, fork left at the sign for Haytor. Price guide: Single £50–£55; double/twin £77.50–£110.

WOOLLEY GRANGE

WOOLLEY GREEN, BRADFORD-ON-AVON, WILTSHIRE BA15 1TX
TEL: 01225 864705 FAX: 01225 864059 E-MAIL: Woolley@luxury-hotel.demon.co.uk

Woolley Grange is a 17th century Jacobean stone manor house set in 14 acres of formal gardens and paddocks. Standing on high ground, it affords southerly views of the White Horse at Westbury and beyond. Furnished with flair and an air of eccentricity, the interior décor and paintings echo the taste of owners Nigel and Heather Chapman. Woolley Grange has gained a reputation for outstanding cuisine. Using local farm produce and organically grown fruit and vegetables from the Victorian kitchen gardens, the chef has created a sophisticated style of country house food which aims to revive the focus on flavours. Children are particularly welcome; the owners have four of their own and they do not expect their young visitors to be 'seen but not heard'. In the Victorian coach house there is a huge games room and a well-equipped nursery with a full-time nanny available to look after guests' children 10–6pm every day. A children's lunch and tea are provided daily. Nearby attractions include medieval Bradford-on-Avon, Georgian Bath, Longleat and prehistoric Stonehenge. Riding can be arranged. **Directions:** From Bath on A363, fork left at Frankleigh House after town sign. From Chippenham, A4 to Bath, fork left on B3109; turn left after town sign. Price guide: Single £95; double/twin £105–£200; suite from £170–£260.

FARLAM HALL HOTEL

BRAMPTON, CUMBRIA CA8 2NG
TEL: 016977 46234 FAX: 016977 46683 E-MAIL: farlamhall@dial.pipex.com

Farlam Hall was opened in 1975 by the Quinion and Stevenson families who over the years have managed to achieve and maintain consistently high standards of food, service and comfort. These standards have been recognised and rewarded by all the major guides and membership of Relais et Châteaux. This old border house, dating in parts from the 17th century, is set in mature gardens which can be seen from the elegant lounges and dining room, creating a relaxing and pleasing environment. The fine silver and crystal in the dining room complement the quality of the English country house cooking produced by Barry Quinion and his team of chefs. There are 12 individually decorated bedrooms varying in size and shape, some having Jacuzzi baths, one an antique four-poster bed and there are two ground floor bedrooms. This area offers many different attractions: miles of unspoiled countryside for walking, eight golf courses within 30 minutes of the hotel, Hadrian's Wall, Lanercost Priory and Carlisle with its castle, cathedral and museum. The Lake District, Scottish Borders and Yorkshire Dales each make an ideal day's touring. Winter and spring breaks are offered. Closed Christmas. **Directions:** Farlam Hall is 2½ miles east of Brampton on the A689, not in Farlam village. Price guide (including dinner): Single £120–£140; double/twin £220–£260.

CHAUNTRY HOUSE HOTEL AND RESTAURANT

HIGH STREET, BRAY, BERKSHIRE SL6 2AB
TEL: 01628 673991 FAX: 01628 773089

Tucked between the local church and cricket club in the small, delightful Thames-side village of Bray, and a minutes walk to the famous Roux's Waterside Inn, Chauntry House is comfortable, friendly and has a plentiful supply of charm and character. With a spacious and secluded garden in which to lounge it is a fine example of an early 18th century country house: an ideal place to relax. The 15 en suite bedrooms are individually appointed in the best English designs and all have cable television, radio, direct dial telephones and tea and coffee making facilities. The public rooms offer comfort in the traditional country house manner and the welcoming drawing room, with an open fire for the winter months, is an ideal and comfortable environment in which to enjoy a pre-dinner aperitif. Modern English and Continental specialities with a distinctively oriental influence are served in the stylish restaurant. The hotel can accommodate conferences and meetings in the Dower House for up to 20 delegates, boardroom style. Maidenhead, Royal Windsor, Eton, Henley, Ascot, Marlow, London and Heathrow Airport are within easy reach. River cruises, golf, fishing, riding and tennis can be arranged locally. **Directions:** From M4, exit at junction 8/9 and take A 308 (M) towards Maidenhead and Windsor. Then join B3028 to Bray village, just before M4 overhead bridge. Price guide: Single £102–£110; double/twin £130–£145.

MONKEY ISLAND HOTEL

BRAY-ON-THAMES, MAIDENHEAD, BERKSHIRE SL6 2EE
TEL: 01628 623400 FAX: 01628 784732 E-MAIL: monkeyisland@btconnect.com

The name Monkey Island derives from the medieval Monk's Eyot. Circa 1723 the island was purchased by Charles Spencer, the third Duke of Marlborough, who built the fishing lodge now known as the Pavilion and the fishing temple, both of which are Grade I listed buildings. The Pavilion's Terrace Bar, overlooking acres of riverside lawn, is an ideal spot for a relaxing cocktail and the Pavilion Restaurant, awarded 2 AA Rosettes, perched on the island's narrowest tip with fine views upstream, boasts fine English cuisine, an award-winning cellar and friendly service. The River Room is suitable for weddings or other large functions, while the Regency-style boardroom is perfect for smaller parties. It is even possible to arrange exclusive use of the whole island for a truly memorable occasion. The Temple houses 26 comfortable bedrooms and suites, the Wedgwood Room, with its splendid ceiling in high-relief plaster, the octagonal Temple Room and gymnasium. Monkey Island is one mile downstream from Maidenhead, within easy reach of Royal Windsor, Eton, Henley and London. Closed from 26 December to mid-January. Weekend breaks from £85 p.p. **Directions:** Take A308 from Maidenhead towards Windsor; turn left following signposts to Bray. Entering Bray, go right along Old Mill Lane, which goes over M4; the hotel is on the left. Price guide: Single £89–£127; double/twin £129–£159; suites from £184.

THE OLD SHIP HOTEL

KINGS ROAD, BRIGHTON, EAST SUSSEX BN1 1NR
TEL: 01273 329001 FAX: 01273 820718 E-MAIL: oldship@paramount–hotels.co.uk

The Old Ship overlooks the beach and promenade and is Brighton's most historic hotel with a tradition of hospitality dating back to 1559. The Prince Regent regularly visited the hotel in the 19th century and it became a favourite with the aristocracy and celebrities. It is now undergoing a major refit from top to bottom with a complete, £2million re-styling of the ground floor. When work is completed in spring 2000, guests will enjoy the highest standards of accommodation, comfort, service and cuisine. There is to be a new spacious reception area and all 152 bedrooms are being refurbished to offer greater comfort and the most up-to-date facilities. Many of the bedrooms are enhanced by having magnificent sea views. The Old Ship has been a fine venue for dinners and banquets and will be even more so with the introduction of a new kitchen, a restaurant opening onto the street and a second off-street restaurant. A variety of versatile meetings rooms will be on offer to the business world, backed up by a full range of high-tech equipment and business centre services. The Old Ship is just a short stroll from the Royal Pavilion, the Palace Pier and The Lane's famous antique shops, cafe bars and restaurants. Glyndebourne, Arundel, Chichester, Lewes and the scenic South Downs are within easy reach. **Directions:** From the M23 join the A23. The hotel is on the sea front between the piers. Price guide: Single from £70; double/twin £95–£200.

HOTEL DU VIN & BISTRO

THE SUGAR HOUSE, NARROW LEWINS MEAD, BRISTOL BS1 2NU
TEL: 0117 925 5577 FAX: 0117 925 1199 E-MAIL: admin@bristol.hotelduvin.co.uk

This hotel is scheduled to open in November 1999. The publishers therefore do not base their recommendation on an inspection visit in this case, although the reputation of the owners would suggest that this establishment will offer very high standards similar to those earned at their other properties, situated in Winchester and Royal Tunbridge Wells. Set around a courtyard dating from the 1700's, this hotel comprises six listed warehouses that have been used for a number of industrial purposes over the centuries. The imposing 100ft chimney is a lasting testimony to the buildings' impressive past and other distinctive vestiges relating to this period feature inside. The individually named bedrooms are decorated with fine fabrics such as Egyptian linen and offer a good range of facilities including oversized baths and power showers. Guests may relax in the convivial Cocktail bar with its walk-in Cigar humidor or enjoy a glass of wine in the well-stocked cellar before dining in the Bistro. The traditional menu has been created using the freshest local ingredients and is complemented by an excellent wine list. Throughout the property the cool, understated elegance is evident as is the owners attention to even the smallest detail. **Directions:** Follow the M32 towards City Centre through to Lewins Mead. Price guide: Single £99; double/twin £99–£120; suite £150–£175.

SWALLOW ROYAL HOTEL

COLLEGE GREEN, BRISTOL BS1 5TA
TEL: 0117 9255200 FAX: 0117 9251515 E-MAIL: bristol@swallow–hotels.co.uk

The Swallow Royal Hotel enjoys a central position near to Bristol Cathedral and overlooking College Green. It was much admired by Queen Victoria and Sir Winston Churchill and it survived Second World War bombs. Today it is restored to its former glory and is Bristol's leading luxury hotel. The warmest welcomes await guests, who are invited to savour the combined experience of Victorian elegance and modern day comfort being air conditioned throughout. There are 242 rooms including 17 suites, all individually designed and furnished to the highest standards and many offer views over the city and harbour. Chef Giles Stonehouse oversees two restaurants; the imposing Victorian Palm Court with its spectacular glass roof awarded 2 AA Rosettes. or the less formal Terrace Restaurant overlooking Cathedral Square. The Swallow Leisure Club, designed with Ancient Rome in mind, has hand-painted murals, mosaics and Roman columns and offers an ideal environment for those seeking energetic pursuits or relaxation. Facilities include a heated indoor swimming pool, sauna, spa bath, steam room, sunbeds and fitness room. The hotel has its own internal "pub", the Queen Vic where you can "surf the net" and watch sport on satellite TV. The hotel has its own car park. **Directions:** At the end of the M32 keep right and follow the signs for the City Centre. Price guide: Single from £140; double/twin from £160; suites £200–£375.

DANESWOOD HOUSE HOTEL

CUCK HILL, SHIPHAM, NR WINSCOMBE, SOMERSET BS25 1RD
TEL: 01934 843145 FAX: 01934 843824 E-MAIL: 113626,3540@COMPUSERVE.COM

A small country house hotel, Daneswood House overlooks a leafy valley in the heart of the Mendip Hills – on a clear day, the views stretch as far as Wales. It was built by the Edwardians as a homeopathic health hydro and under the enthusiastic ownership of David and Elise Hodges it has been transformed into a charming hotel. Each bedroom is well furnished and individually decorated with striking fabrics. The honeymoon suite, with its king-sized bed, frescoed ceiling and antiques, is particularly comfortable. First-class cooking places equal emphasis on presentation and taste. Each dish is carefully prepared in a style that combines traditional English and French cooking. Awarded 2

AA Rosettes. During the summer, guests can dine alfresco and enjoy barbecued dishes such as Indonesian duck and baked sea bass with fennel and armagnac. There is a carefully selected wine list and a wide choice of liqueurs. The private conference lounge makes a quiet setting for meetings, while private functions can be catered for with ease. Cheddar Gorge is 2 miles away and Wells, Glastonbury, Bristol and Bath are nearby. Guide dogs accommodated only. **Directions:** Shipham is signposted from the A38 Bristol–Bridgwater road. Go through the village towards Cheddar; the hotel drive is on the left leaving the village. Price guide: Single £69.50–£89; double/twin £85–£99.50; suite £140.

DORMY HOUSE

WILLERSEY HILL, BROADWAY, WORCESTERSHIRE WR12 7LF
TEL: 01386 852711 FAX: 01386 858636 E-MAIL: reservations@dormyhouse.co.uk

This former 17th century farmhouse has been beautifully converted into a delightful hotel which retains much of its original character. With its oak beams, stone-flagged floors and honey-coloured local stone walls it imparts warmth and tranquillity. Dormy House provides a wealth of comforts for the most discerning guest. Each bedroom is individually decorated – some are furnished with four-poster beds – and suites are available. Head Chef, Alan Cutler, prepares a superb choice of menus and Tapestries Restaurant offers an extensive wine list with a diverse range of half bottles. The versatile Dormy Suite is an ideal venue for conferences, meetings or private functions –

professionally arranged to individual requirements. The hotel has its own leisure facilities which include a games room, gym, sauna/steam room, croquet lawn and putting green. Mountain bikes are available for hire. Broadway Golf Club is adjacent. The locality is idyllic for walkers. Stratford-upon-Avon, Cheltenham Spa, Hidcote Manor Garden and Sudeley Castle are all within easy reach. USA representative: Josephine Barr, 1-800-323-5463. Closed 2 days at Christmas. **Directions:** Hotel is ½ mile off A44 between Moreton-in-Marsh and Broadway. Taking the turning signposted Saintbury, the hotel is first on left past picnic area. Price guide: Single £73–£97; double/twin £146–£174.

THE LYGON ARMS

BROADWAY, WORCESTERSHIRE WR12 7DU
TEL: 01386 852255 FAX: 01386 858611 E-MAIL: info@the-lygon-arms.co.uk

The Lygon Arms, a magnificent Tudor building with numerous historical associations, stands in Broadway, acclaimed by many as 'the prettiest village in England', in the heart of the North Cotswolds. Over the years much restoration has been carried out, emphasising the outstanding period features, such as original 17th century oak panelling and an ancient hidden stairway. All the bedrooms are individually and tastefully furnished and offer guests every modern luxury, even telephone voice-mail, combined with the elegance of an earlier age. The Great Hall, complete with a 17th century minstrels' gallery and the smaller private dining rooms provide a fine setting for a well-chosen and imaginative menu. Conference facilities including the state-of-the-art Torrington Room are available for up to 80 participants. Guests can enjoy a superb range of leisure amenities including all-weather tennis, indoor pool, spa bath, gymnasium, billiard room, beauty salons, steam room, solarium and saunas. Golf can be arranged locally. The many Cotswold villages; Stratford-upon-Avon, Oxford and Cheltenham are nearby, while Broadway itself is a paradise for the antique collector. **Directions:** Set in the centre of Broadway High Street. Price guide: Single from £112; double/twin from £180 including Continental breakfast, excluding VAT.

THE BALMER LAWN

LYNDHURST ROAD, BROCKENHURST, NEW FOREST, HAMPSHIRE SO42 7ZB
TEL: 01590 623116 FAX: 01590 623864 E-MAIL: blh@btinternet.com

The Balmer Lawn enjoys a commanding position in Brockenhurst, an enchanting village nestling in the heart of Hampshire's New Forest. The famous New Forest ponies and deer graze in the surrounding area where the hotel has stood since its days as a coaching inn in the mid 1800s. Recently under new ownership, an extensive programme of improvements has been undertaken, resulting in a new garden, landscaped grounds, upgraded bedrooms and a refurbished restaurant and function rooms. The 55 en suite bedrooms feature televisions, beverage facilities, direct dial television and many other amenities. In the restaurant, recently awarded an AA Rosette, the emphasis is on fresh, local produce and the inspired menu offers a choice of both traditional and modern English dishes. The carefully chosen wine list has been compiled with the flavours in mind. With a capacity for 90 diners, special occasions may be celebrated in the large restaurant. Active guests may utilise the indoor and outdoor swimming pools, squash and tennis courts and gymnasium. There is an array of activities including wagon rides in the Forest, hot-air ballooning, horse-riding, sailing at Lymington or simply hiring a bicycle and discovering the beauty of the New Forest. Places of interest nearby include Beaulieu Motor Museum, Marwell Zoo and Salisbury. **Directions:** Leave M27 at junction 1 and take A337 via Lyndhurst to Brockenhurst. Price guide: Single £72–£88; double/twin £108–£135.

CAREYS MANOR HOTEL

BROCKENHURST, NEW FOREST, HAMPSHIRE SO42 7RH
TEL: 01590 623551 FAX: 01590 622799 E-MAIL: careysmanorhotel@btinternet.com

Careys Manor, dates from 1888 and is built on the site of a royal hunting lodge used by Charles II. Situated in landscaped grounds and close to the glorious New Forest countryside, the hotel is proud of the personal welcome and care it extends to its visitors. The comfortably furnished bedrooms are well-appointed. In the Garden Wing, there is a choice of bedrooms, some opening directly onto the lawns and others with a balcony overlooking the pretty gardens. The restaurant offers fine English and French cuisine. A prestigious sports complex comprises a large indoor swimming pool with Jacuzzi, sauna and a Turkish steam room. In addition, guests can work out in the professionally supervised fitness suite, where there are also rooms for massage, sports injury and beauty treatments. Windsurfing, riding and sailing can all be enjoyed locally, while Stonehenge, Beaulieu, Broadlands, Salisbury and Winchester are a short distance away. Business interests can be catered for – there are comprehensive self-contained conference facilities. **Directions:** From M27 junction 1, follow A337 signed to Lymington. Careys Manor is on the left after 30 mph sign at Brockenhurst. Price guide from: Single £79–£89; double/twin £129–£149; suite £179.

NEW PARK MANOR

LYNDHURST ROAD, BROCKENHURST, NEW FOREST, HAMPSHIRE SO42 7QH
TEL: 01590 623467 FAX: 01590 622268

Escape from the crowds to one of the New Forest's finest country house hotels. A former hunting lodge of Charles II, the building is grade II listed and dates back to the 16th century. It stands in a very fine position a good distance from the road to Lyndhurst, the capital of the New Forest, where "Alice in Wonderland's" grave, and Rufus Stone are curiosities to be visited. The en suite bedrooms are all individually decorated, keeping in mind the style and grandeur of the old manor; most offer superb views over the surrounding parklands with its wandering ponies and deer. Enjoy a romantic evening with fine wines and French influenced cuisine in the Restaurant or relax with a good book from the library in front of the open log fire in the historic Rufus Bar. The New Forest suite creates a wonderful setting for all types of functions – tailor-made to suit your personal requirements. For the more energetic, New Park Manor offers riding from its own equestrian centre with BHS trained stable crew, a tennis court and an outdoor heated swimming pool. There is something for everyone so why not get away from it all and escape to the peace and tranquillity, topped with service par excellence, of the New Park Manor? **Directions:** New Park Manor is 1/2 mile off the A337 between Lyndhurst and Brockenhurst easily reached from M27 junction 1. Price guide: Single from £85; double/twin £110–£190.

RHINEFIELD HOUSE HOTEL

RHINEFIELD ROAD, BROCKENHURST, NEW FOREST, HAMPSHIRE SO42 7QB
TEL: 01590 622922 FAX: 01590 622800

Known locally as the 'jewel in the forest', at first sight the sheer grandeur of Rhinefield House surpasses all expectations. A hint of Italian Renaissance sweeps across ornamental gardens, with canals reflecting the mellow stonework. Lovingly restored to their original 1890s design, over 5,000 yew trees form the maze and formal parterres where a grass amphitheatre has been carved out of the western slopes for summer evening concerts. The interiors are equally impressive, the journey through the rooms is a voyage of discovery. Authentically created in the style of a Moorish Palace, the Alhambra Room has Islamic inscriptions, onyx pillars and mosaic flooring. Fine cuisine is served in the elegant Armada Restaurant – so called after its splendid carving depicting the Spanish Armada. An airy sunlit conservatory and attractive bedrooms appointed in accordance with the style of the house all add to Rhinefield's appeal. The Grand Hall is a model replica of Westminster Hall – an ideal setting for balls, society weddings and stylish banquets. A wide range of conference rooms and equipment is available for business events. Guests may unwind in the Atlantis Leisure Club with its plunge pool, sauna, steam room and small gymnasium. **Directions:** A35 West from Lyndhurst the hotel is signed in about 3 miles. Price guide: Single from £110; double/twin from £140; suite from £175.

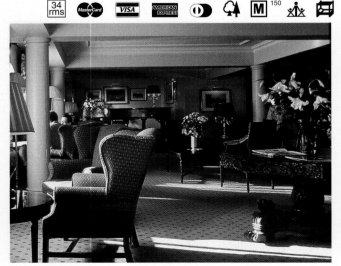

GRAFTON MANOR COUNTRY HOUSE HOTEL

GRAFTON LANE, BROMSGROVE, WORCESTERSHIRE B61 7HA
TEL: 01527 579007 FAX: 01527 575221 E-MAIL: steven@grafman.u-net.com

Closely associated with many of the leading events in English history, Grafton Manor's illustrious past can be traced back to Norman times. Commissioned in 1567, the present manor is set in several acres of gardens leading to a lake. Modern comfort and style are combined with the atmosphere of an earlier age. Pot-pourri from the hotel's 19th century rose gardens scent the rooms and over 100 herbs are grown in a unique, chessboard-pattern garden. All the herbs are in regular use in the restaurant kitchen, where Simon Morris aims to 'produce only the best' for guests. Preserves made from estate produce are on sale. Meals are served in the 18th century dining room, the focal point of Grafton Manor. Damask-

rose petal and mulberry sorbets are indicative of the inspired culinary style. Indian cuisine is Simon's award-winning hobby and Asian dishes often complement the traditional English cooking. The fully equipped bedrooms have been meticulously restored and furnished, some with open fires on cooler evenings. Grafton Manor is ideally placed for Birmingham, the NEC and the International Conference Centre. It is an equally good base from which to explore the Worcestershire countryside. **Directions:** From M5 junction 5 proceed via A38 towards Bromsgrove. Bear left at first roundabout; Grafton Lane is first left after $1/2$ mile. Price guide: Single £85; double/twin from £105; suite £150.

THE BAY TREE HOTEL

SHEEP STREET, BURFORD, OXON OX18 4LW
TEL: 01993 822791 FAX: 01993 823008 E-MAIL: bookings@cotswold–inns–hotels.co.uk

The Bay Tree has been expertly refurbished so that it retains all its Tudor splendour while offering every modern facility. The oak-panelled rooms have huge stone fireplaces and a galleried staircase leads upstairs from the raftered hall. All the bedrooms are en suite, three of them furnished with four-poster beds and two of the five suites have half-tester beds. In the summer, guests can enjoy the delightful walled gardens, featuring landscaped terraces of lawn and flower beds. A relaxing atmosphere is enhanced by the staff's attentive service in the flagstoned dining room where the head chef's creative cuisine is complemented by a comprehensive selection of fine wines. Light meals are served in a country-style bar. Burford, often described as the gateway to the Cotswolds, is renowned for its assortment of antique shops and the Tolsey Museum of local history. The Bay Tree Hotel makes a convenient base for day trips to Stratford-upon-Avon, Stow-on-the-Wold and Blenheim Palace. Golf, clay pigeon shooting and riding can be arranged locally. **Directions:** Burford is on the A40 between Oxford and Cheltenham. Proceed halfway down the hill into Burford, turn left into Sheep Street and The Bay Tree Hotel is 30 yards on your right. Price guide: Single £90; double/twin £135–£210.

NEW

THE HOSTE ARMS HOTEL

THE GREEN, BURNHAM MARKET, NORFOLK PE31 8HD
TEL: 01328 738777 FAX: 01328 730103 E-MAIL: TheHosteArms@compuserve.com

Overlooking the green in the picturesque village of Burnham Market, The Hoste Arms dates back to the 17th century. Deservedly The Hoste has received many awards including Johansens Inn of the Year and the Inn of the Year César Award from the Good Hotel Guide. The en suite bedrooms are individually decorated, some offering views of the village, others of the landscaped garden. Paul Whittome continues his quest constantly to improve and upgrade services and facilities, recently enhancing the enjoyment of his guests with the addition of a very stylish and relaxed lounge and also the new Gallery Restaurant. His wife Jeanne has decorated the rooms throughout the hotel in a simple yet elegant style. A small panelled restaurant offers scope for private dinner parties and conferences. All the main dining areas are air-conditioned. The excellent menu, created by head chef Stephen David and his team, features an extensive amount of seafood and has British, French and Oriental touches. A selection of well priced wines is offered to guests alongside a private collection of Paul's favourites. The Hoste Arms is well situated to cater for most interests. There are several stately homes in the area such as Holkham Hall, Houghton Hall and Sandringham. For nature lovers there are bird sanctuaries and boat trips. Golf enthusiasts have Hunstanton, Brancaster and Cromer. **Directions:** Burnham Market is 2 miles from A149 on B1155. Price guide: Singles £50–£60; doubles £60–£90.

NORTHCOTE MANOR COUNTRY HOUSE HOTEL

BURRINGTON, UMBERLEIGH, DEVON EX37 9LZ
TEL: 01769 560501 FAX: 01769 560770 E-MAIL: rest@northcotemanor.co.uk

This 18th century manor, set in grounds high above the Taw River Valley offers its guests an ambience of timeless tranquillity. Situated in the Devonshire countryside, Northcote Manor is an ideal venue for those seeking a relaxing and peaceful retreat. The extensive refurbishment has culminated in the creation of 11 luxurious and well-appointed bedrooms and suites. This, complemented by a total redesign of the décor of the large sitting rooms, hall and restaurant has resulted in a series of accolades. Cuisine is an important criterion and Chef Chris Dawson has been awarded three Rosettes for his menus. The proprietors are constantly striving to create the West Country's finest country house hotel and are undertaking work in the 20 acre grounds and gardens to complete their endeavour. North Devon is a delight to explore whilst Exmoor and Dartmoor are within easy reach. Guests may spend their days visiting RHS Rosemoor and the many National Trust properties nearby or practising outdoor pursuits. The area hosts some of the best shoots in the country and excellent fishing from the Taw at the bottom of the drive can be arranged with the Gillie. A challenging 18-hole golf course is next to the Manor whilst the tennis court and croquet lawn are on site. **Directions:** About 25m from Exeter on A377 to Barnstaple. Private drive opposite the Portsmouth Arms pub/railway station. Price guide (incl. dinner): Single £100–£200; double/twin £150–£285; suite £205–£350.

         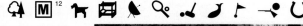

THE ANGEL HOTEL

BURY ST EDMUNDS, SUFFOLK IP33 1LT
TEL: 01284 753926 FAX: 01284 750092 E-MAIL: sales@angel.co.uk

Immortalised by Charles Dickens as the hostelry where Mr Pickwick enjoyed an excellent roast dinner, The Angel Hotel is renowned for its first-class service to travellers, continuing the tradition since first becoming an inn in 1452. Visitors have the immediate impression of a hotel that is loved and nurtured by its owners. In the public rooms, guests will appreciate the carefully chosen ornaments and pictures, fresh flowers and log fires. Bedrooms are individually furnished and decorated and all have en suite bathrooms. The elegant dining room has been awarded 2 Rosettes by the AA for excellent food and service. Overlooking the ancient abbey, the restaurant serves classic English cuisine, including local speciality dishes and succulent roasts. The Angel can offer a wide range of quality conference and banqueting facilities catering for private dinners, meetings and weddings from 10–60 persons. The hotel is within an hour of the east coast ferry ports and 45 minutes from Stansted Airport. Nearby there is racing at Newmarket and several golf courses within easy reach. Bury St Edmunds is an interesting and historic market town and an excellent centre for touring East Anglia. **Directions:** The hotel is situated in the centre of the town. Price guide: Single from £68; double/twin from £86; suite from £100. Weekend rates £53 per person bed and breakfast.

RAVENWOOD HALL

ROUGHAM, BURY ST EDMUNDS, SUFFOLK IP30 9JA
TEL: 01359 270345 FAX: 01359 270788

Nestling within 7 acres of lovely lawns and woodlands deep in the heart of Suffolk lies Ravenwood Hall. Now an excellent country house hotel, this fine Tudor building dates back to 1530 and retains many of its original features. The restaurant, still boasting the carved timbers and huge inglenook from Tudor times, creates a delightfully intimate atmosphere in which to enjoy imaginative cuisine. The menu is a combination of adventurous and classical dishes, featuring some long forgotten English recipes. The Hall's extensive cellars are stocked with some of the finest vintages, along with a selection of rare ports and brandies. A cosy bar offers a less formal setting in which to enjoy some unusual snacks. Comfortable bedrooms are furnished with antiques, reflecting the historic tradition of the Hall, although each is equipped with every modern facility. A wide range of leisure facilities is available for guests, including a hard tennis court, a croquet lawn and heated swimming pool. There are golf courses and woodland walks to enjoy locally; hunting and shooting can be arranged. Places of interest nearby include the famous medieval wool towns of Lavenham and Long Melford; the historic cities of Norwich and Cambridge are within easy reach. **Directions:** 2 miles East of Bury St. Edmunds off the A14. Price guide: Single £67–£89; double/twin: £87–£121.

BUXTED PARK COUNTRY HOUSE HOTEL

BUXTED, NR UCKFIELD, EAST SUSSEX TN22 4AY
TEL: 01825 732711 FAX: 01825 732770

Buxted Park's rural environment, close to Ashdown Forest, provides a calm and peaceful atmosphere in which to relax. The attractive Georgian mansion, built in 1725, has recently been sympathetically restored to reclaim its former glory. Years ago, when Buxted was a private residence, Queen Victoria and Queen Mary were both regular visitors. There are 44 spacious bedrooms with all the amenities required for a comfortable stay. Most of them have superb views over the extensive grounds and undulating landscape. The Orangery Restaurant – a converted Victorian conservatory – provides an elegant surrounding in which to enjoy the excellent food and fine wines. There are several salons which

may also be used for meetings, as well as a grand Ballroom which opens out into the Coat-of-Arms drawing room – ideal for pre-dinner drinks at events in the Ballroom. Unique to the hotel is a 54 seater cinema with back projection. The hotel is justifiably proud of its Health Club which has a well-equipped gym, sauna, steam rooms, Jacuzzi and a lovely outdoor heated swimming pool (open during the Summer). There is a snooker room, too. **Directions:** The entrance to the hotel is located on the A272, east of its junction with the A22. Price guide Single from £85; double/twin from £90; suites from £135. Two night leisure breaks include 4 course dinner from £75 per person per night.

THE LEE WOOD HOTEL & RESTAURANT

THE PARK, BUXTON, DERBYSHIRE SK17 6TQ
TEL: 01298 23002 FAX: 01298 23228 E-MAIL: leewoodhotel@btinternet.com

Charm, character and warmth are evident the moment you enter the curved drive leading to the wide entrance steps of this elegant Georgian hotel. The Lee Wood is situated close to the centre of the historic spa town of Buxton, set amidst mature, lawned grounds that are enhanced with heather-filled borders. In the background are beautiful wooded sheltering hills and the rugged and lushly pastured Peak District. The Lee Wood has everything a visitor could expect from a family-owned, three-star hotel. Each of the 40 en suite bedrooms have been tastefully and stylishly decorated and refurbished to provide every home comfort and facility. A number of executive and non smoking bedrooms have views over the famous

Pooles Cavern and Country Park. The hotel has consistently achieved two AA Red Rosettes for the quality of its traditional and international à la carte and table d'hôte cuisine served with panache in the sunny Garden Restaurant. There are several golf courses, sailing and pony trekking nearby. Chatsworth House and Haddon Hall are among some of the many stately homes within easy driving distance. Other attractions include Alton Towers, Crich Tramway, the Potteries and Buxton Opera House with its programme of music festivals and productions. **Directions:** From the north leave M6 Jct19 and take A537; from the south leave M6 Jct15 and take A53. From M1 Jct28 take A6. Price guide: Single £70; double/twin £92.

THE PALACE HOTEL

PALACE ROAD, BUXTON, DERBYSHIRE SK17 6AG
TEL: 01298 22001 FAX: 01298 72131 E-MAIL: palace@paramount-hotels.co.uk

At 1,007 feet above sea level, Buxton is one of the highest towns in England and the 19th century Palace Hotel stands at its highest point, commanding magnificent panoramic views over the historic spa town with its famous Crescent, the beautiful wooded sheltering hills and the rugged and lushly pastured Peak District National Park. This impressive hotel has been awarded four RAC stars. All 122 en suite bedrooms enjoy superb views, many of them overlooking local beauty spots such as Solomon's Temple and Grinlow Woods. They have been tastefully decorated and refurbished to provide guests with every home comfort and facility. The elegant yet informal Dovedale Restaurant provides a superb selection of English and international cuisine and there is a delightful tearoom in which to enjoy a light afternoon snack. The Palace Hotel has its own exclusive health and fitness club with an indoor swimming pool and extensive range of leisure activities. There are several golf courses nearby, rambling routes, sailing, cycling and riding. Chatsworth House, Haddon Hall, Bolsover Castle and Alton Towers are within easy reach. **Directions:** From the north, leave M6 at junction 20 and take M56 to Stockport and then A6 to Buxton. From the south, exit M6 at junction 15 and take A53 to Leek and Buxton. Price guide: Single £99; double/twin £116.

HOWFIELD MANOR

CHARTHAM HATCH, NR CANTERBURY, KENT CT4 7HQ
TEL: 01227 738294 FAX: 01227 731535 E-MAIL: enquiries@howfield.invictanet.co.uk

Set in the heart of the glorious Kent countryside and surrounded by five acres of attractive landscaped gardens, Howfield Manor has a fine tradition of hospitality dating back to 1181. The welcome afforded by the Towns family and their gracious staff is one associated with bygone times. The Manor is the essence of comfort and this is evident in the excellent standard of accommodation. Furnished in a stylish blend of modern and traditional décor, the bedrooms are individually appointed and are well-equipped with colour televisions, direct dial telephones and other thoughtful extras. Originally part of the Priory of St. Gregory, vestiges of the hotel's historic past include the authentic priest hole and the ferned ancient well under the floor of the Old Well Restaurant which was the main source of water for the monks who lived here 800 years ago. Today, an extensive menu created with the very best of fresh, local produce is served alongside an excellent and carefully compiled wine list. Howlett's Zoo Park, Leeds and Dover Castles, Rye with its charming, cobbled streets and the gardens at Sissinghurst are only a stone's throw away. Special weekend breaks are available. **Directions:** From A2 London–Dover road, follow signs for Chartham Hatch after the Gate Service Station, then follow straight on for 2¼ miles. Hotel is on left at Jct with A28. Price guide: Single £72.50; double/twin £92.50–£100.

THE MANOR HOUSE HOTEL & GOLF CLUB

CASTLE COMBE, CHIPPENHAM, WILTSHIRE SN14 7HR
TEL: 01249 782206 FAX: 01249 782159 E-MAIL: enquiries@manor-house.co.uk.

Nestling in the heart of one of England's prettiest villages deep in the Southern Cotswolds, the 14th century Manor House at Castle Combe is one of Britain's most architecturally beautiful and idyllically set country house hotels. Ivy clad stone walls and mullioned windows, oak panelling, log fires and antique furniture blend sympathetically with the individually designed bedrooms, many of which feature four poster beds, original beams and exposed walls. Designed by Peter Alliss and Clive Clark and set in 200 acres of woodland valley and downland, the 6340 yard par 73, championship golf course is one of the most spectacular and challenging courses in the South of England. Delightful walks in the surrounding countryside or a stroll through Castle Combe, unchanged for almost 200 years, is a magical experience with 26 acres of gardens and parkland, a gently flowing trout stream and the romance of a terraced Italian garden, The Manor House provides tranquillity in enchanting surroundings, together with a friendly atmosphere and award-winning cuisine and hospitality.

Directions: 15 minutes' drive from junctions 17 & 18 of the M4, or 20 minutes from the M5/M4 intersection. 12 miles from the beautiful Georgian city of Bath and only 2 hours drive from central London. Approached directly from A420 and B4039. Price guide: Single/double/twin from £120; suite £265–£350.

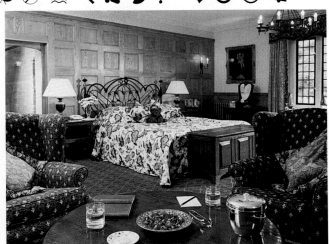

BROCKENCOTE HALL

CHADDESLEY CORBETT, NR KIDDERMINSTER, WORCESTERSHIRE DY10 4PY
TEL: 01562 777876 FAX: 01562 777872

The Brockencote estate consists of 70 acres of landscaped grounds surrounding a magnificent hall. There is a gatehouse, half-timbered dovecote, lake, some fine European and North American trees and an elegant conservatory. The estate dates back over three centuries and the style of the building reflects the changes which have taken place in fashion and taste over the years. The hotel has been awarded 3 AA Red Stars and is Heart of England Tourist Board Midlands Hotel of the Year. At present, the interior combines classical architectural features with contemporary creature comforts. As in most country houses, each of the bedrooms is different: all have their own character, complemented by tasteful furnishings and décor. The friendly staff provide a splendid service under the supervision of owners Alison and Joseph Petitjean. Head chef, Didier Philipot specialises in traditional French cuisine with occasional regional and seasonal specialities. Brockencote Hall is an ideal setting for those seeking peace and quiet in an unspoiled corner of the English countryside. Located a few miles south of Birmingham, it is convenient for business people and sightseers alike and makes a fine base for touring historic Worcestershire. **Directions:** Exit 4 from M5 or exit 1 from M42. Brockencote Hall is set back from A448 at Chaddesley Corbett between Bromsgrove and Kidderminster. Price guide: Single £105; double/twin £125–£150.

GIDLEIGH PARK

CHAGFORD, DEVON TQ13 8HH
TEL: 01647 432367 FAX: 01647 432574 E-MAIL: gidleighpark@gidleigh.co.uk

Gidleigh Park enjoys an outstanding international reputation among connoisseurs for its comfort and gastronomy. It has collected a clutch of top culinary awards including 2 Michelin stars for its imaginative cuisine and the Gidleigh Park wine list is one of the best in Britain. Service throughout the hotel is faultless. The en suite bedrooms – two of them in a converted chapel – are luxuriously furnished with antiques. The public rooms are elegantly appointed and during the cooler months, a fire burns merrily in the lounge's impressive fireplace. Set amid 45 secluded acres in the Teign Valley, Gidleigh Park is 1½ miles from the nearest public road. Two croquet lawns, an all-weather tennis court, a bowling lawn and a splendid water garden can be found in the grounds. A 360 yard long, par 52 putting course designed by Peter Alliss was opened in 1995. Guests can swim in the river or explore Dartmoor on foot or in the saddle. There are 14 miles of trout, sea trout and salmon fishing, as well as golf facilities nearby. Gidleigh Park is a Relais et Châteaux member. **Directions:** Approach from Chagford: go along Mill Street from Chagford Square. Fork right after 150 yards, cross into Holy Street at factory crossroads and follow lane for two miles. Price guide (including dinner): Single £250–£400; double/twin £365–£450.

PONTLANDS PARK COUNTRY HOTEL

WEST HANNINGFIELD ROAD, GREAT BADDOW, NR CHELMSFORD, ESSEX CM2 8HR
TEL: 01245 476444 FAX: 01245 478393

Pontlands Park is a fine Victorian mansion, originally built for the Thomasin-Foster family in 1879. It became a hotel in 1981. The Victorian theme is still much in evidence, tempered with the best of contemporary interior styling. Immaculate public rooms – the conservatory-style Garden Room, the Residents' Lounge with its deep sofas and the relaxed ambience of the Victorian bar – are designed with guests' comfort in mind. Beautifully furnished bedrooms have co-ordinated fabrics and well-defined colour schemes. Diners are offered a selection of imaginative menus, with fine wines and attentive service in our Conservatory Restaurant. Within the grounds, Reflections Leisure Centre has indoor and outdoor swimming pools, Jacuzzis, sauna and steamroom. The Beauty Salon offers many figure-toning, hairstyling and beauty treatments. Meetings and private dinners from 2 to 100 guests can be accommodated and functions for up to 200 guests can be held in the marquee. Closed 27 December to 1 January (but open for New Year's Eve). **Directions:** Pontlands Park is only about 30 miles from London. From A12 Chelmsford bypass take Great Baddow intersection (A130). Take first slip-road off A130 to Sandon/Great Baddow; bear left for Great Baddow, then first left for West Hanningfield Road. Price guide: Single £98; double/twin £120.

THE CHELTENHAM PARK HOTEL

CIRENCESTER ROAD, CHARLTON KINGS, CHELTENHAM, GLOUCESTERSHIRE GL53 8EA
TEL: 01242 222021 FAX: 01242 254880 E-MAIL: cheltenhampark@paramount–hotels.co.uk

Set against the picturesque background of the rolling Cotswold hills, this elegant Georgian hotel rises high and majestically from beautifully lawned and flower-filled gardens ensconcing a tranquil lake. Whilst retaining echoes of its early heritage, The Cheltenham Park Hotel combines a relaxing and welcoming ambience with all the comforts expected by today's discerning visitor. The 144 en suite bedrooms are individually styled, tastefully furnished and have every facility to help occupants enjoy a comfortable and restful stay. Superior rooms have splendid views over the gardens and beyond to Lilley Brook Golf Course. Similar views are enjoyed by diners in the intimate Lakeside Restaurant where the best local produce is prepared with imagination and flair to create cuisine of international appeal. For relaxation there is a well equipped leisure club complete with heated swimming pool, gym, sauna, spa bath, steam room and solarium. Fishing, quad biking, clay and air-rifle shooting can be arranged. Cheltenham, with its Regency architecture, attractive promenade, exclusive shops and famous racecourse is just a short drive away. **Directions:** Exit the M5 at junction 11a and follow the A417, the A436 and the A435 to Cheltenham. The hotel is on the left two miles south of the town. Price guide: Single £99; double/twin from £128; suite £195.

THE GREENWAY

SHURDINGTON, CHELTENHAM, GLOUCESTERSHIRE GL51 5UG
TEL: 01242 862352 FAX: 01242 862780 E-MAIL: relax@greenway–hotel.demon.co.uk

Set amidst gentle parkland with the rolling Cotswold hills beyond, The Greenway is an Elizabethan country house with a style that is uniquely its own – very individual and very special. Renowned for the warmth of its welcome, its friendly atmosphere and its immaculate personal service, The Greenway is the ideal place for total relaxation. The public rooms with their antique furniture and fresh flowers are elegant and spacious yet comfortable, with roaring log fires in winter and access to the formal gardens in summer. The 19 bedrooms all have private bathrooms and are individually decorated with co-ordinated colour schemes. Eleven of the rooms are located in the main house with a further eight rooms in the converted Georgian coach house immediately adjacent to the main building. The award-winning conservatory dining room overlooks the sunken garden and lily pond, providing the perfect backdrop to superb cuisine of international appeal complemented by an outstanding selection of wines. Situated in one of Britain's most charming areas, The Greenway is well placed for visiting the spa town of Cheltenham, the Cotswold villages and Shakespeare country.
Directions: On the outskirts of Cheltenham off the A46 Cheltenham–Stroud road, 2 1/2 miles from the town centre. Price guide: Single from £95; double/twin £150–£240.

HOTEL ON THE PARK

EVESHAM ROAD, CHELTENHAM, GLOUCESTERSHIRE GL52 2AH
TEL: 01242 518898 FAX: 01242 511526 E-MAIL: stay@hotelonthepark.co.uk

Set in the Regency town of Cheltenham, Hotel on the Park is an attractive town house hotel which combines the attentive service of bygone times with an excellent standard of accommodation. The impressive façade, dominated by the grand pillared doorway, hints at the splendour that lies inside. Each of the 12 bedrooms are individually styled and decorated with interesting antiques and exquisite fabrics. Every possible comfort has been provided. Throughout the property the theme of understated elegance prevails and this is truly evident in The Bacchanalian Restaurant, with its high ceilings and beautiful hand-detailed cornice work. Guests may enjoy the glorious views of Pittville Park whilst sampling the inspired creations from the extensive menu along with a selection from the detailed wine list. The well-appointed Library is an ideal venue for board meetings or seminars. Special occasions including private banquets or wedding receptions can be arranged. Synonymous with National Hunt Racing, the spa town of Cheltenham is particularly popular during the racing season and hosts the Gold Cup. The town is also renowned for its Regency architecture, attractive promenade and exclusive boutiques. Historic properties, museums and theatres abound whilst other activities include golf, horse-riding, rambling and exploring the Cotswolds. **Directions:** Opposite Pittville Park, 5 mins walk from town centre. Price guide: Single from £84.75; double/twin from £111.

BROXTON HALL COUNTRY HOUSE HOTEL

WHITCHURCH ROAD, BROXTON, CHESTER, CHESHIRE CH3 9JS
TEL: 01829 782321 FAX: 01829 782330

Built in 1671 by a local landowner, Broxton Hall is a black and white half-timbered building set in five acres of grounds and extensive gardens amid the rolling Cheshire countryside. The medieval city of Chester is eight miles away. The hotel provides every modern comfort while retaining the ambience of a bygone age. The reception area reflects the character of the entire hotel, with its magnificent Jacobean fireplace, plush furnishings, oak panelled walls and carved mahogany staircase. On cool evenings log fires are lit. The small but well-appointed bedrooms are furnished with antiques and have en suite bathrooms as well as every modern comfort. Overlooking the gardens, the restaurant receives constant praise from regular diners. French and English cuisine is served, using local game in season and freshly caught fish. There is an extensive wine list. Breakfast may be taken in the sunny conservatory overlooking the lawned gardens. The hotel is an ideal venue for business meetings and conferences. Broxton Hall is the perfect base from which to visit the North Wales coast and Snowdonia. There are a number of excellent golf courses nearby and racecourses at Chester and Bangor-on-Dee. **Directions:** Broxton Hall is on the A41 Whitchurch–Chester road, eight miles between Whitchurch and Chester. Price guide: Single £60–£70; double/twin £80–£110.

CARDEN PARK

CARDEN, CHESTER, CHESHIRE CH3 9DQ
TEL: 01829 731000 FAX: 01829 731032 E-MAIL: reservations@cardenpark.co.uk

Standing long, low and majestically in 750 acres of the beautiful grounds of a 17th century Cheshire estate, Carden Park is a superb modern hotel combining the best in golfing facilities with the style, luxury and exclusiveness desired by discerning guests. Fine fabrics, exquisite furnishings, deep carpets, oak panelling, open fireplaces and spectacular window views add to the opulence and tranquillity of the surroundings. The 192 spacious en suite bedrooms are furnished to a high standard and offer every comfort. Some have log fires and whirlpool baths. For complete privacy, there is a selection of rooms arranged around three landscaped courtyards. Golfers have the choice of two 18-hole championship courses, a 9-hole course and a driving range. Carden Park is home to Europe's first Nicklaus Residential Teaching School. Diners enjoy stunning views in a choice of restaurants where tempting dishes are complemented by excellent service. The fully-equipped health club has a 20 metre heated swimming pool, 15 treatment rooms and a range of health, beauty and fitness facilities. Outdoor pursuits include bowls, tennis, archery, horse-riding and driving on the 4x4 off-road course. **Directions:** From Chester, take the A41 towards Whitchurch. Turn right at Broxton roundabout onto the A543. Carden Park is on the left after half a mile. Price guide: Single £121–£156; double £147–177; suite £197–£282.

THE CHESTER GROSVENOR

EASTGATE, CHESTER CH1 1LT
TEL: 01244 324024 FAX: 01244 313246 E-MAIL: chesgrov@chestergrosvenor.co.uk

The Chester Grosvenor is in the heart of the historic city of Chester beneath the famous Queen Victoria Clock. The hotel is owned by the Duke of Westminster's Grosvenor Estate. It is renowned for its fabulous cuisine and has two restaurants – the Arkle and La Brasserie. The Arkle is an award winning gourmet restaurant, named after the famous racehorse. La Brasserie is an informal Parisian style restaurant which is open all day, every day. The Chester Grosvenor has an extensive cellar with over 600 bins of fine wine. There are 85 bedrooms of which 11 are suites. All are beautifully appointed, fully air-conditioned with 24 hour room service provided and each room is equipped with all the amenities

expected in a deluxe hotel awarded 5 Stars from both the AA and RAC. The hotel has its own leisure suite with a multi-gymnasium, sauna and solarium and membership of an exclusive local country club which has indoor and outdoor swimming pools, tennis and gymnasium. Adjacent are the famous Roman Walls and the Chester Rows with their boutiques and exclusive shops. A short stroll away is Chester Cathedral, Chester racecourse and the River Dee. **Directions:** In the centre of Chester on Eastgate. 24-hour NCP car parking – follow signs to Grosvenor Precinct Car Park. Price guide: Single from £170; double/twin from £260; suites from £440. Weekend break rates available on request.

CRABWALL MANOR

PARKGATE ROAD, MOLLINGTON, CHESTER, CHESHIRE CH1 6NE
TEL: 01244 851666 FAX: 01244 851400 E-MAIL: sales@crabwall.com

Crabwall Manor can be traced back to Saxon England, prior to the Norman Conquest. Set in 11 acres of mature woodland on the outskirts of Chester, this Grade II listed manor house has a relaxed ambience, which is enhanced by staff who combine attentive service with friendliness and care. The interior boasts elegant drapes complemented by pastel shades which lend a freshness to the décor of the spacious lounge and reception areas, while the log fires in the inglenook fireplaces adds warmth. The hotel has won several awards for their renowned cuisine, complemented by an excellent selection of fine wines and outstanding levels of accommodation. Three meeting suites, accommodating up to 100 delegates, have been specifically designed and a further ten syndicate rooms are available. The new 'Spa at Crabwall' features a 17 metre pool, gymnasium, dance studio, sauna, spa pool, juice bar. Those wishing to be pampered will enjoy the three beauty treatment rooms. Shooting, off-road driving and fishing may be enjoyed. The ancient city of Chester with its many attractions is only 1½ miles away. **Directions:** Go to end of M56, ignoring signs to Chester. Follow signs to Queensferry and North Wales, taking A5117 to next roundabout. Left onto A540, towards Chester for 2 miles. Crabwall Manor is on the right. Price guide: Single £116–£140; double/twin £140–£175; suite £185–£270. Weekend breaks available.

NUNSMERE HALL

TARPORLEY ROAD, OAKMERE, NORTHWICH, CHESHIRE CW8 2ES
TEL: 01606 889100 FAX: 01606 889055 E-MAIL: nunsmere@aol.com.uk

Set in peaceful Cheshire countryside and surrounded on three sides by a lake, Nunsmere Hall epitomises the elegant country manor where superior standards of hospitality still exist. Wood panelling, antique furniture, exclusive fabrics, Chinese lamps and magnificent chandeliers evoke an air of luxury. The 30 bedrooms and 6 suites most with spectacular views of the lake and gardens, and are beautifully appointed with king-size beds, comfortable breakfast seating and marbled bathrooms containing soft bathrobes and toiletries. The Brocklebank, Delamere and Oakmere business suites are air-conditioned, soundproofed and offer excellent facilities for boardroom meetings, private dining and seminars. The Restaurant has a reputation for fine food and uses only fresh seasonal produce. Twice County Restaurant of the Year in the Good Food Guide. A snooker room is available and there are several championship golf courses nearby. Oulton Park racing circuit and the Cheshire Polo Club are next door. Golf pitch and putt is available in the grounds. Archery and air rifle shooting by arrangement. Although secluded, Nunsmere is convenient for major towns and routes. AA 3 Red Star and Three Rosettes. **Directions:** Leave M6 at junction 19, take A556 to Chester (approximately 12 miles). Turn left onto A49. Hotel is 1 mile on left. Price guide: Single £110–£120; double/twin £150–£195; suite from £225.

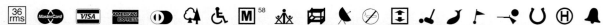

ROWTON HALL HOTEL

WHITCHURCH ROAD, ROWTON, CHESTER, CHESHIRE CH3 6AD
TEL: 01244 335262 FAX: 01244 335464 E-MAIL: rowtonhall@rowtownhall.co.uk

Standing in eight acres of award winning gardens and pastureland on the outskirts of the city of Chester, Rowton Hall enjoys far-reaching views across the Cheshire Plains to the Welsh hills. Built as a private residence in 1779, the hall is renowned for the informal country-house atmosphere which welcomes all its guests. It retains many original features, including a Robert Adam fireplace and superb carved staircase. The conservatory-style Hamilton Lounge, overlooking the garden, is the perfect place to enjoy morning coffee, afternoon tea or cocktails, while the Cavalier Bar is ideal for a lunchtime snack. The bedrooms are individually designed and have en suite bathrooms. In the Langdale Restaurant, which has earned a first-class reputation, Executive Chef, Anthony O'Hare's à la carte and table d'hôte menus can be sampled in elegant and restful surroundings. Fresh vegetables and herbs are supplied by the hall's kitchen garden. Hotel guests have complimentary use of the Leisure Club – facilities include a swimming pool, state-of-the-art gymnasium, sauna, solarium, steam room and two floodlit tennis courts. There are five conference/meeting rooms accommodating up to 200. The hotel offers special weekend rates. **Directions:** From the centre of Chester, take A41 towards Whitchurch. After 3 miles, turn right to Rowton village. The hotel is in the centre of the village. Price guide: Single £140; double/twin £150; suites £199–£220.

THE MILLSTREAM HOTEL

BOSHAM, NR CHICHESTER, WEST SUSSEX PO18 8HL
TEL: 01243 573234 FAX: 01243 573459

A village rich in heritage, Bosham is depicted in the Bayeux Tapestry and is associated with King Canute, whose daughter is buried in the local Saxon church. Moreover, sailors from the world over navigate their way to Bosham, which is a yachtsman's idyll on the banks of Chichester Harbour. The Millstream consists of a restored 18th-century malthouse and adjoining cottages linked to The Grange, a small English manor house. Individually furnished bedrooms are complemented by chintz fabrics and pastel décor. Period furniture, a grand piano and bowls of freshly cut flowers feature in the drawing room. A stream meanders past the front of the delightful gardens, where traditional herbs are grown for use by the *chef de cuisine*. Whatever the season, care is taken to ensure that the composition and presentation of the dishes reflect high standards. An appetising luncheon menu is offered and includes local seafood specialities such as: dressed Selsey crab, home-cured and smoked salmon and grilled fresh lemon sole. During the winter, good-value 'Hibernation Breaks' are available. **Directions:** South of the A259 Between Chichester and Havant. Price guide: Single £69–£99; double/twin £112–£122; suite £142.

THE COTSWOLD HOUSE

HIGH STREET, CHIPPING CAMPDEN, GLOUCESTERSHIRE GL55 6AN
TEL: 01386 840330 FAX: 01386 840310 E-MAIL: reception@cotswold-house.demon.co.uk

Chipping Campden is a nostalgic Cotswold town, unspoilt by the twentieth century, and Cotswold House is a splendid 17th century mansion facing the town square, impressive with colonnades flanking the front door and built in the lovely soft local stone. The interior has been sensitively decorated and modernised so there is no distraction from the graceful pillared archway and staircase. Lovely antiques, fine paintings and fabrics reminiscent of the Regency era blend easily with comfortable sofas in the elegant drawing room. The bedrooms are very individual, with memorabilia appropriate to their theme, but all are peaceful, decorated in harmonious colours and have 'country house' style furnishings.

Cotswold House is deservedly proud of its kitchen, which has won many accolades. The attractive Garden Room Restaurant has a splendid menu and a cellar book of 150 wines. Informal meals are in The Brasserie. Private functions and small conferences can be held in the secluded Courtyard Room. Guests enjoy exploring Chipping Campden's intriguing shops and alleyways. The hotel is a superb base for Stratford-on-Avon, Oxford and visiting famous houses and gardens throughout the Cotswolds. **Directions:** Chipping Campden is 2 miles north-east of A44, on the B4081. The hotel has parking facilities. Price guide: Single from £55; double/twin from £120; four poster from £160.

CHARINGWORTH MANOR

NR CHIPPING CAMPDEN, GLOUCESTERSHIRE GL55 6NS
TEL: 01386 593555 FAX: 01386 593353

The ancient manor of Charingworth lies amid the gently rolling Cotswold countryside, just a few miles from the historic towns of Chipping Campden and Broadway. Beautiful old stone buildings everywhere recall the flourishing wool trade that gave the area its wealth. The 14th century manor house overlooks its own 50 acre grounds and offers peace and enthralling views. Inside, Charingworth is a historic patchwork of intimate public rooms with log fires burning during the colder months. There are 26 individually designed bedrooms, all furnished with antiques and fine fabrics. Outstanding cuisine is regarded as being of great importance and guests at Charingworth are assured of imaginative dishes. Great emphasis is placed on using only the finest produce and the AA has awarded the cuisine two Rosettes. There is an all-weather tennis court within the grounds, while inside, a beautiful swimming pool, sauna, steam room, solarium and billiard room are available, allowing guests to relax and unwind. Warwick Castle, Hidcote Manor Gardens, Batsford Arboretum, Stratford-upon-Avon, Oxford and Cheltenham are all within easy reach. Short break rates are available on request. **Directions:** Charingworth Manor is on the B4035 between Chipping Campden and Shipston-on-Stour. Price guide: (including full breakfast) Single from £105; double/twin from £170.

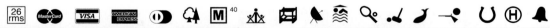

THE NOEL ARMS HOTEL

HIGH STREET, CHIPPING CAMPDEN, GLOUCESTERSHIRE GL55 6AT
TEL: 01386 840317 FAX: 01386 841136 E-MAIL: bookings@cotswold–inns–hotels.co.uk

A long tradition of hospitality awaits you at the Noel Arms Hotel. In 1651 the future Charles II rested here after his Scottish army was defeated by Cromwell at the battle of Worcester and for centuries the hotel has entertained visitors to the ancient and unspoilt, picturesque Cotswold Village of Chipping Campden. Many reminders of the past; fine antique furniture, swords, shields and other mementoes can be found around the hotel. There are 26 en suite bedrooms in either the main house or in the tastefully constructed new wing, some of which boast luxurious antique four-poster beds and all offering the standards you expect from a country hotel. The impressive oak panelled, restaurant, awarded 2 AA Rosettes, offers an excellent menu including a seasonal selection of fresh local produce. You may be tempted to choose from the extensive range of bar snacks available in the conservatory or Dovers Bar. The fine selection of wines from around the world are delicious accompaniments to any meal. Try some of the traditional cask ales and keg beers. Browse around the delightful array of shops in Chipping Campden or many of the enchanting honey-coloured Cotswold Villages, Hidcote Manor Gardens, Cheltenham Spa, Worcester, Oxford and Stratford-upon-Avon which are all close by. **Directions:** The Noel Arms is in the centre of Chipping Campden, which is on the B4081, 2 miles east of the A44. Price guide: Single £75; double £105–120.

THE BEAR OF RODBOROUGH

**RODBOROUGH COMMON, STROUD, NR CIRENCESTER, GLOUCESTERSHIRE GL5 5DE
TEL: 01453 878522 FAX: 01453 872523 E-MAIL: bookings@cotswold-inns-hotels.co.uk**

This 17th century former Ale House offers comfortable accommodation in an area of outstanding beauty. Nestling on the top of a steep hill, The Bear of Rodborough is situated in the verdant landscape of the western Cotswolds, described by the author, Laurie Lee, as "vegetative virginity". The inn has recently undergone a careful and precise restoration, at the request of the new owners, yet many of its past features such as the original archway entrance have been retained. The refurbished bedrooms are exquisite, adorned with plush carpets and beautiful fabrics. All have en suite facilities and several thoughtful extras. The superb bar, popular with the locals, is renowned for its large selection of traditional beers. Elegantly furnished, the restaurant is enhanced by the ceiling beams with a 'running bear' design. Specialities include the full English breakfast, made with fresh local produce, whilst the light luncheons and sumptuous dinners must also be savoured. Special breaks include the charming two day 'Cider with Rosie' breaks, based on the famous novel by Laurie Lee. Badger breaks designed for those with a passion for wildlife give an insight into the behavioural patterns of these fascinating creatures. **Directions:** The nearest motorway is the M5, junction 13. Price guide: Single £65–£75; double/twin £110; suite £150.

THE PLOUGH AT CLANFIELD

BOURTON ROAD, CLANFIELD, OXFORDSHIRE OX18 2RB
TEL: 01367 810222 FAX: 01367 810596

The Plough at Clanfield is an idyllic hideaway for the romantic at heart. Set on the edge of the village of Clanfield, typical of the Oxfordshire Cotswolds, The Plough dates from 1560 and is a fine example of well-preserved Elizabethan architecture. The hotel is owned and personally run by John and Rosemary Hodges, who have taken great care to preserve the charm and character of this historic building. As there are only 12 bedrooms, guests can enjoy an intimate atmosphere and attentive, personal service. All the bedrooms are beautifully appointed to the highest standard and all have en suite bathrooms. At the heart of the hotel is the two AA Rosette Shires Restaurant, regarded as one of the finest in the area. The cuisine is superbly prepared and impeccably served, with an interesting selection of wines. Two additional dining rooms are available for private entertaining. The hotel is an ideal base from which to explore the Cotswolds or the Thames Valley. There are many historic houses and gardens in the area, as well as racing at Newbury and Cheltenham. Hotel closed 25th to 29th December. **Directions:** The hotel is located on the edge of the village of Clanfield, at the junction of the A4095 and B4020, between the towns of Witney and Faringdon, some 15 miles to the west of the city of Oxford. Price guide: Single £80; Double £115–£135.

COBHAM (Stoke D'Abernon)

WOODLANDS PARK HOTEL

WOODLANDS LANE, STOKE D'ABERNON, COBHAM, SURREY KT11 3QB
TEL: 01372 843933 FAX: 01372 842704

Set in 15 acres of wooded lawns, Woodlands Park Hotel is an ideal location for touring the surrounding Surrey and Berkshire countryside or for those seeking a base on the edge of Greater London. At the turn of the century, the then Prince of Wales and the famous actress Lillie Langtry were frequent visitors to this splendid Victorian mansion. Well-equipped en suite bedrooms retain an appealing Victorian theme and ambience, despite having been refurbished to the highest modern standards. Each offers its guests luxury, comfort and every up-to-date amenity. The Oak Room Restaurant, awarded 2 AA Rosettes, serves English and French cuisine in elegant surroundings, whilst in the newly refurbished Quotes Brasserie you will discover a wide selection of dishes from the speciality menu, designed for those who prefer less formal dining. Small meeting rooms can be reached from the Grand Hall and can accommodate between 10 and 60 for private dinners or meetings, while the modern Prince of Wales Suite seats up to 280. Nearby are Wisley Gardens, Hampton Court and Brooklands Museum. Kempton Park, Epsom and Sandown are within a short distance for those who enjoy racing. **Directions:** On the M25, take junction 9 or 10. The hotel is east of Cobham at Stoke d'Abernon on the A245. Price guide: (Room only) Single £125–£155; twin/double £155–£215; suites £255.

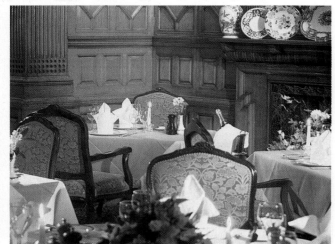

FIVE LAKES HOTEL, GOLF, COUNTRY CLUB & SPA

COLCHESTER ROAD, TOLLESHUNT KNIGHTS, MALDON, ESSEX CM9 8HX
TEL: 01621 868888 FAX: 01621 869696

Set in 320 acres, Five Lakes is a superb 21st century hotel which combines the latest in sporting, leisure and health activities with state-of-the-art conference, meeting and banqueting facilities. The 114 bedrooms are furnished to a high standard and offer every comfort and convenience. With its two 18-hole golf courses – one of them, The Lakes Course, designed by Neil Coles MBE and used annually by the PGA European Tour – the hotel is already recognised as one of East Anglia's leading golf venues. Guests are also invited to take advantage of the championship standard indoor tennis courts; outdoor tennis; squash; indoor pool with Jacuzzi, steam and sauna; gymnasium; jogging trail; snooker and Viverano's health and beauty spa. There is a choice of restaurants, where good food is complemented by excellent service. Lounges and cocktail bars provide a comfortable environment in which to relax and enjoy a drink. Extensive facilities for conferences, meetings, exhibitions and functions include 18 meeting rooms and a 3,500 sqm exhibition hall, suitable for over 3,000 people. All rooms are air-conditioned or comfort-cooled, with 16 rooms having natural daylight. **Directions:** M25 Junction 28, A12 north to Kelvedon exit B1024. Follow Five Lakes signs via Tiptree (B1023). Price guide: (room only) Single £99; double/twin £142; suites £194.

COOMBE ABBEY

BRINKLOW ROAD, BINLEY, WARWICKSHIRE CV3 2AB
TEL: 01203 450450 FAX: 01203 635101

Coombe Abbey is approached by travelling along a lovely avenue of lime trees and chestnuts, crossing a moat and passing through a cloistered entrance. Originally a Cistercian Abbey dating back to the 11th century, this hotel lies in the heart of 500 acres of parkland and formal gardens. Deep colours, carefully selected fabrics and antique furnishing and lighting are all features of its restful bedrooms. Room designs, often eccentric or mischievous, include hidden bathrooms, four poster beds and the occasional hand-painted Victorian bath in the centre of the room. Many bedrooms overlook the grounds with their splendid 80 acre lake. The restaurants and private dining rooms each have their individual charm and offer a variety of settings suitable for all occasions. Sophisticated and creative menus provide a good choice of delightful dishes and the service is attentive but never intrusive. The hotel is an ideal venue for conferences and weddings. Among the local attractions are Warwick Castle and Stratford and the surrounding area is excellent for walking and bird-watching. **Directions:** Leave the M40 at junction 15 and take the A46 towards Binley. Coombe Abbey is on the B4027. Price guide: Single £120–£125; twin/double £130–£135; Feature £180; Grand Feature £305; suite £350. Special weekend rates available.

NAILCOTE HALL

NAILCOTE LANE, BERKSWELL, NR SOLIHULL, WARWICKSHIRE CV7 7DE
TEL: 024 76466174 FAX: 024 76470720 E-MAIL: info@nailcotehall.co.uk

Nailcote Hall is a charming Elizabethan country house hotel set in 15 acres of gardens and surrounded by Warwickshire countryside. Built in 1640, the house was used by Cromwell during the Civil War and was damaged by his troops prior to the assault on Kenilworth Castle. Ideally located in the heart of England, Nailcote Hall is within 15 minutes' drive of the castle towns of Kenilworth and Warwick, Coventry Cathedral, Birmingham International Airport/Station and the NEC. Situated at the centre of the Midlands motorway network, Birmingham city centre, the ICC and Stratford-upon-Avon are less than 30 minutes away. Leisure facilities include indoor swimming pool, gymnasium, solarium and sauna. Outside there are all-weather tennis courts, pétanque, croquet, a challenging 9-hole par-3 golf course and putting green (host to the British Championship Professional Short Course Championship). In the intimate Tudor surroundings of the Oak Room restaurant, the chef will delight you with superb cuisine, while the cellar boasts an extensive choice of international wines. En suite bedrooms offer luxury accommodation and elegant facilities are available for conferences, private dining and corporate hospitality. **Directions:** Situated 6 miles south of Birmingham International Airport/ NEC on the B4101 Balsall Common–Coventry road. Price guide: Single £140; double/twin £150; suite £185–£265.

CRATHORNE HALL HOTEL

CRATHORNE, NR YARM, NORTH YORKSHIRE TS15 0AR
TEL: 01642 700398 FAX: 01642 700814

Part of the Virgin group, Richard Branson's Crathorne Hall was the last great stately home built in the Edwardian era. Now a splendid country house hotel, it is set in 15 acres of woodland overlooking the River Leven and the Cleveland Hills. True to their original fashion, the interiors have elegant antique furnishings complementing the grand architectural style. There is no traffic to wake up to here: just the dawn chorus, all the comforts of a luxury hotel and if desired, a champagne breakfast in bed. From a simple main course to a gastronomic dinner, the food is of the highest quality, complemented by a comprehensive wine list. Whether catering for conferences, product launches, wedding receptions or a quiet weekend for two, professional, courteous service is guaranteed. In the grounds, guests can play croquet, follow the jogging trail or try clay-pigeon shooting with a tutor on a layout designed to entertain the beginner and test the expert. Leisure activities such as clay shooting, golf, ballooning and racing circuit driving can be arranged. The Yorkshire Dales, Durham and York are nearby. **Directions:** From A19 Thirsk–Teesside road, turn to Yarm and Crathorne. Follow signs to Crathorne village; hotel is on left. Teesside Airport and Darlington rail station are both seven miles; a courtesy collection service is available. Price guide: Single £120–£145; double/twin £160–£240. Special rates available.

OCKENDEN MANOR

OCKENDEN LANE, CUCKFIELD, WEST SUSSEX RH17 5LD
TEL: 01444 416111 FAX: 01444 415549 E-MAIL: ockenden@hshotels.co.uk

Set in 9 acres of gardens in the centre of the Tudor village of Cuckfield on the Southern Forest Ridge, this hotel is an ideal base from which to discover Sussex and Kent, the Garden of England. First recorded in 1520, Ockenden Manor has become a hotel of great charm and character. The bedrooms all have their own individual identity: climb your private staircase to Thomas or Elizabeth, look out across the glorious Sussex countryside from Victoria's bay window or choose Charles, with its handsome four-poster bed. The restaurant, with its beautifully painted ceiling, is a dignified setting in which to enjoy acclaimed cuisine. 'Modern English' is how the chef describes his culinary style, offering an à la carte menu with a daily table d'hôte choice to include fresh seasonal produce and herbs from the hotel garden. An outstanding, extensive wine list offers, for example, a splendid choice of first-growth clarets. Spacious and elegantly furnished, the Ockenden Suite welcomes private lunch and dinner parties. A superb conservatory is part of the Ockenden Suite, this opens on to the lawns, where marquees can be set up for summer celebrations. The gardens of Nymans, Wakehurst Place and Leonardslee are nearby, as is the opera at Glyndebourne. **Directions:** In the centre of Cuckfield on the A272. Less than 3 miles east of the A23. Price guide: Single from £99; double/twin from £185; suite from £250.

HEADLAM HALL

HEADLAM, NR GAINFORD, DARLINGTON, COUNTY DURHAM DL2 3HA
TEL: 01325 730238 FAX: 01325 730790 E-MAIL: admin@headlamhall.co.uk

This magnificent 17th century Jacobean mansion stands in four acres of formal walled gardens. The grand main lawn, ancient beach hedges and flowing waters evoke an air of tranquillity. Located in the picturesque hamlet of Headlam and surrounded by over 200 acres of its own rolling farmland, Headlam Hall offers guests a special ambience of seclusion and opulence. The traditional bedrooms are all en suite and furnished to a high standard, many with period furniture. The restaurant offers the very best of classic English and Continental cuisine with our kitchen team enjoying a fine reputation for their dishes. An extensive well-chosen wine list highlights the dining experience. Guests may dine in the tasteful surroundings of either the Panelled room, the Victorian room, the Patio room or Conservatory. The main hall features huge stone pillars and the superb original carved oak fireplace, which has dominated the room for over 300 years. The elegant Georgian drawing room opens on to a stepped terrace overlooking the main lawn. The hotel also offers extensive conference facilities and a fine ballroom, the Edwardian Suite with its oak floor and glass ceiling, suitable for up to 150 people. The vast range of leisure facilities include a swimming pool, mini gym, croquet lawn and snooker room with eight golf courses nearby. **Directions:** Headlam is 2 miles N of Gainford off A67 Darlington–Barnard Castle road. Price guide: Single £65–£75; double/twin £80–£90; suite £105.

ROWHILL GRANGE

WILMINGTON, DARTFORD, KENT DA2 7QH
TEL: 01322 615136 FAX: 01322 615137 E-MAIL: admin@rowhillgrange.com

An unexpected find on the outer edge of London bordering on the Kent countryside, Rowhill Grange nestles in nine acres of woodlands and mature gardens descending to a picturesque lake. A combination of top service and friendliness makes Rowhill Grange the perfect venue for everything from weekend breaks to special occasions such as weddings and anniversaries. All the luxurious bedrooms are named after flowers and boast individual character and decoration, with a full range of facilities available to ensure maximum comfort and convenience for guests. The à la carte Restaurant is supplemented with the delightful Topiary Brasserie. From late spring and through the summer months guests may take dinner on the terrace, sharing a scenic view with the swans and ducks. For special occasions, business meetings or dinners the private oak panelled dining room is available. The Clockhouse Suite is a self contained functions annexe with a dining/dancing area, comfortable lounge and a bar. The Utopia Health and Leisure Spa is outstanding with all the latest equipment for women and for men including the UK's first therapy pool of its kind. **Directions:** M20 junction 1/M25 junction 3. Take the B2173 into Swanley and B258 north at Superstore roundabout. After Hextable Green the entrance is almost immediately on the left. Price guide (room only): Single £99–£139; double/twin £109–£159; suite £149–£189.

DARTMOOR (Haytor Vale)

BEL ALP HOUSE

HAYTOR, NR BOVEY TRACEY, SOUTH DEVON TQ13 9XX
TEL: 01364 661217 FAX: 01364 661292

Peace and seclusion are guaranteed at the Bel Alp House with its spectacular outlook from the edge of Dartmoor across a rolling patchwork of fields and woodland to the sea, 20 miles away. Built as an Edwardian country mansion and owned in the 1920s by millionairess Dame Violet Wills, Bel Alp has been lovingly restored and the personal attention of new owners Jack, Mary and Rachael Twist ensures their guests' enjoyment and comfort in the atmosphere of a private home. The set dinner is changed nightly, using only the best local produce and the meals are accompanied by a well-chosen and comprehensive wine list. Of the eight en suite bedrooms, two still have their original Edwardian basins and

baths mounted on marble plinths and all bedrooms have views over the gardens. An abundance of house plants, open log fires and restful colours complements the family antiques and pictures to create the perfect environment in which to relax. Awarded an AA Rosette. Bel Alp is ideally situated for exploring Devon and parts of Cornwall: Plymouth, famed for Drake and the Pilgrim Fathers, Exeter with its Norman cathedral and National Trust properties Castle Drogo and Cotehele Manor House are all within an hour's drive. **Directions:** Bel Alp is off the B3387 Haytor road, 2½ miles from Bovey Tracey. Price guide: Single £65–£75; double/twin £130–£160. Discounts may be available on room rate.

FAWSLEY HALL HOTEL

FAWSLEY, NR DAVENTRY, NORTHAMPTONSHIRE NN11 3BA
TEL: 01327 892000 FAX: 01327 892001 E-MAIL: fawsley@compuserve.com

Set in the beautiful Northamptonshire countryside and surrounded by acres of rolling parkland with lakes landscaped by Capability Brown, Fawsley Hall combines the charm and character of a gracious manor with the facilities and comforts of a modern hotel. The original Tudor Manor house opened as a hotel in 1998 but many traces of its illustrious past have been retained such as the vaulted hall and Queen Elizabeth I chamber. The hotel accommodation comprises 30 wonderfully decorated rooms offering an extraordinary range of Tudor, Georgian and Victorian styles, many of which include four-poster beds. The former Tudor kitchen has been transformed into a restaurant that has established a reputation for one of the finest in Northamptonshire. There are seven conference and syndicate rooms that can accommodate up to 80 delegates and the attractive Salvin Suite can seat up to 80 for a private banquet or wedding reception. The surrounding countryside offers a host of activities for both the energetic and the more relaxed visitor, whilst places of historic interest abound: Sulgrave Manor, ancestral home of George Washington, Althorp, Canons Ashby, an Elizabethan manor house and Warwick Castle. Oxford, Stratford-upon-Avon and Blenheim Palace are nearby as are Silverstone and Towcester Racecourse. **Directions:** Motorways are M40, Jct11 or M1, Jct16: both 10 miles from Fawsley Hall. Price guide: Single from £185; double/twin from £215; suite from £425.

MAISON TALBOOTH

STRATFORD ROAD, DEDHAM, COLCHESTER, ESSEX CO7 6HN
TEL: 01206 322367 FAX: 01206 322752 E-MAIL: mtreception@talbooth.co.uk

In the north-east corner of Essex, where the River Stour borders with Suffolk, is the Vale of Dedham, an idyllic riverside setting immortalised in the early 19th century by the paintings of John Constable. One summer's day in 1952, the young Gerald Milsom enjoyed a 'cuppa' in the Talbooth tearoom and soon afterwards took the helm at what would develop into Le Talbooth Restaurant. Business was soon booming and the restaurant built itself a reputation as one of the best in the country. In 1969 Maison Talbooth was created in a nearby Victorian rectory, to become, as it still is, a standard bearer for Britain's premier country house hotels. Indeed, in 1982 Gerald Milsom became the founder of the Pride of Britain group. With its atmosphere of opulence, Maison Talbooth has ten spacious guest suites which all have an air of quiet luxury. Every comfort has been provided. Breakfast is served in the suites. The original Le Talbooth Restaurant is about half a mile upstream on a riverside terrace reached by leisurely foot or courtesy car. It has recently been awarded the coveted Booker Sword of Excellence for quality, flair and renown. 'Which' Hotel of the Year for Essex. The hotel arranges special Constable tours. **Directions:** Dedham is about a mile from the A12 between Colchester and Ipswich. Price guide: Single £90–£130; double/twin £115–£175. Telephone for details of special short breaks. Exclusive use available.

MAKENEY HALL COUNTRY HOUSE HOTEL

MAKENEY, MILFORD, NEAR BELPER, DERBYSHIRE DE56 0RS
TEL: 01332 842999 FAX: 01332 842777

Set in a restful location on the River Derwent, Makeney Hall is surrounded by over 6 acres of beautifully landscaped gardens just 10 minutes' drive from Derby, a historic city famous for its china, its silk and Rolls Royce. Built originally by the Strutt family this capacious and restful hotel, with its mid-Victorian features, offers guests a warm, distinctive welcome. The carefully chosen décor imparts an air of bygone comfort. Bedrooms in the main house are spacious and individually appointed and many overlook the gardens. A splendid covered courtyard gives access to a further eighteen new rooms. Guests dine in Lavinia's AA Rosetted restaurant, where expert cooking and fresh produce create cuisine of the highest standard. The fare is British in flavour and a selection of fine wines is available. The hotel is now firmly established as one of Derbyshire's favourite, year-round venues for wedding ceremonies and receptions. Conference and banqueting suites accommodate up to 180 visitors. Places of interest locally include the Derwent Valley – an area of outstanding natural beauty – the Peak District, the stately homes of Chatsworth and Haddon Hall and Alton Towers. **Directions:** From M1 (exits 25 or 28) head for Derby and A38 northbound. Follow A6 (signposted Matlock). Makeney is signposted at Milford, 6 miles NW of Derby. Price guide: Double/twin: from £80; suite: from £150.

MICKLEOVER COURT

ETWALL ROAD, MICKLEOVER, DERBYSHIRE DE3 5XX
TEL: 01332 521234 FAX: 01332 521238 E-MAIL: enquiries@mickleovercourt.com

This unusual, modern hotel located in Derbyshire but only 2 miles from Derby city centre offers impressive, air conditioned, pleasantly furnished bedrooms, each with its own balcony. There are welcoming finishing touches including fresh fruit, bathrobes, in-house movies and satellite television. There is a choice of dining; modern brasserie-style in Avesbury using freshly sourced local produce and classical and regional Italian in the lively, informal Trattoria in the hotel's atrium. The two distinctive bars offer a delightful setting for a pre-dinner drink or post prandial night-cap. Castaways Leisure Club has state-of-the-art gymnasium equipment, a large tropical pool, steam room, sauna, a coffee shop serving an all day snack menu and the 'Castaways' hair and beauty salon. The hotel's extensive conference and banqueting facilities are extremely versatile and can accommodate up to 200 guests. The wide range of activities and country pursuits include golf, hot-air ballooning, gliding, racing car tuition and water-skiing. Alton Towers, Uttoxeter Race Course and the Peak District are nearby. **Directions:** From M1 southbound, exit Jct28, A38 south past Derby, on to A516 towards Uttoxeter. Hotel is on right. From M1 northbound, exit 24 A50 exit Jct5 on to A516. 1st roundabout right, 2nd roundabout on to A516, follow brown sign. From M6, exit 15 to A50 exit Jct5 A516, follow brown sign. Hotel is on left. Price guide: Single from £120; double/twin from £145.

THE PRIEST HOUSE ON THE RIVER

KINGS MILLS, CASTLE DONINGTON, DERBYSHIRE DE74 2RR
TEL: 01332 810649 FAX: 01332 811141

Magnificently situated on the banks of the River Trent, The Priest House is surrounded by 54 acres of mature unspoilt woodland. Each of the bedrooms have been individually styled and the splendid Heron and Stocker suites are designed within the original Gothic Tower. Opening onto the private courtyard garden, the elegant library provides a perfect environment in which to read and relax. The traditional Waterside Inn offers a selection of real ales and is a popular venue for guests and non-residents alike, along with the Malt Bar which boasts over 50 different malt whiskies. The Mille Fleame Restaurant enjoys a growing reputation for the imaginative cuisine that it provides at both lunch and dinner, complemented by an excellent wine list. A number of spacious suites are available for banquets, receptions, weddings and private parties. A variety of leisure activities are available within the hotel, including clay-pigeon shooting, coarse fishing and go-karting (all by arrangement). Places of interest nearby include Calke Abbey and Donington Park race circuit. **Directions:** From M1, junction 23A, follow signs for Donington Park then Castle Donington. At Castle Donington go left at traffic lights and follow road marked Kings Mills to the Priest House. Price guide: Single from £89, double/twin from £109; four-poster from £125; suite from £175.

RISLEY HALL COUNTRY HOUSE HOTEL

DERBY ROAD, RISLEY, DERBYSHIRE DE72 3SS
TEL: 0115 939 9000 FAX: 0115 939 7766

The former glory of Risley Hall is evident once more as this country house hotel has recently undergone a careful and extensive restoration. A grade II listed building, Risley Hall Country House Hotel is an ideal retreat for those seeking a peaceful atmosphere. The beautiful gardens were laid out in Elizabethan times and are quite spectacular with colourful floral arrangements and an old moat. Inside, the décor is rather charming with comfortable furnishings, oak beams and ornate fireplaces. The bedrooms, individually designed and all tastefully decorated in period style, offer every modern amenity including a television, hairdryer and tea/coffee making facilities. Guests recline in the cosy Drawing Room with their afternoon tea or enjoy an after dinner coffee, whilst the Cocktail Lounge serves lunchtime drinks or pre-dinner apéritifs. Within close proximity of junction 25 of the M1 midway between Nottingham and Derby, Risley Hall has the perfect surroundings for corporate meetings or any special occasions. The area is surrounded by historic buildings such as Chatsworth House, Nottingham Castle and Kedleston Hall and is also known for its literary connections with Lord Byron and DH Lawrence. **Directions:** The nearest motorway is the M1. Exit at junction 25 towards Sandiacre. Price guide: Single £75–£95; double/twin £95–£115.

LUMLEY CASTLE HOTEL

CHESTER-LE-STREET, COUNTY DURHAM DH3 4NX
TEL: 0191 389 1111 FAX: 0191 387 1437

This magnificent 14th century castle offers an exciting blend of ancient history and modern convenience. The bedrooms are each individually styled and appointed to a high standard. The King James Suite is Lumley's hallmark of taste and distinction. The public areas of the hotel, amply supported by medieval pillars, captivate the attention and imagination of all visitors. The subdued lighting and hidden corridors enhance the exciting atmosphere that pervades this amazing building. The Black Knight Restaurant will please the most experienced palate. Lumley Castle's Medieval Memories special weekend breaks offer a magnificent 'getaway' opportunity. These include an evening at the award-winning Elizabethan Banquet, full of fun, feasting (5-course meal) and merriment. The sharp wit and musical talent of the Castle's entertainers in their striking costumery offer a night to remember. There are 25 golf courses within 25 minutes drive. The Riverside Health Club offers 'full' facilities for Hotel guests at a discounted rate. For the more serious minded, Lumley has a number of conference and meeting rooms which provide an unusual setting for business matters. **Directions:** From A1(M) northbound take A693/A167 to Chester-le-Street and Durham. At the second roundabout take first left to Lumley Castle. Price guide: Single £98–£140; double/twin £142–£195; suite £242.

GRINKLE PARK HOTEL

EASINGTON, SALTBURN-BY-THE-SEA, CLEVELAND TS13 4UB
TEL: 01287 640515 FAX: 01287 641278 E-MAIL: hotel@leeds.taverns.bass.co.uk

Cleveland means 'cliff-land' and cliffs predominate both along the coast and inland where the great scarp of the Cleveland Hills drops down to the lowlands south of the Tees. This is where the imposing, grey granite-stoned Grinkle Park Hotel with its tall majestic tower stands, between unspoiled coastline and the wild North York Moors National Park. Midway between Saltburn-on-Sea and picturesque, historic Whitby, home port of Captain Cook, this 19th century mansion is surrounded by 35 acres of magnificent parkland and gardens overflowing with azaleas and rhododendrons. Peacocks strut the grounds and wildfowl flock to the hotel's lake. Grinkle Park's 20 en suite bedrooms are all named after the many species of birds and

wonderful flora abundant in the surrounding moorland countryside. Each spacious bedroom offers panoramic views and has every comfort and luxury the discerning guest could wish for. Chef Tim Backhouse provides gastronomic table d'hôte and à la carte delights in the elegant dining room, where the emphasis is on presentation and quality. For relaxation there is a billiards room, croquet lawn and a tennis court. The more active guest can clay pigeon shoot, play golf locally, sail, climb, fish or stroll the moorland pathways. **Directions**: Grinkle Park Hotel is situated 9 miles from Guisborough, signed left, off the main A171 Guisborough – Whitby road. Price guide: Single: £79–£99; double/twin: £97–£118.

THE GRAND HOTEL

KING EDWARD'S PARADE, EASTBOURNE, EAST SUSSEX BN21 4EQ
TEL: 01323 412345 FAX: 01323 412233

The Grand Hotel is a fine property, steeped in history, which evokes the charm and splendour of the Victorian era. The majestic facade complements the elegant interior whilst the reception rooms are beautifully appointed with rich fabrics and ornaments. Many of the 152 bedrooms are of vast proportions: all being refurbished to include every comfort with attractive bathrooms. The hotel has numerous areas in which to relax and a good choice of restaurants and bars. The array of new leisure facilities includes both indoor and outdoor pools, gymnasium, sauna, solarium, spa bath, steam room, snooker tables and a hair salon and 8 beauty rooms. Guests may enjoy membership of nearby racquet and golf clubs. For the meeting organiser, the hotel offers an impressive range of rooms which can cater for a number of business purposes from a board meeting for 12 to a larger conference for up to 300 delegates. Those seeking a peaceful retreat will be pleased with the tranquil atmosphere of Eastbourne. Pastimes include walks along the Downs, sea fishing and trips to the two nearby theatres. **Directions:** Follow signs on M25 for M23 (Gatwick Airport/Brighton) then take A27 onto the A22 to Eastbourne, or A259 from the East or West. At Eastbourne follow the signs to the seafront. Turn right towards the western end of the front, The Grand Hotel is situated opposite the Western Lawns. Price guide: Single £115–£220; double/twin £145–£245; suite £285–£385.

GREAT FOSTERS

STROUDE ROAD, EGHAM, SURREY TW20 9UR
TEL: 01784 433822 FAX: 01784 472455 E-MAIL: GreatFosters@compuserve.com

Probably built as a Royal Hunting lodge in Windsor Forest, very much a stately home since the 16th century, today Great Fosters is a prestigious hotel within half an hour of both Heathrow Airport and central London. Its past is evident in the mullioned windows, tall chimneys and brick finials, while the Saxon moat – crossed by a Japanese bridge – surrounds three sides of the formal gardens, complete with topiary, statuary and a charming rose garden. Within are fine oak beams and panelling, Jacobean chimney pieces, superb tapestries and a rare oakwell staircase leading to the Tower. Some of the guest rooms are particularly magnificent – one Italian styled with gilt furnishings and damask walls, others with moulded ceilings, beautiful antiques and Persian rugs. Guests relax in the bar, then enjoy good English and French cooking and carefully selected wines, either in the Tudor Dining Room or the Tithe Barn with its vaulted roof. Celebrations, meetings and weddings take place in the elegant Orangery and impressive Painted Hall, the ceiling a riot of exotic birds and animals. Great Fosters is close to polo in Windsor Great Park, racing at Ascot, golf at Wentworth, boating in Henley and pageantry at Windsor Castle, Runnymede and Hampton Court. **Directions:** M25/J13, head for Egham and watch for brown 'Historic Buildings' signs. Price guide: Single from £85; double/twin from £105; suite from £225.

SUMMER LODGE

SUMMER LANE, EVERSHOT, DORSET DT2 0JR
TEL: 01935 83424 FAX: 01935 83005 E-MAIL: sumlodge@sumlodge.demon.co.uk

A charming Georgian building, idyllically located in Hardy country, the Summer Lodge was formerly the dower house of the Earls of Ilchester. Now it is a luxurious hotel where owners Nigel and Margaret Corbett who have now been joined by their daughter Tara, and son-in-law Daniel who acts as General Manager offer their guests a genuinely friendly welcome, encouraging them to relax as if in their own home. The bedrooms have views over the 4-acre sheltered gardens or overlook the village rooftops across the meadowland. In the dining room, with its French windows that open on to the garden, the cuisine is highly regarded. Fresh local produce is combined with the culinary expertise of chef Tim Ford to create a distinctive brand of English cooking. The unspoiled Dorset countryside and its coastline, 12 miles south, make for limitless exploration and bring to life the setting of *Tess of the d'Urbervilles, The Mayor of Casterbridge, Far from the Madding Crowd* and the other Hardy novels. Many National Trust properties and gardens in the locality are open to the public. There are stables, golf courses and trout lakes nearby. **Directions:** The turning to Evershot leaves the A37 halfway between Dorchester and Yeovil. Once in the village, turn left into Summer Lane and the hotel entrance is 150 yards on the right. Price guide: Single £125; double/twin £175–£285.

THE EVESHAM HOTEL

COOPERS LANE, OFF WATERSIDE, EVESHAM, WORCESTERSHIRE WR11 6DA
TEL: 01386 765566 RESERVATIONS: 0800 716969 FAX: 01386 765443

It is the somewhat unconventional atmosphere at the Evesham Hotel that stays in the memory. Originally a Tudor farmhouse, the hotel was extended and converted into a Georgian mansion house in 1809. Unusually, it combines an award-winning welcome for families with the relaxed but efficient style required by business users. For the past quarter of a century it has been successfully run by the Jenkinson family. Each of the 39 en suite bedrooms is furnished complete with a teddy bear and a toy duck for the bath. The restaurant offers delicious cuisine from a very imaginative and versatile menu, accompanied by a somewhat unique "Euro-sceptic" wine list (everything but French and German!). The drinks selection is an amazing myriad. The indoor swimming pool has a seaside theme. The peace of the 2½ acre garden belies the hotel's proximity to the town – a 5 minute walk away. In the gardens are six 300 year-old mulberry trees and a magnificent cedar of Lebanon, planted in 1809. The hotel is a good base from which to explore the Cotswolds, Stratford-upon-Avon and the Severn Valley. Closed at Christmas. **Directions:** Coopers Lane lies just off Waterside (the River Avon). Price guide: Single £64–£72; double/twin £96–£100.

WOOD NORTON HALL

WOOD NORTON, EVESHAM, WORCESTERSHIRE WR11 4YB
TEL: 01386 420007 FAX: 01386 420190 E-MAIL: Woodnorton.hall@BBC.co.uk

Wood Norton Hall is a glorious Grade II listed Victorian country house standing in 170 acres of beautiful Worcestershire countryside. A short drive from the historic market town of Evesham, 8 miles from Broadway and the Cotswolds with Stratford-upon-Avon only 15 miles away. French connections dating back to 1872 culminated in the wedding of Princess Louise of Orleans and Prince Charles of Bourbon in 1907. Original fleur-de-lys carved oak panelling lines the walls, grand fireplaces, elegant furniture and beautiful tapestries add comfort and colour. The en suite rooms are furnished to the very highest standards. The ground floor public rooms reflect the grandeur of the Victorian era with voluptuous window drapes framing magnificent views to the Vale of Evesham and the River Avon. The award-winning Duc's Restaurant provides the perfect ambience to savour a fine culinary tradition and a small, intimate bar offers pre and post dining relaxation. The hall offers eight rooms suitable for conferences, private banquets and is an ideal venue for incentive programmes. Extensive leisure facilities include a swimming pool, billiard room, fitness suite and golf at a nearby championship course. **Directions:** Evesham is reached from M5 via Jct7 and then south east on A44, or via Jct9 and then NE on A435. Price guide: Single from £115; double/twin from £155; suite from £160. Weekend breaks and themed weekends feature throughout the year; details available on request.

COMBE HOUSE AT GITTISHAM

HONITON, NR EXETER, DEVON EX14 0AD
TEL: 01404 540400 FAX: 01404 46004 E-MAIL: stay@combe–house.co.uk

Tucked away in a glorious East Devon country estate of 3500 acres at the head of a secluded valley lies Combe House, a beautiful Elizabethan mansion. Offering award-winning cuisine, interesting wines and warm hospitality, the house is one of the finest settings in Devon. The welcoming atmosphere of a large family house is enhanced with treasured antiques, family portraits, burning log fires and fresh country flowers. The fifteen bedrooms vary in size and feature en suite bathrooms and comfortable furnishings. They, along with the various sitting and dining rooms, afford fine views across the lush countryside, where magnificent Arabian horses and pheasants traverse the grounds freely. Guests must sample the cuisine which has been awarded two AA Rosettes. With its excellent standards of accommodation and service, Combe House is becoming an increasingly popular choice for relaxing breaks, special occasions, weddings, house parties, business meetings and corporate hospitality. Once described by HRH Prince Charles as "the ideal English Village", Gittisham lies at the end of the 3/4 mile drive. The A30 and Honiton are within two miles. Combe House is an ideal base for those visiting Exeter and the West Country. **Directions:** From the M5 junction 28 take A373, M5 junction 29 take A30, towards Honiton, then follow signs to Gittisham. Price guide: Single £85–£115; double/twin £102–£146.

ST OLAVES COURT HOTEL

MARY ARCHES STREET, EXETER, DEVON EX4 3AZ
TEL: 01392 217736 FAX: 01392 413054

St Olaves Court, famous for its restaurant and home-from-home atmosphere, stands just 400 yards from Exeter Cathedral. It is a lovely Georgian building which is secluded in its own walled garden; an oasis in the city centre. The rooms are very well-cared for and range from single and twins to luxurious double bedrooms with Jacuzzi. The hotel has been discreetly furnished, partly with antiques and the public rooms are spacious and comfortable. A particularly attractive cocktail bar overlooks the garden. The level of service provided is first rate and reassuringly old fashioned. Central to the enjoyment of St Olaves is the excellence of the cooking. The candlelit restaurant, one of the best in south west England, is renowned for its outstanding cuisine. St Olaves Court Hotel is ideally placed for visiting famous National Trust gardens like Killerton and for exploring the City of Exeter as well as the South Devon coastline and the beauties of Dartmoor National Park. **Directions:** From Exeter city centre follow signs to 'Mary Arches P'. The hotel entrance is directly opposite. Price guide: Single £70–£90; double/twin £75–£110.

BUDOCK VEAN GOLF & COUNTRY HOUSE HOTEL

HELFORD RIVER, MAWNAN SMITH, FALMOUTH, CORNWALL TR11 5LG
TEL: 01326 250288 FAX: 01326 250892 RESERVATIONS: 01326 252100

The elegant 4 star Budock Vean Golf and Country House Hotel is set in 65 acres of beautiful gardens and parklands, with a private foreshore leading to the Helford River. Most of the comfortably furnished bedrooms enjoy stunning views over the hotel's subtropical gardens, some have adjoining sitting rooms and all are well-equipped with modern amenities. Keen appetites will be well-satisfied by the variety of dishes offered on the hotel's excellent and original menus. Seafood, including local lobsters and oysters, is an obvious speciality. In addition to traditional food, there is a choice of dishes with an international flavour. The hotel has its own tennis courts, golf course, health spa and swimming pool and activities including water sports, horse-riding, yachting, boating and fishing are all within easy reach of the hotel. Numerous places of interest nearby include the Seal Sanctuary at Gweek, several heritage sites and many magnificent gardens and properties of the National Trust. **Directions:** Follow A39 to Falmouth, at Hillhead roundabout follow signs for Trebah Gardens and Mawnan Smith. Take the right at the Red Lion. Pass Trebah Gardens and the turning for Helford Passage – Budock Vean is on the left. Price guide: Single £39–£89; double/twin £98–£178; suites £138–£218. (Add £10 per person for 5-course dinner in the 2 AA Rosette restaurant).

MEUDON HOTEL

MAWNAN SMITH, NR FALMOUTH, CORNWALL TR11 5HT
TEL: 01326 250541 FAX: 01326 250543 E-MAIL: info@meudon.co.uk

Set against a delightfully romantic backdrop of densely wooded countryside between the Fal and Helford Rivers, Meudon Hotel is a unique, superior retreat: a luxury, family-run establishment which has its origins in two humble 17th century coastguards' cottages. The French name comes from a nearby farmhouse built by Napoleonic prisoners of war and called after their eponymous home village in the environs of Paris. Set in nearly nine acres of subtropical gardens coaxed annually into early bloom by the mild Cornish climate – Meudon is safely surrounded by 200 acres of beautiful National Trust land and the sea. All bedrooms in a modern wing are en suite and enjoy spectacular views over subtropical gardens. Many a guest is enticed by the cuisine to return: in the restaurant (or the gardens during warm weather), fresh seafood and kitchen garden produce are served with wines from a judiciously compiled list. There are opportunities locally for fishing, sailing and walking. Golf is free at nearby Falmouth Golf Club and eight others in Cornwall. **Directions:** From Truro A39 to Hillhead roundabout turn right and the hotel is four miles on the left. Price guide (including dinner): Single £105; double/twin £190; suite £250.

PENMERE MANOR

MONGLEATH ROAD, FALMOUTH, CORNWALL TR11 4PN
TEL: 01326 211411 FAX: 01326 317588 E-MAIL: reservations@penmere.demon.co.uk

Set in five acres of subtropical gardens and woodlands, this elegant Georgian country house is an oasis of gracious living and fine food. From arrival to departure the Manor's attentive staff ensure that guests have everything they need to enjoy their stay. Bedrooms offer every comfort and are furnished to maintain the country house ambience. The spacious Garden rooms (as illustrated) are delightful. Each is named after a famous Cornish garden and has either king or queen size beds and a lounge area. The restaurant serves excellent international cuisine that includes an extensive lobster speciality menu. Light snacks and substantial lunchtime dishes are also provided in the bar which overlooks the garden and terrace. There is a heated outdoor swimming pool in the old walled garden and a splendid indoor pool, together with Jacuzzi spa, sauna, solarium and gym. Golfers can make use of the hotel's practice net and benefit from reduced green fees at Falmouth Golf Course. Cornish gardens, National Trust and English Heritage properties are within reach. Flambards Theme Park, Poldark Mine and Gweek Seal Sanctuary are less than ten miles away. **Directions:** From Truro follow the A39 towards Falmouth. Turn right at Hillhead roundabout and after 1 mile turn left into Mongleath Road. Price guide: Single £53–£60.50; double/twin £80–£119.

ASHDOWN PARK HOTEL AND COUNTRY CLUB

WYCH CROSS, FOREST ROW, EAST SUSSEX RH18 5JR
TEL: 01342 824988 FAX: 01342 826206 E-MAIL: reservations@ashdownpark.co.uk

Ashdown Park is a grand, rambling 19th century mansion overlooking almost 200 acres of landscaped gardens to the forest beyond. Built in 1867, the hotel is situated within easy reach of Gatwick Airport, London and the South Coast and provides the perfect backdrop for every occasion, from a weekend getaway to a honeymoon or business convention. The hotel is subtly furnished throughout to satisfy the needs of escapees from urban stress. The 95 en suite bedrooms are beautifully decorated – several with elegant four-poster beds, all with up-to-date amenities. The Anderida restaurant offers a thoughtfully compiled menu and wine list, complemented by discreetly attentive service in soigné surroundings. Guests seeking relaxation can retire to the indoor pool and sauna, pamper themselves with a massage, before using the solarium, or visiting the beauty salon. Alternatively, guests may prefer to amble through the gardens and nearby woodland paths; the more energetic can indulge in tennis, croquet or use the Fitness Studio and Beauty Therapy. There is also an indoor driving range, a lounge/bar and an 18-hole par 3 golf course with an outdoor driving range. **Directions:** East of A22 at Wych Cross traffic lights on road signposted to Hartfield. Price guide: Single £115–£285; double/twin £145–£305; suite £305.

FOWEY HALL HOTEL & RESTAURANT

HANSON DRIVE, FOWEY, CORNWALL PL23 1ET
TEL: 01726 833866 FAX: 01726 834100

Situated in five acres of beautiful grounds overlooking the Estuary, Fowey Hall Hotel is a magnificent Victorian mansion renowned for its excellent service and comfortable accommodation. The fine panelling and superb plasterwork ceilings add character to the spacious public rooms. Located in either the main house or the Court, the 25 bedrooms include suites and interconnecting rooms. All are well-proportioned with a full range of modern comforts. The panelled dining rooms provide an intimate atmosphere where guests may savour the local delicacies. Using the best of regional produce, the menu comprises tempting seafood and fish specialities. The hotel offers a full crèche service. Guests may swim in the indoor swimming pool or play croquet in the gardens. Older children have not been forgotten and the cellars of the mansion are well-equipped with table tennis, table football and many other games. Outdoor pursuits include sea fishing, boat trips and a variety of water sports such as sailing, scuba-diving and windsurfing. There are several coastal walks for those who wish to explore Cornwall and its beautiful landscape. **Directions:** On reaching Fowey, go straight over the mini roundabout and turn right into Hanson Drive. Fowey Hall Drive is on the right. Price guide: Double/twin £125–£140; superior double £160; suite £175–£245.

ALEXANDER HOUSE

TURNER'S HILL, WEST SUSSEX RH10 4QD
TEL: 01342 714914 FAX: 01342 717328

A previous winner of Johansens Most Excellent Service award, Alexander House is a magnificent mansion with its own secluded 135 acres of parkland, including a gently sloping valley which forms the head of the River Medway. Records trace the estate from 1332 when a certain John Atte Fen made it his home. Alexander House is now a modern paragon of good taste and excellence. Spacious rooms throughout this luxurious hotel are splendidly decorated to emphasise their many original features and the bedrooms are lavishly furnished to the highest standards of comfort. The House is renowned for its delicious classic English and French cuisine, rare wines and vintage liqueurs.

Music recitals and garden parties feature among a full programme of special summer events and the open fires and cosy atmosphere make this the ideal place to pamper yourself in winter. The many facilities include a resident beautician. Courtesy transport can take guests to Gatwick Airport in under 15 minutes. Antique shops, National Trust properties, museums and the Royal Pavilion in Brighton are nearby. **Directions:** Alexander House lies on the B2110 road between Turner's Hill and East Grinstead, six miles from junction 10 of the M23 motorway. Price guide: Single £120; double/twin £155; suites £195–£285.

GATWICK (Horley)

LANGSHOTT MANOR

LANGSHOTT, HORLEY, SURREY RH6 9LN

TEL: 01293 786680 FAX: 01293 783905 E-MAIL: admin@langshottmanor.com

The peace and seclusion of this beautiful Manor House belies its close proximity to London's Gatwick Airport, 8 minutes away by car. Retaining the essential feel of a fine Elizabethan home, Langshott offers stylish bedrooms and an intimate dining room with every provision for your comfort. The Manor becomes the perfect beginning or end to your holiday in Britain. Free car parking is offered locally for one week and a complimentary car is made available to guests travelling to Gatwick. Although Langshott Manor is situated near to the airport, the house is tucked away down a quiet country lane amidst 3 acres of beautiful gardens and enchanting ponds. A peaceful ambience pervades the manor, ensuring complete relaxation for all its guests. For a longer stay, the area is also a haven for sport enthusiasts with racing at Epsom and Goodwood and polo at Cowdray and Gaurds. Many National Trust gardens and properties are clustered around Langshott Manor such as Hever Castle, Chartwell and Knole Park. Central London is 30 minutes away via the Gatwick/Victoria Express. **Directions:** From A23 in Horley take Ladbroke Road (Chequers Hotel roundabout) to Langshott. The manor is three quarters of a mile (one kilometre) on the right. Price guide: Single from £125; double/twin from £155–£210; suite £250.

THE WIND IN THE WILLOWS

DERBYSHIRE LEVEL, GLOSSOP, DERBYSHIRE SK13 7PT
TEL: 01457 868001 FAX: 01457 853354 E-MAIL: twitwh@aol.com

"Not so much a hotel, more a delightful experience" wrote a guest of this charming, small, family-run hotel on the edge of the Peak District. It won the AA Greatest Courtesy and Care in the North of England award 1996/97. The mother-and-son team of Anne and Peter Marsh have added lavish care, attention to detail and a sincere courtesy to their recipe of antiques, Victorian bric-à-brac and delightful charm that is characteristic of The Wind in the Willows. If you don't know how it gets its name, stay there and read your bedside book! The marvellous scenery of the National Park is, literally, at the doorstep. All of the twelve, en suite bedrooms enjoy superb views and all are full of character, even the newer ones, opened in 1995, having their share of antique furniture and traditional décor that embellishes the whole house. There are some very special features, too – huge antique mahogany beds, a Victorian style bath and individual touches created by Anne in various rooms. Hilary Barton presides in the kitchen from where delicious home-cooking is served to both the private dining room and the purpose-built meeting room. Many activities can be arranged locally, including pot-holing, horse-riding, gliding and para/hang gliding. **Directions:** One mile east of Glossop on the A57, 400 yards down the road opposite the Royal Oak. Price guide: Single £70–£90; double/twin £88–£115.

GRAYTHWAITE MANOR

FERNHILL ROAD, GRANGE-OVER-SANDS, CUMBRIA LA11 7JE
TEL: 015395 32001 FAX: 015395 35549

This beautifully furnished, traditionally run country house has been run by the Blakemore family since 1937 and extends a warm welcome to its guests. It enjoys a superb setting in eight acres of private landscaped gardens and woodland on the hillside overlooking Morecambe Bay. Each bedroom is decorated and furnished in the best of taste and many offer superb views across the gardens and bay to the Pennines beyond. Elegant, spacious lounges with fresh flowers and antiques provide an exclusive setting and log fires are lit to add extra cheer on cooler nights. The Manor enjoys an excellent reputation for its cuisine and guests can look forward to a six-course dinner comprising carefully prepared dishes complemented by the right wine from the extensive cellar. A few miles inland from Grange-over-Sands are Lake Windermere and Coniston Water and some of the most majestic scenery in the country. Nearby are the village of Cartmel, Holker Hall, Levens Hall and Sizergh Castle. The area abounds with historic buildings, gardens and museums. **Directions:** Take M6 to junction 36 and then the A65 towards Kendal, followed by the A590 towards Barrow. At roundabout take B5277 to Grange-over-Sands and go through town turning right opposite the fire station into Fernhill Road. The hotel is on the left. Price guide: Single £47.50–£60; double/twin £85–£104.

MICHAELS NOOK

GRASMERE, CUMBRIA LA22 9RP
TEL: 015394 35496 FAX: 015394 35645 E-MAIL: m.nook@wordsworth–grasmere.co.uk

Built in 1859 and named after Michael the eponymous shepherd of Wordsworth's poem, Michael's Nook has long been established as one of Britain's leading country house hotels. Opened as a hotel in 1969 by Reg and Elizabeth Gifford, it overlooks Grasmere Valley and is surrounded by gardens and trees. The hotel's interior reflects Reg's appreciation of antique English furniture, rugs, prints and porcelain. There are two suites and twelve individually designed bedrooms. Reg's hobby of showing Great Danes has brought him many awards, including Best of Breed at Crufts. In the acclaimed restaurant, polished tables are set with fine Stuart crystal and Wedgwood china. The best ingredients are used to create dishes memorable for their delicate flavours and artistic presentation. An extensive and high quality wine list compliments the food. The panelled Oak Room, with its stone fireplace and gilt furnishings, can be booked for private parties and executive meetings. Leisure facilities at the nearby Wordsworth Hotel are available to guests, as is free golf Mon–Fri at Keswick Golf Club. Michael's Nook is, first and foremost, a home where comfort is the watchword. Awarded AA Best Hotel Restaurant in North England with 4 rosettes and a Michelin Star. **Directions:** Michaels Nook is on the hillside behind the Swan Hotel – East of A591. Price guide (including 5 course dinner): Single from £140; double/twin £180–£290; suite £320–£370.

THE WORDSWORTH HOTEL

GRASMERE, NEAR AMBLESIDE, CUMBRIA LA22 9SW
TEL: 015394 35592 FAX: 015394 35765 E-MAIL: enquiry@wordsworth–grasmere.co.uk

In the very heart of the English Lakeland, The Wordsworth Hotel combines AA 4 Star standards with the magnificence of the surrounding fells. Set in its own grounds in the village of Grasmere, the hotel provides first-class, year-round facilities for both business and leisure travellers. It has a reputation for the high quality of its food, accommodation and hospitality. The comfortable bedrooms have well-equipped bathrooms and there are two suites with whirlpool baths. 24-hour room service is available for drinks and light refreshments. Peaceful lounges overlook landscaped gardens and the heated indoor pool opens on to a sun-trap terrace. There is a Jacuzzi, mini-gym, sauna and solarium. As well as a Cocktail Bar, the hotel has its own pub, "The Dove and Olive Branch", which has received accolades from The Good Pub Guide. In "The Prelude Restaurant", which has 2 AA Rosettes, menus offer a good choice of dishes, prepared with skill and imagination from the freshest produce. The Wordsworth Hotel is a perfect venue for conferences, incentive weekends and corporate entertaining. Three function rooms are available with highly professional back-up. Lakeland's principal places of interest are all within easy reach. **Directions:** The hotel is located next to Grasmere village church. Price guide: Single £65–£80; double/twin £130–£170; suite £200–£210.

GRAYSHOTT HALL HEALTH FITNESS RETREAT

HEADLEY ROAD, GRAYSHOTT, NEAR HINDHEAD, SURREY GU26 6JJ
TEL: 01428 602000 RESERVATIONS: 01428 602020 FAX: 01428 602001

Grayshott Hall, cocooned within 47 acres, surrounded by 700 acres of National Trust woodland is set in a beautiful corner of rural England. Once the home of Victorian poet Lord Tennyson, the house abounds with creature comforts and exudes a friendly atmosphere. On arrival, guests meet a medical and treatments consultant to agree an individual programme to meet their objectives: whether these are to lose weight, start on a new fitness regime or relax, revitalise and invigorate. Non-invasive diagnostic tests complement the 80 available treatments that focus on natural therapies, combined with nutritional advice, personal fitness training and beauty treatments to achieve these objectives. The impressive spa features 37 treatment rooms, hydrotherapy suite, sauna and relaxation rooms, indoor pool and Jacuzzi. There are two superb indoor tennis courts, while outside facilities include tennis and badminton courts and a 9-hole par 3 golf course. Other features of the Hall include an exercise studio, gym and a snooker room. Bedrooms range from tastefully decorated individually designed suites to stylish and comfortable doubles or singles. A low fat, calorie counted buffet is offered at lunch and in the evenings, following healthy cocktails, a 3-course dinner includes a delicious selection of organic, nutritionally balanced dishes. Price guide (p.p. incl. initial consultation, 40mins daily massage, meals, exercise and relaxation classes and evening lectures): Single from £180; double/twin from £160; suites from £250.

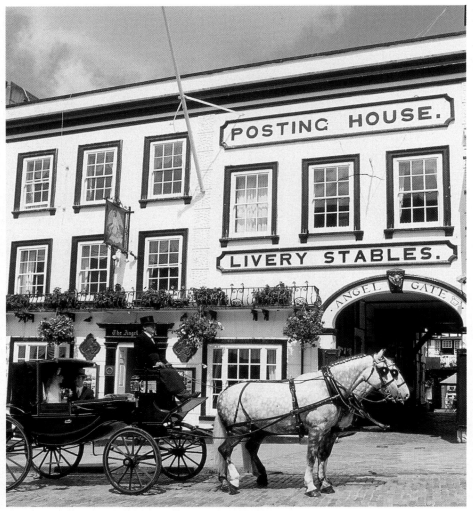

THE ANGEL POSTING HOUSE AND LIVERY

91 THE HIGH STREET, GUILDFORD, SURREY GU1 3DP
TEL: 01483 564555 FAX: 01483 533770

The Angel, a delightful historic coaching inn on the old Portsmouth road, now a luxurious small hotel, has stood on the cobbled High Street in the centre of Guildford since the 16th century. This timber-framed building has welcomed many famous visitors, including Lord Nelson, Sir Francis Drake, Jane Austen and Charles Dickens. Today, with easy access to Gatwick, Heathrow, the M4, M3 and M25, The Angel is ideally placed for both business and leisure weekends. Relax with afternoon tea in the galleried lounge with its oak-beamed Jacobean fireplace and 17th-century parliament clock; a welcome retreat from the bustle of the nearby shops. The No. 1 Angel Gate Restaurant, with its vaulted ceiling and intimate atmosphere, serves a wide choice of superb English and Continental cuisine together with fine wines and impeccable service. The charming bedrooms and suites, decorated with soft furnishings and fabrics, are all unique and named after a famous visitor. Excellent communications, presentation facilities and 24-hour service make this a good choice for business meetings. Private dinners, buffets, dances and wedding receptions can also be catered for. **Directions:** From M3 junction 3 take the A322; or from M25 junction 10 take the A3. The Angel is in the centre of Guildford, within the pedestrian priority area – guests should enquire about vehicle access and parking when booking. Price guide (room only): Double/twin £135–£150; suite £180–£250.

WEST LODGE PARK

**COCKFOSTERS ROAD, HADLEY WOOD, BARNET, HERTFORDSHIRE EN4 0PY
TEL: 0181 216 3900 FAX: 0181 216 3937 E-MAIL: beales–westlodgepark@compuserve.com**

West Lodge Park is a country house hotel which stands in 34 acres of Green Belt parklands and gardens. These include a lake and an arboretum with hundreds of mature trees. Despite the advantages of this idyllic setting, the hotel is only 1 mile from the M25 and within easy reach of London. Run by the Beale family for over 50 years, West Lodge Park was originally a gentleman's country seat, rebuilt in 1838 on the site of an earlier keeper's lodge. In the public rooms, antiques, original paintings and period furnishings create a restful atmosphere. All the bright and individually furnished bedrooms, many of which enjoy country views, have a full range of modern amenities. Well presented cuisine is available in the elegant restaurant. Residents enjoy free membership and a free taxi to the nearby David Lloyd leisure centre, which has excellent facilities. Hatfield House and St Albans Abbey are 15 minutes' drive. The hotel is credited with AA 4 stars and 2 Rosettes, RAC 4 stars plus 3 merit awards and was the 1995 County Hotel of the Year in the Which? Hotel Guide. **Directions:** The hotel is on A111 one mile north of Cockfosters underground station and one mile south of junction 24 on M25. Price guide: Single £95–£140; double/twin from £135–£190; suites £250.

HOLDSWORTH HOUSE

HOLDSWORTH ROAD, HOLMFIELD, HALIFAX, WEST YORKSHIRE HX2 9TG
TEL: 01422 240024 FAX: 01422 245174

Holdsworth House is a retreat of quality and charm standing three miles north of Halifax in the heart of Yorkshire's West Riding. Built in 1633, it was acquired by the Pearson family over 30 years ago. With care, skill and professionalism they have created a hotel and restaurant of considerable repute. The interior, with its polished panelling and open fireplaces, has been carefully preserved and embellished with fine antique furniture and ornaments. The comfortable lounge opens onto a pretty courtyard and overlooks the herb garden and gazebo. The restaurant comprises three beautifully furnished rooms, ideal for private dinner parties. Exciting modern English and Continental cuisine is meticulously prepared and presented, complemented by a thoughtfully-compiled wine list. The restaurant has two AA Rosettes and the new Head Chef, Neal Birtwell and his talented team are constantly striving to attain a third. Each cosy bedroom has its own style, from the four split-level suites to the two single rooms designed for wheelchair access. This is the perfect base from which to explore the Pennines, the Yorkshire Dales and Haworth, home of the Brontë family. Closed at Christmas. **Directions:** From M1 Jct42 take M62 west to Jct26. Follow A58 to Halifax (ignore signs to town centre). At Burdock Way roundabout take A629 to Keighley; after 1½ miles go right into Shay Lane; hotel is 1 mile on right. Price guide: Single £85–£120; double/twin £101–£125; suite £130. Weekend breaks.

SANDRINGHAM HOTEL

3 HOLFORD ROAD, LONDON NW3 1AD
TEL: 020 7435 1569 FAX: 020 7431 5932 E-MAIL: sandringham.hotel@virgin.net

Just minutes' walk from the heart of Hampstead Village, Sandringham Hotel is tucked away in a quiet residential side street. This lively, cosmopolitan London suburb is a historic haunt of artists and writers, containing these days a wealth of restaurants, bars, galleries and boutiques. Yet to the rear of this friendly and welcoming hotel is somewhere to relax. The walled garden is a charming oasis with its miniature pool and abundant greenery: here is the ideal spot to unwind after a day's work or sightseeing. In less clement weather the stylish and serenely comfortable lounge with its open hearth and draped bay window provides a more than adequate alternative. The bedrooms are cosy with rich fabrics and soft furnishings, comfortable beds and gold-tapped bathrooms. One room at the top of the house enjoys views as far distant as London's Millennium Dome, while the quietest bedrooms and an informal breakfast room overlook the garden. The hotel has no restaurant, but refreshments and light meals are available all day and the room service is excellent. There is a multifarious choice of dining venues within walking distance. London's West End with its theatres and attractions is only 15 minutes by Underground on the Northern Line. **Directions:** From Hampstead Underground station, turn uphill into Heath Street. The fourth turning on the right leads into Holford Road. Price guide: Single £75–£90; double/twin £120–£135; suite £145.

THE CARLTON MITRE HOTEL

HAMPTON COURT ROAD, HAMPTON COURT, SURREY KT8 9BN
TEL: 0181 979 9988 FAX: 0181 979 9777 E-MAIL: mitre@carltonhotels.co.uk

Set on the banks of the River Thames, this impressive hotel enjoys glorious views over Hampton Court Palace, the Thames and the courtyard. Built in 1665 at the request of Charles II, The Mitre Hotel maintains a fine equilibrium between tradition and modernity. The elegant en suite bedrooms are individually furnished and include all the latest amenities such as satellite television and tea and coffee facilities. Guests must savour the chef's creations in the superb Mitre Restaurant, overlooking the river, and indulge in the vintage wines. The recently refurbished Landings Brasserie serves light snacks and imaginative Mediterranean cuisine and is renowned for its fine Jazz Brunch on Sundays. The courtyard is particularly convivial during the summer months, when cocktails and other refreshments are served by the riverside as the boats pass by. The hotel's private terrace and jetty are perfect for guests wishing to relax and unwind. An excellent standard of service is offered throughout the hotel. Nearby attractions include the neighbouring Hampton Court Palace, the beautiful Kew Gardens and the racecourses of Kempton Park, Sandown Park and Epsom Downs. Golf enthusiasts will be pleased with the number of excellent courses close by. **Directions:** Leave M3 at Jct1 and take A308 following signs for Hampton Court. The hotel is beside Hampton Court bridge opposite the Palace. Price guide: Single £125–135; double/twin £150–£170; suite £195.

THE BALMORAL HOTEL

FRANKLIN MOUNT, HARROGATE, NORTH YORKSHIRE HG1 5EJ
TEL: 01423 508208 FAX: 01423 530652 E-MAIL: INFO@BALMORALHOTEL.CO.UK

The Balmoral is a delightful privately owned individual hotel with an award-winning garden, near the heart of the elegant spa town of Harrogate. All the bedrooms are luxurious with individual decoration and furnishings offering the highest standards of comfort. Nine rooms have four-posters, each in a different style. For ultimate luxury, The Windsor Suite even boasts its own whirlpool. Guests enjoy the fascinating memorabilia on various themes throughout the Hotel and they can relax in the exquisite Harry's Bar or enjoy a quiet drink in the cosy Snug before taking dinner in Villu Toots. The extensive modern Mediterranean menu embraces both the traditional and unexpected, popular with non-residents. The wine list is equally diverse with fine vintages rubbing shoulders with more youthful newcomers. Guests can enjoy the use of the Academy – one of the finest Health & Fitness Centres in the North, five minutes from the Hotel. Special Spa Breaks throughout the year. Harrogate is famed for its antique and fashion shops, art galleries and Herriot country and the many historic homes and castles in the area. **Directions:** From Harrogate Conference Centre, follow the Kings Road up and the hotel is ½ mile on the right. Price guide: Single £90–£100; double/twin £114–£130; suites £137–£185. Special Breaks available.

THE BOAR'S HEAD HOTEL

THE RIPLEY CASTLE ESTATE, HARROGATE, NORTH YORKSHIRE HG3 3AY
TEL: 01423 771888 FAX: 01423 771509 E-MAIL: boarshead@ripleycastle.co.uk

Imagine relaxing in a four star hotel at the centre of a historic private country estate in England's incredibly beautiful North Country. The Ingilby family who have lived in Ripley Castle for 28 generations invite you to enjoy their hospitality at The Boar's Head Hotel. There are 25 luxury bedrooms, individually decorated and furnished, most with king-size beds. The restaurant menu is outstanding, presented by a creative and imaginative kitchen brigade and complemented by a wide selection of reasonably priced, good quality wines. There is a welcoming bar serving traditional ales straight from the wood and popular bar meal selections. When staying at The Boar's Head, guests can enjoy complimentary access to the delightful walled gardens and grounds of Ripley Castle, which include the lakes and a deer park. A conference at Ripley is a different experience – using the idyllic meeting facilities available in the castle, organisers and delegates alike will appreciate the peace and tranquillity of the location which also offers opportunities for all types of leisure activity in the Deer Park. **Directions:** Ripley is very accessible, just 10 minutes from the conference town of Harrogate, 20 minutes from the motorway network, and Leeds/Bradford Airport, and 40 minutes from the City of York. Price guide: Single £100–£120; double £120–£140.

GRANTS HOTEL

SWAN ROAD, HARROGATE, NORTH YORKSHIRE HG1 2SS
TEL: 01423 560666 FAX: 01423 502550 E-MAIL: enquiries@grantshotel–harrogate.com

Towards the end of the last century, Harrogate became fashionable among the gentry, who came to 'take the waters' of the famous spa. Today's visitors have one advantage over their Victorian counterparts – they can enjoy the hospitality of Grants Hotel, the creation of Pam and Peter Grant. Their friendly welcome, coupled with high standards of service, ensures a pleasurable stay. All the bedrooms are attractively decorated and have en suite bathrooms. Downstairs, guests can relax in the comfortable lounge or take refreshments out to the terrace gardens. Drinks and light meals are available at all times from Harry Grant's Bar and dinner is served in the French café-style Chimney Pots Bistro, complete with brightly coloured check blinds and cloths and lots of humorous 'Beryl Cook' pictures. Cuisine is basically traditional rustic with a smattering of Oriental influence complemented by the mouth-watering home-made puddings. Located less than five minutes' walk from Harrogate's Conference and Exhibition Centre, Grants offers its own luxury meeting and syndicate rooms, the Herriot Suite. The Royal Pump Room Museum and the Royal Baths Assembly Rooms are nearby. Guests have free use of 'The Academy Health and Leisure Club'. **Directions:** Swan Road is in the centre of Harrogate, off the A61 to Ripon. Price guide: Single £96.50–£108; double/twin £108–£150; suites £160. Super value breaks available.

HOB GREEN HOTEL AND RESTAURANT

MARKINGTON, HARROGATE, NORTH YORKSHIRE HG3 3PJ
TEL: 01423 770031 FAX: 01423 771589

Set in 870 acres of farm and woodland this charming 'country house' hotel is only a short drive from the spa town Harrogate and the ancient city of Ripon. The restaurant has an excellent reputation locally with only the finest fresh local produce being used, much of which is grown in the hotel's own garden. The interesting menus are complemented by an excellent choice of sensibly priced wines. All twelve bedrooms have been individually furnished and tastefully equipped to suit the most discerning guest. The drawing room and hall, warmed with log fires in cool weather, are comfortably furnished with the added attraction of fine antique furniture, porcelain and pictures.

Situated in the heart of some of Yorkshire's most dramatic scenery guests can enjoy magnificent views of the valley beyond from all the main rooms. York is only 23 miles away. There is a wealth of cultural and historical interest nearby with Fountains Abbey and Studley Royal water garden and deer park a few minutes' drive. The Yorkshire Riding Centre is in Markington Village. Above all, Hob Green provides a tranquil and relaxing place to stay where your every comfort is catered for. **Directions**: Turn left signposted Markington off the A61 Harrogate to Ripon road, the hotel is one mile after the village on the left. Price guide: Single £85; double/twin £95–£110; suite £120.

RUDDING PARK HOUSE & HOTEL

RUDDING PARK, FOLLIFOOT, HARROGATE, NORTH YORKSHIRE HG3 1JH
TEL: 01423 871350 FAX: 01423 872286 E-MAIL: sales @rudding–park.co.uk

Voted Best Hotel 1998 by the Yorkshire Tourist Board this splendid new hotel is just 2 miles from Harrogate town centre. Rudding Park House, built in the early 19th century, is a fine conference and banqueting centre. The new hotel has been brilliantly designed and built to harmonise with the original mansion. Its setting is superb, surrounded by 230 acres of parkland. The hotel has an elegant façade and entrance, approached by a sweeping driveway. A warm welcome awaits guests in the pleasant foyer, with its big fireplace and easy chairs. The bedrooms are spacious, with contemporary cherry wood furniture, relaxing colour schemes, many modern accessories and lovely views over the estate. The stylish two AA

Rosetted Clocktower Restaurant and Bar are inviting and on sunny days they extend onto the terrace. The food is delicious and the wine list extensive. Leisure facilities are excellent – there is an 18-hole par 72 parkland golf course and golf academy on the estate, which has won accolades for its environmental sensitivity. 9000 new trees, lakes, roaming deer and bird-watching hideaways have increased the estate's beauty. Croquet, fishing and riding are available close by. **Directions:** Rudding Park is accessible from the A1 north or south, via A661, being just off A658. Price guide: Single £110–£135; double/twin £140–£180; suite from £240.

LYTHE HILL HOTEL

PETWORTH ROAD, HASLEMERE, SURREY GU27 3BQ
TEL: 01428 651251 FAX: 01428 644131 E-MAIL: lythe@lythehill.co.uk

Cradled by the Surrey foothills in a tranquil setting is the enchanting Lythe Hill Hotel. It is an unusual cluster of ancient buildings – parts of which date from the 14th century. While most of the beautifully appointed accommodation is in the more recently converted part of the hotel, there are five charming bedrooms in the Tudor House, including the Henry VIII room with a four-poster bed dated 1614! There are two delightful restaurants, the Auberge de France offers classic French cuisine in the oak-panelled room which overlooks the lake and parklands, and the 'Dining Room' has the choice of imaginative English fare. An exceptional wine list offers over 200 wines from more than a dozen countries.

Its situation, easily accessible from London, Gatwick and Heathrow. An excellent train service at Haslemere makes both central London and Portsmouth less than one hour away. National Trust hillside adjoining the hotel grounds provides interesting walking and views over the surrounding countryside. The area is steeped in history, with the country houses of Petworth, Clandon and Uppark to visit as well as racing at Goodwood and polo at Cowdray Park. Brighton and the south coast are only a few miles away. **Directions:** Lythe Hill lies about $1\frac{1}{2}$ miles from the centre of Haslemere, east on the B2131. Price guide (excluding breakfast): Single from £98; double/twin from £120; suite from £140.

GEORGE HOTEL

MAIN ROAD, HATHERSAGE, DERBYSHIRE S32 1BB
TEL: 01433 650436 FAX: 01433 650099 E-MAIL: info@george–hotel.net

The George dates back to the end of the middle ages when it would have been an alehouse serving the packhorse road. Later it was well-known to Charlotte Brontë and it features anonymously in *Jane Eyre*. The present owner, an experienced hotelier, is ably backed by a team of professional senior personnel who guarantee guests a warm welcome and excellent personal service. In its latest hands the building has undergone extensive renovation. However, great care has been taken to preserve the character of the old inn and the stone walls, oak beams, open fires and antique furniture all remain as reminders of a distant age. The simple and pleasant bedrooms offer every modern amenity, including power showers and luxuriously enveloping bath sheets. There is a well-equipped bar in which to relax and enjoy a drink before moving on to the brasserie-style restaurant with its regularly changed menu. Places of interest nearby include Chatsworth and Haddon Halls, Buxton and Bakewell. The area provides some of the most picturesque countryside for walking including renowned Stanage Ridge (with stunning views overlooking the Derwent Reservoirs) and Hope Valley. "Great for the energetic, relaxing for the not-so-energetic". **Directions:** From the M1 Jct29 take the A617 to Baslow, then the A623 and B6001 to Hathersage. The George is in the main street of the village. Price guide: Single £59.50–£69.50; double/twin £89.50–£119.50.

SIMONSTONE HALL

HAWES, NORTH YORKSHIRE DL8 3LY
TEL: 01969 667255 FAX: 01969 667741 E-MAIL:email@simonstone.demon.co.uk

Fine cuisine, comfort, peace and tranquillity combine with breathtaking scenery to make any stay at Simonstone Hall totally memorable. This former 18th century hunting lodge has been lovingly restored and furnished with antiques to create an idyllic retreat for its guests. The Hall stands in 5 acres of beautiful landscaped gardens with an adjacent 14,000 acres of grouse moors and upland grazing. Many period features have been retained such as the panelled dining room, mahogany staircase with ancestral stained glass windows and a lounge with ornamental fireplace and ceilings. The bedrooms are of the highest standards and offer every modern comfort including four-poster and sleigh beds. In the restaurant, guests savour the freshest local produce presented with flair and imagination, whilst enjoying stunning views across Upper Wensleydale. An excellent wine list is available to complement any dish. Informal meals are served in the Game Tavern which provides a particularly warm and local atmosphere. Simonstone Hall, with its fine views, is the perfect base for enjoying and exploring the hidden Yorkshire Dales. The area abounds with ancient castles, churches and museums. Hardraw Force, England's highest single drop waterfall which can be heard from the gardens, is only a walk away. **Directions:** Hawes is on A684. Turn north on Buttertubs Pass towards Muker. Simonstone Hall is ½m on the left. Price guide: Single £55–£80; double/twin £110–£160.

HAZLEWOOD CASTLE HOTEL

PARADISE LANE, HAZLEWOOD, NEAR TADCASTER, NORTH YORKSHIRE LS24 9NJ
TEL: 01937 535353 FAX: 01937 530630

Hazlewood Castle dates back to the late 13th century and was once a fortified knights residence. Standing on a limestone ridge in 77 acres of its own parkland, it is built of white limestone from the famous Thevesdale Quarry and enjoys an idyllic pastoral location. Extensive restoration work, along with some notable additions, has been carried out over the centuries and the Castle has its own 13th century chapel. The Castle recently opened as a luxurious country house hotel. Guests arrive in the courtyard and are greeted at the steps before being shown into the impressive Flemish Hall. There are nine beautifully furnished bedrooms in the main house and 12 similarly luxurious across the courtyard. The Restaurant '1086'(formerly the Old Orangery) provides a fine dining experience. Linked to the Castle via a secret door from the library, '1086' embraces a style and design of the new with respect for the classic and traditional. The cuisine is under the direction of award-winning Chef/Director John Benson-Smith who also supervises the Hazlewood Cookery School, which is based at the Castle. Yorkshire, with its rural villages, splendid beaches and magnificent countryside, offers a host of entertainment and leisure opportunities. Guests can take advantage of nearby York with its excellent shops and beautiful Minster, Leeds and Harrogate. **Directions:** The Castle is just off A64 east of A1 Leeds/York intersection. Price guide: Single £105; double/twin £145–£185; suites £195–£300.

STOKE PARK

PARK ROAD, STOKE POGES, BUCKINGHAMSHIRE SL2 4PG
TEL: 01753 717171 FAX: 01753 717181 E-MAIL: info@stokepark.co.uk

This impressive Palladian mansion was built in 1791 and Capability Brown was responsible for the magnificent landscaped grounds. The Estate, featured in The Doomsday Book, can truly boast that Queen Elizabeth I and King Charles I slept here. It is the clubhouse of Stoke Poges Golf Club and also a splendid hotel, close to Heathrow and only 30 minutes from London, wonderfully secluded and surrounded by extensive parkland. The interior is palatial, with fine tall ceilings, fine antiques and art with original etchings. The bedrooms are lavishly decorated, with stunning exquisite fabrics and elegant period furniture. The bathrooms are luxurious with every possible 'extra'. The Golf Club shares its spacious drawing rooms and traditional President's Bar with residents. The Dining Room is classical and the menu lists great English and French dishes. The cellar is superb! Stoke Park has many well equipped meeting rooms, including the attractive Ballroom, quickly transformed into attractive venues for special celebrations. Croquet and snooker are house sports, shooting and fishing nearby. Windsor, Ascot and Henley are in easy reach. **Directions:** From the M4/J6 or the M40/J2 take the A344; at the double roundabout at Farnham Royal take the B416. The entrance is just over a mile on the right. Price guide: Single £225; suite £375.

THE PHEASANT

HAROME, HELMSLEY, NORTH YORKSHIRE YO62 5JG
TEL: 01439 771241/770416 FAX:01439 771744

The Pheasant, rich in oak beams and open log fires, offers two types of accommodation, some in the hotel and some in a charming, 16th century thatched cottage. The Binks family, who built the hotel and now own and manage it, have created a friendly atmosphere which is part of the warm Yorkshire welcome all guests receive. The bedrooms and suites are brightly decorated in an attractive, cottage style and all are complete with en suite facilities. Traditional English cooking is the speciality of the restaurant, many of the dishes prepared using fresh fruit and vegetables grown in the hotel gardens. During the summer, guests may chat or relax on the terrace overlooking the pond. The opening of a new indoor heated swimming pool is an added attraction. Other sporting activities available locally include swimming, riding, golf and fishing. York is a short drive away, as are a host of historic landmarks including Byland and Rievaulx Abbeys and Castle Howard of *Brideshead Revisited* fame. Also nearby is the magnificent North York Moors National Park. Dogs by arrangement. Closed Christmas, January and February. **Directions:** From Helmsley, take the A170 towards Scarborough; after ¼ mile turn right for Harome. Hotel is near the church in the village. Price guide: Single £62–£69; double/twin £124–£138. (Including five-course dinner).

   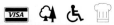   

PHYLLIS COURT CLUB

MARLOW ROAD, HENLEY-ON-THAMES, OXFORDSHIRE RG9 2HT
TEL: 01491 570500 FAX: 01491 570528 E-MAIL: sueg@phylliscourt.co.uk

Founded in 1906 by the owner of the house and a group of friends and London businessmen, the Club has an intriguing history spanning six centuries and involving royal patronage. Phyllis Court occupies an unrivalled position on the banks of the Thames and overlooking the Henley Royal Regatta course. Phyllis Court prides itself on retaining the traditions of its illustrious past while guests today who now stay in this fine historic residence can, in modern times, enjoy the highest standards of up to date hospitality. Oliver Cromwell slept here and he built the embankment wall; and it was here that William II held his first Royal Court. Years later, when the name Henley became synonymous with rowing, there came as patrons of the Royal Regatta Prince Albert, King George V and Edward, Prince of Wales. The character of the place remains unaltered in its hallowed setting, but the comfortable bedrooms, the restaurant, the "cellar" and the entire complement of amenities are of the latest high quality. What is more, they are available for all. Likely to be fully booked far ahead during the season. Ideal for meetings, functions and wedding parties. **Directions:** M40 junction 4 to Marlow or M4 junction 8/9 then follow signposts to Henley-on-Thames. Price guide: Single £92; twin/double £108.

NUTHURST GRANGE

HOCKLEY HEATH, WARWICKSHIRE B94 5NL
TEL: 01564 783972 FAX: 01564 783919 E-MAIL: info@nuthurst.grange.co.uk

The most memorable feature of this friendly country house hotel is its outstanding restaurant. Chef-patron David Randolph and his team have won many accolades for their imaginative menus, described as 'English, cooked in the light French style'. Diners can enjoy their superb cuisine in one of the three adjoining rooms which comprise the restaurant and form the heart of Nuthurst Grange. The rest of the house is no less charming – the spacious bedrooms have a country house atmosphere and are appointed with extra luxuries such as an exhilarating air-spa bath, a trouser press, hairdryer and a safe for valuables. For special occasions there is a room furnished with a four-poster bed and a marble bathroom. There are fine views across the 7½ acres of landscaped gardens. Executive meetings can be accommodated at Nuthurst Grange – within a 12 mile radius of the hotel lie central Birmingham, the NEC, Stratford-upon-Avon, Coventry and Birmingham International Airport. Sporting activities available nearby include golf, canal boating and tennis. **Directions:** From M42 exit 4 take A3400 signposted Hockley Heath (2 miles, south). Entrance to Nuthurst Grange Lane is ¼ mile south of village. Also, M40 (exit 16 – southbound only), take first left, entrance 300 yards. Price guide: Single £120; double/twin £140–£155; suite £165.

SOUTH LODGE HOTEL

LOWER BEEDING, NR HORSHAM, WEST SUSSEX RH13 6PS
TEL: 01403 891711 FAX: 01403 891766 E-MAIL: inquiries@southlodgehotel.dial.iql.co.uk

South Lodge is a magnificent country house hotel, which has successfully captured the essence of Victorian elegance. With one of the most beautiful settings in rural Sussex, unrivalled views may be enjoyed over the South Downs from the hotel's elevated position. The mansion was originally built by Frederick Ducane Godman, a 19th century botanist and explorer, and the hotel's wonderful 90 acre grounds are evidence of his dedication. Many original features have been preserved, wood panelling throughout the hotel and open fires in the reception rooms. The 41 individually designed bedrooms are luxuriously equipped with every modern day requirement. The Camellia Restaurant has menus which change with the seasons and are complemented by a wine list from many countries. The private rooms are perfect for both social and business functions. A variety of leisure facilities, including croquet, tennis and clay pigeon shooting, are available on site (shooting and archery by prior arrangement), also golf at South Lodge's two spectacular 18 hole championship courses just minutes from the hotel. Nearby attractions include Glyndebourne, Chartwell and the Royal Pavilion in Brighton. **Directions:** On A281 at Lower Beeding, south of Horsham. Gatwick airport 12 miles. Nearest motorway M23 junction 11. Price guide: Single from £140; double/twin £165–£205; suite £285–£315.

THE WORSLEY ARMS HOTEL

HOVINGHAM, YORK, NORTH YORKSHIRE YO6 4LA
TEL: 01653 628234 FAX: 01653 628130 E-MAIL: worsleyArm@aol.com

The Worsley Arms is an attractive stone-built Victorian coaching inn in the heart of Hovingham, a pleasant and unspoiled Yorkshire village with a history stretching back to Roman times. The hotel, which overlooks the village green and is set amid delightful gardens, was built in 1841 by the baronet Sir William Worsley. Hovingham Hall, the Worsley family and childhood home of the Duchess of Kent, is nearby. Elegant furnishings and open fires create a welcoming atmosphere. The spacious sitting rooms are an ideal place to relax over morning coffee or afternoon tea. The award-winning Restaurant (2 AA Rosettes) offers creatively prepared dishes, including game from the estate, cooked and presented with flair. The Cricketers Bistro (also 2 AA Rosettes) provides a more informal setting to enjoy modern cooking at its best. The en suite bedrooms range in size and are all prettily decorated with room service available. There is plenty to do nearby, including tennis, squash, jogging, golf and scenic walks along nature trails. Guests can explore the beauty of the Dales and the spectacular coastline or discover the historic abbeys, stately homes and castles nearby like Castle Howard just five miles away. **Directions:** Hovingham is on the B1257, eight miles from Malton and Helmsley. Price guide: Single £60–£80; double/twin £80–£90. Special breaks available.

BAGDEN HALL HOTEL & GOLF COURSE

WAKEFIELD ROAD, SCISSETT, NR HUDDERSFIELD, WEST YORKSHIRE HD8 9LE
TEL: 01484 865330 FAX: 01484 861001 E-MAIL: info@bagdenhall.demon.co.uk

Bagden Hall is set in 40 acres of parkland, yet less than 10 minutes from the M1. It was built in the mid-19th century by local mill owner George Norton as a home for his family, whose portraits still hang in the foyer. Lovingly restored by current owners, the Braithwaite family, Bagden has been transformed into an elegant hotel. The grounds comprise magnificent lawns, superb landscaped gardens, a lake and an 18th century boathouse. Inside, the hotel has recently undergone a major programme of renovation and now has all the attributes one would expect of a modern hotel while retaining its original character. Each of the 17 bedrooms – one with four-poster – has en suite facilities. The oak-panelled lounge bar and conservatory have views over the lawns to the lake, an ideal setting for a drink before moving on to the Glendale Restaurant. Here, traditional and modern English food with classical French influences is served amid tasteful surroundings. There is a fine wine list to complement the food. For golfers, there is a 9-hole par 3/4 golf course on site. Conference facilities are available. **Directions:** From south, leave M1 at junction 38, taking A637 towards Huddersfield. Take A636 to Denby Dale. From north, leave M1 at junction 39, taking A636 to Denby Dale. Hotel is $^1/_2$ mile through Clayton West on left. Price guide: Single £65; double/twin £84–£110.

WILLERBY MANOR HOTEL

WELL LANE, WILLERBY, HULL, EAST YORKSHIRE HU10 6ER
TEL: 01482 652616 FAX: 01482 653901 E-MAIL: info@willerbymanor.co.uk

Originally the home of the Edwardian shipping merchant, Sir Henry Salmon, Willerby Manor was bought in the early 1970s by John Townend, a Wine Merchant from Hull. The elegance of the hotel, as its stands today, is testament to the careful work of the Townend family over the years. Furnished in a stylish manner, the public rooms are the essence of comfort. The 51 bedrooms are beautifully decorated with colour co-ordinated fabrics and soft furnishings. Every modern amenity is provided as well as an array of thoughtful extras such as fresh floral arrangements. The formal Restaurant Lafite serves modern English food and is complemented by an extensive well-chosen wine list of nearly 200 bins. A more informal ambience pervades the Everglades Brasserie where guests may savour bistro-style meals and beverages. Fitness enthusiasts will be delighted with the well-equipped Health Club which includes a spacious gymnasium, whirlpool spa bath, an exercise studio with daily classes and a beauty treatment room. The hotel is in a convenient location for those wishing to explore the cities of Hull and York. **Directions:** Take the M62 towards Hull which runs into the A63, turn off onto the A164 in the direction of Beverley. Follow the signs to Willerby and then Willerby Manor. Price guide: Single £42–£82; double/twin £67–£108.

ROMBALDS HOTEL

WEST VIEW, WELLS ROAD, ILKLEY, WEST YORKSHIRE LS29 9JG
TEL: 01943 603201 FAX: 01943 816586 E-MAIL: reception@rombalds.demon.co.uk

Ilkley Moor has been famous in song. Today the town is singing the praises of Rombalds Hotel, a lovely Georgian townhouse, on the edge of the Moor and within walking distance of the town centre. The owners, Colin and Jo Clarkson, are proud of its history, and the furnishings are appropriate to its 19th century architecture – an elegant facade with tall windows, and, inside, high ceilings, archways and fireplaces. The quiet and extremely comfortable bedrooms range from suites to the more compact with showers. The hotel is pristine throughout, following extensive redecoration. The lounge is a peaceful retreat, guests mingle in the bar while studying the menu for the Restaurant, awarded 2 AA Rosettes. The diverse wine list includes some good half bottles. While business people may want to use the Rombalds' excellent conference and office facilities, others will enjoy Ilkley's intriguing Victorian shopping arcade or Harrogate's boutiques, visiting Fountains Abbey, Bolton Abbey, Castle Howard or Harewood House and exploring the Brontë and Herriot country. Sporting visitors are offered golf, tennis, fishing and riding. **Directions:** M1 Leeds exit, taking A65 to Ilkley and then follow signs to Ilkley Moor. Hotel set back 50 yards before the Moor. Leeds Airport 18 minutes. Price guide: Single £55–£88; double/twin £80–£110; suites £100–£130.

ILSINGTON COUNTRY HOTEL

ILSINGTON, NEWTON ABBOT, DEVON TQ13 9RR
TEL: 01364 661452 FAX: 01364 661307 E-MAIL: hotel@ilsington.co.uk

The Ilsington Hotel stands in ten acres of beautiful private grounds within the Dartmoor National Park. Run by friendly proprietors, Tim and Maura Hassell, the delightful furnishings and ambience offer a most comfortable environment in which to relax. Stylish bedrooms and suites all boast outstanding views across the rolling pastoral countryside and every comfort and convenience to make guests feel at home, including English toiletries. The distinctive candle-lit dining room is perfect for savouring the superb cuisine, awarded an AA Rosette, created by talented chefs from fresh local produce. The library is ideal for an intimate dining party or celebration whilst the Victorian conservatory is the place for morning coffee or a Devon cream tea. There is a fully equipped purpose built gymnasium, heated indoor pool, sauna and spa – also experienced masseurs. Some of England's most idyllic and unspoilt scenery surrounds Ilsington, with the picturesque villages of Lustleigh and Widecombe-in-the-Moor close by. Footpaths lead from the hotel on to Dartmoor. Riding, fishing and many other country pursuits can be arranged. **Directions:** From M5 join A38 at Exeter following Plymouth signs. After approximately 12 miles exit for Moretonhampstead and Newton Abbot. At roundabout follow signs for Ilsington. Price guide: (including dinner) Single £80; double/twin £135.

HINTLESHAM HALL

HINTLESHAM, IPSWICH, SUFFOLK IP8 3NS
TEL: 01473 652268 FAX: 01473 652463 E-MAIL: reservations@hintlesham–hall.co.uk

The epitome of grandeur, Hintlesham Hall is a house of evolving styles: its splendid Georgian façade belies its 16th-century origins, to which the red-brick Tudor rear of the hall is a testament. The Stuart period also left its mark, in the form of a magnificent carved-oak staircase leading to the north wing of the hall. The combination of styles works extremely well, with the lofty proportions of the Georgian reception rooms contrasting with the timbered Tudor rooms. The décor throughout is superb – all rooms are individually appointed in a discriminating fashion. Iced mineral water, toiletries and towelling robes are to be found in each of the comfortable bedrooms. The herb garden supplies many of the flavours for the well-balanced menu which will appeal to the gourmet and the health-conscious alike, complemented by a 300-bin wine list. Bounded by 175 acres of rolling countryside, leisure facilities include the Hall's own 18-hole championship golf course, gymnasium, sauna, steam room, spa bath, tennis, croquet and snooker. Guests can also explore Suffolk's 16th-century wool merchants' villages, its pretty coast, 'Constable country' and Newmarket. **Directions:** Hintlesham Hall is 4 miles west of Ipswich on the A1071 Sudbury road. Price guide: Single £89–£105; double/twin £115–£230; suite £230–£350.

THE MARLBOROUGH HOTEL

HENLEY ROAD, IPSWICH, SUFFOLK IP1 3SP
TEL: 01473 257677 FAX: 01473 226927 E-MAIL: sales@themarlborough.co.uk

Set in a stunning residential area in the environs of Ipswich, the Marlborough is a renovated Victorian hotel whose owners, the Gough family, guarantee a friendly and hospitable ambience. The interior is a model of modern stylishness, with rich coloured décor complementing the comfortable furnishings, freshly picked flowers and breathtaking pictures. Chef Simon Barker serves Rosette-winning fare, emphasising the freshness of the local produce, in an elegant and beautifully-decorated room which overlooks the magnificent garden. Some of the hotel's individually-designed bedrooms have delightful balconies with views of the garden, while all are spacious and have modern bathrooms. Visitors can take advantage of windsurfing and walking at Alton, with nearby Woodbridge a haven for sailing. Christchurch Park and its Tudor mansion, formerly the home of Thomas Wolsey, are practically next door. Within easy driving distance are the rugged Suffolk coastline, historic Aldeburgh and the world-famous Snape Maltings. The Marlborough Hotel is also on the edge of beautiful Constable Country. **Directions:** From Ipswich, take the road towards Woodbridge. Take the A1214 and cross 5 roundabouts until a set of traffic lights. Henley Road is the turning to the left. Price guide: Single from £64; double/twin from £84; suite from £104.

SWALLOW BELSTEAD BROOK HOTEL

BELSTEAD ROAD, IPSWICH, SUFFOLK IP2 9HB
TEL: 01473 682891 FAX: 01473 681249

An oasis on the edge of Ipswich, Belstead Brook Hotel is surrounded by eight acres of landscaped gardens and woodlands. It combines the charm and tranquillity of the original 16th century country house with every modern day comfort. Bedrooms are pleasantly furnished and many overlook the garden where resident peacocks stroll. Guests may use the luxurious swimming pool with sauna, steam room, large Jacuzzi, separate pool for children and a well-equipped gymnasium. There are new executive garden rooms with allocated parking. The award-winning restaurant offers a choice of menus, complemented by a comprehensive cellar. For weddings, conferences or banquets, the hotel offers private dining rooms and a choice of purpose-built meeting and syndicate rooms to accommodate up to 130 guests or delegates. The hotel is an ideal base from which to explore the delights of Suffolk. These include Southwold, Aldeburgh, Woodbridge, the estuaries of the Deben and the Orwell, the wool towns of Lavenham and Long Melford and the countryside of the Stour Valley, made famous by John Constable. **Directions:** From A12/A14 junction take A1214 to Ipswich West. At first roundabout turn right to Belstead and follow the brown signs to the hotel. Price guide: Double/twin £95–£105; suites £140.

THE BORROWDALE GATES COUNTRY HOUSE HOTEL

GRANGE-IN-BORROWDALE, KESWICK, CUMBRIA CA12 5UQ
TEL: 017687 77204 FAX: 017687 77254

Built in 1860, Borrowdale Gates is surrounded on all sides by the rugged charm of the Lake District National Park. It affords a panoramic vista of the Borrowdale Valley and glorious fells and nestles in two acres of wooded gardens on the edge of the ancient hamlet of Grange, close to the shores of Derwentwater. Tastefully decorated bedrooms offer every modern comfort and command picturesque views of the surrounding scenery. The comfortable lounges and bar, decorated with fine antiques and warmed by glowing log fires in cooler months, create the perfect setting in which to enjoy a drink and forget the bustle of everyday life. Fine food is served in the restaurant, with menus offering a wide and imaginative selection of dishes. The cuisine is complemented by a thoughtfully chosen wine list and excellent service. This Lakeland home is a haven of peace and tranquillity and is ideally located for walking, climbing and touring. There are also many places of literary and historical interest within easy reach, for example Wordsworth's birthplace in Cockermouth. The hotel is closed throughout January. **Directions:** M6 junction 40 A66 into Keswick. B5289 to Borrowdale. After four miles right into Grange over double hump back bridge. Price guide: Single £60–£87; double/twin £115–£175 (Including dinner). Special breaks available.

KETTERING PARK HOTEL

KETTERING PARKWAY, KETTERING, NORTHAMPSHIRE NN15 6XT
TEL: 01536 416666 FAX: 01536 416171 E-MAIL: kpark@shireinns.co.uk

This purpose built hotel excellently combines modern architecture with traditional styling. It creates a timeless atmosphere with its Jacobean-style interior of natural stone and slate, furnished with easy chairs and sofas, warm rugs, tiled floors and richly patterned fabrics. Open fires, opulent décor and unobtrusive but attentive staff reflect the character of a well run country house and help provide a relaxing environment. The bedrooms are thoughtfully equipped with all amenities. These include a suitably lit desk space. Kettering Park Hotel has a reputation for its excellent cuisine served in the elegant, tastefully decorated Langberry's Restaurant. Chef Darren Winder provides a superb selection of eclectic dishes which reflect the latest trends in dining. Guests can relax or dine alfresco on the well furnished patio and pergola of the landscaped garden, featuring an attractive waterfall feature. Leisure facilities include a pool, children's splash pool, snooker room with two full-size tables, saunas, solarium, steam room, gym and squash courts. Wicksteed Fun Park, golf, riding, shooting and angling are nearby as are Althorp, Burghley House, Kirby Hall and Silverstone. **Directions:** From A1 and M1 (South) follow link road (A14); from M1 (North) follow A43 to A14, then at Jct 9(A509) take exit signed Venture Park and Hotel. Price guide: Weekend fully inclusive p.p. double/twin £70; Midweek fully inclusive p.p. £95, single B&B £125. Late availability offers on enquiry.

STONE MANOR HOTEL

STONE, KIDDERMINSTER, WORCESTERSHIRE DY10 4PJ
TEL: 01562 777555 FAX: 01562 777834

Built as a private home in the mid 1920s, this sprawling black and white timber-framed house opened as a hotel nearly forty years later. The warmth and character of bygone times have been retained and blend harmoniously with the modern facilities. Upon entering the hotel, guests will be pleased by the traditional furnishings and layout. The public rooms are decorated with soft fabrics whilst the 52 bedrooms are individually styled and offer every modern amenity. The heart of Stone Manor is Fields Restaurant, where memorable dishes are served and the speciality is flambé cuisine. The à la carte menu makes fine use of the seasonal produce and is complemented by the wine list, comprising both New World and European vintages. Three banqueting suites, catering for between 50 and 250 guests, have full self-contained facilities, including dance floors and bars, making Stone Manor Hotel an ideal venue for weddings, conferences and other private functions. Birmingham Indoor Arena and the NEC are renowned for their extensive programmes of entertainment and Worcester Cathedral is also within easy reach. **Directions:** Stone Manor Hotel is situated in the village of Stone, on the A448 Kidderminster to Bromsgrove road, approximately two miles from Kidderminster town centre. Price guide: All rooms from £70–£120.

MILL HOUSE HOTEL

KINGHAM, OXFORDSHIRE OX7 6UH
TEL: 01608 658188 FAX: 01608 658492 E-MAIL: stay@millhouse–hotel.co.uk

Superbly converted Cotswold stone Mill House, listed in the *Domesday Book* and set in nine tranquil acres with its own trout stream, lies in the heart of the Cotswolds between Burford, Chipping Norton and Stow-on-the-Wold. The 23 en suite bedrooms are all elegantly appointed and overlook the surrounding Cotswold countryside. There is a comfortable lounge with deep armchairs and sofas and the bar features the ancient beamed ceiling and original bread ovens of the landfall flour mill. Open log fires are a feature throughout the winter; in summer, all rooms are enhanced by beautiful flower arrangements and fragrant pot-pourri. The heart of the hotel is the Marionette

Room restaurant which provides cuisine of the highest standards. The menus are changed daily to take advantage of the very best of fresh, seasonal produce. With the whole of the Cotswolds within easy reach, the Mill House is the ideal base from which to explore Broadway, Chipping Campden, Moreton-in-Marsh, the Slaughters and Bourton-on-the-Water are all within 30 minutes drive. The Mill House has RAC 3 Stars with Hospitality, Comfort and Restaurant Awards. **Directions:** South of Kingham village midway between Chipping Norton and Stow-on-the-Wold just off the B4450. Price guide: Single £65–£75; double/twin £100–£120.

CONGHAM HALL

GRIMSTON, KING'S LYNN, NORFOLK PE32 1AH
TEL: 01485 600250 FAX: 01485 601191

Dating from the mid-18th century, this stately manor house is set in 30 acres of paddocks, orchards and gardens. The conversion from country house to luxury hotel in 1982 was executed with care to enhance the elegance of the classic interiors. Proprietors Christine and Trevor Forecast have, however, retained the atmosphere of a family home. Christine's particular forte is the herb garden and flower arranging and her displays enliven the décor throughout, while the delicate fragrance of home-made pot-pourri perfumes the air. Winners of the Johansens Hotel Award for Excellence 1993. Light lunches available in the bar, lounge, restaurant and terrace. In the Orangery restaurant, guests can relish modern English cooking. The origin of many of the flavours is explained by the herb garden, with over 100 varieties for the chef's use. Even the most discerning palate will be delighted by the choice of wines. Congham Hall is an ideal base for touring the countryside of West Norfolk, as well as Sandringham, Fakenham races and the coastal nature reserves. **Directions:** Go to the A149/A148 interchange northeast of King's Lynn. Follow the A148 towards Sandringham/Fakenham/Cromer for 100 yards. Turn right to Grimston. The hotel is then 2½ miles on the left. Price guide: Single £95–£140; double/twin £125–£165; suites from £205.

BUCKLAND-TOUT-SAINTS

GOVETON, KINGSBRIDGE, DEVON TQ7 2DS
TEL: 01548 853055 FAX: 01548 856261 E-MAIL: buckland@tout–saints.co.uk

Buckland-Tout-Saints is an impressive Grade II listed manor house, built in 1690 when William of Orange and Mary were on the throne of England. Situated in the South Hams in rural South Devon, the hotel is located in a peaceful and secluded area surrounded by beautiful well-established gardens and woodlands. Spectacular beaches, rivers and estuaries, together with dramatic cliffs and moorland scenery abound within a 10 mile radius. De luxe rooms and suites in period styles, many enjoying splendid views across the surrounding landscape, combine with the exquisite English and French cuisine served in the Queen Anne restaurant to create a most memorable stay. An extensive range of wines and the extremely friendly staff complete the pleasure. Buckland-Tout-Saints is an outstanding small hotel located in a tranquil setting eminently suitable for corporate events, meetings and seminars. Weddings, receptions and dinner parties are also catered for and children and dogs are welcome by prior arrangement. Several renowned golf courses and the famous sailing centres of Dartmouth and Salcombe also lie within this area. Guests can explore the countryside or visit Dartington Hall and other historic properties close by. **Directions:** Signed from A381 between Totnes and Kingsbridge. Price guide: Single from £95; double/twin from £190; suite from £240.

MERE COURT HOTEL

WARRINGTON ROAD, MERE, KNUTSFORD, CHESHIRE WA16 0RW
TEL: 01565 831000 FAX: 01565 831001 E-MAIL: sales@merecourt.co.uk

This attractive Edwardian house stands in seven acres of mature gardens and parkland in one of the loveliest parts of Cheshire. Maintained as a family home since being built in 1903, Mere Court has been skilfully restored into a fine country house hotel offering visitors a peaceful ambience in luxury surroundings. Comforts and conveniences of the present mix excellently with the ambience and many original features of the past. The bedrooms have views over the grounds and ornamental lake. All are individually designed and a number of them have a four-poster beds, Jacuzzi spa bath, mini bar and separate lounge. Facilities include safes, personalised voice mail telephones and modem points. Heavy ceiling beams, polished oak panelling and restful waterside views are features of the elegant Aboreum Restaurant which serves the best of traditional English and Mediterranean cuisine. Lighter meals can be enjoyed in the Lounge Bar. The original coach house has been converted into a designated conference centre with state of the art conference suites and syndicate rooms accommodating up to 120 delegates. Warrington, Chester, Cheshire Oaks Designer Outlet Village and many National Trust properties are within easy reach. **Directions:** From M6, exit at junction 19. Take A556 towards Manchester. After 1 mile turn left at cross-roads onto A50 towards Warrington. Mere Court is on the right. Price guide: Single £60–£124; double/twin £70–£153.

BEECHFIELD HOUSE

BEANACRE, MELKSHAM, WILTSHIRE SN12 7PU
TEL: 01225 703700 FAX: 01225 790118

Beechfield House stands in a classical English landscape within an easy walk of the beautiful and historic National Trust village of Lacock with its winding streets of Gothic-arched grey-stone houses and half-timbered cottages. Built in 1878, this imposing, privately owned hotel is a fine example of late Victorian splendour and is surrounded by eight acres of secluded gardens and grounds. Each of the bedrooms is traditionally furnished to a high standard, combining the benefits and facilities of a hotel room with the atmosphere of a charming private country house. Well-defined colour schemes lend an uplifting brightness, particularly in the relaxing morning room, elegant drawing room and the splendid Bay Tree Restaurant where diners enjoy chef Geoffrey Bell's imaginative English cuisine. In a sheltered corner of the colourful, formal walled garden there is a heated swimming pool. Private functions, conferences and meetings can be accommodated. Four golf courses are in the vicinity and shooting, riding, hunting and fishing can be arranged. The Georgian city of Bath and the country houses of Bowood, Corsham Court and Longleat are close by. Beechfield House is closed between Christmas and New Year. **Directions:** From M4, exit at junction 17 and take A350 towards Melksham. The hotel is on the left one mile south of Lacock. Price guide: Single from £80; double/twin from £100.

RAMPSBECK COUNTRY HOUSE HOTEL

WATERMILLOCK, LAKE ULLSWATER, NR PENRITH, CUMBRIA CA11 0LP
TEL: 017684 86442 FAX: 017684 86688

A beautifully situated hotel, Rampsbeck Country House stands in 18 acres of landscaped gardens and meadows leading to the shores of Lake Ullswater. Built in 1714, it first became a hotel in 1947, before the present owners acquired it in 1983. Thomas and Marion Gibb, with the help of Marion's mother, Marguerite MacDowall, completely refurbished Rampsbeck with the aim of maintaining its character and adding only to its comfort. Most of the well-appointed bedrooms have lake and garden views. Three have a private balcony and the suite overlooks the lake. In the elegant drawing room, a log fire burns and French windows lead to the garden. Guests and non-residents are welcome to dine in the intimate candle-lit restaurant. Imaginative menus offer a choice of delicious dishes, carefully prepared by head chef Andrew McGeorge and his team. A good bar lunch menu offers light snacks as well as hot food. Guests can stroll through the gardens, play croquet or fish from the lake shore, around which there are designated walks. Lake steamer trips, riding, golf, sailing, windsurfing and fell-walking are available nearby. Closed from end of January to mid-February. Dogs by arrangement only. **Directions:** Leave M6 at junction 40, take A592 to Ullswater. At T-junction at lake turn right; hotel is 1½ miles on left. Price guide: Single £60–£110; double/twin £98–£190; suite £190.

SHARROW BAY COUNTRY HOUSE HOTEL

HOWTOWN, LAKE ULLSWATER, PENRITH, CUMBRIA CA10 2LZ
TEL: 017684 86301/86483 FAX: 017684 86349 E-MAIL: enquiries@sharrow–bay.com

Now in its 52nd year, Sharrow Bay is known to discerning travellers the world over, who return again and again to this magnificent lakeside hotel. It wasn't always so. The late Francis Coulson arrived in 1948. He was joined by Brian Sack in 1952 and the partnership flourished, to make Sharrow Bay what it is today. They were joined by the Managing Director, Nigel Lightburn, who is carrying on the tradition with Brian Sack. All the bedrooms are elegantly furnished and guests are guaranteed the utmost comfort. In addition to the main hotel, there are four cottages nearby which offer similarly luxurious accommodation. All the reception rooms are delightfully decorated. Sharrow Bay is universally renowned for its wonderful cuisine. The team of chefs led by Johnnie Martin and Colin Akrigg ensure that each meal is a special occasion, a mouth-watering adventure! With its private jetty and 12 acres of lakeside gardens Sharrow Bay offers guests boating, swimming and fishing. Fell-walking is a challenge for the upwardly mobile. Sharrow Bay is the oldest British member of Relais et Châteaux. Closed in December, January and February. **Directions:** M6 junction 40, A592 to Lake Ullswater, into Pooley Bridge, then take Howtown road for 2 miles. Price guide: (including 7-course dinner and full English breakfast) Single £130–£250; double/twin £230–£400; suite from £390.

MALLORY COURT

**HALBURY LANE, BISHOPS TACHBROOK, LEAMINGTON SPA, WARWICKSHIRE CV33 9QB
TEL: 01926 330214 FAX: 01926 451714 E-MAIL: reception@mallory.co.uk**

Surrounded by ten acres of attractive gardens, Mallory Court affords a stunning vista across the beautiful Warwickshire countryside. Offering every home comfort, arriving guests are enveloped by the welcoming ambience and peace and quiet of a private house rather than a hotel. The public rooms are bedecked with floral arrangements and during the winter season, afternoon tea may be enjoyed in the comfortable lounges beside the burning log fires. The luxurious bedrooms are enhanced by soft fabrics, thick carpets and en suite facilities. The sun lounge is at its most inviting throughout the summer months when it opens onto the terrace. Guests may enjoy a chilled drink whilst listening to the soft tones of the piano before rambling through the gardens which feature a rose garden, herbaceous border and an ornamental stream. The dishes served in the elegant restaurant are a fusion of classical and modern British flavours. Diners may begin with chicken liver and foie gras parfait with truffle dressing, followed by pan-fried monkfish with mussels and a saffron sauce and ending with a baked custard tart with plum compôte. The hotel is set in a particularly historic area: stately homes, castles and gardens abound. **Directions:** 2 miles south of Leamington Spa on Harbury Lane, just off B4087 Bishops Tachbrook-Leamington Spa road, Harbury Lane runs from B4087 towards Fosse Way. M40 Jct13 from London/Jct14 from Birmingham. Price guide: Single £165; double/twin £185; suite £295.

42 THE CALLS

42 THE CALLS, LEEDS, WEST YORKSHIRE LS2 7EW
TEL: 0113 244 0099 FAX: 0113 234 4100 E-MAIL: 42thecalls@co.uk

This remarkable hotel is absolutely unique. Converted from an old riverside corn mill, it is run as a very personal and luxurious hotel by Jonathan Wix with General Manager Belinda Dawson and a dedicated team of staff in a peaceful location in the centre of Leeds. Shops, offices and theatres are within a few minutes' walk. The bedrooms have been individually decorated and furnished, taking full advantage of the many original features from small grain shutes to massive beams, girders and old machinery. Each room has 10 channel TV, a fresh filter coffee machine, complimentary sweets and cordials, luxury toiletries, trouser press and hair dryer. Stereo CD players are fitted in all the bedrooms and a library of disks is available to guests. Every comfort has been provided with full-size desks, handmade beds and armchairs, a liberal scattering of eastern rugs and beautiful bathrooms. Inexpensive valet car parking and 24-hour room service are offered. Next door to the hotel is the simple but stylish Brasserie 44 and the superb Michelin Starred Pool Court at 42. **Directions:** M621 junction 4, follow signs to Harrogate, turn right after Tetley's Brewery, go over bridge. Turn left onto City Centre Loop, following City signs. Take junction 15 off loop, 42 The Calls is immediately in front of you. Price guide: Single £106.50–£161.50; double/twin £151–£173; suite from £208.

HALEY'S HOTEL & RESTAURANT

SHIRE OAK ROAD, HEADINGLEY, LEEDS, WEST YORKSHIRE LS6 2DE
TEL: 0113 278 4446 FAX: 0113 275 3342

Just two miles from Leeds City Centre, yet set in a quiet leafy lane in the Headingley conservation area close to the cricket ground and the university, Haley's is truly the Country House Hotel in the City. Each of the 29 guest rooms offers the highest levels of comfort and is as individual as the fine antiques and rich furnishings which grace the hotel. A new edition to the existing accommodation is Bedford House, the elegant Victorian Grade II listed building next door which contains seven outstandingly furnished and beautifully equipped modern bedrooms, including two suites, one with its own private entrance. The Bramley Room and Library are popular venues for private meetings, lunch or dinner parties. Haley's

Restaurant has an enviable reputation, holding two AA Rosettes. An imaginative menu of modern English cuisine is accompanied by a fine wine list. Leeds offers superb shopping (including Harvey Nichols) and the Victorian Arcades. Opera North and the theatres combine with Haley's superb accommodation and food to provide entertaining weekends. Haley's is an independently owned member of Richard Branson's Virgin Hotel Collection. **Directions:** Two miles north of Leeds City Centre off the main A660 Otley Road – the main route to Leeds/Bradford Airport, Ilkley and Wharfedale. Price guide: Single £110–£130; double/twin £130–£150; suite £220–£230. Weekend rates from £85.

OULTON HALL

ROTHWELL LANE, OULTON, LEEDS, WEST YORKSHIRE LS26 8HN
TEL: 0113 282 1000 FAX: 0113 282 8066

Oulton Hall stands majestically amid acres of woodland and rolling Yorkshire dales. Its 19th century formal gardens are on the English Heritage Register of Historic Gardens. A Grade II listed building, the Hall has a long and fascinating history. In 1850 it was re-built in the neoclassical style. Restored and extended as a 5-star hotel with traditional character and unique charm it combines today the elegance of a Victorian mansion with impeccable service and the most modern facilities for business and leisure. These include 145 superb, en suite bedrooms complemented by 7 de luxe suites above the Great Hall. Guests can enjoy excellent cuisine in the intimate Brontë Restaurant, or comfortably relax in the softly furnished lounges or the panelled library. The conference facilities have been carefully constructed to a demanding professional standard. There is a large indoor swimming pool, Jacuzzi, sauna, steam room, solarium, fully equipped gymnasium, new aerobics studio and health and beauty suite. Adjacent to the hotel are the 9-hole and 18-hole Oulton Park golf courses. Shooting, fishing and riding are nearby. Special leisure breaks available. **Directions:** From M62, exit at junction 30 and take A642 north. After 2 miles, turn left at roundabout onto Rothwell Lane and the hotel is on the left. Price guide: Single from £140; double/twin from £160; suite from £245.

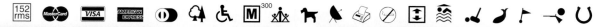

SKETCHLEY GRANGE HOTEL

SKETCHLEY LANE, BURBAGE, HINCKLEY, LEICESTERSHIRE
TEL: 01455 251133 FAX: 01455 631384 E-MAIL: sketchleygrange@btinternet.com

Situated in the rural countryside on the borders of Leicestershire and Warwickshire, Sketchley Grange is an attractive country house hotel with elegant accommodation and good facilities. The bedrooms and suites, some of which are enhanced by four-poster beds, feature soft furnishings and are beautifully appointed. Seventeen new bedrooms have recently been added and are furnished in a most stylish manner. Affording a panoramic views across the pleasant gardens, the award-winning Willow Restaurant offers the very highest standards of cuisine, presentation and service. A more informal ambience may be enjoyed in the new Terrace Bistro and Bar which is decorated in a contemporary style and serves appetising dishes, influenced by the flavours of the Mediterranean. The addition of the superb Romans Health and Leisure Club will delight fitness enthusiasts. Guests may take a dip in the swimming pool or relax in a sauna, spa, whirlpool or Jacuzzi. Those wishing to be pampered must visit the beauty therapy suites and hairdressing salon. There are a number of places of interest nearby from Bosworth Battlefield, the scene of the final War of the Roses, to the charming Stratford-upon-Avon, the birthplace of William Shakespeare. **Directions:** Leave the M6 at junction 2 to join the M69 Leicester. Take the first exit at junction 1. Price guide (room only): From £85.

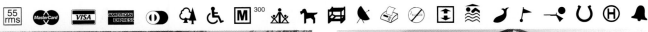

LEWTRENCHARD MANOR

LEWDOWN, NR OKEHAMPTON, DEVON EX20 4PN
TEL: 01566 783 256 FAX: 01566 783 332 E-MAIL: s&j@lewtrenchard.co.uk

Nestling in the soft green Devon countryside just below Dartmoor, Lewtrenchard Manor is a beautiful 17th century grey stone manor house standing on the site of an earlier dwelling, recorded in the Doomsday Book. Once the home of The Reverend Sabine Baring Gould, best remembered as a hymn writer and novelist, the Manor is rich in ornate ceilings, oak panelling, carvings and large open fireplaces. Personally run by owners James and Sue Murray, the warm atmosphere of a large family house has been enhanced with the introduction of family antiques, fine paintings, warm colours and comfortable furniture. Nine spacious and light bedrooms have uninterrupted views through leaded windows over the peaceful countryside. The oak panelled dining room is the perfect setting in which to enjoy excellent dishes that combine superb flavour and delicacy with artistic presentation. There are lovely walks through the Lewtrenchard Estate, which also offers shooting and trout fishing nearby. Exeter, wild Dartmoor and quaint Devon villages are within easy reach and there are good facilities nearby for riding and golf. **Directions:** From Exeter and the M5 take A30 towards Okehampton and then join A386. At T-junction turn right and then left on to old A30 signposted to Bridestowe. Turn left at Lewdown for Lewtrenchard. Price guide: Single £85–£100; double/twin £110–£155; suite from £165.

NEWICK PARK

NEWICK, NEAR LEWES, EAST SUSSEX BN8 4SB
TEL: 01825 723633 FAX: 01825 723969 E-MAIL: newick-park@msn.com

This magnificent Grade II listed Georgian country house, set in over 200 acres of breath-taking parkland and landscaped gardens, overlooks the Longford River and lake and the South Downs. Whilst situated in a convenient location near to the main road and rail routes and only 30 minutes away from Gatwick Airport, Newick Park maintains an atmosphere of complete tranquillity and privacy. The en suite bedrooms are decorated in a classic style and contain elegant antique furnishings. The exquisite dining room offers a wide choice of culinary delights, carefully devised by the Head Chef, Timothy Neal. The convivial bar complements the restaurant with its delicate style and understated elegance. The friendly staff ensure that guests receive a warm welcome and an outstanding level of comfort. The house and grounds are ideal for weddings or conferences and may be hired for exclusive use by larger groups. The Dell gardens, planted primarily in Victorian times, include a rare collection of Royal Ferns. Vibrant and diverse colours saturate the lawns during the changing seasons, courtesy of the various flowers and shrubs encompassing the gardens. The activities on the estate itself include fishing, shooting and tennis, whilst nearby distractions include the East Sussex Golf Club and racing at Goodwood. **Directions:** The nearest motorway is the M23, jct 11. Price guide: Single £95–£120; double/twin £160–225.

HOAR CROSS HALL HEALTH SPA RESORT

HOAR CROSS, NR YOXALL, STAFFORDSHIRE DE13 8QS
TEL: 01283 575671 FAX: 01283 575652 E-MAIL: info@hoarcross.co.uk

Hoar Cross Hall is a health spa resort in a stately home, hidden in the Staffordshire countryside with all the facilities of a 4 star hotel. Built in the 1860s it is a graceful listed residence. Today's guests want more than just to languish in beautiful surroundings, they also wish to rejuvenate their mind and body. Water-based treatments are behind their successful philosophy; from hydro-therapy baths and blitz jet douches, floatation therapy, saunas and steam rooms, to the superb hydrotherapy swimming pool, with over 50 therapists to pamper you with your choice of over 80 treatments. Peripheral activities are extensive. Partake of a full fitness assessment, a new hairstyle or venture into the 100 acres of woodlands and formal gardens. Play tennis, croquet and boules, or bicycle through the countryside. A Golf Academy with a PGA professional will teach you to play or improve your golf. Delight in the à la carte dining room where mouth watering dishes are served. Bedrooms and suites are exquisite with priceless views. Enjoy a day of relaxed luxury or a week of professional pampering (minimum guest age is sixteen years). Price includes accommodation, breakfast, lunch, dinner, unlimited use of facilities and treatments according to length of stay. **Directions:** From Lichfield turn off A51 onto A515 towards Ashbourne. Go through Yoxall and turn left to Hoar Cross. Price guide (fully inclusive, see above): Single £125; double/twin £260.

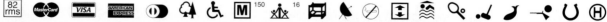

THE ARUNDELL ARMS

LIFTON, DEVON PL16 0AA
TEL: 01566 784666 FAX: 01566 784494 E-MAIL: ArundellArms@btinternet.com

In a lovely valley close to the uplands of Dartmoor, the Arundell Arms is a former coaching inn which dates back to Saxon times. Its flagstone floors, cosy fires, paintings and antiques combine to create a haven of warmth and comfort in an atmosphere of old world charm. One of England's best-known sporting hotels for more than half a century, it boasts 20 miles of exclusive salmon and trout fishing on the Tamar and five of its tributaries and a famous school of Fly Fishing. Guests also enjoy a host of other country activities, including hill walking, shooting, riding and golf. The hotel takes great pride in its elegant 3 AA Rosette restaurant, presided over by Master Chef Philip Burgess, formerly of L'Ecu de France in London. His gourmet cuisine has won the restaurant an international reputation. A splendid base from which to enjoy the wonderful surfing beaches nearby, the Arundell Arms is also well placed for visits to Tintagel and the historic houses and gardens of Devon and Cornwall. Only 45 minutes from Exeter and Plymouth, it is also ideal for the business executive, reached by fast roads from all directions. A spacious conference suite is available. **Directions:** Lifton is approximately 1/4 mile off A30 2 miles east of Launceston and the Cornish Border. Price guide: Single £72–£87; double/twin £110–£114.

QUORN COUNTRY HOTEL

66 LEICESTER ROAD, QUORN, LEICESTERSHIRE LE12 8BB
TEL: 01509 415050 FAX: 01509 415557

Originally Leicestershire's most exclusive private club, created around the original 17th century listed building, this award winning 4 star hotel is set in 4 acres of landscaped gardens. For the tenth consecutive year the hotel has received all 3 RAC merit awards for excellence in cuisine, hospitality and comfort and was also a recipient of a second AA Rosette Award in 1997. The bedrooms are equipped to the very highest standard with attention given to every detail. Suitable for both the business traveller or for weekend guests seeking those extra 'touches' which help create the ideal peaceful retreat. Ladies travelling alone can feel reassured that their special needs are met and indeed exceeded. Particular emphasis is given to the enjoyment of food with a declared policy of using, whenever possible, the freshest local produce. Guests' stay will be enhanced by the choice of two different dining experiences. They can choose between the Shires Restaurant with its classical cuisine with a modern style or the Orangery Brasserie with its changing selection of contemporary dishes. **Directions:** Situated just off the A6 Leicester to Derby main road, in the bypassed village of Quorn (Quorndon), five miles from junction 23 of the M1 from North, junction 21A from South, East and West. Price Guide: Single £98; double/twin £110; suite £130.

KENWICK PARK HOTEL & LEISURE CLUB

KENWICK PARK, LOUTH, LINCOLNSHIRE LN11 8NR
TEL: 01507 608806 FAX: 01507 608027 E-MAIL: kenwick–park.co.uk

Kenwick Park stands in magnificent, extensive parkland with sweeping views over the rolling hills, deep valleys, quiet streams and hanging birchwoods of the beautiful Lincolnshire Wolds. It is a four-star luxury hotel with spacious rooms furnished and serviced in grand, Georgian country house style. Peace, tranquillity and comfort combine with the finest facilities for both the leisure and business guest. Each of the 24 en suite bedrooms is furnished and decorated in the best of taste and many offer superb views over the gardens to the estate's acclaimed international standard golf course beyond. Guests have access to the Par 72 course on a green fee basis. The hotel is justifiably proud of its two Rosettes for its fine dining and gourmet menus. Chef Paul Harvey produces excellent, imaginative à la carte cuisine to suit the most discerning palate in the elegant Fairway Restaurant and delicious, less formal and carvery meals are served in the Keepers Bar. Kenwick Park has full high-tech facilities for the corporate visitor, including three meeting rooms. The leisure club features a 20-metre swimming pool, gymnasium, sauna and steam rooms. There are also squash and tennis courts and nearby there is horse racing at Market Rasen and motor racing at Cadwell Park. **Directions:** From the Louth Bypass (A16) follow the signs to Manby. Kenwick Park is one mile from Louth. Price guide: Single £79.50; double/twin £98–£120; suite £130.

WASHBOURNE COURT HOTEL

LOWER SLAUGHTER, GLOUCESTERSHIRE GL54 2HS
TEL: 01451 822143 FAX: 01451 821045

Now under the private ownership of Roy and Daphne Vaughan, together with Buckland Manor and Lower Slaughter Manor, the Washbourne Court Hotel is in the heart of the tranquil and beautiful Cotswold village of Lower Slaughter, on the banks of the River Eye. The four acres of private gardens have been lovingly re-landscaped with lawns and many delightful features. With just twenty eight bedrooms, it has parts dating back to the 17th century. The recent additions to the hotel, a spacious new dining room and a further six guest rooms with comfortable and elegant furnishings, blend in perfectly with the original building. Always full of freshly picked flowers and planted bowls, the hotel has the feel of a private house with the many personal touches. The modern English cuisine offers an abundance of fresh local produce, concentrating on good textures and intense flavours combined with outstanding presentation. Head Chef Chris Short now oversees the running of the kitchen. Drinks, light lunches and traditional afternoon tea are also served on the garden terrace during the summer months. **Directions:** The hotel is situated 1/2 a mile from the main A429 Fosseway between Stow-on-the-Wold and Bourton-on-the-Water (signed To the Slaughters). Price guide (including dinner): Single from £155; double/twin £210–£235; suite £270.

28 rms MasterCard VISA AMERICAN EXPRESS M 20 7

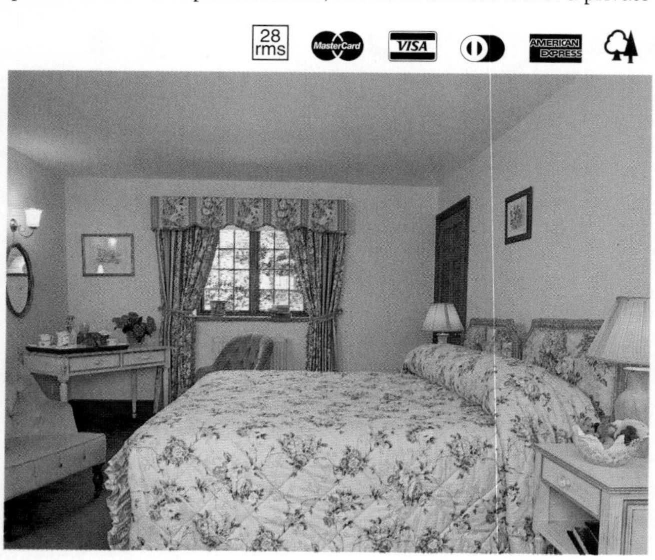

DINHAM HALL

LUDLOW, SHROPSHIRE SY8 1EJ
TEL: 01584 876464 FAX: 01584 876019

Built in 1792 Dinham Hall is situated in the historic town of Ludlow. It lies only 40 metres from the Castle which, having played an important part in England's history, today hosts the Shakespearian productions which form the major part of the annual Ludlow Festival. Dinham's enviable location provides its guests with the combination of ready access to the town and picturesque views over the open Shropshire countryside. There is a magnificent fireplace in the sitting room, with log fires in the winter. In the restaurant flowers help to provide a subtle atmosphere in which to enjoy prize-winning cuisine while the Merchant Suite, with its 14th century timbers, is an ideal setting for private dinners and meetings. During the summer afternoon teas are served on the terrace overlooking the walled garden. The décor of the bedrooms is a harmony of modern facilities and period design, a number of rooms having four-poster beds. The restaurant and many bedrooms command views over the gardens and Teme Valley to wooded hills. Guests may also enjoy a visit to Ludlow races or spend a few hours browsing in the town's antique shops. South Shropshire is one of the most beautiful parts of the country with Ludlow itself being one of the finest market towns. **Directions:** In the centre of Ludlow overlooking the castle. Price guide: Single £70–£80; double/twin £105–£135.

PASSFORD HOUSE HOTEL

MOUNT PLEASANT LANE, LYMINGTON, HAMPSHIRE SO41 8LS
TEL: 01590 682398 FAX: 01590 683494

Set in nine acres of picturesque gardens and rolling parkland, the Passford House Hotel lies midway between the charming New Forest village of Sway and the Georgian splendour of Lymington. Once the home of Lord Arthur Cecil, it is steeped in history and the traditions of leisurely country life. Pleasantly decorated bedrooms include a number of de luxe rooms, while comfort is the keynote in the four public lounges. The hotel prides itself on the standard and variety of cuisine served in its delightful restaurant and the extensive menu aims to give pleasure to the most discerning of palates. Meals are complemented by a speciality wine list. The hotel boasts a compact leisure centre, catering for all ages and activities. In addition to two heated swimming pools, there is a multi-gym, sauna, solarium, pool table, croquet lawn, pétanque and tennis court. Just a short drive away are Beaulieu, the cathedral cities of Winchester and Salisbury and ferry ports to the Isle of Wight and France. The New Forest has numerous golf courses, riding and trekking centres, cycling paths, beautiful walks, and of course sailing on the Solent. Milford-on-Sea, four miles away, is the nearest beach. **Directions:** At Lymington leave the A337 at the Tollhouse Inn, then take the first turning right and the hotel is on the right. Price guide: single from £85: double/twin from £115.

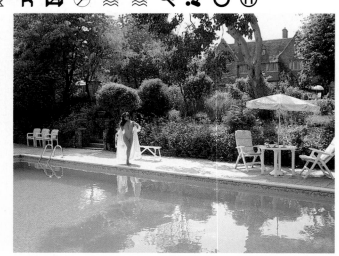

STANWELL HOUSE

HIGH STREET, LYMINGTON, NEW FOREST, HAMPSHIRE SO41 9AA
TEL: 01590 677123 FAX: 01590 677756

The Stanwell House Hotel is a fine example of Georgian architecture and great care has been taken in its restoration. Set on Lymington's fine wide High Street, which still hosts a Saturday market, it combines luxury with style, informal comfort and unobtrusive personal service. The 31 bedrooms include three beautifully refurbished suites and 10 executive rooms and there is an intimate bar and bistro and a delightful conservatory leading onto a flower filled patio and charming walled garden. The award-winning chef and his team prepare exciting fish and other dishes. Adjacent to the hotel, in a quiet courtyard off the street, is Elgars Cottage. This pretty period cottage is furnished to a very high standard and offers a full range of amenities. The house yacht Alpha is available for corporate or private charter, overnight stays or cruising. Lymington is a charming Regency town, close to the New Forest and the magnificent Solent with all its yachting facilities. There are opportunities for walking, riding and golf and river or sea fishing. Crossings by car ferry from Lymington to Yarmouth bring the Isle of Wight within a 30 minute journey. **Directions:** From the M27 junction 1 through Lyndhurst and Brockenhurst. Price guide: Single £75; double/twin £95–£110; suites £120–£140; Stanwell Cottage £500 per week for two people.

PARKHILL COUNTRY HOUSE HOTEL

BEAULIEU ROAD, LYNDHURST, NEW FOREST, HAMPSHIRE SO43 7FZ
TEL: 01703 282944 FAX: 01703 283268

Reached by a winding drive through glorious parkland from the scenic route between Lyndhurst and Beaulieu, Parkhill, situated in an elevated position with superb views across open forest and heathland, is perfect for a restful break or holiday and makes the ideal venue for special business meetings and small conferences, offering a charming New Forest remoteness coupled with an excellence of standards and service. Dining at Parkhill is very much an integral part of your overall pleasure. The award-winning restaurant offers a most tranquil setting with fine views across the lawns, where deer can occasionally be seen grazing. Cuisine is a delicious blend of modern and classical English cooking, where local fresh produce is used to create appetising menus, balanced by a carefully chosen and well-stocked cellar. Parkhill is also an ideal base for touring not only the delightful surrounding areas, but also the many places of interest which are all within easy driving distance, including Exbury Gardens, home to one of the world's finest collections of rhododendrons and azaleas, Broadlands, the old home of Lord Mountbatten, the *Mary Rose* in Portsmouth Dockyard and the graceful cathedral cities of Salisbury and Winchester. **Directions:** From Lyndhurst take the B3056 toward Beaulieu; Parkhill is about 1 mile from Lyndhurst on your right. Price guide: Single £80–£105; double £100–£145; suite £145–£160.

SHRIGLEY HALL HOTEL, GOLF & COUNTRY CLUB

SHRIGLEY PARK, POTT SHRIGLEY, NR MACCLESFIELD, CHESHIRE SK10 5SB
TEL: 01625 575757 FAX: 01625 573323 E-MAIL: shrigleyhall@paramounthotels.co.uk

Built in 1825 for a Lancashire businessman, Shrigley Hall has been a family home, Roman Catholic missionary college and since the 1980s, a hotel. Many alterations and extensions have taken place over the years, but today's splendid building still retains features from its original form. This exclusive country house skilfully blends traditional values and architectural styles with modern day technological advances. All 150 bedrooms include satellite TV with interactive Guestlink, radio, telephone, hairdryer, trouser press and tea and coffee-making facilities. Many overlook the rolling hills and parkland estate. A wide and imaginative selection of English and international dishes is offered in the classical Oakridge Restaurant. Glorious relaxation is secured with an escape to The Retreat Leisure Club with its heated indoor swimming pool, sauna, solarium, steam room, spa bath and beauty salon. For the energetic, there is also a high-tech gym with resistance and cardio-vascular equipment. Alternatively, guest can take advantage of a challenging opportunity presented by the hotel's 18-hole Championship length golf course and new club house. This part of the world offers a huge range of leisure activities, including sight-seeing, riding, rambling, walking and quad-biking. **Directions:** From Macclesfield, take A523 towards Stockport. After 2½ miles turn right at Legh Arms to Pott Shrigley – the hotel is 2 miles on the left. Price guide: Single £110–£135; double/twin £140–£170; suites £195.

CLIVEDEN

TAPLOW, BERKSHIRE SL6 0JF
TEL: 01628 668561 FAX: 01628 661837 E-MAIL: Reservations@clivedenhouse.co.uk

Cliveden, Britain's only 5 Red AA star hotel that is also a stately home, is set in 376 acres of gardens and parkland, overlooking the Thames. As the former home of Frederick, Prince of Wales, three Dukes and the Astor family, Cliveden has been at the centre of Britain's social and political life for over 300 years. It is exquisitely furnished in a classic English style; oil paintings, antiques and *objets d'art* abound. The spacious guest rooms and suites are appointed to the most luxurious standards. The choice of dining rooms and the scope of the menus are superb. The French Dining Room, with its original Madame de Pompadour rococo decoration, is the finest 18th century *boiserie* outside France. Relish the Michelin-starred cuisine of Waldo's Restaurant. The

newly restored Spring Cottage, secluded in its own gardens on the edge of the Cliveden Reach of the River Thames, is truly a cottage for a Queen, boasting a 20 feet domed Gothic ceiling within the drawing room. The Pavilion offers a full range of health and fitness facilities and beauty therapies. Guests enjoy horse-riding over the estate or a river cruise on an Edwardian launch. Well-equipped, the two secure private boardrooms provide self-contained business meeting facilities. Exclusive use of the hotel can be arranged. Cliveden's style may also be enjoyed at the Cliveden Town House, London and the Royal Crescent, Bath. **Directions:** Situated on B476, 2m north of Taplow. Price guide: Double/twin £310; suites from £590.

FREDRICK'S HOTEL & RESTAURANT

SHOPPENHANGERS ROAD, MAIDENHEAD, BERKSHIRE SL6 2PZ
TEL: 01628 581000 FAX: 01628 771054 E-MAIL: reservations@fredricks–hotel.co.uk

'Putting people first' is the guiding philosophy behind the running of this sumptuously equipped hotel and indeed, is indicative of the uncompromising service guests can expect to receive. Set in two acres of grounds, Fredrick's overlooks the fairways and greens of Maidenhead Golf Club beyond. The immaculate reception rooms are distinctively styled to create something out of the ordinary. Minute attention to detail is evident in the 37 bedrooms, all immaculate with gleaming, marble-tiled bathrooms, while the suites have their own patio garden or balcony. A quiet drink can be enjoyed in the light, airy Wintergarden lounge before entering the air-conditioned restaurant. Amid the elegant décor of crystal chandeliers and crisp white linen, fine gourmet cuisine is served which has received recognition from leading guides for many years. Particularly suited to conferences, four private function rooms with full secretarial facilities are available. Helicopter landing can be arranged. Easily accessible from Windsor, Henley, Ascot, Heathrow and London. Closed 24 Dec to 3 Jan. **Directions:** Leave M4 at exit 8/9, take A404(M) and leave at first turning signed Cox Green/White Waltham. Turn into Shoppenhangers Road; Fredrick's is on the right. Price guide: Single £175–£195; double/twin £210–£230; suite £375.

TAPLOW HOUSE HOTEL

BERRY HILL, TAPLOW, NR MAIDENHEAD, BERKSHIRE SL6 0DA
TEL: 01628 670056 FAX: 01628 773625 E-MAIL: taplow@wrensgroup.com

Elegance and splendour are the hallmarks of this majestic hotel which stands in six acres of land adorned by a historic and protected landscape. Taplow House dates back to 1598 and was given by James I to the first Governor of Virginia in 1628. Most of the house was destroyed by fire in the early 1700s but was rebuilt and purchased by the Grenfell family, famed for their equestrian activities, who commissioned the renowned gardener, Springhall, to landscape the grounds. The results can be seen today in the great trees, one of which is reputed to have been planted by Queen Elizabeth I. When the Marquess of Thomond took over the house in 1838 he had architect George Basevi redesign it to introduce the magnificent Doric columns to the reception hall and the elaborate chiselled brass banisters to the staircase which greet today's guests. It was last a private residence in 1958. Taplow House is splendid inside and out. It has recently had a £1.5 million refurbishment which has further enhanced its traditional charm and luxurious comfort. All 32 en suite bedrooms have every comfort. Chef Chris Couborough produces creative cuisine to please every palate. His outstanding menus are complemented by an excellent and extensive wine list. Windsor, Henley, Ascot and Cliveden are close by. **Directions:** From the M40, exit at junction 4. Price guide (room only): Single £130; double/twin £160; suite £200.

CHILSTON PARK

SANDWAY, LENHAM, NR MAIDSTONE, KENT ME17 2BE
TEL: 01622 859803 FAX: 01622 858588

This magnificent Grade I listed mansion, one of England's most richly decorated hotels, was built in the 13th century and remodelled in the 18th century. Now sensitively refurbished, the hotel's ambience is enhanced by the lighting, at dusk each day, of over 200 candles. The drawing room and reading room offer guests an opportunity to relax and to admire the outstanding collection of antiques. The entire hotel is a treasure trove full of many interesting *objets d'art*. The opulently furnished bedrooms are fitted to a high standard and many have four-poster beds.

Good, fresh English cooking is offered in each of Chilston's five dining rooms, where outstanding menus are supported by an excellent wine list. In keeping with the traditions of a country house, a wide variety of sporting activities are available, golf and riding nearby, fishing in the natural spring lake and punting. **Directions:** Take junction 8 off the M20, then A20 to Lenham Station. Turn left into Boughton Road. Go over the crossroads and M20; Chilston Park is on the left. Price guide: Single £110–£195; double/twin £125–£195; suite £250.

CRUDWELL COURT HOTEL

CRUDWELL, NR MALMESBURY, WILTSHIRE SN16 9EP
TEL: 01666 577194 FAX: 01666 577853 E-MAIL: Crudwellcrt@compuserve.com

Crudwell Court is a 17th century rectory, set in three acres of Cotswold walled gardens. The pretty, well-established grounds have lily ponds and a garden gate leading through to the neighbouring Saxon church of All Saints. Completely refurbished in recent years, the old rectory has been decorated with bright, cheery colours. Sunshine yellow in the sitting room, warm apricot in the drawing room and shades of buttercream and blue in the bedrooms lend a fresh feel to this hotel. Visitors enter through a flagstoned hall to discover rooms with comfortable seating and plenty of books to read. In the panelled dining room guests will find a weekly changing menu, which is best described as modern Anglo-French. Cooked to order, the meals are a feast for the eye as well as the palate. The restaurant has recently been extended by proprietor Nick Bristow into a new conservatory, which also hosts private functions. Malmesbury has a magnificent Norman abbey church and a curious market cross. Nearby are the towns of Tetbury and Cirencester, the picturesque villages of Castle Combe and Lacock and numerous stately homes. **Directions:** Crudwell Court is on the A429. Travelling towards Cirencester, when you reach the village of Crudwell turn right (signposted Oaksey) opposite the Plough Inn. The hotel is on the left. Price guide: Single £50–£60; double/twin £95.

THE OLD BELL

ABBEY ROW, MALMESBURY, WILTSHIRE SN16 0AG
TEL: 01666 822344 FAX: 01666 825145 E-MAIL: Woolley@luxury-hotel.demon.co.uk

The Old Bell was established by the Abbot of Malmesbury during the reign of King John as a place to refresh guests who came to consult the Abbey's library. Situated at the edge of the Cotswolds, this Grade I listed building may well be England's most ancient hotel. Inside, the Great Hall boasts a medieval stone fireplace, while each bedroom is decorated and furnished with an individual style and character. In the main house, a classic and imaginative menu exemplifies the best in English cooking, with meals ranging from four-course dinners complemented by fine wines in the Edwardian dining room, to informal snacks on the terrace. The Coach House features bedrooms styled on an oriental theme and many of these are suitable for families as interconnecting pairs of suites. Families are particularly welcomed at The Old Bell; there is no charge for children sharing parents' rooms and children's menus are available. The 'Den' is equipped with a multitude of toys and open every day. Malmesbury is only 30 minutes from Bath and is close to a number of other beautiful villages such as Castle Combe, Bourton-on-the-Water and Lacock. Other places of interest include the mysterious stone circle at Avebury and the Westonbirt Arboretum. **Directions:** Near the market cross in the centre of Malmesbury. Price guide: Single £75; double/twin £95–£150; suites £150–£180.

WHATLEY MANOR

NR EASTON GREY, MALMESBURY, WILTSHIRE SN16 0RB
TEL: 01666 822888 FAX: 01666 826120

This Grade II listed manor, set around a central courtyard, stands in 12 acres of grounds running down to a peaceful stretch of the River Avon. Originally built in the 17th century, Whatley Manor was refurbished by a wealthy sportsman in the 1920s and many of the present buildings date from that period. While the hotel's interior is furnished to a high standard, an emphasis has always been placed on maintaining a relaxed, informal atmosphere, enhanced by pine and oak panelling, log fires and the effect of warm colours in the lounge and drawing room. The dining room similarly combines elegance with intimacy and it overlooks the gardens. Ten of the bedrooms are in the 'Courthouse'. Snooker and table-tennis facilities are provided in the original saddle rooms and there are also a sauna, a solarium and a Jacuzzi. Close for gardening enthusiasts is Hodges Barn at Shipton Moyne. With the Cotswolds, the cities of Bath and Bristol, Tetbury, Cirencester, Westonbirt Arboretum, Longleat, Stourhead Gardens and many places of historic interest nearby. Stays of 2 nights or longer are at a reduced tariff. **Directions:** The hotel is on the B4040 three miles west of Malmesbury. Price guide: Single £82–£92; double/twin £96–£132.

THE COLWALL PARK HOTEL

COLWALL, NEAR MALVERN, WORCESTERSHIRE WR13 6QG
TEL: 01684 540206 FAX: 01684 540847 E-MAIL: colwallparkhotel@hotmail.com

This delightful hotel is in the centre of the village and set against a background of the Malvern Hills – to which it has direct access from its mature gardens. It also has the privilege of almost a private railway station, with two trains a day (just 2 hours from Paddington). The hotel is thriving under new management who have undertaken a thorough renovation of the hotel without spoiling its character. The bedrooms are pristine and comfortable and suites have been introduced – including one for families with an amusing children's bedroom. A bottle of the local Malvern water is always at hand. Residents enjoy the library (which can accommodate private dinners for 8 people), the first floor 'video' snug and the inviting panelled lounge bar where light meals are ordered from attentive waiters. The Edwardian Restaurant has table settings of delicate china and fine crystal. A pianist plays twice weekly. The kitchen is in the hands of a creative chef, offering à la carte and full vegetarian menus to 2 AA Rosette standard. Interesting international wines are listed. The ballroom, ideal for corporate events, leads onto the garden where wedding groups pose by the beautiful plane tree. Special breaks feature Cheltenham Races. Hotel sports are boules and croquet. **Directions:** M5/J7, A442 then A449. Colwall village is on B4218 between Malvern and Ledbury. Price guide: Single £64.50–£85; double/twin £105–£130; suite £140 including champagne & flowers.

THE COTTAGE IN THE WOOD

HOLYWELL ROAD, MALVERN WELLS, WORCESTERSHIRE WR14 4LG
TEL: 01684 575859 FAX: 01684 560662

The Malvern Hills once the home and inspiration for England's most celebrated composer Sir Edward Elgar, are the setting for The Cottage in the Wood. With its spectacular outlook across the Severn Valley plain, this unique hotel won acclaim from the Daily Mail for the best view in England. The main house was originally the Dower House to the Blackmore Park estate and accommodation is offered here and in Beech Cottage, an old scrumpy house – and the Coach House. The cottage-style furnishings give an intimate and cosy impression and the smaller Coach House rooms have suntrap balconies and patios. Owned and run by the Pattin family for over 12 years, the atmosphere is genuinely warm and relaxing. A regularly changing modern English menu is complemented by an almost obsessional wine list of 600 bins. If this causes any over-indulgence, guests can walk to the tops of the Malvern Hills direct from the hotel grounds. Nearby are the Victorian spa town of Great Malvern, the Three Counties Showground and the Cathedral cities of Worcester, Gloucester and Hereford. **Directions:** Three miles south of Great Malvern on A449, turn into Holywell Road by post box and hotel sign. Hotel is 250 yards on right. Price guide: Single £75; double/twin £89–£145. Bargain short breaks available.

THE STANNEYLANDS HOTEL

STANNEYLANDS ROAD, WILMSLOW, CHESHIRE SK9 4EY
TEL: 01625 525225 FAX: 01625 537282

Privately owned and managed, Stanneylands is a handsome country house set in several acres of impressive gardens with an unusual collection of trees and shrubs. Some of the bedrooms offer lovely views over the gardens while others overlook the undulating Cheshire countryside. A sense of quiet luxury prevails in the reception rooms, where classical décor and comfortable furnishings create a relaxing ambience. In the restaurant, contemporary English cooking is prepared to a very high standard both in terms of composition and presentation, while live occasional music adds to the atmosphere. For meetings and parties, a private oak-panelled dining room can accommodate up to 60 people, while a larger suite is available for conferences and larger personal celebrations. The Stanneylands Hotel is conveniently located for tours of the rolling Cheshire plain or the more rugged Peak District, as well as the bustling market towns and notable industrial heritage of the area. Special corporate and weekend rates are available. **Directions:** Three miles from Manchester International Airport. Come off at Junction 5 on the M56 (airport turn off). Follow signs to Wilmslow, turn left into station road, bear right onto Stanneylands Road. Hotel on right. Price guide: Single £104; double/twin £125–£149; suite £149.

ETROP GRANGE
THORLEY LANE, MANCHESTER AIRPORT M90 4EG
TEL: 0161 499 0500 FAX: 0161 499 0790

Hidden away near Manchester Airport lies Etrop Grange, a beautiful country house hotel and restaurant. The original house was built in 1780 and more than 200 years on has been lovingly restored. Today, the hotel enjoys a fine reputation for its accommodation, where the luxury, character and sheer elegance of the Georgian era are evident in every feature. The magnificent restaurant offers a well balanced mix of traditional and modern English cuisine, complemented by an extensive selection of fine wines. Attention to detail ensures personal and individual service. In addition to the obvious advantage of having an airport within walking distance, the location of Etrop Grange is ideal in many other ways. With a comprehensive motorway network and InterCity stations minutes away, it is accessible from all parts of the UK. Entertainment for visitors ranges from the shopping, sport and excellent nightlife offered by the city of Manchester to golf, riding, clay pigeon shooting, water sports and outdoor pursuits in the immediate countryside. Cheshire also boasts an abundance of stately homes, museums and historical attractions. **Directions:** Leave M56 at junction 5 towards Manchester Airport. Follow signs for Terminal 2. Go up the slip road. At roundabout take first exit, take immediate left and hotel is 400yds on the right. Price guide: Single £80–£150; double/twin £95–£170; suites £125–£175.

THE IVY HOUSE HOTEL

HIGH STREET, MARLBOROUGH, WILTSHIRE SN8 1HJ
TEL: 01672 515333 FAX: 01672 515338 E-MAIL: ivy.house@btconnect.com

Owners David Ball and Josephine Scott and manager Julian Roff welcome their guests to this 18th century Grade II listed property overlooking Marlborough High Street. The original building contains period features in its reception and lounge areas overlooking the cobbled courtyard and sun terrace. The recently appointed Beeches Wing provides additional accommodation of superior quality. Scotts restaurant serves delicious modern cuisine such as rillette of duck or steamed rabbit and leek pudding. Whilst the informal Courtyard Bar offers a good selection of light lunches and snacks. Business meetings and seminars may be held in either the dedicated conference suite or the small boardroom in the main house. Private parking is available. The ancient sites of Silbury Hill, Stonehenge and Avebury are easily accessible by car, as are the stately homes of Bowood House, Corsham Court and Blenheim Palace and also Newbury Race Course. **Directions:** The hotel is in Marlborough High Street, just off the A4 Bath–London road. Price guide: Single £69–£79; double/twin £84–£110.

DANESFIELD HOUSE

HENLEY ROAD, MARLOW-ON-THAMES, BUCKINGHAMSHIRE SL7 2EY
TEL: 01628 891010 FAX: 01628 890408

Danesfield House is set in 65 acres of gardens and parkland overlooking the River Thames and offering panoramic views across the Chiltern Hills. It is the third house since 1664 to occupy this lovely setting and it was designed and built in sumptuous style at the end of the 19th century. After years of neglect the house has been fully restored, combining its Victorian splendour with the very best modern hotel facilities. Among the many attractions of its luxury bedrooms, all beautifully decorated and furnished, are the extensive facilities they offer. These include two telephone lines (one may be used for personal fax), satellite TV, in-room movies, mini bar, trouser press, hair dryers, bath robes and toiletries. Guests can relax in the magnificent drawing room with its galleried library or in the sunlit atrium. There is a choice of two restaurants the Oak Room and Orangery Brasserie both of which offer a choice of international cuisine. The hotel also has six private banqueting and conference rooms. Leisure facilities include a swimming pool, croquet and jogging and walking trails. The new fully equipped health spa with treatment rooms and 20m indoor pool are due to open in January 2000. Windsor Castle, Disraeli's home at Hughenden Manor, Milton's cottage and the caves of West Wycombe are nearby. **Directions:** Between M4 and M40 on A4155 between Marlow and Henley-on-Thames. Price guide: Single £135; double/twin £165; suites £195.

NEW

THE OLDE BARN HOTEL

TOLL BAR ROAD, MARSTON, LINCOLNSHIRE NG32 2HT
TEL: 01400 250909 FAX: 01400 250130

Deep in the luscious Lincolnshire countryside, The Olde Barn Hotel is a charming and stylish hideaway, ideally positioned for exploring the cultural sites and golf courses in the area, or simply ambling in this idyllic corner of rural England. Each of the attractive 46 bedrooms is spacious and well-equipped and has an en suite bathroom. The hotel also offers three luxurious suites for families and long term guests. Guests can dine by candlelight in the romantic surroundings of the lofty restaurant, adorned with fresh flowers and rustic memorabilia. Less formal meals can be taken in the traditional bar, which has a welcoming and hospitable ambience. A superb fitness centre and swimming pool are also available, while the Olde Barn Hotel also offers state-of-the-art facilities for conferences and business meetings. The charming market town of Newark is close by and visitors can explore its bustling antiques and agricultural fairs. Nearby, there are eight golf courses, including two 18-hole championship stretches at the New Belton Woods complex. Guests can also satisfy their historical curiosity with visits to the fascinating Belvoir Castle, Belton House and Burghley House, all within easy driving distance of the Olde Barn Hotel. **Directions:** Four miles north of Grantham off the southbound carriageway. The Olde Barn Hotel is signposted from Marston. Price guide: Single £54.95–£89.95; double/twin £69.95–£104.95.

RIBER HALL

MATLOCK, DERBYSHIRE DE4 5JU
TEL: 01629 582795 FAX: 01629 580475 E-MAIL: info@riber-hall.co.uk

Relax in this tranquil and historic Derbyshire country house, which dates from the 1400's. Set in peaceful and picturesque countryside, Riber Hall is recommended by all major hotel and restaurant guides and has been nominated as "One of the most romantic hotels in Britain". Many original features have been preserved – magnificent oak beams, exposed stone work and period fireplaces. Acknowledged as a restaurant of distinction, English Classical, French Provincial cuisine – game when in season is served on bone china in elegant dining rooms. Superb wines, especially New World, are enjoyed in fine crystal glasses. Quietly located around an attractive courtyard and in the Old Hall, the bedrooms are appointed to a high standard with antiques throughout, including four poster beds and many thoughtful extras. The tranquil setting can be appreciated in the secluded old wall garden and orchard which is full of bird life, whilst energetic guests can pit their skills against the tennis trainer ball machine on the all weather tennis court. Conferences, weddings, wedding receptions and small dinner parties are catered for to the highest standard. Nearby are Chatsworth House, Haddon Hall, Hardwick Hall and Calke Abbey; and the Peak National Park. **Directions:** 20 minutes from junction 28 of M1, off A615 at Tansley; 1 mile further to Riber. Price guide: Single £92.50; double/twin £118.50.

STAPLEFORD PARK, AN OUTPOST OF THE CARNEGIE CLUB

NR MELTON MOWBRAY, LEICESTERSHIRE LE14 2EF
TEL: 01572 787 522 FAX: 01572 787 651 E-MAIL: reservations@stapleford.co.uk

A Stately Home and Sporting Estate where casual luxury is the byword. This pre-eminent 16th century house was once coveted by Edward, The Prince of Wales, but his mother Queen Victoria forbade him to buy .it for fear that his morals would be corrupted by the Leicestershire hunting society! Today, Stapleford Park offers house guests and club members a "lifestyle experience" to transcend all others in supremely elegant surroundings with panoramic views over 500 acres of parkland. Voted Top UK Hotel for Leisure Facilities' Conde Nast Traveller, 1998 Readers' Travel Awards, Stapleford has received innumerable awards for its unique style and hospitality. Individually designed bedrooms and a four-bedroom cottage have been created by famous names such as Mulberry, Wedgewood, Liberty and Crabtree & Evelyn. English cuisine with regional specialities are carefully prepared to the highest standards and complemented by an adventurous wine list. Sporting pursuits include fishing, falconry, riding, tennis and golf for all levels at The Stapleford Golf Academy. The Carnegie Clarins Spa with indoor pool, Jacuzzi, sauna and fitness room is a luxurious oasis offering an array of health therapies. Eleven elegant function and dining rooms are eminently suited to private dinners, special occasions and corporate hospitality. **Directions:** By train Kings Cross/Grantham in one hour. A1 north to Colsterworth then B676 via Saxby. Price guide: Double/twin £189–£415; suites from £580.

PERITON PARK HOTEL

MIDDLECOMBE, NR MINEHEAD, SOMERSET TA24 8SN
TEL: 01643 706885 FAX: 01643 706885

Some of the joys of staying in a small independent hotel are the individuality of the rooms, the interesting and varied food and the personal care and attention given to guests by its owners. Periton Park is just such a hotel which Richard and Angela Hunt run in an efficient, yet friendly way. Unusually perhaps today, the large bedrooms are very spacious and well-appointed, with warm colours creating a restful atmosphere. From its secluded and quiet position guests may enjoy wonderful views of the Exmoor National Park in all directions and the early riser may well be rewarded by the sight of a herd of red deer grazing on the surrounding countryside. The wood panelled restaurant, with its double aspect views, is the perfect place to enjoy some of the best food on Exmoor. Fresh fish, local game, delicately cooked vegetables, local cheeses and Somerset wine have all helped the restaurant to achieve an AA Red Rosette. Exmoor is very much for country lovers with miles of varied, unspoilt and breathtaking landscape. Riding is available from stables next to the hotel. Shooting is available in season. **Directions:** Periton Park is situated off the A39 on the left just after Minehead, in the direction of Lynmouth and Porlock. Price guide: Single £65; double/twin £99.

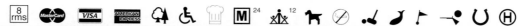

THE ANGEL HOTEL

NORTH STREET, MIDHURST, WEST SUSSEX GU29 9DN
TEL: 01730 812421 FAX: 01730 815928 E-MAIL: i.fleming@virgin.net

The Angel Hotel is a stylishly restored 16th century coaching inn which has earned widespread praise from its guests, the national press and guidebooks. Sympathetically renovated to combine contemporary comfort with original character, The Angel bridges the gap between town house bustle and country house calm. To the front, a handsome Georgian façade overlooks the High Street, while at the rear, quiet rose gardens lead to the parkland and ruins of historic Cowdray Castle. There are 28 bedrooms, all offering private bathrooms and modern amenities. Individually furnished with antiques, many rooms feature original Tudor beams. The hotel has been widely acclaimed for the quality of its food. For corporate guests the hotel offers two attractive meeting rooms, a business suite, presentation aids and secretarial services. Racegoers will find it very convenient for Goodwood and theatregoers for the internationally acclaimed Chichester Festival Theatre. The historic market town of Midhurst is well placed for visits to Petworth House, Arundel Castle and the South Downs. **Directions:** From the A272, the hotel is on the left as the town centre is approached from the east. Price guide: Single from £85; double/twin from £120–£180.

THE SPREAD EAGLE HOTEL & HEALTH SPA

SOUTH STREET, MIDHURST, WEST SUSSEX GU29 9NH
TEL: 01730 816911 FAX: 01730 815668 E-MAIL: i.fleming@virgin.net

Dating from 1430, when guests were first welcomed here, The Spread Eagle Hotel is one of England's oldest hotels and is steeped in history. Following a recent refurbishment, the hotel is the essence of opulence and those wishing to be pampered will enjoy the superb fitness facilities and excellent standard of service. Located in either the main building or the market house, the 39 en suite bedrooms, some with four-poster beds, are well-appointed with soft furnishings and fine ornaments. A roaring log fire attracts guests into the historic lounge bar, ideal for relaxing in the afternoons or enjoying an apéritif. Sumptuous modern British cuisine may be savoured in the candlelit restaurant, complemented by an extensive wine list.

Weddings, banquets and meetings are held in the Jacobean Hall and Polo Room. The Aquila Health Spa is an outstanding facility featuring a blue tiled swimming pool as its centrepiece. A Scandinavian sauna, Turkish steam room, hot tub, fitness centre and a range of beauty treatments, aromatherapy and massage are also offered. The stately homes at Petworth, Uppark and Goodwood are all within a short drive, with Chichester Cathedral, the Downland Museum and Fishbourne Roman Palace among the many local attractions. Cowdray Park Polo Club is only 1 mile away. **Directions:** Midhurst is on the A286 between Chichester and Milford. Price guide: Single £89–£130; double/twin £120–£198.

MOORE PLACE HOTEL

THE SQUARE, ASPLEY GUISE, MILTON KEYNES, BEDFORDSHIRE MK17 8DW
TEL: 01908 282000 FAX: 01908 281888

This elegant Georgian mansion was built by Francis Moore in the peaceful Bedfordshire village of Aspley Guise in 1786. The original house, which is set on the village square, has been sympathetically extended to create extra rooms. The additional wing has been built around an attractive courtyard with a rock garden, lily pool and waterfall. The pretty Victorian-style conservatory restaurant, awarded 2 AA Rosettes, serves food that rates among the best in the area. Vegetarian options and special diets can always be found on the menus, which offer dishes prepared in the modern English style and balanced with a selection of fine wines. The 54 bedrooms are well-appointed with many amenities, including a trouser press, hairdryer, welcome drinks and large towelling bathrobes. Banquets, conferences and dinner parties can be accommodated in five private function rooms: all are decorated in traditional-style yet are equipped with the latest audiovisual facilities. The hotel is close to Woburn Abbey, Silverstone, Whipsnade Zoo, Stowe and Milton Keynes. The convenient location and accessibility to the motorway network makes Moore Place Hotel an attractive choice, whether travelling on business or for pleasure. **Directions:** Only two minutes' drive from the M1 junction 13. Price guide: Single from £80; double/twin £95–£175; suite £185.

THE MANOR HOUSE HOTEL

MORETON-IN-MARSH, GLOUCESTERSHIRE GL56 0LJ
TEL: 01608 650501 FAX: 01608 651481

This former 16th century manor house and coaching inn is set in beautiful gardens in the Cotswold village of Moreton-in-Marsh. The Manor House Hotel has been tastefully extended and restored, yet retains many of its historic features, among them a priest's hole and secret passages. The 38 well-appointed bedrooms have been individually decorated and furnished. The restaurant offers imaginative and traditional English dishes using only the freshest ingredients, accompanied by an expertly selected wine list. For the guest seeking relaxation, leisure facilities include an indoor heated swimming pool, spa bath and sauna. Sports enthusiasts will also find that tennis, golf, riding and squash can be arranged locally. The spacious conference facilities are set apart from the rest of the hotel. Modern business facilities, combined with the peaceful location, make this an excellent venue for executive meetings. It is also an ideal base for touring, with many attractions nearby, including Stratford-upon-Avon, Warwick and the fashionable centres of Cheltenham, Oxford and Bath. **Directions:** The Manor House Hotel is on the A429 Fosse Way near the junction of the A44 and A429 north of Stow, on the Broadway side of the intersection. Price guide: Single £65; double/twin £90–£125.

ROOKERY HALL

WORLESTON, NANTWICH, NR CHESTER, CHESHIRE CW5 6DQ
TEL: 01270 610016 FAX: 01270 626027 E-MAIL: rookery@co.com

Rookery Hall enjoys a peaceful setting where guests can relax, yet is convenient for road, rail and air networks. The hotel also has a chauffeur driven Bentley to take guests for local journeys or further afield. Within the original house are elegant reception rooms and the mahogany and walnut panelled restaurant, which is renowned for its cuisine. Dine by candlelight in the intimate dining room overlooking the lawns. Over 300 wines are in the cellar. Private dining facilities are available for meetings and weddings – summer lunches can be taken alfresco on the terrace. Companies can hire the hotel as their own "Country House", with leisure pursuits such as archery, clay pigeon shooting and off road driving available within the grounds. Tennis or croquet, fishing, golf and riding can be arranged. All of the bedrooms are individually designed and luxuriously furnished with spacious marbled bathrooms. Many afford views over fields and woodlands. Suites are available including the self-contained stable block. Special breaks and celebrations packages are offered with gourmet evenings in the restaurant. The hotel is ideally situated for historic Chester and North Wales. **Directions:** From M6 junction 16 take A500 to Nantwich, then B5074 to Worleston. Price guide: Single £125–£190; double/twin £150–£210; suite £220–£310.

DONNINGTON VALLEY HOTEL & GOLF COURSE

OLD OXFORD ROAD, DONNINGTON, NEWBURY, BERKSHIRE RG14 3AG
TEL: 01635 551199 FAX: 01635 551123 E-MAIL: general@donningtonvalley.co.uk

Uncompromising quality is the hallmark of this hotel built in contrasting styles in 1991 with its own golf course. The grandeur of the Edwardian era has been captured by the interior of the hotel's reception area with its splendid wood-panelled ceilings and impressive overhanging gallery. Each individually designed bedroom has been thoughtfully equipped to guarantee comfort and peace of mind. In addition to the standard guest rooms Donnington Valley offers a number of non-smoking rooms, family rooms, superior executive rooms and luxury suites. With its open log fire and elegant surroundings, the Piano Bar is an ideal place to meet friends or enjoy the relaxed ambience. Guests lunch and dine in the Gallery Restaurant which offers fine international cuisine complemented by an extensive choice of wines and liqueurs. The 18-hole, par 71, golf course is a stern test for golfers of all abilities, through a magnificent parkland setting. Special corporate golfing packages are offered and tournaments can be arranged. Seven purpose-built function suites provide the flexibility to meet the demands of corporate and special events. Donnington Castle, despite a siege during the Civil War, still survives for sight-seeing. **Directions:** Leave the M4 at junction 13, go south towards Newbury on A34, then follow signs for Donnington Castle. Price guide: Single from £120; double/twin from £120; suite from £200.

HOLLINGTON HOUSE HOTEL

WOOLTON HILL, NR NEWBURY, BERKSHIRE RG20 9XA
TEL: 01635 255100 FAX: 01635 255075 E-MAIL: hollington.house@newbury.net

Hollington House Hotel, one of England's foremost luxury country house hotels, opened in July 1992. The Elizabethan-style house, built in 1904, is set in 14 acres of Gertrude Jekyll woodland gardens, adjacent to 250 acres of private parkland. Prior to returning to the UK after an absence of 32 years, John and Penny Guy created and owned Burnham Beeches Hotel, near Melbourne, which became Australia's first Relais et Châteaux hotel. No expense has been spared in their successful endeavours to maintain similar standards of excellence here. The 20 individually designed bedrooms are furnished with antiques and paintings and have sumptuous bathrooms. Elegant reception rooms, an oak-panelled, galleried hall and private boardroom are among the many splendid features of the house. The Chef serves a modern style of cooking with flair and innovation, based on traditional English and French cuisine. Indoors, there is a swimming pool and a full-size snooker table, outdoors, a solar-heated swimming pool, a tennis court and a croquet lawn. The surrounding countryside offers opportunities for walking, shooting, hunting and horse-racing. Conference, wedding and weekend packages available. **Directions:** From M4 junction 13, south of Newbury, leave A343 Andover road, follow signs for Hollington House. Price guide: Single from £105; spa feature room £195; king-size double/twin £145; junior suite from £275.

THE VINEYARD AT STOCKCROSS

NEWBURY, BERKSHIRE RG20 8JU
TEL: 01635 528770 FAX: 01635 528398 E-MAIL: general@the-vineyard.co.uk

The Vineyard at Stockcross, Sir Peter Michael's 'restaurant-with-suites' is a European showcase for the finest Californian wines including those from the Peter Michael Winery. Head Sommelier, Edoardo Amadi, has selected the best from the most highly-prized, family owned Californian wineries, creating one of the widest, most innovative, international wine lists. Awarded 4 Red Stars and 3 Rosettes by the AA, the classical French cuisine with a modern British twist matches the calibre of the wines. Pure flavours, fresh ingredients and subtle design blend harmoniously with the fine wines. A stimulating collection of paintings and sculpture includes the keynote piece, Fire and Water by William Pye FRBS and

'Deconstructing the Grape', a sculpture commissioned for the opening of The Vineyard Spa. A vine-inspired, steel balustrade elegantly dominates the restaurant and the luxurious interior is complemented by subtle attention to detail throughout with stunning china and glass designs. The 33 well-appointed bedrooms include 13 suites offering stylish comfort with distinctive character. The Vineyard Spa features an indoor pool, spa bath, sauna, steam room, gym and treatment rooms. **Directions:** From M4, exit Jct13, A34 towards Newbury, then Hungerford exit. 1st roundabout Hungerford exit, 2nd roundabout Stockcross exit. Hotel on right. Price guide: Double/twin £188–£276; suite £276–£511.

LINDEN HALL HOTEL, HEALTH SPA & GOLF COURSE

LONGHORSLEY, MORPETH, NEWCASTLE-UPON-TYNE, NORTHUMBERLAND NE65 8XF
TEL: 01670 516611 FAX: 01670 788544

Ivy-clad, hidden away among 450 acres of fine park and woodland in mid-Northumberland, Linden Hall is a superb Georgian country house within easy reach of Newcastle-upon-Tyne. An impressive mile-long drive sweeps up to its main door where, upon entering, the visitor will discover a relaxed, dignified atmosphere enhanced by gracious marble hearths, antiques and period pieces. Those wishing to escape the urban stress will be delighted to find every fitness and relaxation requirement catered for on the 18-hole golf course or at the health and beauty spa. Beauty therapy treatments, fitness and steam room, swimming pool, sun terrace and solarium are all available on the premises. The 50 bedrooms are individually and elegantly furnished. Some rooms have four-poster beds; each has its own private bathroom, supplied with thoughtful extras. The Linden Tree Bar and Grill serves informal drinks and bar meals and the Dobson Restaurant, with panoramic views of the Northumberland coastline, serves delicious food, imaginatively prepared. Wedding receptions, banquets, dinner parties and business conferences can be held in comfort in any one of Linden Hall's conference and banqueting suites. **Directions:** From Newcastle take A1 north for 15 miles, then A697 toward Coldstream and Wooler. The hotel is 1 mile north of Longhorsley. Price guide: Single £97.50–£147.50; double/twin £125–£195; suite: £195.

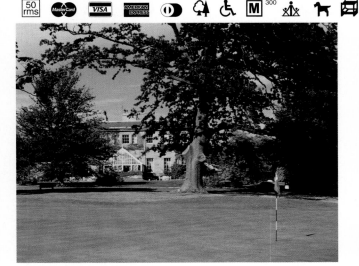

SWYNFORD PADDOCKS HOTEL AND RESTAURANT

SIX MILE BOTTOM, NR NEWMARKET, SUFFOLK CB8 0UE
TEL: 01638 570234 FAX: 01638 570283 E-MAIL: info@swynford.paddocks.com

This classical white mansion standing in glorious gardens and idyllic countryside with racehorses grazing its pastures has a romantic history. In 1813 it was the scene of a passionate love affair between Lord Byron and the wife of the owner, Colonel George Leigh. Swynford was converted into a luxury hotel 20 years ago. It has a country house atmosphere with antique furniture, open fires and attention to detail of times gone by. Each individually decorated, en suite bedroom has colour television, clock radio alarm, telephone, mini-bar and many other amenities. The lounge bar overlooks the gardens and the dining room offers an imaginative menu, changed regularly to incorporate the season's fresh produce. Awarded AA

Rosette for food alongside The Romantic Hotel award 1997. There is a conference room for up to 25 delegates and a luxury marquee for private and special functions. Tennis, putting and croquet are within the grounds and guided tours of Newmarket with a look at the horseracing world can be arranged. Heliquisine: For a special occasion guests are chauffeur driven in a limousine to Cambridge airport for a helicopter ariel view of the surrounding towns, then land for a superb lunch at the hotel. **Directions:** From M11, exit at jct 9 and take A11 towards Newmarket. After 10 miles join A1304 signed Newmarket. Hotel is on left after $^3/_4$ of a mile. Price guide: Single £90; double/twin £127–£148.

REDWORTH HALL HOTEL & COUNTRY CLUB

REDWORTH, NEWTON AYCLIFFE, COUNTY DURHAM DL5 6NL

TEL: 01388 772442 FAX: 01388 775112 CONFERENCE OFFICE FAX: 01388 775660 E-MAIL: rhh@scottishhighlandhotel.co.uk

Redworth Hall, winner of the Pride of Northumberland 'Best Hotel 1998' award, is a 17th century, tastefully converted manor house situated in 25 acres of woodland. There are 100 en suite bedrooms, several of which are suitable for guests who are disabled. The furnishings throughout range from antique to fine reproduction. The hotel's health club won the 'Flame Award Best Health Club in Great Britain 1998', and includes a heated indoor swimming pool, with a hoist for guests with disabilities, a spa bath, sunbeds, steam bath, squash courts, sauna, all-weather tennis courts and a fully-equipped gymnasium. There is an indoor play area and an outdoor adventure playground for children. There are 16 function rooms which can accommodate from 3 to 300 guests, making the hotel ideal for conferences, training courses and weddings. Guests may choose between two restaurants: the elegant Blue Room offering innovative cuisine or the airy Conservatory which features a table d'hôte and contemporary à la carte menu. Redworth Hall, was awarded 2 AA Rosettes for food and service and has achieved the coveted Investor in People Standard. **Directions:** A1(M) exit 58, A68 to Corbridge, then A6072 to Redworth. The hotel is two miles on left. Price guide (room only): Single £95–£115; double/twin £115–£145; four-poster £165–£195.

PARK FARM COUNTRY HOTEL & LEISURE

HETHERSETT, NORWICH, NORFOLK NR9 3DL
TEL: 01603 810264 FAX: 01603 812104

Park Farm Hotel occupies a secluded location in beautifully landscaped grounds south of Norwich, once the second greatest city in England. There are executive rooms for additional comforts, with four poster beds and Jacuzzi baths. Additional bedrooms have been sympathetically converted from traditional and new buildings to reflect the style of the six rooms available in the main house. A superb leisure complex to suit all ages has been carefully incorporated alongside the original Georgian house to include heated swimming pool, sauna, steam room, solarium, spa bath, gymnasium, aerobics studio and a new beauty therapy area. The croquet lawn and putting green are situated in the grounds. The delightful Georgian restaurant is renowned for high standards of cuisine and service, awarded 1 Rosette, with a wide selection of dishes and fine choice of wines. Conference facilities cater for up to 120 candidates, (24 hour and daily delegate rates available). Ideal location for wedding receptions. The Norfolk broads, the coast, Norwich open market, Castle museum and Cathedral are nearby. **Directions:** By road, just off A11 on B1172, Norwich Airport eight miles, Norwich rail station six miles and Norwich bus station five miles. Price guide: Single £70–£100; double/twin £90–£120; suite £130.

PETERSFIELD HOUSE HOTEL

LOWER STREET, HORNING, NR NORWICH, NORFOLK NR12 8PF
TEL: 01692 630741 FAX: 01692 630745

Petersfield House Hotel is set back from one of the most attractive reaches of the River Bure in the area known as the Norfolk Broads. The original property was built in the twenties on a prime site as a large private residence in two acres of gardens with its own moorings on a grassy bank of the river. Today it is a secluded family run hotel whose reputation is based on traditional comfort and hospitality. Guests can be sure of receiving personal attention at all times. The bedrooms are bright and welcoming – most rooms overlook the well-kept landscaped gardens which feature an ornamental pond, a putting green and a flintstone moon gate. Varied fixed-price and extensive à la carte menus are served in the restaurant where a list of over 60 wines provides an ideal accompaniment. Regular Saturday night dinner-dances are held with the hotel occupying one of the choicest positions on the Norfolk Broads. Sailing is the popular local pastime and open regattas are held during the summer. Golf is within easy driving distance. Other local attractions include Norwich with its famous art gallery and "Ten Ancient Monuments" and Blickling Hall with its interesting furniture and gardens. **Directions:** From Norwich ring road, take A1151 to Wroxham. Cross bridge, turn right at Hoveton on A1062 to Horning; hotel is beyond centre of the village. Price guide: Single £60; double £75.

SWALLOW SPROWSTON MANOR HOTEL

SPROWSTON PARK, WROXHAM ROAD, NORWICH, NORFOLK NR7 8RP
TEL: 01603 789409 FAX: 01603 423911

This imposing country house, built in 1559, stands in 10 acres of grounds at the end of an oak-lined driveway and is situated just 3 miles from Norwich. The bedrooms, all en suite and some with four-posters, have views over the hotel's own 18 hole golf course and surrounding parkland, and are spacious and comfortable. The 2 AA Rosette award winning Manor Restaurant has been restored to classic splendour with mahogany columns, oil paintings and crystal chandeliers. The à la carte menu offers an excellent choice of dishes. The health spa with large indoor swimming pool and leisure club, with spa bath, pool bar, fitness studio, steam rooms and sauna, are open to hotel residents free of charge. Solarium and beauty salon treatments are charged as taken. It is advisable to pre-book treatments and golf tee-off times. With its well-equipped conference rooms, the hotel is an excellent venue for both social and business functions. The city of Norwich is rich with art and history, whilst Sandringham, the Norfolk Broads and the Norfolk coast are all within easy reach. **Directions:** From Norwich, take the Wroxham Road (A1151) and follow signs to Sprowston Park. Price guide: Single £105–£145; double/twin £115–£155; suite £160.

LANGAR HALL

LANGAR, NOTTINGHAMSHIRE NG13 9HG
TEL: 01949 860559 FAX: 01949 861045 E-MAIL: langarhall–hotel@direct.co.uk

Set in the Vale of Belvoir, mid-way between Nottingham and Grantham, Langar Hall is the family home of Imogen Skirving. Epitomising "excellence and diversity" it combines the standards of good hotel-keeping with the hospitality and style of country house living. Having received a warm welcome, guests can enjoy the atmosphere of a private home that is much loved and cared for. The en suite bedrooms are individually designed and comfortably appointed. The public rooms feature fine furnishings and most rooms afford beautiful views of the garden, park and moat. Imogen and her kitchen team collaborate to produce an excellent, varied menu of modern British food. This is an ideal venue for exclusive 'House party' bookings and private dinner parties. Celebrations may include a choice of in–house entertainment, opera, theatre, music or a murder mystery dinner. Langar Hall is an ideal venue for small boardroom meetings. It is also an ideal base from which to visit Belvoir Castle, to see cricket at Trent Bridge, to visit students at Nottingham University and to see Robin Hood's Sherwood Forest. Dogs can be accommodated by arrangement. **Directions:** Langar is accessible via Bingham on the A52, or via Cropwell Bishop from the A46 (both signposted). The house adjoins the church and is hidden behind it. Price guide: Single £75–£95; double/twin £95–£150; suite £175.

HAMBLETON HALL

HAMBLETON, OAKHAM, RUTLAND LE15 8TH
TEL: 01572 756991 FAX: 01572 724721 E-MAIL: hotel@hambletonhall.com

Winner of Johansens Most Excellent Country Hotel Award 1996, Hambleton Hall, originally a Victorian mansion, became a hotel in 1979. Since then its renown has continually grown. It enjoys a spectacular lakeside setting in a charming and unspoilt area of Rutland. The hotel's tasteful interiors have been designed to create elegance and comfort, retaining individuality by avoiding a catalogue approach to furnishing. Delightful displays of flowers, an artful blend of ingredients from local hedgerows and the London flower markets colour the bedrooms. In the restaurant, the chef and his enthusiastic team offer a menu which is strongly seasonal. Grouse, Scottish ceps and chanterelles, partridge and woodcock are all available at just the right time of year, accompanied by the best vegetables, herbs and salads from the Hall's garden. The dishes are beautifully presented and supported by a list of interesting wines at reasonable prices. For the energetic there are lovely walks around the lake and opportunities for tennis and swimming, golf, riding, bicycling, trout fishing, and sailing. Burghley House and Belton are nearby, as are the antique shops of Oakham, Uppingham and Stamford. Hambleton Hall is a Relais & Châteaux member. **Directions:** In the village of Hambleton, signposted from the A606, 1 mile east of Oakham. Price guide: Single £145; double/twin £170–£295.

CHEVIN LODGE COUNTRY PARK HOTEL

YORKGATE, OTLEY, WEST YORKSHIRE LS21 3NU
TEL: 01943 467818 FAX: 01943 850335 FREEPHONE RESERVATIONS 0500 340560

A quite unique hotel – you would probably need to travel to Scandinavia to discover a similar hotel to Chevin Lodge. Built entirely of Finnish logs and surrounded by birch trees, it is set in 50 acres of lake and woodland in the beauty spot of Chevin Forest Park. The spacious, carefully designed bedrooms are tastefully furnished with pine and some have patio doors leading to the lakeside gardens. In addition, there are several luxury lodges tucked away in the woods, providing alternative accommodation to the hotel bedrooms. Imaginative and appetising meals are served in the beautiful balconied restaurant, which overlooks the lake. Chevin Lodge offers conference facilities in the Woodlands Suite which is fully- equipped for all business requirements. The Leisure Club has a 11 x 7 metres swimming pool, spa bath, sauna, solarium and gym. There is also a games room, all weather tennis court and jogging and cycling trails that wind through the woods. Leeds, Bradford and Harrogate are within 20 minutes' drive. Special weekend breaks are available. **Directions:** From A658 between Bradford and Harrogate, take the Chevin Forest Park road, then left into Yorkgate for Chevin Lodge. Price guide: Single £95–£120; double/twin £110–£130. Special breaks available.

FOXHILLS

STONEHILL ROAD, OTTERSHAW, SURREY KT16 0EL
TEL: 01932 704500 FAX: 01932 874762

This magnificent 400 acre estate is a delightful environment for any discerning traveller, whatever their interests may be. Named after the 18th century foreign secretary, Charles James Fox, Foxhills comprises of a large Manor House, elegant suites, three golf courses, numerous tennis courts, indoor and outdoor swimming pools, three restaurants and a host of health and fitness facilities including a gymnasium and a sauna. The 38 bedrooms, located in a superb courtyard setting, are the essence of comfort; elegantly furnished and offering all the latest amenities, they are designed in a number of styles; some have gardens whilst others are on two floors. The three restaurants pride themselves in their culinary excellence. Inside the Manor itself, the award-winning restaurant serves fine cuisine and is renowned for the Sunday buffet – a gourmet's delight! The sport and health facilities at Foxhills are particularly impressive and with 20 qualified instructors on hand, guests may wish to acquire a new skill such as racquetball or T'ai Chi. Those wishing to be pampered will enjoy the sauna, steamroom and the fine beauty salon. **Directions:** From M25 Jct 11, follow signs to Woking. After a dual carriageway, turn left into Guildford Road. 3rd exit at roundabout and immediately right into Foxhills Road. Turn left at the end of the road, Foxhills is on the right. Price guide (room only): Double/twin £120–£175; suite £225–£250.

FALLOWFIELDS

KINGSTON BAGPUIZE WITH SOUTHMOOR, OXON OX13 5BH
TEL: 01865 820416 FAX: 01865 821275 E-MAIL: stay@fallowfields.com

Fallowfields, once the home of Begum Aga Khan, dates back more than 300 years. It has been updated and extended over past decades and today boasts a lovely early Victorian Gothic southern aspect. The house is set in two acres of gardens, surrounded by ten acres of grassland. The guests' bedrooms, which offer a choice of four poster or coroneted beds, are large and well appointed and offer every modern amenity to ensure maximum comfort and convenience. The house is centrally heated throughout and during the winter months, there are welcoming log fires in the elegant main reception rooms. The walled kitchen garden provides most of the vegetables and salads for the table and locally grown organic produce is otherwise used wherever possible. Places of interest nearby: Fallowfields is close to Stratford, the Cotswolds, Stonehenge, Bath and Bristol to the west, Oxford, Henley on Thames, the Chilterns and Windsor to the east. Heathrow airport is under an hour away. **Directions:** Take the Kingston Bagpuize exit on the A420 Oxford to Swindon. Fallowfields is at the west end of Southmoor and just after the Longworth sign. Price guide: Single £85–105; double/twin £110–£145.

LE MANOIR AUX QUAT' SAISONS

GREAT MILTON, OXFORDSHIRE OX44 7PD
TEL: 01844 278881 FAX: 01844 278847

Situated in secluded grounds a few miles south of the historic city of Oxford in rural Cotswold countryside, the restaurant and the contemporary classic hotel of Le Manoir aux Quat' Saisons are among the finest in Europe. Le Manoir is the inspired creation of Raymond Blanc whose extraordinary cooking has received the highest tributes from all international guides to culinary excellence. The Times uniquely gives Blanc's cooking 10 out of 10 and rates it 'the best in Britain'. The atmosphere throughout is one of understated elegance while all 32 bedrooms and suites offer guests the highest standards of comfort and luxury. Every need is anticipated, for service is a way of life here, never intrusive but always present. For dedicated 'foodies', Raymond Blanc's highly successful cookery school, is a must. Four-day courses are run from August to April and participation is restricted to ten guests to ensure the highest level of personal tuition. Participants stay at Le Manoir and their partners are welcome to stay free of charge although their meals and drinks are charged separately. **Directions:** From London, M40 and turn off at junction 7 (A329 to Wallingford). From the North, leave M40 at junction 8A and follow signs to Wallingford (A329). After 1½ miles, turn right, follow the brown signs for Le Manoir aux Quat' Saisons. Price guide: Double/twin £230–£340; suites £395–£550. Midweek Escape rates available.

STUDLEY PRIORY

HORTON HILL, HORTON-CUM-STUDLEY, OXFORD, OXFORDSHIRE OX33 1AZ
TEL: 01865 351203 FAX: 01865 351613 USA/CANADA TOLL FREE: 800 437 2687 E-MAIL: res@studley-priory

Studley Priory, its exterior little altered since Elizabethan days, is conveniently located only 7 miles from both the main London–Oxford road and the dreaming spires of Oxford. There is a sense of timeless seclusion in the setting of 13 acres of wooded grounds with their fine views of the Cotswolds, the Chilterns and the Vale of Aylesbury. The bedrooms range from single rooms to the Elizabethan Suite, which has a half-tester bed dating from around 1700. Cots are available for young children. The restaurant, offering the best of English and French cuisine, provides a seasonally changing menu created from fresh local produce and complemented by an extensive and well-balanced wine list. Good conference facilities are available and wedding parties and banquets can be accommodated. Studley Priory is ideally placed for visits to Blenheim Palace, the Manors of Waddesdon and Milton, Broughton Castle, the Great Western Museum of Railways and also horse-racing at Ascot, Newbury and Cheltenham. Many activities can be arranged at the hotel. Riding facilities and the Studley Wood 18 hole golf course are nearby. **Directions:** From London leave M40 at Jct8. Follow A40 toward Oxford. Turn right for Horton-cum-Studley. Hotel is at the top of the hill. Price guide: Single £105–£135; double/twin £130–£200; suite £200–£250.

WESTON MANOR

WESTON-ON-THE-GREEN, OXFORDSHIRE OX6 8QL
TEL: 01869 350621 FAX: 01869 350901

Imposing wrought-iron gates flanked by sculptured busts surmounting tall grey stone pillars lead into the impressive entrance to this delightful old manor house, the showpiece of the lovely village of Weston-on-the Green since the 11th century. The ancestral home of the Earls of Abingdon and Berkshire, and once the property of Henry VIII, Weston Manor stands regally in 13 acres of colourful gardens restored as a unique country house hotel of character. A peaceful retreat for visitors wishing to discover the delights of the surrounding Cotswold countryside and of Oxford, Woodstock, Blenheim Palace and Broughton Castle. Many of the Manor's 34 charming bedrooms, including four in a cottage and 14 in the old coach-house, retain antique furniture and all have garden views, private bathrooms and elegant surroundings. There is a squash court, croquet lawn and a secluded, heated outdoor swimming pool. Golf and riding are nearby. At the heart of the Manor is the restaurant, a magnificent vaulted and oak panelled Baronial Hall where delectable cuisine is served. Dining in such historic splendour is very much the focus of a memorable stay. **Directions:** From the M40, exit at junction 9 onto the A34. Leave A34 on 1st exit, towards Oxford. After approximately one mile turn right onto the B340. Weston Manor is on the left. Price guide: Single £105; double/twin £125; suite £165.

THE PAINSWICK HOTEL

KEMPS LANE, PAINSWICK, GLOUCESTERSHIRE GL6 6YB
TEL: 01452 812160 FAX: 01452 814059

The village of Painswick stands high on a hill overlooking the beautiful rolling valleys of the Cotswolds. Dating back to the 14th century, the village was an old wool community, medieval cottages mingle gracefully with elegant Georgian merchants' houses. A feature of the village is the church, with its ancient churchyard graced by 99 Yew trees planted in 1792 and 17th century table tombs in memory of the wealthy clothiers. Situated majestically within these architectural gems is the Palladian-style Painswick Hotel, built in 1790 and formerly the home of affluent village rectors. Each of the luxury en suite bedrooms have modern amenities, beautiful fabrics, antique furniture and objets d'art; creating a restful atmosphere and the impression of staying in a comfortable private house. The stylish restaurant, with its pine panelling, offers delicious cuisine with an emphasis upon regional produce such as locally reared Cotswold meat, game, wild Severn salmon, Gloucestershire cheeses and fresh shellfish from the seawater tank. The private Dining Room accommodates quiet dinner parties, wedding occasions and business meetings. **Directions:** M5 Jct13. Painswick is on A46 between Stroud and Cheltenham, turn into road by the church and continue round the corner, taking the first right. The hotel is at the bottom of the road on the right hand side. Price guide: Single from £90; double/twin from £120–£195.

THE HAYCOCK

WANSFORD-IN-ENGLAND, PETERBOROUGH, CAMBRIDGESHIRE PE8 6JA
TEL: 01780 782223 FAX: 01780 783031

The Haycock is a handsome old coaching inn of great charm, character and historic interest. It was host to Mary Queen of Scots in 1586 and Princess Alexandra Victoria, later Queen Victoria, in 1835. Overlooking the historic bridge that spans the River Nene, the hotel is set in a delightful village of unspoilt cottages. All the bedrooms are individually designed, equipped to the highest standards and graced by Italian hand-painted furniture. The Restaurant is renowned for the quality of its traditional English cooking, with dishes utilising the freshest possible ingredients. It is also famed for its outstanding wine list. A purpose-built ballroom, with lovely oak beams and its own private garden, is a popular venue for a wide range of events, from May Balls, wedding receptions and Christmas parties. The Business Centre has also made its mark; it is well equipped with every facility required and offers the flexibility to cater for meetings, car launches, product seminars and conferences. Places of interest nearby include Burghley House, Nene Valley Railway, Elton Hall, Rutland Water and Peterborough Cathedral. **Directions:** Clearly signposted on A1 a few miles south of Stamford, on A1/A47 intersection west of Peterborough. Price guide: Single £85–£115; double/twin room £115–£130; Four posters £140.

TALLAND BAY HOTEL

TALLAND-BY-LOOE, CORNWALL PL13 2JB
TEL: 01503 272667 FAX: 01503 272940

This lovely old Cornish manor house, parts of which date back to the 16th century, enjoys a completely rural and unspoilt setting. The hotel is surrounded by over two acres of beautiful gardens with glorious views over the two dramatic headlands of Talland Bay itself. Bedrooms are individually furnished to a high standard, some having lovely sea views. Sitting rooms open to the south-facing terrace by a heated outdoor swimming pool. In keeping with the period of the house, the newly refurbished restaurant, bar and lounges are tastefully decorated. Dinner menus are imaginative and incorporate seafood from Looe, Cornish lamb and West Country cheeses. A choice of à la carte supplementary dishes changes with the seasons. Meals are complemented by a list of about 100 carefully selected wines. Leisure pursuits at the hotel include putting, croquet, table tennis, sauna, painting courses and other special interest holidays. Talland Bay is a magically peaceful spot from which to explore this part of Cornwall: there are breathtaking coastal walks at the hotel's doorstep and many National Trust houses and gardens to visit locally – but most people come here just to relax and enjoy the view. This hotel provides old fashioned comfort in beautiful surroundings at exceptionally moderate prices. Resident owners: Barry and Annie Rosier. Closed Jan–late Feb. **Directions:** The hotel is signposted from the A387 Looe–Polperro road. Price guide: Single £47–£76; double/twin £84–£152.

THE BRIDGE HOTEL

PRESTBURY, MACCLESFIELD, CHESHIRE SK10 4DQ
TEL: 01625 829326 FAX: 01625 827557

The Bridge Hotel is situated in the centre of the village of Prestbury, one of the prettiest villages in the North West of England. Originally dating from 1626, The Bridge today combines the old world charm of an ancient and historic building with the comfort and facilities of a modern hotel, yet within easy reach of Manchester Airport and major motorways. The public rooms have retained much of the former inn's original character, with oak panelling and beams in the bar and reception area. The bedrooms, many of which overlook the River Bollin, are decorated to the highest standard, five of which are in the original building. In the attractive galleried dining room, table d'hôte and à la carte menus offer traditional English cuisine. There is an extensive selection of wines to accompany your meal. It is also the perfect place for business with three conference suites. While enjoying a quiet location, the hotel is convenient for Manchester, just 30 minutes away and Manchester Airport only 15 minutes away. The Peak District National Park and Cheshire are nearby with Stately Homes including Chatsworth, Tatton Park and Capesthorne. **Directions:** In the centre of the village next to the church. Prestbury is on the A538 from Wilmslow to Macclesfield. Price guide: Single £85–£90; double/twin £90–£100; suite £110. Special weekend rates available.

282

THE GIBBON BRIDGE HOTEL

NR CHIPPING, FOREST OF BOWLAND, LANCASHIRE PR3 2TQ
TEL: 01995 61456 FAX: 01995 61277 E-MAIL: reception@gibbon–bridge.co.uk

This award-winning hotel, in the heart of Lancashire in the Forest of Bowland provides a welcoming and peaceful retreat. The area, a favourite of the Queen, is now famous for being recognised officially as the centre of the Kingdom! Created in 1982 by resident proprietor Janet Simpson and her late Mother Margaret, the hotel buildings combine traditional architecture with interesting Gothic masonry. Individually designed, furnished and equipped to the highest standard, the seven bedrooms and twenty two suites include four-posters, half-testers, Gothic brass beds and whirlpool baths. The restaurant overlooks the garden and is renowned for traditional and imaginative dishes incorporating home-grown vegetables and herbs. The splendid garden bandstand is perfect for any musical repertoire or civil wedding ceremony. Inside the hotel elegant rooms and lounges are available for private dinner parties and wedding receptions. For executive meetings and conference facilities the hotel will offer you that 'something a bit different'. Leisure facilities include a beauty salon, gymnasium, solarium, steam room, all weather tennis court and countryside pursuits. **Directions:** From the South: M6 Exit 31A, follow signs for Longridge. From the North: M6 Exit 32, follow A6 to Broughton and B5269 to Longridge – follow signs for Chipping – in the village turn right a T-junction, the hotel is ¼ miles on the right. Price guide: Single £70–£100; double/twin £100; suite £120–£225.

NUTFIELD PRIORY

NUTFIELD, REDHILL, SURREY RH1 4EN
TEL: 01737 824400 FAX: 01737 823321 E-MAIL: nutpriory@aol.com.uk

Built in 1872 by the millionaire MP, Joshua Fielden, Nutfield Priory is an extravagant folly embellished with towers, elaborate carvings, intricate stonework, cloisters and stained glass, all superbly restored to create an unusual country house hotel. Set high on Nutfield Ridge, the priory has far-reaching views over the Surrey and Sussex countryside, while being within easy reach of London and also Gatwick Airport. The elegant lounges and library have ornately carved ceilings and antique furnishings. Unusually spacious bedrooms – some with beams – enjoy views over the surrounding countryside. Fresh fruit is a thoughtful extra. The Cloisters Restaurant provides a unique environment in which to enjoy the high standard of cuisine, complemented by an extensive wine list. Conferences and private functions can be accommodated in the splendid setting of one of the hotel's 10 conference rooms. The Priory Health and Leisure Club, adjacent to the hotel, provides all the facilities for exercise and relaxation that one could wish for, including a swimming pool, sauna, spa, solarium, gym, steam room, beauty & hairdressing and billiard room. **Directions:** Nutfield is on the A25 between Redhill and Godstone and can be reached easily from junctions 6 and 8 of the M25. From Godstone, the Priory is on the left just after the village. Price guide: Single from £115; double/twin £140–£160; suite from £220.

THE RICHMOND GATE HOTEL AND RESTAURANT

RICHMOND HILL, RICHMOND-UPON-THAMES, SURREY TW10 6RP
TEL: 020 8940 0061 FAX: 020 8332 0354

This former Georgian country house stands on the crest of Richmond Hill close to the Royal Park and Richmond Terrace with its commanding views over the River Thames. The 68 stylishly furnished en suite bedrooms combine every comfort of the present with the elegance of the past and include several luxury four-poster rooms and suites. Exceptional and imaginative cuisine, complemented by an extensive wine list offering over 100 wines from around the world is served in the sophisticated surroundings of 'Gates On The Park Restaurant'. Through the week a less formal alternative is available in the Bistro in the Victorian conservatory, overlooking the hotel's beautiful walled garden. Weddings, business meetings and private dining events can be arranged in a variety of rooms. Cedars Health and Leisure Club is accessed through the hotel and includes a 20 metre pool, 6 metre spa, sauna, steam room, aerobics studio, cardiovascular and resistance gymnasia and a health and beauty suite. Richmond is close to London and the West End yet in a country setting. The Borough offers a wealth of visitor attractions, including Hampton Court Palace, Syon House and Park and the Royal Botanic Gardens at Kew. **Directions:** Opposite the Star & Garter Home at the top of Richmond Hill. Price guide: Single £100–£175; double/twin £130–£185; suite £185.

THE CHASE HOTEL

GLOUCESTER ROAD, ROSS-ON-WYE, HEREFORDSHIRE HR9 5LH
TEL: 01989 763161 FAX: 01989 768330

The Chase Hotel, just a few minutes' walk from the historic market town of Ross-on-Wye, is a handsome Georgian Country House Hotel situated in 11 acres of beautiful grounds and landscape gardens. The 38 en suite bedrooms contain all the latest amenities, including satellite television. The bedrooms and lounge areas, preserve the original Georgian style of the Hotel. Guests wishing to relax will enjoy the convivial ambience and comfortable décor in the Chase Lounge and Bar. Overlooking Chase Hill, the tall elegant windows of the Lounge expose the splendour of the surrounding landscape. The delightful Chase Restaurant, with its delicate peach furnishings, is renowned for its superb traditional cuisine and excellent service and has won several accolades and awards including two AA Rosettes. The hotel is an ideal venue for conferences, exhibitions, training activities, weddings including civil ceremonies and events for up to 300 guests. A diverse range of activities is available within the locality and include water sports, theatre, countryside rambles, fascinating antique centres or perusing the shops in either the historic city of Hereford or Regency Cheltenham. **Directions:** From the M50 (Jct 4) turn left for Ross-on-Wye, take A40 Gloucester at the second roundabout and turn right for town centre at third roundabout. The Hotel is ½ mile on the left. Price guide: Single £60; double/twin £75; suite £100.

PENGETHLEY MANOR

PENGETHLEY PARK, NR ROSS-ON-WYE, HEREFORDSHIRE HR9 6LL
TEL: 01989 730211 FAX: 01989 730238 E-MAIL: reservations@pengethleymanor.co.uk

The first Baron Chandos, a favourite of Mary I Queen of England is reputed to have acquired Pengethley Estate in 1544 and here he built the original Tudor house. Although much of the building was ravaged by fire in the early 19th century, some parts survived – notably the oak panelling in the entrance hall – and it was rebuilt as a Georgian manor house in 1820. The en suite bedrooms reflect the traditional character of a former nobleman's country home. Drawing on the best produce that rural Herefordshire can offer, the varied menu in the AA 2 Rosetted restaurant reflects the creations of our experienced chefs. The manor's own vineyard flourishs within the boundaries of the estate and the delicious product may be sampled in the hotel. Throughout their stay at Pengethley, guests will find the service always attentive, but never intrusive. Chandos House is a purpose-built conference suite which can cater for business and social events. For leisure, there are numerous countryside walks, trout lake, a 9-hole golf improvement course, an outdoor heated pool and croquet lawn. Riding, hot-air ballooning, river fishing and golfing can be arranged. The Wye Valley and Welsh border are not very far away and the Malvern Hills are nearby. **Directions:** 4 miles from Ross-on-Wye, 10 miles from Hereford on the A49. Price guide: Single £75–£115; double/twin £120–£160.

GHYLL MANOR COUNTRY HOTEL

HIGH STREET, RUSPER, NEAR HORSHAM, WEST SUSSEX RH12 4PX
TEL: 01293 871571 FAX: 01293 871419

Ghyll Manor Country Hotel dates back to the 17th century and was once the family home of Sir Geoffrey and Lady Kitchen. The manor house and stable mews were converted in the early 1980's and still retain many of the original features such as beamed ceilings and charming log fires. Over the past two years the hotel has undergone an extensive restoration, resulting in a splendid hotel with excellent facilities. Guests have the choice of staying in the house itself, the Stable Mews complex or in seven delightful self-contained cottages. Attractive covered walkways connect the cottages and the complex to the main house. All the 29 bedrooms have been individually furnished and have en suite facilities. A relaxing atmosphere may be found in the library lounge and orangery, whilst those wishing to relax outdoors will enjoy the open terraces overlooking the beautiful grounds and lakes. The award-winning Benedictine Restaurant serves fine cuisine and is renowned for its excellent Sunday lunches. The tennis court and croquet lawn are on site whilst golf and riding can be arranged nearby. Ghyll Manor is an ideal location for those wishing to discover Sussex and Surrey and is in an area surrounded by National Trust houses and famous gardens such as Nymans. **Directions:** Leave M23 at junction 11 and follow A264 to Horsham. Turn off at roundabout signed Faygate and Rusper. Price guide: Single £110; double/twin £157.

BARNSDALE LODGE

THE AVENUE, RUTLAND WATER, NR OAKHAM, RUTLAND, LEICESTERSHIRE LE15 8AH
TEL: 01572 724678 FAX: 01572 724961 E-MAIL: barnsdale.lodge@btconnect.com

Situated in the ancient county of Rutland, amid unspoiled countryside, Barnsdale Lodge overlooks the rippling expanse of Rutland Water. After nine years, the expansion is finally complete and guests are invited to enjoy the hospitality offered by hosts The Hon. Thomas Noel and Robert Reid. A restored 17th century farmhouse, the atmosphere and style are distinctively Edwardian. This theme pervades throughout, from the courteous service to the furnishings, including chaises-longues and plush, upholstered chairs. The 45 en suite bedrooms, mostly on the ground floor, including two superb rooms specifically designed for disabled guests, evoke a mood of relaxing comfort. Traditional English cooking and fine wines are served. The chef makes all the pastries and cakes as well as preserves. Elevenses, buttery lunches, afternoon teas and suppers are enjoyed in the garden, conservatory, courtyard and à la carte dining rooms. There are 5 conference rooms and facilities for wedding receptions and parties. Interconnecting bedrooms, a baby-listening service and safe play area are provided for children. Robert Reid has strived to maintain the friendly intimacy of the lodge and is often on hand, offering advice and suggestions. Belvoir and Rockingham Castles are nearby. Rutland Water, a haven for nature lovers, offers several water sports. **Directions:** The Lodge is on A606 Oakham–Stamford road. Price guide: Single £65; double/twin £85; junior suite £99.50–£109.50.

BROOMHILL LODGE

RYE FOREIGN, RYE, EAST SUSSEX TN31 7UN
TEL: 01797 280421 FAX: 01797 280402

Imposing and ivy-bedecked, Broomhill is a dramatic mock-Jacobean construction towering above three green acres and dating back to the 1820s, when it was commissioned by a prominent local banker. Giving pleasing views over rolling East Sussex terrain, the hotel has been renovated with care by its owners to offer a standard of accommodation as impressive as the architecture. Relaxed, informal, yet unerringly professional, the management and staff have quickly established an elegant, comfortable and warm place to stay. All 12 rooms are equipped with en suite bath or shower rooms and all modern conveniences. A splendid new conservatory-style restaurant serves innovative cuisine expertly prepared. A fixed-price menu offers a wide choice (dinner £21.50) and a typical menu might include calamares, then venison with cranberries followed by chocolate torte. Special tariffs apply for bookings of two or more nights. The hotel has its own mini-gym and sauna. Sports available locally include windsurfing, sailing, angling, clay-pigeon shooting and golf on the famous links nearby. Hastings, Winchelsea, Rye itself, Romney Marsh and Battle Abbey are not far away and worth visiting. **Directions:** $1\frac{1}{2}$ miles north of Rye on A268. Price guide: Single from £48; double/twin from £84–£140.

ROSE-IN-VALE COUNTRY HOUSE HOTEL

MITHIAN, ST AGNES, CORNWALL TR5 0QD
TEL: 01872 552202 FAX: 01872 552700 E-MAIL: reception@rose–in–vale–hotel.co.uk

This 18th century Cornish manor house, hiding in 11 acres of glorious gardens, woodlands and pastures in a wooded valley of great natural beauty, successfully blends the old with the new. There is a sense of timelessness: a world apart from the bustle of modern living. Restrained floral décor contrasts with dark mahogany throughout the elegant public rooms and tasteful bedrooms, many of which have outstanding views across the valley gardens. Three ground floor rooms have level access. The Rose Suite and Master Rooms feature four-poster/half-tester beds and separate sitting rooms. Chef Phillip Sims serves imaginative, international cuisine in the intimate restaurant where sweeping, softly-draped bay windows overlook lawns and flower-beds. The gardens feature ponds with a collection of waterfowl, a secluded, heated swimming pool, croquet, badminton, dovecote and summer house. There is a four-seater light aircraft for hire or for scenic coastal flights. Massage, aromatherapy and reflexology can be arranged. National Trust properties abound and special walks, to and from the hotel, are available. Six golf courses, riding, fishing, gliding, swimming and water sports are close by. A converted chapel in a nearby village is also available on a self-catering basis. **Directions:** A30 through Cornwall. Two miles beyond Zelah turn right onto B3284. Cross A3075 and take third left turn signposted Rose-in-Vale. Price guide: Single £50–£66; double/twin £110–£126; suite £150.

291

SOPWELL HOUSE HOTEL, COUNTRY CLUB & SPA

COTTONMILL LANE, SOPWELL, ST ALBANS, HERTFORDSHIRE AL1 2HQ
TEL: 01727 864477 FAX: 01727 844741/845636

Once the country home of Lord Mountbatten, surrounded by a peaceful and verdant 13 acre estate, Sopwell House is an oasis just minutes away from the motorways. The classical reception rooms reflect its illustrious past and the grand panelled ballroom opens out onto the terraces and gardens. The bedrooms, many with four-posters, are charming and well-equipped. Superb English cuisine and fine wines are served in the enchanting Magnolia Conservatory Restaurant amidst the trees after which it is named whilst Bejerano's Brasserie in the Country Club offers an informal ambience. The recent conversion of farm buildings has resulted in beautifully designed mews suites, ideal for long-stay executives and bridal parties. These are complemented by 30 new bedrooms, featuring the latest amenities and the new conference and banqueting suites, overlooking the splendid gardens and terrace, are popular venues for weddings and special events. The new business centre provides guests with facilities such as photocopier, fax and e-mail. The Country Club & Spa, dedicated to health and relaxation, has a full range of fitness facilities and highly qualified beauty therapists. **Directions:** Close to M25, M1, M10, M11 & A1(M). 22m from Heathrow. From A414 take A1081 to St Albans. Turn left at Mile House pub. Cross mini-roundabout. Hotel is ¼m on left. Price guide: Single £79.75–£144.75; double/twin £109.75–£154.75; suites from £184.75. Breakfast: Full English £11.50, continental £9.50.

THE GARRACK HOTEL & RESTAURANT

BURTHALLAN LANE, ST IVES, CORNWALL TR26 3AA

TEL: 01736 796199 FAX: 01736 798955 FREEPHONE: 08000 197 393 E-MAIL: Garrack@accuk.co.uk

This family-run hotel, secluded and full of character, ideal for a family holiday, is set in two acres of gardens with fabulous sea views over Porthmeor Beach, the St Ives Tate Gallery and the old town of St Ives. The bedrooms in the original house are in keeping with the style of the building. The additional rooms are modern in design. All rooms have private bathrooms and baby-listening facilities. Superior rooms have either four-poster beds or whirlpool baths. A ground-floor room has been fitted for guests with disabilities. Visitors return year after year to enjoy informal yet professional service, good food and hospitality. The restaurant specialises in seafood especially fresh lobsters. The wine list includes over 70 labels from ten regions. The lounges have books, magazines and board games for all and open fires. The small attractive leisure centre contains a small swimming pool with integral spa, sauna, solarium and fitness area. The hotel has its own car park. Porthmeor Beach, just below the hotel, is renowned for surfing. Riding, golf, bowls, sea-fishing and other activities can be enjoyed locally. St Ives, with its harbour, is famous for artists and for the new St Ives Tate Gallery. Dogs by prior arrangement. **Directions:** A30–A3074–B3311–B3306. Go ½ mile, turn left at mini-roundabout, hotel signs are on the left as the road starts down hill. Price guide: Single £59.50; double/twin £103–£145.

THE WELL HOUSE

ST KEYNE, LISKEARD, CORNWALL PL14 4RN
TEL: 01579 342001 FAX: 01579 343891

The West Country is one corner of England where hospitality and friendliness are at their most spontaneous and nowhere more so than at The Well House, just beyond the River Tamar. New arrivals are entranced by their first view of this lovely Victorian country manor. Its façade wrapped in rambling wisteria and jasmine trailers is just one of a continuous series of delights including top-quality service, modern luxury and impeccable standards of comfort and cooking. The hotel is professionally managed by proprietor Nick Wainford, whose attention to every smallest detail has earned his hotel numerous awards, among them the AA 2 Red Stars. From the tastefully appointed bedrooms there are fine rural views and each private bathroom offers luxurious bath linen, soaps and gels by Neutrogena. Continental breakfast is served in bed – or a traditional English breakfast may be taken in the dining room. Chef John Lyons selects fresh, seasonal produce to create his superbly balanced and presented cuisine. Tennis and swimming are on site and the Cornish coastline offers matchless scenery and walking territory. The Well House is a Pride of Britain member. **Directions:** Leave A38 at Liskeard, take A390 to town centre, then take B3254 south to St Keyne Well and hotel. Price guide: Single from £80; double/twin £100–£165; family suite from £170.

THE ROSEVINE HOTEL

PORTHCURNICK BEACH, PORTSCATHO, ST MAWES, TRURO, CORNWALL TR2 5EW
TEL: 01872 580206 FAX: 01872 580230 E-MAIL: info@makepeacehotels.co.uk

Positioned at the heart of Cornwall's breathtaking Roseland Peninsula, the Rosevine is an elegant and gracious late Georgian hotel that offers visitors complete comfort and peace. The Rosevine stands in its own landscaped grounds overlooking Portscatho Harbour, a traditional Cornish fishing village. The superbly-equipped bedrooms are delightfully designed, with some benefiting from direct access into the gardens and from their own private patio. Awarded two Rosettes, the restaurant serves exceptional food, utilising the freshest seafood and locally grown produce. After dining, guests can relax in any of the three tasteful and comfortably presented lounges, bathe in the spacious heated swimming pool, or read in the hotel's well stocked library. Drinks are served in the convivial bar which offers a dizzy array of top quality wines and spirits. The Rosevine is the only hotel in Cornwall to have been awarded the RAC Blue Ribbon. Visitors to the region do not forget the walks to the charming villages dotted along the Roseland Peninsula, and the golden sand of the National Trust maintained beach. Visitors can also take river trips on small ferries, once the only means of travel around the peninsula. The region is awash with National Trust gardens and the beautiful town of Truro is easily reached. **Directions:** From Exeter take A30 towards Truro. Take the St. Mawes turn and the hotel is on the left. Price guide: Single £65–£110; double/twin £130–£160; suite from £190.

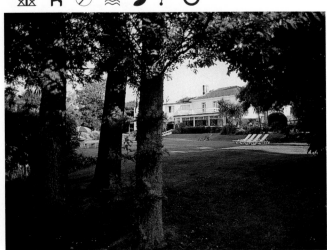

BOLT HEAD HOTEL

SOUTH SANDS, SALCOMBE, SOUTH DEVON TQ8 8LL
TEL: 01548 843751 FAX: 01548 843061 E-MAIL: info@bolthead-salcombe.co.uk

Bolt Head Hotel occupies a spectacular position overlooking Salcombe Estuary, where the mild climate ensures a lengthy holiday season. The bedrooms are furnished to a high standard, all with good en suite bathrooms and there are family suites available, complete with a baby-listening service. The light and sunny lounge, refurbished in unique Roman style, is ideal for relaxation, or guests may sit on the adjoining sun terrace with sweeping views of the sea. In the air-conditioned restaurant special care is taken to cater for all tastes. Both English and French cuisine are prepared, with freshly caught fish, lobster and crab delivered daily, as well as wholesome farm produce and local cheeses. Palm trees surround the heated outdoor swimming pool on the sunny terrace. There is a good golf course within a few miles. Riding, sailing and wind-surfing can be arranged. Sea fishing trips can be organised and private moorings are available. The hotel is adjacent to miles of magnificent National Trust cliff land at Bolt Head, including Overbecks, an unusual house and garden with rare plants. Dogs by arrangement. Closed mid-November to mid-March. **Directions:** Contact the hotel for directions. Price guide (including dinner): Single from £69; double/twin from £138; superior rooms available, as illustrated.

SOAR MILL COVE HOTEL

SOAR MILL COVE, SALCOMBE, SOUTH DEVON TQ7 3DS
TEL: 01548 561566 FAX: 01548 561223 E-MAIL: info@makepeacehotels.co.uk

Owned and loved by the Makepeace family who, for over 21 years, have provided a special blend of friendly yet professional service. The hotel's spectacular setting is a flower-filled combe, facing its own sheltered sandy bay and entirely surrounded by 2000 acres of dramatic National Trust coastline. While it is perhaps one of the last truly unspoiled corners of South Devon, Soar Mill Cove is only 15 miles from the motorway system (A38). The hotel has been awarded the prestigious RAC Blue Ribbon. All the bedrooms are at ground level, each with a private patio opening onto the gardens, which in spring or summer provides wonderful alfresco opportunities. In winter, crackling log fires and efficient double glazing keeps cooler weather at bay. A strict "no conference policy" guarantees that the peace of guests shall not be compromised. Both the indoor and outdoor pools are spring-water fed, the former being maintained all year at a constant 88°F. Here is Keith Stephen Makepeace's award winning cuisine, imaginative and innovative, reflecting the very best of the West of England; fresh crabs and lobster caught in the bay are a speciality. Soar Mill Cove is situated midway between the old ports of Plymouth and Dartmouth. **Directions:** A384 to Totnes, then A381 to Soar Mill Cove. Price guide: Single £70–£120; double/twin £140–£180; suite from £210.

THE TIDES REACH HOTEL

SOUTH SANDS, SALCOMBE, DEVON TQ8 8LJ
TEL: 01548 843466 FAX: 01548 843954 E-MAIL: enquire@tidesreach.com

This luxuriously appointed hotel is situated in an ideal position for those wishing to enjoy a relaxing or fun-filled break. Facing south in a tree-fringed sandy cove just inside the mouth of the Salcombe Estuary it has an extensive garden on one side, the sea and a safe bathing sandy beach a few steps opposite and, to the rear, a sheltering hill topped by the subtropical gardens of Overbecks. The Tides Reach has been under the supervision of owners, Mr and Mrs Roy Edwards, for more than 30 years and they have built up a reputation for hospitality and courteous service. The atmosphere is warm and friendly, the décor and furnishings tasteful and comfortable. All 38 spacious bedrooms are en suite, well equipped and decorated with flair and originality. The lawned garden centres around an ornamental lake with waterfall and fountain which is surrounded by landscaped tiers of colourful plants, shrubs and palms. Overlooking it is the restaurant where chef Finn Ibsen's excellent gourmet cuisine has earned two AA Rosettes. A superb indoor heated swimming pool is the nucleus of the hotel's leisure complex which includes a sauna, solarium, spa bath, gymnasium, squash court and snooker room. The hotel has facilities for windsurfing, water skiing, sailing and canoeing. **Directions:** From the M5, exit at junction 30 and join the A38 towards Plymouth. Exit for Totnes and then take the A381. Price guide: Single £70–£86; double/twin £120–£200.

HOWARD'S HOUSE

TEFFONT EVIAS, SALISBURY, WILTSHIRE SP3 5RJ
TEL: 01722 716392 FAX: 01722 716820 E-MAIL: paul.firmin@virgin.net

Tucked away in the depths of rural Wiltshire and surrounded by two acres of glorious gardens, stone-built Howard's House is a haven of tranquillity for all those seeking to escape the noise and stress of the modern world. An inscribed date in the East Gable shows that the house was built in 1623. In 1837 it was extended and roofed in Swiss style for a member of the Mayne family, who have owned the village of Teffont Evias since 1692. After extensive renovations, present owner and chef Paul Firmin opened the house as a hotel in 1990 and has built a reputation for hospitality, friendliness and attentive service. His restaurant, decorated in cool greens and whites, is the height of elegance and serves modern British cuisine. Paul cooks with flair and imagination, using the best local ingredients supplemented with herbs and vegetables from the hotel's garden. The nine bedrooms are luxuriously equipped and their floral prints and pastel shades enhance the feeling of informality and relaxation. The sitting room with its bold flower patterns, warm yellows, ceiling beams and open log fire is also wonderfully comfortable. Howard's House is ideally situated for visiting Stonehenge, Old Sarum, Salisbury Cathedral, Wilton House and Stourhead Gardens. **Directions:** From London, turn left off the A303 two miles after the Wylye intersection. Follow signs to Teffont and on entering the village join B3089. Howard's House is signposted. Price guide: Single £75; double/twin £125–£145.

HACKNESS GRANGE

NORTH YORK MOORS NATIONAL PARK, SCARBOROUGH, NORTH YORKSHIRE YO13 0JW
TEL: 01723 882345 FAX: 01723 882391 E-MAIL: hacknessgrange@englishrosehotels.co.uk

The attractive Georgian Hackness Grange country house lies at the heart of the dramatic North York Moors National Park – miles of glorious countryside with rolling moorland and forests. Set in acres of private grounds, overlooking a tranquil lake, home to many species of wildlife, Hackness Grange is a haven of peace and quiet for guests. There are charming bedrooms in the elegant courtyard together with de luxe rooms in the main house. For leisure activities, guests can enjoy 9-hole pitch 'n' putt golf, tennis, private fishing on the River Derwent and an indoor heated swimming pool. Hackness Grange is an ideal meeting location for companies wishing to have exclusive use of the hotel for VIP gatherings. The attractive Derwent Restaurant with its quality décor and paintings, is the setting for lunch and dinner and you will enjoy creatively prepared delicious cuisine, which is partnered by a wide choice of international wines. When you choose to stay at Hackness Grange you will find you have chosen well – a peaceful and relaxing location with so much to see and do: for example, visit Great Ayton, birthplace of Captain Cook. **Directions:** Take A64 York road until left turn to Seamer on to B1261, through to East Ayton and Hackness. Price guide: Single £78–£90; double/twin £135–£190; suite £190.

WREA HEAD COUNTRY HOTEL

SCALBY, NR SCARBOROUGH, NORTH YORKSHIRE YO13 0PB
TEL: 01723 378211 FAX: 01723 355936 E-MAIL: wreahead@englishrosehotels.co.uk

Wrea Head Country Hotel is an elegant, beautifully refurbished Victorian country house built in 1881 and situated in 14 acres of wooded and landscaped grounds on the edge of the North York Moors National Park, just three miles from Scarborough. The house is furnished with antiques and paintings and the oak-panelled front hall with its inglenook fireplace with blazing log fires in the winter, is very welcoming. All the bedrooms are individually decorated to the highest standards, with most having delightful views of the gardens. The elegant Four Seasons Restaurant is renowned for serving the best traditional English fare using fresh local produce and has an AA Rosette for outstanding cuisine. There are attractive meeting rooms, each with natural daylight, ideal for private board meetings and training courses requiring privacy and seclusion. Scarborough is renowned for its cricket, music and theatre. Wrea Head is a perfect location from which to explore the glorious North Yorkshire coast and country and you can take advantage of special English Rose breaks throughout the year. **Directions:** Follow the A171 north from Scarborough, past the Scalby Village, until the hotel is signposted. Follow the road past the duck pond and then turn left up the drive. Price guide: Single from £75; double/twin £120–£190; suite £190.

THE PRIORY BAY HOTEL

PRIORY DRIVE, SEAVIEW, ISLE OF WIGHT PO34 5BU
TEL: 01983 613146 FAX: 01983 616539 E-MAIL: reception@priorybay.co.uk

From decades gone by this beautiful site has been built upon by Medieval monks, Tudor farmers and Georgian gentry. Now its medley of buildings has been sympathetically restored and brought to life as a quite splendid hotel. Situated in gorgeous open countryside to the south of Seaview, the Priory Bay overlooks its own private beach. Everything about it is stylish and elegant, from the massive arched stone entrance with magnificent carved figures to the delightful, flower-filled gardens with their shady corners and thatched roofed tithe barns. The public rooms are a delight. Exquisitely and comfortably furnished, their tall windows are framed by rich curtains and they are liberally filled with vases of flowers. Log fires blaze in open fireplaces during colder months. Each of the 19 bedrooms is individually decorated, comfortable and has picturesque window views over the gardens. The dining room has an established reputation for first-class gastronomy, complemented by a fine wine list. Guests can relax under shady umbrellas in the garden or on the surrounding terraces. For the more energetic guest, there is an outdoor pool and the hotel's adjoining 9-hole golf course. Butterfly World, a tiger sanctuary, Carisbrook Castle and Osborne House are all nearby. **Directions:** Ferry from Portsmouth, Lymington or Southampton to Fishbourne, Yarmouth. Ryde, East or West Cowes. The hotel is on the B3330. Price guide: Single £65–£130; double/twin £100–£195.

CHARNWOOD HOTEL

10 SHARROW LANE, SHEFFIELD, SOUTH YORKSHIRE S11 8AA
TEL: 0114 258 9411 FAX: 0114 255 5107 E-MAIL: king@charnwood.force9.co.uk

The Charnwood Hotel is a listed Georgian mansion dating from 1780. Originally owned by John Henfrey, a Sheffield Master Cutler, it was later acquired by William Wilson of the Sharrow Snuff Mill. Restored in 1985, this elegant 'country house in town' is tastefully furnished, with colourful flower arrangements set against attractive décor. The bedrooms are decorated in a country style, with the Woodford suite designed specifically to meet the requirements of a family. Brasserie Leo has a relaxed atmosphere serving traditional English and French cuisine. The Library and Henfrey's are ideal for private dining or small meetings and larger functions are catered for in the Georgian Room and Coach House. While approximately a mile from Sheffield city centre, with its concert hall, theatre and hectic night-life, Charnwood Hotel is also convenient for the Peak District National Park. Meadowhall shopping centre and Sheffield Arena are nearby. **Directions:** Sharrow Lane is near the junction of London Road and Abbeydale Road, 1½ miles from city centre. Junction 33 from the M1. Price guide: Single £50–£85; double/twin £65–£105.

HELLABY HALL HOTEL

OLD HELLABY LANE, HELLABY, NR SHEFFIELD, SOUTH YORKSHIRE S66 8SM
TEL: 01709 702701 FAX: 01709 700979 E-MAIL: hhh@scottishhighlandhotels.co.uk

Built in 1692 by Ralph Fretwell on his return from Barbados, Hellaby Hall has a fine tradition and history of welcoming guests. Set in private gardens, the hall has been carefully restored to reflect its Dutch Colonial influence and the estate has been developed; resulting in one of the finest four star hotel's in South Yorkshire. The 52 bedrooms, three of which are in the original hall, feature en suite facilities and an array of modern comforts. A number of bedrooms are designated for non-smokers and disabled guests. A quiet corner can always be found in the Library or Drawing Room, while the oak panelled bar overlooks the gardens where guests can enjoy putting or croquet. The Attic Restaurant with its wall of mirrors and vibrant colours provides an innovative backdrop for varied menus and an extensive wine list. The former barns of the estate have been converted into Rizzio's Italian Restaurant/Bar, serving authentic Italian cuisine amidst a most convivial ambience. The excellent conference facilities comprise a range of meeting and function rooms which feature the most up-to-date audiovisual equipment. Fitness enthusiasts will be pleased with the facilities at the Bodysense Health and Leisure Club whilst those wishing to be spoilt must visit the on-site hairdressing salon and beauty treatment rooms. **Directions:** Exit M18 at Jct1. Take A631 towards Bawtry. The hotel is ½ mile on the left. Price guide: Single £45–£95; double/twin £79–£125; suite £145.

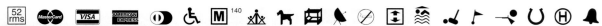

WHITLEY HALL HOTEL

ELLIOTT LANE, GRENOSIDE, SHEFFIELD, SOUTH YORKSHIRE S35 8NR
TEL: 0114 245 4444 FAX: 0114 245 5414 E-MAIL: whitley.hall@btinternet.com

Carved into the keystone above one of the doors is the date 1584, denoting the start of Whitley Hall's lengthy country house tradition. In the bar is a priest hole, which may explain the local belief that a tunnel links the house with the nearby 11th century church. In the 18th century, the house was a prestigious boarding school, with Gothic pointed arches and ornamentation added later by the Victorians. Attractively refurbished, Whitley Hall is now a fine hotel with all the amenities required by today's visitors. Stone walls and oak panelling combine with richly carpeted floors and handsome decoration. A sweeping split staircase leads to the bedrooms, all of which have en suite bathrooms. Varied yet unpretentious cooking is served in generous portions and complemented by a wide choice from the wine cellar, including many clarets and ports. Peacocks strut around the 30 acre grounds, which encompass rolling lawns, mature woodland and two ornamental lakes. Banquets and private functions can be held in the conference suite. **Directions:** Leave M1 at junction 35, following signs for Chapeltown (A629), go down hill and turn left into Nether Lane. Go right at traffic lights, then left opposite Arundel pub, into Whitley Lane. At fork turn right into Elliott Lane; hotel is on left. Price guide: Single £57–£82; double/twin £73–£105; suite £150.

CHARLTON HOUSE AND THE MULBERRY RESTAURANT

CHARLTON ROAD, SHEPTON MALLET, NEAR BATH, SOMERSET BA4 4PR
TEL: 01749 342008 FAX: 01749 346362 E-MAIL: reservations–charltonhouse@btinternet.com

This grand 17th century country manor, is now owned by Roger and Monty Saul, founders of the Mulberry Design Co. They have lovingly and skilfully created an exquisite hotel of the highest international standards without detracting from Charlton's own history and architecture. The reception rooms have wonderful proportions and are not overwhelmed by the sumptuous furnishings, fine antiques, brilliant rugs on polished floors, witty memorabilia and exciting paintings adorning their walls – veritable Aladdin's Caves! The bedrooms, some in the adjacent Coach House, are equally magical, totally luxurious and yet restful, with opulent bathrooms. Professional yet friendly staff play an important part both in the

drawing room, with its marvellous intimate atmosphere and in the dramatic dining room presided over by award-winning chef, Adam Fellows. Fantastic cooking and sublime wines make every meal a sybaritic experience. The hotel prides itself on catering for "special occasions". Charlton House recreations include shove-halfpenny(!), croquet, a trout lake, tennis, a sauna and pool and strolling in the landscaped gardens. Nearby are Bath, Wincanton Races, sailing, golf, the Mendip Hills – and the Mulberry factory shop. Directions: A303, then A37 to Shepton Mallet. Take A361 towards Frome and find hotel drive on the right. Price guide: Single £100–£135; double/twin £135–£200; suite £225–£340.

ALBRIGHTON HALL HOTEL & RESTAURANT

ALBRIGHTON, SHREWSBURY, SHROPSHIRE SY4 3AG
TEL: 01939 291000 FAX: 01939 291123

Albrighton Hall is a handsome 300 year old house standing in 15 acres of secluded grounds with terraced gardens stepping down to a large ornamental pond which attracts a variety of wildlife. Five minutes from the centre of the historic market town of Shrewsbury, ornamented by its pink sandstone castle and superb black and white buildings. Careful restoration and sympathetic development have helped maintain the Hall's country house character. There is an abundance of rich panelling, open fires and fine paintings. The bedrooms are individually styled and feature every modern facility from satellite television to a welcoming bottle of mineral water. Some have four-poster beds and most have stunning views over the gardens. The lounges are elegantly and comfortably furnished and decorated with appealing fabrics. Traditional and contemporary cuisine can be enjoyed in the Restaurant. Excellent leisure facilities include a heated indoor swimming pool, squash court, gymnasium and snooker room. Ludlow, the Midland Motor Museum, Ironbridge Gorge and Wyle Cop are within easy reach. **Directions:** Exit the M6 at junction 10a (if travelling from the north, exit junction 12). Follow the M54, A5 and A49 towards Whitchurch. Then join the A528 signposted Ellesmere. The hotel is one mile ahead. Price guide: Single £60–£85; double/twin £80–£95; suite £115–135.

HAWKSTONE PARK HOTEL

WESTON-UNDER-REDCASTLE, SHREWSBURY, SHROPSHIRE SY4 5UY
TEL: 01939 200611 FAX: 01939 200311 E-MAIL: info@hawkstone.co.uk

Hawkstone Park is a golfer's paradise. Set in 400 acres of idyllic Shropshire parkland the hotel is bounded on all sides by two contrasting 18-hole championship courses, on one of which British golfing star Sandy Lyle first learned the game. Supporting these courses is a 6-hole par 3 Academy Course, a driving range, practice area and a purpose-built Golf Centre. The top floor Terrace Room offers all-day bar and restaurant facilities with wonderful, panoramic views over the courses. The hotel's 65 en suite bedrooms, all newly refurbished, have tea and coffee making facilities, radio and satellite television, trouser press, iron and hairdryer. In the elegant restaurant which overlooks the landscaped gardens, chef John Robinson offers a high standard of traditional British and classical French cuisine. There is a large, comfortable snooker room with two tables, a card room and private bar and a variety of comprehensively equipped meeting and conference rooms. Hawkstone Historic Park and Follies complements the Hotel and Golf courses situated on 400 acres of English Heritage designated Grade I landscape. Places of interest nearby include Shrewsbury Castle, Ironbridge, Chester and Nantwich. Clay shooting, archery, croquet and hot-air ballooning are available. **Directions:** From M54, join A5 and then A49 north towards Whitchurch. Weston is signposted after approximately 11 miles. Price guide: Single/double/twin £67.50–£105.

ROWTON CASTLE

SHREWSBURY, SHROPSHIRE SY5 9EP
TEL: 01743 884044 FAX: 01743 884949 E-MAIL: *rowtoncastle@go2.co.uk*

Set in 17 acres of grounds, Rowton Castle Hotel and Restaurant is just ten minutes from the medieval town of Shrewsbury. The entrance to the Grade II listed building is dominated by an impressive Cedar of Lebanon, reputed to be the largest of its kind in Europe. A Victorian walled garden and two recently restored trout lakes are some of the many pleasures that await guests wishing to stroll through the tranquil grounds. Fishing enthusiasts can even hire equipment and catch their own dinner! Situated within the walls of the historic castle, the 19 en suite bedrooms are well appointed. There are three four-poster beds and a four-poster Jacuzzi bath. The tastefully refurbished Cedar Restaurant features a 17th century carved oak fireplace and offers a wide range of mouthwatering cuisine, whilst the oak-panelling provides a cosy and convivial ambience. The Georgian Dining Room, with its hand painted murals, gilt panelling and crystal chandeliers, caters for private dinners for up to 10 guests. The Cardeston Suite can accommodate up to 110 banquet style and has private bar facilities. The hotel may be booked exclusively for large groups and special occasions. Places of interest nearby include Shrewsbury Castle, Ironbridge and Llangollen. Golf, shooting, fishing and croquet are available. **Directions:** Five miles from Shrewsbury on the A458 Welshpool road. Price guide: Single £64.50; double/twin £80–£160.

HOTEL RIVIERA

THE ESPLANADE, SIDMOUTH, DEVON EX10 8AY
TEL: 01395 515201 FAX: 01395 577775 E-MAIL: enquiries@hotelriviera.co.uk

A warm welcome awaits guests arriving at this prestigious award-winning hotel. With accolades such as the AA Courtesy and Care Award and more recently, the Which? Hotel Guide's Hotel of the Year 1999, it comes as no surprise that Peter Wharton's Hotel Riviera is arguably one of the most comfortable and most hospitable in the region. The exterior, with its fine Regency façade and bow fronted windows complements the elegance of the interior comprising handsome public rooms and beautifully appointed bedrooms, many with sea views. Perfectly located at the centre of Sidmouth's historic Georgian esplanade and awarded four stars by both the AA and the RAC, the Riviera is committed to providing the very highest standard of excellence which makes each stay at the property a totally pleasurable experience. Guests may dine in the attractive salon, which affords glorious views across Lyme Bay, and indulge in the superb cuisine, prepared by Swiss and French trained chefs. The exceptional cellar will please the most discerning wine connoisseur. Activities include coastal walks, golf, bowling, croquet, putting, tennis, fishing, sailing, riding and exploring the breathtaking surroundings with its gardens, lush countryside and stunning coastline. **Directions:** The hotel is situated at the centre of the esplanade. Price guide (including seven-course dinner): Single £84–£109; double/twin £148–£198; suite £198–£218.

THE FRENCH HORN

SONNING-ON-THAMES, BERKSHIRE RG4 OTN
TEL: 01189 692204 FAX: 01189 442210 E-MAIL: TheFrenchHorn@Compuserve.com

For over 150 years The French Horn has provided a charming riverside retreat from the busy outside world. Today, although busier on this stretch of the river, it continues that fine tradition of comfortable accommodation and outstanding cuisine in a beautiful setting. The hotel nestles beside the Thames near the historic village of Sonning. The well-appointed bedrooms and suites are fully-equipped with modern amenities and many have river views. The old panelled bar provides an intimate scene for pre-dinner drinks and the restaurant speciality, locally reared duck, is spit roasted here over an open fire. By day the sunny restaurant is a lovely setting for lunch, while by night diners can enjoy the floodlit view of the graceful weeping willows which fringe the river. Dinner is served by candlelight and the cuisine is a mixture of French and English cooking using the freshest ingredients. The French Horn's wine list is reputed to be amongst the finest in Europe. Places of interest include Henley, Stratfield Saye, Oxford, Blenheim Palace and Mapledurham. There are numerous golf courses and equestrian centres in the area.
Directions: Leave the M4 at J8/9. Follow A404/M then at Thickets Roundabout turn left on A4 towards Reading for 8 miles. Turn right for Sonning. Cross Thames on B478. Hotel is on right. Price guide: Single £100–£145; double/twin £110–£165.

WHITECHAPEL MANOR

NR SOUTH MOLTON, NORTH DEVON EX36 3EG
TEL: 01769 573377 FAX: 01769 573797

Built in 1575 by Robert de Bassett, pretender to the English throne, Whitechapel Manor, a Grade I listed building, is a vision of the past with terraced and walled gardens of manicured lawns, roses and clipped yew hedges offering peace and tranquillity. The entrance hall has a perfect Jacobean carved oak screen. Elsewhere, William & Mary plasterwork and panelling along with painted overmantles have been preserved. The large bedrooms at the front overlooking the gardens and the smaller, cosy rooms which overlook the woodlands are thoughtfully appointed for comfort. The grounds teem with wildlife including numerous varieties of birds and the native Red Deer which are unique to Exmoor. The restaurant combines international flavours producing an exciting dining experience and is recognised as one of the best in the West Country. All around is tranquil, unspoilt countryside rising up to Exmoor National Park and the most dramatic coastline in England. Whitechapel is the ideal base from which to explore the moors, coast, ancient woodland valleys, Exmoor's villages and its wildlife. Also nearby are the RHS Gardens at Rosemoor, Dartington Crystal and many National Trust properties. **Directions:** Leave M5 at junction 27. Follow signs to Barnstaple. After 30 minutes turn right at roundabout to Whitechapel. Price guide: Single £70–£85; double/twin £110–£170. Special breaks and events all year round.

THE SWAN HOTEL

MARKET PLACE, SOUTHWOLD, SUFFOLK IP18 6EG
TEL: 01502 722186 FAX: 01502 724800

Rebuilt in 1659, following the disastrous fire which destroyed most of the town, The Swan was remodelled in the 1820s, with further additions in 1938. The hotel provides all modern services while retaining its classical dignity and elegance. Many of the antique-furnished bedrooms in the main hotel offer a glimpse of the sea, while the garden rooms – decorated in a more contemporary style – are clustered around the old bowling green. The Drawing Room has the traditional character of an English country house and the Reading Room upstairs is perfect for quiet relaxation or as the venue for a private party. The daily menu offers dishes ranging from simple, traditional fare through the English classics to the chef's personal specialities. An exciting selection of wines is offered. Almost an island, Southwold is bounded on three sides by creeks, marshes and the River Blyth – making it a paradise for birdwatchers and nature lovers. Hardly changed for a century, the town, built around a series of greens, has a fine church, lighthouse and golf course. Music lovers flock to nearby Snape Maltings for the Aldeburgh Festival. Winner of Country Living Gold Award for the Best Hotel 1993/94. **Directions:** Southwold is off the A12 Ipswich–Lowestoft road. The Swan Hotel is in the town centre. Price guide: Single £62–£69; double/twin £100–£165.

THE GEORGE OF STAMFORD

ST MARTINS, STAMFORD, LINCOLNSHIRE PE9 2LB
TEL: 01780 750750 RESERVATIONS: 01780 750700 FAX: 01780 750701 E-MAIL: georgehotelofstamford@btinternet.com

The George, a beautiful, 16th century coaching inn, retains the charm of its long history, as guests will sense on entering the reception hall with its oak travelling chests and famous oil portrait of Daniel Lambert. Over the years, The George has welcomed a diverse clientèle, ranging from highwaymen to kings – Charles I and William III were both visitors. At the heart of the hotel is the lounge, its natural stone walls, deep easy chairs and softly lit alcoves imparting a cosy, relaxed atmosphere, while the blazing log fire is sometimes used to toast muffins for tea! The flair of Julia Vannocci's interior design is evident in all the expertly styled, fully appointed bedrooms. Exotic plants, orchids,

orange trees and coconut palms feature in the Garden Lounge, where a choice of hot dishes and an extensive cold buffet are offered. Guests may also dine alfresco in the courtyard garden. The more formal, oak-panelled restaurant serves imaginative but traditional English dishes and an award-winning list of wines. Superb facilities are incorporated in the Business Centre, converted from the former livery stables. Special weekend breaks available. **Directions:** Stamford is 1 mile from the A1 on the B1081. The George is in the town centre opposite the gallows sign. Car parking is behind the hotel. Price guide: Single from £78–£105; double/twin from £103–£135; suite £140–£220.

WHITEHALL

CHURCH END, BROXTED, ESSEX CM6 2BZ
TEL: 01279 850603 FAX: 01279 850385

Set on a hillside overlooking the delightful rolling countryside of north-west Essex is Whitehall, one of East Anglia's leading country hotels. While its origins can be traced back to 1151, the manor house is ostensibly Elizabethan in style, with recent additions tastefully incorporated. Traditional features such as beams, wide fireplaces and log fires blend well with the contemporary, fresh pastel shades and subtle-hued fabrics. A spectacular vaulted ceiling makes the dining room an impressive setting for dinner, with an à la carte or six-course set menu offering many a delicious bonne-bouche. For large private functions, the timbered Barn House is an ideal venue, where guests can enjoy the same high standards of cuisine found in the restaurant. Overlooked by the old village church is the attractive Elizabethan walled garden. Whitehall is only a short drive from London's most modern international airport at Stansted, opened in 1989 and easily accessible from the M11 motorway, while Cambridge and Newmarket are only 30 minutes' drive away. **Directions:** Take junction 8 from the M11, follow Stansted Airport signs to new terminal building and then signs for Broxted. Price guide (Room only): Single £90; double/twin £115–£220.

STONEHOUSE COURT

STONEHOUSE, GLOUCESTERSHIRE GL10 3RA

TEL: 01453 825155 FAX: 01453 824611 E-MAIL: stonehousecourt@pageant.co.uk

This outstanding Grade II listed manor house is set in six acres of magnificent gardens on the edge of the Cotswolds. All of the bedrooms which have recently been totally refurbished are individually decorated, with many in the main house featuring original fireplaces and mullion windows. The highly acclaimed award winning John Henry Restaurant provides the perfect setting for either an intimate candlelit dinner, a family gathering or a formal business luncheon. The cuisine, although primarily English, has a rustic Mediterranean influence and is complemented by many fine wines. Outdoor pursuits include golf at Minchinhampton golf club, while activity days within the grounds can include laser shooting, archery, quad-biking and team-building exercises. The conference facilities at Stonehouse Court are designed for all styles of meetings, from informal to boardroom. The self-contained Caroline Suite is well-suited to holding product launches, training courses and conferences whilst the oak panelled Crellin Room is ideal for small meetings or private dining. Nearby are Cheltenham, Berkeley Castle and Slimbridge Wildfowl Trust, also Cheltenham Races, polo at Cirencester or the Badminton horse trials. **Directions:** From Jct13 of the M5 Stonehouse Court is two miles on the A419 towards Stroud. Price guide: Single from £79; double/twin from £110.

THE GRAPEVINE HOTEL

SHEEP STREET, STOW-ON-THE-WOLD, GLOUCESTERSHIRE GL54 1AU
TEL: 01451 830344 FAX: 01451 832278 E-MAIL: enquiries@vines.co.uk

Set in the pretty town of Stow-on-the-Wold, regarded by many as the jewel of the Cotswolds, The Grapevine Hotel has an atmosphere which makes visitors feel welcome and at ease. The outstanding personal service provided by a loyal team of staff is perhaps the secret of the hotel's success. This, along with the exceptionally high standard of overall comfort and hospitality, earned The Grapevine the 1991 *Johansens Hotel Award for Excellence* – a well-deserved accolade. Beautifully furnished bedrooms, including six superb garden rooms across the courtyard, offer every facility. Visitors can linger over imaginative cuisine in the relaxed and informal atmosphere of the conservatory restaurant, with its unusual canopy of trailing vines.

Awarded two AA Rosettes for food. The restaurant, like all of the bedrooms, is non-smoking. The hotel has its own tennis court, 1.5 miles away. Whether travelling on business or pleasure, guests will wish to return to The Grapevine again and again. The local landscape offers unlimited scope for exploration, whether to the numerous picturesque villages tucked away in the Cotswolds or to the towns of Oxford, Cirencester and Stratford-upon-Avon within easy reach. Nature enthusiasts must visit the beautiful gardens of Hidcote, Kifsgate and Barnsley House nearby. Open over Christmas. **Directions:** Sheep Street is part of A436 in the centre of Stow-on-the-Wold. Price guide: Single from £80.50; double/twin from £124.

LORDS OF THE MANOR HOTEL

UPPER SLAUGHTER, NR BOURTON-ON-THE-WATER, GLOUCESTERSHIRE GL54 2JD
TEL: 01451 820243 FAX: 01451 820696 E-MAIL: lordsofthemanor@btinternet.com

Situated in the heart of the Cotswolds, on the outskirts of one of England's most unspoiled and picturesque villages, stands the Lords of the Manor Hotel. Built in the 17th century of honeyed Cotswold stone, the house enjoys splendid views over the surrounding meadows, stream and parkland. For generations the house was the home of the Witts family, who historically had been rectors of the parish. It is from these origins that the hotel derives its distinctive name. Charming, walled gardens provide a secluded retreat at the rear of the house. Each bedroom bears the maiden name of one of the ladies who married into the Witts family; each room is individually and imaginatively decorated with period furniture. The reception rooms are magnificently furnished with fine antiques, paintings, traditional fabrics and masses of fresh flowers. Log fires blaze in cold weather. The heart of this English country house is its dining room, where truly memorable dishes are created from the best local ingredients. Nearby are Blenheim Palace, Warwick Castle, the Roman antiquities at Bath and Shakespeare country. **Directions:** Upper Slaughter is 2 miles west of the A429 between Stow-on-the-Wold and Bourton-on-the-Water. Price guide: Single from £98; double/twin £138–£295.

WYCK HILL HOUSE

WYCK HILL, STOW-ON-THE WOLD, GLOUCESTERSHIRE GL54 1HY
TEL: 01451 831936 FAX: 01451 832243

Wyck Hill House is a magnificent Cotswold mansion built in the early 1700s, reputedly on the site of an early Roman settlement. It is set in 100 acres of wooded and landscaped gardens, overlooking the beautiful Windrush Valley. The hotel has been elegantly restored and the bedrooms, some of which are located in the Coach House and Orangery, are individually furnished to combine superb antiques with modern comforts. There is a suite with a large, antique four-poster bed, which is perfect for a honeymoon or for other special occasions. The cedar-panelled library is an ideal room in which to read, if you wish, and to relax with morning coffee or afternoon tea. The award-winning restaurant provides the highest standards of modern British cuisine from the freshest seasonally available local produce. The menus are complemented by a superb wine list. Wyck Hill House hosts several special events, including opera, travel talks, cultural weekends and a variety of theme activities. The hotel is an ideal base from which to tour the university city of Oxford and the Georgian city of Bath. Cheltenham, Blenheim Palace and Stratford-upon-Avon are just a short drive away. Special price 2-night breaks are available. **Directions:** 1½ miles south of Stow-on-the-Wold on A424 Stow–Burford road. Price guide: Single £105; double/twin £150; suite £250.

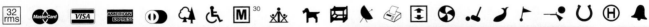

BILLESLEY MANOR

BILLESLEY, ALCESTER, NR STRATFORD-UPON-AVON, WARWICKSHIRE B49 6NF
TEL: 01789 279955 FAX: 01789 764145

This magnificent 16th century Manor House is set in 11 acres of its own private parkland and has a unique topiary garden and sun terrace. Centuries of history and tradition welcome guests to this beautiful hotel. An impressive indoor heated swimming pool, tennis courts, six hole pitch and putt course, croquet lawn and rough ground are available. The organisation of corporate events such as clay pigeon shooting, archery and quad biking are also on offer. The hotel has 41 beautiful bedrooms, including four-poster rooms and suites, all of which are en suite and many with stunning gardens views. A selection of rooms for private dining are available for family, friends or business guests – the cuisine is of the highest standards with the Stuart restaurant having been awarded 2 AA Rosettes. Billesley Manor is a fine venue for residential conferences and meetings, offering self-contained amenities and seclusion. Weekend breaks are available – ideal for visiting the Royal Shakespeare Theatre, Warwick Castle, Ragley Hall and the Cotswolds. Situated in the very heart of England, minutes away from Shakespeare's Stratford upon Avon and only 23 miles from Birmingham International Airport. The hotel is set in some of England's finest countryside and can be easily accessed by air, rail and road. **Directions:** Leave M40 at exit 15, follow A46 towards Evesham and Alcester. 3 miles beyond Stratford-upon-Avon turn right to Billesley. Price guide: Single £125; double/twin £180; suite £240.

ETTINGTON PARK

ALDERMINSTER, STRATFORD-UPON-AVON, WARWICKSHIRE CV37 8BU
TEL: 01789 450123 FAX: 01789 450472

The foundations of Ettington Park date back at least 1000 years. Mentioned in the *Domesday Book*, Ettington Park rises majestically over 40 acres of Warwickshire parkland, surrounded by terraced gardens and carefully tended lawns, where guests can wander at their leisure to admire the pastoral views. The interiors are beautiful, their striking opulence enhanced by flowers, beautiful antiques and original paintings. Amid these elegant surroundings guests can relax totally, pampered with every luxury. On an appropriately grand scale, the 48 bedrooms and superb leisure complex, comprising an indoor heated swimming pool, spa bath, solarium and sauna, make this a perfect choice for the sybarite.

The menu reflects the best of English and French cuisine, served with panache in the dining room, with its elegant 18th century rococo ceiling and 19th century carved family crests. The *bon viveur* will relish the fine wine list. Splendid conference facilities are available: the panelled Long Gallery and 14th century chapel are both unique venues. Riding is a speciality, while clay pigeon shooting, archery and fishing can also be arranged on the premises.
Directions: From M40 junction 15 (Warwick) take A46, A439 signposted Stratford, then left-hand turn onto A3400. Ettington Park is five miles south of Stratford-upon-Avon off the A3400. Price guide: Single £125; double/twin from £185; suites from £235.

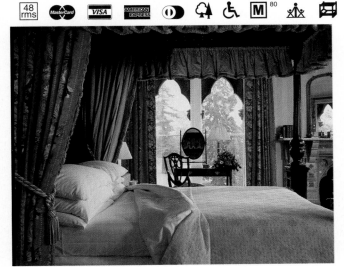

SALFORD HALL HOTEL

ABBOT'S SALFORD, NR EVESHAM, WORCESTERSHIRE WR11 5UT
TEL: 01386 871300 FAX: 01386 871301 E-MAIL: reception@salfordhall.co.uk

Between Shakespeare's Stratford-upon-Avon, the rolling Cotswolds and the Vale of Evesham is the Roman village of Abbot's Salford. Steeped in history, Salford Hall is a romantic Grade I listed manor house. It was built in the late 15th century as a retreat for the monks of Evesham Abbey and the imposing stone wing was added in the 17th century. Essentially unchanged, stained glass, a priest hole, exposed beams, oak panelling and original decorative murals are examples of the well-preserved features of the interior. The period charm is doubly appealing when combined with modern comforts, gracious furnishings, delicious food and an extensive selection of fine wines. Reflecting the past associations of the hall, the bedrooms are named after historical figures and all are individually appointed with oak furniture and luxury fittings. Guests may relax in the conservatory lounge or on the sunny terrace within the walled flower garden. The Hawkesbury room was formerly a medieval kitchen. Facilities include snooker, a sauna and a solarium. Special weekends are arranged for hot-air ballooning, horse-racing, touring the Cotswolds, discovering Shakespeare and murder mysteries. Closed for Christmas. **Directions:** Abbot's Salford is 8 miles west of Stratford-upon-Avon on B439 towards The Vale of Evesham. Price guide: Single £80; double/twin £115–£150.

WELCOMBE HOTEL AND GOLF COURSE

WARWICK ROAD, STRATFORD-UPON-AVON, WARWICKSHIRE CV37 0NR
TEL: 01789 295252 FAX: 01789 414666 E-MAIL: sales@welcombe.co.uk

A splendid Jacobean-style mansion dating from 1869, the aptly named Welcombe Hotel stands in 157 acres of rolling parkland, much of which was owned by Shakespeare. One of the foremost hotels in the heart of England, it is also renowned for its championship 18-hole golf course and director of golf Carl Mason. The magnificent lounge, with its striking black marble fireplace, ornate oak panelling, deep armchairs and bright flower arrangements, typifies the immaculate style of the hotel's interior. Exquisitely decorated, the restaurant is light, airy and spacious – an elegant setting overlooking the extensive formal gardens. The finest English and French cuisine, awarded two AA Rosettes, is impeccably prepared, with particular emphasis on delicate sauces and presentation. A well-balanced wine list includes a wide selection of half bottles. Whether staying in one of the suites, gallery rooms or bedrooms, guests will find the accommodation appointed to the highest standards. For small meetings or large scale conferences, the Welcombe Hotel can offer every amenity to support the event. Guests will be delighted with the health and beauty salon, solarium and fitness room. Floodlit tennis courts are on site with superb country walks in the Welcombe Hills and boating nearby. Warwick Castle and Blenheim Palace are close by. **Directions:** 5m from exit 15 of M40, on A439. 1m from Stratford-upon-Avon. Price guide: Single £110–£160; double/twin £140–£295; suite £275–£650.

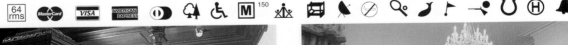

THE SWAN DIPLOMAT

STREATLEY-ON-THAMES, BERKSHIRE RG8 9HR
TEL: 01491 878800 FAX: 01491 872554 E-MAIL: sales@swan–diplomat.co.uk

In a beautiful setting on the bank of the River Thames, this hotel offers visitors comfortable accommodation. All of the 46 bedrooms, many of which have balconies overlooking the river, are appointed to high standards with individual décor and furnishings. Chef Damian Bradley's fine food maintains the hotels well earned two AA rosettes and guests may choose to dine in the attractive Dining Room or in the relaxing Club Room – both with views of the river. In summer, guests may also dine on the river terrace. Business guests are well catered for with six conference suites – all with natural light. Moored alongside the hotel is the Magdalen College Barge – a unique venue for small meetings and cocktail parties. Special themed programmes are arranged such as Bridge weekends and Lifestyle weekends. Reflexions leisure club is equipped with a heated 'fit' pool, sauna, spa bath, steam room and a wide range of exercise equipment. Cruising on the river may be arranged by the hotel and golf, horse riding, and clay pigeon shooting are available locally. Events in the locality include Henley Regatta, Ascot and Newbury Races, while Windsor Castle, Blenheim Palace, Oxford and London's airports are easily accessible. **Directions:** The hotel lies just off the A329 in Streatley village. Price guide: Single from £74–£140; double/twin from £112–£174.

PLUMBER MANOR

STURMINSTER NEWTON, DORSET DT10 2AF
TEL: 01258 472507 FAX: 01258 473370 E-MAIL: enquiries@plumbermanor.com

An imposing Jacobean building of local stone, occupying extensive gardens in the heart of Hardy's Dorset, Plumber Manor has been the home of the Prideaux-Brune family since the early 17th century. Leading off a charming gallery, hung with family portraits, are six very comfortable bedrooms. The conversion of a natural stone barn lying within the grounds, as well as the courtyard building, has added a further ten spacious bedrooms, some of which have window seats overlooking the garden and the Develish stream. Three interconnecting dining rooms comprise the restaurant, where a good choice of imaginative, well-prepared dishes is presented, supported by a wide-ranging wine list. Chef

Brian Prideaux-Brune's culinary prowess has been recognised by all the major food guides. Open for dinner every evening and Sunday lunch. The Dorset landscape, with its picture-postcard villages such as Milton Abbas and Cerne Abbas, is close at hand, while Corfe Castle, Lulworth Cove, Kingston Lacy and Poole Harbour are not far away. Riding can be arranged locally: however, if guests wish to bring their own horse to hack or hunt with local packs, the hotel provides free stabling on a do-it-yourself basis. Closed during February. **Directions:** Plumber Manor is two miles south west of Sturminster Newton on the Hazelbury Bryan road, off the A357. Price guide: Single from £75; double/twin from £95.

THE PEAR TREE AT PURTON

CHURCH END, PURTON, SWINDON, WILTSHIRE SN5 9ED
TEL: 01793 772100 FAX: 01793 772369 E-MAIL: peartreepurton@msn.com

Dedication to service is the hallmark of this excellent honey-coloured stone hotel nestling in the Vale of the White Horse between the Cotswolds and Marlborough Downs. Owners Francis and Anne Young are justly proud of its recognition by the award of the RAC's Blue Ribbon for excellence. Surrounded by rolling Wiltshire farmland, The Pear Tree sits majestically in 7½ acres of tranquil grounds on the fringe of the Saxon village of Purton, famed for its unique twin towered Parish Church and the ancient hill fort of Ringsbury Camp. Each of the 18 individually and tastefully decorated bedrooms and suites is named after a character associated with the village, such as Anne Hyde, mother of Queen

Mary II and Queen Anne. All are fitted to a high standard and have satellite television, hairdryer, trouser press and a host of other luxuries. The award-winning conservatory restaurant overlooks colourful gardens and is the perfect setting in which to enjoy good English cuisine prepared with style and flair. Cirencester, Bath, Oxford, Avebury, Blenheim Palace, Sudeley Castle and the Cotswolds are all within easy reach. **Directions:** From M4 exit 16 follow signs to Purton and go through the village until reaching a triangle with Spar Grocers opposite. Turn right up the hill and the Pear Tree is on the left after the Tithe Barn. Price Guide: Single/double/twin £95–£135; suite/4 poster £115.

BINDON COUNTRY HOUSE HOTEL

LANGFORD BUDVILLE, WELLINGTON, SOMERSET TA21 0RU
TEL: 01823 400070 FAX: 01823 400071 E-MAIL: BindonHouse@msn.com

This splendid baroque country house has a motto over the west wing door which, although put there in the 1860s, is appropriate today. 'Je trouve bien' is the perfect sentiment for this hotel, albeit in an old setting. Mark and Lynn Jaffa have meticulously restored Bindon. It is tranquil and private, surrounded by seven acres of gardens and woodland. New arrivals immediately have a feeling of well-being, as they respond to greetings from their hosts and drop into sofas in the charming lounge. There are just twelve beautifully proportioned, luxurious bedrooms, all extremely comfortable with many 'extras' including robes in the well-designed bathrooms. The handsome panelled Jacobean bar is convivial and it is advisable to reserve a table in the Wellesley Restaurant, as its reputation is far flung. The graceful setting and excellent wines accompanying the exquisitely presented gourmet dishes make dining a memorable occasion. Country pursuits – fishing, riding, shooting and golf are nearby and Bindon has its own pool, tennis court and croquet lawn. Wells Cathedral and stately homes are there to visit. **Directions:** 15 minutes from M5/J26, drive to Wellington take B3187 to Langford Budville, through village, right towards Wiveliscombe, then right at junction. Pass Bindon Farm and after 450 yards turn right. Price guide: Single £85; double/twin £95–£155; suite from £125.

THE CASTLE AT TAUNTON

CASTLE GREEN, TAUNTON, SOMERSET, TA1 1NF
TEL: 01823 272671 FAX: 01823 336066 E-MAIL: reception@the-castle-hotel.com

Winner of Johansens 1997 Town & City Award for Excellence, The Castle at Taunton is steeped in the romance of history. Once a Norman fortress, it has been welcoming travellers to the town since the 12th century. In 1685, the Duke of Monmouth's officers were heard "roystering at the Castle Inn" before their defeat by the forces of King James II at Sedgemoor. Shortly after, Judge Jeffreys held his Bloody Assize in the Great Hall of the Castle. Today, the Castle lives at peace with its turbulent past but preserves the atmosphere of its ancient tradition. The Chapman family have been running the hotel for 50 years and in that time it has acquired a worldwide reputation for the warmth of its hospitality. Laurels in Egon Ronay, AA and the RAC also testify to the excellence of the Castle's kitchen and cellar. Located in the heart of England's beautiful West Country, the Castle is the ideal base for exploring a region rich in history. This is the land of King Arthur, King Alfred, Lorna Doone's Exmoor and the monastic foundations of Glastonbury and Wells. Roman and Regency Bath, the majestic gardens of Stourhead and Hestercombe all within easy driving distance of Taunton. **Directions:** Exit M5 junction 25 and follow signs for town centre. Alternatively from the south go by A303 and A358. Price guide: Single from £88; double/twin from £139; club room from £149; suites from £230.

MOUNT SOMERSET COUNTRY HOUSE HOTEL

HENLADE, TAUNTON, SOMERSET TA3 5NB
TEL: 01823 442500 FAX: 01823 442900

This elegant Regency residence, awarded 2 Rosettes and 3 Stars, stands high on the slopes of the Blackdown Hills, overlooking miles of lovely countryside. The hotel is rich in intricate craftsmanship and displays fine original features. Its owners have committed themselves to creating an atmosphere in which guests can relax, confident that all needs will be catered for. The bedrooms are sumptuously furnished and many offer excellent views over the Quantock Hills. Most of the luxurious en suite bathrooms have spa baths. Tea, coffee and home-made cakes can be enjoyed in the beautifully furnished drawing room, while in the evening the finest food and wines are served in the dining room. A team of chefs work together to create dishes to meet the expectations of the most discerning gourmet. The President's Health Club is close by and its pool and equipment can be used by hotel guests by arrangement. Somerset is a centre for traditional crafts and exhibitions of basket making, sculpture, wood turning and pottery abound. Places of interest nearby include Glastonbury Abbey and Wells Cathedral. **Directions:** At M5 exit at junction 25 and join A358 towards Ilminster. Just past Henlade turn right at sign for Stoke St Mary. At T-junction turn left, the hotel drive is 150 yards on the right. Price guide: Single from £85–£105; double/twin from £100–£125; suites £145–£170; 3 Course Luncheon from £16.95 and 3 Course Dinner from £24.50.

THE HORN OF PLENTY

GULWORTHY, TAVISTOCK, DEVON PL19 8JD
TEL/FAX: 01822 832528 E-MAIL: enquiries@thehornofplenty.co.uk

This elegant, square, solidly built Georgian hotel nestles in the foothills of Dartmoor overlooking the scenic delights of the beautiful Tamar Valley. Built by the Duke of Bedford nearly 200 years ago it is surrounded by four acres of wonderful gardens and orchards which are ablaze with colour and laden with fruit all summer long. The Horn of Plenty has a character and charm of its own and its peaceful, comfortable, warm and welcoming atmosphere have earned several accolades. They include three AA Rosettes and the prestigious title of Good Food Guide County Restaurant of the Year. The smell of polished woodwork and fresh flowers and fruit delightfully pervades the interior and competes with the tang of wood smoke from log fires in winter months. A spacious suite and a large double room are within the main house with six comfortable, en suite bedrooms in the converted coach house. These have balconies which command uninterrupted views over the garden and valley to the brooding Tors of Bodmin Moor beyond. The tastefully decorated and intimate restaurant where excellent cuisine is prepared by chef Peter Gorton, also shares these delightful views. Riding, fishing and golf are available nearby. **Directions:** Take the A390 from Tavistock and after three miles turn right at Gulworthy Cross. Follow signs to the hotel. Price guide: Single £105–£140; double/twin £115–£150, suite £250.

MADELEY COURT

TELFORD, SHROPSHIRE TF7 5DW
TEL: 01952 680068 FAX: 01952 684275

Madeley is a veritable gem of a residence. Its characteristic manor house façade stands virtually unaltered since the 16th century when it was mainly built, while its interior has been recently expertly rejuvenated – with respect for its history – to provide accommodation suitable for all who stay there whether for pleasure or on business. Furnishings have been judiciously selected to enrich Madeley's period appeal: scatterings of fine fabrics, handsome antique pieces and elaborate fittings all accentuate the historic atmosphere and ensure that every guest leaves with an indelible impression. Bedrooms, whether located in the old part of the Court or in the newer wing, are quiet and full of character; some offer whirlpool baths and views over the lake, all are en suite. At the heart of Madeley is the original 13th century hall where the restaurant is now located, serving inventive food of the highest standard with a wine list to match. The Cellar Bar offers a more informal setting. Business meetings and private functions are happily catered for in the three rooms available. Places of interest nearby include Ironbridge Gorge, Shrewsbury, Powys Castle and Weston Park. **Directions:** Four miles from junction 4 of M54; follow A442 then B4373. Signposted Dawley then Madeley. Price guide (room only): Single from £105; double/twin £120–£145; historic £137.

CALCOT MANOR

NR TETBURY, GLOUCESTERSHIRE GL8 8YJ
TEL: 01666 890391 FAX: 01666 890394 E-MAIL: reception@calcotmanor.com

This delightful old manor house, built of Cotswold stone, offers guests tranquillity amidst acres of rolling countryside. Calcot Manor is situated in the southern Cotswolds close to the historic town of Tetbury. The building dates back to the 15th century and was a farmhouse until 1983. Its beautiful stone barns and stables include one of the oldest tithe barns in England, built in 1300 by the Cistercian monks from Kingswood Abbey. These buildings form a quadrangle and the stone glistening in the dawn or glowing in the dusk is quite a spectacle. Calcot achieves the rare combination of professional service and cheerful hospitality without any hint of over formality. The atmosphere is one of peaceful relaxation. All the cottage style rooms are beautifully appointed as are the public rooms. Recent additions are a discreet conference facility and charming cottage providing nine family suites with the sitting areas convertible into children's bedrooms. At the heart of Calcot Manor is its elegant conservatory restaurant where dinner is very much the focus of a memorable stay. There is also the congenial Gumstool Bistro and bar offering a range of simpler traditional food and local ales. **Directions:** From Tetbury, take the A4135 signposted Dursley; Calcot is on the right after 3 1/2 miles. Price guide: Double/twin £120–£165; family rooms £165; family suites £170.

THE CLOSE HOTEL

LONG STREET, TETBURY, GLOUCESTERSHIRE GL8 8AQ
TEL: 01666 502272 FAX: 01666 504401 E-MAIL: central.reservations@oldenglishpub.co.uk

This distinctive town house, built over 400 years ago as a successful wool merchant's home, has been turned into a delightful hotel. It retains great character while boasting the facilities expected of a first class hotel. The Close is renowned for luxurious accommodation – individually styled bedrooms that are truly elegant, with hand-painted bathrooms and antique furniture. The award winning cuisine, served in the stylish restaurant with its Adam style ceilings, is delicious, imaginative and well complemented by an outstanding wine list, including some excellent vintages. The restaurant overlooks a traditional Cotswold walled garden and in fine weather, you can take drinks or even dinner on the terrace. The Close offers a variety of rooms for conferences accommodating up to 24 guests. The hotel is extremely popular for wedding receptions and ceremonies and can be booked for exclusive use. Many famous sporting venues are close by, including Cheltenham Racecourse and Badminton House. Tetbury itself is a must for shoppers and antique lovers, while the Cotswolds are just on the doorstep. **Directions:** The Close is on Long Street, the main street of Tetbury which can be found on the A433 – minutes from the M4 and M5. Private parking is at the rear of the hotel in Close Gardens. Price guide: Single £75; double/twin £130.

CORSE LAWN HOUSE HOTEL

CORSE LAWN, NR TEWKESBURY, GLOUCESTERSHIRE GL19 4LZ
TEL: 01452 780479/771 FAX: 01452 780840 E-MAIL: hotel@corselawnhouse.u–net.com

Although only 6 miles from the M5 and M50, Corse Lawn is a completely unspoiled, typically English hamlet in a peaceful Gloucestershire backwater. The hotel, an elegant Queen Anne listed building set back from the village green, stands in 12 acres of gardens and grounds and still displays the charm of its historic pedigree. Visitors can be assured of the highest standards of service and cooking: Baba Hine is famous for the dishes she produces, while Denis Hine, of the Hine Cognac family, is in charge of the wine cellar. The service here, now in the hands of son Giles, is faultlessly efficient, friendly and personal. As well as the renowned restaurant, there are three comfortable drawing rooms, a large lounge bar, a private dining-cum-conference room for up to 45 persons and a similar, smaller room for up to 20. A tennis court, heated swimming pool and croquet lawn adjoin the hotel and most sports and leisure activities can be arranged. Corse Lawn is ideal for exploring the Cotswolds, Malverns and Forest of Dean. **Directions:** Corse Lawn House is situated on the B4211 between the A417 (Gloucester–Ledbury road) and the A438 (Tewkesbury–Ledbury road). Price guide: Single £75; double/twin £100; four-poster £120; suites £135. Good reductions for short breaks.

THE SPREAD EAGLE HOTEL

CORNMARKET, THAME, OXFORDSHIRE OX9 2BW
TEL: 01844 213661 FAX: 01844 261380

The historic market town of Thame with its mile long main street is a delightful town just six miles from the M40 and surrounded by beautiful countryside speckled with tiny, charming villages, many of them with cosy thatched cottages. The Spread Eagle has stood tall, square and imposingly in the heart of Thame since the 16th century and over the years has played host to Charles II, French prisoners from the Napoleonic wars, famous politicians and writers such as Evelyn Waugh. The former proprietor John Fothergill introduced haute cuisine to the provinces and chronicled his experiences in the best seller, 'An Innkeeper's Diary'. The book is still available at The Spread Eagle and the restaurant is named after him. It serves excellent English and French cuisine made with the freshest local produce. Seasonal changing menus are complemented by a well balanced wine list which includes some superb half-bottles of unusual vintages. Guests have 33 bedrooms to choose from, comprising two suites, 23 doubles, three twins and five singles. All are en suite, well equipped and tastefully decorated. Good conference facilities are available. The Spread Eagle is ideally situated for visits to many fascinating historic places such as Blenheim Palace and Waddesdon Manor. **Directions:** Exit M40 at junction 6. Take B4009 to Chinnor and then B4445 to Thame. The hotel is on the left after the roundabout at the west end of Upper High Street. Price guide: Single £95; double/twin from £110.

CRAB MANOR

ASENBY, THIRSK, NORTH YORKSHIRE YO7 3QL
TEL: 01845 577286 FAX: 01845 577109 E-MAIL: reservations@crabandlobster.co.uk

Set in seven acres of landscaped gardens encompassing a formal garden, two attractive ponds and a full-size par three golf hole, Crab Manor is a beautiful Georgian Manor House. After purchasing the unusual property over five years ago, the owners have carefully refurbished the Manor and it was opened in December 1998. Nine sumptuous bedrooms are situated in the house itself and are individually furnished, each incorporating the theme of a different world-famous hotel from the Cipriani in Venice to Sharrow Bay in the Lake District. The same exacting standards are evident in the three bedrooms located in the Thatched Cottage. There is a veritable array of dining options at Crab Manor, from the large barbecue area at the rear of the house to the creperie van with its freshly made treats. Breakfast is served in the Conservatory Dining Room and guests may choose to dine here during mealtimes or stroll down through the gardens to the adjacent Crab and Lobster Dining Pub and Bistro. As the name implies, seafood is a speciality and the menu offers some exciting interpretations such as Moroccan fish tagine alongside traditional favourites including poached salmon. Crab Manor is ideally located for equestrians as it is in the centre of the Yorkshire Horse Racing Circle. **Directions:** Crab Manor is on the outskirts of Asenby, which is signposted off A168 (A19) north of the intersection with A1(M). Price guide: Single £60–£100; double/twin £80–£120.

DALE HILL

TICEHURST, WADHURST, EAST SUSSEX TN5 7DQ
TEL: 01580 200112 FAX: 01580 201249 E-MAIL: info@dalehill.co.uk

Situated in over 300 acres of fine grounds, high on the Kentish Weald, Dale Hill is a modern hotel which combines the best in golfing facilities with the style and refinement desired by discerning guests. The décor is enhanced by soft coloured fabrics and carpets, creating a summery impression throughout the year. The 26 spacious bedrooms, all with en suite facilities, are furnished to a high standard and offer every comfort and convenience. Golfers have the choice of two 18-hole courses, a gently undulating, 6,093 yards par 70 and a new, challenging championship-standard course designed by former U.S. Masters champion Ian Woosnam. Tuition is available from a PGA professional. Diners enjoy glorious views in a choice of restaurants where traditional cuisine is complemented by a fine wine list and service. The fully equipped health club features a heated swimming pool and a range of health, beauty and fitness facilities. Dale Hill is only a short drive from Tunbridge Wells and its renowned Pantiles shopping walk. Also nearby are medieval Scotney Castle, which dates back to 1380, Sissinghurst, a moated Tudor castle with gardens and Bewl Water, renowned for fly-fishing and water sports. **Directions:** From the M25, junction 5, follow the A21 to Flimwell. Then turn right onto the B2087. Dale Hill is on the left. Price guide: Single from £64; double/twin £108–£170.

THE OSBORNE HOTEL & LANGTRY'S RESTAURANT

MEADFOOT BEACH, TORQUAY, DEVON TQ1 2LL
TEL: 01803 213311 FAX: 01803 296788

The combination of Mediterranean chic and the much-loved Devon landscape has a special appeal which is reflected at The Osborne. The hotel is the centrepiece of an elegant recently refurbished Regency crescent in Meadfoot, a quiet location within easy reach of the centre of Torquay. Known as a 'country house by the sea', the hotel offers the friendly ambience of a country home complemented by the superior standards of service and comfort expected of a hotel on the English Riviera. Most of the 25 bedrooms have magnificent views and are decorated in pastel shades. Overlooking the sea, Langtry's acclaimed award-winning restaurant provides fine English cooking and tempting regional specialities, while the Brasserie has a menu available throughout the day. Guests may relax in the attractive 5-acre gardens and make use of indoor and outdoor swimming pools, gymnasium, sauna, solarium, tennis court and putting green – all without leaving the grounds. Sailing, archery, clay pigeon shooting and golf can be arranged. Devon is a county of infinite variety, with its fine coastline, bustling harbours, tranquil lanes, sleepy villages and the wilds of Dartmoor. The Osborne is ideally placed to enjoy all these attractions. **Directions:** The hotel is in Meadfoot, to the east of Torquay. Price guide: Single £55–£95; double/twin £78–£135; suite £98–£170.

THE PALACE HOTEL

BABBACOMBE ROAD, TORQUAY, DEVON TQ1 3TG
TEL: 01803 200200 FAX: 01803 299899 E-MAIL: mail2@palacetorquay.co.uk

Once the residence of the Bishop of Exeter, the privately owned Palace Hotel is a gracious Victorian building set in 25 acres of beautifully landscaped gardens and woodlands. The comfortable bedrooms are equipped with every modern amenity and there are also elegant, spacious suites available. Most rooms overlook the hotel's magnificent grounds. The main restaurant provides a high standard of traditional English cooking, making full use of fresh, local produce, as well as offering a good variety of international dishes. The cuisine is complemented by a wide selection of popular and fine wines. Light meals are also available from the lounge and during the summer months, a barbecue and buffet are served on the terrace. A host of sporting facilities has made this hotel famous. These include a short par 3 9-hole championship golf course, indoor and outdoor swimming pools, two indoor and four outdoor tennis courts, two squash courts, saunas, snooker room and a well equipped fitness suite. Places of interest nearby include Dartmoor, South Hams and Exeter. Paignton Zoo, Bygone's Museum and Kent's Cavern are among the local attractions. **Directions:** From seafront follow signs for Babbacombe. Hotel entrance is on the right. Price guide: Single £70–£80; double/twin £160–£180; executive £190; suites £230–£270. Leisure breaks and special weekly rates on request.

PENDLEY MANOR HOTEL & CONFERENCE CENTRE

COW LANE, TRING, HERTFORDSHIRE HP23 5QY
TEL: 01442 891891 FAX: 01442 890687 E-MAIL: sales@pendley–manor.co.uk

The Pendley Manor was commissioned by Joseph Grout Williams in 1872. His instructions to architect John Lion were to build it in the Tudor style, reflecting the owner's interest in flora and fauna on the carved woodwork and stained glass panels. It stayed in the Williams family for three generations, but in 1987 the Manor was purchased by an independent hotel company, Craydawn Ltd. A refurbishment programme transformed it to its former glory and today's guests can once again enjoy the elegance and beauty of the Victorian era. The bedrooms are attractively furnished and well-equipped, while the cuisine is appealing and well presented. Pendley Manor offers flexible conference facilities for up to 200 people. For indoor recreation, a snooker room with a full-size table has been added to the amenities. On its estate, which lies at the foot of the Chiltern Hills, sporting facilities include tennis courts, gymnasium, snooker room with full size table, games rooms, buggy riding, laser shooting, archery and hot-air balloon rides. Places of interest nearby include Woburn, Winslow Hall, Chenies Manor, Tring Zoological Museum and Dunstable Downs. **Directions:** Leave M25 at Jct20 and take new A41, pass exits for Berkhamsted and Chesham. Take exit marked 'Tring'. At the roundabout, take the road to Berkhamsted. The first right turn is signed Tring Station and Pendley Manor. Then take first right turn. Price guide: Single £90; double/twin £120–£130; suites £150.

HOTEL DU VIN & BISTRO

CRESCENT ROAD, ROYAL TUNBRIDGE WELLS, KENT TN1 2LY
TEL: 01892 526455 FAX: 01892 512044 E-MAIL: reception@tunbridgewells.hotelduvin.co.uk

Set in the historic town of Tunbridge Wells, this Grade II sandstone mansion dates back to 1762 and although in the centre, it enjoys spectacular views over Calverley Park. An inviting ambience is present throughout the property, from the convivial bar to the sunny terrace. The 32 en suite bedrooms have been individually decorated and are enhanced by the superb Egyptian linen, CD players and satellite television. The spacious bathrooms feature power showers, large baths and fluffy robes and towels. The hotel takes great pride in its excellent bistro cuisine and the outstanding wine list. The imaginative dishes are prepared using the freshest local ingredients and are exceptionally good value. Fine wine dinners are often held at the hotel, whilst private tastings may be organised given prior notice. There are many castles, gardens and stately homes within the vicinity, such as Chartwell, Groombridge Place and Hever Castle. Guests can work up their appetites by rambling through the orchards and hop fields, perusing the shops and boutiques in the Pantiles or playing golf nearby. **Directions:** From M25 take A21 south in the direction of Hastings. to Tunbridge Wells. The hotel has excellent parking facilities. Price guide: Double/twin £75–109.

THE SPA HOTEL

MOUNT EPHRAIM, ROYAL TUNBRIDGE WELLS, KENT TN4 8XJ
TEL: 01892 520331 FAX: 01892 510575 E-MAIL: info@spahotel.co.uk

The Spa was originally built in 1766 as a country mansion with its own landscaped gardens and two beautiful lakes. A hotel for over a century now, it retains standards of service reminiscent of life in Georgian and Regency England. All the bedrooms are individually furnished and many offer spectacular views. Above all else, The Spa Hotel prides itself on the excellence of its cuisine. The grand, award winning Chandelier restaurant features the freshest produce from Kentish farms and London markets, complemented by a carefully selected wine list. Within the hotel is Sparkling Health, a magnificent health and leisure centre which is equipped to the highest standards. Leisure facilities include an indoor heated swimming pool, a fully equipped state-of-the-art gymnasium, cardiovascular gymnasium, aerobics dance studio, steam room, sauna, beauty clinic, hairdressing salon, flood-lit hard tennis court and $^{1}/_{2}$ mile jogging track. The hotel is perfectly positioned for exploring the castles, houses and gardens of Kent and Sussex. Special weekend breaks are offered, with rates from £70 per person per night – full details available on request. **Directions:** Facing the common on the A264 in Tunbridge Wells. Price guide (room only): Single £79–£89; double/twin £95–£150.

HORSTED PLACE HOTEL

LITTLE HORSTED, NR UCKFIELD, EAST SUSSEX TN22 5TS
TEL: 01825 750581 FAX: 01825 750459 E-MAIL: hotel@horstedplace.co.uk

Horsted Place enjoys a splendid location amid the peace of the Sussex Downs. This magnificent Victorian Gothic Mansion, which was built in 1851, overlooks the East Sussex National golf course and boasts an interior predominantly styled by the celebrated Victorian architect, Augustus Pugin. In former years the Queen and Prince Philip were frequent visitors. Guests today are invited to enjoy the unobtrusive but excellent service offered by a committed staff. The bedrooms in this lovely hotel are luxuriously decorated and furnished and offer every modern day comfort. Dining at Horsted is guaranteed to be a memorable experience. Chef Allan Garth offers a number of fixed price and seasonally changing menus with his eclectic style of cooking. The Horsted Management Centre is a suite of air-conditioned rooms which have been specially designed to accommodate theatre-style presentations and training seminars or top level board meetings. Places of interest nearby include Royal Tunbridge Wells, Lewes and Glyndebourne. For golfing enthusiasts there is the added attraction of the East Sussex National Golf Club, one of the finest golf complexes in the world. **Directions:** The hotel entrance is on the A26 just short of the junction with the A22, two miles south of Uckfield and signposted towards Lewes. Price guide: Double/twin from £75–£105; suites from £155.

THE LAKE ISLE

16 HIGH STREET EAST, UPPINGHAM, RUTLAND LE15 9PZ
TEL: 01572 822951 FAX: 01572 822951

This small personally run restaurant and town house hotel is situated in the pretty market town of Uppingham, dominated by the famous Uppingham School and close to Rutland Water. The entrance to the building, which dates back to the 18th century, is via a quiet courtyard where a wonderful display of flowering tubs and hanging baskets greets you. In winter, sit in the bar where a log fire burns or relax in the upstairs lounge which overlooks the High Street. In the bedrooms, each named after a wine growing region in France and all of which are en suite, guests will find fresh fruit, home-made biscuits and a decanter of sherry. Those in the courtyard are cottage-style suites. Under the personal direction of chef-patron David Whitfield, the restaurant offers small weekly changing menus using fresh ingredients from far afield. There is an extensive wine list of more than 300 wines ranging from regional labels to old clarets. Special 'Wine Dinners' are held throughout the year, enabling guests to appreciate this unique cellar. Burghley House, Rockingham and Belvoir Castles are within a short drive. **Directions:** Uppingham is near the intersection of A47 and A6003. The hotel is on the High Street and is reached on foot via Reeves Yard and by car via Queen Street. Price guide: Single £47–£55; double/twin £67–£77; suite £77–£87.

THE NARE HOTEL

CARNE BEACH, VERYAN-IN-ROSELAND, TRURO, CORNWALL TR2 5PF
TEL: 01872 501279 FAX: 01872 501856 E-MAIL: office@narehotel.co.uk

The Nare Hotel overlooks the fine sandy beach of Gerrans Bay, facing south and is sheltered by The Nare and St Mawes headlands. In recent years extensive refurbishments have ensured comfort and elegance without detracting from the country house charm of this friendly hotel. All the bedrooms are within 100 yards of the sea, many with patios or balconies to take advantage of the outlook. While dining in the restaurant, with its colour scheme of soft yellow and green, guests can enjoy the sea views from three sides of the room. Local seafood such as lobster and delicious home-made puddings, served with Cornish cream, are specialities, complemented by an interesting range of wines. The

Nare is one of the only AA 4 star hotels in the South West with two Rosettes for its food. Surrounded by subtropical gardens and National Trust land, the peaceful seclusion of The Nare is ideal for lazing or for exploring the coastline and villages of the glorious Roseland Peninsula and is also central for many of Cornwall's beautiful houses and gardens including the famous Heligan. Guests arriving by train can be met by prior arrangement at Truro. Christmas and New Year house parties. **Directions:** Follow road to St Mawes; 3 miles after Tregony Bridge turn left for Veryan. The hotel is 1 mile from Veryan. Price guide: Single £75–£154; double/twin £150–£278; suite £324–£500.

THE SPRINGS HOTEL & GOLF CLUB

NORTH STOKE, WALLINGFORD, OXFORDSHIRE OX10 6BE
TEL: 01491 836687 FAX: 01491 836877 E-MAIL: info@thespringshotel.co.uk

The Springs is a grand old country house which dates from 1874 and is set deep in the heart of the beautiful Thames valley. One of the first houses in England to be built in the Mock Tudor style, it stands in six acres of grounds. The hotel's large south windows overlook a spring fed lake, from which it takes its name. Many of the luxurious bedrooms and suites offer beautiful views over the lake and lawns, while others overlook the quiet woodland that surrounds the hotel. Private balconies provide patios for summer relaxation. The Lakeside restaurant has an intimate atmosphere inspired by its gentle décor and the lovely view of the lake. The award winning restaurant's menu takes advantage of fresh local produce and a well stocked cellar of international wines provides the perfect accompaniment to a splendid meal. Leisure facilities include a new 18 hole par 72 golf course, Clubhouse and putting green, a swimming pool, sauna and touring bicycles. Oxford, Blenheim Palace and Windsor are nearby and the hotel is convenient for racing at Newbury and Ascot and the Royal Henley Regatta. **Directions:** From the M40, take exit 6 onto the B4009, through Watlington to Benson; turn left onto A4074 towards Reading. After $^1/_2$ mile go right onto B4009. The hotel is $^1/_2$ mile further, on the right. Price guide: Single from £85; double/twin from £115; suite from £160.

HANBURY MANOR

WARE, HERTFORDSHIRE SG12 0SD
TEL: 01920 487722 FAX: 01920 487692

An outstanding 5 star hotel, Marriott Hanbury Manor combines palatial grandeur with the most up-to-date amenities. Designed in 1890 in a Jacobean style, the many impressive features include elaborately moulded ceilings, carved wood panelling, leaded windows, chandeliers, portraits and huge tapestries. These create an elegant and comfortable environment. The two dining rooms vary in style from the formal Zodiac Restaurant to the informal Vardon Restaurant. All the cuisine is under the inspired guidance of Executive Chef Robert Gleeson. The health club includes a 17m indoor swimming pool, spa bath, resistance gymnasium, cardiovascular suite, dance studio, crèche, sauna and steam rooms.

Professional treatments include herbal wraps, aromatherapy, mineral baths and massage, while specialists can advise on a personal fitness programme. There is an 18-hole golf course *par excellence* designed by Jack Nicklaus II, host to the PGA European Tour English Open. Outdoor pursuits include shooting, archery, horse-riding and hot-air ballooning. Ideal for conferences, twelve rooms offer versatile business meetings facilities, with fax, photocopying, secretarial services and full professional support available. Stansted Airport is 16 miles away. **Directions:** On the A10 25 miles north of London and 32 miles south of Cambridge. Price guide: Single/double/twin from £135; suites £235–£460.

THE PRIORY HOTEL

CHURCH GREEN, WAREHAM, DORSET BH20 4ND
TEL: 01929 551666 FAX: 01929 554519 E-MAIL: reception@theprioryhotel.co.uk

Dating from the early 16th century, the one-time Lady St Mary Priory has, for hundreds of years, offered sanctuary to travellers. In Hardy's Dorset, 'far from the madding crowd', it placidly stands on the bank of the River Frome in four acres of immaculate gardens. Steeped in history, The Priory has undergone a sympathetic conversion to a hotel which is charming yet unpretentious. Each bedroom is distinctively styled, with family antiques lending character and many rooms have views of the Purbeck Hills. A 16th century clay barn has been transformed into the Boathouse, consisting of four spacious luxury suites at the river's edge. Tastefully furnished, the drawing room,

residents' lounge and intimate bar together create a convivial atmosphere. The Garden Room Restaurant is open for breakfast and lunch, while splendid dinners are served in the vaulted stone cellars. There are moorings for guests arriving by boat. Dating back to the 9th century, the market town of Wareham has more than 200 listed buildings. Corfe Castle, Lulworth Cove, Poole and Swanage are all close by with superb walks and beaches. **Directions:** Wareham is on the A351 to the west of Bournemouth and Poole. The hotel is beside the River Frome at the southern end of the town near the parish church. Price guide: Single £80–£125; double/twin £115–£210; suite £240.

BISHOPSTROW HOUSE

WARMINSTER, WILTSHIRE BA12 9HH
TEL: 01985 212312 FAX: 01985 216769 E-MAIL: enquiries@bishopstrow.co.uk

Bishopstrow House is the quintessential Georgian mansion. It combines the intimacy of a grand country hotel retreat with all the benefits of modern facilities and the luxury of the new Ragdale spa, offering a superb range of beauty, fitness and relaxation therapies in addition to Michaeljohn's world class hair styling. A Grade II listed building, Bishopstrow House was built in 1817 and has been sympathetically extended to include indoor and outdoor heated swimming pools, a high-tech gymnasium and a sauna. The attention to detail is uppermost in the Library, Drawing Room and Conservatory with their beautiful antiques and Victorian oil paintings. Grandly furnished bedrooms are festooned with fresh orchids and some have opulent marble bathrooms and whirlpool baths. The Mulberry Restaurant serves skilfully prepared modern British food, with lighter meals available in the Mulberry Bar and the Conservatory which overlooks 27 acres of gardens. There is fly–fishing on the hotel's private stretch of the River Wylye, golf at five nearby courses, riding, game and clay-pigeon shooting. Longleat House, Wilton House, Stourhead, Stonehenge, Bath, Salisbury and Warminster are within easy reach. **Directions:** Bishopstrow House is south–east of Warminster on the B3414 from London via the M3. Price guide: Single £90–£99; double/twin £170–£225; suite from £230.

THE GLEBE AT BARFORD

CHURCH STREET, BARFORD, WARWICKSHIRE CV35 8BS
TEL: 01926 624218 FAX: 01926 624625

"Glebe" means belonging to the Church, which explains why this beautiful Georgian country house is in a unique and quiet position next to the church in Barford, one of the most attractive villages in Warwickshire. It is a Grade II listed building, dating back to 1820, with an unusual central atrium and surrounded by landscaped gardens. The bedrooms are spacious, comfortable and peaceful. They have all the accessories expected by today's travellers. The restaurant is in an elegant, conservatory, green plants adding cool colour. There are excellent table d'hôte and à la carte menus and the wine list has been carefully selected to complement the dishes. The Glebe is an ideal venue for private celebrations and corporate events as it has several well-equipped conference rooms – the Bentley Suite seats 120 people for a banquet and the Directors Suite, with leather armchairs, is ideal for a discreet strategy meeting. Those wishing to be pampered will be pleased with the two new beauty rooms and hair salon. Guests appreciate the Glebe Leisure Club with a pool, air-conditioned gymnasium, sauna, steam room and spa facilities. They can play croquet in the garden, or tennis and golf nearby. **Directions:** M40 exit Junction 15 A429 signed Barford & Wellesbourne. Turning left at mini-roundabout, the hotel is on the right just past the church. Price guide: Single £90; double/twin £110; suite £125.

WOOD HALL

TRIP LANE, LINTON, NR WETHERBY, WEST YORKSHIRE LS22 4JA
TEL: 01937 587271 FAX: 01937 584353

Off the A1 about 15 miles due west of York, built of stone from the estate, Wood Hall is an elegant Georgian house overlooking the River Wharfe. Its grounds, over 100 acres in all, are approached along a private drive that winds through a sweep of parkland. The sumptuously furnished drawing room and the oak-panelled bar, with its gentlemen's club atmosphere, lead off the grand entrance hall. Superb floral displays, gleaming chandeliers and immaculately designed interiors hint at the careful attention that has been lavished on Wood Hall. Gastronomes will relish the excellent à la carte menu, which combines contemporary Anglo-French style with attractive presentation. The mile-long private stretch of the Wharfe offers up trout and barbel to the keen angler, while miles of walks and jogging paths encompass the estate. There is a leisure club including a swimming pool, spa bath, steam room, gymnasium, solarium and treatment salon. Near to the National Hunt racecourse at Wetherby, York, Harrogate, Leeds, the Dales and Harewood House are only a short distance away. **Directions:** From Wetherby, take the A661 towards Harrogate. Take turning for Sicklinghall and Linton, then left for Linton and Wood Hall. Turn right opposite the Windmill public house; hotel is 1½ miles further on. Price guide: Single £115–£170; double/twin £125–£190; suite £190.

OATLANDS PARK HOTEL

146 OATLANDS DRIVE, WEYBRIDGE, SURREY KT13 9HB
TEL: 01932 847242 FAX: 01932 842252 E-MAIL: oatlandspark@btinternet.com

Records of the Oatlands estate show that Elizabeth I and the Stuart kings spent time in residence in the original buildings. The present mansion dates from the late-18th century and became a hotel in 1856: famous guests included Émile Zola, Anthony Trollope and Edward Lear. The hotel stands in acres of parkland overlooking Broadwater Lake, with easy access to Heathrow, Gatwick and central London. Although it caters for the modern traveller, the hotel's historic character is evident throughout. The accommodation ranges from superior rooms to large de luxe rooms and suites. The elegant, high-ceilinged Broadwater Restaurant is the setting for creative à la carte menus with dishes to suit all tastes. A traditional roast is served every Sunday lunchtime. The six air-conditioned meeting rooms and up-to-date facilities include video conferencing and are complemented by the professional conference team. Theme evenings, such as Henry VIII banquets, are a speciality. Many sporting and leisure activities are offered including a new 9 hole, par 27, golf course. **Directions:** From M25 junction 11, follow signs to Weybridge. Follow A317 through High Street into Monument Hill to mini-roundabout. Turn left into Oatlands Drive; hotel is 50 yards on left. Price guide: Single £117–£141; double/twin £163–£183; suite from £162. Special Break rate: Single £60; double/twin £90.

MOONFLEET MANOR

FLEET, WEYMOUTH, DORSET DT3 4ED
TEL: 01305 786948 FAX: 01305 774395

Overlooking Chesil Beach, a unique feature of the Dorset coast, Moonfleet Manor is both a luxury hotel and a family resort. The owners have applied the same flair for design evident in their other properties, Woolley Grange and the Old Bell at Malmesbury. The use of a variety of unusual antiques and objects from around the world lends a refreshing and individual style to this comfortable and attractive hotel. Refurbished bedrooms are beautifully decorated and furnished and a range of amenities ensures that guests enjoy standards of maximum comfort and convenience. An enthusiastic and attentive staff works hard to ensure that guests feel at home, whatever their age. Moonfleet's dining room, whose décor and style would do credit to a fashionable London restaurant, offers an excellent and varied menu based on fresh local produce but bringing culinary styles from around the world. Facilities at the hotel include an indoor swimming pool with squash and tennis courts for the more energetic. Key places of interest nearby include Abbotsbury, Dorchester, Corfe Castle and Lulworth Cove, while in Weymouth itself the Sea Life Park, The Deep Sea Adventure and The Titanic Story are worth a visit. **Directions:** Take B3157 Weymouth to Bridport Road, then turn off towards the sea at sign for Fleet. Price guide: Single from £75; double/twin £95–£180; suite from £180–£200.

HOTEL DU VIN & BISTRO

SOUTHGATE STREET, WINCHESTER, HAMPSHIRE SO23 9EF
TEL: 01962 841414 FAX: 01962 842458 E-MAIL: admin@winchester.hotelduvin.co.uk

Relaxed, charming and unpretentious are words which aptly describe the stylish and intimate Hotel du Vin & Bistro. This elegant hotel is housed in one of Winchester's most important Georgian buildings, dating back to 1715. It is jointly run by Gerard Basset, perhaps the UK's most famous sommelier, and Robin Hutson, whose successful career includes experience in other similarly fine hotels. The 23 individually decorated bedrooms feature superb beds made up with crisp, Egyptian cotton and offer every modern amenity, including trouser press, mini bar and CD players. Each bedroom is sponsored by a wine house whose vineyard features in its decorations. Bathrooms boasting power showers, oversized baths and fluffy towels and robes add to guests' sense of luxury and comfort. Quality food cooked simply with fresh ingredients is the philosophy behind the Bistro, where an excellent and reasonably priced wine list is available. There are also 2 function rooms available for special occasions. A welcoming and enthusiastic staff cater for every need. The hotel is a perfect base for exploring England's ancient capital, famous for its cathedral, its school and antique shops. The New Forest is a short drive away. **Directions:** M3 to Winchester. Southgate Street leads from the City centre to St. Cross. Price guide: Single/double/twin £89–£125; suite £185.

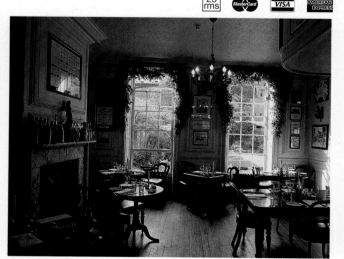

LAINSTON HOUSE HOTEL

SPARSHOLT, WINCHESTER, HAMPSHIRE SO21 2LT
TEL: 01962 863588 FAX: 01962 776672

The fascinating history of Lainston House is well documented, some of its land having been recorded in the *Domesday Book* of 1087. Set in 63 acres of superb downland countryside, this graceful William and Mary country house has been sympathetically restored to create a beautiful hotel with a stately home atmosphere. From the individually designed bedrooms to the main reception rooms, elegant and comfortable furnishings are the hallmark of Lainston House. Freshly prepared food, attentive service and views over the lawn make the restaurant one of the most popular in Hampshire. Facilities are available for small meetings in the Mountbatten Room or larger functions in the recently converted 17th century Dawley Barn. The charming grounds hold many surprises – an ancient chapel, reputedly haunted by the legendary Elizabeth Chudleigh, an 18th century herb garden and a dovecote. Historic Winchester is only 2½miles south, while Romsey Abbey, Salisbury and the New Forest are a short drive away. Other local activities include riding, country walking and good trout fishing on the River Test at nearby Stockbridge. **Directions:** Lainston House is well signposted off the B3049 Winchester–Stockbridge road, at Sparsholt 2½ miles from Winchester. Price guide: Single from £95; double/twin from £145; suite from £265.

GILPIN LODGE

CROOK ROAD, NEAR WINDERMERE, CUMBRIA LA23 3NE

TEL: 015394 88818 FREEPHONE: 0800 269460 FAX: 015394 88058 E-MAIL: hotel@gilpin-lodge.co.uk

Gilpin Lodge is a small, friendly, elegant, relaxing country house hotel set in 20 acres of woodlands, moors and country gardens 2 miles from Lake Windermere, yet just 12 miles from the M6. The original building, tastefully extended and modernised, dates from 1901. A profusion of flower arrangements, picture-lined walls, antique furniture and log fires in winter are all part of John and Christine Cunliffe's perception of hospitality. The sumptuous bedrooms all have en suite bathrooms and every comfort. Some have four-poster beds, split levels and whirlpool baths. The exquisite food, created by a team of 7 chefs, has earned 3 rosettes from the AA. The award winning wine list contains 175 labels from 13 different countries. The beautiful gardens are the perfect place in which to muse while savouring the lovely lake-land scenery. Windermere golf course is ½ a mile away. There is almost every kind of outdoor activity imaginable. Guests have free use of a nearby private leisure club. This is Wordsworth and Beatrix Potter country and nearby there are several stately homes, gardens and castles. England for Excellence Silver award 1997 Hotel of the year, English Tourist Board Gold award and RAC Blue Ribbon award. **Directions:** M6 exit 36. A591 Kendal bypass then B5284 to Crook. Price guide: Single £60–£110; double/twin £80–£180. Dinner inclusive and year-round short-break rates available.

LAKESIDE HOTEL ON LAKE WINDERMERE

LAKESIDE, NEWBY BRIDGE, CUMBRIA LA12 8AT
TEL: 0541 541586 FAX: 015395 31699 E-MAIL: sales@lakesidehotel.co.uk

Lakeside Hotel offers you a unique location on the water's edge of Lake Windermere. It is a classic, traditional Lakeland hotel offering four star facilities and service. All the bedrooms are en suite and enjoy individually designed fabrics and colours, many of the rooms offer breathtaking views of the lake. Guests may dine in either the award-winning Lakeview Restaurant or Ruskin's Brasserie, where extensive menus offer a wide selection of dishes including Cumbrian specialities. The Lakeside Conservatory serves drinks and light meals throughout the day – once there you are sure to fall under the spell of this peaceful location. Berthed next to the hotel there are cruisers which will enable you to explore the lake from the water. Guests enjoy free use of the Cascades Leisure Club at Newby Bridge until Summer 2000 when the hotels Health Club with 17m pool will be complete. The hotel offers a fully equipped conference centre and many syndicate suites allowing plenty of scope and flexibility. Most of all you are assured of a stay in an unrivalled setting of genuine character. The original panelling and beams of the old coaching inn create an excellent ambience, whilst you are certain to enjoy the quality and friendly service. **Directions:** From M6 junction 36 join A590 to Newby Bridge, turn right over bridge towards Hawkshead; hotel is one mile on right. Price guide: Single from £95; double/twin £135–£190; suites £210–£230.

LANGDALE CHASE

WINDERMERE, CUMBRIA LA23 1LW
TEL: 015394 32201 FAX: 015394 32604

Langdale Chase stands in five acres of landscaped gardens on the shores of Lake Windermere, with panoramic views over England's largest lake to the Langdale Pikes beyond. Visitors will receive warm-hearted hospitality in this well-run country home, which is splendidly decorated with oak panelling, fine oil paintings and ornate, carved fireplaces. A magnificent staircase leads to the well-appointed bedrooms, many overlooking the lake. One unique bedroom is sited over the lakeside boathouse, where the traveller may be lulled to sleep by the gently lapping waters below. The facilities also include a private boat mooring which is available on request. For the energetic, there is a choice of water-skiing, swimming or sailing from the hotel jetty. Guests can stroll through the gardens along the lake shore, in May the gardens are spectacular when the rhododendrons and azaleas are in bloom. Being pampered by attentive staff will be one of the many highlights of your stay at Langdale Chase. The variety of food and wine is sure to delight the most discerning diner. Combine this with a panoramic tableau across England's largest and loveliest of lakes and you have a truly unforgettable dining experience. **Directions:** Situated on the A591, three miles north of Windermere, two miles south of Ambleside. Price guide: Single £50–£120; double/twin £100–£190; suite £180.

LINTHWAITE HOUSE HOTEL

CROOK ROAD, BOWNESS-ON-WINDERMERE, CUMBRIA LA23 3JA
TEL: 015394 88600 FAX: 015394 88601 E-MAIL: admin@linthwaite.com

Situated in 14 acres of gardens and woods in the heart of the Lake District, Linthwaite House overlooks Lake Windermere and Belle Isle, with Claife Heights and Coniston Old Man beyond. Here, guests will find themselves amid spectacular scenery, yet only a short drive from the motorway network. The hotel combines stylish originality with the best of traditional English hospitality. The superbly decorated en suite bedrooms, most of which have lake or garden views. The comfortable lounge is the perfect place to unwind and there is a fire on winter evenings. In the restaurant, excellent cuisine features the best of fresh, local produce, accompanied by a fine selection of wines. Within the hotel grounds, there is a 9-hole putting green and a par 3 practice hole. Fly fishermen can fish for brown trout in the hotel tarn. Guests have complimentary use of a private swimming pool and leisure club nearby, while fell walks begin at the hotel's front door. The area around Linthwaite abounds with places of interest: this is Beatrix Potter and Wordsworth country, and there is much to interest the visitor. **Directions:** From the M6 junction 36 follow Kendal by-pass (A590) for 8 miles. Take B5284 Crook Road for 6 miles. 1 mile beyond Windermere Golf Club, Linthwaite House is signposted on left. Price guide: Single £85–£100; double/twin £90–£200; suite £240–£250.

MILLER HOWE

RAYRIGG ROAD, WINDERMERE, CUMBRIA LA23 1EY
TEL: 015394 42536 FAX: 015394 45664 E-MAIL: lakeview@millerhowe.com

One of the finest views in the entire Lake District is from the restaurant, conservatory and terrace of this lovely hotel which stands high on the shores of Lake Windermere. Lawned gardens bedded with mature shrubs, trees and borders of colour sweep down to the water's edge. It is a spectacular scene. Visitors receive warm hospitality from this well-run and splendidly decorated hotel now owned by Charles Garside, the former Editor-in-Chief of the international newspaper 'The European' and his brother Iain from Fayrer Garden Hotel. Previous owner John Tovey, the celebrated chef and author, remains as a consultant. All 12 en suite bedrooms are furnished in a luxurious style, the majority of which have views over the lake to the mountains beyond. They feature every modern amenity amongst the antiques. Chef Susan Elliott's imaginative menus will delight the most discerning guest, while the panoramic tableau across England's largest lake as the sun sets, presents an unforgettable dining experience. Guests can enjoy a range of water sports or boat trips on Lake Windermere and there are many interesting fell walks close by. **Directions:** From the M6 junction 36 follow the A591 through Windermere, then turn left onto the A592 towards Bowness. Miller Howe is ½ mile on the right. Price guide (including 4-course dinner): Single £95–£175; double/twin £140–£250.

STORRS HALL

WINDERMERE, CUMBRIA LA23 3LG
TEL: 015394 47111 FAX: 015394 47555

From the windows, terrace and gardens of this magnificent listed Georgian manor house not another building can be seen. Just a spectacular, seemingly endless, panoramic view over beautiful Lake Windermere. Built in the 18th century for a Lancashire shipping magnate, Storrs Hall stands majestically in an unrivalled peninsular position surrounded by 17 acres of landscaped, wooded grounds which slope gently down to half a mile of lakeside frontage. Once frequented by Wordsworth, it is owned by Les Hindle, a property developer and Richard Livock, a fine art and antiques dealer, who rescued the manor from decay and lovingly restored it to its former glory, furnishing the rooms throughout with sumptuous antiques and objets d'art. They include the owner's private collection of ship models, reflecting the maritime fortunes which built the hall and a grand piano, once played by the great virtuosos. Opened as a hotel in 1998, the Hall has 18 beautifully furnished bedrooms. Each is en suite, spacious and offers every possible comfort. Most have unparalleled views over the lake, which was once the property of the Hall. Equally splendid views are enjoyed from an exquisite lounge, library, writing room and cosy bar. The Terrace Restaurant is renowned for the superb cuisine prepared by chef David Baruthio whose menus reflect the grandeur of the setting. **Directions:** On A592 two miles south of Bowness and 5 miles north of Newby Bridge. Price guide: Single £125; double/twin £155–£300.

SIR CHRISTOPHER WREN'S HOUSE

THAMES STREET, WINDSOR, BERKSHIRE SL4 1PX
TEL: 01753 861354 FAX: 01753 860172

A friendly and homely atmosphere makes Sir Christopher Wren's House a perfect location for guests seeking a break from the hectic pace of modern life. Built by the famous architect in 1676, it nestles beneath the ramparts and towers of Windsor Castle, beside the River Thames and Eton Bridge. With a quiet charm and dignity of its own, the hotel combines fine furnishings from the past with every comfort and convenience associated with life today. Additions to the original house have been made at different times over the centuries and there are now 70 bedrooms available for guests. These have all recently been refurbished to the highest standards and while some feature a balcony and river views, others overlook the famous castle. All offer a full range of amenities, including direct dial telephone, cable TV, trouser press, tea and coffee-making facilities, mineral water and an air cooling system. There are two restaurants to choose from – Stroks Riverside Restaurant or the Café Wren. Both offer a good selection of beautifully cooked and well-presented dishes. The Windsor area has a great deal to offer, for those with time to explore. Among the many attractions within easy reach are Windsor Castle, Eton College, Royal Ascot, Thorpe park, Henley, Saville Gardens and Legoland. **Directions:** Windsor is just 2 miles from junction 6 of the M4. Price guide: Single from £145, double/twin from £185, suite from £275.

THE BEDFORD ARMS

GEORGE STREET, WOBURN, MILTON KEYNES, BEDFORDSHIRE MK17 9PX
TEL: 01525 290441 FAX: 01525 290432

The Bedford Arms was built in 1724 to serve the Royal Mail coaches staging north and replaced the George Inn which was destroyed when Woburn village was ravaged by fire. Over the years it has been altered, extended and refurbished but still retains many original features and its old world charm and elegance. The Bedford Arms is tastefully decorated, furnished in country house style and has a reputation for hospitality, friendliness and comfort. The 53 en suite bedrooms are spacious, attractive, individual and offer a high standard of decor and furnishings. There are a number of Executive Rooms, one with a four-poster bed. Holland's Restaurant, named after the architect Henry Holland who built both the hotel and remodelled Woburn Abbey in 1787–8, serves tasty and imaginative cuisine with chef Kevin Christman using the best and freshest local produce whenever possible. The cosy, timber beamed Tavistock bar, decorated with horse brasses and racing memorabilia from the Woburn Estate's Bloomsbury Stud, is popular with guests for its homely character, conditioned ales and substantial meals and snacks. Close by are many places of historical interest, particularly Woburn Abbey with its priceless antiques, silver, porcelain, paintings and 3,000 acre Deer Park. **Directions:** Exit M1 at junction 13 and follow signs to Woburn. Price guide: Single £105-£125; double/twin £120-£148; suites £180.

FLITWICK MANOR

CHURCH ROAD, FLITWICK, BEDFORDSHIRE MK45 1AE
TEL: 01525 712242 FAX: 01525 718753 E-MAIL: flitwick@menzies–hotels.co.uk

Flitwick Manor is a Georgian gem, classical in style, elegant in décor, comfortable in appointment, a country house hotel that remains true to the traditions of country house hospitality. Nestling in acres of glorious rolling parkland complete with lake, grotto and church, the manor has the intimacy and warmth that make it the ideal retreat for both pleasure and business. The seventeen bedrooms, with their distinctive characters and idiosyncrasies, add to the charm of the reception rooms: a soothing drawing room, a cosy library and pine panelled morning room, the latter two doubling up as both meeting and private dining rooms. Fine antiques and period pieces, easy chairs and

inviting sofas, winter fires and summer flowers, they all blend effortlessly together to make a perfect combination. The restaurant is highly acclaimed by all the major food guides and indeed the AA, with its bestowal of three Rosettes, rated Flitwick Manor as the county's best and amongst the top one hundred establishments in the country. Outside pleasures are afforded by the all-weather tennis court, croquet lawns and putting green as well as a range of local attractions such as Woburn Abbey and Safari Park. **Directions:** Flitwick is on the A5120 just north of the M1 junction 12. Price guide: Single £120–£190; double/twin/suite £145–£225. Special weekend rates available.

THE OLD VICARAGE HOTEL

WORFIELD, BRIDGNORTH, SHROPSHIRE WV15 5JZ
TEL: 01746 716497 FAX: 01746 716552 E-MAIL: admin@the-old-vicarage.demon.co.uk

Standing in 2 acres of mature grounds, this Edwardian parsonage has hardly been altered since its days as a turn of the century Parsonage. An extensive, subtle refurbishment has created an exceptional Country House Hotel offering guests a peaceful retreat in countryside of outstanding beauty. The spacious bedrooms are sensitively furnished in Victorian and Edwardian styles to complement the period features of the house. Four Coach House rooms offer complete luxury and comfort and the Leighton suite has been specially designed with the disabled guest in mind. Award-winning imaginative menus include fresh and organic produce carefully sourced from local suppliers and small farmers. The hotel's wine list was awarded the AA

Regional Wine List in 1998. The Ironbridge Gorge Museum Complex and The Severn Valley Railway are just two of the many visitor attractions within easy reach of the hotel as well as the splendour of the border towns and villages nearby. Two-day breaks are available from £72.50 per person, per day, which includes half price golf at Worfield Golf Club and free entrance to Attingham Park. The hotel's many accolades and awards include AA 3 Star 79%, AA 3 Rosettes and the Egon Ronay Regional Cheeseboard of the Year 1997. **Directions:** 8 miles west of Wolverhampton, 1 mile off A454, 8 miles south of junction 4 of M54. Price guide including breakfast: Single £70–£105; double/twin £107.50–£170.

SECKFORD HALL

WOODBRIDGE, SUFFOLK IP13 6NU
TEL: 01394 385678 FAX: 01394 380610 E-MAIL: reception@seckford.co.uk

Seckford Hall dates from 1530 and it is said that Elizabeth I once held court there. The hall has lost none of its Tudor grandeur. Furnished as a private house with many fine period pieces, the panelled rooms, beamed ceilings, carved doors and great stone fireplaces are displayed against the splendour of English oak. Local delicacies such as the house speciality, lobster, feature on the à la carte menu. The original minstrels gallery can be viewed in the banqueting hall, which is now a conference and function suite designed in keeping with the general style. The Courtyard area was converted from a giant Tudor tithe barn, dairy and coach house. It now incorporates ten charming cottage-style suites and a modern leisure complex, which includes a heated swimming pool, exercise machines, solarium and spa bath. The hotel is set in 34 acres of tranquil parkland with sweeping lawns and a willow-fringed lake and guests may stroll about the grounds or simply relax in the attractive terrace garden. There is a 18-hole golf course, where equipment can be hired, and a gentle walk along the riverside to picturesque Woodbridge, with its tide mill, antique shops, yacht harbours and the rose-planted grave of Edward Fitzgerald. Constable country and the Suffolk coast are nearby. **Directions:** Remain on the A12 Woodbridge bypass until the blue-and-white hotel sign. Price guide: Single £79–£125; double/twin £110–£165; suite £140–£165.

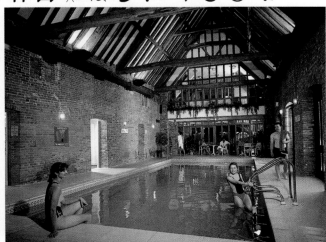

THE FEATHERS HOTEL

MARKET STREET, WOODSTOCK, OXFORDSHIRE OX20 1SX
TEL: 01993 812291 FAX: 01993 813158 E-MAIL: enquiries@feathers.co.uk

The Feathers is a privately owned and run country house hotel, situated in the centre of Woodstock, a few miles from Oxford. Woodstock is one of England's most attractive country towns, constructed mostly from Cotswold stone and with some buildings dating from the 12th century. The hotel, built in the 17th century, was originally four separate houses. Antiques, log fires and traditional English furnishings lend character and charm. There are 21 bedrooms, all of which have private bathrooms and showers. Public rooms, including the drawing room and study, are intimate and comfortable. The small garden is a delightful setting for a light lunch or afternoon tea and guests can enjoy a drink in the cosy courtyard bar, which has an open fire in winter. The antique-panelled restaurant is internationally renowned for its fine cuisine, complemented by a high standard of service and recently awarded 3 AA Rosettes. The menu changes daily and offers a wide variety of dishes, using the finest local ingredients. Blenheim Palace, seat of the Duke of Marlborough and birthplace of Sir Winston Churchill, is just around the corner. The Cotswolds and the dreaming spires of Oxford are a short distance away. **Directions:** From London leave the M40 at junction 8; from Birmingham leave at junction 9. Take A44 and follow the signs to Woodstock. The hotel is on the left. Price guide: Single £95; double/twin £105–£169; suite £220–£275.

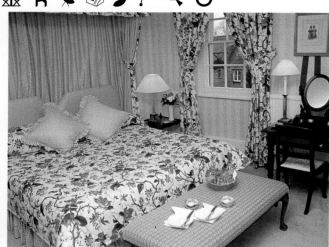

WATERSMEET HOTEL

MORTEHOE, WOOLACOMBE, DEVON EX34 7EB

TEL: 01271 870333 FAX: 01271 870890 RESERVATIONS: 0800 731 7493 E-MAIL: watersmeethotel@compuserve.com

Watersmeet personifies the comfortable luxury of a country house hotel. Majestically situated on The National Trust's rugged North Atlantic coastline the hotel commands dramatic views across the waters of Woolacombe Bay past Hartland Point to Lundy Island. The gardens reach down to the sea and nearby steps lead directly to the beach. Attractive décor, combined with soft coloured fabrics, creates a summery impression all year round. The main bedrooms look out to sea and guests can drift off to sleep to the sound of lapping waves or rolling surf. Morning coffee, lunch and afternoon tea can be served in the relaxing comfort of the lounge, on the terrace or by the heated outdoor pool. The splendid new indoor pool and spa is a favourite with everyone. Tempting English and international dishes are served in the award-winning Watersmeet Restaurant where each evening candles flicker as diners absorb a view of the sun slipping below the horizon. The hotel has been awarded an AA Rosette for cuisine, the AA Courtesy and Care Award and all three RAC Merit awards for excellent hospitality, restaurant and comfort. There is a grass tennis court and locally surfing, riding, clay pigeon shooting and bracing walks along coastal paths. Open February to December. **Directions:** From M5, J27, follow A361 towards Ilfracombe, turn left at roundabout and follow signs to Mortehoe. Price guide (including dinner): Single £91–£134; double/twin £152–£238.

WOOLACOMBE BAY HOTEL

SOUTH STREET, WOOLACOMBE, DEVON EX34 7BN
TEL: 01271 870388 FAX: 01271 870613

Woolacombe Bay Hotel stands in 6 acres of grounds, leading to three miles of golden sand. Built by the Victorians, the hotel has an air of luxury, style and comfort. All rooms are en suite with satellite TV, baby listening, ironing centre, some with a spa bath or balcony. Traditional English and French dishes are offered in the dining room. Superb recreational amenities on site include unlimited free access to tennis, squash, indoor and outdoor pools, billiards, bowls, croquet, dancing and films, a health suite with steam room, sauna, spa bath with heated benches and high impulse shower. Power-boating, shooting and riding can be arranged and preferential rates are offered for golf at the Saunton Golf Club. The "Hot House" aerobics studio, cardio vascular weights room, solariums, masseur and beautician. However, being energetic is not a requirement for enjoying the qualities of Woolacombe Bay. Many of its regulars choose simply to relax in the grand public rooms and in the grounds, which extend to the rolling surf of the magnificent bay. A drive along the coastal route in either direction will guarantee splendid views. Exmoor's beautiful Doone Valley is an hour away by car. Closed January. **Directions:** At centre of village, off main Barnstaple–Ilfracombe road. Price guide (including dinner): Single £80–£110; double/twin £160–£220.

THE GEORGE HOTEL

QUAY STREET, YARMOUTH, ISLE OF WIGHT PO41 0PE
TEL: 01983 760331 FAX: 01983 760425 E-MAIL: res@thegeorge.co.uk

This historic 17th century town house is superbly located just a few paces from Yarmouth's ancient harbour. Built for Admiral Sir Robert Holmes, a former governor of the island, it once welcomed Charles II through its doors. With the cosy ambience of a well-loved home, The George is the perfect place for self-indulgence. Beautifully furnished and well-equipped bedrooms complement the luxurious surroundings. Enjoy either the 3 AA Rosette cuisine in the elegant restaurant or opt for a more informal à la carte meal in the lively brasserie with its lovely sea views. The excellent cellar contains particularly good claret. The hotel has its own private beach and there is no shortage of leisure opportunities in the near vicinity, including world class sailing on the Solent. Yarmouth remains the gateway to the downs and villages of the West Wight and there are countless opportunities to make the most of this area of outstanding natural beauty by walking, hiking or enjoying a host of other country pursuits, golf too. Historic places of interest include Carisbrook Castle and Osborne House. **Directions:** From the M3/M27, exit at junction 1 and take the A377 to Lymington and then the ferry to Yarmouth. Alternatively, ferry services run regularly to the island from Southampton and Portsmouth. The A3054 leads direct to Yarmouth. Price guide: Single £95–£115; double/twin £140–£185.

THE GRANGE HOTEL

1 CLIFTON, YORK, NORTH YORKSHIRE YO30 6AA
TEL: 01904 644744 FAX: 01904 612453 E-MAIL: grangehotel.co.uk

Set near the ancient city walls, 4 minutes' walk from the famous Minster, this sophisticated Regency town house has been carefully restored and its spacious rooms richly decorated. Beautiful stone-flagged floors in the corridors of The Grange lead to the classically styled reception rooms. The flower-filled Morning Room is welcoming, with its blazing log fire and deep sofas. Double doors between the panelled library and drawing room can be opened up to create a dignified venue for parties, wedding receptions or business entertaining. Prints, flowers and English chintz in the bedrooms reflect the proprietor's careful attention to detail. The Ivy Restaurant has an established reputation for first-class gastronomy, incorporating the best in French and country house cooking. The Seafood bar has two murals depicting racing scenes. The Brasserie is open for lunch and dinner until after the theatre closes in the evening. For conferences, a computer and fax are available as well as secretarial services. Brimming with history, York's list of attractions includes the National Railway Museum, the Jorvik Viking Centre and the medieval Shambles. **Directions:** The Grange Hotel is on the A19 York–Thirsk road, 1/2 mile from the centre on the left. Price guide: Single £99–£160; double/twin £120–£180; suites £210.

MIDDLETHORPE HALL

BISHOPTHORPE ROAD, YORK YO23 2GB

TEL: 01904 641241 FAX: 01904 620176 E-MAIL: info@middlethorpe.u-net.com

Middlethorpe Hall is a delightful William III house, built in 1699 for Thomas Barlow, a wealthy merchant and was for a time the home of Lady Mary Wortley Montagu, the 18th century writer of letters. The house has been immaculately restored by Historic House Hotels who have decorated and furnished it in its original style and elegance. There are beautifully designed bedrooms and suites in the main house and the adjacent 18th century courtyard. The restaurant, which has been awarded 3 Rosettes from the AA, offers the best in contemporary English cooking. A health and leisure Spa with an indoor swimming pool opened in 1999. Middlethorpe Hall, which is a member of Relais & Chateaux Hotels, stands in 26 acres of parkland and overlooks York Racecourse yet is only 1½ miles from the medieval city of York with its fascinating museums, restored streets and world-famous Minster. From Middlethorpe you can visit Yorkshire's famous country houses, like Castle Howard, Beningbrough and Harewood, the ruined Abbeys of Fountains and Rievaulx and explore the magnificent Yorkshire Moors. Helmsley, Whitby and Scarborough are nearby. **Directions:** Take A64 (T) off A1 (T) near Tadcaster, follow signs to York West, then smaller signs to Bishopthorpe. Price guide: Single £112–£140; double/twin £170–£260; suite from £210–£290.

MONK FRYSTON HALL

MONK FRYSTON, NORTH YORKSHIRE LS25 5DU
TEL: 01977 682369 FAX: 01977 683544 E-MAIL: monkfryston.hall@virgin.net

A short distance from the A1 and almost equidistant from Leeds and York, this mellow old manor house hotel, built in 1109, is ideal for tourists, business people and those looking for an invitingly secluded spot for a weekend break. The mullioned and transom windows and the family coat of arms above the doorway are reminiscent of Monk Fryston's fascinating past. In 1954 the Hall was acquired by the Duke of Rutland, who has created an elegant contemporary hotel, while successfully preserving the strong sense of heritage and tradition. The bedrooms, ranging from cosy to spacious, have private en suite bathrooms and are appointed to a high standard. A generous menu offers a wide choice of traditional English dishes with something to suit all tastes. From the Hall, the terrace leads down to an ornamental Italian garden which overlooks a lake and is a delight to see at any time of year. Wedding receptions are held in the oak-panelled Haddon Room with its splendid Inglenook fireplace. The Rutland Room provides a convenient venue for meetings and private parties. York is 17 miles, Leeds 13 miles and Harrogate 18 miles away. **Directions:** The Hall is three miles off the A1, on the A63 towards Selby in the centre of Monk Fryston. Price guide: Single £80–£98; double/twin £99–£150.

MOUNT ROYALE HOTEL

THE MOUNT, YORK, NORTH YORKSHIRE YO2 2DA
TEL: 01904 628856 FAX: 01904 611171 E-MAIL: Reservations@mountroyale.co.uk

Two elegant William IV houses have been restored to their former glory to create the Mount Royale Hotel, which is personally run by the Oxtoby family. Comfortable bedrooms are furnished with imagination, all in an individual style. Each of the garden rooms opens onto the garden and has its own verandah. Downstairs, the public rooms are filled with interesting items of antique furniture, *objets d'art* and gilt-framed paintings. To the rear of the building, overlooking the gardens, is the restaurant, where guests can enjoy the best of traditional English cooking and French cuisine. Amenities include a snooker room with a full-sized table, steam room, sauna, solarium and health and beauty treatment centre.

With a delightful English garden and heated outdoor pool, the one acre grounds are a peaceful haven just minutes from York's centre. York is a historic and well-preserved city, famous for its Minster and medieval streets. Also within walking distance is York racecourse, where the flat-racing season runs from May to October. Lovers of the great outdoors will find the Yorkshire Dales and North York Moors a 45 minute drive away. Only small dogs by arrangement. **Directions:** From A64, turn onto the A1036 signposted York. Go past racecourse; hotel is on right before traffic lights. Price guide: Single £85–£99; double/twin £95–£145; suites £145.

Johansens Recommended Hotels
Wales

Breathtaking scenery, a rich variety of natural, cultural and modern leisure attractions, and the very best accommodation awaits the Johansens visitor in Wales.

Harlech Castle

What's new in Wales?

• Llangollen International Musical Eisteddfod – the 54th International Musical Eisteddfod held at the Royal International Pavilion, Llangollen, between 4th and 9th July 2000. Participants from around 50 countries are drawn together by their love of music, song and dance. A unique cultural festival to be enjoyed by all.
Tel: 01978 860236

• Royal Welsh Show – exhibition of livestock, cattle, horses, machinery, handicrafts, tradestands, sheepdog trials, tug of war plus much more. Held at the Royal Welsh Showground between 24th and 27th July 2000.
Tel: 01982 553683

• Ladies Home International Matches – Golf – annual competition between ladies golf teams from England, Ireland, Scotland & Wales. Held between 13th and 15th September 2000 at the Royal St David's Golf Club.
Tel: 01334 475811

• Welsh International Film Festival – premier welsh film event celebrating the industry in an international context. Held at various venues in Cardiff between 10th and 19th November 2000.
Tel: 01970 617995

For more information please contact:-

Wales Tourist Board
Dept GN
PO Box 1
Cardiff CF1 2XN
Tel: 01222 475226

North Wales Tourism
Tel: 01492 531731

Mid Wales Tourism
Tel: 0800 273747

Tourism South & West Wales
Tel: 01792 781212

TY NEWYDD COUNTRY HOTEL

PENDERYN ROAD, HIRWAUN, MID-GLAMORGAN CF44 9SX
TEL: 01685 813433 FAX: 01685 813139

Surrounded by undisturbed woodland and beautiful, mature gardens this attractive hotel stands serenely midway between Cardiff and Swansea on the southern edge of the magnificent 520 square miles of the Brecon Beacons National Park. The original house was built by a coal baron, William Llewellyn, uncle of Sir Harry Llewellyn who rode Foxhunter to a gold medal in the 1956 Olympic Games. Peace, comfort and a warm welcome are the hallmarks of Ty Newydd, which offers guests all modern facilities whilst retaining the character and ambience of a fine Georgian country house. The lounges with their open fires are particularly comfortable while the individually styled bedrooms are a delight. Each is en suite and tastefully furnished with a mixture of antique and locally made traditional pieces. There are connecting rooms for families and cots, high chairs and baby listening service are available. For lovers of good food, the spacious restaurant with an adjoining conservatory overlooking the landscaped gardens serves superb traditional favourites alongside varied and seasonal international cuisine. The hotel is an excellent base for exploring the many historic properties nearby, including the 13th century castle at Caerphilly, the largest in Wales. **Directions:** Leave M4 at junction 32. and take the A470 and A465 to Hirwaun. Then follow the A4059 Brecon road towards Penderyn. Price guide: Single £47–£70; double/twin £62–£90.

ALLT-YR-YNYS HOTEL

WALTERSTONE, NR ABERGAVENNY HEREFORDSHIRE HR2 0DU
TEL: 01873 890307 FAX: 01873 890539 E-MAIL: allthotel@compuserve.com

Nestling in the foothills of the Black Mountains, on the fringes of the Brecon Beacons National park, Allt-yr-Ynys is an impressive Grade II 16th century manor house hotel. The Manor was the home of the Cecil family whose ancestry dates back to Rhodri Mawr, King of Wales in the 8th century. A more recent Cecil was Lord Burleigh, Chief Minister to Queen Elizabeth I, portrayed by Sir Richard Attenborough in the recent film, 'Elizabeth'. Features of this interesting past still remain and include moulded ceilings, oak panelling and beams and a 16th century four-poster bed in the Jacobean suite. However, whilst the charm and the character of the period remains, the house has been sympathetically adapted to provide all the comforts expected of a modern hotel. The former outbuildings have been transformed into spacious and well-appointed guest bedrooms. Fine dining is offered in the award-winning restaurant and the conference/function suite accommodates up to 200 guests. Facilities include a heated pool, Jacuzzi, clay pigeon shooting range and private river fishing. Pastimes include exploring the scenery, historic properties and plethora of tourist attractions. **Directions:** 5 miles north of Abergavenny on A465 Abergavenny/ Hereford trunk road, turn west at Old Pandy Inn in Pandy. After 400 metres turn right down lane at grey/green barn. The hotel is on the right after 400 metres. Price guide: Single £70–£95; double/twin £90–£120.

LLANSANTFFRAED COURT HOTEL

LLANVIHANGEL GOBION, ABERGAVENNY, MONMOUTHSHIRE NP7 9BA
TEL: 01873 840678 FAX: 01873 840674 E-MAIL: Llansantff@aol.com

Llansantffraed Court is a perfect retreat from the fast pace of modern life. This elegant Georgian-style country house hotel, part of which dates back to the 14th century, is set in spacious grounds on the edge of the Brecon Beacons and the Wye Valley. Guests are welcomed with warmth and provided with the highest level of personal, yet unobtrusive service. Most of the tastefully decorated and luxuriously furnished bedrooms offer views over the hotel's garden, and ornamental trout lake. While one has a four poster bed, others feature oak beams and dormer windows. An excellent reputation is enjoyed by the restaurant, which offers menus reflecting the changing seasons and the availability of fresh local produce. AA Two Rosettes. Exquisite cuisine is complemented by a fine wine list. Afternoon tea can be taken in the lounge, with guests warming themselves in front of the blazing log fire during the cooler months and savouring the views of the South Wales countryside. A range of excellent facilities is available for functions, celebrations and meetings. Llansantffraed Court is an ideal base for exploring the diverse history and beauty of this area and there are plenty of opportunities to take advantage of energetic or relaxing pursuits, including, golf, trekking, walking, and salmon and trout fishing. **Directions:** From M4 J24 (Via A449) off B4598 (formerly A40 old road) Leave A40 D/C at Abergavenny or Raglan. Price guide: Single £68–£80; double/twin £85–£95; suites £155.

PORTH TOCYN COUNTRY HOUSE HOTEL

ABERSOCH, PWLLHELI, GWYNEDD LL53 7BU
TEL: 01758 713303 FAX: 01758 713538

This is a rare country house seaside hotel – family owned for three generations, the first of whom had the inspiration to transform a row of miners' cottages into an attractive low white building, surrounded by enchanting gardens, with glorious views over Cardigan Bay and Snowdonia. The Fletcher-Brewer family have created a unique ambience that appeals to young and old alike. Children are welcome – the younger ones have their own sitting room and high tea menu. Nonetheless, Porth Tocyn's charm is appreciated by older guests, with its Welsh antiques and delightful, comfortable sitting rooms. Most of the pretty bedrooms have sea views, some are family oriented and three on the ground floor are ideal for those with mobility problems. All have en suite bathrooms. Enjoy cocktails in the intimate bar, anticipating a fabulous meal, for dining at Porth Tocyn is a memorable experience every day of the week (the menu changes completely every day). Scrumptious dishes and mellow wines are served in great style on antique tables. Lunch is informal, on the terrace or by the pool. Glorious beaches, water sports, golf, tennis, riding and exploring the coast provide activities for all ages. **Directions:** The hotel is 2 miles from Abersoch on the Sarn Bach road. Watch for bilingual signs – Gwesty/hotel – then the hotel name. Price guide: Single £48–£63; double/twin £74–£116.

CONRAH COUNTRY HOUSE HOTEL

RHYDGALED, CHANCERY, ABERYSTWYTH, CEREDIGION SY23 4DF
TEL: 01970 617941 FAX: 01970 624546 E-MAIL: hotel@conrah.freeserve.co.uk

One of Wales' much loved country house hotels, the Conrah is tucked away at the end of a rhododendron-lined drive, only minutes from the spectacular rocky cliffs and sandy bays of the Cambrian coast. Set in 22 acres of rolling grounds, the Conrah's magnificent position gives views as far north as the Cader Idris mountain range. Afternoon tea and Welsh cakes or pre-dinner drinks can be taken at leisure in the quiet writing room or one of the comfortable lounges, where antiques and fresh flowers add to the relaxed country style. The acclaimed restaurant uses fresh local produce, together with herbs and vegetables from the Conrah kitchen garden, to provide the best of both classical and modern dishes. The hotel is owned and run by the Heading family who extend a warm invitation to guests to come for a real 'taste of Wales', combined with old-fashioned, high standards of service. For recreation, guests may enjoy a game of table-tennis in the summer house, croquet on the lawn or a walk around the landscaped gardens. The heated swimming pool and sauna are open all year round. Golf, pony-trekking and sea fishing are all available locally, while the university town of Aberystwyth is only 3 miles away. Closed Christmas. **Directions:** The Conrah lies 3 miles south of Aberystwyth on the A487. Price guide: Single £68–£78; double/twin £90–£125.

TREARDDUR BAY HOTEL

LON ISALLT, TREARDDUR BAY, NR HOLYHEAD, ANGLESEY LL65 2UN
TEL: 01407 860301 FAX: 01407 861181 E-MAIL: the–trearddur–bay–hotel.com

This seaside hotel enjoys a magnificent location on the Anglesey coast, overlooking Trearddur Bay and close to a medieval chapel dedicated to the nun St Brigid. An extensive refurbishment programme in recent years has given the hotel a completely new look. Many of the spacious bedrooms, all of which are en suite, have panoramic views over the bay. All are furnished to a high standard. There are also fifteen studio suites, including one with a four-poster bed. The comfortable lounge is the perfect place to relax and read the papers over morning coffee or afternoon tea. Before dinner, enjoy an apéritif in one of the hotel bars. Superb views apart, the hotel restaurant enjoys a reputation for excellent food – including locally caught fish and seafood – complemented by fine wines. Table d'hôte and à la carte menus offer a good choice of dishes. For those who find the Irish Sea too bracing, the hotel has an indoor pool. The beach is just a short walk away and there is an 18-hole golf course nearby. Anglesey is a haven for water sports enthusiasts and bird-watchers. Places of interest include Beaumaris Castle and the Celtic burial mound at Bryn Celli Ddu. Snowdonia is a little further afield. **Directions:** From Bangor, take A5 to Valley crossroads. Turn left onto B4545 for 3 miles, then turn left at garage. Hotel is 350 yards on right. Price guide: Single £70–£105; double/twin £108–£130; executive suite £130.

PALÉ HALL

LLANDDERFEL, BALA, GWYNEDD LL23 7PS
TEL: 01678 530285 FAX: 01678 530220 E-MAIL: palehall@fsbdial.co.uk

One of the ten best-kept private residences throughout Wales, Palé Hall's stunning interiors include its magnificent entrance hall, a 32 foot high galleried staircase and ornate hand-painted ceilings in the Boudoir. Built in 1870 at no spared expense for Henry Robertson, a Scottish gentleman responsible for construction of the local railways, the Hall's notable guests have included Queen Victoria – who described the house as enchanting – and Winston Churchill. The Hall stands in 150 acres of mature woodland on the fringe of the Snowdonia National Park above the Vale of Edeinion. The comfortable lounges (including 2 non-smoking lounges) enable quiet relaxation and contemplation. Each of the 17 suites is individually decorated and contains en suite bathroom, television, hospitality tray and luxury toiletries, all sharing magnificent views of the surrounding scenery. The restaurant offers seasonal table d'hôte menus (AA 2 rosettes) and is complemented by an extensive cellar. Outdoor pursuits include walking, riding, golf and white-water rafting. Fishing rights on the River Dee are included in the rates. The hotel has its own clay shooting and can organise shooting parties. Exclusive use of the hotel is available for executive conferences and weddings. **Directions:** Palé Hall is situated off the B4401 Corwen to Bala road, four miles from Llandrillo. Price guide: Single £69–£120; double/twin £95–£155.

BONTDDU HALL

BONTDDU, NR BARMOUTH, GWYNEDD LL40 2UF
TEL: 01341 430661 FAX: 01341 430284

Solid and grey-stoned, with a rampart-topped tower and slim, arched windows, Bontddu Hall looks in every way like a small fairytale castle. Situated in the beautiful Southern Snowdonia National Park, the hotel stands majestically in 14 acres of gardens and woodlands overlooking the picturesque magnificence of the Mawddach Estuary. It is a superb example of Gothic architecture, reflected inside by the grandeur, elegance and tradition of high, beamed ceilings, huge fireplaces, handsome portraits and rich furnishings. Peace, privacy and relaxation are guaranteed with owner Michael Ball and his wife ensuring that guests receive the very best service and hospitality. Period furniture and Victorian style wallpapers add to the country-house ambience of the bedrooms, each named after a past visiting Prime Minister. Each bedroom is en suite, delightfully decorated and has all modern facilities. Four rooms in the Lodge have balconies from which occupants can enjoy mountain views. There are two comfortable lounges and a Victorian-style bar where local artists regularly exhibit their work. Lunch and tea are served in the brasserie or on the sun-catching garden terrace. The devoted team of chefs produce traditional cuisine using fresh, local produce in the Mawddach Restaurant. **Directions:** Bontddu Hall is on A496 between Dolgellau and Barmouth. Price guide: Single £65–£75; double/twin £100–£120; suite £160.

YE OLDE BULL'S HEAD

CASTLE STREET, BEAUMARIS, ISLE OF ANGLESEY LL58 8AP
TEL: 01248 810329 FAX: 01248 811294

Situated in the town centre of Beaumaris, Ye Olde Bull's Head is a Grade II listed building and is the original posting house of the borough. Many vestiges of the hotel's 17th century past are evident, for example, the single hinged gate which closes the courtyard of the Inn is listed as the largest in Britain. Despite a history dating back to 1472, the Bull retains a more Dickensian feel with bedrooms named after the author's characters. All have been built or refurbished in the last five years and offer comfortable furnishings, en suite facilities and modern amenities such as direct dial telephone, television and radio. Guests relax in the intimate lounge with its chintz furnishings and roaring open fire and then can choose to dine in the superb restaurant or the ground floor brasserie. Chef proprietor Keith Rothwell ensures the highest quality standards are maintained in both restaurant and brasserie. Creative dishes in the modern British style make full use of the finest local produce and are complemented by the carefully selected wine list. Guests and townsfolk alike enjoy the ambience of the inn's historic bar with a glass of real ale by the open fire. Sports include sailing, climbing in Snowdonia and fishing in The Menai Straits and Conwy Coast. Beaumaris Castle is 100 yards away whilst Plas Newydd and Anglesey Sea Zoo are worth a visit. **Directions:** From Britannia Road Bridge (A5), follow A545 for approx 5m to Beaumaris. Price guide: Single £53; double/twin £83; suite £92.

LLANGOED HALL

LLYSWEN, BRECON, POWYS, WALES LD3 0YP

TEL: 01874 754525 FAX: 01874 754545 E-MAIL: Llangoed_Hall_Co_Wales_UK@compuserve.com

The history of Llangoed Hall dates back to 560 AD when it is thought to have been the site of the first Welsh Parliament. Inspired by this legend, the architect Sir Clough Williams-Ellis, transformed the Jacobean mansion he found here in 1914 into an Edwardian country house. Situated deep in a valley of the River Wye, surrounded by a walled garden, the hotel commands magnificent views of the Black Mountains and Brecon Beacons beyond. The rooms are warm and welcoming, furnished with antiques and oriental rugs and on the walls, an outstanding collection of paintings acquired by the owner, Sir Bernard Ashley. The luxurious and spacious bedrooms enjoy fine views of the Wye Valley. Llangoed's restaurant is one of the principal reasons for going there. Classic but light, the Michelin starred menus represent the very best of modern cuisine, complemented by a cellar of more than 300 wines. Exclusive use of the entire hotel can be made available for board meetings. Outdoor pursuits include golf, riding, shooting and some of the best mountain walking and gliding in Britain. For expeditions, there are Hay-on-Wye and its bookshops, the border castles, Hereford and Leominster. Children over 8 are welcome. There are 3 heated kennels for dogs. The hotel is a member of Welsh Rarebits and Small Luxury Hotels of the World. **Directions:** 9 miles west of Hay, 11 miles north of Brecon on A470. Price guide: Single from £155; double/twin from £185; suite from £325.

COED-Y-MWSTWR HOTEL

COYCHURCH, NEAR BRIDGEND, VALE OF GLAMORGAN CF35 6AF
TEL: 01656 860621 FAX: 01656 863122 E-MAIL: hotel.reservations@virgin.co.uk

Coed-y-Mwstwr is a country mansion of Victorian origin set in 17 acres of mature woodland, which is also home to an abundance of wildlife – overlooking the Vale of Glamorgan (easy access from Cardiff Airport – 25 minutes). Much thought has gone into ensuring that the décor and furnishings are in keeping with the style of the house. High ceilings, chandeliers and large fireplaces feature in the elegant public rooms. The 23 luxurious bedrooms all have en suite facilities and wonderful views. The elegant oak-panelled restaurant enjoys a good reputation locally and offers a blend of traditional and modern cuisine, with both table d'hôte and à la carte menus with an AA Rosette. The wine list has more than 80 wines. Private functions for up to 130 people may be held in the Hendre Suite. In addition, there are two private dining rooms. A heated outdoor swimming pool and all-weather tennis court are available for guests' use. For golfers, Royal Porthcawl and Southerndown courses are a short drive away from the hotel. The beautiful Gower and Pembrokeshire coastline and Brecon Beacons National Park are within easy reach. Open all year. **Directions:** Leave M4 at junction 35, take A473 towards Bridgend for 1 mile, turn right into Coychurch. At filling station turn right and follow signs uphill. Price guide: Single £97.50; double/twin £135; suite £150.

MISKIN MANOR COUNTRY HOUSE HOTEL

MISKIN, NR CARDIFF CF72 8ND
TEL: 01443 224204 FAX: 01443 237606 E-MAIL: info@miskin–manor.co.uk

Although its history dates back to the 11th century, Miskin Manor first became a hotel only in 1986, following extensive restoration and refurbishment. Only 20 minutes' drive from central Cardiff and Cardiff Bay and set amid 22 acres of undisturbed parkland, criss-crossed with streams, peace and seclusion are guaranteed. The uncommonly spacious reception rooms have fine fireplaces, panelled walls and elaborate plasterwork ceilings, all enhanced by rich drapery and comfortable furniture. All of the bedrooms have en suite bathrooms and full facilities. In the 1920s, one of the de luxe suites was occupied by the Prince of Wales (later King Edward VIII), a room which is now aptly named the Prince of Wales suite. First-class Welsh cuisine is served in the restaurant, awarded two AA Rosettes and complemented by a comprehensive wine list. Just a short walk away from the hotel, within the grounds, the popular Sports and Leisure Club boasts two glass-backed squash courts, badminton, swimming pool and 2 gymnasiums while more gentle pursuits are provided by the solarium, sauna and steam room as well as refreshment facilities and a crèche. Celebrations, conferences and functions can be catered for at Miskin Manor, with reliable, professional support assured. Corporate activities can be held on site. **Directions:** From junction 34 of the M4, towards Llantrisant. Drive is one mile north of the M4. Price guide: Single from £85; double/twin £110–£130; suite £145–£195.

ST DAVID'S PARK HOTEL

EWLOE, FLINTSHIRE CH5 3YB
TEL: 01244 520800 FAX 01244 520930 E-MAIL: reservations@st.davids–park–hotel.co.uk

A magnificent three-tiered fountain welcomes visitors on arrival at this large, modern hotel at the crossroads of North Wales. Crowned by a glistening white clock tower, St David's stands regally in extensive landscaped gardens with its gracious Georgian-style façade designed around an attractive inner courtyard. Inside the hotel the ambience is truly elegant, from the furnishings, fabrics and floor coverings to the pictures, ornaments and accessories in every room. The en suite bedrooms are particularly well-appointed and extremely spacious. There are a number of suites and studio rooms, family and adjoining rooms and rooms especially for disabled guests. The air-conditioned

Fountains Restaurant is the heart of the hotel and the international choice of cuisine from Head Chef Graham Wilson leaves nothing to be desired. Light snacks are available at the hotel's Health Club where facilities include an indoor pool, gymnasium, steam and sauna rooms. There is also a children's Fun Club where the little ones can be safely left to play. Golfers and tennis players enjoy the nearby Northop Country Park Golf Club. **Directions:** From M56 take A5117 to North Wales. Turn on to A550 for 1 mile and then join A494 to Queensbury/Mold. After 4 miles take B5219 to Buckley. Price guide: Single £90–£118; double/twin £109–£150, Suite £154–£175.

TYDDYN LLAN COUNTRY HOUSE HOTEL

LLANDRILLO, NR CORWEN, DENBIGHSHIRE LL21 0ST
TEL: 01490 440264 FAX: 01490 440414 E-MAIL: tyddynllanhotel@compuserve.com

Set in beautifully tended gardens amid some of mid-Wales' finest scenery, Tyddyn Llan is a Georgian country house built in Welsh stone and slate that was once used by the Dukes of Westminster as a shooting lodge. It is the home today of Peter and Bridget Kindred who have brought to its modernised interior just the right degree of comfortable elegance, enhanced by Peter's skill in interior design and enriched by his own paintings that adorn the hall and lounges. Individually decorated, the bedrooms are filled with fine antiques and period furniture and enjoy fine views of the garden and surrounding hills. Dining has always been a highlight at Tyddyn Llan and the nightly dinner menus are complemented by a carefully selected wine list. Quality local ingredients, from salmon caught on the Dee to lamb, beef and dairy products, make for memorable dishes to partner the fresh vegetables and herbs from the kitchen garden. Three AA Rosettes constitute well-earned recognition of Tyddyn Llan's unique attention to detail. The hotel has rights to four miles of fly-fishing on the River Dee. Keen walkers can trace the ancient Roman road, Ffordd Gam Elin, which traverses the Berwyn Mountains. Here naturalists will find many species of birds and wild flowers. **Directions:** Llandrillo is midway between Corwen and Bala on B4401, 4 miles from A5 at Corwen. Price guide (bed and breakfast): Single £65–£82; double/twin £100–£134.

BRON EIFION COUNTRY HOUSE HOTEL

CRICCIETH, GWYNEDD LL52 0SA
TEL: 01766 522385 FAX: 01766 522003

This magnificent baronial Grade II listed mansion stands within five acres of glorious gardens and woodlands, yet only minutes from the sea. It was built by the millionaire slate owner John Greaves whose master craftsmen carved the spectacular pitch and Oregon pine panelled hallway, minstrels gallery and vaulted ceiling. The Conservatory Restaurant, which overlooks the floodlit gardens, serves innovative cuisine complemented by a superb selection of wines. All 19 bedrooms are en suite and are individually decorated, offering king-sized and four-poster beds, or you could choose a standard or superior room. The gardens provide interesting walks, from the stone walled terraces to the secluded herb garden. Perhaps you would like to laze on the verandah overlooking the lawns which abound in a variety of wildlife. Small dogs by arrangement. Golf, shooting, riding and fishing are all nearby. A short car drive will take you to the pretty villages of Criccieth, Bedde Gelert or the Italiante village of Portmeirion. The rugged beauty of the mountains of Snowdonia, together with castles, stately homes, Lloyd George's Museum and Ffestiniog Railway are all close by. **Directions:** The hotel is on the A497 on the outskirts of Criccieth and stands at the top of a tree-lined drive, nestled in Woodland. Price guide: Single £61–£68; double/twin £92–£120. Superior supplement £15 per room per night.

GLIFFAES COUNTRY HOUSE HOTEL

CRICKHOWELL, POWYS NP8 1RH

TEL: 01874 730371 FAX: 01874 730463 FREEPHONE: 0800 146719 E-MAIL: calls@gliffaeshotel.com

Visitors may be surprised to discover a hotel featuring distinctive Italianate architecture midway between the Brecon Beacons and the Black Mountains. Gliffaes Country House Hotel is poised 150 feet above the River Usk and commands glorious views of the surrounding hills and valley. The elegantly furnished, Regency style drawing room is an ideal place to relax and leads to a large sun room and on to the terrace, from which guests may enjoy the magnificent scenery. In addition to a panelled sitting room, there is a billiard room with a full-size table. In the dining room a wide choice from an imaginative menu covers the best of National dishes and Mediterranean specialities. The Gliffaes fishery includes every type of water, from slow-flowing flats to fast-running rapids, on 2½ miles of the River Usk renowned for its wild brown trout and salmon fishing. The 33 acre hotel grounds have rare trees and shrubs as well as lawns for putting and croquet. There are two Golf courses within easy reach. Riding can be arranged nearby. Open throughout the year. There are now conference facilities available in the grounds. **Directions:** Gliffaes is signposted from the A40, 2½ miles west of Crickhowell. Price guide: Single from £50.30; double/twin from £60.70.

PENMAENUCHAF HALL

PENMAENPOOL, DOLGELLAU, GWYNEDD LL40 1YB
TEL: 01341 422129 FAX: 01341 422787 E-MAIL: penhall@tinyonline.co.uk

The splendour of Cader Idris and the Mawddach Estuary forms the backdrop for this handsome Victorian mansion which is an exceptional retreat. Set within the Snowdonia National Park, the 21-acre grounds encompass lawns, a formal sunken rose garden, a water garden and woodland. The beautiful interiors feature oak and mahogany panelling, stained-glass windows, log fires in winter, polished Welsh slate floors and freshly cut flowers. There are 12 luxurious bedrooms, some with four-poster and half-tester beds and all with interesting views. In the Gothic-style conservatory restaurant, guests can choose from an imaginative menu prepared with the best seasonal produce and complemented by an extensive list of wines. An elegant panelled dining room can be used for private dinners or meetings. Penmaenuchaf Hall is perfect for a totally relaxed holiday. For recreation, guests can fish for trout and salmon along ten miles of the Mawddach River or take part in a range of water sports. They can also enjoy scenic walks, visit sandy beaches and historic castles and take trips on narrow-gauge railways. **Directions:** The hotel is off the A493 Dolgellau–Tywyn road, about two miles from Dolgellau. Price guide: Single £70–£110; double/twin £100–£160.

HOTEL MAES-Y-NEUADD

TALSARNAU, NR HARLECH, GWYNEDD LL47 6YA
TEL: 01766 780200 FAX: 01766 780211 E-MAIL: maes@neuadd.com

This part-14th century house, built of granite and slate, is cradled by eight acres of landscaped mountainside. Michael and June Slatter, joint owners of this much-loved hotel since 1981, have been joined in partnership by Peter Jackson and his wife Lynn. Peace and tranquillity are all-pervasive, whether relaxing in the pretty, beamed lounge or reclining in a leather Chesterfield in the bar while enjoying an apéritif. Peter's team of talented chefs create delicious English and Welsh dishes using fresh produce such as lamb, fish and a variety of Welsh farmhouse cheeses, along with vegetables and herbs from the kitchen garden. The hotel hosts "Steam and Cuisine" formal dinners on the world famous Ffestiniog railway. The hotel produces its own oils and vinegars which are stylishly presented for sale. Spring and autumn breaks are available and the hotel is licensed for weddings. The bedrooms vary in style, from early beams and dormers to later Georgian elegance with full-length windows. For golfers, the Royal St David's Golf Course is located three miles away. Nearby attractions include the Italianate village of Portmeirion, slate caverns, beautiful beaches, Snowdonia, Edward I's castle at Harlech and the Ffestiniog railway. **Directions:** Hotel is 3^1/$_2$ miles north of Harlech, off the B4573, signposted at the end of the lane. Price guide: Single £80; double/twin £159–£230 (including dinner).

LAKE VYRNWY HOTEL

LAKE VYRNWY, LLANWDDYN, MONTGOMERYSHIRE SY10 0LY
TEL: 01691 870 692 FAX: 01691 870 259 E-MAIL: res@lakevyrnwy.com

Situated high on the hillside within the 24,000 acre Vyrnwy Estate the hotel commands breathtaking views of mountains, lakes and moorland. It is also surrounded by lawns, an abundance of rhododendrons, woods and meadowlands. Built in 1860, its heritage has been maintained for well over a hundred years as a retreat for all lovers of nature and fine dining. There are 35 bedrooms, all individually furnished and decorated, many with antiques and some with special features such as Jacuzzis, balconies, four-posters or suites. There are also dedicated meeting and private dining facilities. The award-winning candlelit restaurant has a seasonally changing menu. Everything from the marmalade to the *petits fours* at dinner are created in the Vyrnwy kitchens. The hotel owns some of Wales' best fishing together with some 24,000 acres of sporting rights. Other pursuits include sailing, cycling, tennis, quad trekking and some beautiful walking trails. Also an RSPB sanctuary, the estate provides a wealth of wildlife and represents true peace and tranquillity. **Directions:** From Shrewsbury take the A458 to Welshpool, then turn right onto B4393 just after Ford (signposted to Lake Vyrnwy 28 miles). Price guide: Single from £75; double/twin £100–£150; suite £170.

BODIDRIS HALL

LLANDEGLA, WREXHAM, DENBIGHSHIRE LL 11 3AL
TEL: 01978 790434 FAX: 01978 790335 E-MAIL: bodidrishall@micro–plus–web.net

Ivy-clad Bodidris Hall, amid the wild hills, forests and moorlands of North Wales, is steeped in history and legend. A fortified building has stood on the site since two Crusaders were granted the estate by their Prince, Gryffydd ap Madoc, as a reward for valour. It later became the Tudor hunting lodge of Lord Robert Dudley, controversial favourite of Elizabeth I. The Hall still harbours many historical features inside its thick, grey-stone walls, including a former prison cell, a priest hole and a narrow staircase on which duels were fought. Spacious bedrooms, some with four-poster beds, are individually designed with magnificent views over 50 acres of rugged countryside, landscaped lawns and the Hall's own trout filled pond that is a haven for wildfowl. The heavily beamed bar with its mullion windows is welcoming with nooks that beckon you to relax and unwind, and the intimate restaurant with its excellent British and Continental cuisine features a huge open fireplace built to roast a whole lamb. The Hall is excellent value for money and an ideal base for exploring North Wales, or enjoying walks on nearby Offa's Dyke. Riding, cycling, pony trekking, trout fishing, archery, clay pigeon and driven shooting are available. **Directions**: Bodidris Hall is ½ mile off the main A5104 Chester-Corwen road, 2 miles west of the junction with the A525. Price guide: Single £80–£99; double/twin £96–£140.

BODYSGALLEN HALL

LLANDUDNO LL30 1RS
TEL: 01492 584466 FAX: 01492 582519 E-MAIL: info@bodysgallen.u-net.com

Bodysgallen Hall, owned and restored by Historic House Hotels, lies at the end of a winding drive in 200 acres of wooded parkland and beautiful formal gardens. Magnificent views encompass the sweep of the Snowdonia range of mountains and the hotel looks down on the imposing medieval castle at Conwy. This Grade I listed house was built mainly in the 17th century, but the earliest feature is a 13th century tower, reached by a narrow winding staircase, once used as a lookout for soldiers serving the English kings of Conwy and now a safe place from which to admire the fabulous views. The hotel has 19 spacious bedrooms in the house and 16 delightful cottage suites in the grounds. Two of the finest rooms in the house are the large oak-panelled entrance hall and the first floor drawing room, both with splendid fireplaces and mullioned windows. The restaurant has been awarded 3 Rosettes by the AA and menus feature delicious dishes using fresh local ingredients. The Bodysgallen Spa comprises a spacious swimming pool, steam room, sauna, solaria, gym, beauty salons and a club room. The hotel is ideally placed for visiting the many historic castles and stately homes in North Wales. Famous golf courses adorn the coastline. Bodysgallen Hall is a member of Relais & Chateaux Hotels **Directions:** On A470 1 mile from the intersection with the A55. Llandudno is a mile further on the A470. Price guide: Single £105–£155; double/twin £145–£225; suite £180–£235.

ST TUDNO HOTEL

PROMENADE, LLANDUDNO LL30 2LP
TEL: 01492 874411 FAX: 01492 860407 E-MAIL: sttudnohotel@btinternet.com

Without doubt one of the most delightful small hotels to be found on the coast of Britain, St Tudno Hotel, a former winner of the *Johansens Hotel of the Year Award for Excellence*, certainly offers a very special experience. The hotel, which has been elegantly and lovingly furnished with meticulous attention to detail, offers a particularly warm welcome from owners, Martin and Janette Bland and their caring and friendly staff. Each beautifully co-ordinated bedroom has been individually designed with many thoughtful extras provided to ensure guests' comfort. The bar lounge and sitting room, which overlook the sea, have an air of Victorian charm. Regarded as one of Wales' leading restaurants, the air-conditioned Garden Room has won three AA Rosettes for its excellent cuisine. This AA Red Star hotel has won a host of other awards, including *Best Seaside Resort Hotel in Great Britain, Welsh Hotel of the Year,* national winner of the AA's *Warmest Welcome Award,* the British Tea Council *'Tea places award of excellence 1996–1998'* and even an accolade for having the *Best Hotel Loos in Britain*! St Tudno is ideally situated for visits to Snowdonia, Conwy and Caernarfon Castles, Bodnant Gardens and Anglesey. Golf, riding, swimming and dry-slope skiing and tobogganing can be enjoyed locally. **Directions:** On the promenade opposite the pier entrance and gardens. Price guide: Single from £75; double/twin £95–£185; suite £260.

THE LAKE COUNTRY HOUSE

LLANGAMMARCH WELLS, POWYS LD4 4BS
TEL: 01591 620202 FAX: 01591 620457 E-MAIL: lakehotel@ndirect.co.uk

A welcoming Welsh Country house set in its own 50 acres with rhododendron lined pathways, riverside walks and a large well stocked trout lake. Within the hotel, airy rooms filled with fine antiques, paintings and fresh flowers make this the perfect place to relax. Delicious home-made teas are served everyday beside log fires. From the windows, ducks and geese can be glimpsed wandering in the gardens which cascade down to the river. In the award winning restaurant, fresh produce and herbs from the gardens are used for seasonal Country House menus, complemented by one of the finest wine lists in Wales. Each of the supremely comfortable bedrooms or suites with beautifully appointed sitting rooms are furnished with the thoughtful attention to details seen throughout the hotel. Guests can fish for trout or salmon on the four miles of river which runs through the grounds and the 3 acre lake regularly yields trout of five pounds and over. The grounds are a haven for wildlife: herons, dippers and kingfishers skim over the river, there are badgers in the woods and swans and waterfowl abound. There is a large billiard room in the hotel and a 9 hole par three golf course, tennis court, croquet lawn and putting green. Awarded an AA 3 Red star and RAC Blue Ribbon. **Directions:** From the A483, follow signs to Llangammarch Wells and then to the hotel. Price guide: Single £90–£120; double/twin £130–£140; suite £160–£230.

YNYSHIR HALL

EGLWYSFACH, MACHYNLLETH, CEREDIGION SY20 8TA
TEL: 01654 781209 FAX: 01654 781366 E-MAIL: info@ynyshir–hall.co.uk

Once owned by Queen Victoria, Ynyshir Hall is a captivating Georgian manor house that perfectly blends modern comfort and old-world elegance. Its 12 acres of picturesque, landscaped gardens are set alongside the Dovey Estuary, one of Wales' most outstanding areas of natural beauty and the hotel is surrounded by the Ynyshir Bird Reserve. Hosts Rob and Joan Reen offer guests a warm welcome and ensure a personal service, the hallmark of a good family-run hotel. Period furniture and opulent fabrics enhance the ten charming bedrooms. The suites are particularly luxurious and along with a four-poster room and ground floor room, are popular with many guests. The interiors are exquisitely furnished throughout with comfortable sofas, antiques, contemporary colour schemes, oriental rugs and original paintings. These works of art are the creation of Rob, an established and acclaimed artist. The artistry continues in the kitchen where local seafood, game and vegetables from the kitchen garden are used to create superb modern interpretations of classic French cuisine. The imaginative dishes prepared by Welsh Chef of the Year, Chris Colmer, comprise a wonderful balance of colours, textures and flavours. Winner of Johansens 'Most Excellent Restaurant Award 1999'. Landmarks include Cader Idris, Wales' 2nd most popular mountain. Closed in Jan. **Directions:** Off main road between Aberystwyth and Machynlleth. Price guide: Single £110–£135; double/twin £120–£170; suite £195.

THE COURT HOTEL AND RESTAURANT

LAMPHEY, NR TENBY, PEMBROKESHIRE SA71 5NT
TEL: 01646 672273 FAX: 01646 672480 E-MAIL: thecourthotel.lamphey@btinternet.com

This magnificent Georgian mansion, is idyllically situated in acres of grounds bordered by the beautiful Pembrokeshire National Park and just one mile from some of Britain's finest coastal scenery and beaches. Warm, friendly and efficient service is enriched by comfortable furnishings and decor. There are deluxe and superior bedrooms within the hotel and purpose built Coach House studios provide the extra space required by families. The restaurant has a prestigious AA Rosette. Traditional flavours and local produce include such pleasures as Teifi salmon and Freshwater Bay lobster. Lighter meals and snacks can be taken in the elegant conservatory. The wide range of facilities in the superb leisure centre include an indoor heated swimming pool, Jacuzzi, sauna and a gymnasium. There are aerobics classes, massage and a beautician by appointment. Golf, sailing and fishing are nearby and the hotel's private yacht is available for charter. Well worth a visit is picturesque Tenby, the cliffside chapel of St Govan's, the Bishops Palace at Lamphey and Pembroke's impressive castle. **Directions:** From M4, exit at Junction 49 onto the A48 to Carmarthen. Then follow the A477 and turn left at Milton Village for Lamphey. Price guide: Single £69–£79; double/twin £85–£135. Bargain breaks from £43–£71 per person per night, dinner, bed and breakfast, all year.

THE HOTEL PORTMEIRION

PORTMEIRION, GWYNEDD LL48 6ET
TEL: 01766 770000 FAX: 01766 771331 E-MAIL: hotel@portmeirion.wales.com

Portmeirion is a private Italianate village, designed by the renowned architect Sir Clough Williams-Ellis. The unique avant-garde complex was started in 1925 and completed in the 1970s. It enjoyed a celebrated clientèle from the start – writers such as George Bernard Shaw, H G Wells, Bertrand Russell and Noel Coward were habitués. It is set in 120 acres of beautiful gardens and woodland, including two miles of tranquil sandy beaches and provides accommodation for visitors either in the village or in the main hotel. The Hotel Portmeirion, originally a mansion house, has been sensitively restored, retaining striking features from the past, such as the Victorian Mirror Room. The bedrooms are furnished to the highest standards, 14 rooms being in the hotel and 25 rooms and suites in the village. Designated conference facilities newly completed adjacent to the main hotel can accommodate up to 100 people. The restaurant offers the best French and Welsh cooking, the seasonal menu relying on fresh, locally produced ingredients. Swimming and tennis are available on site as well as complimentary golf at Porthmadog and sailing is close at hand. The Ffestiniog and Snowdon mountain railways, slate caverns and Bodnant Gardens are nearby. Closed Saturday 8 January–4 February **Directions:** Portmeirion lies off the A487 between Penrhyndeudrath and Porthmadog. Price guide: Single £105–£140; double/twin £105–£145; suite £125–£210.

WARPOOL COURT HOTEL

ST DAVID'S, PEMBROKESHIRE SA62 6BN
TEL: 01437 720300 FAX: 01437 720676 E-MAIL: warpool@enterprise.net

Originally built as St David's Cathedral Choir School in the 1860s, Warpool Court enjoys spectacular scenery at the heart of the Pembrokeshire National Park, with views over the coast and St Bride's Bay to the islands beyond. First converted to hotel use over 40 years ago, continuous refurbishment has ensured all its up-to-date comforts are fit for the next century. All 25 bedrooms have immaculate en suite bathrooms and over half enjoy glorious sea views. The hotel restaurant enjoys a splendid reputation. Imaginative menus, including vegetarian, offer a wide selection of modern and traditional dishes. Local produce, including Welsh lamb and beef, is used whenever possible, with crab, lobster, sewin and sea bass caught just off the coast. Salmon and mackerel are smoked on the premises and a variety of herbs are grown. The hotel gardens are ideal for a peaceful stroll or an after-dinner drink on a summer's evening. There is a covered heated swimming pool (open April to end of October) and all-weather tennis court in the grounds. A path from the hotel leads straight on to the Pembrokeshire Coastal Path, with its rich variety of wildlife and spectacular scenery. Boating and water sports are available locally. St David's Peninsula offers a wealth of history and natural beauty and has inspired many famous artists. **Directions:** The hotel is signposted from St David's town centre. Price guide: Single £74–£90; double/twin £106–£170.

PENALLY ABBEY

PENALLY, TENBY, PEMBROKESHIRE SA70 7PY
TEL: 01834 843033 FAX: 01834 844714 E-MAIL: penally.abbey@btinternet.com

Penally Abbey, a beautiful listed Pemrokeshire country house, offers comfort and hospitality in a secluded setting by the sea. Standing in five acres of gardens and woodland on the edge of Pembrokeshire National Park, the hotel overlooks Carmarthen Bay and Caldey Island. The bedrooms in the main building and in the adjoining coach house are well furnished, many with four-poster beds. The emphasis is on relaxation – enjoy a late breakfast and dine at leisure. Fresh seasonal delicacies are offered in the candlelit restaurant, with its chandeliers and colonnades. Guests can enjoy a game in the snooker room or relax in the elegant sunlit lounge, overlooking the terrace and gardens. In the grounds there is a wishing well and a ruined chapel – the last surviving link with the hotel's monastic past. Water-skiing, surfing, sailing, riding and parascending are available nearby. Sandy bays and rugged cliffs are features of the Pembrokeshire coastal park. As the rates include the cost of dinner, this friendly hotel offers splendid value for money. **Directions:** Penally Abbey is situated adjacent to the church on Penally village green. Price guide (including dinner): Single £118; double/twin £152; suite £176.

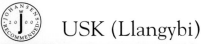

THE CWRT BLEDDYN HOTEL

LLANGYBI, NEAR USK, MONMOUTHSHIRE, SOUTH WALES NP5 1PG
TEL: 01633 450521 FAX: 01633 450220 E-MAIL: hotel.reservations@virgin.co.uk

Set in 17 acres of wooded grounds, this 14th century manor house, not far from the Roman town of Caerleon, is the perfect location from which to explore the Wye Valley and Forest of Dean. The hotel is a fine example of the traditional and the modern under one roof. Carved panelling and huge fireplaces in the lounge lend an air of classic country-house comfort. The 33 en suite bedrooms are spacious and offer guests every amenity, and most have wonderful views over the surrounding countryside. Cwrt Bleddyn's restaurant, Jesters, offers a wide à la carte menu with plenty of provision for vegetarians and those on special diets. Light meals are also served in the hotel's lounge and country club. Here, extensive leisure facilities include an indoor heated swimming pool, floodlite tennis courts, sauna, solarium, steam room and beauty salon. Alternatively, guests may just wish to stroll and relax in the grounds. Nearby is the local beauty spot of Llandegfedd, with its 434 acre reservoir. The hotel is open all year round and licensed for weddings. Private dining/function rooms are available. **Directions:** From Cardiff/Bristol, leave M4 at Jct 26. Hotel is 3 miles north of Caerleon on the road to Usk. From the Midlands, take M5, then A40 to Monmouth. Turn off A449, through Usk, over stone bridge, then left towards Caerleon for 4 miles. Price guide: Single £99; double/twin £150.

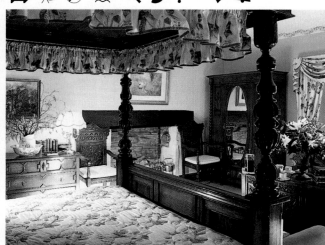

LLYNDIR HALL HOTEL

LLYNDIR LANE, ROSSETT, NR CHESTER, WALES LL12 0AY
TEL: 01244 571648 FAX: 01244 571258 E-MAIL: llyndir.hall@pageant.co.uk

This attractive hotel is individual in style and strong in charm and hospitality. It is peacefully situated in acres of parkland midway between Chester and Wrexham. A graceful country house with a 19th century Strawberry Gothic façade, Llyndir Hall has been tastefully refurbished and extended to offer guests every comfort. The 38 bedrooms are individually decorated and their tall, wide windows beautifully framed with heavy, rich curtains. Every bedroom is en suite with bath and shower and has satellite television, direct dial telephone and hair dryer. Chef Jeremy Stone's extensive menus are imaginative and the hotel has a high reputation for formal dinners and special event dining. For informal eating, Redwoods Brasserie and Bar is a lively venue for enjoying a range of dishes and desserts. At the hotel's leisure club you can swim in a heated pool, workout in the fully equipped gym or rest in the steam room/spa or solarium. Adjacent to the hotel is a purpose built Business Training Centre, which is an ideal venue for residential or non-residential conferences. Golf, shooting and riding are nearby. The Roman City of Chester with it's bustling shopping centre, racecourse and Cathedral are just a 15 minutes drive away. North Wales with it's Snowdonia National Park is within easy reach. **Directions:** From Chester take A483 to Wrexham. At junction with A55 follow signs to Pulford B5445. Continue on to Rossett. Price guide: Single £79; double/twin £115; suites £120.

TALISKER.
A PLACE WHERE THE THUNDER ROLLS OVER YOUR TONGUE.

Of all the islands that defend Scotland's west coast from the Atlantic, Skye is the most dramatic. How fitting then that this is the home of the fiery Talisker. Standing on Skye's western shore, the distillery lies in the shadow of The Cuillins. Jagged mountains that rise out of the sea to skewer the clouds for a thunderous retort. In the shadow of these peaks, next to a fearsome sea, Talisker takes its first breath and draws it all in. Skye's explosive fervour captured forever in its only single malt. That Talisker is not a whisky for the faint-hearted is beyond dispute. Indeed even when one seasoned whisky taster once went as far as calling it "The lava of The Cuillins", no one disagreed.

TALISKER IS THE ISLAND MALT FROM THE CLASSIC MALTS RANGE. TO FIND OUT MORE ABOUT ALL SIX DEFINITIVE EXPRESSIONS OF SCOTLAND'S MAIN MALT-PRODUCING REGIONS, WRITE TO: THE FRIENDS OF THE CLASSIC MALTS, P.O. BOX 87, GLASGOW, SCOTLAND G14 0JF.

Johansens Recommended Hotels
Scotland

Myths and mountains, lochs and legends – Scotland's scenic splendour acts as a magnet for visitors from all over the globe. Superb as it is, Scotland's charismatic charm is more than just visual.

Dunrobin Castle

What's new in Scotland?

• The Big Idea – aiming to be open in the spring of 2000, a state-of-the-art permanent exhibition will be launched on the west coast of Scotland on the Ardeer peninsula. This is a visitor experience, not a science museum, nor an exploratorium but a gigantic workshop where visitors are encouraged to have their own big ideas.

•Scottish Seabird Centre – expected to open in May 2000 in North Berwick, offers visitors an amazing insight into the some of the largest seabird colonies in Europe.

•Our Dynamic Earth – this new visitor attraction opened in July 1999 directly opposite the site of the new Scottish parliament and close to the Palace of Holyroodhouse and tells the story of our planet. Using dramatic special effects this attraction takes the visitor through the fascinating journey from the Earth's creation through to the future (whatever it may be!) Travel through time and step aboard a spaceship and see the creation of earth and the splendour of the natural world.

For further information, please contact:-

The Scottish Tourist Board
23 Ravelston Terrace
Edinburgh
EH4 3TP

Tel: 0131 332 2433

ARDOE HOUSE HOTEL AND RESTAURANT

SOUTH DEESIDE ROAD, BLAIRS, ABERDEEN AB12 5YP
TEL: 01224 867355 FAX: 01224 861283 E-MAIL: info@ardoe.macdonald-hotels.co.uk

Built in 1878 by a local manufacturer for his wife, the majestic, turreted Ardoe House is designed in the Scottish Baronial style favoured by Queen Victoria for Balmoral Castle. Situated within its own beautifully landscaped grounds with magnificent views over the River Dee and open countryside, Ardoe House has the style of an elegant country mansion with all modern comforts. Rich oak panelling, ornate ceilings and stained glass windows abound. The Great Hall reception area is truly spectacular, the richly furnished public rooms are relaxing and there are various small secluded areas where guests can privately enjoy a glass of malt whisky. Every bedroom has a pleasant and comfortable atmosphere and whatever your taste in cuisine, the fare available in the hotel's 2 AA Rosettes award-winning restaurant will more than match expectations. Ardoe House is only 10 minutes from Aberdeen City Centre yet is a fine gateway to tour Royal Deeside. Guests will enjoy complimentary use of a new fully equipped leisure centre, opening in January 2000, which comprises an 18m x 8m swimming pool, sauna, steam room, state-of-the-art gymnasium, aerobics studio, blitz room and four health and beauty treatment rooms. **Directions:** Leave Aberdeen on A92 south and join B9077 south Deeside Road at the Bridge of Dee. Price guide: Single £85–£170; double/twin £120–£165; suite £160–£225. Short break rates to include dinner and breakfast on request.

THAINSTONE HOUSE HOTEL & COUNTRY CLUB

INVERURIE, BY ABERDEEN, ABERDEENSHIRE AB51 5NT
TEL: 01467 621643 FAX: 01467 625084 E-MAIL: info@thainstone.macdonald–hotels.co.uk

An avenue of tall, whispering beech and sycamore trees culminates at a gracious portal leading into the grandeur of the galleried reception area of this historic Palladian mansion. Standing resplendent in 40 acres of lush meadowland, surrounded by richly wooded valleys, heather-clad moors and a magnificent series of castles, Thainstone House offers visitors the opportunity to enjoy the style of a bygone area, combined with all the modern comforts of a first-class hotel. Rebuilt in the 19th century after being torched by 18th century Jacobites, the hotel radiates a relaxed ambience and a regal atmosphere confirmed by the elegance of its public rooms. Superb meals can be enjoyed in the sumptuous

Georgian restaurant. Informally, you can dine in Cammie's Bar with its light-hearted charm. All the bedrooms have been created for comfort and restfulness. There is even a welcoming decanter of sherry and a tray of shortbread awaiting arrivals. Extensive leisure facilities include a trimnasium and a heated swimming pool designed in the style of an ancient Roman bath. Outdoor activities range from golf and fishing to clay pigeon shooting and falconry. Walkers can tramp the famed Grampian castle and whisky trails. **Directions:** From Aberdeen, take A96 towards Inverurie and turn left at Thainstone Mart roundabout. Price guide: Single £115–£130; double/twin £145–£165; suite £180.

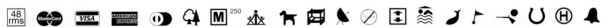

ABERFOYLE (Trossachs)

FOREST HILLS HOTEL

KINLOCHARD BY ABERFOYLE, THE TROSSACHS FK8 3TL
TEL: 01877 387277 FAX: 01877 387307

The tall, rambling, majestic Forest Hills hotel is delightfully situated in 25 acres of gardens and woodland overlooking beautiful Loch Ard in the foothills of the Trossachs, scattered with tumbling burns, rocky waterfalls, winding pathways and meandering forest trails. It is a stunning, history-steeped scenic location where hotel guests can unwind and enjoy sumptuous comfort, warm to winter log fires and thrill to the summer sun illuminating Ben Lomond across the waters as they sip cooling drinks on the terrace. Forest Hills is excellent in every way, particularly so in its service, friendliness and hospitality. Each of the 55 elegantly furnished en suite bedrooms has every facility that visitors could wish for. The lounges are a joy and the restaurant is renowned for its sumptuous cuisine prepared by award winning chefs. Grills, pastas and salads are offered in the New Rafters Bar and Bistro, which stages a weekly Ceilidh with Scottish music and dancing. For the more active visitor, the Hotel's leisure centre has a heated swimming pool, gym, billiards and a curling rink which converts into an extensive children's play area with go-karts. There are also tennis courts and for the more adventurous, canoeing, windsurfing and sailing on the Loch. The Hotel also specialises in guided walks, fishing trips and its now famous Ghost Walk. **Directions:** From M9, exit at Jct10. Take A873 to Aberfoyle and then join B892 to Kinlochard. Price guide: Double/twin £45–£65 per person.

LETHAM GRANGE RESORT

COLLISTON, BY ARBROATH, ANGUS DD11 4RL
TEL: 01241 890373 FAX: 01241 890725 E-MAIL: lethamgrange@sol.co.uk

Letham Grange is a beautifully renovated Victorian mansion with its original sculptured ceilings, panelling, antique staircase, fireplaces and period paintings faithfully restored to their former splendour. With its splendid scenery, it is a perfect country retreat for either a sporting or leisure break. The sumptuous luxury of country house living that the hotel provides is enhanced by two excellent golf courses and a four-lane curling rink. The bedrooms are individually designed and spacious, with charming décor which reflects the original character of this lovely building. Dining in the restful Rosehaugh Restaurant is a gourmet experience. The finest fresh local foods are selected to create table d'hôte and à la carte menus of international standard. Even the most seasoned golfers will enjoy meeting the demands of the 18-hole championship standard Old Course, which surrounds the hotel. The Glens Course offers a more relaxing game. Carnoustie and St Andrews are within easy driving distance. The curling rink is overlooked by the spacious Sweep 'n' Swing lounge. **Directions:** International flights to Edinburgh, Glasgow and Aberdeen. From Dundee take A92 and on the outskirts of Arbroath follow A933 to Colliston village. Turn right, signposted Letham Grange and at T-junction turn right and follow sign for half a mile. Prices on application according to season.

BALCARY BAY HOTEL

AUCHENCAIRN, NR CASTLE DOUGLAS, DUMFRIES & GALLOWAY DG7 1QZ
TEL: 01556 640217 FAX: 01556 640272

The hotel takes its name from the bay on which it stands, in an area of Galloway that is romantic in its isolation and which was once full of intrigue. Heston Isle, the hide-out of 17th century smugglers, fronts the hotel's view across the Solway coast and the Cumbrian Hills beyond. Originally owned by a shipping firm, the hotel was known to harbour illegal loot in its secret underground passages. Nowadays, Scottish hospitality at Balcary Bay includes the provision of modern facilities with a traditional atmosphere. It offers local delicacies such as lobsters, prawns and salmon imaginatively prepared, plus the reassuring intimacy of a family-run hotel. Despite its northerly aspect, Galloway benefits from the Gulf Stream and enjoys a mild and long holiday season. The area has great coastal and woodland walks. Closed from mid November to early March. Nearby are several 9 and 18 hole golf courses at Colvend, Kirkcudbright, Castle Douglas, Southerness and Dumfries. There are also salmon rivers and trout lochs, sailing, shooting, riding and bird-watching facilities. The area abounds with National Trust historic properties and gardens.
Directions: Located off the A711 Dumfries–Kirkcudbright road, two miles out of Auchencairn on the Shore Road. Price guide: Single £59; double/twin £104–£118. Seasonal short breaks and reduced inclusive rates for 3 and 7 nights.

AUCHTERARDER HOUSE

AUCHTERARDER, PERTHSHIRE PH3 1DZ
TEL: 01764 663646 FAX: 01764 662939 E-MAIL: auchterarder@wrensgroup.com

This splendid mansion, set amidst the rolling hills and glens of Perthshire, is a 19th century Scottish Baronial style house. Built over 150 years ago as a family home, the mansion retains its elegance whilst providing all the modern facilities. The opulent bedrooms are beautifully appointed, overlooking either the surrounding countryside or the grounds. All are double rooms and offer colour satellite television, radio, telephone and en suite facilities. The fine public rooms are enhanced by warming log fires and crystal chandeliers and the oak-panelled walls are adorned with paintings. This beautiful house has a warm, informal ambience that is omnipresent. In the traditional dining room, guests indulge in the sumptuous cuisine, a fusion of Scottish recipes and exquisite French presentation. The original cellars boast an extensive selection of both New World and European wines, but specialising in vintage Bordeaux. The 17½ acre grounds will delight nature lovers, with brilliant colour emanating from the various species of azaleas and rhododendrons. Traditional country pursuits such as fishing and shooting are readily available whilst croquet and golf may be played on site, or at the Gleneagles courses. **Directions:** From the A9, junction 8, drive into Auchterarder. Take the B8062 signposted Crieff for 1½ miles, the hotel is on the right. Price guide: Double/twin from £160; suite from £300.

BALLANTRAE (Ayrshire)

GLENAPP CASTLE

BALLANTRAE, SCOTLAND KA26 0NZ
TEL: 01465 831212 FAX: 01465 831000 E-MAIL: castle@glenapp.demon.co.uk

Glenapp Castle with its high sandstone walls and fairytale turrets and towers is a magnificent and romantic sight. Standing high above the village of Ballantrae, overlooking the Irish Sea towards Ailsa Craig, Arran and the Mull of Kintyre, this spectacular Scottish Baronial Castle, formerly the home of the Earls of Inchcape, opens this year, after complete restoration and refurbishment, as a luxury hotel exclusively for resident guests. Proprietors Graham and Fay Cowan offer a truly Scottish welcome to their glorious Ayrshire home and Glenapp is the ideal venue for a peaceful break from the stresses of modern living. The castle retains many of its original features as well as personally selected oil paintings and antique furnishings throughout bedrooms, lounges and oak panelled hallways. The 17 en suite bedrooms are spacious, individually decorated, and furnished to the highest standard. All bedrooms offer either garden views or panoramic views of the coastline. The castle's 30 acre gardens contain many rare and unusual trees and shrubs in both formal and woodland settings and an impressive Victorian glasshouse and walled garden. Tennis and croquet are available in the grounds. Guests may play golf on the many local courses including championship courses and shoot or fish on local estates. **Directions:** Glenapp Castle is approximately 15 miles north of Stranraer or 35 miles south of Ayr on A77. Price guide (All inclusive): Double/twin £410; suite £450; master room £500.

DARROCH LEARG HOTEL

BRAEMAR ROAD, BALLATER, ABERDEENSHIRE AB35 5UX
TEL: 013397 55443 FAX: 013397 55252

Four acres of leafy grounds surround Darroch Learg, sited on the side of the rocky hill which dominates Ballater. The hotel, which was built in 1888 as a fashionable country residence, offers panoramic views over the golf course, River Dee and Balmoral Estate to the fine peaks of the Grampian Mountains. Oakhall, an adjacent mansion built in Scottish baronial style and adorned with turrets, contains five of the 18 bedrooms ideal for private groups. All are individually furnished and decorated, providing modern amenities. The reception rooms in Darroch Learg are similarly elegant and welcoming, a comfortable venue in which to enjoy a relaxing drink. Log fires create a particularly cosy atmosphere on chilly nights. The beautifully presented food has been awarded 3AA Rosettes. A wide choice of wines, AA "Wine List of the Year for Scotland", complements the cuisine, which is best described as modern and Scottish in style. To perfect the setting, there is a wonderful outlook south towards the hills of Glen Muick. The wealth of outdoor activities on offer include walking, riding, mountain-biking, loch and river fishing, gliding and skiing. Ballater itself is interesting with an old ruined Kirk and ancient Celtic stones. A few miles away stands Balmoral Castle, the Highland residence of the British sovereign. **Directions:** At the western edge of Ballater on the A93. Price guide: Single £47–£62; double/twin £95–£140.

RAEMOIR HOUSE HOTEL

BANCHORY, ROYAL DEESIDE, ABERDEENSHIRE AB31 4ED
TEL: 01330 824884 FAX: 01330 822171 E-MAIL: raemoirhse@aol.com

This lovely 18th century mansion, part of a 3,500 acre estate, was converted from a private house into a hotel in 1943 and is now under new ownership. Spacious, liberally wooded grounds surround the hotel, with the Hill of Fare rising some 1,500 feet behind it. All the bedrooms are individually furnished with antique furniture and several feature beautiful tapestried walls. Many face south and offer fine views of the surrounding countryside. In the listed 16th century Ha' Hoose at the rear of the mansion there are some ground floor rooms suitable for wheelchairs. Outstanding and creative dishes prepared by the head chef and his team, feature the best local Scottish produce and have gained the hotel an Egon Ronay Restaurant entry, an RAC Restaurant Award and 2 AA Rosettes. The hotel welcomes conferences and private dinner parties for up to 50 people. Self-catering apartments (in converted stables and coach house) on site. Many beautiful walks can be enjoyed in the grounds and there are numerous castles to visit nearby, such as Balmoral and Crathes. **Directions:** Raemoir House is 2^1/$_2$ miles north of Banchory on the A980. Price guide: Single from £50; double/twin from £80.

ARISAIG HOUSE

BEASDALE, BY ARISAIG, INVERNESS-SHIRE PH39 4NR
TEL: 01687 450622 FAX: 01687 450626 E-MAIL: ArisaiGHse@aol.com

Princely redwoods rising above the sudden abundance of Arisaig's oak and rhododendron declare your journey done: now it is time to relax and enjoy the hospitality offered by your hosts, the Smither and Wilkinson families. Natural light floods into the house, streaming through tall windows into the inner hall to warm the oak staircase and cast a gleam across polished furniture. The chef's epicurean offerings – supported by a lineage of fine château bottlings – give promise of the restoration of body and soul. Comprising game in season, crisp local vegetables, fruits de mer and pâtisserie baked daily, the cuisine is always a gastronomic delight. High above the ponticum and crinodendrons, the 12 spacious bedrooms afford a magnificent vista of mountains, sea and ever-changing sky. On some days, the clink of billiard balls or the clunk of croquet from the beautiful grounds are the only sounds to thread their way across the rustle of a turning page. On other days guests are hard to find, taking trips on ferries to Skye and the Inner Hebrides or discovering the landscape that has barely changed since Bonnie Prince Charlie's passage through these parts many years ago. Closed early November to Easter. Arisaig House is a Relais et Châteaux member. **Directions:** Three miles from Arisaig village on the A830 Mallaig road. Price guide: Single £80–£130; double/twin £160–£220; suite £220–£275.

SHIELDHILL–INCORPORATING THE MENNOCK VALLEY SHOOT

QUOTHQUAN, BIGGAR, LANARKSHIRE ML12 6NA
TEL: 01899 220035 FAX: 01899 221092 E-MAIL: enquiries@shieldhill.co.uk

Shieldhill, an 800 year old castle hotel offering true Scottish hospitality, is the ancestral home of the Chancellor family. The old keep, turreted roof and secret stairs are all romantic reminders of a past age. Individually designed, spacious bedrooms boast king, queen, twin or four poster beds and en suite facilities – many with Jacuzzis. The well-stocked Gun Room offers over 90 tempting malts, whilst the Oak Room with its open fires and fine panelling is the perfect place to relax. In the Chancellor Restaurant, with its glorious views to Tinto Hill and enormous fine wine glasses, guests may sample the creations of the Executive and Head Chefs, Chris and Trevor Williams. The imaginative menu served in this historic setting uses the best of fresh local produce and is complemented by the finest wine list in the south of Scotland. Shieldhill has a permanent marquee – ideal for up to 200 wedding guests and is the perfect venue for business meetings and conferences. The property has its own high-bird pheasant shoot and offers clay shooting, archery and hot-air ballooning within the hotel's grounds. Walking, horse-riding, fishing and golf are all but a stone's throw away. Glasgow 30 miles, Edinburgh 28 miles, Stirling 45 minutes and Carlisle is only an hour away. **Directions:** From Biggar take B7016 (signed Carnwath), after 2 miles turn left into Shieldhill Road. The hotel is 1½ miles on the right. Price guide: Single £75–£228; double/twin £114–£238; suite £170–£250.

KINLOCH HOUSE HOTEL

BY BLAIRGOWRIE, PERTHSHIRE PH10 6SG
TEL: 01250 884237 FAX: 01250 884333 E-MAIL: reception@kinlochhouse.com

Winner of the 1994 Johansens Country Hotel Award, Kinloch House is an elegant example of a Scottish country home built in 1840. Set in 25 acres, including a magnificent walled garden and wooded parkland grazed by Highland cattle, it offers panoramic views to the south over Marlee Loch to the Sidlaw Hills beyond. It has a grand galleried hall with an ornate glass ceiling and fine paintings and antiques in the reception rooms. Chef Bill McNicoll and his team have established Kinloch House as one of the top dining venues in Scotland and his daily changing menus are complemented by the very extensive wine list. The cocktail bar, which stocks over 155 malt whiskies, is adjacent to the conservatory and is a focal point of the hotel. In August 1997 a fully equipped Health and Fitness Centre was opened for the exclusive use of guests. The Shentall Family offer a warm personal welcome to all their guests, whether they come simply to enjoy the beauty of the area, or to take advantage of the local pursuits of golf, hill walking, fishing and shooting. For the sightseer, Glamis Castle, Scone Palace and Blair Castle are among the area's attractions. 3 AA Rosettes and 3 AA Red Stars. Closed at Christmas. **Directions:** The hotel is 3 miles west of Blairgowrie, off the A923 Dunkeld road. Price guide (including dinner): Single £98; double/twin £178–£225; suite £255.

          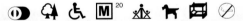

ROMAN CAMP HOTEL

CALLANDER, PERTHSHIRE FK17 8BG
TEL: 01877 330003 FAX: 01877 331533

Roman Camp Hotel, originally built in 1625 as a hunting lodge for the Dukes of Perth, takes its name from a nearby Roman encampment. Reminiscent of a French château, the hotel's turrets house a myriad of period features, including a tiny chapel, linenfold wood panelling and ornate moulded ceilings. Set on the banks of the River Teith, the hotel is surrounded by 20 acres of superb grounds including a listed walled garden where herbs and flowers are grown for the hotel. The public rooms, drawing room, sun lounge and library are characterised by grand proportions, antique furnishings and fine views over the river and gardens. The bedrooms, many of which have been refurbished, are individually and most becomingly decorated. The large oval dining room with its fine tapestries and real log fire is truly spectacular due to its vast proportions and unusual shape. Awarded two AA Red Rosettes, the delicious food is accompanied by a long and tempting wine list. Guests are welcome to fish free of charge on the private stretch of the river, while all around there are plenty of interesting walks. Callander is an ideal tourist centre for Central Scotland. Within easy reach are the Trossachs, Doune Motor Museum and Aberfoyle. Dogs are welcome by prior arrangement. **Directions:** Approaching Callander on A84, the entrance to hotel is between two cottages in Callander's main street. Price guide: Single £65–£95; double/twin from £89–£145; suite £129–£160.

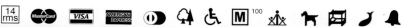

CRAIGELLACHIE HOTEL

CRAIGELLACHIE, BANFFSHIRE AB38 9SR
TEL: 01340 881204 FAX: 01340 881253 E-MAIL: info@craigellachie.com

Overlooking the River Spey, with direct access to the Speyside Walk, Craigellachie Hotel is located in the centre of Scotland's famous Malt Whisky and Castle Trails, in one of the most picturesque villages in Moray. This Victorian hotel opened in 1893 and has recently undergone a meticulous restoration to incorporate all the amenities of a first-class hotel while retaining the charm and elegance of a Scottish country house. Many of the 26 individually designed bedrooms and suites overlook the River Spey and several have a view of the local landmark, Thomas Telford's slender iron bridge. The Ben Aigan, Ben Rinnes and Livet Rooms have firmly established a good reputation for their modern Scottish cuisine with an international twist. Only fresh local produce is used in the preparation of dishes, which are always beautifully presented and accompanied by an extensive wine list. After dinner, guests can choose from a wide selection of over 400 malt whiskies in the internationally renowned Quaich Bar. Craigellachie specialises in personalised packages including traditional Scottish Christmas and New Year events. Sporting holidays can include golf with private tuition, salmon and trout fishing, deer stalking, game shooting, falconry and pony-trekking. There is also a Beauty Salon and an old-fashioned games room. **Directions:** Just off A95 between Grantown-on-Spey (24 miles) and Elgin (12 miles). Price guide: Single £80–£130; double/twin £90–£180.

KINNAIRD

KINNAIRD ESTATE, BY DUNKELD, PERTHSHIRE PH8 0LB
TEL: 01796 482440 FAX: 01796 482289 E-MAIL: enquiry@kinnairdestate.com

Offering a panoramic vista across the moors and the Tay valley, Kinnaird is surrounded by a beautiful estate of 9000 acres and is ideally located for those seeking a relaxing break or enthusiasts of outdoor pursuits. Built in 1770, the house has been privately owned by the Ward family since 1927 and was completely renovated by Mrs Constance Ward in 1990. The nine bedrooms are individually decorated with exquisite fabrics, gas log fires and opulent bathrooms. Throughout the house, rare pieces of antique furniture, china and fine paintings abound. The panelled Cedar Room is the essence of comfort, where guests may relax before enjoying gourmet cuisine in the restaurant, enhanced by hand-painted Italian frescoes. The private dining room is furnished in a stylish manner and affords magnificent views of the surrounding Perthshire countryside. The original wine cellars are stocked with an extensive range of wines, liqueurs and malt whiskies. An array of sporting facilities is available from salmon and trout fishing to bird-watching and shooting of pheasant, grouse, duck and partridge. The estate also features an all-weather tennis court and croquet and bowling lawns. During the months of January and February, the hotel will be closed on Monday, Tuesday and Wednesday. **Directions:** Two miles north of Dunkeld on A9, take B898 for 4½ miles. Price guide: Double/twin £235–£350. Special winter rates on application.

ENMORE HOTEL

MARINE PARADE, KIRN, DUNOON, ARGYLL PA23 8HH
TEL: 01369 702230 FAX: 01369 702148 E-MAIL: enmorehotel@btinternet.com

Known as the jewel on the Clyde, the waterfront town of Dunoon on the Cowal peninsula is often regarded as the gateway to the Western Highlands yet only ¾ hour from Glasgow airport. Enmore Hotel is an attractive house, built in 1785 as a summer retreat for a wealthy cotton merchant. It has since been fully restored by owners David and Angela Wilson. Pretty country wallpaper and bright fabrics characterise the bedrooms, with fluffy towelling robes and flowers among the extras. One of the bedrooms has a water bed and an invigorating whirlpool bath and another has a four-poster bed with a Jacuzzi. In the restaurant, the emphasis is on the use of fresh, local produce to create traditional Scottish dishes. Typical choices may include Arbroath smokies, haggis soup, kippers or steak served in a Drambuie and cream sauce. Chef-patron David Wilson offers a five-course table d'hôte menu each evening. Two international-standard squash courts are available. Dunoon is well equipped with recreational amenities, including bowling, tennis, sailing and a championship golf course. **Directions:** Kirn is on the A815, north-west of Dunoon (A885). A car-ferry crosses to and from Gourock across the Firth of Clyde. Price guide: Single £45–£75; double/twin £80–£138.

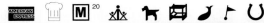

EAST KILBRIDE (Glasgow)

MACDONALD CRUTHERLAND HOUSE HOTEL

STRATHAVEN ROAD, EAST KILBRIDE G75 0QZ
TEL: 01355 577000 FAX: 01355 220855 E-MAIL: info@crutherland.macdonald–hotels.co.uk

Standing in 37 acres of garden and lush woodland just outside the attractive market town of Strathaven, which became prosperous in the middle ages because of the silk industry, the Crutherland is a fine example of a great Scottish house restored in superb style. It is extravagantly decorated and boasts every luxury whilst evoking an age of elegance. The Crutherland House was built in 1705 as a dower house for the Lady Dowager from Torrance Castle, which was situated in what is now Calderglen Country Park. After being home to many families it was converted into a hotel in 1964 and recently had a £6million refurbishment which has enhanced and added to every facility. Each of the 76 bedrooms has views over the grounds, is spacious and has all comforts from satellite television to hospitality tray and 24-hour service. The best of Scottish and international cuisine is attentively served in the attractive restaurant and less formal meals can be enjoyed in the lively Peligrino's Cafe Bar. A new leisure club features an 18-metre swimming pool, high-tech gymnasium, sauna and four beauty treatment rooms. The hotel also offers extensive business meeting facilities that include 11 conference suites. Glasgow is within easy reach and Caldergren Country Park and Strathclyde Park are worth relaxing visits. **Directions**: From M74, exit at junction 5. Take A726 to East Kilbride and follow signs for Strathaven. Price guide: Single £110; double/twin £140; suites £160.

THE BONHAM

35 DRUMSHEUGH GARDENS, EDINBURGH EH3 7RN
RESERVATIONS: 0131 623 6060 TEL: 0131 226 6050 FAX: 0131 226 6080 E-MAIL: reserve@thebonham.com

The Bonham is a fine new hotel built by the owners of Edinburgh's Channings and The Howard. A £3 million investment has converted this four-storey Victorian building – formerly a university halls of residence – into a unique and contemporary town house, equally suitable for a restful weekend or a high intensity business trip. Rich and imaginative use of colours, fabrics and furnishings have been used to create the individually designed and impressive guest rooms. In addition to superb décor, each offers access to ISDN, DDI lines with voice mail, international modem ports, direct internet access and DVD facility. Purely for pleasure, 55 channel cable TV, a mini bar and a CD system are also available. Interesting use of lighting, designed by specialist Jonathan Spiers, adds atmosphere to the beautifully furnished public areas. The hotel has a modern bistro style restaurant, offering a wide range of snacks as well as full midday and evening meals. The excellent standard of cuisine and service enjoyed by guests reflects the owner's extensive experience in restaurants. The Bonham also offers the Events Room, catering for 10 to 50 delegates. Along with its famous castle and numerous shops, Edinburgh houses Scotland's national galleries and some splendid museums. **Directions:** The hotel is situated in the city's West End. Price guide: Single: £125–£155; double/twin £158–£198; suite £225–£255.

BORTHWICK CASTLE

BORTHWICK, NORTH MIDDLETON, MIDLOTHIAN EH23 4QY
TEL: 01875 820514 FAX: 01875 821702

To the south of Edinburgh, off the A7, stands historic Borthwick Castle Hotel, a twenty minute drive from Scotland's capital. Built in 1430 by the Borthwick family, this ancient stronghold has witnessed many of the great events of Scotland's history at first hand. Notably, the safe keeping of Mary Queen of Scots following her wedding to the Earl of Bothwell and a forceful visitation by Oliver Cromwell in 1650. At Borthwick Castle there are 10 bedchambers, each with en suite facilities and five with four-poster beds. In the evening, guests dine in the magnificent setting of the candle-lit Great Hall where a four-course set menu is prepared by the chef. The cooking is traditional Scottish, serving fresh local produce. A comprehensive wine list is complemented by a fine selection of malt whiskies. While the castle caters for banquets of up to 65 guests, it especially welcomes those in search of that intimate dinner for two. In either case, the experience is unforgettable. Open from March to January 3rd. **Directions:** 12 miles south of Edinburgh on the A7. At North Middleton, follow signs for Borthwick. A private road then leads to the castle. Price guide: Single £80–£180; double/twin £115–£195.

CHANNINGS

SOUTH LEARMONTH GARDENS, EDINBURGH EH4 1EZ

RESERVATIONS: 0131 332 3232 TEL: 0131 315 2226 FAX: 0131 332 9631 E-MAIL: reserve@channings.co.uk

Channings is located on a quiet cobbled street only 10 minutes' walk from the centre of Edinburgh, with easy access to the host of shops on Princes Street and the timeless grandeur of Edinburgh Castle. Formerly five Edwardian town houses, the original features have been restored with flair and consideration and the atmosphere is like that of an exclusive country club. Guests can relax in one of the lounges with coffee or afternoon tea. For those who like to browse, the hotel has an interesting collection of antique prints, furniture, *objets d'art*, periodicals and books. Five ground floor suites provide versatile accommodation for corporate requirements, small seminars and presentations, while both the Kingsleigh Suite and oak-panelled

Library make an ideal venue for cocktail parties and private dinners. This year the recently renovated Brasserie and new Conservatory and Wine Bar were opened at Channings. Retaining its Edwardian nuances, the Brasserie is a traditional dining area offering fine cuisine for business lunches or informal dinners whilst the Conservatory and Wine Bar exude a more contemporary ambience. Closed for Christmas. **Directions:** Go north-west from Queensferry Street, over Dean Bridge on to Queensferry Road. Take 3rd turning on right down South Learmonth Avenue, turn right at end into South Learmonth Gardens. Price guide: Single £110–£130; double/twin £135–£175; four poster from £170–£195; junior suite £220–£235.

DALHOUSIE CASTLE

NR EDINBURGH, BONNYRIGG EH19 3JB

TEL: 01875 820153 FAX: 01875 821936 CONFERENCE FAX: 01875 823365 E-MAIL: enquiries@dalhousiecastle.co.uk

For over 700 years Dalhousie Castle has nestled in beautiful parkland, providing warm Scottish hospitality. Recent restoration has weaved history back into the sandstone walls whilst retaining elegant touches of the past. There are fascinating reminders of a rich and turbulent history, such as the Vaulted Dungeon Restaurant; a delightful setting in which to enjoy classical French and traditional Scottish 'Castle Cuisine'. 10 of the 29 bedrooms are historically themed and include the James VI, Robert the Bruce, Victoria and William Wallace and are complemented by the 5 en suite bedrooms in the 100 year old Lodge. The new "de Ramseia" suite houses the 500 year old "Well" in the sitting room. Five carefully renovated function rooms provide a unique setting for conferences, banquets and weddings for up to 120 guests or delegates. Extensive parking and a helipad are on site. Only 20 mins drive from Edinburgh City Centre and just 14m from the International Airport. The Castle is a Scottish Tourist Board 4 Stars classification. It is Taste of Scotland approved. A new Medieval Spa is planned for Summer 2000, to include a swim-spa bath, sauna, steam room and therapy rooms and an Orangery for "modern" dining. Activities include falconry, clay pigeon shooting and nearby golf courses plus championship course a ½hr drive away. **Directions:** From Edinburgh A7 south, through Newtongrange. Right at Jct onto B704, hotel is ¾mile. Price guide: Single £95–£125; double £118–£220.

THE HOWARD

34 GREAT KING STREET, EDINBURGH EH3 6QH
RESERVATIONS: 0131 315 2220 **TEL:** 0131 557 3500 **FAX:** 0131 557 6515 **E-MAIL:** reserve@thehoward.com

Since its conversion from private residence to hotel, The Howard has been sumptuously appointed throughout and offers a service to match the surroundings. The original character of this Georgian town house still prevails. The 15 bedrooms, including two suites, are beautifully furnished with antiques, while the drawing-room centres on an elaborate crystal chandelier. The Oval and Cumberland suite offers quiet and elegant surroundings for either meetings or private dining, accommodating 12–30 guests. The Howard is an integral part of the largest classified historical monument in Britain: Edinburgh's New Town. Having a private car park to the rear, The Howard is a superb city centre base from which to explore Edinburgh's cultural heritage, being in close proximity to such monuments as Edinburgh Castle, the Palace of Holyrood and the Royal Mile. Equally it is just minutes from much of the city's business community. **Directions:** Turn off Princes Street, into South Charlotte Street, turn left into Queen Street. Take 2nd left into Dundas Street, then 2nd right into Great King Street. The hotel is on the left. Price guide: Single £130–£165; double £245–£275; Junior suite £325.

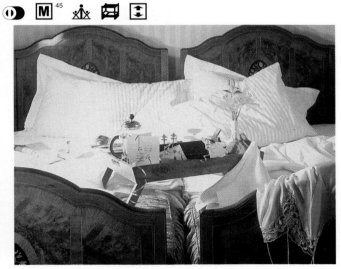

THE NORTON HOUSE HOTEL

INGLISTON, EDINBURGH EH28 8LX
TEL: 0131 333 1275 FAX: 0131 333 5305

This Victorian mansion, dating back to 1840, is a part of the Virgin Hotel Collection. Situated in 55 acres of mature parkland, Norton House combines modern comforts with elegance. The 47 en suite bedrooms are bright and spacious, with many facilities, including a video channel and satellite TV. Influenced by the best Scottish and French traditions, the menu offers a balanced choice. Moments away, through leafy woodlands, a former stable block has been converted into The Gathering Bistro and Bar, where drinks and snacks are available to family and friends. Set in a walled garden, it is an ideal venue for the barbecues which are a regular feature in the summer months. The Patio, Veranda and Usher Room lend a sense of occasion to small gatherings, while the Linlithgow Suite can cater for large-scale events such as banquets, weddings and conferences. Norton House is conveniently 1 mile from Edinburgh Airport and 6 miles from the city centre, it is also a base from which to explore the Trossachs, Borders and Lothians. **Directions:** From Edinburgh take A8 past airport and hotel is ½ mile on left. From Glasgow, follow M8 to junction 2, take the first exit off the roundabout following signs for Ratho, take the first left, then left again following the signs to Ratho, then turn left at the top of the hill where hotel is signposted. Price guide: Single £120–£190; double/twin £145–£165; suite from £180.

PRESTONFIELD HOUSE

PRIESTFIELD ROAD, EDINBURGH EH16 5UT
TEL: 0131 668 3346 FAX: 0131 668 3976 E-MAIL: prestonfield_house@compuserve.com

13 acres of landscaped gardens and a challenging golf course encompass the grounds and parklands of this fine estate. Built in 1687 for the Lord Provost of Edinburgh, Prestonfield House is one of Scotland's finest historic mansions and part of its great architectural heritage. The interior has retained many of its original 17th and 18th century features and houses the family's collection of paintings and antique furniture. An ornate ceiling forms the centrepiece in the Tapestry Room whilst the next door room is entirely panelled in 17th century Spanish leather. The spacious bedrooms are beautifully appointed and are located in either the original house or in the new extension. Every room enjoys spectacular views across the surrounding landscape and gardens which makes it hard to believe that Prestonfield is a city centre hotel, only five minutes by taxi from the centre of Edinburgh. The Old Dining Room serves a mouth-watering à la carte menu comprising traditional cuisine such as grilled turbot steak and fillet of guinea fowl. Five private rooms, varying in size, may be hired for parties, meetings or special occasions. **Directions:** Approaching Edinburgh from the south, follow the City bypass to the Sheriffhall roundabout and take the A7. At Cameron Toll roundabout go straight across and turn right at third set of traffic lights onto Priestfield Road. Price guide: Single/double/twin £125–£245; suite £350.

THE SCOTSMAN

20 NORTH BRIDGE, EDINBURGH, EH1
TEL: 0113 244 0099 FAX: 0113 234 4100 E-MAIL: Scotsman@42thecalls.co.uk

This hotel is scheduled to open at the end of the year 2000. The publishers therefore base their recommendation in this case on an inspection visit carried out before the hotel was fully operational although the reputation of their sister property, 42 The Calls in Leeds, would suggest that The Scotsman will offer the highest standards required of a Johansens property. Set in the very heart of Edinburgh, within walking distance of the new Parliament, the castle, the galleries and shops that exude the magic of this vibrant city, the Scotsman is one of the city's landmark buildings. Built at the start of the 20th century as the headquarters of The Scotsman Newspaper, this historic building is a splendid example of late Victorian Scottish architectural style. The interiors reflect the owners' love of combining the very best of the existing 'listed' public areas with fine contemporary art, on loan from a neighbouring museum. Scottish materials have been used whenever possible with the hotel having commissioned its own tweeds and contemporary materials from one of the country's finest mills. The Scotsman is enveloped by the air of a Town House Hotel and with 68 rooms and suites it offers an exceptional range of room types, sizes and styles. **Directions:** Set in the city centre, on North Bridge between Princes Street and High Street. Price guide: Double/twin £110–£175; junior suite £195; suite £225–£400.

MANSION HOUSE HOTEL

THE HAUGH, ELGIN, MORAY IV30 1AW
TEL: 01343 548811 FAX: 01343 547916

Set within tranquil grounds and overlooking the River Lossie stands the grand Mansion House Hotel. This former baronial mansion is only a minute's walk from the centre of the ancient city of Elgin. A welcoming entrance hall boasts oak-panelled walls, fresh flowers and many antique curiosities. Its majestic staircase leads to the well-appointed bedrooms, featuring four-poster beds. The Piano Lounge is an ideal place to relax before entering the elegant restaurant which has been awarded an AA Rosette. Here the cuisine is creative, delicious and beautifully presented. The "Wee Bar" is in the centre of the house, well placed next to the Snooker Room, while a unique collection of whiskies gives the name to the Still Room. A purpose-built function room, called the Haugh Room, has its own entrance, bar, cloakrooms and dance area. Guests at the hotel are invited to use the Country Club facilities which include a swimming pool, gymnasium, spa, steam room, sauna and sunbed. Complementing this is the Beauty Spot, which provides a multitude of unisex services. There is a choice of ten golf courses within ten miles, the opportunity to fish on the Spey and unlimited water sports in Findhorn Bay. **Directions:** In Elgin, turn off the main A96 road into Haugh Road. The hotel is at the end of this road by the river. Price guide: Single £75–£95; double/twin £130–£160; suite £200.

GLENSPEAN LODGE

ROY BRIDGE, BY FORT WILLIAM, INVERNESS-SHIRE PH31 4AW
TEL: 01397 712223 FAX: 01397 712660 E-MAIL: Wdgsl@aol.com

This former Victorian Hunting Lodge with a splendid conical tower stands high and serenely in the Spean Valley just north of Fort William. It is surrounded by magnificent Highland scenery, with the impressive 4,406ft mass of Ben Nevis dominating a glen of rivers and waterfalls. Glenspean stands in five acres of landscaped gardens and woodland and was extensively reconstructed and refurbished to the highest standards in 1993. Its 15 en suite bedrooms offer spectacular panoramic views of the Nevis range and each is decorated in relaxing pastel shades. Pinewood furnishings create a warm and comfortable ambience. Two bedrooms have king-size posters and the luxurious Braveheart

Suite incorporates a corner bath and lounge area. A country house atmosphere prevails in the traditionally furnished lounge and restaurant where diners can gaze out over Aonach Mor and the Spean Valley as they enjoy beautifully prepared traditional Scottish cuisine. Local activities are climbing, walking, mountaineering, sailing and skiing. Fort William, with its romantic Jacobite Steam Train, is just 20 minutes away and 13th century Inverlochy Castle just a little further onwards. **Directions**: From Fort William take the A82 road toward Inverness. At Spean Bridge turn right onto the A86 and the hotel is five miles further on. Single: £49–£53; double/twin: £80–£96; suite: £130.

CALLY PALACE HOTEL

GATEHOUSE OF FLEET, DUMFRIES & GALLOWAY DG7 2DL
TEL: 01557 814341 FAX: 01557 814522 E-MAIL: cally@cphotel.demon.co.uk

Set in over 100 acres of forest and parkland, on the edge of Robert Burns country, this 18th century country house has been restored to its former glory by the McMillan family, the proprietors since 1981. On entering the hotel, guests will initially be impressed by the grand scale of the interior. Two huge marble pillars support the original moulded ceiling of the entrance hall. All the public rooms have ornate ceilings, original marble fireplaces and fine reproduction furniture. Combine these with grand, traditional Scottish cooking and you have a hotel *par excellence*. The 56 en suite bedrooms have been individually decorated. Some are suites with a separate sitting room; others are large enough to accommodate a sitting area. An indoor leisure complex, completed in the style of the marble entrance hall, includes heated swimming pool, Jacuzzi, saunas and solarium. The hotel has an all-weather tennis court, a putting green, croquet and a lake for private fishing or boating. Also, for exclusive use of hotel guests is an 18-hole golf course, par 70, length 5,802 yards set around the lake in the 150 acre grounds. Special weekend and over-60s breaks are available out of season. Closed January. **Directions:** Sixty miles west of Carlisle, 1–1½ miles from Gatehouse of Fleet junction on the main A75 road. Price guide: (including dinner): Single £77–£120; double/twin £144–£168 per night (min 2 nights).

CARLTON GEORGE HOTEL

44 WEST GEORGE STREET, GLASGOW G2 1DH
TEL: 0141 353 6373 FAX: 0141 353 6263 E-MAIL: george@carltonhotels.co.uk

This splendid new hotel is situated in the commercial heart of Glasgow surrounded by the city's major shops, designer outlets, restaurants, galleries and the entertainment world. It is a fine modern building with a traditional style façade and is an ideal venue for leisure and business visitors. The whole of Glasgow is at hand with Queen Street Station next to the hotel, Central Station a four minute walk away, the motorway half a mile and the airport eight miles. Carlton George has 65 stylish, air-conditioned bedrooms, all with king-size beds and every modern facility. The seventh floor Windows restaurant offers panoramic views over the city. The Executive lounge is ideal for relaxation in front of the open fire and is available 24 hours a day for visitors who can take advantage of its advanced telecommunications facilities including free use of a computer with Internet link, printer, photocopy service, telephone and fax. An open bar offers complimentary hot and cold drinks and spirits. **Directions:** From Edinburgh, exit M8 at junction 18. Drive along Sauchiehall Street, then turn right onto West George Street. From Glasgow International Airport, exit eastbound M8 at junction 19 onto Bothwell Street. Turn left up Douglas Street and then onto West George Street. Price guide: Executive room £150; weekend rate £99. Breakfast £11.

GLEDDOCH HOUSE

LANGBANK, RENFREWSHIRE PA14 6YE
TEL: 01475 540711 FAX: 01475 540201

Once the home of a Glasgow shipping baron, Gleddoch House stands in 360 acres, with dramatic views across the River Clyde to Ben Lomond and the hills beyond. The individually appointed bedrooms all have en suite facilities and some have four-poster beds. Executive rooms and suites and family rooms are also available. There are also self-catering lodges on the estate. Other amenities include a range of meeting rooms to cater for up to 120 delegates theatre style. The Restaurant is renowned for its award-winning modern Scottish cuisine and is complemented by a comprehensive wine list. On the estate a series of activities are available such as golf, clay pigeon shooting, archery and off-road driving, making Gleddoch an ideal venue to host corporate events. Additionally the equestrian centre caters for all levels, from trekking to pony rides and individual tuition. Gleddoch's location offers an experience of a bygone era yet amid the sophistication that today's traveller requires. A range of short breaks, golfing packages and gourmet events are available throughout the year. Glasgow Airport is only 10 minutes drive away and the City Centre, 20 minutes. **Directions:** M8 towards Greenock; take B789 Langbank/ Houston exit. Follow signs to left and then right after ½ mile; hotel is on left. Price guide: Single £99; double/twin £150; suite £185.

DALMUNZIE HOUSE

SPITTAL O'GLENSHEE, BLAIRGOWRIE, PERTHSHIRE PH10 7QG
TEL: 01250 885224 FAX: 01250 885225 E-MAIL: dalmunzie@aol.com

Dalmunzie House is beautifully tucked away high in the Scottish Highlands, 18 miles north of Blairgowrie and 15 miles south of Braemar. Standing in its own mountainous 6,000-acre sporting estate, it is run by Simon and Alexandra Winton. Guests come to enjoy the relaxed family atmosphere which, together with unobtrusive service and attention, ensures a comfortable stay. The bedrooms are individual in character, some with antiques, others romantically set in the turrets of the house, all tastefully decorated. Delicately cooked traditional Scottish fare is created from local ingredients fresh from the hills and lochs. The restaurant now has 1 AA Rosette. The menu changes daily and meals are served in the dining room, accompanied by wines from the well-stocked cellar. Among the sporting activities available on site are golf (the 9-hole course is one of the highest in Britain) and shooting for grouse, ptarmigan and black game. Other country pursuits include river and loch fishing, clay pigeon shooting, mountain biking, stalking for red deer and pony-trekking. Glenshee Ski Centre is 6 miles away: it offers cross-country and downhill skiing. Closer to home, the hotel games room provides more sedate pastimes for all the family. Closed late November to 28 December. Special winter/skiing rates. **Directions:** Dalmunzie is on the A93 at the Spittal O'Glenshee, south of Braemar. Price guide: Single £42–£59; double/twin £64–£100.

MUCKRACH LODGE HOTEL & RESTAURANT

DULNAIN BRIDGE, BY GRANTOWN-ON-SPEY, MORAYSHIRE PH26 3LY
TEL: 01479 851257 FAX: 01479 851325 E-MAIL: muckrach.lodge@sol.co.uk

A visit to the charming Muckrach Lodge is the ideal antidote to the strains of modern urban living. Set in 10 acres of secluded gardens above the River Dulnain, visitors to Muchrach are enchanted by its views of the Cairngorms massif and the valley of the River Spey, an untouched environment for recreation and rare wildlife at the heart of the Scottish Highlands. The area is dominated by ancient forests, mountains and fragrant heather moors, making it a paradise for low-ground walkers, climbers and wild game hunters. The less energetic visitor can play golf at the magnificent links and inland courses in the vicinity. Anglers can test their skills on the Spey, one of the best salmon fishing rivers in Scotland. Nearby Aberneth Forest is home to the protected Loch Garten Osprey, as well as a host of other rare birds. The Malt Whisky Trail, Culloden Battlefield and historic castles are among the other attractions. Owners James and Dawn Macfarlane and their hospitable staff emphasise warm and personal service. The food, using only the finest, fresh, local ingredients, is truly excellent, and guests will want to spend their evenings reclining on a sofa next to a crackling log fire, sipping a dram or two of rare malt whisky from Muckrach's distinguished cellar. **Directions:** On A938, 3 miles from Granton-on-Spey, 11 miles from Aviemore. Price guide: Single £55–£75; double/twin £110–£130.

GREYWALLS

MUIRFIELD, GULLANE, EAST LOTHIAN EH31 2EG
TEL: 01620 842144 FAX: 01620 842241

Greywalls, neighbouring Muirfield golf course, the home of the Honourable Company of Edinburgh Golfers, was designed by Sir Edwin Lutyens. King Edward VII was a frequent visitor. The hotel is a beautiful crescent shaped building made of warm, honey coloured stone from the local quarry. A delightful garden, believed to be the work of Gertrude Jekyll, provides secret enclaves where guests can escape to enjoy a good book and savour the delightful scents of roses and lavender. The hotel's bedrooms, all of varying size and design, are individually furnished and include many fine antiques. Downstairs is the peaceful panelled library, Edwardian tearoom and small bar stocked with a selection of excellent brandies and whiskies. Hearty breakfasts of porridge, kippers from Achiltibuie, tasty sausages and freshly-made croissants make an ideal start to the day while dinner is an outstanding feast provided by dedicated chefs. East Lothian has excellent golf courses, including Muirfield, where The Open is held regularly. Beautiful sandy beaches are within easy reach, along with nature reserves, ruined castles, villages, market towns and stately homes. The hotel is closed from November through to March. **Directions:** On A198 from city bypass which links to the M8, M9 and M90. Price guide: Single £100; double/twin £175–£205.

BUNCHREW HOUSE HOTEL

INVERNESS, SCOTLAND IV3 8TA

TEL: 01463 234917 FAX: 01463 710620 E-MAIL: welcome@bunchrew–inverness.co.uk

This splendid 17th century Scottish mansion, owned by Graham and Janet Cross, is set amidst 20 acres of landscaped gardens and woodlands on the shores of the Beauly Firth. Guests can enjoy breathtaking views of Ben Wyvis and the Black Isle, while just yards from the house the sea laps at the garden walls. Bunchrew has been carefully restored to preserve its heritage, while still giving its guests the highest standards of comfort and convenience. A continual schedule of refurbishment is on-going. The luxury suites are beautifully furnished and decorated to enhance their natural features. The elegant panelled drawing room is the ideal place to relax at any time, while during the winter log fires lend it an added appeal which has given the hotel 4 Star status. In the candle-lit restaurant the traditional cuisine includes prime Scottish beef, fresh lobster and langoustines, locally caught game and venison and freshly grown vegetables which has been rewarded with one AA Rosette. A carefully chosen wine list complements the menu. Local places of interest include Cawdor Castle, Loch Ness, Castle Urquhart and a number of beautiful glens. For those who enjoy sport there is skiing at nearby Aviemore, sailing, cruising and golf. **Directions:** From Inverness follow signs to Beauly, Dingwall on the A862. One mile from the outskirts of Inverness the entrance to Bunchrew House is on the right. Price guide: Single £70–£120; double/twin £90–£160; suites £115–£175.

CULLODEN HOUSE HOTEL

INVERNESS, INVERNESS-SHIRE IV2 7BZ

TEL: 01463 790461 FAX: 01463 792181 E-MAIL: info@cullodenhouse.co.uk

A majestic circular drive leads to the splendour of this handsome Georgian mansion, battle headquarters of Bonnie Prince Charlie 253 years ago. Three miles from Inverness this handsome Palladian country house stands in 40 acres of beautiful gardens and peaceful parkland roamed by roe deer. Princes past and present and guests from throughout the world have enjoyed the hotel's ambience and hospitality. Rich furnishings, sparkling chandeliers, impressive Adam fireplaces and ornate plaster reliefs add to the grandness of the hotel's luxurious, high-ceilinged rooms. The bedrooms are appointed to the highest standard many having four-poster beds and Jacuzzis. Four non-smoking suites are in the Pavilion Annex which overlooks

a three-acre walled garden and two in the newly renovated West Pavilion. In the Dining Room guests can savour superb cuisine prepared by chef Michael Simpson, who trained at the Gleneagles Hotel and the Hamburg Conference Centre. There is an outdoor tennis court and indoor sauna. Shooting, fishing and pony-trekking can be arranged, while nearby are Cawdor Castle, the Clava Cairns Bronze Age burial ground and Culloden battlefield. AA 4 stars and 2 Rosettes, Scottish Tourist Board 4 stars. From USA Toll Free Fax/Phone 0800 980 4561 **Directions:** Take the A96 going east from Inverness and turn right to Culloden. Price guide: Single £135–£145; double/twin £190–£235; suite: £250–£270.

SWALLOW KINGSMILLS HOTEL

CULCABOCK ROAD, INVERNESS, INVERNESS-SHIRE IV2 3LP
TEL: 01463 237166 FAX: 01463 225208 E-MAIL: inverness@swallow–hotels.co.uk

Built in the capital of The Highlands in 1785, this historic 4 star hotel has been extended and it offers guests both comfort and elegance. It is only a mile from the town centre, in three acres of gardens, adjacent to Inverness Golf Course. There is a choice of attractively appointed bedrooms, all with modern amenities. In addition to the standard rooms, there are 7 beautifully furnished suite-style rooms, also family rooms with bunk beds and 6 self-catering villas. The Inglis Restaurant is highly regarded both locally and by guests, with the finest of Scottish ingredients put to succulent and inventive use by the hotel's chefs. The Leisure Club incorporates a heated swimming pool, spa bath, steam cabin, sauna, sunbeds, mini-gym and pitch-and-putt. Business guests have the perfect excuse for enjoying the comforts of the Kingsmills, with 6 function suites for up to 100 people. Throughout the year exceptionally good value is offered by special breaks which include seasonal attractions. Golf, fishing, skiing, riding and pony-trekking can all be enjoyed nearby and arranged as part of an activity holiday. Christmas, Easter and New Year packages are available. The Kingsmills Hotel is well placed for visiting the Highlands, Loch Ness, Culloden battlefield and Cawdor Castle. **Directions:** Turn left off A9 signed Kingsmills and Culcabock. Turn right at first roundabout, left at second. Hotel is on left just past golf course. Price guide: Single £115–£140; double/twin £165–£195; suite £195.

PITTODRIE HOUSE

CHAPEL OF GARIOCH, BY INVERURIE, ABERDEENSHIRE AB51 5HS
TEL: 01467 681444 FAX: 01467 681648 US TOLL FREE: 1 800 365 6537 E-MAIL: info@pittodrie.macdonald–hotels.co.uk

The dramatic landscape of Bennachie and the Eastern Edge of the Highlands surround this 17th century mansion. Pittodrie House, a family home, is renowned for its excellent standards of comfort and service and each visitor is treated as an important guest. The hotel has retained many of its original features and the public rooms are adorned with the family's paintings and antiques; evoking the charming ambience of a country house. The en suite bedrooms offer a full range of facilities including satellite television, radio and telephones. The comfort of the individually furnished bedrooms are enhanced by soft fabrics and thoughtful additions such as fresh flowers and courtesy trays. Guests can relax in front of the roaring log fires in the Drawing Room and Library or savour one of the ninety malt whiskies in the cosy Bar. The daily changing menu features the best of local seasonal produce including game, smoked fish and Aberdeen Angus beef which has resulted in an AA Rosette. Specialising in clarets and New World vintages, the wine list is extensive. Guests may enjoy playing on the hotel's own squash courts, pony-trekking and fishing for salmon or trout on the Dee, Don and Deveron rivers. The Castle and Whisky Trails are enjoyed by those wishing to explore the Scottish countryside. **Directions:** From Aberdeen, take A96 to Inverness. 2 miles past Inverurie, turn left and follow signs to Chapel of Garioch. Price guide: Single £120; double/twin £140; suite £160.

FLODIGARRY COUNTRY HOUSE HOTEL

STAFFIN, ISLE OF SKYE IV51 9HZ
TEL: 01470 552203 FAX: 01470 552301

This imposing 19th century mansion stands amidst the dramatic scenery of north-east Skye where the Golden Eagle is a frequent visitor and otters inhabit the shoreline. It has a panoramic vista across the waters of Staffin Bay to the Torridon mountains and the towering pinnacles of the Quiraing provide a remarkable skyline to the views inland. Set in five acres of gardens and woodland, Flodigarry has strong Jacobite associations. It was built in 1895 as a private house by Alexander Livingston MacDonald on a site adjacent to the cottage where his legendary ancestor, Flora MacDonald, once lived. Flora, who helped Bonnie Prince Charlie escape in 1746 following the Battle of Culloden, lived in the cottage from 1751–59. The cottage has been sympathetically renovated to provide seven self-contained bedrooms each furnished in period style. All bedrooms in the hotel are well-appointed and enjoy splendid sea or mountain views. The award-winning highland hospitality of Flodigarry extends to its cuisine which comprises traditional Scottish dishes and other tempting specialities. All bedrooms, the restaurant and conservatory are no smoking areas. Open all year. Explore the countryside with its unspoilt landscapes and abundant wildlife and visit Duntulm and Dunvegan Castles, Flora MacDonald's monument and Staffin Museum, with its remarkable collection of fossils. **Directions:** Flodigarry is just off A855 about 20 miles from Portree. Price guide: Single £49–£59; double/twin £98–150.

EDNAM HOUSE HOTEL

BRIDGE STREET, KELSO, ROXBURGHSHIRE TD5 7HT
TEL: 01573 224168 FAX: 01573 226319

Overlooking the River Tweed, in 3 acres of gardens, Ednam House is one of the region's finest examples of Georgian architecture. This undulating, pastoral countryside was immortalised by Sir Walter Scott. Ednam House has been owned and managed by the Brooks family for over 70 years, spanning four generations. Although the grandiose splendour may seem formal, the warm, easy-going atmosphere is all-pervasive. The lounges and bars are comfortably furnished and command scenic views of the river and grounds. All 32 bedrooms are en suite, individually decorated and well equipped. In the elegant dining room which overlooks the river, a blend of traditional and creative Scottish cuisine, using fresh local produce, is served. The wine list is very interesting and reasonably priced. Ednam House is extremely popular with fishermen, the Borders being renowned for its salmon and trout. Other field sports such as stalking, hunting and shooting can be arranged as can riding, golfing and cycling. Local landmarks include the abbeys of Kelso, Melrose, Jedburgh and Dryburgh. Closed Christmas and New Year. **Directions:** From the south, reach Kelso via A698; from the north, via A68. Hotel is just off market square by the river. Price guide: Single from £58; double/twin £76–£107.

THE ROXBURGHE HOTEL & GOLF COURSE

KELSO, ROXBURGHSHIRE TD5 8JZ
TEL: 01573 450331 FAX: 01573 450611 E-MAIL: sunlaws.roxgc@virgin.net

Converted by its owners, the Duke and Duchess of Roxburghe, into a luxury hotel of character and charm, The Roxburghe is situated in over 200 acres of rolling grounds on the bank of the River Teviot. There are 22 bedrooms, including four poster rooms and suites, and like the spacious reception rooms, they are furnished with care and elegance. The menu, which is changed daily, reflects the hotel's position at the source of some of Britain's finest fish, meat and game – salmon and trout from the waters of the Tweed, or grouse, pheasant and venison from the Roxburghe estate – complemented with wines from the Duke's own cellar. Fine whiskies are served in the Library Bar, with its log fire and leather-bound tomes. The Beauty Clinique *Elixir* brings to guests the régimes of Decleor, Paris. Surrounding the hotel is the magnificent Roxburghe Golf Course, designed by Dave Thomas. This parkland course is the only championship standard golf course in the Scottish Borders. A full sporting programme can be arranged, including fly and coarse fishing, and falconry. The shooting school offers tuition in game and clay shooting. Seven great country houses are within easy reach including Floors Castle, the home of the Duke and Duchess of Roxburghe. **Directions:** The hotel is at Heiton, just off the A698 Kelso–Jedburgh road. Price guide: Single £110; double/twin £165; 4-poster £205; suite £255.

ARDANAISEIG

KILCHRENAN BY TAYNUILT, ARGYLL PA35 1HE
TEL: 01866 833333 FAX: 01866 833222

This romantic small luxury hotel, built in 1834, stands alone in a setting of almost surreal natural beauty at the foot of Ben Cruachan. Directly overlooking Loch Awe and surrounded by wild wooded gardens, Ardanaiseig is evocative of the romance and history of the Highlands. Skilful restoration has ensured that this lovely old mansion has changed little since it was built. The elegant drawing room has log fires, bowls of fresh flowers, superb antiques, handsome paintings and marvellous views of the islands in the Loch and of faraway mountains. The traditional library, sharing this outlook, is ideal for postprandial digestifs. The charming bedrooms are peaceful, appropriate to the era of the house, yet equipped thoughtfully with all comforts. True Scottish hospitality is the philosophy of the Ardanaiseig Restaurant, renowned for its inspired use of fresh produce from the Western Highlands. The wine list is magnificent. Artistic guests enjoy the famous 100 acre Ardanaiseig gardens and nature reserve, filled with exotic shrubs and trees brought back from the Himalayas over the years. Brilliant rhododendrons and azaleas add a riot of colour. The estate also offers fishing, boating, tennis and croquet (snooker in the evenings) and exhilarating hill or lochside walks. **Directions:** Reaching Taynuilt on A85, take B845 to Kilchrenan. Price guide: Single £80–£119; double/twin £108–£230.

KILDRUMMY CASTLE HOTEL

KILDRUMMY, BY ALFORD, ABERDEENSHIRE AB33 8RA
TEL: 019755 71288 FAX: 019755 71345

In the heart of Donside near to the renowned Kildrummy Castle Gardens and overlooking the ruins of the original 13th century castle from which it takes its name, Kildrummy Castle Hotel offers a rare opportunity to enjoy the style and elegance of a bygone era combined with all the modern comforts of a first-class hotel. Recent improvements have not detracted from the turn-of-the century interior, featuring the original wall tapestries and oak-panelled walls and high ceilings. The bedrooms, some with four-poster beds, all have en suite bathrooms. All have been refurbished recently to a high standard. The hotel restaurant was runner-up for Johansens 1996 Restaurant Award. Chef Kenneth White prepares excellent menus using regional produce that includes local game and both fish and shellfish from the Moray Firth. Kildrummy Castle is ideally located for touring Royal Deeside and Balmoral, the Spey Valley, Aberdeen and Inverness, while the surrounding Grampian region has more castles than any other part of Scotland – 8 of the National Trust for Scotland's finest properties are within an hour's drive of the hotel. Also within an hour's drive are more than 20 golf courses. Visitors can discover the 'Scotch Whisky Trail' and enjoy a tour of some of Scotland's most famous distilleries. **Directions:** Off the A97 Ballater/Huntly road, 35 miles west of Aberdeen. Price guide: Single £80–£85; double/twin £130–£170.

CROMLIX HOUSE

KINBUCK, BY DUNBLANE, PERTHSHIRE FK15 9JT
TEL: 01786 822125 FAX: 01786 825450 E-MAIL: reservations@cromlixhouse.com

Set in a 2,000 acre estate in the heart of Perthshire, just off the A9, the STB 5 Star Cromlix House is a rare and relaxing retreat. Built as a family home in 1874, much of the house remains unchanged including many fine antiques acquired over the generations. Proprietors David and Ailsa Assenti are proud of their tradition of country house hospitality. The individually designed bedrooms and spacious suites have been redecorated with period fabrics to enhance the character and fine furniture whilst retaining the essential feeling of a much loved home. Unpretentious, restful and most welcoming, the large public rooms have open fires. In the restaurant, the finest local produce is used. Cromlix is an ideal venue for small exclusive conferences and business meetings. The private Chapel is a unique feature and perfect for weddings. Extensive sporting and leisure facilities include trout and salmon fishing and game shooting in season. There are several challenging golf courses within easy reach including Gleneagles, Rosemount, Carnoustie and St Andrews. The location is ideal for touring the Southern Highlands, with Edinburgh and Glasgow only an hour away. **Directions:** Cromlix House lies four miles north of Dunblane, north of Kinbuck on B8033 and four miles south of Braco. Price guide: Single £100–£170; double/twin £185–£225; suite with private sitting room £215–£310.

INVER LODGE HOTEL

LOCHINVER, SUTHERLAND IV27 4LU
TEL: 01571 844496 FAX: 01571 844395 E-MAIL: inverlodge@compuserve.com

The Highlands have a unique appeal for those who appreciate country pursuits and magnificent landscapes. The Inver Lodge Hotel not only meets these criteria, but also offers luxurious accommodation. From Inverness Airport it is two hours drive through dramatic Highland landscapes, the Lodge stands above the fishing village of Lochinver, with spectacular views across Inver Loch to the Western Isles. A warm welcome awaits new arrivals in the reception hall and the Residents Lounge has a big fireplace and comfortable chairs. The spacious bedrooms, each named after a loch or mountain, have magnificent views. Beautifully decorated with period furniture and providing every modern amenity, they have extra big beds, coffee tables and an aura of serenity. The handsome Cocktail Bar stocks the Lodge's own malt whisky. In the traditional Dining Room, discerning guests feast on local fish, lobsters, wild salmon and Highland beef and imbibe excellent wines. The Lodge has 10 rods on local rivers and access to deer forests. Ornithologists study innumerable wild birds, while country lovers explore the waterfalls, subtropical gardens and castles. Children enjoy the loch's sandy beach. Golf, climbing and snooker provide other diversions. **Directions:** A9 north to Dornoch, left onto A949, then A837 to Lochinver. Price guide: Single £80–£120; double/twin £120–£200.

KIRROUGHTREE HOUSE

NEWTON STEWART, WIGTOWNSHIRE DG8 6AN
TEL: 01671 402141 FAX: 01671 402425

Winner of the Johansens Most Excellent Service Award 1996, Kirroughtree House is situated in the foothills of the Cairnsmore of Fleet, on the edge of Galloway Forest Park. The hotel stands in eight acres of landscaped gardens, where guests can relax and linger over the spectacular views. This striking mansion was built by the Heron family in 1719 and the oak-panelled lounge with open fireplace reflects the style of that period. From the lounge rises the original staircase, from which Robert Burns often recited his poems. Each bedroom is well furnished – guests may choose to spend the night in one of the hotel's spacious de luxe bedrooms with spectacular views over the surrounding countryside. Many guests are attracted by Kirroughtree's culinary reputation – only the finest produce is used to create meals of originality and finesse. This is a good venue for small conferences. Pitch-and-putt, lawn tennis and croquet can be enjoyed in the grounds. Residents can play golf on the many local courses and also have use of our sister hotel's exclusive 18-hole course at Gatehouse of Fleet. Trout and salmon fishing can be arranged nearby, as can rough shooting and deer stalking during the season. Closed 3 January to mid February. **Directions:** The hotel is signposted one mile outside Newton Stewart on the A75. Price guide: Single £65–£90; double/twin £120–£130; suite £150.

KNIPOCH HOTEL

BY OBAN, ARGYLL PA34 4QT
TEL: 01852 316251 FAX: 01852 316249 E-MAIL: reception@knipochhotel.co.uk

Six miles south of Oban lies Knipoch, an elegant Georgian building with a history dating from 1500, set halfway along the shore of Loch Feochan with an arm of the sea stretching 4 miles inland. Wildlife is abundant in this area – rare birds of prey, deer and otters can often be seen. The hotel is owned and personally run by the Craig family, who go out of their way to ensure that their guests enjoy their stay. All the bedrooms are fully-equipped and offer splendid views either of the loch or the surrounding hills. High standards of cooking are proudly maintained here. The daily menu features many Scottish specialities, prepared with imaginative flair. Not only is the choice of wines extensive – there are over 350 labels – but the list is informative too. Guests are given a copy to peruse at leisure rather than to scan hurriedly before ordering. In addition, the bar stocks a wide range of malt whiskies. Sporting activities available locally include fishing, sailing, yachting, golf, tennis, pony-trekking and skiing. A traditional Scottish event, the Oban Highland Games, is particularly renowned for its solo piping competition. The Knipoch Hotel makes a good base from which to visit the Western Isles and explore the spectacular scenery of the area. Closed mid-December to mid-February. **Directions:** On the A816, 6 miles south of Oban. Price guide: Single £40–£75; double/twin £80–£154; suite £195–£250

CRINGLETIE HOUSE HOTEL

PEEBLES EH45 8PL
TEL: 01721 730233 FAX: 01721 730244 E-MAIL: cringletie@wrensgroup.com

This distinguished mansion, turreted in the Scottish baronial style, stands in 28 acres of beautifully maintained gardens and woodland. Designed by Scottish architect David Bryce, Cringletie was built in 1861 for the Wolfe Murray family, whose ancestor, Colonel Alexander Murray, accepted the surrender of Quebec after General Wolfe was killed. All of the bedrooms have fine views and many have been redesigned with attractively co-ordinated curtains and furnishings. The splendid panelled lounge has an impressive carved oak and marble fireplace, a painted ceiling and many oil portraits. The imaginative cooking, prepared with flair, attracts consistently good reports including the Border Chef of the Year award in 1998.

Opera recitals are held in the 2-acre walled garden during the summer and the range and quality of fruit and vegetables grown make this the only Scottish garden recommended in Geraldene Holt's *The Gourmet Garden*. On-site facilities include a new hard tennis court, croquet lawn and putting green. Golf can be played at Peebles and fishing is available by permit on the River Tweed. Cringletie, the winner of the AA Country and Care award 1998 is a good base from which to discover the rich historic and cultural heritage of the Borders and is convenient for visiting Edinburgh. **Directions:** The hotel is on the A703 Peebles–Edinburgh road, $2^{1}/_{2}$ miles from Peebles. Price guide: Single £75; double/twin £130–£160.

BALLATHIE HOUSE HOTEL

KINCLAVEN, STANLEY, PERTHSHIRE PH1 4QN
TEL: 01250 883268 FAX: 01250 883396 E-MAIL: email@ballathiehousehotel.com

Set in an estate overlooking the River Tay near Perth, Ballathie House Hotel offers Scottish hospitality in a house of character and distinction. Dating from 1850, this mansion has a French baronial façade and handsome interiors. Overlooking lawns which slope down to the riverside, the drawing room is an ideal place to relax with coffee and the papers, or to enjoy a malt whisky after dinner. The premier bedrooms are large and elegant, while the standard rooms are designed in a cosy, cottage style. On the ground floor there are several bedrooms suitable for guests with disabilities. Local ingredients such as Tay salmon, Scottish beef, seafood and piquant soft fruits are used by chef Kevin MacGillivray winner of the title Scottish "Chef of the Year" 1999–2000, to create menus catering for all tastes. The hotel has two rosettes for fine Scottish cuisine. Activities available on the estate include salmon fishing, river walks, tennis, croquet and putting. The Sporting Lodge adjacent to the main house is designed to accommodate sporting parties. The area has many good golf courses. Perth, Blairgowrie and Edinburgh are within an hour's drive. STB 4 star. Dogs in certain rooms only. **Directions:** From the A93 at Beech Hedges, signposted for Kinclaven and Ballathie, or off the A9, 2 miles north of Perth, take the Stanley Road. The hotel is 8 miles north of Perth. Price guide: Single £65–£120; double/twin £130–£200; suite £180–£220.

HUNTINGTOWER HOTEL

CRIEFF ROAD, PERTH, SCOTLAND PH1 3JT
TEL: 01738 583771 FAX: 01738 583777

When staying at this splendid country house, guests soon forget that they are just 5 minutes from the busy city of Perth. Once the home of wealthy mill owners and mentioned in Sir Walter Scott's Ivanhoe, it has an ambience of gracious living. There is a delightful burn in the four acre grounds which surround the hotel and ensure privacy and tranquillity, so valued by people today. Huntingtower has splendid Victorian interiors, with high ceilings and elaborate panelling. Tartan carpeting brightens the entrance hall and staircase. The bedrooms are also evocative of its past, with elaborate chintz drapes and period furniture. They are all individually decorated and have well-designed bathrooms. The handsome bar is well-stocked, an ideal rendezvous for drinks at the end of a long day. The Restaurant is quite formal, but the menu covers a spectrum of traditional Scottish dishes through to French regional specialities. Superb wines are listed. The charming Conservatory, overlooking the gardens, is a more relaxed brasserie restaurant. The Huntingtower Suite, opening onto the gardens, is ideal for corporate functions or private celebrations. Marvellous golf, shooting and fishing are nearby and it is easy to travel to Edinburgh, Glasgow and St Andrews or set off to tour the Highlands. **Directions:** The hotel is west of Perth, 500 yards off the A9 dual carriageway. Price guide: Single £85–£90; double/twin £99–£129; suite £125.

KINFAUNS CASTLE

NR PERTH, PERTHSHIRE PH2 7JZ

TEL: 01738 620777 FAX: 01738 620778 E-MAIL: email@kinfaunscastle.co.uk

Set within 26 acres of parkland and landscaped gardens, Kinfauns Castle stands on a promontory overlooking the River Tay. The castle, built by Lord Gray in the 1820s is located immediately off the A90 Dundee Road, just two miles from Perth. The new Directors, Mr and Mrs James A. Smith, made a commitment to the restoration of the wonderful building, the historical seat of Lord Gray. James Smith was until recently Vice-President of Central Asia for Hilton International. The 16 suites and rooms are individually decorated and reflect the quality, comfort and ambience one expects of a luxury country house. The public rooms feature the rich Victorian décor which has survived the Castle's 70 years as a hikers' hotel. One particular lounge sports a William Morris hunting scene paper whilst another contains a Dragon Boat Bar, brought back from Taipai by the present owner. Jeremy Wares, Scottish Restaurant Chef of the Year 99, leads an award-winning brigade serving an exquisite fusion of modern Scottish and classical French cuisine produced from the finest locally-sourced ingredients. The area abounds with castles and sites of historic interest: Scone Palace and Glamis Castle are only a few miles away. Salmon fishing on the River Tay, golf, shooting and riding are easily available. **Directions:** The hotel is two miles from Perth on the A90 Dundee Road. Price guide: Single £110–£140; double £170–£250; suite £250–£280.

PINE TREES HOTEL

STRATHVIEW TERRACE, PITLOCHRY, PERTHSHIRE PH16 5QR
TEL: 01796 472121 FAX: 01796 472460 E-MAIL: info@pinetrees–hotel.demon.co.uk

Pine Trees has an established reputation for its standards of hospitality amid beautiful Highlands scenery. Historic sites and castles abound in the surrounding countryside and the Pass of Killiecrankie – famed for the battle in 1689 – lies just a few miles to the north. The hotel was built as a family mansion in 1892, enclosed by 10 acres of mature grounds that include a putting green. The public rooms are attractive and furnished in country house style. Each of the 19 en suite bedrooms is spacious and equipped with every comfort. Pine Trees is known for its cuisine. In the AA Rosette awarded Garden Restaurant, where Chef Lesley Ferguson provides expertly prepared menus, the freshest of local produce is the basis of all the meals. The hotel has good facilities for weddings and conferences. Exclusive hire of the entire building can be arranged out of season. Guests can use our courtesy transport to and from Pitlochry's Festival Theatre and also within walking distance is an 18-hole golf course and the salmon run at Loch Faskally. Fishing, horse-riding and shooting can be arranged. **Directions:** From the A9 out of Perth take the A924 to Pitlochry. Pine Trees is at the north end of the town. Price guide: Single £56–£60; double/twin £72–£124.

FERNHILL HOTEL

HEUGH ROAD, PORTPATRICK, WIGTOWNSHIRE DG9 8TD
TEL: 01776 810220 FAX: 01776 810596 E-MAIL: *fernhill@portpatrick.demon.co.uk*

Modern civilisation has left almost untouched a rich store of beauty and relics of the past in this half-forgotten corner of Scotland where the Gulf Stream warmly washes the cliffs and sandy beaches giving a gentle climate in which frost is rare. Historic Portpatrick, with its snug little fishing and yacht harbour, was, until the mid 19th century, the main ferry port to Northern Ireland and today is justifiably the jewel in the crown of Galloway. The Fernhill Hotel stands in secluded grounds and subtropical gardens just above the village. It is owned and run by the McMillan family who are proud of its four-star rating, Rosetted conservatory restaurant and stunning panoramic views over the sea. The hotel is particularly famed for its cuisine. Chef John Henry's menus change daily but always offer the house speciality of delicious, fresh Mull of Galloway lobster, caught by local fishermen. Guests can relax and enjoy true Scottish hospitality in two comfortable lounges and an attractive bar which also serves less formal meals. All 20 en suite bedrooms are well equipped with every facility and comfort. The challenging cliff-top Portpatrick (Dunskey) Golf Course is a five minutes stroll away, there are four internationally famous gardens within a 15 miles radius and deep sea angling, game fishing, shooting, pony trekking and a variety of water sports are nearby. **Directions:** From Dumfries, take A75 to Stranraer and then A77 south. Price guide: Single £58–£90; double/twin £85–£110.

ST ANDREWS GOLF HOTEL

40 THE SCORES, ST ANDREWS, FIFE KY16 9AS
TEL: 01334 472611 FAX: 01334 472188 E-MAIL: thegolfhotel@standrews.co.uk

St Andrews Golf Hotel stands tall and handsomely on the coast road of the old town with commanding views of St Andrews Bay and the vast, world famous links. Fashioned from two solid, grey stone Victorian houses, the hotel is family owned and extends friendly and personal true Scottish hospitality to guests. The interior décor of warm browns and deep greens, rich oak panelling and beautifully framed scenic and golfing prints enhance the comfortable ambience. All 22 luxuriously draped bedrooms are individually designed and have every modern amenity. Most enjoy panoramic sea views. The elegant bar opens onto a patio and small garden, an ideal place for pre-dinner apéritifs prior to sampling the cuisine provided by chef Colin Masson in his award-winning restaurant which now has 2 AA Rosettes. Featured on the menus are the finest quality Scottish meats, pheasant and East Neuk seafood. More casual eating can be enjoyed throughout the day in the bistro bar. St Andrews is not only famous for its golf courses but also for its early 15th century university, predated in Britain only by Oxford and Cambridge and the ruined splendour of a 15th century cathedral and 14th century castle. Among the many places of interest nearby are the British Golf Museum and Crail Harbour. **Directions:** From the M90, exit at junction 8 and take the A91 east to St Andrews. Price guide: Single £85–£92.50; double/twin £140–£155; suites £175.

DRYBURGH ABBEY HOTEL

ST BOSWELLS, MELROSE, SCOTTISH BORDERS TD6 0RQ
TEL: 01835 822261 FAX: 01835 823945 E-MAIL: enquiries@dryburgh.co.uk

This Scottish country house, set on the banks of the Tweed, overlooks the magnificent Borders countryside and landscape. Situated next to the historic ruins from which it takes its name, the Dryburgh Abbey Hotel is furnished with a touch of elegance. There are two cosy lounges, one for non-smokers, with wooden coffee tables and large plush armchairs; perfect for reclining and relaxing. The spacious bedrooms have private bathrooms and offer every modern amenity. The formal Tweed Restaurant enjoys a tranquil atmosphere, serving inspired recipes using local produce, such as haggis in a whisky cream sauce whilst the bistro-style Courtyard Bar is the height of conviviality. The wine list has been compiled as a complement to the cuisine, with the 150 wines chosen personally by the owner. Guests will enjoy the luxurious indoor pool. There are several outdoor pursuits including shooting, salmon and trout fishing or playing golf at one of the nearby courses. Kelso Abbey, Traquair House and the statue of Wallace are within easy reach. **Directions:** Take the A68 from Edinburgh to St Boswells then turn onto the B6404. Continue on this road for two miles then turn left onto the B6356 signposted Scott's view and Earlston. The hotel entrance is approximately 2 miles further on this road. Price guide: Single £63.50–£103.50; double/twin £60–£80; suite £80–£103.50.

STIRLING HIGHLAND HOTEL

SPITTAL STREET, STIRLING FK8 1DU
TEL: 01786 272727 FAX: 01786 272829

With its tall tower, turret, balustrades and historic façade the Stirling Highland Hotel is a magnificent and welcoming sight in the heart of Scotland's ancient capital. Close by is the massive and imposing 15th century castle which overlooks the battlefield of Bannockburn where Robert the Bruce put the English, under Edward II, to flight. The hotel embraces an atmosphere of true Scottish spirit, hospitality and tradition. A Grade A listed building, dating back to 1854, it was formerly the High School of Stirling. It has been meticulously transformed and refurbished with many of the original features retained alongside the installation of every modern convenience. A grand entrance sweeps guests into a superb and stylish hotel to enjoy excellent accommodation, cuisine and service. All bedrooms and suites are furnished and equipped to a high standard, the lounge areas are beautifully appointed and relaxing and there is a choice of cuisine in the sophisticated, wood-panelled Scholars Restaurant or in the lively atmosphere of Rizzios, an Italian themed restaurant. A well-equipped leisure club enables guests to exercise in a 17-metre swimming pool, gymnasium or squash court, or to relax in a sauna, spa, or solarium. **Directions:** Stirling is reached from Glasgow via the A80 and M80 and from Edinburgh direct on the M9. Price guide (room only): Single £104; double/twin £140.

CORSEWALL LIGHTHOUSE HOTEL

STRANRAER, SCOTLAND DG9 OQG
TEL: 01776 853220 FAX: 01776 854231

The charm and romance of a 19th century lighthouse have been combined with every modern day comfort to create this unique and delightful luxury hotel and restaurant. Remaining a listed building of national importance, with a light still beaming a warning for ships approaching the mouth of Loch Ryan, the Corsewall Lighthouse Hotel promises its guests the ultimate in peace and relaxation. Extensive restorations have taken place to provide eight charming bedrooms, all equipped with a full range of amenities. The restaurant features flickering candlelight and a blazing log fire and the menu caters for a wide variety of tastes including local beef, lamb, seafood and vegetarian dishes. Savour a plump breast of duck, gently pan-fried and masked in peach and cherry sauce, or perhaps one of the Corsewall House specialities such as roasted loin of lamb, scented with garlic and rosemary and served with a rich pickled walnut sauce. Within the hotel's 20-acre grounds and further afield can be found some of Scotland's most spectacular coastline, along with unique rock forms, seals, birds, deer and a wide variety of flora. Outdoor activities available by arrangement include golf, horse-riding, windsurfing, sailing and day trips to Ireland. **Directions:** The hotel is located 15 minutes from Stranraer. Take A718 signposted to Kirkcolm and then the B738 to Corsewall and the Lighthouse. Price guide: Single £75–£210; Double/twin £70–£220.

STRATHPEFFER (Contin)

COUL HOUSE HOTEL

CONTIN, BY STRATHPEFFER, ROSS-SHIRE IV14 9EY
TEL: 01997 421487 FAX: 01997 421945

Coul House is an attractive country house in secluded grounds with magnificent, uninterrupted views. Owners Martyn and Ann Hill have a reputation for their friendly, personal service and high standards, both of food and accommodation. Refurbishments of the decor and furnishings have enhanced the lovely interiors. All bedrooms are en suite, individually designed and each has a colour television, clock radio, trouser press, hairdryer, iron and hospitality tray. One has a four-poster bed. There are three elegant lounges with log burning fires, a cocktail bar and a Kitchen Bar where there is regular evening entertainment. A piper entertains during summer months. In the dining room guests can savour "Taste of Scotland"

cuisine such as fresh salmon and venison or eat in the new Tartan Bistro. Conferences and private functions can be accommodated. A cruise on Loch Ness or a sailing trip to to the Summer Isles can be arranged while nearby are Cawdor Castle, Culloden battlefield, fishing, pony-trekking, shooting and golf. The hotel has its own 9 hole pitch and putt course. Numerous routes lead to lovely glens.
Directions: From the south, bypassing Inverness, continue on A9 over Moray Firth Bridge and after 5 miles take second exit at roundabout onto A835. Follow to Contin. The hotel is 1/2 mile along a private drive to the right. Price guide (including dinner): Single £66–£94; double/twin £102–£182; suite £138–£206.

466

MANSFIELD HOUSE HOTEL

SCOTSBURN ROAD, TAIN, ROSS-SHIRE IV19 1PR

TEL: 01862 892052 FAX: 01862 892260 US TOLL FREE: 1 800 365 6537 E-MAIL: mansfield@cali.co.uk

Built in the 1870s, this Victorian mansion has won many accolades and enjoys an excellent reputation for its high standards of service and cordial atmosphere. Many of the hotel's original features have been retained such as the pine panelling and ornate plaster ceilings. All the bedrooms have recently been refurbished and offer every modern amenity whilst the array of thoughtful extras include complimentary sherry. Mansfield House Hotel provides a diverse choice of restaurants with a bar-style bistro serving traditional Scottish food in a relaxed environment and formal dining in the à la carte restaurant which now has 2 AA Rosettes. The international dishes comprise the best of fresh regional produce and are popular with the locals. Those seeking a postprandial drink may try one of the eighty malt whiskies stocked in the convivial bar. Country pursuits include river and sea angling, deer stalking and shooting for game birds. The Highlands are a delight to explore with beautiful walks through the countryside and marine wildlife such as dolphins to be admired, close to Tain. Golf enthusiasts will be pleased with the opportunities which include eight courses within easy reach including Royal Dornoch. **Directions:** Heading North, ignore the first turning to Tain off the A9. Continue for ½ mile and take the turning signposted "police station". The hotel is then signposted. Price guide: Single £65–£80; double/twin £110–£150.

LOCH TORRIDON COUNTRY HOUSE HOTEL

TORRIDON, BY ACHNASHEEN, WESTER-ROSS IV22 2EY
TEL: 01445 791242 FAX: 01445 791296 E-MAIL: enquiries@lochtorridonhotel.com

The Loch Torridon Hotel is gloriously situated at the foot of wooded mountains on the shores of the loch from which it derives its name. The hotel was built as a shooting lodge for the first Earl of Lovelace in 1887 in a 58 acre estate containing formal gardens, mature trees and resident Highland cattle. David and Geraldine Gregory acquired the hotel in March 1992 and have since brought in their daughter Rohaise and son-in-law Dan Rose-Bristow to take over management of the hotel. Winner of the AA Scottish 'Hotel of the Year' award in 1998, Loch Torridon has 20 bedrooms, all of which are furnished in a stylish manner. During the summer months the hotel is bedecked with flowers from the attractive garden. The Victorian kitchen garden provides the chef, Ross Duncan, with fresh herbs, salad, potatoes, broad beans, apples and many other fruits and vegetables. Dinner is served between 7.15pm and 8.30pm and guests may begin with home-cured gravadlax with honey and mustard dressed leaves and lemon basil sorbet followed by peppered highland venison on 'bubble and squeak' with roasted vegetables and game jus. There is a vast array of outdoor pursuits including walking in the mountains, boating, fishing and the opportunity to watch otters, seals and whales. **Directions:** Ten miles from Kinlochewe on the A896. Do not turn off to Torridon village. Price guide: Single £50–£90; double/twin £110–£260; suites £220–£260.

MARINE HIGHLAND HOTEL

TROON, AYRSHIRE KA10 6HE, SCOTLAND
TEL: 01292 314444 FAX: 01292 316922 E-MAIL: GrahamT@scottishhighlandhotel.co.uk

With peerless views of the Firth of Clyde and overlooking the championship Royal Troon Golf Course, the Marine Highland Hotel offers the golf-loving traveller an unparalleled base from which to explore Scotland's finest links courses. Dating back to the late 19th century, the Marine is an imposing edifice, but once inside the visitor is immediately struck by the friendly hospitality for which the Highlands are renowned. As befits a hotel which has been official host to Open Championships in 1989 and 1997, famous golfers photographs adorn the walls. One can almost feel the presence of champions past in its hallowed halls. The restaurant, which serves superb home-cooked fare, affords views over Royal Troon, while many of the individually designed rooms also have vistas over the course. There is also an Italian restaurant where the emphasis is on style and sophistication. The hotel boasts of one the finest health and fitness clubs in Scotland. After a long day on the links, visitors can soak in the 50ft pool, play squash or work out in the gym. Lazing in the steam room, sauna or solarium is an option for the more indolent guest. The conference and function facilities are the height of luxury, with the main Portland Suite comfortably housing up to 200 guests. **Directions:** From Glasgow follow A77, A78, A79 to Prestwick Airport. Leave A79 at B749 to Troon. Over railway bridge, hotel is visible on the left. Price guide (room only): Single £96; double/twin £156; suite £236.

PIERSLAND HOUSE HOTEL

CRAIGEND ROAD, TROON, AYRSHIRE KA10 6HD
TEL: 01292 314747 FAX: 01292 315613

This historic listed house, built for the grandson of Johnnie Walker, founder of the Scottish whisky brand, is as attractive inside as out. All the public rooms are spacious and inviting, with original features such as oak panelling and a frieze of Jacobean embroidery. Retaining their original charm, the bedrooms are formally decorated in a period style with soft colourings. Afternoon cream teas are served on the verandah overlooking the beautiful gardens. The landscaped grounds include an oriental garden. Guests can enjoy classically prepared 2 AA Rosettes gourmet dishes and Continental-style cooking in the warm, intimate atmosphere of our two restaurants. The wine list is compiled from labels supplied by one of Scotland's oldest-established wine firms. For golfers, Royal Troon, venue of the British Open 1997, is situated across the road. Turnberry, Old Prestwick and numerous championship courses are nearby. Ayr, the county town and birthplace of Robert Burns, our national poet and Culzean Castle, Seat of the Kennedy Clan are also close at hand. Glasgow, Edinburgh and the beautiful island of Arran are easily accessible, as are Loch Lomond and the Trossachs. **Directions:** The hotel is just off the A77 on the B749, beside Royal Troon Golf Club. Price guide: Single £62.50–£82.50; double/twin £114–£140.

HOUSTOUN HOUSE

UPHALL, WEST LOTHIAN, SCOTLAND EH52 6JS
TEL: 01506 853831 FAX: 01506 854220

Houstoun House is a beautiful and unspoilt example of a 17th century Scottish laird's house. The fine gardens were laid out in the 1700s and include a great cedar tree which was grown from seed brought from the Lebanon by one of the early lairds. The 20 acres of gardens and woodland are adjacent to Uphall Golf Course where guests can play by arrangement. The house is divided into three distinct buildings – the Tower, containing the dining rooms and vaulted bars; the Woman House, a 16th century manor house joined to the Tower by a stone-flagged courtyard; and The Steading, formerly the estate factor's house. The bedrooms all offer a range of modern facilities and overlook the historic gardens. The standard bedrooms are mostly modern in style,

while the traditional bedrooms are generally larger and feature antique furnishings. Executive bedrooms are all non-smoking and elegantly decorated. Houstoun House enjoys an excellent reputation for its cuisine, with the best of Scottish and international dishes served in wood-panelled dining rooms situated in the old Drawing Room, the Library and the Great Hall. Italian flavours may be sampled in the restaurant within the grounds. The health and fitness facilities include a 20 metre pool and well-equipped gymnasium. **Directions:** From M8 Jct 3 (Livingston), turn right at first roundabout, follow signs for Broxburn – A89 left at traffic lights on A899 to Uphall. Price guide (exclusive of Breakfast): Single £120–£140 double/twin £160–£180.

HONDA

First man, then machine

The Honda Accord has won critical acclaim from both the public and press alike.

What Car? Magazine voted it best in class in their 1999 Car of the Year Awards.

Now there's the choice of a 5 door model within the range, offering increased versatility.

Like all Accords, the 5 door is one of the quietest and most refined in its class.

It's powered by Honda's Formula One bred VTEC engine, which combines high power with high economy (147ps and 32.8mpg* from the 2.0i).

With multi-link double-wishbone suspension- which keeps the wheels as vertical as possible, thereby maximising road grip-plus ABS and air conditioning, it's a pleasure to drive.

Call 0345 159 159 or visit www.honda.co.uk

Same story, different ending.
The Honda Accord.

*COMBINED FIGURE FOR THE 2.0i MANI

Johansens Recommended Hotels

Ireland

Celtic legends, medieval architecture, racecourses and golf courses, great art collections and a rich history of literature are all to be found amongst the green landscapes of Ireland.

Whiterocks, Co. Antrim, N. Ireland

What's happening in Ireland?

• Wexford Festival Opera – one of Ireland's most internationally renowned festivals and has been held in this small coastal town for almost half a century. Held in Wexford from 14th – 31st October 1999.

• Guinness Cork Jazz '99 Festival – one of Ireland's best known international festivals and has attracted a galaxy of jazz greats over the years. Held in Cork from 22nd – 25th October 1999.

• The Belfast Festival at Queens University – this festival takes place in numerous different venues from the Grand Opera House to the new Waterfront Hall. Held from 29th October – 14th November, this festival includes over four hundred shows of international theatre, dance, classical and pop music, film and arts, jazz and folk.

For more information about Ireland and Northern Ireland please contact:

The Irish Tourist Board
St Andrews Church
Suffolk Street
Dublin 2
Tel: 00 353 1 602 4000

Northern Ireland Tourist Board
St Anne's Court
59 North Street
Belfast BT1 1NB
Tel: 01232 246609

ADARE MANOR HOTEL & GOLF CLUB

ADARE, CO LIMERICK

TEL: 00 353 61 396566 FAX: 00 353 61 396124 E-MAIL: Reservations@adaremanor.com

Adare Manor is a wonderful example of 18th century gothic architecture, set in 840 acres around the River Maigue in the charming village of Adare. The splendour of the hotel is evident upon entering as elegant chandeliers, rich décor and plush furnishings adorn the lobby and reception. The luxurious bedrooms are the essence of comfort with soft fabrics and individually designed wood panellings, created by local craftsmen. Afternoon tea is served in the cosy Drawing Room whilst a postprandial drink may be enjoyed in the Library, with its fine collection of books and imposing fireplace. Guests dine by candlelight in the enchanting restaurant, indulging in a fusion of European cuisine and traditional Irish flavours. This is a magnificent venue for golf enthusiasts with a 7138 yard championship course within the estate. There are a number of sporting facilities available on site including an indoor swimming pool, sauna and fitness centre and lakes for fishing. Clay pigeon shooting and horse-riding may also be practised within the grounds. The hotel is in an ideal location for those visiting the many picturesque areas of Ireland such as the magnificent cliffs of Moher, Clare Glens, the lakes of Killarney and the Dingle Peninsula. **Directions:** The hotel is situated 20 miles away from Shannon airport on the N21. Price guide: double/twin from IR£145; state room from IR£265.

THE McCAUSLAND HOTEL

34-38 VICTORIA STREET, BELFAST BT1 3GH
TEL: 028 9022 0200 FAX: 028 9022 0220 E-MAIL: info@mccauslandhotel.com

Located in the heart of Belfast centre, this classic Italianate hotel of contemporary design is the essence of opulence with an ornate carved façade. The McCausland Hotel has 60 bedrooms, all of which are beautifully appointed with fine fabrics and soft carpets. From mini bars and room safes to direct dial telephones with voice mail, the rooms offer every modern convenience. Wheelchair users, non smokers and lady travellers have not been forgotten. Guests may indulge in a pre or postprandial drink in the Café Marco Polo. Merchants, the hotel's gourmet restaurant, serves an inspired menu, using the best of fresh regional produce. Guests may start with the tartelette of Irish cheeses served with deep fried parsley salad, followed by the roast monkfish with garlic and muscadet sauce and finally indulge in the crêpe with orange butter and a rum-scented crème anglais. Business meetings and seminars are held in the well-equipped conference rooms, combining state-of-the-art facilities with an excellent support team. There are ten golf courses within easy reach including the Royal Belfast. Galleries, theatres and boutiques abound and the hotel is only steps away from the internationally-renowned Waterfront Hall. The hotel is the sister property to The Hibernian Hotel in Dublin. **Directions:** The hotel is located on Victoria Street between Anne Street and the Albert Clock Tower. Price guide (room only): Single £120; double/twin £150; junior suite £200.

NUREMORE HOTEL AND COUNTRY CLUB

CARRICKMACROSS, CO MONAGHAN, IRELAND

TEL: 00 353 42 9661438 FAX: 00 353 42 9661853 E-MAIL: nuremore@tinet.ie

Set in 200 acres of glorious countryside on the fringe of Carrickmacross, the Nuremore Hotel offers guests all-round enjoyment, a vast array of activities and facilities and all that is best in a first-class country hotel. The bedrooms are well-appointed and attractively designed to create a generous sense of personal space. Lunch and dinner menus, served in an elegant dining room, emphasise classic European cooking with French and Irish dishes featured alongside. For sport, fitness and relaxation, guests are spoiled for choice. A major feature is the championship-length, par 71, 18-hole golf course designed by Eddie Hackett to present an exciting challenge to beginners and experts alike. Maurice Cassidy has been appointed as resident professional and is on hand to give tuition. Riding nearby in Carrickmacross. The leisure club has a superb indoor pool, modern gymnasium, squash and tennis courts, sauna, steam room and whirlpool bath. Meetings and seminars held here are guaranteed a professional support service. Recent additions include a private dining room, 13 executive rooms and three purpose built syndicate rooms with air-conditioning and blackout facilities. Dublin is 75 minutes' drive away, while Drogheda and Dundalk are nearby for shopping. **Directions:** The hotel is on main N2 road between Dublin and Monaghan. Price guide: Single IR£90–IR£115; double/twin IR£140–IR£180; suite IR190.

THE LODGE & SPA AT INCHYDONEY ISLAND

CLONAKILTY, WEST CORK

TEL: 00 353 23 33143 FAX: 00 353 23 35229 E-MAIL: reservations@inchdoneyisland.com

Set on the island of Inchydoney with its causeway linking it to the mainland, this opulent hotel offers comfortable accommodation in an area of breathtaking beauty. The Lodge and Spa at Inchydoney Island is only 30 miles from Cork and is situated above two of the finest beaches in Ireland, ideal for coastal walks or relaxing along the beachfront. The sense of natural beauty pervades the interior of the hotel, where natural materials blend harmoniously with warm earth tones. The 67 bedrooms are beautifully appointed with a vast array of modern amenities. All offer a panoramic vista across the coast. The Lodge features a superb Thalassotherapy Spa comprising an aquamarine spa, aeromarine baths, cryotherapy, underwater massages and other treatments. Fitness enthusiasts may use the steam room, sauna and fully equipped gymnasium. French and Mediterranean flavours can be savoured in the elegant Gulfstream Restaurant, which enjoys glorious views across the Atlantic Ocean and Irish coast. Featuring fresh seafood and local produce, the menu offers dishes which are both healthy and satisfying. A warm Irish welcome is extended to all guests at The Nautical Theme Pub, serving traditional meals. Canoeing, deep sea-angling, cycling and hill walking can be practised nearby while golfers try the course at Old Head of Kinsale. **Directions:** The hotel is 3 miles from Clonakilty in West Cork. Price guide: Single IR£85; double/twin IR£140; suite IR£180.

ASHFORD CASTLE

CONG, CO MAYO

TEL: 00 353 92 46003 FAX: 00 353 92 46260 E-MAIL: ashford@ashford.ie

Ashford Castle is set on the northern shores of Lough Corrib amidst acres of beautiful gardens and forests. Once the country estate of Lord Ardilaun and the Guinness family, it was transformed into a luxury hotel in 1939. The castle's Great Hall is lavishly decorated with rich panelling, fine period pieces, *objets d'art* and masterpiece paintings. Guest rooms are of the highest standards and many feature high ceilings, enormous bathrooms and delightful lake views. The main dining room offers superb continental and traditional menus, while the gourmet restaurant, The Connaught Room, specialises in excellent French cuisine. Before and after dinner in the Dungeon Bar guests are entertained by a harpist or pianist. Ashford Castle offers a full range of country sports, including fishing on Lough Corrib, clay pigeon shooting, riding and an exclusive 9-hole golf course. The hotel has a modern health centre comprising a whirlpool, sauna, steam room, fully equipped gymnasium and conservatory. Ashford is an ideal base for touring the historic West Ireland, places like Kylemore Abbey and Westport House, Sligo and Drumcliffe Churchyard, the burial place of W.B. Yeats. **Directions:** 30 minutes from Galway on the shore of Lough Corrib, on the left when entering the village of Cong. Price guide: Single/twin/double IR£140–IR£312; suite IR£330–IR£650.

RENVYLE HOUSE HOTEL

CONNEMARA, CO GALWAY

TEL: 00 353 95 43511 FAX: 00 353 95 43515 FREEPHONE: 00 800 77335555 E-MAIL: renvyle@iol.ie

Renvyle House Hotel has occupied its rugged, romantic position on Ireland's west coast for over four centuries. Set between mountains and sea on the unspoilt coast of Connemara, this hardy, beautiful building with its superlative views over the surrounding countryside is just an hour's drive from Galway or Sligo. Originally constructed in 1541, Renvyle has been an established hotel for over 100 years, witnessing in that time a procession of luminaries through its doors – Augustus John, Lady Gregory, Yeats and Churchill, drawn no doubt by an atmosphere as warm and convivial then as it is today. Renvyle now welcomes visitors with turf fires glowing in public areas, wood-beamed interiors and comfortable, relaxed furnishings in the easy rooms. The bedrooms too are comfortably appointed and all have been refurbished in the past three years. In the dining room, meals from a constantly-changing menu are served with emphasis on local fish and Renvyle lamb. In the grounds activities include tennis, croquet, riding, bowls and golf. Beyond the hotel, there are walks in the heather-clad hills, or swimming and sunbathing on empty beaches. **Directions:** On the N59 from Galway turn right at Recess, take the Letterfrack turning to Tully Cross and Renvyle is signposted. Price guide: Single IR£50–IR£120; double/twin IR£100–IR£180.

HAYFIELD MANOR HOTEL

PERROTT AVENUE, COLLEGE ROAD, CORK, IRELAND
TEL: 00 353 21 315600 FAX: 00 353 21 316839 E-MAIL: enquiries@hayfieldmanor.ie

From the tall, pillared entrance and richly curtained sash windows to the two acres of mature formal gardens this hotel is the essence of style. Hayfield Manor Hotel is a veritable country manor estate within a comfortable walk of the heart of Ireland's second largest city. Situated adjacent to University College Cork, the hotel provides seclusion and privacy and maintains the atmosphere of unhurried tranquillity that has been established since its Georgian days. The magnificently furnished lounge, with its soft sofas and chairs, ornate open fire and vases of fragrant fresh flowers, is particularly restful. Every modern comfort is to hand and none more so than in the 87 spacious and elegant guest rooms. Furnishings and décor are excellent,

matched by marble bathrooms with fluffy robes and baskets brimming with toiletries. Directly linked to the bedrooms is a health club exclusive to hotel residents only where even the palm-surrounded pool has views across the garden. Before or after a swim you can work out in the gym, enjoy the steam room or relax in the outdoor Jacuzzi. Gourmet cuisine is served in the intimate Manor Room restaurant where owners Joe and Margaret Scaly ensure that, like the hotel throughout, ambience and service is of the highest. Golf, riding and fishing are nearby as are Blarney Castle, Kinsale and Cobh Heritage Centre. **Directions:** 1 mile from city centre. Price guide: Single IR£120–£150; double/twin IR£195–IR£240; suite IR245–IR£700.

BROOKS HOTEL

59–62 DRURY STREET, DUBLIN 2
TEL: 00 353 1 670 4000 FAX: 00 353 1 670 4455 E-MAIL: reservations@brookshotel.ie

Brooks Hotel, sister hotel to the Connemara Coast Hotel in Galway, offers a delightful fusion of fine décor, excellent service and comfortable accommodation. Located on a quiet street in the heart of Dublin, the hotel is distinctly avant-garde with a spacious interior and beautifully appointed public rooms. The Drawing Room is dominated by an impressive fireplace creating a warm and intimate atmosphere, perfect for reclining with a good book or enjoying a postprandial drink. The 75 bedrooms are the essence of opulence featuring elegant furnishings and every modern comfort. Well-equipped with air conditioning, personal safes and computer points with ISDN telephone connections, these rooms are ideal for both the leisure and business traveller. Guests may converse in the attractive Piano Bar before dining in the stylish restaurant, where the menu comprises modern Irish dishes and specialities include fresh fish. Those seeking a more informal ambience may relax and converse in the welcoming bar. Business meetings and seminars can be held in the fully-equipped meeting room which can accommodate up to 70 delegates. Childcare facilities are available. **Directions:** Brooks is located within easy reach of Grafton Street, Stephen Green and Trinity College. Price guide: (room only) Single IR£125–IR£145; double IR£165–IR£185; executive rooms IR£210. Weekend rates also available, please enquire at hotel.

THE FITZWILLIAM HOTEL

ST STEPHEN'S GREEN, DUBLIN 2, IRELAND
TEL: 00 353 1 478 7000 FAX: 00 353 1 478 7878 E-MAIL: enq@fitzwilliamh.com

Overlooking the elegant, tranquil gardens of St Stephen's Green in the centre of historic Dublin the Fitzwilliam is the ultimate in hotel chic, a 'designer hotel' representing both a cosmopolitan landmark for the city and a stylish retreat from the bustle of everyday life. Style is at the heart of the Fitzwilliam, which was designed by Sir Terence Conran's group. Traditional hotel trappings of chintz and four-poster beds have given way to modernistic architecture entitled 'Baronial Modern'. The interior of the hotel features many themes often found in country houses but updated and given a contemporary feel. Solid yet simple furnishings, well-made in walnut or oak and complemented by carefully chosen accessories, offer elegance with comfort. Each bedroom has every modern amenity and luxury from stereo CD player and satellite television to a minibar, multi-line telephone facility, modem line, personal fax and voice mail. In addition to Christopher's all-day brasserie-style restaurant superb cuisine is served in leading chef Conrad Gallagher's Restaurant, Peacock Alley. The Fitzwilliam also has a popular cocktail bar, Ireland's largest roof garden and secure indoor car parking. Condé Nast's Traveller Magazine voted the Fitzwilliam in the top 21 of the World's Coolest Hotels. **Directions:** In the centre of the city adjacent to the top of Grafton Street. Price guide: Single IR£190–IR£225; double/twin IR£210–IR£260; suite IR£325–IR£475.

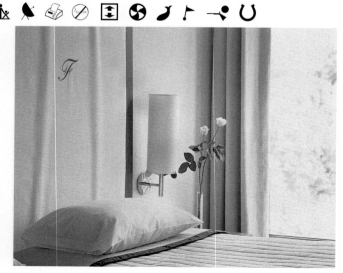

THE HIBERNIAN HOTEL

EASTMORELAND PLACE, BALLSBRIDGE, DUBLIN 4
TEL: 00 353 1 668 7666 FAX: 00 353 1 660 2655 E-MAIL: info@hibernianhotel.com

In bustling downtown Dublin, the Hibernian Hotel is a magnificent architectural feat constructed just before the turn of the century in the commercial heart of the city. Refurbished and reopened in 1993 as a grand town house hotel, The Hibernian now prides itself on the elegance, style and warmth of service it can offer visitors to this vibrant metropolis. David Butt and Siobhan Maher are ably assisted by a professional team who ensure that the needs of both business and holiday guests are met quickly and efficiently. The Hibernian was awarded hotel of the year 1997 from Small Luxury Hotels of the World and also received the AA Courtesy and Care Ireland award 2000. Luxury prevails at The Hibernian in soft furnishings, rich fabrics and deep upholstery; in each of the 40 individually designed bedrooms and suites. En suite bathrooms with a full range of toiletries are standard, as are fax/modem points, drinks facilities, individually controlled thermostats and hairstyling appliances. In the Patrick Kavanagh Room the virtuoso chef, David Foley, creates menus full of gastronomic dishes, from locally caught, artfully interpreted seafood to modern cuisine and wines to accompany them. The hotel makes an ideal base from which to explore the city. The McCausland Hotel in Belfast is The Hibernian's sister hotel. **Directions:** Turn right from Mespil Road into Baggot Street Upper, then left into Eastmoreland Place. Price guide (room only): Single IR£120; double/twin IR£150; suite IR£185.

THE KILDARE HOTEL & COUNTRY CLUB

AT STRAFFAN, CO KILDARE
TEL: 00 353 1 601 7200 FAX: 00 353 1 601 7299

Straffan House is one of Ireland's most elegant 19th century manor houses, set in 330 acres of beautiful countryside and overlooking the River Liffey. Just 17 miles from Dublin, this is an international world class resort with its graceful reception rooms, totally luxurious bedrooms and palatial en suite bathrooms, also a superb leisure club with a sybaritic indoor pool. The public areas of the hotel are a treasure trove of contemporary paintings and works of art. There are excellent conference areas for business meetings, while corporate entertaining is dominated by facilities which include the Arnold Palmer course, which is the venue for The Smurfit European since 1995 and venue for the 2005 Ryder Cup Matches, indoor tennis and squash courts, a gymnasium, clay target shooting, fishing and riding, croquet. Formal entertaining, meeting in the bar followed by a magnificent meal in the prestigious Byerley Turk Restaurant, with table d'hôte and à la carte menus complemented by an extensive wine list, is effortless The Legend Bar and Restaurant in the Country Club offer less formality. The Arnold Palmer Room is available for gala functions and conferences at the Clubhouse. **Directions:** Leave Dublin on N7 driving south for 17 miles. Straffan is signposted on the left. Price guide: Double/twin IR£310–IR£380; suite IR£450–£1,000. Conference rates on request.

THE MERRION HOTEL

UPPER MERRION STREET, DUBLIN 2, IRELAND
TEL: 00 353 1 603 0600 FAX: 00 353 1 603 0700 E-MAIL: info@merrionhotel.com

Dublin has an élite hotel. The Merrion is the city's historic landmark. It has been imaginatively and brilliantly conceived, four superb Grade I Georgian terrace houses meticulously restored. There is also an elegant new Garden Wing. The interior decorations are impressive, authentically reflecting the Georgian era by the choice of wall colours, specially commissioned fabrics and well researched antiques. By contrast, a private collection of 20th century art is displayed throughout the hotel, and the neo-classic stairwell has a series of contemporary murals. Every guest room is luxurious, some situated in the Garden Wing, with views over the two gardens – delightful with box hedges, statuary and fountains, approached from the drawing rooms in summer. The Merrion offers a choice of two handsome bars, the larger a fascinating 18th century cellar, the other more intimate and two restaurants, the legendary Restaurant Patrick Guilbaud in a dramatic new setting and the Morningtons Brasserie, offering traditional dishes with an Irish influence. The Merrion has a state-of-the-art meeting and private dining facility, perfect for hosting banquets. Guests relax in The Tethra Spa, which has an 18m pool, gymnasium and salons for pampering. **Directions:** City Centre. The hotel has valet parking. Price guide: Single IR£200–IR£240; double/twin IR£220–IR£265; suite IR£375–IR£675.

PORTMARNOCK HOTEL AND GOLF LINKS

STRAND RD, PORTMARNOCK, CO. DUBLIN, IRELAND
TEL: 00 353 1 846 0611 FAX: 00 353 1 846 2442

This magnificent hotel is a golfer's paradise for it is on the new golf links designed by Bernhard Langer in 1995. It also has two famous championship courses in the vicinity, Portmarnock Golf Club and the Royal Dublin Golf Club. The mansion was the home of the Jameson whiskey family and has been transformed into a magnificent hotel. The Jamesons hosted many prestigious visitors, and in its new guise, the guest book is once again filling with distinguished names. Skilled restoration has rediscovered the beauty of the reception rooms. Extensions to the hotel have been carefully designed to blend with the old house and today, big picture windows look out onto the course. The charming bedrooms have modern comforts and efficient bathrooms. Executive Suites have balconies overlooking Dublin Bay and a number of Jameson Suites have four-poster beds. Guests mingle in the traditional drawing room, on the terrace or in the inviting bar before feasting in the elegant restaurant which has an excellent wine list. The smart Golf Clubhouse is adjacent to the hotel and the atmosphere is more relaxed. It has a pleasant bar where players review the day's round. The informal restaurant is very popular. When not golfing, visitors fish or explore the delights of Dublin. **Directions:** Follow signs to Portmarnock from Dublin airport or city centre. Price guide: Single IR£135; double/twin IR£195; suite IR£300.

CONNEMARA COAST HOTEL

FURBO, GALWAY
TEL: 00 353 91 592108 FAX: 00 353 91 592065

This modern resort hotel, sister hotel of Brooks in Dublin, is located just 6 miles from Galway city centre on the shores of Galway Bay. With magnificent views, The Connemara Coast Hotel combines a friendly and welcoming atmosphere with elegant décor and a picturesque landscape. The stylish interior is bedecked with fresh floral arrangements whilst the reception rooms are spacious with plush furnishings, comfortable armchairs and rich fabrics. The 112 bedrooms, all with views across the Bay, are well-appointed with attractive colour schemes and a range of thoughtful extras including tea/coffee making facilities. Guests indulge in a preprandial drink in the typically Irish Bar, which exudes character and charm, before dining in the fine restaurant. The imaginative menu uses the best of regional produce and is complemented by an excellent wine list. There are well-equipped conference rooms and the hotel provides additional services including fax, typing and photocopying services. The Leisure Centre features an indoor pool and fitness facilities including a gymnasium. This is an ideal base for exploring Galway City and Connemara. Attractions include the Spanish Arch, Pearse's Cottage, Kylemore Abbey and Coole Park. Fishing enthusiasts must visit Lough Corrib with its plentiful supply of salmon, trout and pike. **Directions:** The hotel is 10 minutes out of Galway on R336. Price guide: Single IR£55–IR£85; double/twin IR£90–IR£170.

MARLFIELD HOUSE

GOREY, CO WEXFORD

TEL: 00 353 55 21124 FAX: 00 353 55 21572 E-MAIL: marlf@iol.ie

Staying at Johansens award-winning Marlfield House is a memorable experience. Set in 34 acres of woodland and gardens, this former residence of the Earl of Courtown preserves the Regency lifestyle in all its graciousness. Built in 1820, it is recognised as one of the finest country houses in Ireland and is supervised by its welcoming hosts and proprietors, Raymond and Mary Bowe and their daughter Margaret. The State Rooms have been built in a very grand style and have period fireplaces where open fires burn even in the cooler weather. All of the furniture is antique and the roomy beds are draped with sumptuous fabrics. The bathrooms are made of highly polished marble and some have large freestanding bathtubs. There is an imposing entrance hall, luxurious drawing room and an impressive curved Richard Turner conservatory. The kitchen's gastronomic delights have earned it numerous awards. Located two miles from fine beaches and Courtown golf club, the house is central to many touring high points: Glendalough, Waterford Crystal and Powerscourt Gardens and the medieval city of Kilkenny. Closed mid-December to the end of January. **Directions:** On the Gorey–Courtown road, just over a mile east of Gorey. Price guide: Single from IR£85; double/twin IR£158–IR£170; state rooms from IR£270–IR£490.

PARK HOTEL KENMARE

KENMARE, CO. KERRY

TEL: 00 353 64 41200 FAX: 00 353 64 41402 E-MAIL: phkenmare@iol.ie

Eleven acres of beautiful gardens surround this charming Victorian hotel, built in 1897. Retaining the character and ambience of a past era, the hotel combines elegant accommodation and superb amenities with glorious views across the countryside. The 40 bedrooms and 9 suites are furnished in a traditional style with fine antiques skilled by craftsmen from Ireland and England. Innovative cuisine, made with the best of fresh, regional produce is served in the classic dining room. Guests may indulge in the delicious seafood specialities featuring Wild salmon and lobsters from the bay. A vast array of rare wines and smooth whiskies may be found in the cellar, one of the most highly regarded in Ireland. There is a wide range of sports facilities available on site including an all-weather tennis court, executive fitness studio and 18-hole golf course. Riding, shooting, croquet and fishing are other outdoor pursuits which may be practised nearby. The hotel is located in the picturesque town of Kenmare, close to the prestigious golf club. Park Hotel Kenmare is well-situated for those wishing to tour the Ring of Kerry, Beara Peninsula, Dingle and other historic towns. **Directions:** The hotel is in the centre of Kenmare on the N70 or the N71, just 27 miles away from Kerry International Airport. Price guide: Single IR£132–IR£152; double/twin IR£244–IR£350; suite IR£410–IR£484.

SHEEN FALLS LODGE

KENMARE, CO. KERRY, IRELAND
TEL: 00 353 64 41600 FAX: 00 353 64 41386 E-MAIL: info@sheenfallslodge.ie

You could be forgiven for expecting a magic carpet instead of a plane to land you at Sheen Falls Lodge – one of the Emerald Isle's most romantic and luxurious hotels. Standing amidst a vast estate of green countryside and well-kept gardens, with the sparkling Sheen River tumbling down the falls. The Lodge is a magnificent mansion, built in the attractive local stone, with a slate roof and the interior of this prestigious hotel is evocative of the past, with its country house ambience. The Library, with traditional leather furniture, holds many fine books and the spacious lounges have warm colour schemes, log fires and generous sofas. Flowers, lovely antiques and memorabilia enhance the atmosphere. The guest rooms are exquisite, luxuriously appointed and decorated in soft restful shades. They have opulent bathrooms. Dining here starts with the privilege of touring the extensive wine cellar with the sommelier to select a great vintage to accompany a magnificent meal – local salmon, lobster or duck perhaps. Riding, tennis, croquet, fishing, shooting and billiards are 'house' sports. The Lodge also has a superb fitness centre, with indoor heated swimming pool. Nearby are several excellent golf courses, marvellous walking, bikes to hire and deep sea fishing can be arranged. **Directions:** The hotel is signed from the junction of N70 and N71 at Kenmare. Helipad. Price guide: Deluxe Room IR£168–IR£258; suite IR£320–IR£378.

AGHADOE HEIGHTS HOTEL

AGHADOE, KILLARNEY, CO KERRY
TEL: 00 353 64 31766 FAX: 00 353 64 31345 E-MAIL: aghadoeheights@tinet.ie

In the heart of beautiful County Kerry overlooking stunning panoramic views of the lakes and mountains of Killarney, stands the recently refurbished Aghadoe Heights Hotel. It reflects owner Patrick Currans' influence: rich tapestries, crystal chandeliers, paintings and antiques. Much attention has been given to the bedrooms. The furniture is of mahogany, ash or cherry wood, with soft drapes and deep carpets. Excellent cuisine and fine wines are served in the rooftop restaurant. Chef Robin Suter uses the freshest local ingredients to create innovative dishes. Three function rooms offer good conference facilities. A leisure club includes an indoor pool, Jacuzzi, sauna, plunge pool, solarium, fitness room and now by appointment, a massage and beauty treatment service in the hotel. Aghadoe Heights is a good departure point for tours of Kerry or for playing south-west Ireland's premier golf courses, such as Killarney, Waterville and Ballybunion. The hotel has its own stretch of river for salmon and trout fishing and there is also a tennis court within the eight acre gardens. Pony-trekking, lake and sea fishing are also offered locally. **Directions:** The hotel is ten miles south of Kerry Airport, three miles north of Killarney. It is situated off the N22 Tralee road. Price guide: Single IR£105–IR£180; double/twin IR£160–IR£245; suite IR£220–£390.

MUCKROSS PARK HOTEL

MUCKROSS, KILLARNEY, CO KERRY

TEL: 00 353 64 31938 FAX: 00 353 64 31965 – FROM USA TOLL FREE 800 223 6510 E-MAIL: muckrossparkhotel@tinet.ie

Muckross Park stands in the heart of beautiful County Kerry surrounded by the 25,000 acre Killarney National Park with its lakes, mountains and peaceful gardens with giant rhododendrons and tropical plants. It is a redevelopment of an 18th century hotel with stone wall interiors, wooden panelling and exposed beams. Fine antiques and paintings, deep carpets and glittering chandeliers combine the luxurious ambience of a traditional country house with the comfort of a modern four star hotel. All the en suite bedrooms are charmingly old-world. Each has satellite television, direct dial telephone, trouser press and hairdryer. Innovative cuisine and fine wines are served in the bright, sunny Blue Pool Restaurant which looks out over two acres of landscaped gardens that lead down to the hotel's river frontage. Adjacent to the hotel is Molly's, a famous, award-winning traditional Irish pub and restaurant, where bare wooden floors, beamed ceilings, open fires and live entertainment recreate the pleasures of bygone days. Muckross Park is a good base from which to tour Kerry, to explore Killarney National Park, or play south west Ireland's premier golf courses. Boating, fishing, tennis, clay pigeon shooting, riding and hill walking can all be arranged. **Directions:** The hotel is $2^{1}/2$ miles south of Killarney on N71 towards Kenmare. Price guide: Single IR£85; double/twin IR£130; suite IR£200–IR£300.

RANDLES COURT HOTEL

MUCKROSS ROAD, KILLARNEY, CO. KERRY
TEL: 00 353 64 35333 FAX: 00 353 64 35206 E-MAIL: randles@iol.ie

A warm ambience envelopes this Victorian hotel, set in the picturesque countryside of Killarney, renowned for its challenging golf courses. Randles Court Hotel has retained the friendly and welcoming atmosphere of a family home whilst offering the luxury and comforts of a modern hotel. The reception area is spacious with marble floors and exquisite Persian rugs. The 49 bedrooms are beautifully appointed with opulent en suite bathrooms. The fresh flowers and soft bathrobes are thoughtful additions. Guests may relax by the open fires in the comfortable drawing room, furnished with objet d'art murals, antiques and Japanese table lamps. A preprandial drink may be enjoyed in the cosy bar before indulging in the creative dishes served in the elegant Court Restaurant. Seafood specialities are included on the inspired à la carte and table d'hôte menus which are also served in the new black and white themed 'checkers' restaurant . The lakes of Killarney and the Rivers Laune and Flesk provide excellent salmon and trout fishing. Boats are also available for hire whilst the two championship courses are a must for golfers. Places of interest nearby include Ross Castle, St Mary's Cathedral and Demesne. Excursions include trips by pony and trap to Killarney's natural wonder, the Gap of Dunloe. The hotel has its own fleet of self-drive cars. **Directions:** Situated on Muckross Road, only 5 mins walk from the town centre. Price guide: Single IR£80–140; double/twin IR£100–185; suite IR£120–200.

HUMEWOOD CASTLE

KILTEGAN, CO. WICKLOW

TEL: 00 353 508 73215 FAX: 00 353 508 73382 E-MAIL: humewood@iol.ie

Humewood Castle, a magnificent Victorian mansion, offers a panoramic vista across the Wicklow mountains and the surrounding countryside. This is an ideal venue for enthusiasts of country pursuits as there are many opportunities for outdoor sports within the estate. The 14 bedrooms, each with its own specific theme, have been carefully restored and are luxurious with four-poster beds, en suite facilities and plush fabrics. Guests savour the excellent cuisine, accompanied by a superb wine list, in the castle's dining room which is complemented by the friendly and enthusiastic staff. The menu comprises the very best of local produce such as wild duck and fresh fish. Conferences, business meetings, weddings and other private events may be held in the ballroom, billiard room and other smaller rooms, perfect for seminars. Clay pigeon shooting may be practised at the well-designed Sporting Clay Course whilst golfers will enjoy the three championship courses within the area. The castle holds its own simulated pheasant shooting days throughout the year and duck and driven pheasant shooting, in season. The 4 lakes within the estate provide good trout fishing. Beginner or experienced riders may try the three-day event course or play on the polo field. Other activities include hill-walking, cycling, hunting and deer stalking. **Directions:** The Castle is one hour south of Dublin, on the N81. Price guide: (including VAT) Double/twin IR£160–IR£200; suite IR£240–IR£360.

LONGUEVILLE HOUSE & PRESIDENTS' RESTAURANT

MALLOW, CO CORK, IRELAND

TEL: 00 353 22 47156 FAX: 00 353 22 47459 E-MAIL: info@longuevillehouse.ie

Set in a 500 acre estate renowned for its salmon and brown trout fishing, Longueville House is a family-run listed Georgian Manor providing comfortable accommodation in peaceful surroundings. Dominated by a glowing log fire, the Drawing Room exudes a cosy and welcoming atmosphere and the large armchairs with soft cushions are perfect for reclining. The 20 bedrooms, all with en suite facilities, are beautifully appointed with stylish fabrics and plush furnishings. Each room offers an array of thoughtful extras including fresh flowers. Food is an important criterion and The Presidents' Restaurant with its glowing log fires and silver candelabra is renowned for its superb cuisine. The talented Chef, William O'Callaghan, uses many of the flavours and produce from the estate's farm and the specialities include traditional Irish dishes such as Irish Mist sorbet with House smoked salmon and seafood terrine with a squid ink vinaigrette. Sports enthusiasts enjoy the many activities available nearby such as hill walking, cycling, horse-riding and clay pigeon shooting. This is an ideal base for those wishing to explore the South West and its many attractions. Mallow Golf and Race Courses and a number of historic properties are all within easy reach. **Directions:** Longueville House is three miles west of Mallow on the N72 to Killarney. Price guide: Single from IR£80; double/twin from IR£125; suite from IR£160.

DROMOLAND CASTLE

NEWMARKET-ON-FERGUS, SHANNON AREA, CO CLARE
TEL: 00 353 61 368144 FAX: 00 353 61 363355 E-MAIL: sales@dromoland.ie

Dromoland Castle, just 8 miles from Shannon Airport, is one of the most famous baronial castles in Ireland, dating from the 16th century. Dromoland was the ancestral seat of the O'Briens, direct descendants of Irish King Brian Boru. Priceless reminders of its past are everywhere: in the splendid wood and stone carvings, magnificent panelling, oil paintings and romantic gardens. The 99 en suite guest rooms and suites are all beautifully furnished. Stately halls and an elegant dining room are all part of the Dromoland experience. The new Dromoland International Centre is one of Europe's most comprehensive conference venues, hosting groups of up to 450. Classical cuisine is prepared by award-winning chef David McCann. Fishing, 18 hole golf, clay pigeon shooting and Full Health and Beauty Centre are all available on the estate, whilst activities nearby include horse riding and golf on some of Ireland's other foremost courses. The castle is an ideal base from which to explore this breathtakingly beautiful area. Dromoland Castle is a member of Preferred Hotels & Resorts World Wide. **Directions:** Take the N18 to Newmarket-on-Fergus, go two miles beyond the village and the hotel entrance is on the right-hand side. Price guide: Double/twin IR£140–IR£312; suite IR£401–IR£808.

PARKNASILLA HOTEL

GREAT SOUTHERN HOTEL, PARKNASILLA, CO. KERRY, IRELAND
TEL: 00 353 64 45122 FAX: 00 353 64 45323 E-MAIL: res@parknasilla.gsh.ie

County Kerry has an equitable climate from the warm Gulf Stream. Parknasilla is a splendid Victorian mansion surrounded by extensive parkland and subtropical gardens leading down to the seashore. New arrivals appreciate the graceful reception rooms which, like the luxurious bedrooms, look out on the mountains, across the verdant countryside or down to Kenmare Bay. Wonderful damask and chintz harmonize with the period furniture and thoughtful 'extras' have been provided. The bathrooms are lavishly appointed. George Bernard Shaw's many visits are reflected in the names of the inviting Doolittle Bar and the elegant Pygmalion Restaurant. The sophisticated menus always include fish fresh from the sea and the international wine list will please the most discerning guests. Corporate activities and private celebrations are hosted in the traditional Shaw Library or handsome Derryquin Suite. Leisure facilities abound: a private 9-hole golf course with challenging championship courses close by, riding, water sports, sailing, clay pigeon shooting and archery. Parknasilla has 7 recommended walks through the estate and its own motor yacht for cruises round the coast. Indoors there is a superb pool, sauna, steam room, Jacuzzi, hot tub, hydrotherapy seaweed baths, aromatherapy and massage. **Directions:** The hotel is south west of Killarney off N70. Price guide: Single IR£105–IR£120; double/twin IR£168–IR£197; suite (room only) IR£300.

HUNTER'S HOTEL

NEWRATH BRIDGE, RATHNEW, CO WICKLOW
TEL: 00 353 404 40106 FAX: 00 353 404 40338 E-MAIL: reception@hunters.ie

Hunter's Hotel, one of Ireland's oldest coaching inns, has been established since the days of post horses and carriages. Run by the Gelletlie family for five generations, the hotel has a long-standing reputation for hospitality, friendliness and excellent food. The restaurant is known for its roast joints, its locally caught fish and its home-grown vegetables. The hotel gardens above the river Vartry are a delightful scene for enjoying afternoon tea, lunch or dinner. All the reception rooms retain the character of bygone days with antique furniture, open fires, fresh flowers and polished brass. Most of the 16 attractive en suite bedrooms overlook the award-winning gardens. Business meetings and seminars for up to 25 delegates are held in the new Garden Room. Hunter's is an ideal base from which to visit Mount Usher gardens, Powerscourt Gardens, Russborough House, Glendalough, Killruddery House, Avondale House and the other attractions of Co. Wicklow, "The Garden of Ireland", where a Garden Festival is held each year in May/June. Local amenities include twenty 18 hole golf courses within half an hour's drive, most notably Druid's Glen and the highly regarded European. Horse riding and hill walking are other pursuits which can be arranged. **Directions:** Take N11 to Rathnew; turn left just before village on Dublin side. Price guide: Single IR£55–IR£75; double/twin IR£110–IR£125.

KELLY'S RESORT HOTEL

ROSSLARE, CO WEXFORD, IRELAND
TEL: 00 353 53 32114 FAX: 00 353 53 32222 E-MAIL: kellyhot@iol.ie

Situated beside the long, sandy beach at Rosslare, Kelly's is very much a family hotel, now managed by the fourth generation of Kellys. With a firm reputation as one of Ireland's finest hotels, based on a consistently high standard of service, Kelly's extends a warm welcome to its guests, many of whom return year after year. The public rooms are tastefully decorated and feature a collection of carefully selected paintings. All bedrooms have been refurbished and extended in the last three years and have en suite facilities. The hotel restaurant is highly regarded for its superb cuisine, served with great attention to detail. An extensive wine list includes individual estate wines imported directly from France. To complement Chef Aherne's fine cuisine Kelly's have now opened a new French Bar/Bistro "La Marine", which is an inspired assemblage of design and offers the ideal venue for pre-dinner drinks. Ireland's Egon Ronay Hotel of the Year 1995. For exercise and relaxation, guests have the use of the hotel's new Aqua Club, with two swimming pools and a range of water and health facilities including hydro massage, 'swimming lounge', plunge pool and hot tub, also a beauty salon. Golfers have courses at Rosslare and Wexford, which has an excellent shopping centre. Places of interest nearby include the Irish National Heritage Park at Ferrycarrig. **Directions:** Follow signs to Rosslare. Price guide: Single IR£50–IR£65; double/twin IR£88–IR£120.

THE SAND HOUSE HOTEL

ROSSNOWLAGH, DONEGAL BAY, IRELAND
TEL: 00 353 72 51777 FAX: 00 353 72 52100 E-MAIL: Reserv@SandHouse–Hotel.ie

The Sand House has been delightfully converted from a 19th century fishing lodge into a gracious hotel which combines high standards of accommodation, service and cuisine with the charm, luxury and leisurely ambience of bygone days. It is excellent in every way and has been described as one of Ireland's west coast treasures. Situated between Ballyshannon and historic Donegal Town, The Sand House overlooks the blue waters of the Atlantic and a superb three miles crescent of golden sand. Rossnowlagh is regarded as the most scenic and dramatic beach in the North West. Each of the 45 en suite bedrooms are individually styled and offer all home comforts. The elegant restaurant has been awarded two AA Red Rosettes for excellent cuisine which is enhanced by a carefully chosen wine list. Seafood specialities include Donegal Bay salmon, trout, scallops, crab, mussels and fresh oysters. Fishing, horseriding and three championship golf courses are nearby. Being half-way between the wild beauty of Connemara and the North Donegal Highlands, The Sand House provides an ideal base for touring. Places of interest nearby include Glenveagh National Park, Yeats country and Lough Gill. **Directions:** From Dublin follow the N3 via Cavan or the N4 via Sligo. From Galway take the N17 via Sligo, and from Belfast take the M1 and A4 via Enniskillen. Price guide: Single from IR£80; double/twin from IR£55; suite from IR£75 per person.

Johansens Recommended Hotels
Channel Islands

With a wealth of wonderful scenery, magnificent coastlines, historic buildings, natural and man-made attractions plus mouthwatering local produce, the Channel Islands provide a memorable destination that is distinctly different.

St. Aubins Harbour, Jersey

What's happening in Guernsey?

• Millennium Eve Carnival, 31st December 1999 – to start the evening there will be a true Guernsey 'budloe' style boat burning in St Peter Port Harbour, then a torchlit procession, a magical parade of light and music through the streets of St Peter Port. There will also be an Octopussy Big Top with an early evening cabaret, live bands, DJs, sideshows and various artists. The Big Top will be situated on North Beach.

• Gala Millennium Concert – a fantastic musical event featuring the Guernsey Symphony Orchestra, the Guernsey Choral Society, the Guernsey Sinfonia Chorus and the Guernsey Youth Choir all join together for a performance of Beethoven's Symphony No. 9. To be held on 1st July 2000 at Beau Sejour.

For further information, please contact:-

Guernsey Tourist Board
PO Box 23
St Peter Port
Guernsey GY1 3AN
Tel: 01481 723557

What's happening in Jersey?

• Jersey Jazz Festival – taking place at various venues around the Island. Held between 6th and 9th April 2000.

• The Jersey International Food Festival – this event gives visitors the chance to taste the finest local produce and experience the skills of top Jersey Chefs. Held between 13th and 21st May 2000.

• Jersey Battle of Flowers – this parade is held on 10th August 2000 and features floats covered in flowers, musicians, dancers and carnival queens.

For further information, please contact:-

Jersey Tourism
Liberation Square
St Helier
Jersey JE1 1BB
Tel: 01534 500700

ST PIERRE PARK HOTEL

ROHAIS, ST PETER PORT, GUERNSEY, CHANNEL ISLANDS GY1 1FD
TEL: 01481 728282 FAX: 01481 712041 E-MAIL: stppark@itl.net

Conveniently situated only minutes away from the airport and St Peter Port, this superb 5 Crown hotel is an ideal choice for a business function, short break, sporting or family holiday. Nestling in 45 acres of glorious parkland, the estate has its own lake, fountain, driving range and a challenging 9-hole golf course, designed by Tony Jacklin. Following a careful and extensive refurbishment, the en suite bedrooms offer comfortable accommodation and many of the latest amenities. Specialising in delicate seafood recipes, the Victor Hugo is one of Guernsey's finest restaurants and uses the freshest local produce. A more informal ambience may be found in the Café Renoir, where guests may savour brasserie-style snacks and refreshments. Fitness enthusiasts will be pleased with the extensive leisure facilities at the hotel's Le Mirage Health Suite, including an indoor swimming pool and individual saunas and steam rooms. Golf, tennis, croquet and many other sports may also be practised on site. With its French influence and varied coastline, Guernsey has so much to offer. Guests may spend an afternoon exploring the delightful harbour town of St Peter Port and enjoy exclusive VAT free shopping. **Directions:** The hotel is centrally situated, only 10 minutes' drive from the airport and 5 minutes' drive from St Peter Port, Guernsey's main town. Take the Rohais road westbound out of St Peter Port. Price guide: Single from £125; double/twin from £165; suite from £320.

THE ATLANTIC HOTEL

LE MONT DE LA PULENTE, ST BRELADE, JERSEY JE3 8HE
TEL: 01534 744101 FAX: 01534 744102 E–MAIL: atlantic@itl.net

A major refurbishment programme in 1994 has transformed this modern building into one with classical warmth and style internally. Privately owned and supervised, every aspect of the four-star service matches its location overlooking the five-mile sweep of St Ouen's Bay. Situated in three acres of private grounds alongside La Moye Golf Course, there is something here for everyone. General Manager, Simon Dufty and his team provide the highest standards of welcome and service. The 50 bedrooms are furnished in the style of the 18th century and like the public rooms, have co-ordinated colours and fabrics. All have picture windows with views of the sea or the golf course. There are luxury suites and garden studios within the hotel as well. The award-winning restaurant, beautifully situated overlooking the open air pool and terrace, specialises in modern British cooking created by Head Chef, Ken Healy. For the more energetic guest, or those wishing to lose excess calories, The Atlantic has extensive indoor health and leisure facilities in The Palm Club including an indoor ozone treated pool. The hotel is an ideal spot from which to walk on the beach or coast paths, to play golf, go riding or just relax. There are comprehensive meeting facilities. **Directions:** Off a private drive off the A13 at La Pulente, two miles from the airport. Price guide: Single £100; double/twin £125; suite £200.

CHÂTEAU LA CHAIRE

ROZEL BAY, JERSEY JE3 6AJ
TEL: 01534 863354 FAX: 01534 865137 E-MAIL: res@chateau-la-chaire.co.uk

Nestling on the Rozel Valley's sunny slopes is Château La Chaire, an elegantly proportioned Victorian house surrounded by terraced gardens. Built in 1843, the Château has been enhanced and transformed into a luxurious hotel providing its guests with a superb blend of superior comfort, service and cuisine. Each of the bedrooms has been furnished to the highest standards and offers an impressive array of personal comforts; many en suite bathrooms feature Jacuzzis. The same attention to detail is evident in the public rooms, such as the splendid rococo lounge. The atmosphere throughout the hotel is enhanced by the exceptional personal service that its residents receive. Both adventurous and traditional dishes can be enjoyed in the oak panelled setting of La Chaire restaurant. Seafood is a speciality, but there is plenty of choice to cater for all tastes. Awarded 3AA Red Stars and 2 AA Rosettes. A few minutes from the hotel is the picturesque Rozel Bay, a bustling fishing harbour with safe beaches close by. The island's capital, St Helier, is just six miles away. Local tours, golf, fishing and riding are among the many leisure activities that the hotel's staff will be happy to arrange for guests. **Directions:** The hotel is signposted off the main coastal road to Rozel Bay, six miles north east of St Helier. Price guide: Single from £72; double/twin from £107; suites from £172.

HOTEL L'HORIZON

ST BRELADE'S BAY, JERSEY, JE3 8EF, CHANNEL ISLANDS
TEL: 01534 43101 FAX: 01534 46269

A premier hotel in the Channel Islands, L'Horizon is situated on Jersey's lovely St Brelade's Bay. Its south facing position ensures that the hotel enjoys many hours of sunshine. A variety of reception areas provides guests with a choice of environments in which to sit and relax. Comfortable and spacious bedrooms offer every modern amenity and many enjoy a wonderful view across the bay. All sea facing bedrooms have balconies. There are two restaurants, each noted for its individual style, the traditional and elegant Crystal Room and the intimate Grill Room. L'Horizon has won many international accolades and its menus are compiled from the best fresh Jersey produce and from speciality ingredients from the world's top markets. In summer, relax and sip your favourite cocktails enjoying the panoramic views from the terrace. Guests are invited to take advantage of the superb facilities of the Club L'Horizon, which include a mini gym, large swimming pool, steam room, sauna and hairdressing salon. Activities available nearby are swimming, walking and golf. There are two 18-hole golf courses on the island. Seafarers can go on boat trips round the island or across to Guernsey, Alderney, Herm, Sark, even France. **Directions:** In the heart of St Brelade's Bay, ten minutes from the airport. Price guide: Single from £110; double/twin from £160. Special breaks available.

LONGUEVILLE MANOR

ST SAVIOUR, JERSEY JE2 7WF
TEL: 01534 725501 FAX: 01534 731613 E-MAIL: longman@itl.net

For nearly fifty years, three generations of the Lewis family have welcomed guests to Longueville Manor. This 13th century Manor has undergone an extensive conversion, resulting in a fine and prestigious hotel. The rooms are both comfortable and exquisite and are complemented by the enthusiastic and attentive staff. The individually decorated bedrooms contain delicate fabrics and antique furnishings and are provided with fresh flowers, fruit and home-made biscuits, each morning. Sumptuous cuisine is served in Longueville Manor's restaurant, awarded a Michelin star for the sixth year in 1999. Guests may dine in either the elegant oak-panelled room or the spacious garden room. Many of the fruits, vegetables and herbs are grown in the hotel's walled garden and splendid hothouse and provide fresh produce throughout the seasons. The wine list offers a selection by Longueville's Master Sommelier which includes New World wines, vintages from the French châteaux and a superb choice of champagnes. The large heated pool has an adjoining bar, where guest may enjoy a light alfresco meal during the summer. Tennis can be played on the synthetic grass court whilst the lawn is ideal for croquet. Guests wishing to stroll through the magnificent gardens will be delighted with the picturesque lake, home to a black swan and mandarin ducks. **Directions:** On the A3, one mile from St Helier. Price guide: Single from £132.50; double/twin £165; suite £300.

Johansens Recommended Traditional Inns, Hotels & Restaurants in Great Britain

ENGLAND

Aldbury (Ashridge N.T Estate) – The Greyhound Inn, The Greyhound Inn, Stocks Road, Aldbury, Near Tring, Hertfordshire HP23 5RT. Tel: 01442 851228

Aldeburgh – The Dolphin Inn, The Dolphin Inn, Thorpeness, Aldeburgh, Suffolk IP16 4NA. Tel: 01728 454994

Alfriston – Deans Place Hotel, Deans Place Hotel, Seaford Road, Alfriston, East Sussex BN26 5TW. Tel: 01323 870248

Amberley (Near Arundel) – The Boathouse Brasserie, The Boathouse Brasserie, Houghton Bridge, Amberley, Nr Arundel, West Sussex BN18 9LR. Tel: 01798 831059

Ambleside (Great Langdale) – The New Dungeon Ghyll Hotel, The New Dungeon Ghyll Hotel, Great Langdale, Ambleside, Cumbria LA22 9JY. Tel: 015394 37213

Appleby-In-Westmorland – The Royal Oak Inn, The Royal Oak Inn, Bongate, Appleby-In-Westmorland , Cumbria CA16 6UN. Tel: 017683 51463

Ashbourne (Hognaston) – Red Lion Inn, Red Lion Inn, Main Street, Hognaston, Ashbourne, Derbyshire DE6 1PR. Tel: 01335 370396

Ashbourne (Waldley) – Beeches Country Restaurant, Beeches Country Restaurant, Waldley, Doveridge, Nr Ashbourne, Derbyshire DE6 5LR. Tel: 01889 590288

Axminster (Chardstock) – Tytherleigh Cot Hotel, Tytherleigh Cot Hotel, Chardstock, Axminster, Devon EX13 7BN. Tel: 01460 221170

Badby Nr Daventry – The Windmill At Badby, The Windmill At Badby, Main Street, Badby, Nr Daventry, Northamptonshire NN11 6AN. Tel: 01327 702363

Bamburgh – The Victoria Hotel, The Victoria Hotel, Front Street, Bamburgh, Northumberland NE69 7BP. Tel: 01668 214431

Bassenthwaite Lake – The Pheasant, The Pheasant, Bassenthwaite Lake, Nr Cockermouth, Cumbria CA13 9YE. Tel: 017687 76234

Beckington Nr Bath – The Woolpack Inn, The Woolpack Inn, Beckington, Nr Bath, Somerset BA3 6SP. Tel: 01373 831244

Belford – The Blue Bell Hotel, The Blue Bell Hotel, Market Place, Belford, Northumberland NE70 7NE. Tel: 01668 213543

Bibury – The Catherine Wheel, The Catherine Wheel, Bibury, Nr Cirencester, Gloucestershire GL7 5ND. Tel: 01285 740250

Bickleigh (Nr Tiverton) – The Fisherman's Cot, The Fisherman's Cot, Bickleigh, Nr Tiverton, Devon EX16 8RW. Tel: 01884 855237 / 855289

Binfield – Stag & Hounds, Stag & Hounds, Forest Road, Binfield, Berkshire RG12 9HA. Tel: 01344 483553

Blakeney – White Horse Hotel, White Horse Hotel, 4 High Street, Blakeney, Holt, Norfolk NR25 7AL. Tel: 01263 740574

Bourton-On-The-Water – Dial House Hotel, Dial House Hotel, The Chestnuts, High Street, Bourton-On-The-Water , Gloucestershire GL54 2AN. Tel: 01451 822244

Bridport (West Bexington) – The Manor Hotel, The Manor Hotel, West Bexington, Dorchester, Dorset DT2 9DF. Tel: 01308 897616

Bristol – The New Inn, The New Inn, Badminton Road, Mayshill, Nr Frampton Cottrell, Bristol BS36 2NT. Tel: 01454 773161

Bristol (Aust) – The Boars Head, The Boars Head, Main Road, Aust, Bristol BS12 3AX. Tel: 01454 632581

Broadway – The Broadway Hotel, The Broadway Hotel, The Green, Broadway, Worcestershire WR12 7AA. Tel: 01386 852401

Brockenhurst – The Snakecatcher, The Snakecatcher, Lyndhurst, Brockenhurst, Hampshire SO42 7RL. Tel: 01590 622348

Burford – Cotswold Gateway Hotel, Cotswold Gateway Hotel, Cheltenham Road, Burford, Oxfordshire OX18 4HX. Tel: 01993 822695

Burford – The Golden Pheasant Hotel & Restaurant, The Golden Pheasant Hotel & Restaurant, The High Street, Burford, Oxford OX18 4QA. Tel: 01993 823417

Burford – The Lamb Inn, The Lamb Inn, Sheep Street, Burford, Oxfordshire OX18 4LR. Tel: 01993 823155

Burford (The Barringtons) – The Inn For All Seasons, The Inn For All Seasons, The Barringtons, Burford, Oxfordshire OX18 4TN. Tel: 01451 844324

Burnham Market – The Hoste Arms Hotel, The Hoste Arms Hotel, The Green, Burnham Market, Norfolk PE31 8HD. Tel: 01328 738777

Burnley (Fence) – Fence Gate Inn, Fence Gate Inn, Wheatley Lane Road, Fence, Nr Burnley, Lancashire BB12 9EE. Tel: 01282 618101

Burnsall (Skipton) – The Red Lion, The Red Lion, By the bridge at Burnsall, Near Skipton, North Yorkshire BD23 6BU. Tel: 01756 720204

Burton upon Trent – Ye Olde Dog & Partridge, Ye Olde Dog & Partridge, High Street, Tutbury, Burton upon Trent, Staffordshire DE13 9LS. Tel: 01283 813030

Burton Upon Trent (Sudbury) – Boar's Head Hotel, Boar's Head Hotel, Lichfield Road, Sudbury, Derbyshire DE6 5GX. Tel: 01283 820344

Calver (Near Bakewell) – The Chequers Inn, The Chequers Inn, Froggatt Edge, Nr Calver, Derbyshire S30 1ZB. Tel: 01433 630231

Camborne – Tyacks Hotel, Tyacks Hotel, 27 Commercial Street, Camborne, Cornwall TR14 8LD. Tel: 01209 612424

Cambridge (Withersfield) – The White Horse Inn, The White Horse Inn, Hollow Hill, Withersfield, Haverhill, Suffolk CB9 7SH. Tel: 01440 706081

Carlisle (Talkin Tarn) – The Tarn End House Hotel, The Tarn End House Hotel, Talkin Tarn, Brampton, Cumbria CA8 1LS. Tel: 016977 2340

Castle Ashby – The Falcon Hotel, The Falcon Hotel, Castle Ashby, Northampton, Northamptonshire NN7 1LF. Tel: 01604 696200

Chippenham – The Crown Inn, The Crown Inn, Giddea Hall, Yatton Keynell, Chippenham, Wiltshire SN14 7ER. Tel: 01249 782229

Chipping Sodbury – The Codrington Arms, The Codrington Arms, Wapley Road, Codrington, Nr Chipping Sodbury, Bristol BS37 6RY. Tel: 01454 313145

Christchurch (Highcliffe on Sea) – The Lord Bute, The Lord Bute, 181 / 185 Lymington Road, Highcliffe on Sea, Christchurch , Dorset BH23 4JS. Tel: 01425 278884

Cirencester (Coln St-Aldwyns) – The New Inn at Coln, The New Inn at Coln, Coln St-Aldwyns, Nr Cirencester, Gloucestershire GL7 5AN. Tel: 01285 750651

Cirencester (South Cerney) – The Eliot Arms Hotel, The Eliot Arms Hotel, Clarks Hay, South Cerney, Cirencester, Gloucestershire GL7 2UA. Tel: 01285 860215

Clare (Hundon) – The Plough Inn, The Plough Inn, Brockley Green, Sudbury, Nr Hundon, Suffolk CO10 8DT. Tel: 01440 786789

Clavering (Stansted) – The Cricketers, The Cricketers, Clavering, Nr Saffron Walden, Essex CB11 4QT. Tel: 01799 550442

Cleobury Mortimer – Crown At Hopton, Crown At Hopton, Hopton Wafers, Cleobury Mortimer, Shropshire DY14 0NB. Tel: 01299 270372

Cleobury Mortimer – The Redfern Hotel, The Redfern Hotel, Cleobury Mortimer, Shropshire DY14 8AA. Tel: 01299 270 395

Colchester (Coggeshall) – The White Hart Hotel & Restaurant, The White Hart Hotel & Restaurant, Market End, Coggeshall, Essex CO6 1NH. Tel: 01376 561654

Coleford – The New Inn, The New Inn, Coleford, Crediton, Devon EX17 5BZ. Tel: 01363 84242

Dartmouth – The Little Admiral Hotel, The Little Admiral Hotel, Victoria Road, Dartmouth, Devon TQ6 9RT. Tel: 01803 832572

Ditcheat (Nr Wells) – The Manor House Inn, The Manor House Inn, Ditcheat, Somerset BA4 6RB. Tel: 01749 860276

Doncaster – Hamilton's Restaurant & Hotel, Hamilton's Restaurant & Hotel, Carr House Road, Doncaster, South Yorkshire DN4 5HP. Tel: 01302 760770

Dorchester-On-Thames – The George Hotel, The George Hotel, High Street, Dorchester-On-Thames, Oxford OX10 7HH. Tel: 01865 340404

East Witton (Wensleydale) – The Blue Lion, The Blue Lion, East Witton, Nr Leyburn, North Yorkshire DL8 4SN. Tel: 01969 624273

Eccleshall – The George Inn, The George Inn, Eccleshall, Staffordshire ST21 6DF. Tel: 01785 850300

Edenbridge – Ye Old Crown, Ye Old Crown, High Street, Edenbridge, Kent TN8 5AR. Tel: 01732 867896

Egton (Nr Whitby) – The Wheatsheaf Inn, The Wheatsheaf Inn, Egton, Nr Whitby, North Yorkshire YO21 1TZ. Tel: 01947 895271

Eton (Windsor) – The Christopher Hotel, The Christopher Hotel, High Street, Eton, Windsor, Berkshire SL4 6AN. Tel: 01753 811677 / 852359

Evershot – The Acorn Inn Hotel, The Acorn Inn Hotel, Fore Street, Evershot, Nr Dorchester, Dorset DT2 0JW. Tel: 01935 83228

Evesham – The Northwick Hotel, The Northwick Hotel, Waterside, Evesham, Worcestershire WR11 6BT. Tel: 01386 40322

Evesham (Offenham) – Riverside Restaurant And Hotel, Riverside Restaurant And Hotel, The Parks, Offenham Road, Nr Evesham, Worcestershire WR11 5JP. Tel: 01386 446200

Exmoor – The Royal Oak Inn, The Royal Oak Inn, Winsford, Exmoor National Park, Somerset TA24 7JE. Tel: 01643 851455

Falmouth (Constantine) – Trengilly Wartha Country Inn & Restaurant, Trengilly Wartha Country Inn & Restaurant, Nancenoy, Constantine, Falmouth, Cornwall TR11 5RP. Tel: 01326 340332

Fifield (Nr Burford) – The Merrymouth Inn, The Merrymouth Inn, Stow Road, Fifield, Nr Burford, Oxford OX7 6HR. Tel: 01993 831652

Ford, Nr Bath – The White Hart, The White Hart, Ford, Chippenham, Wiltshire SN14 8RP. Tel: 01249 782213

Fordingbridge (New Forest) – The Woodfalls Inn, The Woodfalls Inn, The Ridge, Woodfalls, Fordingbridge, Hampshire SP5 2LN. Tel: 01725 513222

Goring-On-Thames – The Leatherne Bottel Riverside Inn & Restaurant, The Leatherne Bottel Riverside Inn & Restaurant, The Bridleway, Goring-On-Thames, Berkshire RG8 0HS. Tel: 01491 872667

Grimsthorpe (Bourne) – The Black Horse Inn, The Black Horse Inn, Grimsthorpe, Bourne, Lincolnshire PE10 0LY. Tel: 01778 591247

Grindleford – The Maynard Arms, The Maynard Arms, Main Road, Grindleford, Derbyshire S32 2HE. Tel: 01433 630321

Halifax/Huddersfield – The Rock Inn Hotel, The Rock Inn Hotel, Holywell Green, Halifax, West Yorkshire HX4 9BS. Tel: 01422 379721

Handcross (Slaugham) – The Chequers At Slaugham, The Chequers At Slaugham, Slaugham, Nr Handcross, West Sussex RH17 6AQ. Tel: 01444 400239/400996

Harrogate – The George & Newboulds Restaurant, The George & Newboulds Restaurant, Wormald Green, Nr Harrogate, North Yorkshire HG3 3PR. Tel: 01765 677214

Harrogate (Killinghall) – The Low Hall Hotel, The Low Hall Hotel, Ripon Road, Killinghall, Harrogate, North Yorkshire HG3 2AY. Tel: 01423 508598

Harrogate (Knaresborough) – The Dower House, The Dower House, Bond End, Knaresborough, Nr Harrogate, North Yorkshire HG5 9AL. Tel: 01423 863302

Harrogate (Ripley Castle) – The Boar's Head Hotel, The Boar's Head Hotel, Ripley, Harrogate, North Yorkshire HG3 3AY. Tel: 01423 771888

Hartley Wintney (Bramshill) – The Hatchgate, The Hatchgate, Bramshill, Nr Hook, Hampshire RG27 0JX. Tel: 01189 32666

Hathersage – The Plough Inn, The Plough Inn, Leadmill Bridge, Hathersage, Derbyshire S30 1BA. Tel: 01433 650319

Hay-On-Wye – Rhydspence Inn, Rhydspence Inn, Whitney-On-Wye, Nr Hay-On-Wye, Herefordshire HR3 6EU. Tel: 01497 831262

Hayfield (High Peak) – The Waltzing Weasel, The Waltzing Weasel, New Mills Road, Birch Vale, High Peak, Derbyshire SK22 1BT. Tel: 01663 743402

Helmsley – The Feathers Hotel, The Feathers Hotel, Market Place, Helmsley, North Yorkshire YO6 5BH. Tel: 01439 770275

Helmsley (Near York) – The Feversham Arms Hotel, The Feversham Arms Hotel, Helmsley , North Yorkshire YO6 5AG. Tel: 01439 770766

Hindon, Nr Salisbury – The Lamb at Hindon, The Lamb at Hindon, High Street, Hindon, Salisbury, Wiltshire SP3 6DP. Tel: 01747 820573

Hindon (Nr Salisbury) not opposite Lamb – The Grosvenor Arms, The Grosvenor Arms, Hindon, Salisbury, Wiltshire SP3 6DJ. Tel: 01747 820696

Honiton (Wilmington) – Home Farm Hotel, Home Farm Hotel, Wilmington, Nr Honiton, Devon EX14 9JR. Tel: 01404 831278

Huddersfield (Golcar) – The Weavers Shed Restaurant with Rooms, The Weavers Shed Restaurant with Rooms, Knowl Road, Golcar, Huddersfield, West Yorkshire HD7 4AN. Tel: 01484 654284

Ilchester – Northover Manor, Northover Manor, Ilchester, Somerset BA22 8LD. Tel: 01935 840447

Kenilworth – Clarendon House Bar Brasserie Hotel, Clarendon House Bar Brasserie Hotel, High Street, Kenilworth, Warwickshire CV8 1LZ. Tel: 01926 857668

Kingskerswell (Nr Torquay) – The Barn Owl Inn, The Barn Owl Inn, Aller Mills, Kingskerswell, Devon TQ12 5AN. Tel: 01803 872130

Knutsford – Longview Hotel And Restaurant, Longview Hotel And Restaurant, 51/55 Manchester Road, Knutsford, Cheshire WA16 0LX. Tel: 01565 632119

Ledbury – Feathers Hotel, Feathers Hotel, High Street, Ledbury, Herefordshire HR8 1DS. Tel: 01531 635266

Leek (Blackshaw Moor) – The Three Horseshoes Inn & Kirk's Restaurant, The Three Horseshoes Inn & Kirk's Restaurant, Buxton Road, Blackshaw Moor, Nr Leek, Staffordshire ST13 8TW. Tel: 01538 300296

Long Melford – The Countrymen, The Countrymen, The Green, Long Melford, Suffolk CO10 9DN. Tel: 01787 312356

Longleat (Horningsham) – The Bath Arms, The Bath Arms, Horningsham, Warminster, Wiltshire BA12 7LY. Tel: 01985 844308

Lymington – The Angel Inn, The Angel Inn, High Street, New Forest, Hampshire SO41 9AP. Tel: 01590 672050

Lynmouth – The Rising Sun, The Rising Sun, Harbourside, Lynmouth, Devon EX35 6EQ. Tel: 01598 753223

Maidstone (Ringlestone) – Ringlestone Inn, Ringlestone Inn, 'Twixt Harrietsham and Wormshill, Nr Maidstone, Kent ME17 1NX. Tel: 01622 859900

Malmesbury – The Horse And Groom Inn, The Horse And Groom Inn, Charlton, Near Malmesbury, Wiltshire SN16 9DL. Tel: 01666 823904

Mells (Nr Bath) – The Talbot Inn at Mells, The Talbot Inn at Mells, High Street, Mells, Nr Bath, Somerset BA11 3PN. Tel: 01373 812254

Newbury (Gt Shefford) – The Swan Inn, The Swan Inn, Newbury Road, Great Shefford, Newbury, Berkshire RG17 7DS. Tel: 01488 648271

Newby Bridge – The Swan Hotel, The Swan Hotel, Newby Bridge, Nr Ulverston, Cumbria LA12 8NB. Tel: 015395 31681

North Walsham – Elderton Lodge, Elderton Lodge, Gunton Park, Thorpe Market, Nr North Walsham, Norfolk NR11 8TZ. Tel: 01263 833547

Nottingham – Hotel Des Clos, Hotel Des Clos, Old Lenton Lane, Nottingham, Nottinghamshire NG7 2SA. Tel: 01159 866566

Old Hunstanton – The Lodge Hotel & Restaurant, The Lodge Hotel & Restaurant, Old Hunstanton, Norfolk PE36 6HX. Tel: 01485 532896

Oxford (Banbury) – Holcombe Hotel, Holcombe Hotel, High Street, Deddington, Nr Woodstock, Oxfordshire OX15 0SL. Tel: 01869 338274

Oxford (Middleton Stoney) – The Jersey Arms, The Jersey Arms, Middleton Stoney, Oxfordshire OX6 8SE. Tel: 01869 343234

Oxford (Minster Lovell) – The Mill & Old Swan, The Mill & Old Swan, Minster Lovell, Nr Burford, Oxfordshire OX8 5RN. Tel: 01993 774441

Pelynt, Nr Looe – Jubilee Inn, Jubilee Inn, Pelynt, Nr Looe, Cornwall PL13 2JZ. Tel: 01503 220312

Penistone (Ingbirchworth) – The Fountain Inn & Rooms, The Fountain Inn & Rooms, Wellthorne Lane, Ingbirchworth, Nr Penistone, South Yorkshire S36 7GJ. Tel: 01226 763125

Petworth – The Stonemason's Inn, The Stonemason's Inn, North Street, Petworth, West Sussex GU28 9NL. Tel: 01798 342510

Petworth (Coultershaw Bridge) – Badgers, Badgers, Coultershaw Bridge, Petworth, West Sussex GU28 0JF. Tel: 01798 342651

Petworth (Fittleworth) – The Swan Inn, The Swan Inn, Lower Street, Fittleworth, Nr Petworth, West Sussex RH20 1EN. Tel: 01798 865429

Petworth (Sutton) – White Horse Inn, White Horse Inn, Sutton, Nr Pulborough, West Sussex RH20 1PS. Tel: 01798 869 221

Port Gaverne – The Port Gaverne Hotel, The Port Gaverne Hotel, Nr Port Isaac, North Cornwall PL29 3SQ. Tel: 01208 880244

Preston (Goosnargh) – Ye Horn's Inn, Ye Horn's Inn, Horn's Lane, Goosnargh, Nr Preston, Lancashire PR3 2FJ. Tel: 01772 865230

Reading (Streatley) – The Bull at Streatley, The Bull at Streatley, Reading Road, Reading, Berkshire RG8 9TJ. Tel: 01491 875231

Romsey (Greatbridge) – Duke's Head, Duke's Head, Greatbridge, Nr Romsey, Hampshire SO51 0HB. Tel: 01794 514450

Rugby (Easenhall) – The Golden Lion Inn of Easenhall, The Golden Lion Inn of Easenhall, Easenhall, Nr Rugby, Warwickshire CV23 0JA. Tel: 01788 832265

Rye – The George Hotel, The George Hotel, High Street, Rye, East Sussex TN31 7JP. Tel: 01797 222114

Saddleworth (Delph) – The Old Bell Inn Hotel, The Old Bell Inn Hotel, Huddersfield Road, Delph, Saddleworth, Nr Oldham, Greater Manchester OL3 5EG. Tel: 01457 870130

Salisbury (Downton) – The White Horse, The White Horse, Downton, Salisbury, Wiltshire SP5 3LY. Tel: 01725 510408

Sheffield (Dronfield) – Manor House Hotel & Restaurant, Manor House Hotel & Restaurant, High Street, Old Dronfield, Derbyshire S18 1PY. Tel: 01246 413971

Sherborne – The Half Moon Inn, The Half Moon Inn, Half Moon Street, Sherborne, Dorset DT9 3LN. Tel: 01935 812017

Sherborne (Oborne) – The Grange Hotel & Restaurant, The Grange Hotel & Restaurant, Oborne, Nr Sherborne, Dorset DT9 4LA. Tel: 01935 813463

Sherborne (West Camel) – The Walnut Tree, The Walnut Tree, West Camel, Nr Sherborne, Somerset BA22 7QW. Tel: 01935 851292

Shifnal (Telford) – Naughty Nell's, Naughty Nell's, 1 Park Street, Shifnal, Shropshire TF11 9BA. Tel: 01952 411412

Shipton Under Wychwood – The Shaven Crown Hotel, The Shaven Crown Hotel, High Street, Shipton Under Wychwood, Oxfordshire OX7 6BA. Tel: 01993 830330

Snettisham (Nr King's Lynn) – The Rose & Crown, The Rose & Crown, Old Church Road, Snettisham, King's Lynn, Norfolk PE31 7LX. Tel: 01485 541382

Southport (Formby) – Tree Tops Country House Restaurant & Hotel, Tree Tops Country House Restaurant & Hotel, Southport Old Road, Formby, Nr Southport, Lancashire L37 0AB. Tel: 01704 572430

Stafford (Ingestre) – The Dower House, The Dower House, Ingestre Park, Great Haywood, Staffordshire ST18 0RE. Tel: 01889 270707

Stamford – The Crown Hotel, The Crown Hotel, All Saints Place, Stamford, Lincolnshire PE9 2AG. Tel: 01780 763136

Stamford (Nr Grantham) – Black Bull Inn, Black Bull Inn, Lobthorpe, Nr Grantham, Lincolnshire NG33 5LL. Tel: 01476 860086

Stow-on-the-Wold – The Unicorn Hotel, The Unicorn Hotel, Sheep Street, Stow-on-the-Wold, Gloucestershire GL54 1HQ. Tel: 01451 830257

Stow-On-The-Wold (Bledington) – The Kings Head Inn & Restaurant, The Kings Head Inn & Restaurant, The Green, Bledington, Oxfordshire OX7 6XQ. Tel: 01608 658365

Stratford-upon-Avon – The Coach House Hotel & Cellar Restaurant, The Coach House Hotel & Cellar Restaurant, 16/17 Warwick Road, Stratford-upon-Avon, Warwickshire CV37 6YW. Tel: 01789 204109 / 299468

Stroud (Frampton Mansell) – The Crown Inn, The Crown Inn, Frampton Mansell, Stroud, Gloucestershire GL6 8JG. Tel: 01285 760601

Sudbury (Long Melford) – The Bull Hotel, The Bull Hotel, Hall Street, Long Melford, Suffolk CO10 9JG. Tel: 01787 378494

Taunton (Staple Fitzpaine) – Greyhound Inn, Greyhound Inn, Staple Fitzpaine, Nr Taunton, Somerset TA3 5SP. Tel: 01823 480227

Telford (Hadley Park) – Hadley Park House Hotel, Hadley Park House Hotel, Hadley Park, Telford, Shropshire TF1 4UL. Tel: 01952 677269

Telford (Norton) – The Hundred House Hotel, The Hundred House Hotel, Bridgnorth Road, Norton, Nr Shifnal, Telford, Shropshire TF11 9EE. Tel: 01952 730353

Tenterden – The White Lion Hotel, The White Lion Hotel, The High Street, Tenterden, Kent TN30 6BD. Tel: 01580 765077

Thaxted – Recorders House Restaurant (With Rooms), Recorders House Restaurant (With Rooms), 17 Town Street, Thaxted, Essex CM6 2LD. Tel: 01371 830438

Thirsk – Crab & Lobster, Crab & Lobster, Asenby, North Yorkshire YO7 3QL. Tel: 01845 577286

Thornham – The Lifeboat Inn, The Lifeboat Inn, Ship Lane, Thornham, Norfolk PE36 6LT. Tel: 01485 512236

Thorpe Market – Green Farm Restaurant And Hotel, Green Farm Restaurant And Hotel, North Walsham Road, Thorpe Market, Norfolk NR11 8TH. Tel: 01263 833602

Tintagel (Trebarwith Strand) – The Port William, The Port William, Trebarwith Strand, Nr Tintagel, Cornwall PL34 0HB. Tel: 01840 770230

Totnes (Bow Bridge, Ashprington) – The Watermans Arms, The Watermans Arms, Bow Bridge, Ashprington, Nr Totnes, Devon TQ9 7EG. Tel: 01803 732214

Totnes (Staverton) – The Sea Trout Inn, The Sea Trout Inn, Staverton, Nr Totnes, Devon TQ9 6PA. Tel: 01803 762274

Troutbeck (Near Windermere) – The Mortal Man Hotel, The Mortal Man Hotel, Troutbeck, Nr Windermere, Cumbria LA23 1PL. Tel: 015394 33193

Upton-Upon-Severn, Nr Malvern – The White Lion Hotel, The White Lion Hotel, High Street, Upton-Upon-Severn, Nr Malvern, Worcestershire WR8 0HJ. Tel: 01684 592551

Warminster (Upton Scudamore) – The Angel Inn, The Angel Inn, Upton Scudamore, Warminster, Wiltshire BA12 0AG. Tel: 01985 213225

Wells – The Market Place, Wells, Somerset BA5 2RW. Tel: 01749 672616

Weobley – The Salutation Inn, The Salutation Inn, Market Pitch, Weobley, Herefordshire HR4 8SJ. Tel: 01544 318443

West Auckland – The Manor House Hotel & Country Club, The Manor House Hotel & Country Club, The Green, West Auckland, County Durham DL14 9HW. Tel: 01388 834834

West Witton (Wensleydale) – The Wensleydale Heifer Inn, The Wensleydale Heifer Inn, West Witton, Wensleydale, North Yorkshire DL8 4LS. Tel: 01969 622322

Whitewell – The Inn At Whitewell, The Inn At Whitewell, Forest Of Bowland, Clitheroe, Lancashire BB7 3AT. Tel: 01200 448222

Witney (Hailey) – The Bird in Hand, The Bird in Hand, Hailey, Witney, Oxfordshire OX8 5XP. Tel: 01993 868321

Wooler – The Tankerville Arms Hotel, The Tankerville Arms Hotel, Wooler, Northumberland NE71 6AD. Tel: 01668 281581

Worthing (Bramber) – The Old Tollgate Restaurant And Hotel, The Old Tollgate Restaurant And Hotel, The Street, Bramber, Steyning, West Sussex BN44 3WE. Tel: 01903 879494

Wroxham – The Barton Angler Country Inn, The Barton Angler Country Inn, Irstead Road, Neatishead, Nr Wroxham, Norfolk NR12 8XP. Tel: 01692 630740

York (Easingwold) – The George at Easingwold, The George at Easingwold, Market Place, Easingwold, York, North Yorkshire YO6 3AD. Tel: 01347 821698

WALES

Chepstow – The Castle View Hotel, The Castle View Hotel, 16 Bridge Street, Chepstow, Monmouthshire NP6 5EZ. Tel: 01291 620349

Llanarmon Dyffryn Ceiriog – The West Arms Hotel, The West Arms Hotel, Llanarmon D C, Nr Llangollen, Denbighshire LL20 7LD. Tel: 01691 600665

Llandeilo (Rhosmaen) – The Plough Inn, The Plough Inn, Rhosmaen, Llandeilo, Carmarthenshire SA19 6NP. Tel: 01558 823431

Machynlleth – The Wynnstay, The Wynnstay, Maengwyn Street, Machynlleth, Powys SY20 8AE. Tel: 01654 702941

Presteigne – The Radnorshire Arms, The Radnorshire Arms, High Street, Presteigne, Powys. Tel: 01544 267406

SCOTLAND

Glendevon (South Perthshire) – Tormaukin Hotel, Tormaukin Hotel, Glendevon, By Dollar, Perthshire FK14 7JY. Tel: 01259 781252

Inverness (Farr) – Grouse & Trout, Grouse & Trout, Flichity, By Farr, Inverness, IV1 2XE. Tel: 01808 521314

Isle Of Skye (Eilean Iarmain) – Hotel Eilean Iarmain, Hotel Eilean Iarmain, Sleat, Isle Of Skye IV43 8QR. Tel: 01471 833332

Isle Of Skye (Uig) – Uig Hotel, Uig Hotel, Uig, Isle Of Skye, Isle Of Skye IV51 9YE. Tel: 01470 542205

Kylesku (Sutherland) – Kylesku Hotel, Kylesku Hotel, Kylesku, Via Lairg, Sutherland IV27 4HW. Tel: 01971 502231/502200

Loch Earn (Perthshire) – Achray House on Loch Earn, Achray House on Loch Earn, Loch Earn, St Fillan, Perthshire PH6 2NF. Tel: 01764 685231

Moffat – Annandale Arms Hotel, Annandale Arms Hotel, High Street, Moffat, Dumfriesshire DG10 9HF. Tel: 01683 220013

Pitlochry – The Moulin Hotel, The Moulin Hotel, Moulin, By Pitlochry, Perthshire PH16 5EW. Tel: 01796 472196

Plockton (By Kyle of Lochalsh) – The Plockton Hotel & Garden Restaurant, The Plockton Hotel & Garden Restaurant, Harbour Street, Plockton, Wester Ross IV52 8TN. Tel: 01599 544274

Poolewe (Wester Ross) – Pool House Hotel, Pool House Hotel, Poolewe, Achnasheen, Wester Ross IV22 2LD. Tel: 01445 781272

CHANNEL ISLANDS

Guernsey (St Peter Port) – Les Rocquettes Hotel, Les Rocquettes Hotel, Les Gravees, St Peter Port, GY1 1RN. Tel: 01481 722176

Johansens Recommended Country Houses & Small Hotels – Great Britain & Ireland

ENGLAND

Alcester (Arrow) – Arrow Mill Hotel And Restaurant, Arrow Mill Hotel And Restaurant, Arrow, Nr Alcester, Warwickshire B49 5NL. Tel: 01789 762419

Ambleside (Clappersgate) – Nanny Brow Country House Hotel & Restaurant, Nanny Brow Country House Hotel & Restaurant, Clappersgate, Ambleside, Cumbria LA22 9NF. Tel: 015394 32036

Ampleforth – Shallowdale House, Shallowdale House, Ampleforth, York, North Yorkshire YO62 4DY. Tel: 01439 788325

Appleton-Le-Moors – Appleton Hall, Appleton Hall, Appleton-Le-Moors, North Yorkshire YO6 6TF. Tel: 01751 417227

Arundel (Burpham) – Burpham Country House Hotel, Burpham Country House Hotel, Old Down, Burpham, Nr Arundel, West Sussex BN18 9RJ. Tel: 01903 882160

Atherstone – Chapel House, Chapel House, Friars' Gate, Atherstone, Warwickshire CV9 1EY. Tel: 01827 718949

Bakewell (Rowsley) – East Lodge Country House Hotel, East Lodge Country House Hotel, Rowsley, Matlock, Derbyshire DE4 2EF. Tel: 01629 734474

Bakewell (Rowsley) – The Peacock Hotel at Rowsley, The Peacock Hotel at Rowsley, Rowsley, Near Matlock, Derbyshire DE4 2EB. Tel: 01629 733518

Bamburgh – Waren House Hotel, Waren House Hotel, Waren Mill, Bamburgh, Northumberland NE70 7EE. Tel: 01668 214581

Barnstaple (Bishops Tawton) – Downrew House Hotel, Downrew House Hotel, Bishops Tawton, Barnstaple, Devon EX32 0DY. Tel: 01271 342497

Bath – Apsley House, Apsley House, 141 Newbridge Hill, Bath, Somerset BA1 3PT. Tel: 01225 336966

Bath – Bloomfield House, Bloomfield House, 146 Bloomfield Road, Bath, Somerset BA2 2AS. Tel: 01225 420105

Bath – Duke's Hotel, Duke's Hotel, Great Pulteney Street, Bath, Somerset BA2 4DN. Tel: 01225 463512

Bath – Eagle House, Eagle House, Church Street, Bathford, Somerset BA1 7RS. Tel: 01225 859946

Bath – Oldfields, Oldfields, 102 Wells Road, Bath, Somerset BA2 3AL. Tel: 01225 317984

Bath – Paradise House, Paradise House, Holloway, Bath, Somerset BA2 4PX. Tel: 01225 317723

Bath – Villa Magdala, Villa Magdala, Henrietta Road, Bath, Somerset BA2 6LX. Tel: 01225 466329

Bath (Bradford-On-Avon) – Widbrook Grange, Widbrook Grange, Trowbridge Road, Bradford-On-Avon, Wiltshire BA15 1UH. Tel: 01225 864750 / 863173

Bath (Midsomer Norton) – The Old Priory Hotel, The Old Priory Hotel, Church Square, Midsomer Norton, Somerset BA3 2HX. Tel: 01761 416784

Bath (Norton St Philip) – Bath Lodge Hotel, Bath Lodge Hotel, Norton St Philip, Bath, Somerset BA3 6NH. Tel: 01225 723040

Bath (Woolverton) – Woolverton House, Woolverton House, Woolverton, Nr Bath, Somerset BA3 6QS. Tel: 01373 830415

Belper (Shottle) – Dannah Farm Country Guest House, Dannah Farm Country Guest House, Bowman's Lane, Shottle, Nr Belper, Derbyshire DE56 2DR. Tel: 01773 550273 / 630

Beverley (Walkington) – The Manor House, The Manor House, Northlands, Walkington, East Yorkshire HU17 8RT. Tel: 01482 881645

Bibury – Bibury Court, Bibury Court, Bibury , Gloucestershire GL7 5NT. Tel: 01285 740337

Bicester (Chesterton) – Bignell Park Hotel, Bignell Park Hotel, Chesterton, Nr Bicester, OX6 8UE. Tel: 01869 241444

Bideford (Northam) – Yeoldon House Hotel, Yeoldon House Hotel, Durrant Lane, Northam, Nr Bideford, Devon EX39 2RL. Tel: 01237 474400

Biggin-By-Hartington – Biggin Hall, Biggin Hall, Biggin-By-Hartington, Buxton, Derbyshire SK17 0DH. Tel: 01298 84451

Blockley (Chipping Campden) – Lower Brook House, Lower Brook House, Blockley, Nr Moreton-In-Marsh, Gloucestershire GL56 9DS. Tel: 01386 700286

Bolton (Edgworth) – Pelton Fold Farm, Pelton Fold Farm, Bury Road, Edgworth, Bolton, Lancashire BL7 0BS. Tel: 01204 852207

Bolton (Edgworth) – Quarlton Manor Farm, Quarlton Manor Farm, Plantation Road , Edgworth, Turton, Bolton , Lancashire BL7 0DD. Tel: 01204 852277

Bridgnorth – Cross Lane House Hotel, Cross Lane House Hotel, Cross Lane Head, Bridgnorth, Shropshire WV16 4SJ. Tel: 01746 764887

Brighton – The Granville, The Granville, 124 Kings Road, Brighton, East Sussex BN1 2FA. Tel: 01273 326302

Broadway – The Broadway Hotel, The Broadway Hotel, The Green, Broadway, Worcestershire WR12 7AA. Tel: 01386 852401

Broadway – Collin House Hotel, Collin House Hotel, Collin Lane, Broadway, Worcestershire WR12 7PB. Tel: 01386 858354

Broadway (Willersey) – The Old Rectory, The Old Rectory, Church Street, Willersey, Broadway, Gloucestershire WR12 7PN. Tel: 01386 853729

Brockenhurst – Thatched Cottage Hotel & Restaurant, Thatched Cottage Hotel & Restaurant, 16 Brookley Road, Brockenhurst, New Forest, Hampshire SO42 7RR. Tel: 01590 623090

Brockenhurst – Whitley Ridge & Country House Hotel, Whitley Ridge & Country House Hotel, Beaulieu Road, Brockenhurst, New Forest, Hampshire SO42 7QL. Tel: 01590 622354

Buttermere (Lorton Vale) – New House Farm, New House Farm, Lorton, Cockermouth, Cumbria CA13 9UU. Tel: 01900 85404

Cambridge (Melbourn) – Melbourn Bury, Melbourn Bury, Melbourn, Cambridgeshire, Nr Royston, Cambridgeshire SG8 6DE. Tel: 01763 261151

Carlisle (Crosby-On-Eden) – Crosby Lodge Country House Hotel, Crosby Lodge Country House Hotel, High Crosby, Crosby-On-Eden, Carlisle, Cumbria CA6 4QZ. Tel: 01228 573618

Cartmel – Aynsome Manor Hotel, Aynsome Manor Hotel, Cartmel, Grange-Over-Sands, Cumbria LA11 6HH. Tel: 015395 36653

Castle Cary – Bond's - Bistro with Rooms, Bond's - Bistro with Rooms, Ansford Hill, Castle Cary, Somerset BA7 7JP. Tel: 01963 350464

Chagford – Easton Court Hotel, Easton Court Hotel, Easton Cross, Chagford, Devon TQ13 8JL. Tel: 01647 433469

Chagford – Mill End Hotel, Mill End Hotel, Dartmoor National Park, Chagford, Devon TQ13 8JN. Tel: 01647 432282

Cheltenham (Charlton Kings) – Charlton Kings Hotel, Charlton Kings Hotel, Charlton Kings, Cheltenham, Gloucestershire GL52 6UU. Tel: 01242 231061

Cheltenham (Withington) – Halewell, Halewell, Halewell Close, Withington, Nr Cheltenham, Gloucestershire GL54 4BN. Tel: 01242 890238

Chester – Green Bough Hotel, Green Bough Hotel, 60 Hoole Road, Chester, Cheshire CH2 3NL. Tel: 01244 326241

Chichester (Apuldram) – Crouchers Bottom Country Hotel, Crouchers Bottom Country Hotel, Birdham Road, Apuldram, Nr Chichester, West Sussex PO20 7EH. Tel: 01243 784995

Chichester (Charlton) – Woodstock House Hotel, Woodstock House Hotel, Charlton, Nr Chichester, West Sussex PO18 0HU. Tel: 01243 811666

Chippenham – Stanton Manor, Stanton Manor, Stanton Saint Quinton, Nr Chippenham, Wiltshire SN14 6DQ. Tel: 01666 837552

Chipping Campden (Broad Campden) – The Malt House, The Malt House, Broad Campden, Gloucestershire GL55 6UU. Tel: 01386 840295

Church Stretton (Little Stretton) – Mynd House Hotel & Restaurant, Mynd House Hotel & Restaurant, Little Stretton, Church Stretton, Nr Shrewsbury, Shropshire SY6 6RB. Tel: 01694 722212

Clearwell – Tudor Farmhouse Hotel & Restaurant, Tudor Farmhouse Hotel & Restaurant, High Street, Clearwell, Nr Coleford, Gloucestershire GL16 8JS. Tel: 01594 833046

Clovelly (Horns Cross) – Foxdown Manor, Foxdown Manor, Horns Cross, Clovelly, Devon EX39 5PJ. Tel: 01237 451325

Coalville (Greenhill) – Abbots Oak, Abbots Oak, Greenhill, Coalville, Leicestershire LE67 4UY. Tel: 01530 832 328

Combe Martin (East Down) – Ashelford, Ashelford, Ashelford, East Down, Nr Barnstaple, Devon EX31 4LU. Tel: 01271 850469

Crediton (Coleford) – Coombe House Country Hotel, Coombe House Country Hotel, Coleford, Crediton, Devon EX17 5BY. Tel: 01363 84487

Dartmoor (Haytor Vale) – Bel Alp House, Bel Alp House, Haytor , Nr Bovey Tracey, Devon TQ13 9XX. Tel: 01364 661217

Diss (Fressingfield) – Chippenhall Hall, Chippenhall Hall, Fressingfield, Eye, Suffolk IP21 5TD. Tel: 01379 588180 / 586733

Diss (Starston) – Starston Hall, Starston Hall, Starston, Harleston, Norfolk IP20 9PU. Tel: 01379 854252

Doncaster – Hamilton's Restaurant & Hotel, Hamilton's Restaurant & Hotel, Carr House Road, Doncaster, South Yorkshire DN4 5HP. Tel: 01302 760770

Dorchester (Lower Bockhampton) – Yalbury Cottage Hotel, Yalbury Cottage Hotel, Lower Bockhampton, Dorchester, Dorset DT2 8PZ. Tel: 01305 262382

Dorchester-On-Thames – The George Hotel, The George Hotel, High Street, Dorchester-On-Thames, Oxford OX10 7HH. Tel: 01865 340404

Dover (Temple Ewell) – The Woodville Hall, The Woodville Hall, Temple Ewell, Dover , Kent CT16 3DJ. Tel: 01304 825256

Dover (West Cliffe) – Wallett's Court, Wallett's Court, West Cliffe, St. Margaret's-at-Cliffe, Nr Dover, Kent CT15 6EW. Tel: 01304 852424

Dulverton – Ashwick Country House Hotel, Ashwick Country House Hotel, Dulverton, Somerset TA22 9QD. Tel: 01398 323868

Enfield (London) – Oak Lodge Hotel, Oak Lodge Hotel, 80 Village Road, Bush Hill Park, Enfield, Middlesex EN1 2EU. Tel: 020 8360 7082

Epsom – Chalk Lane Hotel, Chalk Lane Hotel, Chalk Lane, Epsom, Surrey KT18 7BB. Tel: 01372 721179

Evershot – Rectory House, Rectory House, Fore Street, Evershot, Dorset DT2 0JW. Tel: 0193583 273

Evesham (Harvington) – The Mill At Harvington, The Mill At Harvington, Anchor Lane, Harvington, Evesham, Worcestershire WR11 5NR. Tel: 01386 870688

Exford (Exmoor) – The Crown Hotel, The Crown Hotel, Exford , Exmoor National Park, Somerset TA24 7PP. Tel: 01643 831554/5

Exmoor (Minehead) – The Beacon Country House Hotel, The Beacon Country House Hotel, Beacon Road, Minehead, Somerset TA24 5SD. Tel: 01643 703476

Falmouth (Mawnan Smith) – Trelawne Hotel-The Hutches Restaurant, Trelawne Hotel-The Hutches Restaurant, Mawnan Smith, Nr Falmouth, Cornwall TR11 5HS. Tel: 01326 250226

Fenny Drayton (Leicestershire) – White Wings, White Wings, Quaker Close, Fenny Drayton, Nr Nuneaton, Leicestershire CV13 6BS. Tel: 01827 716100

Gatwick (Charlwood) – Stanhill Court Hotel, Stanhill Court Hotel, Stan Hill , Charlwood, Nr Horley, Surrey RH6 0EP. Tel: 01293 862166

Golant by Fowey – The Cormorant Hotel, The Cormorant Hotel, Golant, Fowey, Cornwall PL23 1LL. Tel: 01726 833426

Grasmere (Rydal Water) – White Moss House, White Moss House, Rydal Water, Grasmere, Cumbria LA22 9SE. Tel: 015394 35295

Great Snoring – The Old Rectory, The Old Rectory, Barsham Road, Great Snoring, Norfolk NR21 0HP. Tel: 01328 820597

Hampton Court (Hampton Wick) – Chase Lodge, Chase Lodge, 10 Park Road, Hampton Wick, Kingston Upon Thames, Surrey KT1 4AS. Tel: 020 8943 1862

Hamsterley Forest (Near Durham) – Grove House, Grove House, Hamsterley Forest, Nr Bishop Auckland, Co.Durham DL13 3NL. Tel: 01388 488203

Harrogate – The White House, The White House, 10 Park Parade, Harrogate, North Yorkshire HG1 5AH. Tel: 01423 501388

Hawes (Wensleydale) – Rookhurst Country House Hotel, Rookhurst Country House Hotel, West End, Gayle, Hawes, North Yorkshire DL8 3RT. Tel: 01969 667454

Hawkshead (Near Sawrey) – Sawrey House Country Hotel, Sawrey House Country Hotel, Near Sawrey, Hawkshead, Ambleside, Cumbria LA22 OLF. Tel: 015394 36387

Helston – Nansloe Manor, Nansloe Manor, Meneage Road, Helston, Cornwall TR13 0SB. Tel: 01326 574691

Hereford (Fownhope) – The Bowens Country House, The Bowens Country House, Fownhope, Herefordshire HR1 4PS. Tel: 01432 860430

Hereford (Ullingswick) – The Steppes, The Steppes, Ullingswick, Nr Hereford, Herefordshire HR1 3JG. Tel: 01432 820424

Holt (Felbrigg) – Felbrigg Lodge, Felbrigg Lodge, Aylmerton, Norfolk NR11 8RA. Tel: 01263 837588

Ilminster (Cricket Malherbie) – The Old Rectory, The Old Rectory, Cricket Malherbie, Ilminster, Somerset TA19 0PW. Tel: 01460 54364

Ilsington (Dartmoor) – Ilsington Country Hotel, Ilsington Country Hotel, Ilsington, Newton Abbot, Devon TQ13 9RR. Tel: 01364 661452

Isle of Wight (Shanklin) – Rylstone Manor, Rylstone Manor, Rylstone Gardens, Shanklin, Isle of Wight PO37 6RG. Tel: 01983 862806

Keswick (LakeThirlmere) – Dale Head Hall Lakeside Hotel, Dale Head Hall Lakeside Hotel, Thirlmere, Keswick, Cumbria CA12 4TN. Tel: 017687 72478

Keswick (Newlands) – Swinside Lodge Hotel, Swinside Lodge Hotel, Grange Road, Newlands, Keswick, Cumbria CA12 5UE. Tel: 017687 72948

Kirkby Lonsdale – Hipping Hall, Hipping Hall, Cowan Bridge, Kirkby Lonsdale, Cumbria LA6 2JJ. Tel: 015242 71187

Lavenham – Lavenham Priory, Lavenham Priory, Water Street, Lavenham, Sudbury, Suffolk CO10 9RW. Tel: 01787 247404

Leominster – Lower Bache House, Lower Bache House, Kimbolton, Nr Leominster, Herefordshire HR6 0ER. Tel: 01568 750304

Lifton (Sprytown) – The Thatched Cottage Country Hotel And Restaurant, The Thatched Cottage Country Hotel And Restaurant, Sprytown, Lifton, Devon PL16 0AY. Tel: 01566 784224

Lincoln (Washingborough) – Washingborough Hall, Washingborough Hall, Church Hill, Washingborough, Lincoln, Lincolnshire LN4 1BE. Tel: 01522 790340

Looe (Widegates) – Coombe Farm, Coombe Farm, Widegates, Looe, Cornwall PL13 1QN. Tel: 01503 240223

Lorton – Winder Hall, Winder Hall, Low Lorton, Nr Cockermouth, Cumbria CA13 9UP. Tel: 01900 85107

Loughborough – The Old Manor Hotel, The Old Manor Hotel, 11-14 Sparrow Hill, Loughborough, Leicestershire LE11 1BT. Tel: 01509 211228

Ludlow (Diddlebury) – Delbury Hall, Delbury Hall, Diddlebury, Craven Arms, Shropshire SY7 9DH. Tel: 01584 841267

Ludlow (Overton) – Overton Grange Hotel, Overton Grange Hotel, Overton, Ludlow, Shropshire SY8 4AD. Tel: 01584 873500

Luton (Little Offley) – Little Offley, Little Offley, Hitchin, Hertfordshire SG5 3BU. Tel: 01462 768243

Lydford (Vale Down) – Moor View House, Moor View House, Vale Down, Lydford, Devon EX20 4BB. Tel: 01822 820220

Lyme Regis (Charmouth) – Thatch Lodge Hotel, Thatch Lodge Hotel, The Street, Charmouth, Nr Lyme Regis, Dorset DT6 6PQ. Tel: 01297 560407

Lymington – Rosefield House, Rosefield House, Sway Road, Lymington, New Forest, Hampshire SO41 8LR. Tel: 01590 671526

Lymington (Hordle) – Hotel Gordleton Mill, Hotel Gordleton Mill, Silver Street, Hordle, Nr Lymington, Hampshire SO41 6DJ. Tel: 01590 682219

Lynton – Hewitt's Hotel, Hewitt's Hotel, North Walk, Lynton, Devon EX35 6HJ. Tel: 01598 752293

Maidstone (Boughton Monchelsea) – Tanyard, Tanyard, Wierton Hill, Boughton Monchelsea, Nr Maidstone, Kent ME17 4JT. Tel: 01622 744705

Malton – Newstead Grange, Newstead Grange, Norton-On-Derwent, Malton, North Yorkshire YO17 9PJ. Tel: 01653 692502

Maxey (Nr Stamford) – Abbey House & Coach House, Abbey House & Coach House, West End Road, Maxey, Cambridge PE6 9EJ. Tel: 01778 344642

Middlecombe (Minehead) – Periton Park Hotel, Periton Park Hotel, Middlecombe, Nr Minehead, Somerset TA24 8SN. Tel: 01643 706885

Middleham (Wensleydale) – Millers House Hotel, Millers House Hotel, Middleham, Wensleydale, North Yorkshire DL8 4NR. Tel: 01969 622630

Middleham (Wensleydale) – Waterford House, Waterford House, 19 Kirkgate, Middleham, North Yorkshire DL8 4PG. Tel: 01969 622090

Minchinhampton – Burleigh Court, Burleigh Court, Minchinhampton, Gloucestershire GL5 2PF. Tel: 01453 883804

Morchard Bishop – Wigham, Wigham, Morchard Bishop, Crediton, Devon EX17 6RJ. Tel: 01363 877350

New Romney (Littlestone) – Romney Bay House, Romney Bay House, Coast Road, Littlestone, New Romney, Kent TN28 8QY. Tel: 01797 364747

North Walsham – Beechwood Hotel, Beechwood Hotel, Cromer Road, North Walsham, Norfolk NR28 0HD. Tel: 01692 403231

Norwich – The Beeches Hotel & Victorian Gardens, The Beeches Hotel & Victorian Gardens, 2-6 Earlham Road, Norwich, Norfolk NR2 3DB. Tel: 01603 621167

Norwich (Coltishall) – Norfolk Mead Hotel, Norfolk Mead Hotel, Coltishall, Norwich, Norfolk NR12 7DN. Tel: 01603 737531

Norwich (Drayton) – The Stower Grange, The Stower Grange, School Road, Drayton, Norfolk NR8 6EF. Tel: 01603 860210

Norwich (Old Catton) – Catton Old Hall, Catton Old Hall, Lodge Lane, Catton, Norwich, Norfolk NR6 7HG. Tel: 01603 419379

Norwich (Thorpe St Andrew) – The Old Rectory, The Old Rectory, 103 Yarmouth Road, Thorpe St Andrew, Norwich, Norfolk NR7 0HF. Tel: 01603 700772

Nottingham – Cockliffe Country House Hotel, Cockliffe Country House Hotel, Nottingham, Nottinghamshire NG5 8PQ. Tel: 01159 680179

Nottingham (Langar) – Langar Hall, Langar Hall, Langar, Nottinghamshire NG13 9HG. Tel: 01949 860559

Nottingham (Redmile) – L'Auberge, L'Auberge, 29 Main Street, Redmile, Nottinghamshire NG13 0GA. Tel: 01949 843086

Nottingham (Ruddington) – The Cottage Country House Hotel, The Cottage Country House Hotel, Easthorpe Street, Ruddington, Nottingham, Nottinghamshire NG11 6LA. Tel: 01159 846882

Ockham – The Hautboy, The Hautboy, Ockham Lane, Ockham, Surrey GU23 6. Tel: 01483 225355

Oswestry – Pen-y-Dyffryn Country Hotel, Pen-y-Dyffryn Country Hotel, Rhydycroesau, Nr Oswestry, Shropshire SY10 7JD. Tel: 01691 653700

Otterburn – The Tower, The Tower, Otterburn, Northumberland NE19 1NS. Tel: 01830 520620

Owlpen – Owlpen Manor, Owlpen Manor, Near Uley, Gloucestershire GL11 5BZ. Tel: 01453 860261

Oxford (Kingston Bagpuize) – Fallowfields, Fallowfields, Kingston Bagpuize With Southmoor, Oxfordshire OX13 5BH. Tel: 01865 820416

Padstow – Cross House Hotel, Cross House Hotel, Church Street, Padstow, Cornwall PL28 8BG. Tel: 01841 532391

Penrith (Temple Sowerby) – Temple Sowerby House Hotel, Temple Sowerby House Hotel, Temple Sowerby, Penrith, Cumbria CA10 1RZ. Tel: 017683 61578

Penzance – The Summer House, The Summer House, Cornwall Terrace, Penzance, Cornwall TR18 4HL. Tel: 01736 363744

Petersfield (Langrish) – Langrish House, Langrish House, Langrish, Nr Petersfield, Hampshire GU32 1RN. Tel: 01730 266941

Petworth – The Old Railway Station, The Old Railway Station, Coultershaw Bridge, Petworth, West Sussex GU28 0JF. Tel: 01798 342346

Porlock Weir – The Cottage Hotel, The Cottage Hotel, Porlock Weir, Porlock, Somerset TA24 8PB. Tel: 01643 863300

Porlock Weir – Porlock Vale House, Porlock Vale House, Porlock Weir, Somerset TA24 8NY. Tel: 01643 862338

Porthleven (Nr Helston) – Tye Rock Country House Hotel, Tye Rock Country House Hotel, Loe Bar Road, Porthleven, Nr Helston, Cornwall TR13 9EW. Tel: 01326 572695

Portsmouth – The Beaufort Hotel, The Beaufort Hotel, 71 Festing Road, Portsmouth, Hampshire PO4 0NQ. Tel: 023 92823707

Preston (Gardstang) – Pickering Park Country House, Pickering Park Country House, Gardstang Road, Catterall, Gardstang, Lancashire PR3 0HD. Tel: 01995 600999

Pulborough – Chequers Hotel, Chequers Hotel, Church Place, Pulborough, West Sussex RH20 1AD. Tel: 01798 872486

Ringwood – Moortown Lodge, Moortown Lodge, 244 Christchurch Road, Ringwood, Hampshire BH24 3AS. Tel: 01425 471404

Ross-On-Wye (Glewstone) – Glewstone Court, Glewstone Court, Nr Ross-On-Wye, Herefordshire HR9 6AW. Tel: 01989 770367

Rye – White Vine House, White Vine House, High Street, Rye, East Sussex TN31 7JF. Tel: 01797 224748

Saham Toney (Thetford) – Broom Hall, Broom Hall, Richmond Road, Saham Toney, Thetford, Norfolk IP25 7EX. Tel: 01953 882125

Saunton – Preston House Hotel, Preston House Hotel, Saunton, Braunton, Devon EX33 1LG. Tel: 01271 890472

Seavington St Mary, Nr Ilminster – The Pheasant Hotel, The Pheasant Hotel, Seavington St Mary, Nr Ilminster, Somerset TA19 0HQ. Tel: 01460 240502

Sherborne – The Eastbury Hotel, The Eastbury Hotel, Long Street, Sherborne, Dorset DT9 3BY. Tel: 01935 813131

Shipton-Under-Wychwood – The Shaven Crown Hotel, The Shaven Crown Hotel, High Street, Shipton-Under-Wychwood, Oxfordshire OX7 6BA. Tel: 01993 830330

Shrewsbury – Upper Brompton Farm, Upper Brompton Farm, Cross houses, Shrewsbury, Shropshire SY5 6LE. Tel: 01743 761629

Simonsbath (Exmoor) – Simonsbath House Hotel, Simonsbath House Hotel, Simonsbath, Exmoor, Somerset TA24 7SH. Tel: 01643 831259

Snape (Butley) – Butley Priory, Butley Priory, Nr Woodbridge, Suffolk IP12 3NR. Tel: 01394 450046

St Ives (Trink) – The Countryman At Trink Hotel, The Countryman At Trink Hotel, Old Coach Road, St Ives, Cornwall TR26 3JQ. Tel: 01736 797571

St Mawes (Ruan Highlanes) – The Hundred House Hotel, The Hundred House Hotel, Ruan Highlanes, Truro, Cornwall TR2 5JR. Tel: 01872 501336

Stanhope (Weardale) – Horsley Hall, Horsley Hall, East Gate, Nr Stanhope, Bishop Auckland, Co.Durham DL13 2LJ. Tel: 01388 517239

Stanwell (Nr Heathrow) – Stanwell Hall, Stanwell Hall, Town Lane, Stanwell, Nr Staines, Middlesex TW19 7PW. Tel: 01784 252292

Staverton (Nr Totnes) – Kingston House, Kingston House, Staverton, Totnes, Devon TQ9 6AR. Tel: 01803 762 235

Stevenage (Hitchin) – Redcoats Farmhouse Hotel & Restaurant, Redcoats Farmhouse Hotel & Restaurant, Redcoats Green, Nr Hitchin, Hertfordshire SG4 7JR. Tel: 01438 729500

Stonor (Henley-on-Thames) – The Stonor Arms Hotel, The Stonor Arms Hotel, Stonor, Nr Henley-on-Thames, Oxfordshire RG9 6HE. Tel: 01491 638866

Stow-on-the-Wold – The Unicorn Hotel, The Unicorn Hotel, Sheep Street, Stow-on-the-Wold, Gloucestershire GL54 1HQ. Tel: 01451 830257

Stow-On-The-Wold (Kingham) – The Tollgate Inn, The Tollgate Inn, Church Street, Kingham, Oxfordshire OX7 6YA . Tel: 01608 658389

Stratford-upon-Avon (Loxley) – Glebe Farm House, Glebe Farm House, Loxley, Warwickshire CV35 9JW. Tel: 01789 842501

Sway – The Nurse's Cottage, The Nurse's Cottage, Station Road, Sway, Lymington, Hampshire SO41 6BA. Tel: 01590 683402

Tarporley (Willington) – Willington Hall Hotel, Willington Hall Hotel, Willington, Near Tarporley, Cheshire CW6 0NB. Tel: 01829 752321

Tewkesbury (Kemerton) – Upper Court, Upper Court, Kemerton, Tewkesbury, Gloucestershire GL20 7HY. Tel: 01386 725351

Thurlestone Sands (Nr Salcombe) – Heron House Hotel, Heron House Hotel, Thurlestone Sands, Nr Salcombe, South Devon TQ7 3JY. Tel: 01548 561308

Tintagel (Trenale) – Trebrea Lodge, Trebrea Lodge, Trenale, Tintagel , Cornwall PL34 0HR. Tel: 01840 770410

Uckfield – Hooke Hall, Hooke Hall, High Street, Uckfield, East Sussex TN22 1EN. Tel: 01825 761578

Wadebridge (Washaway) – Trehellas House & Memories of Malaya Restaurant, Trehellas House & Memories of Malaya Restaurant, Washaway, Bodmin, Cornwall PL30 3AD. Tel: 01208 72700

Wareham (East Stoke) – Kemps Country House Hotel & Restaurant, Kemps Country House Hotel & Restaurant, East Stoke, Wareham, Dorset BH20 6AL. Tel: 01929 462563

Warwick (Claverdon) – The Ardencote Manor Hotel & Country Club, The Ardencote Manor Hotel & Country Club, Lye Green Road, Claverdon, Warwickshire CV35 8LS. Tel: 01926 843111

Wells – Beryl, Beryl, Wells, Somerset BA5 3JP. Tel: 01749 678738

Wells – Glencot House, Glencot House, Glencot Lane, Wookey Hole, Nr Wells, Somerset BA5 1BH. Tel: 01749 677160

Wells (Coxley) – Coxley Vineyard, Coxley Vineyard, Coxley, Wells, Somerset BA5 1RQ. Tel: 01749 670285

Wem – Soulton Hall, Soulton Hall, Near Wem, Shropshire SY4 5RS. Tel: 01939 232786

Wimborne Minster – Beechleas, Beechleas, 17 Poole Road, Wimborne Minster, Dorset BH21 1QA. Tel: 01202 841684

Wincanton (Holbrook) – Holbrook House Hotel, Holbrook House Hotel, Wincanton, Somerset BA9 8BS. Tel: 01963 32377

Windermere – Quarry Garth Country House Hotel, Quarry Garth Country House Hotel, Windermere, Lake District, Cumbria LA23 1LF. Tel: 015394 88282

Windermere (Bowness) – Fayrer Garden House Hotel, Fayrer Garden House Hotel, Lyth Valley Road, Bowness-On - Windermere, Cumbria LA23 3JP. Tel: 015394 88195

Witherslack – The Old Vicarage Country House Hotel, The Old Vicarage Country House Hotel, Church Road, Witherslack, Grange-Over-Sands, Cumbria LA11 6RS. Tel: 015395 52381

Woodbridge – Wood Hall Country House Hotel, Wood Hall Country House Hotel, Shottisham, Woodbridge, Suffolk IP12 3EG. Tel: 01394 411283

York (Escrick) – The Parsonage Country House Hotel, The Parsonage Country House Hotel, Escrick, York, North Yorkshire YO19 6LF. Tel: 01904 728111

Yoxford – Hope House, Hope House, High Street, Yoxford, Saxmundham, Suffolk IP17 3HP. Tel: 01728 668281

WALES

Aberdovey – Plas Penhelig Country House Hotel, Plas Penhelig Country House Hotel, Aberdovey, Gwynedd LL35 0NA. Tel: 01654 767676

Abergavenny (Glangrwyney) – Glangrwyney Court, Glangrwyney Court, Glangrwyney, Nr Crickhowell, Powys NP8 1ES. Tel: 01873 811288

Abergavenny (Govilon) – Llanwenarth House, Llanwenarth House, Govilon, Abergavenny, Monmouthshire NP7 9SF. Tel: 01873 830289

Anglesey (Llangefni) – Tre-Ysgawen Hall, Tre-Ysgawen Hall, Capel Coch, Llangefni, Ynys Yuon LL77 7UR. Tel: 01248 750750

Betws-y-Coed – Tan-y-Foel, Tan-y-Foel, Capel Garmon, Nr Betws-y-Coed, Conwy LL26 0RE. Tel: 01690 710507

Brecon (Three Cocks) – Old Gwernyfed Country Manor, Old Gwernyfed Country Manor, Felindre, Three Cocks, Brecon, Powys LD3 0SU. Tel: 01497 847376

Caernarfon – Ty'n Rhos Country Hotel, Ty'n Rhos Country Hotel, Seion Llanddeiniolen, Caernarfon, Gwynedd LL55 3AE. Tel: 01248 670489

Conwy – The Old Rectory, The Old Rectory, Llanrwst Road, Llansanffried Glan Conwy, Colwyn Bay, Conwy LL28 5LF. Tel: 01492 580611

Dolgellau (Ganllwyd) – Plas Dolmelynllyn, Plas Dolmelynllyn, Ganllwyd, Dolgellau, Gwynedd LL40 2HP. Tel: 01341 440273

Fishguard (Welsh Hook) – Stone Hall, Stone Hall, Welsh Hook, Haverfordwest, Pembrokeshire, Dyfed SA62 5NS. Tel: 01348 840212

Monmouth (Whitebrook) – The Crown At Whitebrook, The Crown At Whitebrook, Restaurant With Rooms, Whitebrook, Monmouth, Monmouthshire NP5 4TX. Tel: 01600 860254

Pwllheli – Plas Bodegroes, Plas Bodegroes, Nefyn Road, Pwllheli, Gwynedd LL53 5TH. Tel: 01758 612363

Swansea (Mumbles) – Norton House Hotel & Restaurant, Norton House Hotel & Restaurant, Norton Road, Mumbles, Swansea, West Glamorgan SA3 5TQ. Tel: 01792 404891

Tenby (Waterwynch Bay) – Waterwynch House Hotel, Waterwynch House Hotel, Waterwynch Bay, Tenby, Pembrokeshire SA70 8JT. Tel: 01834 842464

Tintern – Parva Farmhouse and Restaurant, Parva Farmhouse and Restaurant, Tintern, Chepstow, Monmouthshire NP16 6SQ. Tel: 01291 689411

SCOTLAND

Ballater, Royal Deeside – Balgonie Country House, Balgonie Country House, Braemar Place, Royal Deeside, Ballater, Aberdeenshire AB35 5NQ. Tel: 013397 55482

By Huntly (Bridge of Marnoch) – The Old Manse of Marnoch, The Old Manse of Marnoch, Bridge of Marnoch, By Huntly, Aberdeenshire AB54 7RS. Tel: 01466 780873

Castle Douglas – Longacre Manor, Longacre Manor, Ernespie Road, Castle Douglas, Dumfries & Galloway DG7 1LE. Tel: 01556 503576

Comrie (Perthshire) – The Royal Hotel, The Royal Hotel, Melville Square, Comrie, Perthshire PH6 2DN. Tel: 01764 679200

Dunfries (Thornhill) – Trigony House Hotel, Trigony House Hotel, Closeburn, Thornhill, Dunfriesshire DG3 5EZ. Tel: 01848 331211

Dunkeld – The Pend, The Pend, 5 Brae Street, Dunkeld, Perthshire PH8 0BA. Tel: 01350 727586

Edinburgh (Dunfermline) – Garvock House Hotel, Garvock House Hotel, St. Johns Drive, Transy, Dunfermline, Fife KY12 7TU. Tel: 01383 621067

Fintry (Stirlingshire) – Culcreuch Castle Hotel & Country Park, Culcreuch Castle Hotel & Country Park, Fintry, Loch Lomond, Stirling & Trossachs G63 0LW. Tel: 01360 860555

Glasgow – Nairns, Nairns, 13 Woodside Crescent, Glasgow, G3 7UP. Tel: 0141 353 0707

Glen Cannich (By Beauly) – Mullardoch House Hotel, Mullardoch House Hotel, Glen Cannich, By Beauly, Inverness-shire IV4 7LX. Tel: 01456 415460

Helmsdale (Sutherland) – Navidale House Hotel, Navidale House Hotel, Helmsdale, Sutherland KW8 6JS. Tel: 01431 821 258

Inverness – Culduthel Lodge, Culduthel Lodge, 14 Culduthel Road, Inverness, Inverness-shire IV2 4AG. Tel: 01463 240089

Inverness – Maple Court & Chandlery Restaurant, Maple Court & Chandlery Restaurant, No12 Ness Walk, Inverness, Inverness-shire IV3 5SQ. Tel: 01463 230330

Isle Of Harris – Ardvourlie Castle, Ardvourlie Castle, Aird A Mhulaidh, Isle Of Harris, Western Isles HS3 3AB. Tel: 01859 502307

Isle Of Mull – Killiechronan, Killiechronan, Killiechronan, Isle Of Mull, Argyllshire PA72 6JU. Tel: 01680 300403

Isle of Mull (Tobermory) – Highland Cottage, Highland Cottage, Breadalbane Street, Tobermory, Isle of Mull, Argyll PA75 6PD. Tel: 01688 302030

Isle of Skye (Portree) – Bosville Hotel & Chandlery Seafood Restaurant, Bosville Hotel & Chandlery Seafood Restaurant, Bosville Terrace, Portree, Isle of Skye IV51 9DG. Tel: 01478 612846

Kentallen Of Appin – Ardsheal House, Ardsheal House, Kentallen Of Appin, Argyll PA38 4BX. Tel: 01631 740227

Killiecrankie, By Pitlochry – The Killiecrankie Hotel, The Killiecrankie Hotel, Killiecrankie, By Pitlochry, Perthshire PH16 5LG. Tel: 01796 473220

Kinlochbervie – The Kinlochbervie Hotel, The Kinlochbervie Hotel, Kinlochbervie, By Lairg, Sutherland IV27 4RP. Tel: 01971 521275

Leslie (Fife) – Balgeddie House Hotel, Balgeddie House Hotel, Balgeddie Way, Glenrothes, Fife KY6 3ET. Tel: 01592 742511

Loch Ness (Drumnadrochit) – Polmaily House Hotel, Polmaily House Hotel, Drumnadrochit, Loch Ness, Inverness-shire IV3 6XT. Tel: 01456 450343

Lockerbie – The Dryfesdale Hotel, The Dryfesdale Hotel, Lockerbie, Dumfriesshire DG11 2SF. Tel: 01576 202427

Maybole (Ayrshire) – Culzean Castle, Culzean Castle, Maybole, Ayrshire KA19 8LE. Tel: 01655 760274

Moffat – Well View Hotel, Well View Hotel, Ballplay Road, Moffat, Dumfriesshire DG10 9JU. Tel: 01683 220184

Nairn (Auldearn) – Boath House, Boath House, Auldearn, Nairn, Inverness IV12 5TE. Tel: 01667 454896

Oban – Dungallan House Hotel, Dungallan House Hotel, Gallanach Road, Oban, Argyllshire PA34 4PD. Tel: 01631 563799

Oban – The Manor House Hotel, The Manor House Hotel, Gallanch Road, Oban, Argyllshire PA34 4LS. Tel: 01631 562087

Pitlochry – Knockendarroch House, Knockendarroch House, Higher Oakfield, Pitlochry, Perthshire PH16 5HT. Tel: 01796 473473

Port Of Menteith – The Lake Hotel, The Lake Hotel, Port Of Menteith, Perthshire FK8 3RA. Tel: 01877 385258

Rothiemurchus (Highland) – Corrour House Hotel, Corrour House Hotel, Inverdruie, Aviemore, Inverness-shire PH22 1QH. Tel: 01479 810220

St. Andrews – The Argyle House Hotel, The Argyle House Hotel, 127 Norton Street, St. Andrews, KY16 9AG. Tel: 01334 473387

St. Boswell By Melrose – Clint Lodge, Clint Lodge, St. Boswells, Melrose, Roxburghshire TD6 0DZ. Tel: 01835 822027

St Fillans (Perthshire) – The Four Seasons Hotel, The Four Seasons Hotel, St Fillans , Perthshire PH6 2NF. Tel: 01764 685333

Strathtummel (By Pitlochry) – Queen's View Hotel, Queen's View Hotel, Strathtummel, By Pitlochry, Perthshire PH16 5NR. Tel: 01796 473291

Tain (Ross-shire) – Glenmorangie House at Cadbol, Glenmorangie House at Cadbol, Cadbol, Fearn, By Tain, IV20 1XP. Tel: 01862 871671

The Great Glen (Fort William) – Corriegour Lodge Hotel, Corriegour Lodge Hotel, Loch Lochy, By Spean Bridge, Inverness-shire PH34 4EB. Tel: 01397 712685

IRELAND

Caragh Lake Co Kerry – Caragh Lodge, Caragh Lodge, Caragh Lake, Co Kerry. Tel: 00 353 66 9769115

Cashel Co Tipperary – Cashel Palace Hotel, Cashel Palace Hotel, Cashel, Co Tipperary. Tel: 00 353 62 62707

Connemara (Co Galway) – Ross Lake House Hotel, Ross Lake House Hotel, Rosscahill, Oughterard, Co Galway. Tel: 00 353 91 550109

Craughwell (Co.Galway) – St. Clerans, St. Clerans, Craughwell, Co.Galway. Tel: 00 353 91 846 555

Dublin – Aberdeen Lodge, Aberdeen Lodge, 53-55 Park Avenue, Ailesbury Road, Dublin 4. Tel: 00 353 1 2838155

Dublin – Fitzwilliam Park, Fitzwilliam Park, No5 Fitzwilliam Square, Dublin 2. Tel: 00 353 1 6628 280

Kilkee Co Clare – Halpins Hotel & Vittles Restaurant, Halpins Hotel & Vittles Restaurant, Erin Street, Kilkee, Co Clare. Tel: 00 353 65 9056032

Killarney Co Kerry – Earls Court House, Earls Court House, Woodlawn Junction, Muckross Road, Co Kerry. Tel: 00 353 64 34009

Kilmeaden (Co. Waterford) – The Old Rectory - Kilmeaden House, The Old Rectory - Kilmeaden House, Kilmeaden, Co Waterford. Tel: 00 353 51 384254

Letterkenny (Co Donegal) – Castle Grove Country House, Castle Grove Country House, Ramelton Road, Letterkenny, Co Donegal. Tel: 00 353 745 1118

Riverstown, Co Sligo – Coopershill House, Coopershill House, Riverstown, Co Sligo. Tel: 00 353 71 65108

Sligo, Co Sligo – Markree Castle, Markree Castle, Colooney, Co Sligo. Tel: 00 353 71 67800

Wicklow, Co Wicklow – The Old Rectory, The Old Rectory, Wicklow Town, Co Wicklow. Tel: 00 353 404 67048

CHANNEL ISLANDS

Guernsey (Fermain Bay) – La Favorita Hotel, La Favorita Hotel, Fermain Bay, Guernsey GY4 6SD. Tel: 01481 35666

Guernsey (St Martin) – Bella Luce Hotel & Restaurant, Bella Luce Hotel & Restaurant, La Fosse, St Martin, Guernsey, GY4 6EB. Tel: 01481 38764

Herm Island (Guernsey) – The White House, The White House, Herm Island, Guernsey, GY1 3HR. Tel: 01481 722159

Jersey (St Aubin) – Hotel La Tour, Hotel La Tour, Rue de Croquet, St Aubin, Jersey, JE3 8BR. Tel: 01534 743770

Sark Island (Guernsey) – La Sablonnerie, La Sablonnerie, Little Sark, Sark Island, Guernsey. Tel: 01481 832061

Johansens Recommended Hotels – Europe & The Mediterranean

ANDORRA

Andorra La Vella – Andorra Park Hotel, Les Canals 24, Andorra La Vella. Tel: +376 82 09 79

AUSTRIA

Alpbach – Romantik Hotel Böglerhof, Alpbach 166, 6236. Tel: +43 5336 5227

Altaussee – Landhaus Hubertushof, Puchen, 8992 Altaussee, Steiermark. Tel: +43 36 22 71 280

Bad Gastein – Hotel & Spa Haus Hirt, Kaiserhofstrasse 14, 5640 Bad Gastein. Tel: +43 64 34 27 97

Bad Hofgastein – Grand Park Hotel , Kurgartenstrasse 26, 5630 Bad Hofgastein. Tel: +43 6432 63560

Bad Hofgastein – Kur-Sport & Gourmethotel Moser, Kaiser-Franz-Platz 2, 5630 Bad Hofgastein. Tel: +43 6432 6209

Bad Kleinkirchheim – Almdorf "Seinerzeit", Fellacher Alm, 9564 Patergassen bei Bad Kleinkirchheim. Tel: +43 4275 7201

Baden bei Wien – Grand Hotel Sauerhof, Weilburgstrasse 11-13, 2500 Baden bei Wien. Tel: +43 2252 41251 0

Dürnstein – Hotel Schloss Dürnstein, 3601 Dürnstein. Tel: +43 2711 212

Graz – Schlossberg Hotel, Kaiser-Franz-Josef-Kai 30, 8010 Graz. Tel: +43 316 80700

Grünau Im Almtal – Romantik Hotel Almtalhof, 4645 Grünau Im Almtal. Tel: +43 7616 82040

Igls – Schlosshotel Igls, Viller Steig 2, 6080 Igls, Tirol. Tel: +43 512 37 72 17

Igls – Sporthotel Igls, Hilberstrasse 17, 6080 Igls, Tirol. Tel: +43 512 37 72 41

Kitzbühel – Romantik Hotel Tennerhof, Griesenauweg 26, 6370 Kitzbühel. Tel: +43 53566 3181

Klagenfurt – Hotel Palais Porcia, Neuer Platz 13, 9020 Klagenfurt. Tel: +43 463 51 1590

Lech – Sporthotel Kristiania, Omesberg 331 , 6764 Lech/Arlberg. Tel: +43 55 83 25 610

Oberlech – Hotel Goldener Berg, Lech, 6764. Tel: +43 5583 22050

Pörtschach Am Wörther See – Hotel Schloss Leonstein, Leonstein 1, Pörtschach Am Wörther See. Tel: +43 4272 28160

Salzburg – Hotel Auersperg, Auerspergstrasse 61, 5027 Salzburg. Tel: +43 662 88944

Salzburg – Hotel Schloss Mönchstein, Mönchsberg Park, City Center, 26-Joh, 5020 Salzburg. Tel: +43 662 84 85 55 0

Salzburg – Schloss Haunsperg, Oberalm bei Hallein, 5411 Salzburg. Tel: +43 62 45 80 662

Schwarzenberg im Bregenzerwald – Romantik-Hotel Gasthof Hirschen, Hof 14, 6867 Schwarzenberg. Tel: +43 55 12/29 44 0

Seefeld – Hotel Klosterbräu, 6100 Seefeld Tirol. Tel: +43 5212 26210

Seefeld – Hotel Viktoria, Geigenbühelweg 589 , 6100 Seefeld Tirol. Tel: +43 52 12 44 41

St Christoph – Arlberg Hospiz, St Christoph, 6580. Tel: +43 5446 2611

St Wolfgang am See – Romantik Hotel im Weissen Rössl, 5360 St Wolfgang am See, Salzkammergut. Tel: +43 61 38 23 060

Velden – Seeschlössl Velden, Klagenfurter Strasse 34, 9220 Velden. Tel: +43 4274 2824

Vienna – Ana Grand Hotel Wien, Kärntner Ring 9, 1010, Vienna. Tel: +43 1 515 80 0

Vienna – Hotel im Palais Schwarzenberg, Schwarzenbergplatz 9, 1030 Vienna. Tel: +43 1 798 4515

Zürs – Thurnhers Alpenhof, 6763 Zürs/Arlberg. Tel: +43 5583 2191

BELGIUM

Antwerp – Firean Hotel, Karel Oomsstraat 6, 2018 Antwerp. Tel: +32 3237 02 60

Bruges – Die Swaene, Steenhouwersdijk, 8000 Bruges. Tel: +32-50-34 27 98

Bruges – Hotel Acacia, Korte Zilverstraat 3A, 8000 Bruges. Tel: +32 50 34 44 11

Bruges – Hotel de Orangerie, Kartuizerinnenstraat10, 8000 Bruges. Tel: +32 50 34 16 49

Bruges – Hotel Hansa, N. Desparsstraat 11, 8000 Bruges. Tel: +32 50 33 84 44

Bruges – Hotel Jan Brito, Freren Fonteinstraat 1, 8000 Bruges. Tel: +32 50 33 06 01

Bruges – Hotel Montanus, Nieuwe Gentweg 78, 8000 Bruges. Tel: +32 50 33 11 76

Bruges – Hotel Prinsenhof, Ontvangersstraat 9, 8000 Bruges. Tel: +32-50- 34 26 90

Brussels – L'Amigo, 1-3 Rue de L'Amigo, 1000 Brussels. Tel: +32 2 547 47 47

Florenville – Hostellerie Le Prieuré De Conques, Rue Florenville 176, 6820 Florenville. Tel: +32 61 41 14 17

Lanaken – La Butte Aux Bois, Paalsteenlaan 90, 3620 Lanaken. Tel: +32 89 72 12 86

Malmedy – Hostellerie Trôs Marets, Route Des Trôs Marets , 4960 Malmédy. Tel: +32-80- 33 79 17

Marche-en-Famenne – Château d'Hassonville, 6900 Marche-en-Famenne. Tel: +32 84 31 10 25

Vieuxville – Chateau de Palogne, Route du Palogne 3, 4190 Vieuxville. Tel: +32 86 21 38 74

CYPRUS

Limassol – Le Meridien Limassol, PO Box 56560, 3308, Limassol. Tel: +357 5 634 000

Limassol – The Four Seasons Hotel, PO Box 57222, Limassol. Tel: +35 7 5 310 222

CZECH REPUBLIC

Prague – Hotel Hoffmeister, Pod Bruskou 7, Kralov, 11800 Prague 1. Tel: +420 2 510 17 111

Prague – Sieber Hotel & Apartments, Slezska 55, 130 00, Prague 3. Tel: +420 224 25 00 25

DENMARK

Faaborg – Steensgaard Herregårdspension, Steensgaard, 5600 Millinge, Faaborg. Tel: +45 62 61 94 90

Nyborg – Hotel Hesselet, Christianslundsvej 119, 5800 Nyborg. Tel: +45 65 31 30 29

GREAT BRITAIN

Aylesbury – Hartwell House, Oxford Road, Nr Aylesbury, Buckinghamshire, England HP17 8NL. Tel: +44 1296 747444

Bamburgh – Waren House, Waren Mill, Bamburgh, Northumberland, England NE70 7EE. Tel: +44 1668 214581

Bath – Lucknam Park, Colerne, Nr Bath, Wiltshire, England SN14 8AZ. Tel: +44 1225 742777

Berwick-Upon-Tweed – Tillmouth Park, Cornhill-on-Tweed, Nr Berwick-Upon-Tweed, Northumberland TD12 4UU. Tel: +44 1890 882255

Birmingham – The Burlington, 6 Burlington Arcade, 126 New STreet, Birmingham, West MIdlands, England B2 4JQ. Tel: +44 121 643 9191

Burrington – Northcote Manor, Burrington, Nr Umberleigh, Devon, England EX37 9LZ. Tel: +44 1769 560501

Clanfield – The Plough At Clanfield, Bourton Road, Clanfield, Oxfordshire OX18 2RB. Tel: +44 1367 810222

Jersey – The Atlantic Hotel, La Moye, St Brelade, Jersey JE3 8HE. Tel: +44 1534 44101

London, Chelsea – Draycott House Apartments, 10 Draycott Avenue, Chelsea, London SW3 3AA. Tel: +44 171 584 4659

London, Kensington – Pembridge Court Hotel, 34 Pembridge Gardens, London W2 4DX. Tel: +44 171 229 9977

London, Knightsbridge – Basil Street Hotel, Basil Street, London SW3 1AH. Tel: +44 171 581 3311

London, Knightsbridge – Beaufort House Apartments, 45 Beaufort Gardens, London SW3 1PN. Tel: +44 171 584 2600

London, Knightsbridge – The Beaufort, 33 Beaufort Gardens, Knightsbridge, London SW3 1PP. Tel: +44 171 584 5252

London, Knightsbridge – The Cliveden Town House, 26 Cadogan Gardens, London SW3 2RP. Tel: +44 171 730 6466

London, Mayfair – The Ascott Mayfair, 49 Hill Street, London W1X 7FQ. Tel: +44 171 499 6868

London – Number Eleven Cadogan Gardens, 11 Cadogan Gardens, Sloane Square, London SW3 2RJ. Tel: +44 171 730 7000

London – Swan Hellenic Minerva, 77 New Oxford Street, London WC1 1PP. Tel: +020 7800 2227

London – The Colonnade Town House, 2 Warrington Crescent, London, England W9 1ER. Tel: +44 20 7286 1052

London – The Dorchester, Park Lane, Mayfair, London WIA 2HJ. Tel: +44 171 629 8888

London – The Hempel, Hempel Garden Square, 31-35 Craven Hill Gardens, London W2 3EA. Tel: +44 171 298 9000

London – The Leonard, 15 Seymour Street, London W1H 5AA. Tel: +44 171 935 2010

London – The Lexham, 32–38 Lexham Gardens, Kensington, London, England W8 5JE. Tel: +44 20 7559 4444

London – The Milestone, 1-2 Kensington Court, London W8 5DL. Tel: +44 171 917 1000

London – Twenty Nevern Square, 20 Nevern Square, London, England WC1 1PP. Tel: +44 20 7565 9555

London South Kensington – Number Sixteen, 16 Sumner Place, London SW7 3EG. Tel: +44 171 589 5232

London, Wimbledon Common – Cannizaro House, West Side, Wimbledon Common, London SW19 4UE. Tel: +44 181 879 1464

Lynton – Hewitt's Hotel, North Walk, Lynton, Devon, England EX35 6HJ. Tel: +44 1598 752293

Stapleford – Stapleford Park, Nr Melton Mowbray, Leicestershire LE14 2EF. Tel: +44 1572 787522

Streatley-On-Thames, Reading – Swan Diplomat, Streatley-On-Thames, Reading, Berkshire RG8 9HR. Tel: +44 1491 873737

Windermere – Miller Howe, Rayrigg Road, Windermere, Cumbria LA23 1EY. Tel: +44 15394 42536

Windermere – Storrs Hall, Windermere, Cumbria, England LA23 3LG. Tel: +44 15394 47111

ESTONIA

Tallinn – Park Consul Schlössle, Pühavaimu 13-15, EE 10123 Tallinn. Tel: +372 699 7700

FINLAND

Hämeenlinna – Hotel Vanajanlinna, 13330 Harviala, Hämeenlinna. Tel: +358 3 619 65 65

FRANCE

Amboise – Chateau de Pray, Route De Charge, 37400, Amboise. Tel: +33 2 47 57 23 67

Avallon – Château de Vault de Lugny, 11 Rue de Château, 89200 Avallon. Tel: +33 3 86 34 07 86

Avallon – Hostellerie de la Poste, 13 place Vauban, 89200, Vauban. Tel: +33 3 86 34 16 16

Beaulieu-sur-Mer – La Réserve de Beaulieu, 5 Boulevard Général Leclerc, 06310 Beaulieu-sur-Mer. Tel: +33 4 93 01 00 01

Beaune – Ermitage de Corton, R.N. 74, 21200 Chorey-Les-Beaune. Tel: +33 3 80 22 05 28

Biarritz – Hôtel du Palais, Avenue de L'Impératrice, 64200 Biarritz. Tel: +33 5 59 41 64 00

Billiers – La Domaine de Rochevilaine, Pointe De Pen Lan, 56190 Billiers. Tel: +33 2 97 41 61 61

Boutigny Nr Barbizon – Domaine de Belesbat, Courdimanche-sur-Essonne, 91820, Bourtigny-sur-Essonne. Tel: +33 1 69 23 19 00

Castres – Château d'Aiguefonde, 81200 , Aiguefonde. Tel: +33 563 98 1370

Chambéry-le-Vieux – Château de Candie, Rue du Bois de Candie, 73000 Chambéry-le-Vieux. Tel: +33 47 99 66 300

Champigné – Château des Briottières, 49330 Champigné. Tel: +33 2 41 42 00 02

Chinon – Château de Danzay, RD 749, 37420 Chinon. Tel: +33 2 47 58 46 86

Colmar – Hôtel Les Têtes, 19 Rue De Têtes, 68000 Colmar. Tel: +33 3 89 24 43 43

Connelles – Le Moulin de Connelles, 39 Route d'Amfreville-Sous-Les-Monts, 27430 Connelles. Tel: +33 2 32 59 53 33

Corsica-Porticcio – Hotel Le Maquis, BP 94, 20166 Porticcio-Corsica. Tel: +33 4 95 25 05 55

Courchevel – Hôtel Annapurna, 73120 Courchevel, 1850. Tel: +33 4 79 08 04 60

Divonne-les-Bains – Le Domaine de Divonne, Avenue des Thermes, 01220 Divonne-Les-Bains. Tel: +33 4 50 40 3434

Épernay – Hostellerie La Briqueterie, 4 Route de Sézanne, Vinay, 51530 Epernay. Tel: +33 3 26 59 99 99

Eze Village – Château Eza, Rue De La Pise, 06360 Eze Village. Tel: +33 4 93 41 12 24

Gérardmer – Hostellerie Les Bas Rupts , , 88400 Gérardmer, Vosges. Tel: +33 3 29 63 09 25

Gressy-en-France/Chantilly – Le Manoir de Gressy, 77410 Gressy-en-France, Seine et Marne. Tel: +33 1 60 26 68 00

Grignan – Manoir de la Roseraie, Route de Valreas, 26230, Grignan. Tel: +33 4 75 46 58 15

Honfleur – La Chaumière, Route du Littoral, 14600 Honfleur. Tel: +33 2 31 81 63 20

Honfleur – La Ferme Saint Siméon, Rue Adolphe-Marais, 14600 Honfleur. Tel: +33 2 31 89 23 61

Honfleur – Le Manoir du Butin, Phare du Butin, 14600 Honfleur. Tel: +33 2 31 81 63 00

La Gouesniere/St Malo – Chateau de Bonaban, La Gouesniere, 35350. Tel: +33 299 58 24 50

Langeais – Château de Rochecotte, Saint Patrice, 37130 Langeais. Tel: +00 33 2 47 96 16 16

Les Issambres – Villa Saint Elme, Corniche des Issambres, 83380 Les Issambres. Tel: +33 4 94 49 52 52

Lyon – La Tour Rose, 22 Rue de Boeuf, 69005 Lyon. Tel: +33 4 78 37 25 90

Madieres-Ganges – Chateau de Madieres, Madieres-Ganges, 34170, Ganges. Tel: +33 4 67 73 84 03

Martillac – Les Sources de Caudalie, Chemin de Smith Haut-Lafitte, 33650, Martillac. Tel: +33 5 57 83 83 83

Megève – Hôtel Mont-Blanc, Place de l'Eglise, 74120 Megève. Tel: +33 4 50 21 20 02

Megève – Lodge Park Hôtel, 100 Route d'Arly, 74120 Megève. Tel: +33 4 50 93 05 03

Monestier – Château des Vigiers, 24240 Monestier. Tel: +33 5 53 61 50 00

Paris – Hôtel Buci Latin, 34 Rue de Buci, 75006 Paris. Tel: +33 1 43 29 07 20

Paris – Hôtel de Crillon, 10 Place de la Concorde, 75008 Paris. Tel: +33 1 44 71 15 00

Paris – Hôtel de L'Arcade, 9 Rue de L'Arcade, 75008 Paris. Tel: +33 1 53 30 60 00

Paris – Hotel Franklin D. Roosevelt, 18 rue Clement Marot, 75008, Paris. Tel: +33 1 53 57 49 50

Paris – Hôtel Le Parc, 55-57 avenue Raymond Poincare, 75116, Paris. Tel: +33 1 44 05 66 66

Paris – Hôtel le Saint-Grégoire, 43 Rue de l'Abbé Grégoire, 75006 Paris. Tel: +33 1 45 48 23 23

Paris – Hôtel Le Tourville, 16 Avenue de Tourville, 75007 Paris. Tel: +33 1 47 05 62 62

Paris – L'Hôtel, 13 rue des Beaux Arts, 75006 Paris. Tel: +33 1 43 25 27 22

Paris – L'Hôtel Pergolese, 3 Rue Pergolese, 75116 Paris. Tel: +33 1 53 64 04 04

Paris – La Villa Maillot, 143 Avenue de Malakoff, 75116, Paris. Tel: +33 1 53 64 52 52

Paris – Le Lavoisier, 21 rue Lavoisier, 75008, Paris. Tel: +33 1 53 30 06 06

Pleven – Le Manoir de Vaumadeuc, 22130 Pleven. Tel: +33 2 96 84 46 17

Rochefort-sur-Mer – Hotel De La Corderie Royale, Rue Audebert, BP 275 , 17300. Tel: +33 5 46 99 35 35

Roquebrune Cap-Martin/Monaco – Grand Hôtel Vista Palace , Route De La Grande Corniche, 06190 Roquebrune/Cap-Martin. Tel: +33 4 92 10 40 00

Saint Tropez – Hôtel Sube, 15 Quai Suffren, 83990 St Tropez. Tel: +33 4 94 97 30 04

Saint Tropez – La Résidence de la Pinède, Plage de la Bouillabaisse, 83991 Saint Tropez. Tel: +33 4 94 55 91 00

Saint-Rémy-de-Provence – Château des Alpilles, Route Départementale 31, Ancienne route du Grés, 13210 St-Rémy-de-Provence. Tel: +33 4 90 92 03 33

Sainte- Maxime/Bay Of St Tropez – Hotel Le Beauvallon, Baie de St. Tropez, Beauvallon-Grimaud, 83120 Sainte-Maxime. Tel: +33 4 94 55 78 88

Sarlat-Vitrac – Domaine de Rochebois, Route du Château de Montfort, 24200 Vitrac. Tel: +33 5 53 31 52 52

Sciez sur Leman – Château de Coudrée, Domaine de Coudrée, Bonnatrait, 74140 Sciez sur Leman. Tel: +33 4 50 72 62 33

Serre-Chevalier – L'Auberge du Choucas, 05220, Monetier-Les-Bains, 1550 Serre-Chevalier . Tel: +33 4 92 24 42 73

Vervins – La Tour Du Roy, 45 rue du Général Leclerc, 02140, Vervins. Tel: +33 3 23 98 00 11

GERMANY

Badenweiler – Hotel Römerbad, Schlossplatz 1, 79410, Badenweiler. Tel: +49 76 32 70 0

Göttingen – Burghotel Hardenberg, 37176 Nörten-Hardenberg. Tel: +49 5503 9810

Munich – Hotel Königshof, Karlsplatz 25, 80335 Munich. Tel: +49 89 551 360

Niederstotzingen – Schlosshotel Oberstotzingen, Stettener Strasse 35-37 , 89168 Niederstotzingen. Tel: +49 7325 1030

Oberwesel/Rhein – Burghotel Auf Schönburg, 55430 Oberwesel/Rhein. Tel: +49 67 44 93 93 0

Rothenburg ob der Tauber – Hôtel Eisenhut, Herrngasse 3-7, 91541. Tel: +49 9861 70 50

Triberg – Romantik Parkhotel Wehrle, Gartenstr.24, 78098, Triberg. Tel: +49 7722 86020

Waldeck – Hotel Schloss Waldeck, , 34513 Waldeck. Tel: +49 5623 5890

Wassenberg – Hotel Burg Wassenberg, Kirchstrasse 17, 41849 Wassenberg. Tel: +49 2432 9490

Wernberg-Köblitz – Hotel Burg Wernberg, Schlossberg 10, 92533 Wernberg-Köblitz, Wernberg-Köblitz. Tel: +49 9604 9390

GIBRALTAR

Gibraltar – The Rock Hotel, 3 Europa Road. Tel: +350 73 000

GREECE

Athens – Hotel Pentelikon, 66 Diligianni Street, 14562 Athens. Tel: +30 1 62 30 650 6

Crete – St Nicolas Bay Hotel, Agios Nicholaos, Crete, 72100. Tel: +30 841 25 041

Evritania-Karpenissi – Hotel Club Montana, , Karpenissi 36100. Tel: +30 237 80400

Samos Island – Doryssa Bay Hotel-Village, Pythagorion, Samos Island, Aegean Island, 83103. Tel: +30 273 613 60

Santorini Island – Esperas Traditional Houses, Oia Santorini, 84702. Tel: +30 286 71088

HUNGARY

Budapest – Danubius Hotel Gellért, St.Gellért Tér 1, 1111 Budapest. Tel: +36 1 185 2200

Lake Balaton – Hotel Erika, Bathyany u.6, 8237, Tihany. Tel: +36 87 44 86 44

ISRAEL

Jerusalem – The American Colony, PO Box 19215, Jerusalem. Tel: +972 2 6279 777

ITALY

Assisi – Romantik Hotel Le Silve di Armenzano, Loc. Armenzano, 06081 Assisi. Tel: +39 075 801 90 00

Breuil-Cervinia – Hotel Bucaneve, Piazza Jumeaux 10, 11021 Breuil-Cervinia. Tel: +39 0166 949119/948386

Castellina In Chianti – Romantik Hotel Tenuta Di Ricavo, Localita Ricavo 4, 53011 Castellina In Chianti. Tel: +39 0577 740221

Castello Di Montegridolfo – Palazzo Vivani Castello Di Montegridolfo, Via Roma 38, Montegridolfo 47837. Tel: +39 0541 855350

Como – Albergo Terminus, Lungo Lario Trieste 14, 22100 Como. Tel: +39 031 329111

Como – Hotel Villa Flori, Via Cernobbio 12, 22100 Como. Tel: +39 031 573105

Etna – Hotel Villa Paradiso Dell' Etna, Via per Viagrande 37, 95037 SG La Punta. Tel: +39 751 2409

Ferrara – Albergo Annunziata, Piazza Repubblica 5, 44100 Ferrara. Tel: +39 0532 20 11 11

Ferrara – Ripagrande Hotel, Via Ripagrande 21, 44100 Ferrara. Tel: +39 0532 765250

Florence – Hotel J &J, Via Mezzo 20, 50121 Florence. Tel: +39 55 26312

Ischia – Hotel Miramare E Castello, Via Pontano 9, 80070 Ischia (NA). Tel: +39 081 991333

Italian Riviera – Hotel Punta Est, Via Aurelia 1, Finale Ligure, 17024. Tel: +39 019 600 611

Lido – Albergo Quattro Fontane, 30126, Lido di Venezia. Tel: +39 041 5260227

Lucca – Locanda l'Elisa, Via Nuova per Pisa, 1952, 55050 Massa Pisana, Lucca. Tel: +39 0583 379737

Madonna Di Campiglio – Hotel Lorenzetti, Via Dolomiti Di Campiglio 119, 38084 Madonna Di Campiglio (TN). Tel: +39 0 465 44 1404

Mantova – Albergo San Lorenzo, Piazza Concordia 14, 46100 Mantova. Tel: +39 0376 220500

Marling-Méran – Romantic Hotel Oberwirt, St Felixweg 2, 39020 Marling/Méran. Tel: +39 0473 44 71 11

Mauls – Romantik Hotel Stafler, Mauls 10, 39040 Freienfeld. Tel: +39 0472 771136

Milan – Hotel Auriga, Via Pirella 7, 20124 Milan. Tel: +39 02 66 98 58 51

Novi Ligure – Relais Villa Pomela, Via Serravalle 69, 15067 Novi Ligure (AL). Tel: +39 0143 329910

Pievescola – Hotel Relais La Suvera, 53030 Pievescola, Siena. Tel: +39 0577 960 300

Porto Ercole – Il Pellicano, , Aeralita Cala Dei Santi, 58018 Porto Ercole (GR). Tel: +39 0564 858111

Portobuffolé-Treviso – Romantik Hotel Villa Giustinian, Via Giustiniani 11, 31019 Portobuffolé-Treviso. Tel: +39 0422 850244

Positano – Romantik Hotel Poseidon, Via Pasitea 148, 84017 Positano. Tel: +39 089 81 11 11

Rimini – Il Grand Hotel Di Rimini, Parco Federico Fellini, 47900 Rimini. Tel: +39 0541 56000

Rome – Hotel Farnese, Via Alessandro Farnese 30 , (Anglo Viale Giulio Cesare), 00192 Rome. Tel: +39 06 321 25 53

Rome – Hotel Giulio Cesare, Via Degli Scipioni 287, 00192 Rome. Tel: +39 06 321 0751

Rome – Romantik Hotel Barocco, Piazza Barberini 9, 00187 Rome. Tel: +39 0 6 4872001

Rome-Palo Laziale – La Posta Vecchia, Palo Laziale, 00055 Ladispoli, Rome. Tel: +39 06 9949 501

Salerno-Santa Maria di Castellabate – Hotel Villa Sirio, Via Lungomare De Simone 15, 84072 Santa Maria di Castellabate. Tel: +39 0974 960 162

Saturnia – Hotel Terme Di Saturnia , 58050 Saturnia, Grosseto. Tel: +39 0 564 601061

Sestri Levante – Grand Hotel Villa Balbi, Viale Rimembranza 1, 16039 Sestri Levante. Tel: +39 0185 42941

Sorrento – Grand Hotel Cocumella, Via Cocumella 7, 80065 Sant'Agnello, Sorrento. Tel: +39 081 878 2933

Sorrento – Grand Hotel Excelsior Vittoria, Piazza Tasso 24, Sorrento-(Napoli). Tel: +39 081 80 71 044

South Tyrol Nova Levante – Posthotel Weisses Rössl, Via Carezza 30, 39036 Nova Levante (BZ), Dolomites. Tel: +39 0 471 613113

Südtirol-Völs am Schlern – Romantik Hotel Turm, Piazza Della Chiesa 9, Fié Allo Scilari, Bolzano. Tel: +39 0471 725014

Taormina Mare – Hotel Villa Sant' Andrea, Via Nazionale 137, 98030 Taormina Mare. Tel: +39 0942 23125

Taormina – Hotel Villa Diodoro, Via Bagnoli Croci 75, 98039 Taormina (ME). Tel: +39 0942 23312

Taormina-Sicily – Grande Albergo Capotaormina, Via Nazionale 105, 98039 Taormina. Tel: +39 0942 576015

Torino – Hotel Victoria, Via N.Costa 4, 10123 Torino. Tel: +39 011 56 11 909

Tuscan Riviera – Hotel Villa Undulna, Viale Marina, 54030 Cinquale Di Montignoso. Tel: +39 0585 807788

Varese Lake - Malpensa – Romantik Hotel Locanda Dei Mai Intees, Via Nobile Claudio Riva 2, 21022 Azzate (VA). Tel: +39 0332 457223

Venice – Hotel Metropole, San Marco- Riva Degli Schiavoni 4149, 30122 Venice. Tel: +39 041 52 05 044

Venice – Villa Condulmer, 31020 Zerman Di Mogliani Veneto, Treviso. Tel: +39 041 45 71 00

Vicenza-Arcugnano – Hotel Villa Michelangelo, Via Sacco 19, 36057 Arcugnano (Vicenza). Tel: +39 0444 550300

LATVIA

Riga – Hotel de Rome, Kalkuiela 28, LV 1050 Riga. Tel: +37 1 708 7600

Riga – Hotel Konventa Seta, Kaleju Iela 9/11, LV 1050 Riga. Tel: +371 708 7501

LUXEMBOURG

Luxembourg City – Hotel Albert Premier, 2A rue Albert 1er, 1117. Tel: +352 442 4421

Remich – Hotel Saint Nicolas, 31 Esplanade, 5533 Remich. Tel: +352 69 8888

MONACO

Monte-Carlo – Hotel Hermitage, Square Beaumarchis BP277, MC 98005. Tel: +33 92 16 40 00

Monte Carlo – Monte Carlo Beach Hotel, Avenue Princess Grace, 06190 Roquebrune-Cap-Martin. Tel: +33 4 93 28 66 66

MOROCCO

Marrakech – Les Deux Tours, Douar Abiad- Circuit de la Palmeraie, Municipalite An-Natchil, Marrakech BP 513. Tel: +212 4 32 95 27

THE NETHERLANDS

Amsterdam – Ambassade Hotel, Herengracht 341, 1016 AZ Amsterdam. Tel: +31 20 5550222

Amsterdam – Seven One Seven, Prinsengracht 717, 1017 jw, Amsterdam. Tel: +31 20 42 70 717

Amsterdam – The Canal House Hotel, Keizersgracht 148, 1015 CX, Amsterdam. Tel: +31 20 622 5182

Beetsterzwaag – Bilderberg Landgoed Lauswolt, Van Harinxmawrg 10, Beetsterzwaag 9244 CJ. Tel: +31 512 38 12 45

Bergambacht – Hotel De Arendshoeve, Molenlaan 14, 2861 LB Bergambacht. Tel: +31 182 35 1000

Drunen – Hotel De Duinrand, Steergerf 2, 5151 RB Drunen. Tel: +31 416 372 498

Lattrop – Hotel De Holtwenjde, Spiekweg 7, 7635 LP, Lattrop. Tel: +31 541 229 234

Oisterwijk – Hotel Restaurant de Swaen, De Lind 47, 5061 HT Oisterwijk. Tel: +31 135 23 3233

Ootmarsum – Hotel de Wiemsel, Winhofflaan 2, 7631 HX Ootmarsum. Tel: +31 541 292 155

Voorburg – Restaurant-Hotel Savelberg, Oosteinde 14, 2271 EH Voorburg. Tel: +31 70 387 2081

NORWAY

Balestrand – Kvikne's Hotel, 6898 Balestrand. Tel: +47 57 69 11 01

Bergen – Grand Hotel Terminus, Zander Kaaesgt 6, PO Box 1100 Sentrum, 5001 Bergen. Tel: +47 55 31 16 55

Dalen – Dalen Hotel, PO Boks 123, 3880 Dalen. Tel: +47 35 07 70 00

Honefoss – Grand Hotel Honefoss, Stabellsgate 8, 3500 Honefoss. Tel: +47 32 12 27 22

Lofthus in Hardanger – Hotel Ullensvang, 5787 Lofthus in Hardanger. Tel: +47 53 66 11 00

Moss – Hotel Refsnes Gods, P.O Box 236, 1501, Moss. Tel: +47 69 27 83 00

Oslo – First Hotel Bastion, Postboks 27, Sentrum, Skippergaten 7, 0152 Oslo. Tel: +47 22 47 77 00

Sandane – Gloppen Hotel, 6860 Sandane. Tel: +47 57 86 53 33

Sandnes/Stavanger – Kronen Gaard Hotel, Vatne, 4300 Sandnes. Tel: +47 51 62 14 00

Solvorn – Walaker Hotell, 6879 Solvorn. Tel: +47 576 84 207

Voss) – Fleischers Hotel, 5700 Voss. Tel: +47 56 52 05 00

PORTUGAL

Armacao De Pera – Vilalara Thalasso, Praia das Gaivotas, 8365, Armacao De Pera. Tel: +351 82 320 000

Carvoeiro – Casa Domilu, Estrada De Benagil, Apartado 250, Praia Do Carvoeiro, 8400 Lagoa. Tel: +351 82 358 409

Faro – La Réserve, Santa Bárbara de Nexe, 8000 Faro, Algarve. Tel: +351 89 999474

Faro – Monte do Casal, Cerro do Lobo, Estoi , 8000 Faro, Algarve. Tel: +351 89 91503

Lagos – Romantik Hotel Vivenda Miranda, Porto de Mós, 8600 Lagos, Algarve. Tel: +351 82 763 222

Lisbon – Hotel Tivoli Lisboa, Av da Liberdade 185, 1250 Lisbon. Tel: +351 1 319 89 00

Madeira – Quinta Da Bela Vista, Caminho Do Avista Navios, 4, 9000 Funchal, Madeira. Tel: +351 91 764144

Pinhao – Vintage House Hotel, Lugar da Ponte, 5085 Pinhao. Tel: +351 54 730 230

Redondo – Convento de Sao Paulo, Aldeia Da Serra, 7170, Redondo. Tel: +351 66 98 91 60

Sintra – Hotel Palacio de Seteais, Rua Barbosa de Bocage, 10, Seteais, 2710 Sintra. Tel: +351 1 923 32 00

Sintra – Quinta de Sao Thiago, 2710 Sintra . Tel: +351 1 923 29 23

SPAIN

Almuñecar – Hotel Suites Albayzin Del Mar, Avenida Costa Del Sol, 23-18690 Almuñecar, (Granada). Tel: +34 958 63 21 61

Arcos De La Frontera – Hacienda El Santiscal, Avda. del Santiscal, 129 (Lago de Arcos), 11630 Arcos de la Frontera. Tel: +34 9 56 70 83 13

Barcelona – Hotel Claris, Pau Claris 150, 08009 Barcelona. Tel: +34 93 487 62 62

Barcelona – Hotel Colon, Avenida de la Catedral 7, 08002, Barcelona. Tel: +34 93 301 14 04

Barcelona – The Gallery, Rosselló 249, 08008, Barcelona. Tel: +34 93 415 99 11

Camprodon – Hotel Grevol, Crta. Camprodon A Setcases S/N, Llanars, 17869. Tel: +34 972 74 10 13

El Rocio Almonte – El Cortijo de los Mimbrales, Crta del Rocio A483, KM20, 21.750 Almonte (Huelva). Tel: +34 959 44 22 37

Ibiza – Pikes, San Antonio De Portmany, Isla De Ibiza, Balearic Islands. Tel: +34 971 34 22 22

Lloret de Mar – Hotel Rigat Park, Playa de Fenals, 17310 Lloret de Mar, Costa Brava. Tel: +34 972 36 52 00

Madrid – Villa Real, Plaza De Las Cortes 10, 28014 Madrid . Tel: +34 91420 37 67

Malaga – La Posada Del Torcal, 29230 Villanueva de la Concepción, Malaga. Tel: +34 9 5 203 11 77

Mallorca – Gran Hotel Son Net, Castillo Son Net, 07194 Puigpunyent, Mallorca. Tel: +34 971 147 000

Mallorca – Hotel Monnaber Nou, Possessio de Monnaber Nou, 07310, Campanet, Mallorca. Tel: +34 971 877 176

Mallorca – Hotel Vistamar De Valldemosa, Ctra. Valldemosa, Andratx Km 2, 07170 Valldemosa , Mallorca. Tel: +34 971 61 23 00

Mallorca – Read's, Ca'n Moragues, 07320 Santa Marta, Mallorca. Tel: +34 9 971 140 262

Marbella – Hotel Los Monteros, 29600, Marbella. Tel: +34 952 82 38 46

Marbella – Hotel Puente Romano, P.O Box 204, 29600 Marbella. Tel: +34 9 52 82 09 00

Marbella – Marbella Club Hotel, Boulevard Príncipe Alfonso von Hohenlohe s/n, 29600 Marbella. Tel: +34 95 282 22 11

Marbella/Estepona – Las Dunas Suites, Ctra de Cádiz Km163.5, 29689 Marbella-Estepona, (Malaga). Tel: +34 95 279 43 45

Mijas-Costa – Hotel Byblos Andalus, 29640 Mijas Golf, Apt.138., Fuengirola (Malaga). Tel: +34 95 246 0250

Oviedo – Hotel de la Reconquista, Gil de Jaz 16, 33004 Oviedo, Principado de Asturias. Tel: +34 98524 1100

Pals – Hotel La Costa, Avenida Arenales de Mar 3, 17526 Platja de Pals, Costa Brava. Tel: +34 972 66 77 40

Puerto de Santa Maria-Cádiz – Monasterio de San Miguel, Calte Larga 27, 11500 El Puerto de Santa Maria, Cádiz. Tel: +34 956 54 04 40

Salamanca – Hotel Rector, Rector Esperabe, 10-Apartado 399, 37008 Salamanca. Tel: +34 923 21 84 82

Seville – Cortijo Aguila Real, Crta.Guillena-Burguillos, KM4, 41210 Guillena, Seville. Tel: +34 95 578 50 06

Seville – Hacienda Benazuza, 41800 Sanlúcar la Mayor, Seville. Tel: +34 95 570 33 44

Sitges – Hotel Estela Barcelona, Avda. Port d'Aiguadolc s/n, 08870, Stiges (Barcelona). Tel: +34 938 11 45 45

Sotogrande/San Roque – The San Roque Club Suites Hotel, CN340, KM127, 5, 11360 Sotogrande/San Roque, (Cadiz). Tel: +34 956 613 030

Tarragona – Hotel Termes Montbrío Resort, Spa & Park, Carrer Nou, 38, 43340 Montbrío Del Camp, Tarragona. Tel: +34 9 77 81 40 00

Tenerife – Gran Hotel Bahia Del Duque, 38660 Adeje, Costa Adeje, Tenerife South. Tel: +34 922 74 69 00

Tenerife – Hotel Botánico, Avda. Richard J. Yeoward 1, Urb Botánico, 238400 Puerto de la Cruz, Tenerife. Tel: +34 922 38 14 00

Tenerife – Hotel Jardin Tropical, Calle Gran Bretana, 38670 Costa Adeje, Tenerife, Canary Islands. Tel: +34 922 746 000

Tenerife – Hotel San Roque, C/. Esteban de Ponte 32, 38450, Garachico, Tenerife. Tel: +34 922 13 34 35

Viladrau – Xalet La Coromina, Carretera De Vic S/N, 17406, Viladrau. Tel: +34 93 884 92 64

SWEDEN

Åre – Hotell Åregården, Box 6, 83013 Åre. Tel: +46 647 178 00

Borgholm – Halltorps Gästgiveri, 387 92 Borgholm. Tel: +46 485 85000

Gothenburg – Hotel Eggers, Drottningtorget, Box 323, 401 25 Gothenburg. Tel: +46 31 80 60 70

Lagan – Toftaholm Herrgård, Toftaholm P.A., 34014 Lagan. Tel: +46 370 44055

Söderköping – Romantik Hotel Söderköpings Brunn, Skönbergagatan 35, Box 44, 614 21 Söderköping. Tel: +46 121 109 00

Stockholm – Hotell Diplomat, Strandvägen 7C, Box 14059, 10440 Stockholm. Tel: +46 8 459 68 00

Tällberg – Romantik Hotel Åkerblads, 793 70 Tällberg. Tel: +46 247 50800

Tanndalen – Hotel Tanndalen, 84098 Tanndalen. Tel: +46 684 22020

SWITZERLAND

Burgdorf-Bern – Hotel Stadthaus, Kirchbühl 2, 3402, Burgdorf-Bern. Tel: +41 34 428 8000

Chateau d'Oex – Hostellerie Bon Accueil, 1837 Chateau d'Oex. Tel: +41 26 924 6320

Kandersteg – Royal Park ***** Hotel, 3718 Kandersteg. Tel: +41 33 675 88 88

Lucerne/ Luzern – Romantik Hotel Wilden Mann, Bahnhofstrasse 30, 6000 Lucerne 7. Tel: +41 41 210 16 66

Lugano – Villa Principe Leopoldo & Residence, Via Montalbano, 6900 Lugano. Tel: +41 91 985 8855

Montreux – Villa Kruger, Villas Dubochet 17, 1815, Clarens. Tel: +41 21 98 92 110

Zermatt – Grand Hotel Zermatterhof, 3920, Zermatt. Tel: +41 27 966 66 00

Zuoz – Posthotel Engiadina, Via Maistra, Zouz. Tel: +41 81 85 41 021

TUNISIA

Tunis – La Maison Blanche, 45 Avenue Mohamed V, 1002, Tunis. Tel: +216 1 849 849

TURKEY

Istanbul – Hotel Sari Konak, Mimar Mehmet Aga Cad, No.42-46 34400 Sultanahmet, Istanbul. Tel: +90 212 638 62 58

Kalkan – Hotel Villa Mahal, P.K 4 Kalkan, 07960 Antalya. Tel: +90 242 844 3268

Kas – Club Savile, Cukurbag Yarimadasi, Kas, Antalya. Tel: +90 242 836 1393

Kas – Savile Residence, Cukurbag Yarimidasi, Kas, Antalya. Tel: +90 242 836 2300

Johansens Recommended Hotels – Southern Africa, Mauritius, The Seychelles

BOTSWANA

Kalahari – Jack's Camp, PO Box 173, Francistown. Tel: +27 49 124 575

Okavango – Xugana Island Lodge, C/O Hartley's Safaris, Private Bag 48 Maun. Tel: +267 661806

Okavango Delta – Abu Camp- Elephant Back Safaris, Elephant Back Safaris, Private Bay 332. Tel: +267 661 260

MAURITIUS

Mauritius – Paradis, Mauritius House, 1 Portsmouth Road, GU2 5BL. Tel: +01483 533008

Mauritius – Royal Palm, Mauritius House, 1 Portsmouth Road, GU2 5BL. Tel: +01483 533008

NAMIBIA

Windhoek – Vingerklip Lodge, PO Box 443, Outjo. Tel: +264 61 220 324

SEYCHELLES

Victoria – Fregate Island Private, PO Box 330, Victoria. Tel: +248 324 545

SOUTH AFRICA

Eastern Cape (Graaff-Reinet) – Andries Stockenström Guest House & Restaurant, 100 Cradock Street. Tel: +27 49 892 4575

Eastern Cape (Grahamstown) – Auckland Country House, PO Box 997, Grahamstown 6140. Tel: +27 46 622 2401

Eastern Cape (Port Elizabeth) – Hacklewood Hill Country House, 152 Prospect Road, Walmer, Port Elizabeth. Tel: +27 41 58 11 300

Eastern Cape (Port Elizabeth) – Shamwari Game Reserve, PO Box 32017, Summerstrand. Tel: +27 42 203 1111

Gauteng (Cullinan) – Zebra Country Lodge, PO Box 1090, Montana Park 0159. Tel: +27 12 735 1088/9

Gauteng (Magaliesburg) – De Hoek, PO Box 117, Magaliesburg. Tel: +27 014 577 1198

Gauteng (Pretoria) – Rovos Rail, P.O Box 2837, Pretoria 0001. Tel: +27 12 323 6052

Gauteng (Rozenhof) – Rozenhof Guest House, 525 Alexander Street, Brooklyn, Pretoria. Tel: +27 12 468 075

Kwazulu-Natal (Currys Post) – Old Halliwell Country Inn , PO Box 201, Howick 3290. Tel: +27 33 330 2602

Kwazulu-Natal (Durban) – Ridgeview Lodge, 17 Loudoun Road, Berea, Durban. Tel: +27 31 202 9777

Kwazulu-Natal (Lidgetton) – Happy Hill, Old Main Road, Lidgetton, 3270. Tel: +27 33 234 4380

Kwazulu-Natal (Lidgetton) – Lythwood Lodge, PO Box 17, Lidgetton 3270. Tel: +27 33 234 4666

Kwazulu-Natal (Maputaland) – Makakatana Bay Lodge, PO Box 65, Mtubatuba. Tel: +27 35 550 4189

Kwazulu-Natal (Maputaland) – Shayamoya Game Lodge, PO Box 784, Pongola 3170. Tel: +27 34 435 1110

Kwazulu-Natal (Mooi River Nr Giants Castle) – Hartford House, PO Box 31, Mooi River 3300. Tel: +27 33 263 2713

Kwazulu-Natal (Nottingham Road) – Hawklee Country House, PO Box 27, Nottingham Road 3280. Tel: +27 33 263 6209

Kwazulu-Natal (Pietermaritzburg) – Rehoboth Chalets, 276 Murray Road, Hayfields, Pietermaritzburg 3201. Tel: +27 331 962 312

Kwazulu-Natal (Rorke's Drift) – Fugitives Drift Lodge & Guest House, PO Rorkes Drift. Tel: +27 322 525 5789

Kwazulu-Natal (Shaka's Rock) – Comfort House, 27 Dolphin Crescent, Shaka's Rock. Tel: +27 322 525 5575

Kwazulu-Natal (Shakas Rock) – Lalaria Lodge, 25a Dolphin Crescent, Shakas Rock, Dolphin Coast. Tel: +27 322 525 5789

Kwazulu-Natal (Umhlali) – Isibindi Lodge, P.O. Box 275, Umhlali, 4390. Tel: +27 322 947 0538

Kwazulu-Natal (Umhlali) – Zimbali Lodge & Country Club, PO Box 404, Umhlali 4390. Tel: +27 117 80 7475

Kwazulu-Natal (Underberg) – Penwarn Country Lodge. Tel: +27 33 7011 777

Mozambique (Benguerra Island) – Benguerra Lodge, Box 87416, Houghton 2198. Tel: +27 11 483 27 34

Mpumalanga – Idube Game Reserve, PO Box 2617, Northcliff 2115. Tel: +27 11 888 3713

Mpumalanga (Hazyview) – Casa Do Sol, PO Box 57, Hazyview 1242. Tel: +27 13 737 8111

Mpumalanga (Kruger National Park) – Chitwa Chitwa Game Lodges, Head Office & Central Reservations, P.O Box 781854 Sandton , 2146. Tel: +27 11 883 1354

Mpumalanga (Malelale) – Buhala Country House, Kruger National Park, Box 165, Malelane 1320. Tel: +27 13 790 4372

Mpumalanga (Nelspruit) – Annandale House, 27 Rocket Street, Nelspruit. Tel: +27 82 7745 833

Mpumalanga (Nelspruit) – The Rest Country Lodge, PO Box 5900, Nelspruit. Tel: +27 13 744 9991/2

Mpumalanga (Timbavati) – Kings Camp, PO Box 427, Nelspruit 1200. Tel: +27 83 305 8130

Mpumalanga (White River) – Jatinga Country Lodge, Jatinga Road, White River, Mpumlanga. Tel: +27 13 751 5059

Mpumalanga (White River) – Leopard Hills Private Game Reserve, PO Box 612, Hazyview 1242. Tel: +27 13 737 6626/7

Mpumalanga (White River) – Savanna Tented Safari Lodge, PO Box 3619, White River 1240. Tel: +27 13 751 2205

Northern Cape (Kalahari) – Tswalu Private Desert Reserve, PO Box 420, Kathu. Tel: +27 53 781 9211

Northern Province (Hoedspruit) – Garonga Safari Camp, Makalali Conservancy, Hoedspruit 1380. Tel: +27 11 804 759

Northern Province (Hoedspruit) – Kapama Lodge, P.O Box 1511, Hoedspruit 1380. Tel: +27 12 804 4840

Northern Province (Hoedspruit) – Tshukudu Game Lodge, Main Road to Phalaborwa, Hoedspruit, Northern Province. Tel: +27 15 793 2476

Northern Province (Tzaneen) – Coach House, Tzaneen 0850. Tel: +27 15 307 3641

Northern Province (Waterberg) – Entabeni Game Reserve, PO Box 6349, Weltevreden Park. Tel: +27 11 675 0609

Northern Province (Welgevonden) – Makweti Safari Lodge, Welgevonden Game Reserve, P.O Box 310 , Vaalwater, 0530. Tel: +27 83 458 6122

Western Cape (Cape Town) – Cape Grace Hotel, West Quay, Victoria & Alfred Waterfront, Cape Town. Tel: +27 21 410 7100

Western Cape (Cape Town) – De Waterkant Lodge & Cottages, 20 Loader Street, De Waterkant, Cape Town 8001. Tel: +27 21 419 1097/77

Western Cape (Cape Town) – Villa Belmonte Manor House, 33 Belmont Avenue, Orangezicht, Cape Town. Tel: +27 21 462 1576

Western Cape (Cape Town-Higgovale) – Kensington Place, 38 Kensington Crescent, Higgovale, Cape Town. Tel: +27 21 424 4744

Western Cape (Cape Town-Seapoint) – The Clarendon, 67 Kloof Road, Fresnaye, Cape Town. Tel: +27 21 439 3224

Western Cape (Cape Town-Seapoint) – Huijs Haerlem, 25 Main Drive, Sea Point. Tel: +27 21 434 6434

Western Cape (Cape Town-Seapoint) – Winchester Mansions, 221 Beach Road, Sea Point. Tel: +27 21 434 2351

Western Cape (Cederberg Mountains) – Bushmans Kloof Wilderness Reserve, PO Box 53405 Kenilworth, Cape Town. Tel: +27 21 797 0990

Western Cape (Constantia Valley) – Steenberg Country Hotel, PO Box 10802, Steenberg Estate, Cape Town, 7945. Tel: +27 21 713 2222

Western Cape (Franschhoek) – La Couronne, Robertsvlei Road, Franschhoek 7690. Tel: +27 21 876 2770

Western Cape (Franschhoek) – Le Quartier Francais, 16 Huguenot Road, Franschhoek. Tel: +27 21 876 2151

Western Cape (Greyton) – Greyton Lodge, 46 Main Street, Greyton 7233. Tel: +27 28 254 9876

Western Cape (Hermon) – Bartholomeus Klip Farmhouse, PO Box 36, Hermon 7308. Tel: +27 22 448 1820

Western Cape (Hout Bay) – Tarragona Lodge, Cnr of Disa River Road & Valley Road, PO Box 26887, Hout Bay 7872. Tel: +27 21 790 5080

Western Cape (Knysna) – Belvidere Manor, Duthie Drive Belvedire Estate, Knynsa.

Western Cape (Little Karoo) – Mimosa Lodge, Church Street, Montague. Tel: +27 23 614 23 51

Western Cape (Mossel Bay) – Reins Coastal Nature Reserve, PO Box 298, Albertina. Tel: +27 28 735 3322

Western Cape (Newlands) – The Vineyard Hotel, Colinton Road, Newlands 7700, Cape Town. Tel: +27 21 683 3044

Western Cape (Northern Paarl) – Roggeland Country House, PO Box 7210, Northern Paarl, 7623. Tel: +27 21 868 2501

Western Cape (Oranjezicht) – No.1 Chesterfield, 1 Chesterfield Road, Oranjezicht, 8001 Cape Town. Tel: +27 21 461 7383

Western Cape (Plettenberg Bay) – Hog Hollow Country Lodge, PO Box 503, Plettenberg Bay, 6600. Tel: +27 4457 48879

What does your paper say about you?

Jeremy Hoskins, hotelier, chooses Conqueror* Contour in Oyster, printed in colour.

Starring role. Jeremy Hoskins combed the Conqueror* range to discover the perfect texture for his hotel's letterhead. Ideal for brochures, menus, wine-lists and letterheads, as well as for all corporate and conference stationery, the colours, textures and weights of the Conqueror* range are the best in the business. For a free sample pack or advice on the Conqueror* range and where to find it, call + 44 (0) 1256 728665 or visit www.conqueror.com now. You'll get five stars for presentation.

Star quality. For a free sample pack or advice on the Conqueror* range and where to find it, call + 44 (0) 1256 728665 or visit www.conqueror.com now.

Western Cape (Plettenberg Bay) – Laird's Lodge, PO Box 657, Plettenberg Bay, 6600. Tel: +27 4453 27721

Western Cape (Stellenbosch) – d'Ouwe Werf, 30 Church Street, Stellenbosch. Tel: +27 21 887 4608

Western Cape (Stellenbosch) – Lyngrove Country House, PO Box 7275, Stellenbosch 7599. Tel: +27 21 842 2116

Western Cape (Stellenbosch) – River Manor, No.6 The Avenue, Stellenbosch. Tel: +27 21 887 9944

Western Cape (Tulbagh) – Rijk's Ridge Country House, PO Box 340, Tulbagh. Tel: +27 23 230 1006

ZIMBABWE

Zimbabwe (Chiredzi-South East Lowveld) – Nduna Safari Lodge, Malilangwe Private Wildlife Reserve, Reservations P.O Box MP845 Mount Pleasant. Tel: +263 4 722 983

Zimbabwe (Chiredzi-South East Lowveld) – Pamushana, Malilangwe Private Wildlife Reserve, Reservations P.O Box MP845 Mount Pleasant. Tel: +263 4 722 983

Zimbabwe (Harare) – Meikles Hotel, Jason Moyo Avenue, PO Box 594, Harare. Tel: +263 4 707721

Zimbabwe (Harare) – Wild Geese Lodge, Buckland Lane, Teviotdale, Harare. Tel: +263 4 860466/275

Zimbabwe (Hwange) – The Hide Safari Camp, 27-29 James Martin Drive, PO Box ST274, Southerton. Tel: +263 4 660554

Zimbabwe (Lake Cariba) – Sanyati Lodge, 124 Josiah Chinamano, Harare. Tel: +263 4 72 22 33

Zimbabwe (Nyanga) – Inn on Rupurara, PO Box 337, Juliasdale. Tel: +263 20 67449

Zimbabwe (Victoria Falls) – Victoria Falls Hotel, Mallet Drive, Victoria Falls. Tel: +263 13 4761

Johansens Recommended Hotels – North America, Bermuda & The Caribbean

BERMUDA

Hamilton – Rosedon Hotel, Pitts Bay Road, PO Box HM 290, Hamilton HMCX. Tel: +1 441 295 1640

Paget – The Newstead Hotel, 27 Harbour Road, Paget PG02. Tel: +1 1 441 236 6060

Paget – Harmony Club All Inclusive, PO Box 299, South Shore Road, Paget PG BX. Tel: +1 441 236 3500

Paget – Fourways Inn, PO Box PG 294, Paget PG BX. Tel: +1 441 236 6517

Warwick – Surf Side Beach Club, 90 South Shore Road, PO Box WK 101, Warwick. Tel: +1 441 236 7100

CARIBBEAN

Antigua – The Inn At English Harbour, PO Box 187, St Johns, Antigua. Tel: +1 268 460 1014

Curacao – Avila Beach Hotel, Penstraat 130, Willemstad, Curacao. Tel: +599 9 461 4377

Dominica – Hummingbird Inn, Morne Daniel, Box 1901, Roseau, Dominica. Tel: +1 767 449 1042

Martinique – Manoir De Beauregard, Chemin Des Salines 97227, Sainte Anne, Frenc. Tel: +596 76 73 40

St Lucia – Mago Estate Hotel, PO Box 434. Tel: +

St Vincent – Grand View Beach Hotel, Villa Point, Box 173, St Vincent, West Indies. Tel: +1 809 458 4811

St Vincent & The Grenadines – Camelot Inn, PO Box 787, Kingstown, St Vincent & The Grenadines. Tel: +1 784 456 2100

Tobago – Coco Reef Resort, PO box 434, Scarborough, Tobago, West Indies. Tel: +1 868 639 8571

Turks & Caicos – Grace Bay Club, Grace Bay Road, PO Box 681, Providenciales, Provo Island. Tel: +1 649 946 5199

CANADA

Quebec, Ayer's Cliff – Auberge Ripplecove Inn, 700 Ripplecove Road, Ayer's Cliff, Quebec JOB 1C0. Tel: +1 819 838 4296

Sidney – Seaside Luxury Resort, 8355 Lockside Drive, Sidney, British Columbia. Tel: +1 250 544 1000

Vancouver – The West End Guest House, 1362 Haro Street, Vancouver, British Columbia V6 IG2. Tel: +1 604 681 2889/1302

Vancouver – The Wedgewood Hotel, 845 Hornby Street, Vancouver, British Columbia V6Z 1V1. Tel: +1 604 689 7777

Victoria – Dashwood Manor, 1 Cook Street, Victoria, British Columbia V8V 3W6. Tel: +1 250 385 5517

UNITED STATES OF AMERICA

Arizona (Flagstaff) – Inn at 410, 410 North Leroux Street, Flagstaff, Arizona 86001. Tel: +1 520 774 0088

Arizona (Phoenix) – Maricopa Manor, Box 7186, 15 West Pasadena Avenue, Phoenix, Arizona 85013-2001. Tel: +1 602 274 6302

Arizona (Sedona) – Canyon Villa Inn, 125 Canyon Circle Drive, Sedona, Arizona 86351. Tel: +1 520 284 1226

Arizona (Sedona) – Casa Sedona, 55 Hozoni Drive, Sedona, Arizona 86336. Tel: +1 520 282 2938

Arizona (Tucson) – Tanque Verde Ranch, 14301 East Speedway Boulevard, Tucson, Arizona 85748. Tel: +1 520 296 6275

Arizona (Tucson) – White Stallion Ranch, 9251 West Twin Peaks Road, Tucson, Arizona 85743. Tel: +1 520 297 0252

California (Carmel) – Pine Inn, PO Box 250, Ocean Avenue & Monte Verde, Carmel, California 93921. Tel: +1 408 624 3851

California (Elk) – Elk Cove Inn, 6300 South Highway One, PO Box 367, Elk, California 95432. Tel: +1 707 877 3321

California (Eureka) – Carter House, 301 L Street, Eureka, California 95501. Tel: +1 707 444 8062

California (Ferndale) – Gingerbread Mansion Inn, 400 Berding Street, (PO Box 40), Ferndale, California 95536-0040. Tel: +1 707 786 4000

California (Hollywood) – Le Parc Suite Hotel, 733 North West Knoll Drive, West Hollywood, California 90069. Tel: +1 310 855 8888

California (La Jolla) – The Bed & Breakfast Inn at La Jolla, 7753 Draper Avenue, La Jolla, California 92037. Tel: +1 619 456 2066

California (La Quinta) – Two Angels Inn, 78-120 Caleo Bay, La Quinta, California. Tel: +1 760 564 7332

California (Mendocino) – Joshua Grindle Inn, 44800 Little Lake Road, PO Box 647, Mendocino, California 95460. Tel: +1 707 937 4143

California (Monterey Peninsula) – The Martine Inn, 255 Oceanview Boulevard, Pacific Grove, California 93950. Tel: +1 831 373 3388

California (Muir Beach) – Pelican Inn, Highway 1, Muir Beach, California 94965. Tel: +1 415 383 6000

California (Napa Valley) – The Ink House, 1575 Helena Highway at Whitehall Lane, St Helena, California 94574-9775. Tel: +1 707 963 3890

California (Nevada City) – Red Castle Inn Historic Lodging, 109 Prospect Street, Nevada City, California 95959. Tel: +1 530 265 5135

California (Palm Springs) – The Willows, 412 West Tahquitz Canyon Way, Palm Springs, California 92262. Tel: +1 760 320 0771

California (San Francisco) – Nob Hill Lambourne, 725 Pine Street, San Francisco, California 94108. Tel: +1 415 433 2287

California (San Rafael) – Gerstle Park Inn, 34 Grove Street, San Rafaël, California 94901. Tel: +1 415 721 7611

California (Santa Ana) – Woolley's Petite Suites, 2721 Hotel Terrace Road, Santa Ana, California 92705. Tel: +1 714 540 1111

California (Shasta) – Brigadoon Castle, 9036 Zogg Mine Road, PO Box 324, Igo, California 96047. Tel: +1 530 396 2785

California (Solvang) – The Alisal Guest Ranch & Resort, 1054 Alisal Road, Solvang, California 93463. Tel: +1 805 688 6411

California (Sutters Creek, Gold Country) – The Foxes Inn, 77 Main Street, Sutters Creek, California 95685. Tel: +1 209 267 5882

Colorado (Denver) – Historic Castle Marne, 1572 Race Street, Denver , Colorado 80206. Tel: +1 303 331 0621

Colorado (Durango) – Tall Timber, 1 Silverton Star, Durango, Colorado 81301. Tel: +1 970 259 4813

Connecticut (Deep River) – Riverwind Inn, 209 Main Street, Deep River, Connecticut 06417. Tel: +1 860 526 2014

Connecticut (Greenwich) – The Homestead Inn, 420 Fieldpoint Road, Greenwich, Connecticut 06830. Tel: +1 203 869 7500

Connecticut (New Preston) – The Boulders, East Shore Road, Route 45, PO Box 2575 New Preston, Connecticut 06777. Tel: +1 860 868 0541

Delaware (Montchanin) – The Inn at Montchanin Village, Route 100 & Kirk Road, Montchanin, Delaware 19710. Tel: +1 302 888 2133

Delaware (Rehoboth Beach) – Boardwalk Plaza Hotel, Olive Avenue & The Boardwalk, Rehoboth Beach, Delaware 19971. Tel: +1 302 227 0441

Florida (Duck Key) – Hawk's Cay Resort, 61 Hawk's Cay Blvd, , Duck Key, Florida 33050-3756. Tel: +1 305 743 7000

Florida (Fort Lauderdale) – Lago Mar, 1700 South Ocean Lane, Fort Lauderdale, Florida 33316. Tel: +1 954 523 6511

Florida (Holmes Beach) – Harrington House. Tel: +

Florida (Key West) – Island City House, 411 William Street, Key West, Florida 33040. Tel: +1 305 294 5702

Florida (Key West) – Simonton Court Historic Inn & Cottages, 320 Simonton Street, Key West, Florida 33040. Tel: +1 305 294 6386

Florida (Lake Wales) – Chalet Suzanne, 3800 Chalet Suzanne Drive, Lake Wales, Florida 33853-7060. Tel: +1 941 676 6011

Florida (Miami Beach) – The Richmond, 1757 Collins Avenue, Miami Beach, Florida 33139. Tel: +1 305 538 2331

Florida (Miami Beach) – Hotel Ocean, 1230-1238 Ocean Drive, South Beach, Florida 33139. Tel: +1 305 672 2579

Georgia (Cumberland Island) – Greyfield Inn , Cumberland Island, PO Box 900, Fernandina Beach, Florida 32035-0900. Tel: +1 904 261 6408

Georgia (Little St. Simons Island) – The Lodge on Little St. Simons Island, PO Box 21078, St Simons Island, Georgia. Tel: +1 912 638 7472

Georgia (Perry) – Henderson Village, 125 South Langston Circle, Perry, Georgia 31069. Tel: +1 912 988 8696

Georgia (Savannah) – Foley House Inn, 14 West Hull, Chippewa Square, Savannah, Georgia 31401. Tel: +1 912 232 6622

Georgia (Savannah) – The Eliza Thompson House, 5 West Jones Street, Savannah, Georgia 31401. Tel: +1 912 236 3620

Georgia (Savannah) – Presidents Quarters, 225 East President Street, Savannah, Georgia 31401. Tel: +1 912 233 1600

Georgia (Savannah) – Magnolia Place Inn, 503 Whittaker Street, Savannah, Georgia 31401. Tel: +1 912 236 7674

Georgia (Thomasville) – Melhana Plantation, 301 Showboat Lane, Thomasville, Georgia 31792. Tel: +1 912 266 2290

Hawaii (Kailua-Kona) – Kailua Plantation House, 75-5948 Alii Drive, Kailua-Kona, Hawaii 96740. Tel: +1 808 329 3727

Hawaii (Volcano Village, Big Island) – Chalet Kilauea-The Inn at Volcano, Box 998, Wright Road, Volcano Village, Hawaii 96785. Tel: +1 808 967 7786

Louisiana (Napoleonville) – Madewood Plantation House, 4250 Highway 308, Napoleonville, Louisiana 70390. Tel: +1 504 369 7151

Louisiana (New Orleans) – The Claiborne Mansion, 2111 Dauphine Street, New Orleans, Louisiana 70116. Tel: +1 504 949 7327

Louisiana (New Orleans) – Windsor Court, 300 Gravier Street, New Orleans, Louisiana 70130. Tel: +1 504 523 6000

Maine (Greenville) – The Lodge at Moosehead Lake, Upon Lily Bay Road, Box 1167, Greenville, Maine 04441. Tel: +1 207 695 4400

Maine (Kennebunkport) – Kennebunkport Inn, 1 Dock Square, PO Box 111, Kennebunkport, Maine 04046. Tel: +1 207 967 2621

Maine (Prouts Neck) – Black Point Inn Resort, Prouts Neck, Scarborough, Maine 04074. Tel: +1 207 883 4126

Maryland (Frederick) – Tyler Spite Inn, 112 West Church Street, Frederick, Maryland 21701. Tel: +1 301 831 4455

Maryland (Taneytown) – Antrim 1844, 30 Trevanion Road, Taneytown, Maryland 21787. Tel: +1 410 756 6182

Massachusetts (Boston Area) – A Cambridge House, 2218 Massachusetts Avenue, Cambridge, Massachusetts 02140-1836. Tel: +1 617 491 6300

Massachusetts (Cape Cod) – Wedgewood Inn, 83 Main Street, Route 6A, Yarmouth Port, Massachusetts 02675. Tel: +1 508 362 9178

Massachusetts (Chatham) – Pleasant Bay Village Resort, PO Box 772, Route 28, Chatham, Massachusetts 02633. Tel: +1 508 945 1133

Massachusetts (Chatham) – The Captain's House Inn, 369-377 Old Harbor Road, Chatham, Cape Cod, Massachusetts 02633. Tel: +1 508 945 0127

Massachusetts (Deerfield) – Deerfield Inn, 108 Old Main Street, Deerfield, Massachusetts 01342. Tel: +1 413 774 5587

Massachusetts (Eastham) – The Whalewalk Inn, 220 Bridge Road, Eastham, Massachusetts 02642. Tel: +1 508 255 0617

Massachusetts (Gloucester) – Ocean View Inn, 171 Atlantic Road, Gloucester, Massachusetts 01930. Tel: +1 978 283 6200

Massachusetts (Lenox) – Wheatleigh, Hawthorne Road, Lenox, Massachusetts 01240. Tel: +1 413 637 0610

Massachusetts (Rockport) – Seacrest Manor, 99 Marmion Way, Rockport, Massachusetts 01966. Tel: +1 978 546 2211

Mexico (Ixtapa/Zihuatanejo) – Hotel Villa Del Sol, Playa La Ropa s/n, PO Box 84. Tel: +1 52 755 4 2239

Michigan (Petoskey) – Staffords Perry Hotel, Bay at Lewis Street, Petoskey, Michigan 49770. Tel: +1 616 347 4000

Mississippi (Biloxi) – Father Ryan House, 1196 Beach Boulevard, Biloxi, Mississippi. Tel: +1 228 435 1189

Mississippi (Jackson) – Fairview Inn, 734 Fairview Street, Jackson, Mississippi 39202. Tel: +1 601 948 3429

Mississippi (Vicksburg) – The Duff Green Mansion, 1114 1st East Street, Vicksburg , Mississippi 39180. Tel: +1 601 636 6968

New Hampshire (Bedford) – Bedford Village Inn, 2 Village Inn Lane, Bedford, New Hampshire 03110. Tel: +1 603 472 2001

New Hampshire (Bethlehem) – Adair, 80 Guider Lane, Bethelehem, New Hampshire 03574. Tel: +1 603 444 2600

New Hampshire (Henniker) – Colby Hill Inn, The Oaks, PO Box 779, Henniker, New Hampshire 03242. Tel: +1 603 428 3281

New Hampshire (Jackson) – Inn at Thorn Hill, Thorn Hill Road, Jackson, New Hampshire 03846. Tel: +1 603 383 4242

New Jersey (Cape May) – The Queens Hotel, 601 Columbia Avenue, Cape May, New Jersey 08204. Tel: +1 609 884 1613

New Jersey (Hope) – The Inn at Millrace Pond, PO Box 359, Hope, New Jersey 07844. Tel: +1 908 459 4884

New York – The Iroquois, 49 West 44th Street, New York, New York 10036. Tel: +212 840 3080

New York (Cazenovia) – The Brewster Inn, 6 Ledyard Avenue, Cazenovia, New York 13035. Tel: +1 315 655 9232

New York (Clarence) – Asa Ransom House, 10529 Main Street, Route 5, Clarence, New York 14031-1684. Tel: +1 716 759 2315

New York (East Aurora) – The Roycroft Inn, 40 South Grove Street, East Aurora, New York 14052. Tel: +1 716 652 5552

New York (Ithaca) – Benn Conger Inn, 206 West Cortland Street, Groton, New York 13073. Tel: +1 607 898 5817

North Carolina (Lake Toxaway) – The Greystone Inn, , Lake Toxaway, North Carolina 28747. Tel: +1 828 966 4700

North Carolina (Pittsboro) – The Fearrington House, 2000 Fearrington Village Center, Pittsboro, North Carolina 27312. Tel: +1 919 542 2121

North Carolina (Saluda) – Orchard Inn, Highway 176, Box 725, Saluda, North Carolina 28773. Tel: +1 828 749 5471

North Carolina (Tryon) – Pine Crest, 200 Pine Crest Lane, Tryon, North Carolina 28782. Tel: +1 828 859 9135

North Carolina (Waynesville) – The Swag Country Inn, 2300 Swag Road, Waynesville, North Carolina 28786. Tel: +1 828 926 0430

Oregon (Ashland) – The Winchester Country Inn, 35 South Second Street, Ashland, Oregon 97520. Tel: +1 541 488 1113

Oregon (Eugene) – Campbell House, 252 Pearl Street, Eugene, Oregon 97401. Tel: +1 541 343 1119

Oregon (Hood River) – Columbia Gorge Hotel, 4000 Westcliff Drive, Hood River, Oregon 97031-9970. Tel: +1 541 386 5566

Pennsylvania (South Sterling) – The French Manor, Huckleberry Road (Route 191), BOX 39, South Sterling, Pennsylvania 18460. Tel: +1 717 676 3244

Rhode Island (Newport) – Cliffside Inn, 2 Seaview Avenue, Newport, Rhode Island 02840. Tel: +1 401 847 1811

South Carolina (Beaufort) – The Rhett House Inn, 1009 Craven Street, Beaufort, South Carolina 29902. Tel: +1 843 524 9030

South Carolina (Charleston) – Wentworth Mansion, 149 Wentworth Street, Charleston, South Carolina 29401. Tel: +1 843 853 1886

South Carolina (Pawleys Island) – Litchfield Plantation, Kings River Road, Pawleys Island, South Carolina 29585. Tel: +1 843 237 9121

Utah (Salt Lake City) – The Inn On Capitol Hill, 225 North State Street, Salt Lake City, Utah 84103. Tel: +1 801 575 1112

Utah (Salt Lake City) – La Europa Royale, 1135 East Vine Street, Salt Lake City, Utah 84121. Tel: +1 801 263 7999

Vermont (Chittenden) – Mountain Top Inn & Resort, Mountain Top Road, Chittenden, Vermont 05737. Tel: +1 802 483 2311

Vermont (Chittenden) – Tulip Tree Inn, Chittenden Dan Road, Chittenden, Vermont 05737. Tel: +1 802 483 6213

Vermont (Lower Waterford) – Rabbit Hill Inn, 48 Lower Waterford Road, Lower Waterford, Vermont 05848. Tel: +1 802 748 5168

Vermont (Manchester Village) – 1811 House, PO Box 39, Route 7A, Manchester Village, Vermont 05254. Tel: +1 802 362 1811

Vermont (Stowe) – The Mountain Road Resort, PO Box 8, 1007 Mountain Road, Stowe, Vermont 05672. Tel: +1 802 253 4566

Vermont (Vergennes) – Basin Harbor Club, On Lake Champlain, Vergennes, Vermont 05491. Tel: +1 802 475 2311

Vermont (West Townshend) – Windham Hill Inn, , West Townshend, Vermont 05359. Tel: +1 802 874 4080

Virginia (Charlottesville) – Clifton-The Country Inn & Estate, 1296 Clifton Inn Drive, Charlottesville, Virginia 22941. Tel: +1 804 971 1800

Washington (Orcas Island) – Turtleback Farm Inn, 1981 Crow Valley Road, Eastsound, Washington 98245. Tel: +1 360 376 4914

Washington (Port Townsend) – Ann Starrett Mansion, 744 Clay Street, Port Townsend, Washington 98368. Tel: +1 360 385 3205

Washington (Seattle) – Sorrento Hotel, 900 Madison Street, Seattle, Washington 98104-9742. Tel: +1 206 622 6400

JOHANSENS RECOMMENDED HOTEL
JOHANSENS RECOMMENDED INN OR RESTAURANT
JOHANSENS RECOMMENDED COUNTRY HOUSE

To Dublin/
Dun Laoghaire

To Rosslare

To Rosslare

To Cork

To Santander

To Roscoff

To Guernsey

ISLES OF
SCILLY

0   20   40   60   80   100 Kilometres
0 10 20 30 40 50 Miles

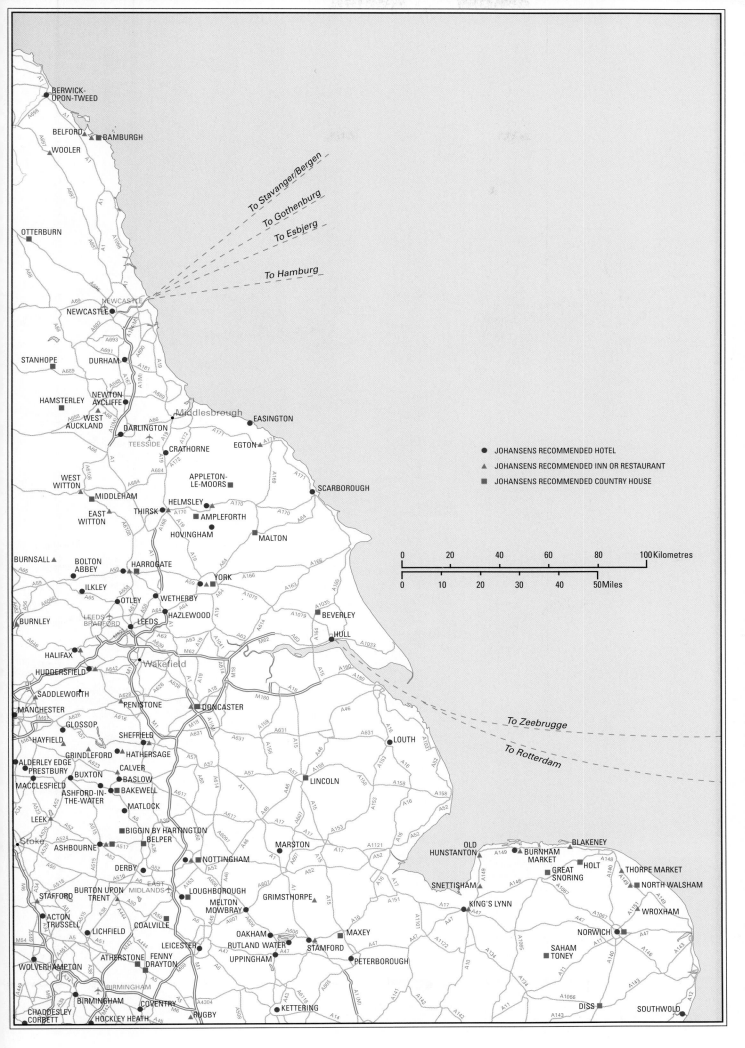

JOHANSENS RECOMMENDED HOTEL

▲ JOHANSENS RECOMMENDED INN OR RESTAURANT

■ JOHANSENS RECOMMENDED COUNTRY HOUSE

To Stavanger/Bergen
To Gothenburg
To Esbjerg
To Hamburg
To Zeebrugge
To Rotterdam

BERWICK-UPON-TWEED
BELFORD
BAMBURGH
WOOLER
OTTERBURN
STANHOPE
HAMSTERLEY
NEWTON AYCLIFFE
DURHAM
WEST AUCKLAND
DARLINGTON
NEWCASTLE
Middlesbrough
EASINGTON
TEESSIDE
CRATHORNE
EGTON
APPLETON-LE-MOORS
SCARBOROUGH
WEST WITTON
MIDDLEHAM
HELMSLEY
THIRSK
AMPLEFORTH
EAST WITTON
HOVINGHAM
MALTON
BURNSALL
BOLTON ABBEY
HARROGATE
ILKLEY
YORK
OTLEY
WETHERBY
BURNLEY
HAZLEWOOD
LEEDS BRADFORD
LEEDS
BEVERLEY
HALIFAX
HULL
HUDDERSFIELD
Wakefield
SADDLEWORTH
PENISTONE
MANCHESTER
DONCASTER
GLOSSOP
HAYFIELD
SHEFFIELD
LOUTH
GRINDLEFORD
HATHERSAGE
ALDERLEY EDGE
PRESTBURY
CALVER
BUXTON
BASLOW
LINCOLN
MACCLESFIELD
BAKEWELL
ASHFORD-IN-THE-WATER
MATLOCK
LEEK
BIGGIN BY HARTINGTON
BELPER
MARSTON
Stoke
ASHBOURNE
DERBY
NOTTINGHAM
BURTON UPON TRENT
EAST MIDLANDS
LOUGHBOROUGH
GRIMSTHORPE
STAFFORD
MELTON MOWBRAY
ACTON TRUSSELL
LICHFIELD
COALVILLE
OAKHAM
MAXEY
LEICESTER
RUTLAND WATER
STAMFORD
WOLVERHAMPTON
ATHERSTONE
FENNY DRAYTON
UPPINGHAM
PETERBOROUGH
BIRMINGHAM
CHADDESLEY CORBETT
COVENTRY
KETTERING
HOCKLEY HEATH
RUGBY

OLD HUNSTANTON
BLAKENEY
BURNHAM MARKET
HOLT
THORPE MARKET
GREAT SNORING
NORTH WALSHAM
SNETTISHAM
KING'S LYNN
WROXHAM
NORWICH
SAHAM TONEY
DISS
SOUTHWOLD

0   20   40   60   80   100 Kilometres
0   10   20   30   40   50 Miles

© Lovell Johns Ltd, Oxford

517

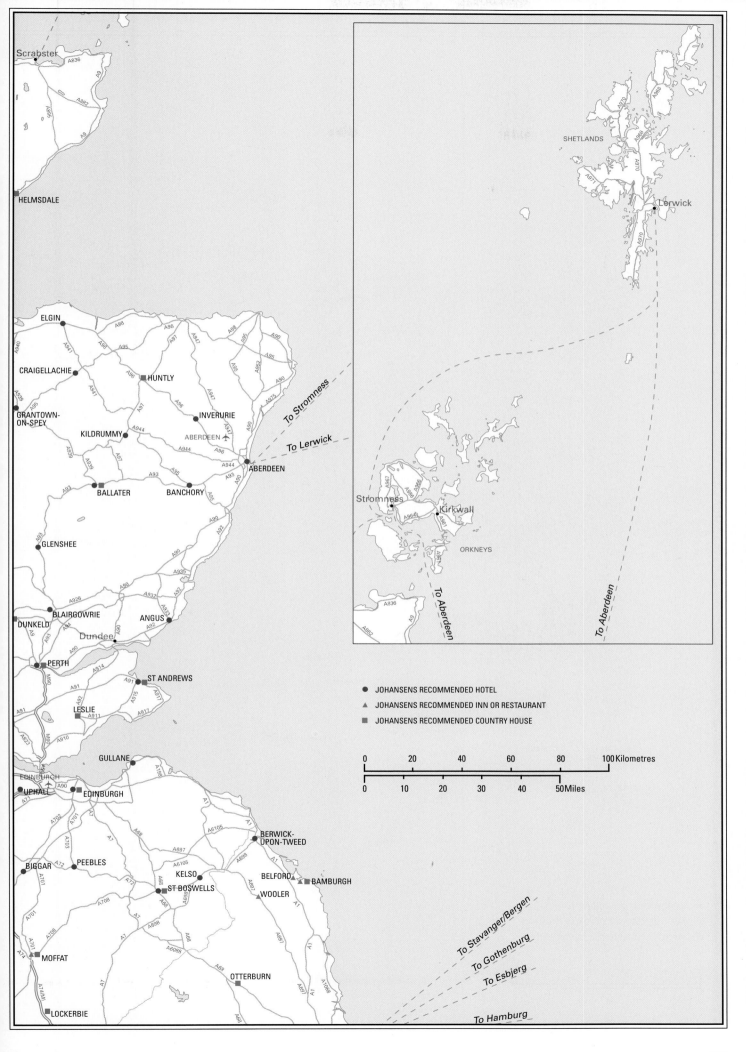

JOHANSENS RECOMMENDED HOTEL
▲ JOHANSENS RECOMMENDED INN OR RESTAURANT
■ JOHANSENS RECOMMENDED COUNTRY HOUSE

| 0 | 20 | 40 | 60 | 80 | 100 Kilometres |

| 0 | 10 | 20 | 30 | 40 | 50 Miles |

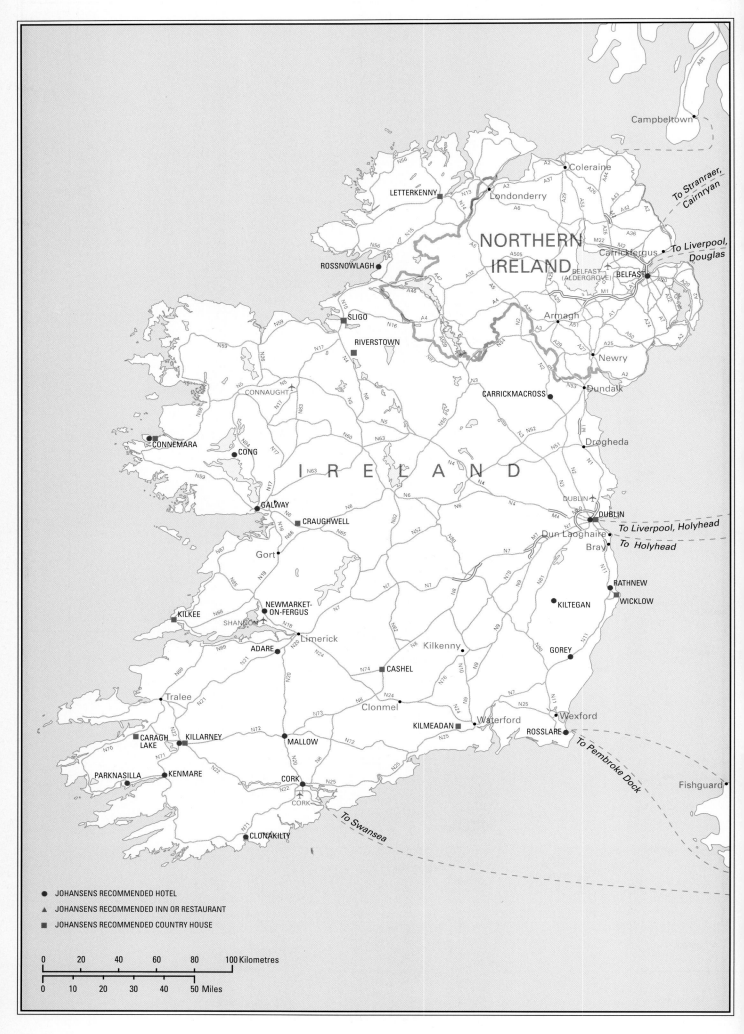

JOHANSENS RECOMMENDED HOTEL
JOHANSENS RECOMMENDED INN OR RESTAURANT
JOHANSENS RECOMMENDED COUNTRY HOUSE

| 0 | 20 | 40 | 60 | 80 | 100 Kilometres |
| 0 | 10 | 20 | 30 | 40 | 50 Miles |

PREFERRED PARTNERS

Preferred partners are those organisations specifically chosen and exclusively recommended by Johansens for the quality and excellence of their products and services for the mutual benefit of Johansens members, readers and independent travellers.

 Barrels & Bottles

 Classic Malts of Scotland

 Conqueror, The Preferred Paper Partner

 Dorlux

 Ercol Furniture Ltd

 Hildon Ltd

 Marsh UK Ltd

 Knight Frank International

 Honda (UK)

 Moët Hennessy

 Pacific Direct

MARSH
An *MMC* Company

Marsh, the world's leading insurance broker, is proud to be the appointed Preferred Insurance Provider to Johansens Members Worldwide

ARE YOU A HOTELIER?

There is never a spare moment when you're running a Hotel, Inn, Restaurant or Country House. If you're not with a customer, your mind is on stocktaking. Sound familiar?

At Marsh, we realise you have little time to worry about your insurance policy, instead, you require peace of mind that you are covered.

That is why for over 20 years Marsh have been providing better cover for businesses like yours.

Our unique services are developed specifically for establishments meeting the high standards required for entry in a Johansens guide.

CONTACT US NOW FOR DETAILS OF THE INSURANCE POLICY FOR JOHANSENS

01892 553160 (UK)

Insurance Policy for Johansens members arranged by:
Marsh UK Ltd.
Mount Pleasant House,
Lonsdale Gardens,
Tunbridge Wells, Kent TN1 1NY

ARE YOU AN INDEPENDENT TRAVELLER?

Insurance is probably the last thing on your mind. Especially when you are going on holiday or on a business trip. But are you protected when travelling? Is your home protected while you are away?

Marsh offer a wide range of insurances that gives you peace of mind when travelling.

FOR DETAILS ON THESE SERVICES RING (UK):

TRAVEL	**01462 428041**
PENSIONS & FINANCIAL	
SERVICES	**0171 357 3307**
HOUSEHOLD	**01462 428200**
MOTOR	**01462 428100**
HEALTHCARE	**01462 428000**

Johansens Recommended Hotels listed by region

To enable you to use your Johansens Recommended Hotels Guide more effectively the following pages of indexes contain a wealth of useful information about the hotels featured in the guide. As well as listing the hotels alphabetically by region and by county, the indexes also show at a glance which hotels offer certain specialised facilities.

The indexes are as follows:

- By region
- By county
- With a heated indoor swimming pool
- With a golf course on site
- With shooting arranged
- With salmon or trout fishing on site
- With health/fitness facilities
- With childcare facilities
- With conference facilities for 250 delegates or more
- Pride of Britain members
- Relais & Châteaux members
- Small Luxury Hotels of the World members
- Johansens Preferred Partners

LONDON

The Ascott Mayfair	London	14
Basil Street Hotel	London	17
The Beaufort	London	15
Beaufort House Apartments	London	16
Blakes Hotel	London	18
Brown's Hotel	London	19
The Cadogan	London	20
Cannizaro House	London	21
Chelsea Green Hotel	London	22
Chequers of Kensington	London	23
Claridge's	London	24
The Cliveden Town House	London	25
The Colonnade Town House	London	26
The Dorchester	London	27
Draycott House Apartments	London	28
Fountains	London	29
Harrington Hall	London	30
The Hempel	London	31
Hendon Hall	London	32
The Leonard	London	33
The Lexham Apartments	London	34
London Bridge Hotel	London	35
The Milestone Hotel	London	36
No 5 Maddox Street	London	37
Number Eleven Cadogan Gardens	London	38
Number Sixteen	London	39
One Aldwych	London	40
Pembridge Court Hotel	London	41
The Royal Horseguards	London	42
Twenty Nevern Square	London	43
Westbury Hotel	London	44
Swan Hellenic Minerva	London	45

ENGLAND

42 The Calls	Leeds	224
Albrighton Hall Hotel	Shrewsbury	307
The Alderley Edge Hotel	Alderley Edge	51
Alexander House	Gatwick	179
Amberley Castle	Amberley	55
The Angel Hotel	Bury St Edmunds	125
The Angel Hotel	Midhurst	257
The Angel Posting House	Guildford	186
Appleby Manor Hotel	Appleby-in-Westmorland	62
The Arundell Arms	Lifton	231
Ashdown Park Hotel	Forest Row	177
Astley Bank Hotel	Blackburn	101
Bagden Hall Hotel	Huddersfield	206
Bailiffscourt	Arundel	64
The Balmer Lawn	Brockenhurst	117
The Balmoral Hotel	Harrogate	191
Barnsdale Lodge	Rutland Water	289
The Bath Priory Hotel	Bath	79
The Bay Tree Hotel	Burford	122
The Bear of Rodborough Hotel	Cirencester	148
The Bedford Arms	Woburn	364
Beechfield House	Lacock	220
Bel Alp House	Dartmoor	158
Billesley Manor	Stratford-Upon-Avon	320
Bindon Country House Hotel	Taunton	327
Bishopstrow House	Warminster	349
The Boar's Head Hotel	Harrogate	192
Bolt Head Hotel	Salcombe	296
The Borrowdale Gates Hotel	Keswick	213
The Bridge Hotel	Prestbury	282
Bridge House Hotel	Beaminster	89
Brockencote Hall	Chaddesley Corbett	132
Broomhill Lodge	Rye	290
Broxton Hall Hotel	Chester	138
Buckland-Tout-Saints	Kingsbridge Estuary	218
Budock Vean Hotel	Falmouth	174
The Burlington Hotel	Birmingham	96
Buxted Park Hotel	Buxted	127
Calcot Manor	Tetbury	332
Callow Hall	Ashbourne	66
Carden Park	Chester	139
Careys Manor Hotel	Brockenhurst	118
The Carlton Mitre Hotel	Hampton Court	190
The Castle At Taunton	Taunton	328
The Cavendish Hotel	Baslow	77
Charingworth Manor	Chipping Campden	146
Charlton House	Shepton Mallet	306
Charnwood Hotel	Sheffield	303
The Chase Hotel	Ross-On-Wye	286
Chauntry House Hotel	Bray-on-Thames	109
The Cheltenham Park Hotel	Cheltenham	135
The Chester Grosvenor	Chester	140
Chevin Lodge Hotel	Otley	273
Chilston Park	Maidstone	243
Cliveden	Maidenhead	240
The Close Hotel	Tetbury	333
The Colwall Park Hotel	Malvern	247
Combe Grove Manor	Bath	80
Combe House at Gittisham	Exeter	172
Congham Hall	King's Lynn	217
Coombe Abbey	Coventry	152
Corse Lawn House Hotel	Tewkesbury	334
The Cotswold House	Chipping Campden	145
The Cottage In The Wood	Malvern Wells	248
Crab Manor	Thirsk	336
Crabwall Manor	Chester	141
Crathorne Hall Hotel	Crathorne	154
Crudwell Court Hotel	Malmesbury	244
Dale Hill	Ticehurst	337
Danesfield House	Marlow-On-Thames	252
Daneswood House Hotel	Bristol South	114
The Devonshire Arms Hotel	Bolton Abbey	102
Dinham Hall	Ludlow	235
Donnington Valley Hotel	Newbury	262
The Dormy	Bournemouth	103
Dormy House	Broadway	115
Down Hall Hotel	Bishop's Stortford	100
Eastwell Manor	Ashford	69
The Edgemoor	Bovey Tracey	106
The Elms	Abberley	48
Esseborne Manor	Andover	60
Etrop Grange	Manchester Airport	250
Ettington Park	Stratford-Upon-Avon	321
The Evesham Hotel	Evesham	170
Fallowfields	Oxford	275
Farlam Hall Hotel	Brampton	108
Fawsley Hall Hotel	Daventry	159
The Feathers Hotel	Woodstock	368
Fifehead Manor	Andover	61
Fischer's	Baslow	78
Five Lakes Hotel	Colchester	151
Flitwick Manor	Woburn	365
Fowey Hall Hotel	Fowey	178
Foxhills	Ottershaw	274
Fredrick's Hotel & Restaurant	Maidenhead	241
The French Horn	Sonning-On-Thames	311
The Garrack Hotel	St. Ives	293
The George Hotel	Yarmouth	371
George Hotel	Hathersage	197
The George Of Stamford	Stamford	314
Ghyll Manor Country Hotel	Rusper	288
The Gibbon Bridge Hotel	Preston	283
Gidleigh Park	Chagford	133
Gilpin Lodge	Windermere	356
The Glebe At Barford	Warwick	350
Grafton Manor Hotel	Bromsgrove	121
The Grand Hotel	Eastbourne	167
The Grange Hotel	York	372
Grants Hotel	Harrogate	193
The Grapevine Hotel	Stow-On-The-Wold	317
Grayshott Hall	Grayshott	185
Graythwaite Manor	Grange-Over-Sands	182
Great Fosters	Egham	168
The Greenway	Cheltenham	136
Grinkle Park Hotel	Easington	166
Hackness Grange	Scarborough	300
Haley's Hotel and Restaurant	Leeds	225
Hambleton Hall	Oakham	272
Hanbury Manor	Ware	347
Hartwell House	Aylesbury	71
Hassop Hall	Bakewell	74
Hawkstone Park Hotel	Shrewsbury	308
The Haycock	Peterborough	280
Hazlewood Castle Hotel	Hazlewood	199
Headlam Hall	Darlington	156
Hellaby Hall Hotel	Sheffield	304
Hintlesham Hall	Ipswich	210
Hoar Cross Hall	Lichfield	230
Hob Green Hotel	Harrogate	194
Holbeck Ghyll Hotel	Ambleside	56
Holdsworth House	Halifax	188
Hollington House Hotel	Newbury	263
Holne Chase Hotel	Ashburton	68
Homewood Park	Bath	81
The Horn Of Plenty	Tavistock	330
Horsted Place Hotel	Uckfield	343
The Hoste Arms Hotel	Burnham Market	123
Hotel Du Vin & Bistro	Winchester	354
Hotel Du Vin & Bistro	Tunbridge Wells	341
Hotel Du Vin & Bistro	Bristol	112
Hotel On The Park	Cheltenham	137
Hotel Riviera	Sidmouth	310
Howard's House	Salisbury	299
Howfield Manor	Canterbury	130
Hunstrete House	Bath	82
Ilsington Country Hotel	Ilsington	209
Ivy House Hotel	Marlborough	251
The Izaak Walton Hotel	Ashbourne	67
Kenwick Park Hotel	Louth	233
Kettering Park Hotel	Kettering	214
Lainston House Hotel	Winchester	355
The Lake Isle	Uppingham	344
Lakeside Hotel On Lake Windermere	Windermere	357
Langar Hall	Nottingham	271
Langdale Chase	Windermere	358
Langdale Hotel	Ambleside	57
Langshott Manor	Gatwick	180
Langtry Manor	Bournemouth	104
Le Manoir aux Quat' Saisons	Oxford	276
The Lee Wood Hotel	Buxton	128
Lewtrenchard Manor	Lewdown	228
Linden Hall Hotel	Newcastle-Upon-Tyne	265
Linthwaite House Hotel	Windermere	359
Lords Of The Manor Hotel	Stow-on-the-Wold	318
Lovelady Shield Hotel	Alston	53
Lucknam Park	Bath	83
Lumley Castle Hotel	Durham	165
The Lygon Arms	Broadway	116
Lythe Hill Hotel	Haslemere	196
Madeley Court	Telford	331
Maison Talbooth	Dedham	160
Makeney Hall Hotel	Derby	161
Mallory Court	Leamington Spa	223
The Manor House Hotel	Moreton-In-Marsh	260
The Manor House Hotel	Castle Combe	131
The Marlborough Hotel	Ipswich	211
Marshall Meadow Hotel	Berwick-Upon-Tweed	93
The Master Builder's House	Beaulieu	90
Mere Court Hotel	Knutsford	219
Meudon Hotel	Falmouth	175
Michaels Nook	Grasmere	183
Mickleover Court	Derby	162
Middlethorpe Hall	York	373
Mill House Hotel	Kingham	216

The Mill House Hotel ... Birmingham ... 97
Miller Howe ... Windermere ... 360
The Millstream Hotel ... Chichester ... 144
The Moat House ... Acton Trussell ... 49
Monk Fryston Hall ... York ... 374
Monkey Island Hotel ... Bray-on-Thames ... 110
The Montagu Arms Hotel ... Beaulieu ... 91
Moonfleet Manor ... Weymouth ... 353
Moore Place Hotel ... Milton Keynes ... 259
Mount Royale Hotel ... York ... 375
The Mount Somerset Hotel ... Taunton ... 329
Nailcote Hall ... Coventry ... 153
Nanny Brow Hotel ... Ambleside ... 58
The Nare Hotel ... Veryan ... 345
Netherfield Place Hotel ... Battle ... 87
New Hall ... Birmingham ... 98
New Park Manor ... Brockenhurst ... 119
Newick Park ... Lewes ... 229
Noel Arms Hotel ... Chipping Campden 147
The Norfolk Royale Hotel ... Bournemouth ... 105
Northcote Manor Hotel ... Burrington ... 124
Nunsmere Hall ... Chester ... 142
Nutfield Priory ... Redhill ... 284
Nuthurst Grange ... Hockley Heath ... 203
Oakley Court ... Windsor ... 362
Oatlands Park Hotel ... Weybridge ... 352
Ockenden Manor ... Cuckfield ... 155
The Old Bell ... Malmesbury ... 245
The Old Ship Hotel ... Brighton ... 111
The Old Vicarage Hotel ... Wolverhampton ... 366
The Olde Barn Hotel ... Marston ... 253
The Osborne Hotel ... Torquay ... 338
Oulton Hall ... Leeds ... 226
The Painswick Hotel ... Painswick ... 279
The Palace Hotel ... Torquay ... 339
The Palace Hotel ... Buxton ... 129
Park Farm Hotel & Leisure ... Norwich ... 268
Parkhill Country House Hotel .. Lyndhurst ... 238
Passford House Hotel ... Lymington ... 236
The Pear Tree at Purton ... Swindon ... 326
Pendley Manor Hotel ... Tring ... 340
Pengethley Manor ... Ross-On-Wye ... 287
Penmere Manor ... Falmouth ... 176
Pennyhill Park Hotel ... Bagshot ... 73
Periton Park Hotel ... Middlecombe ... 256
Petersfield House Hotel ... Norwich ... 269
The Pheasant ... Helmsley ... 201
Phyllis Court Club ... Henley-On-Thames . 202
The Plough at Clanfield ... Clanfield ... 149
Plumber Manor ... Sturminster Newton . 325
Pontlands Park Country Hotel .. Chelmsford ... 134
PowderMills Hotel ... Battle ... 88
The Priest House On the River .. Derby ... 163
The Priory ... Wareham ... 348
The Priory Bay Hotel ... Seaview ... 302
The Priory Hotel ... Aylesbury ... 72
The Queensberry ... Bath ... 84
Quorn Country Hotel ... Loughborough ... 232
Rampsbeck Hotel ... Lake Ullswater ... 221
Ravenwood Hall ... Bury St Edmunds ... 126
Redworth Hall Hotel ... Newton Aycliffe ... 267
Rhinefield House Hotel ... Brockenhurst ... 120
Riber Hall ... Matlock ... 254
The Richmond Gate Hotel ... Richmond-Upon-Thames ... 285
Risley Hall Hotel ... Derby ... 164
Riverside House ... Ashford-In-The-Water ... 70
Rombalds Hotel ... Ilkley ... 208
Rookery Hall ... Nantwich ... 261
Rose-in-Vale Hotel ... St Agnes ... 291
The Rosevine Hotel ... St.Mawes ... 295
Rothay Manor ... Ambleside ... 59
Rowhill Grange ... Dartford ... 157
Rowton Castle ... Shrewsbury ... 309
Rowton Hall Hotel ... Chester ... 143
Royal Berkshire ... Ascot ... 65
The Royal Crescent Hotel ... Bath ... 85
Rudding Park House & Hotel .. Harrogate ... 195
Salford Hall Hotel ... Stratford-Upon-Avon .. 322
Sandringham Hotel ... Hampsetad Village 189
Seckford Hall ... Woodbridge ... 367
Sharrow Bay Hotel ... Lake Ullswater ... 222
Shrigley Hall Hotel ... Macclesfield ... 239
Simonstone Hall ... Hawes ... 198
Sir Christopher Wren's Hotel .. Windsor ... 363
Sketchley Grange Hotel ... Leicester ... 227
Soar Mill Cove Hotel ... Salcombe ... 297
Sopwell House Hotel ... St Albans ... 292
South Lodge Hotel ... Horsham ... 204
The Spa Hotel ... Tunbridge Wells ... 342
The Spread Eagle Hotel ... Thame ... 335
The Spread Eagle Hotel ... Midhurst ... 258
The Springs Hotel & Golf Club .. Wallingford ... 346
St Olaves Court Hotel ... Exeter ... 173
The Stanneylands Hotel ... Manchester ... 249
Stanwell House ... Lymington ... 237
Stapleford Park, An Outpost of The Carnegie Club ... Melton Mowbray ... 255
Stoke Park ... Heathrow ... 200
Ston Easton Park ... Bath ... 86
Stone Manor Hotel ... Kidderminster ... 215
Stonehouse Court ... Stonehouse ... 316
Storrs Hall ... Windermere ... 361
Studley Priory ... Oxford ... 277
Summer Lodge ... Evershot ... 169
Swallow Belstead Brook Hotel .. Ipswich ... 212
The Swallow Hotel ... Birmingham ... 99
Swallow Royal Hotel ... Bristol ... 113
Swallow Sprowston Manor Hotel .. Norwich ... 270
The Swan Diplomat ... Streatley-On-Thames . 324
The Swan Hotel ... Southwold ... 313
The Swan Hotel At Bibury ... Bibury ... 95
Swynford Paddocks Hotel ... Newmarket ... 266
Talland Bay Hotel ... Polperro ... 281
Taplow House Hotel ... Maidenhead ... 242
The Tides Reach Hotel ... Salcombe ... 298
Tillmouth Park ... Berwick-Upon-Tweed .. 94
Tufton Arms Hotel ... Appleby-In-Westmorland ... 63
Tylney Hall ... Basingstoke ... 76
The Vineyard At Stockcross ... Newbury ... 264
Washbourne Court Hotel ... Lower Slaughter ... 234
Watersmeet Hotel ... Woolacombe ... 369
Welcombe Hotel ... Stratford-Upon-Avon .. 323
The Well House ... St Keyne ... 294
Wentworth Hotel ... Aldeburgh ... 50
West Lodge Park ... Hadley Wood ... 187
Weston Manor ... Oxford ... 278
Whatley Manor ... Malmesbury ... 246
White Lodge Hotel ... Alfriston ... 52
Whitechapel Manor ... South Molton ... 312
Whitehall ... Stansted ... 315
Whitley Hall Hotel ... Sheffield ... 305
Willerby Manor Hotel ... Hull ... 207
The Wind In The Willows ... Glossop ... 181
Wood Hall ... Wetherby ... 351
Wood Norton Hall ... Evesham ... 171
Woodland Park Hotel ... Altrincham ... 54
Woodlands Manor ... Bedford ... 92
Woodlands Park Hotel ... Cobham ... 150
Woolacombe Bay Hotel ... Woolacombe ... 370
Woolley Grange ... Bradford-On-Avon . 107
The Wordsworth Hotel ... Grasmere ... 184
The Worsley Arms Hotel ... Hovingham ... 205
Wrea Head Country Hotel ... Scarborough ... 301
Wroxton House Hotel ... Banbury ... 75
Wyck Hill House ... Stow-On-The-Wold . 319

WALES

Allt-Yr-Ynys Hotel ... Abergavenny ... 379
Bodidris Hall ... Llandegla ... 397
Bodysgallen Hall ... Llandudno ... 398
Bontddu Hall ... Barmouth ... 385
Bron Eifion Hotel ... Criccieth ... 392
Coed-Y-Mwstwr Hotel ... Bridgend ... 388
Conrah Country House Hotel .. Aberystwyth ... 382
The Court Hotel & Restaurant Pembroke ... 402
The Cwrt Bleddyn Hotel ... Usk ... 406
Gliffaes Country House Hotel .. Crickhowell ... 393
Hotel Maes-Y-Neuadd ... Harlech ... 395
The Hotel Portmeirion ... Portmeirion Village . 403
The Lake Country House ... Llangammarch Wells 400
Lake Vyrnwy Hotel ... Lake Vyrnwy ... 396
Llangoed Hall ... Brecon ... 387
Llansantffraed Court Hotel ... Abergavenny ... 380
Llyndir Hall Hotel ... Wrexham ... 407
Miskin Manor ... Cardiff ... 389
Palé Hall ... Bala ... 384
Penally Abbey ... Tenby ... 405
Penmaenuchaf Hall ... Dolgellau ... 394
Porth Tocyn Hotel ... Abersoch ... 381
St. David's Park Hotel ... Chester ... 390
St Tudno Hotel ... Llandudno ... 399
Trearddur Bay Hotel ... Anglesey ... 383
Ty Newydd Country Hotel ... Aberdare ... 378
Tyddyn Llan Hotel ... Corwen ... 391
Warpool Court Hotel ... St David's ... 404
Ye Olde Bull's Head ... Beaumaris ... 386
Ynyshir Hall ... Machynlleth ... 401

SCOTLAND

Ardanaiseig ... Kilchrenan by Taynuilt . 450
Ardoe House Hotel ... Aberdeen ... 410
Arisaig House ... Beasdale By Arisaig . 419
Auchterarder House ... Auchterarder ... 415
Balcary Bay Hotel ... Auchencairn ... 414
Ballathie House Hotel ... Perth ... 457
The Bonham ... Edinburgh ... 427
Borthwick Castle ... Edinburgh ... 428
Bunchrew House Hotel ... Inverness ... 443
Cally Palace Hotel ... Gatehouse Of Fleet . 437
Carlton George Hotel ... Glasgow ... 438
Channings ... Edinburgh ... 429
Corsewall Lighthouse Hotel ... Stranraer ... 465
Coul House Hotel ... Strathpeffer ... 466
Craigellachie Hotel ... Craigellachie ... 423
Cringletie House Hotel ... Peebles ... 456
Cromlix House ... Kinbuck ... 452
Culloden House Hotel ... Inverness ... 444
Dalhousie Castle ... Edinburgh ... 430
Dalmunzie House ... Glenshee ... 440
Darroch Learg Hotel ... Ballater ... 417
Dryburgh Abbey Hotel ... St Boswells ... 463
Ednam House Hotel ... Kelso ... 448
Enmore Hotel ... Dunoon ... 425
Fernhill Hotel ... Portpatrick ... 461
Flodigarry Hotel ... Isle Of Skye ... 447
Forest Hills ... Aberfoyle ... 412
Gleddoch House ... Glasgow ... 439
Glenapp Castle ... Ballantrae ... 416
Glenspean Lodge Hotel ... Fort William ... 436
Greywalls ... Gullane ... 442
Houstoun House ... Uphall ... 471
The Howard ... Edinburgh ... 431
Huntingtower Hotel ... Perth ... 458
Inver Lodge Hotel ... Lochinver ... 453
Kildrummy Castle Hotel ... Kildrummy ... 451
Kinfauns Castle ... Perth ... 459
Kinloch House Hotel ... Blairgowrie ... 421
Kinnaird ... Dunkeld ... 424
Kirroughtree House ... Newton Stewart ... 454
Knipoch Hotel ... Oban ... 455
Letham Grange Resort ... Angus ... 413
Loch Torridon Hotel ... Torridon ... 468
Macdonald Crutherland Hotel East Kilbride ... 426
Mansfield House Hotel ... Tain ... 467
Mansion House Hotel ... Elgin ... 435
Marine Highland Hotel ... Troon ... 469
Muckrach Lodge Hotel ... Grantown-on-Spey .. 441
The Norton House Hotel ... Edinburgh ... 432
Piersland House Hotel ... Troon ... 470
Pine Trees Hotel ... Pitlochry ... 460
Pittodrie House ... Inverurie ... 446
Prestonfield House ... Edinburgh ... 433
Raemoir House Hotel ... Banchory ... 418
Roman Camp Hotel ... Callander ... 422
The Roxburghe Hotel ... Kelso ... 449
The Scotsman ... Edinburgh ... 434
Shieldhill ... Biggar ... 420
St. Andrews Golf Hotel ... St. Andrews ... 462
Stirling Highland Hotel ... Stirling ... 464
Swallow Kingsmills Hotel ... Inverness ... 445
Thainstone House Hotel ... Aberdeen ... 411

IRELAND

Adare Manor ... Adare ... 474
Aghadoe Heights Hotel ... Killarney ... 491
Ashford Castle ... Cong ... 478
Brooks Hotel ... Dublin ... 481
Connemara Coast Hotel ... Galway ... 487
Dromoland Castle ... Newmarket-On-Fergus . 496
The Fitzwilliam Hotel ... Dublin ... 482
Hayfield Manor Hotel ... Cork ... 480
The Hibernian ... Dublin ... 483
Humewood Castle ... Kiltegan ... 494
Hunter's Hotel ... Rathnew ... 498
Kelly's Resort Hotel ... Rosslare ... 499
Kildare Hotel ... Dublin ... 484
The Lodge & Spa at Inchydoney Island ... Clonakilty ... 477
Longueville House ... Mallow ... 495
Marlfield House ... Gorey ... 488
The McCausland Hotel ... Belfast ... 475
The Merrion Hotel ... Dublin ... 485
Muckross Park Hotel ... Killarney ... 492
Nuremore Hotel ... Carrickmacross ... 476
The Park Hotel Kenmare ... Kenmare ... 489
Parknasilla Hotel ... Parknasilla ... 497
Portmarnock Hotel ... Dublin ... 486
Randles Court Hotel ... Killarney ... 493
Renvyle House Hotel ... Connemara ... 479
The Sand House Hotel ... Rossnowlagh ... 500
Sheen Falls Lodge ... Kenmare ... 490

CHANNEL ISLANDS

The Atlantic Hotel ... Jersey ... 503
Château La Chaire ... Jersey ... 504
Hotel L'Horizon ... Jersey ... 505
Longueville Manor ... Jersey ... 506
St Pierre Park Hotel ... Guernsey ... 502

Johansens Recommended Hotels by county

ENGLAND

Bath/Avon: Please refer to the Somerset listing

Bedfordshire
The Bedford Arms .... Woburn 364
Flitwick Manor .... Woburn 365
Moore Place Hotel .... Milton Keynes 259
Woodlands Manor .... Bedford 92

Berkshire
Chauntry House Hotel .... Bray-on-Thames 109
Cliveden .... Maidenhead 240
Donnington Valley Hotel .... Newbury 262
Fredrick's Hotel & Restaurant .. Maidenhead 241
The French Horn .... Sonning-On-Thames 311
Hollington House Hotel .... Newbury 263
Monkey Island Hotel .... Bray-on-Thames 110
Oakley Court .... Windsor 362
Royal Berkshire .... Ascot 65
Sir Christopher Wren's Hotel .. Windsor 363
The Swan Diplomat .... Streatley-On-Thames 324
Taplow House Hotel .... Maidenhead 242
The Vineyard At Stockcross .... Newbury 264

Bristol
Hotel Du Vin & Bistro .... Bristol 112
Swallow Royal Hotel .... Bristol 113

Buckinghamshire
Danesfield House .... Marlow-On-Thames 252
Hartwell House .... Aylesbury 71
The Priory Hotel .... Aylesbury 72
Stoke Park .... Heathrow 200

Cambridgeshire
The Haycock .... Peterborough 280

Cheshire
The Alderley Edge Hotel .... Alderley Edge 51
The Bridge Hotel .... Prestbury 282
Broxton Hall Hotel .... Chester 138
Carden Park .... Chester 139
The Chester Grosvenor .... Chester 140
Crabwall Manor .... Chester 141
Mere Court Hotel .... Knutsford 219
Nunsmere Hall .... Chester 142
Rookery Hall .... Nantwich 261
Rowton Hall Hotel .... Chester 143
Shrigley Hall Hotel .... Macclesfield 239
The Stanneylands Hotel .... Manchester 249
Woodland Park Hotel .... Altrincham 54

Cleveland
Grinkle Park Hotel .... Easington 166

Cornwall
Budock Vean Hotel .... Falmouth 174
Fowey Hall Hote .... Fowey 178
The Garrack Hotel .... St. Ives 293
Meudon Hotel .... Falmouth 175
The Nare Hotel .... Veryan 345
Penmere Manor .... Falmouth 176
Rose-in-Vale Hotel .... St Agnes 291
The Rosevine Hotel .... St.Mawes 295
Talland Bay Hotel .... Polperro 281
The Well House .... St Keyne 294

County Durham
Headlam Hall .... Darlington 156
Lumley Castle Hotel .... Durham 165
Redworth Hall Hotel .... Newton Aycliffe 267

Cumbria
Appleby Manor Hotel .... Appleby-in-Westmorland 62
The Borrowdale Gates Hotel .... Keswick 213
Farlam Hall Hotel .... Brampton 108
Gilpin Lodge .... Windermere 356
Graythwaite Manor .... Grange-Over-Sands 182
Holbeck Ghyll Hotel .... Ambleside 56
Lakeside Hotel On Lake Windermere .... Windermere 357
Langdale Chase .... Windermere 358
Langdale Hotel .... Ambleside 57
Linthwaite House Hotel .... Windermere 359
Lovelady Shield Hotel .... Alston 53
Michaels Nook .... Grasmere 183
Miller Howe .... Windermere 360
Nanny Brow Hotel .... Ambleside 58
Rampsbeck Hotel .... Lake Ullswater 221
Rothay Manor .... Ambleside 59
Sharrow Bay Hotel .... Lake Ullswater 222
Storrs Hall .... Windermere 361
Tufton Arms Hotel .... Appleby-In-Westmorland 63
The Wordsworth Hotel .... Grasmere 184

Derbyshire
Callow Hall .... Ashbourne 66
The Cavendish Hotel .... Baslow 77
Fischer's .... Baslow 78
George Hotel .... Hathersage 197
Hassop Hall .... Bakewell 74
The Izaak Walton Hotel .... Ashbourne 67
The Lee Wood Hotel .... Buxton 128
Makeney Hall Hotel .... Derby 161
Mickleover Court .... Derby 162
The Palace Hotel .... Buxton 129
The Priest House On the River .. Derby 163
Riber Hall .... Matlock 254
Risley Hall Hotel .... Derby 164
Riverside House .... Ashford-In-The-Water 70
The Wind In The Willows .... Glossop 181

Devon
The Arundell Arms .... Lifton 231
Bel Alp House .... Dartmoor 158
Bolt Head Hotel .... Salcombe 296
Buckland-Tout-Saints .... Kingsbridge Estuary .. 218
Combe House at Gittisham .... Exeter 172
The Edgemoor .... Bovey Tracey 106
Gidleigh Park .... Chagford 133
Holne Chase Hotel .... Ashburton 68
The Horn Of Plenty .... Tavistock 330
Hotel Riviera .... Sidmouth 310
Ilsington Country Hotel .... Ilsington 209
Lewtrenchard Manor .... Lewdown 228
Northcote Manor Hotel .... Burrington 124
The Osborne Hotel .... Torquay 338
The Palace Hotel .... Torquay 339
Soar Mill Cove Hotel .... Salcombe 297
St Olaves Court Hotel .... Exeter 173
The Tides Reach Hotel .... Salcombe 298
Watersmeet Hotel .... Woolacombe 369
Woolacombe Bay Hotel .... Woolacombe 370

Dorset
Bridge House Hotel .... Beaminster 89
The Dormy .... Bournemouth 103
Langtry Manor .... Bournemouth 104
Moonfleet Manor .... Weymouth 353
The Norfolk Royale Hotel .... Bournemouth 105
Plumber Manor .... Sturminster Newton 325
The Priory .... Wareham 348
Summer Lodge .... Evershot 169

East Riding
Willerby Manor Hotel .... Hull 207

East Sussex
Ashdown Park Hotel .... Forest Row 177
Broomhill Lodge .... Rye 290
Buxted Park Hotel .... Buxted 127
Dale Hill .... Ticehurst 337
The Grand Hotel .... Eastbourne 167
Horsted Place Hotel .... Uckfield 343
Netherfield Place Hotel .... Battle 87
The Old Ship Hotel .... Brighton 111
PowderMills Hotel .... Battle 88
White Lodge Hotel .... Alfriston 52

Essex
Five Lakes Hotel Golf .... Colchester 151
Maison Talbooth .... Dedham 160
Pontlands Park Country Hotel .. Chelmsford 134
Whitehall .... Stansted 315

Gloucestershire
The Bear of Rodborough Hotel .. Cirencester 148
Calcot Manor .... Tetbury 332
Charingworth Manor .... Chipping Campden 146
The Cheltenham Park Hotel .... Cheltenham 135
The Close Hotel .... Tetbury 333
Corse Lawn House Hotel .... Tewkesbury 334
The Cotswold House .... Chipping Campden 145
The Grapevine Hotel .... Stow-On-The-Wold 317
The Greenway .... Cheltenham 136
Hotel On The Park .... Cheltenham 137
Lords Of The Manor Hotel .... Stow-on-the-Wold 318
The Manor House Hotel .... Moreton-In-Marsh 260
Noel Arms Hotel .... Chipping Campden 147
The Painswick Hotel .... Painswick 279
Stonehouse Court .... Stonehouse 316
The Swan Hotel At Bibury .... Bibury 95
Washbourne Court Hotel .... Lower Slaughter 234
Wyck Hill House .... Stow-On-The-Wold 319

Greater Manchester
Etrop Grange .... Manchester Airport 250

Hampshire
The Balmer Lawn .... Brockenhurst 117
Careys Manor Hotel .... Brockenhurst 118
Esseborne Manor .... Andover 60
Fifehead Manor .... Andover 61
Hotel Du Vin & Bistro .... Winchester 354
Lainston House Hotel .... Winchester 355
The Master Builder's House .... Beaulieu 90
The Montagu Arms Hotel .... Beaulieu 91
New Park Manor .... Brockenhurst 119
Parkhill Country House Hotel .. Lyndhurst 238
Passford House Hotel .... Lymington 236
Rhinefield House Hotel .... Brockenhurst 120
Stanwell House .... Lymington 237
Tylney Hall .... Basingstoke 76

Herefordshire
The Chase Hotel .... Ross-On-Wye 286
Pengethley Manor .... Ross-On-Wye 287

Hertfordshire
Down Hall Hotel .... Bishop's Stortford .. 100
Hanbury Manor .... Ware 347
Pendley Manor Hotel .... Tring 340
Sopwell House Hotel .... St Albans 292
West Lodge Park .... Hadley Wood 187

Isle of Wight
The George Hotel .... Yarmouth 371
The Priory Bay Hotel .... Seaview 302

Kent
Chilston Park .... Maidstone 243
Eastwell Manor .... Ashford 69
Hotel Du Vin & Bistro .... Tunbridge Wells 341
Howfield Manor .... Canterbury 130
Rowhill Grange .... Dartford 157
The Spa Hotel .... Tunbridge Wells 342

Lancashire
Astley Bank Hotel .... Blackburn 101
The Gibbon Bridge Hotel .... Preston 283

Leicestershire
Barnsdale Lodge .... Rutland Water 289
Quorn Country Hotel .... Loughborough 232
Sketchley Grange Hotel .... Leicester 227
Stapleford Park, An Outpost of The Carnegie Club .... Melton Mowbray .. 255

Lincolnshire
The George Of Stamford .... Stamford 314
Kenwick Park Hotel .... Louth 233
The Olde Barn Hotel .... Marston 253

London
The Ascott Mayfair .... Mayfair 14
Basil Street Hotel .... Knightsbridge 17
The Beaufort .... Knightsbridge 15
Beaufort House Apartments .... Knightsbridge 16
Blakes Hotel .... South Kensington .. 18
Brown's Hotel .... Londo 19
The Cadogan .... Knightsbridge 20
Cannizaro House .... Wimbledon Common 21
Chelsea Green Hotel .... Chelsea 22
Chequers of Kensington .... Kensington 23
Claridge's .... Mayfair 24
The Cliveden Town House .... Knightsbridge 25
The Colonnade Town House .... Little Venice 26
The Dorchester .... Mayfair 27
Draycott House Apartments .... Chelsea 28
Fountains .... Lancaster Gate 29
Harrington Hall .... Kensington 30
The Hempel .... Lancaster Gate 31
Hendon Hall .... Hendon 32
The Leonard .... Portman Square 33
The Lexham Apartments .... Kensington 34
London Bridge Hotel .... City 35
The Milestone Hotel .... Kensington 36
No 5 Maddox Street .... Mayfair 37
Number Eleven Cadogan Gardens .... Knightsbridge 38
Number Sixteen .... South Kensington .. 39
One Aldwych .... Covent Garden 40
Pembridge Court Hotel .... Kensington 41
The Royal Horseguards .... Whitehall 42
Sandringham Hotel .... London 189
Twenty Nevern Square .... Kensington 43
Westbury Hotel .... Mayfair 44

Swan Hellenic Minerva .... Cruise Ship 45

Norfolk
Congham Hall .... King's Lynn 217
The Hoste Arms Hotel .... Burnham Market .. 123
Park Farm Hotel & Leisure .... Norwich 268
Petersfield House Hotel .... Norwich 269
Swallow Sprowston Manor Hotel .. Norwich 270

North Devon
Whitechapel Manor .... South Molton 312

North Yorkshire
The Balmoral Hotel .... Harrogate 191
The Boar's Head Hotel .... Harrogate 192
Crab Manor .... Thirsk 336
Crathorne Hall Hotel .... Crathorne 154
The Devonshire Arms Hotel .... Bolton Abbey 102
The Grange Hotel .... York 372
Grants Hotel .... Harrogate 193
Hackness Grange .... Scarborough 300
Hazlewood Castle Hotel .... Hazlewood 199

Johansens Recommended Hotels by county continued

Hob Green Hotel ... Harrogate ... 194
Middlethorpe Hall ... York ... 373
Monk Fryston Hall ... York ... 374
Mount Royale Hotel ... York ... 375
The Pheasant ... Helmsley ... 201
Rudding Park House & Hotel ... Harrogate ... 195
The Worsley Arms Hotel ... Hovingham ... 205
Wrea Head Country Hotel ... Scarborough ... 301
Simonstone Hall ... Hawes ... 198

Northamptonshire
Fawsley Hall Hotel ... Daventry ... 159
Kettering Park Hotel ... Kettering ... 214

Northumberland
Linden Hall Hotel ... Newcastle-Upon-Tyne 265
Marshall Meadow Hotel ... Berwick-Upon-Tweed .. 93
Tillmouth Park ... Berwick-Upon-Tweed .. 94

Nottinghamshire
Langar Hall ... Nottingham ... 271

Oxfordshire
The Bay Tree Hotel ... Burford ... 122
Fallowfields ... Oxford ... 275
The Feathers Hotel ... Woodstock ... 368
Le Manoir aux Quat' Saisons ... Oxford ... 276
Mill House Hotel ... Kingham ... 216
Phyllis Court Club ... Henley-On-Thames 202
The Plough at Clanfield ... Clanfield ... 149
The Spread Eagle Hotel ... Thame ... 335
The Springs Hotel ... Wallingford ... 346
Studley Priory ... Oxford ... 277
Weston Manor ... Oxford ... 278
Wroxton House Hotel ... Banbury ... 75

Rutland
Hambleton Hall ... Oakham ... 272
The Lake Isle ... Uppingham ... 344

Shropshire
Albrighton Hall Hotel ... Shrewsbury ... 307
Dinham Hall ... Ludlow ... 235
Hawkstone Park Hotel ... Shrewsbury ... 308
Madeley Court ... Telford ... 331
The Old Vicarage Hotel ... Wolverhampton ... 366
Rowton Castle ... Shrewsbury ... 309

Somerset
The Bath Priory Hotel ... Bath ... 79
Bindon Country House Hotel ... Taunton ... 327
The Castle At Taunton ... Taunton ... 328
Charlton House ... Shepton Mallet ... 306
Combe Grove Manor ... Bath ... 80
Daneswood House Hotel ... Bristol South ... 114
Homewood Park ... Bath ... 81
Hunstrete House ... Bath ... 82
The Mount Somerset Hotel ... Taunton ... 329
Periton Park Hotel ... Middlecombe ... 256
The Queensberry ... Bath ... 84
The Royal Crescent Hotel ... Bath ... 85
Ston Easton Park ... Bath ... 86

South Yorkshire
Charnwood Hotel ... Sheffield ... 303
Hellaby Hall Hotel ... Sheffield ... 304
Whitley Hall Hotel ... Sheffield ... 305

Staffordshire
Hoar Cross Hall ... Lichfield ... 230
The Moat House ... Acton Trussell ... 49

Suffolk
The Angel Hotel ... Bury St Edmunds .. 125
Hintlesham Hall ... Ipswich ... 210
The Marlborough Hotel ... Ipswich ... 211
Ravenwood Hall ... Bury St Edmunds .. 126
Seckford Hall ... Woodbridge ... 367
Swallow Belstead Brook Hotel ... Ipswich ... 212
The Swan Hotel ... Southwold ... 313
Swynford Paddocks Hotel ... Newmarket ... 266
Wentworth Hotel ... Aldeburgh ... 50

Surrey
The Angel Posting House ... Guildford ... 186
The Carlton Mitre Hotel ... Hampton Court ... 190
Foxhills ... Ottershaw ... 274
Grayshott Hall ... Grayshott ... 185
Great Fosters ... Egham ... 168
Langshott Manor ... Gatwick ... 180
Lythe Hill Hotel ... Haslemere ... 196
Nutfield Priory ... Redhill ... 284
Oatlands Park Hotel ... Weybridge ... 352
Pennyhill Park Hotel ... Bagshot ... 73
The Richmond Gate Hotel ... Richmond-Upon-Thames 285
Woodlands Park Hotel ... Cobham ... 150

Sussex
Ghyll Manor Country Hotel ... Rusper ... 288
Newick Park ... Lewes ... 229

Warwickshire
Billesley Manor ... Stratford-Upon-Avon 320
Coombe Abbey ... Coventry ... 152
Ettington Park ... Stratford-Upon-Avon 321
The Glebe At Barford ... Warwick ... 350
Mallory Court ... Leamington Spa ... 223
Nailcote Hall ... Coventry ... 153
Nuthurst Grange ... Hockley Heath ... 203
Welcombe Hotel ... Stratford-Upon-Avon 323

West Midlands
The Burlington Hotel ... Birmingham ... 96
The Mill House Hotel ... Birmingham ... 97
New Hall ... Birmingham ... 98
The Swallow Hotel ... Birmingham ... 99

West Sussex
Alexander House ... Gatwick ... 179
Amberley Castle ... Amberley ... 55
The Angel Hotel ... Midhurst ... 257
Bailiffscourt ... Arundel ... 64
The Millstream Hotel ... Chichester ... 144
Ockenden Manor ... Cuckfield ... 155
South Lodge Hotel ... Horsham ... 204
The Spread Eagle Hotel ... Midhurst ... 258

West Yorkshire
42 The Calls ... Leeds ... 224
Bagden Hall Hote ... Huddersfield ... 206
Chevin Lodge Hotel ... Otley ... 273
Haley's Hotel and Restaurant ... Leeds ... 225
Holdsworth House ... Halifax ... 188
Oulton Hall ... Leeds ... 226
Rombalds Hotel ... Ilkley ... 208
Wood Hall ... Wetherby ... 351

Wiltshire
Beechfield House ... Lacock ... 220
Bishopstrow House ... Warminster ... 349
Crudwell Court Hotel ... Malmesbury ... 244
Howard's House ... Salisbury ... 299
Ivy House Hotel ... Marlborough ... 251
Lucknam Park ... Bath ... 83
The Manor House Hotel ... Castle Combe ... 131
The Old Bell ... Malmesbury ... 245
The Pear Tree at Purton ... Swindon ... 326
Whatley Manor ... Malmesbury ... 246
Woolley Grange ... Bradford-On-Avon 107

Worcestershire
Brockencote Hall ... Chaddesley Corbett ... 132
The Colwall Park Hotel ... Malvern ... 247
The Cottage In The Wood ... Malvern Wells ... 248
Dormy House ... Broadway ... 115
The Elms ... Abberley ... 48
The Evesham Hotel ... Evesham ... 170
Grafton Manor Hotel ... Bromsgrove ... 121
The Lygon Arms ... Broadway ... 116
Salford Hall Hotel ... Stratford-Upon-Avon 322
Stone Manor Hotel ... Kidderminster ... 215
Wood Norton Hall ... Evesham ... 171

WALES

Ceredigion
Conrah Country House Hotel ... Aberystwyth ... 382
Ynyshir Hall ... Machynlleth ... 401

Clwyd
Llyndir Hall Hotel ... Wrexham ... 407

Denbighshire
Bodidris Hall ... Llandegla ... 397
Tyddyn Llan Hotel ... Corwen ... 391

Flintshire
St. David's Park Hotel ... Chester ... 390

Gwynedd
Bodysgallen Hall ... Llandudno ... 398
Bontddu Hall ... Barmouth ... 385
Bron Eifion Country House Hotel ... Criccieth. 392
Hotel Maes-Y-Neuadd ... Harlech ... 395
The Hotel Portmeirion ... Portmeirion Village 403
Palé Hall ... Bala ... 384
Penmaenuchaf Hall ... Dolgellau ... 394
Porth Tocyn Hotel ... Abersoch ... 381
St Tudno Hotel ... Llandudno ... 399
Trearddur Bay Hotel ... Anglesey ... 383
Ye Olde Bull's Head ... Beaumaris ... 386

Herefordshire
Allt-Yr-Ynys Hotel ... Abergavenny ... 379

Mid-Glamorgan
Miskin Manor ... Cardiff ... 389
Ty Newydd Country Hotel ... Aberdare ... 378

Monmouthshire
The Cwrt Bleddyn Hotel ... Usk ... 406
Llansantffraed Court Hotel ... Abergavenny ... 380

Montgomeryshire
Lake Vyrnwy Hotel ... Lake Vyrnwy ... 396

Pembrokeshire
The Court Hotel ... Pembroke ... 402
Penally Abbey ... Tenby ... 405
Warpool Court Hotel ... St David's ... 404

Powys
Gliffaes Country House Hotel ... Crickhowell ... 393
The Lake Country House ... Llangammarch Wells 400
Llangoed Hall ... Brecon ... 387

Vale of Glamorgan
Coed-Y-Mwstwr Hotel ... Bridgend ... 388

SCOTLAND

Aberdeenshire
Ardoe House Hotel ... Aberdeen ... 410
Darroch Learg Hotel ... Ballater ... 417
Kildrummy Castle Hotel ... Kildrummy ... 451
Pittodrie House ... Inverurie ... 446
Raemoir House Hotel ... Banchory ... 418
Thainstone House Hotel ... Aberdeen ... 411

Angus
Letham Grange Resort ... Angus ... 413

Argyll
Ardanaiseig ... Kilchrenan by Taynuilt 450
Enmore Hotel ... Dunoon ... 425
Knipoch Hotel ... Oban ... 455

Ayrshire
Glenapp Castle ... Ballantrae ... 416
Piersland House Hotel ... Troon ... 470
Marine Highland Hotel ... Troon ... 469

Banffshire
Craigellachie Hotel ... Craigellachie ... 423

Borders
Dryburgh Abbey Hotel ... St Boswells ... 463

Dumfries & Galloway
Balcary Bay Hotel ... Auchencairn ... 414
Cally Palace Hotel ... Gatehouse Of Fleet 437
Corsewall Lighthouse Hotel ... Stranraer ... 465

East Lothian
Greywalls ... Gullane ... 442

Edinburgh
Dalhousie Castle ... Edinburgh ... 430
The Howard ... Edinburgh ... 431
Prestonfield House ... Edinburgh ... 433
The Scotsman ... Edinburgh ... 434

Fife
St. Andrews Golf Hotel ... St. Andrews ... 462

Glasgow
Carlton George Hotel ... Glasgow ... 438

Inverness-shire
Arisaig House ... Beasdale By Arisaig 419
Bunchrew House Hotel ... Inverness ... 443
Culloden House Hotel ... Inverness ... 444
Glenspean Lodge Hotel ... Fort William ... 436
Loch Torridon Hotel ... Torridon ... 468
Mansion House Hotel ... Elgin ... 435
Swallow Kingsmills Hotel ... Inverness ... 445

Isle of Skye
Flodigarry Hotel ... Isle Of Skye ... 447

Lanarkshire
Shieldhill ... Biggar ... 420

Mid Lothian
The Bonham ... Edinburgh ... 427
Borthwick Castle ... Edinburgh ... 428
Channings ... Edinburgh ... 429
The Norton House Hotel ... Edinburgh ... 432

Morayshire
Muckrach Lodge Hotel ... Grantown-on-Spey .. 441

Peebleshire
Cringletie House Hotel ... Peebles ... 456

Perthshire
Auchterarder House ... Auchterarder ... 415
Ballathie House Hotel ... Perth ... 457
Cromlix House ... Kinbuck ... 452
Dalmunzie House ... Glenshee ... 440
Huntingtower Hotel ... Perth ... 458
Kinfauns Castle ... Perth ... 459
Kinloch House Hotel ... Blairgowrie ... 421
Kinnaird ... Dunkeld ... 424
Roman Camp Hotel ... Callander ... 422

Renfrewshire
Gleddoch House ... Glasgow ... 439

Ross-shire
Coul House Hotel ... Strathpeffer ... 466
Mansfield House Hotel ... Tain ... 467

Roxburghshire
Ednam House Hotel ....Kelso 448
The Roxburghe Hotel ....Kelso 449

Stirlingshire
Forest Hills ....Aberfoyle 412
Stirling Highland Hotel ....Stirling 464

Strathclyde
Macdonald Crutherland Hotel ..East Kilbride 426

Sutherland
Inver Lodge Hotel ....Lochinver 453

Tayside
Pine Trees Hotel ....Pitlochry..............460

West Lothian
Houstoun House.......................Uphall 471

Wigtownshire
Fernhill Hotel.......................Portpatrick 461
Kirroughtree House ....Newton Stewart 454

IRELAND

Belfast
The McCausland Hotel ....Belfast 475

Co. Clare
Dromoland Castle Newmarket-On-Fergus496

Co Cork
Hayfield Manor Hotel ....Cork 480
Longueville House ....Mallow 495

Co Donegal
The Sand House Hotel.............Rossnowlagh..........500

Co Dublin
Brooks Hotel.......................Dublin 481
The Fitzwilliam Hotel ....Dublin 482
The Hibernian ....Dublin 483
The Merrion Hotel..................Dublin 485
Portmarnock Hotel..................Dublin 486

Co Galway
Renvyle House Hotel ....Connemara...........479

Co Kerry
Aghadoe Heights Hotel ....Killarney..............491
Muckross Park Hotel ....Killarney..............492
The Park Hotel Kenmare ....Kenmare 489
Parknasilla Hotel ....Parknasilla 497
Randles Court Hotel ....Killarney..............493
Sheen Falls Lodge..................Kenmare 490

Co Kildare
Kildare Hotel & Country Club ..Dublin 484

Co Limerick
Adare Manor ....Adare 474

Co Mayo
Ashford Castle ....Cong 478

Co Monaghan
Nuremore Hotel ....Carrickmacross.....476

Co Wexford
Kelly's Resort Hotel ....Rosslare 499
Marlfield House ....Gorey 488

Co Wicklow
Humewood Castle ....Kiltegan 494
Hunter's Hotel ....Rathnew 498

Galway
Connemara Coast Hotel ....Galway 487

West Cork ....
The Lodge & Spa
  at Inchydoney Island.............Clonakilty 477

CHANNEL ISLANDS

Guernsey
St Pierre Park Hotel ....St Peter Port..........502

Jersey
The Atlantic Hotel ....St Brelade 503
Château La Chaire ....Rozel 504
Hotel L'Horizon ....St Brelade 505
Longueville Manor ....St Saviour 506

Hotels with a heated indoor swimming pool

Swimming pools at these hotels are open all year round

LONDON

One Aldwych..................................40

ENGLAND

Albrighton Hall 307
Appleby Manor Hotel 62
Ashdown Park Hotel 177
The Balmer Lawn 117
The Bath Priory Hotel....................79
Billesley Manor 320
Bishopstrow House 349
Budock Vean Hotel 174
Carden Park 139
Careys Manor Hotel 118
Charingworth Manor...................146
Charlton House 306
The Cheltenham Park Hotel......135
Chevin Lodge Hotel 273
Cliveden 240
Combe Grove Manor 80
Crabwall Manor 141
Dale Hill 337
The Devonshire Arms Hotel......102
The Dormy..............................103
Down Hall Hotel 100
Eastwell Manor 69
Ettington Park 321
The Evesham Hotel...................170
Five Lakes Hotel 151
Fowey Hall Hotel 178
Foxhills 274
The Garrack Hotel 293
The Glebe At Barford 350
The Grand Hotel 167
Grayshott Hall 185
Hackness Grange 300
Hanbury Manor 347
Hartwell House 71
Headlam Hall............................156
Hellaby Hall Hotel.....................304
Hoar Cross Hall 230
Hollington House Hotel...........263
Horsted Place Hotel 343
Ilsington Country Hotel 209
Kenwick Park Hotel 233
Kettering Park Hotel 214
Lakeside Hotel On
  Lake Windermere 357
Langdale Hotel 57
Linden Hall Hotel 265
Lucknam Park 83
The Lygon Arms........................116
The Manor House Hotel 260
Mickleover Court 162
Middlethorpe Hall 373
The Mill House Hotel 97
Moonfleet Manor......................353
Nailcote Hall 153
The Nare Hotel 345
The Norfolk Royale Hotel..........105
Nutfield Priory 284
Oakley Court 362
The Olde Barn Hotel..................253
The Osborne Hotel....................338
Oulton Hall 226
The Palace Hotel 339
The Palace Hotel 129
Park Farm Hotel & Leisure........268
Passford House Hotel................236
Penmere Manor 176
The Pheasant 201

Pontlands Park Country Hotel ...134
Redworth Hall Hotel..................267
Rhinefield House Hotel.............120
The Richmond Gate Hotel 285
The Rosevine Hotel 295
Rowhill Grange 157
Rowton Hall Hotel....................143
Royal Berkshire..........................65
Seckford Hall 367
Shrigley Hall Hotel...................239
Sketchley Grange Hotel 227
Soar Mill Cove Hotel................297
Sopwell House Hotel.................292
The Spa Hotel 342
The Spread Eagle Hotel.............258
Stapleford Park, An Outpost
  of The Carnegie Club 255
Swallow Belstead Brook Hotel ...212
The Swallow Hotel......................99
Swallow Royal Hotel 113
Swallow Sprowston Manor Hotel .270
The Swan Diplomat 324
The Tides Reach Hotel 298
Tylney Hall 76
The Vineyard At Stockcross 264
Watersmeet Hotel 369
Willerby Manor Hotel 207
Wood Hall 351
Woolacombe Bay Hotel 370
The Wordsworth Hotel 184

WALES

Allt-Yr-Ynys Hotel 379
Bodysgallen Hall 398
Conrah Country House Hotel 382
The Court Hotel & Restaurant ..402
The Cwrt Bleddyn Hotel...........406
Llyndir Hall Hotel 407
Miskin Manor 389
Penally Abbey..........................405
St. David's Park Hotel 390
St Tudno Hotel..........................399
Trearddur Bay Hotel.................383
Warpool Court Hotel 404

SCOTLAND

Cally Palace Hotel.....................437
Houstoun House 471
Kinloch House Hotel 421
Macdonald Crutherland Hotel...426
Mansion House Hotel................435
Marine Highland Hotel 469
Stirling Highland Hotel 464
Swallow Kingsmills Hotel.........445
Thainstone House Hotel 411

IRELAND

Adare Manor 474
Aghadoe Heights Hotel.............491
Connemara Coast Hotel............487
Hayfield Manor Hotel 480
Kelly's Resort Hotel 499
Kildare Hotel & Country Club ..484
The Lodge & Spa
  at Inchydoney Island 477
The Merrion Hotel....................485
Nuremore Hotel........................476
Parknasilla Hotel 497
Sheen Falls Lodge 490

CHANNEL ISLANDS

The Atlantic Hotel....................503
Hotel L'Horizon 505
St Pierre Park Hotel..................502

Hotels with golf

Hotels with golf on site

ENGLAND

Ashdown Park Hotel 177
Bagden Hall Hotel 206
Budock VeanHotel 174
Carden Park 139
Dale Hill 337
Donnington Valley Hotel...........262
Five Lakes Hotel 151
Foxhills 274
Grayshott Hall 185
Hanbury Manor 347
Hawkstone Park Hotel 308
Hintlesham Hall 210
Kenwick Park Hotel 233
Linden Hall Hote 265
The Manor House Hotel 131
Nailcote Hall 153
New Hall..............................98
Oakley Court 362
Oulton Hall 226
The Palace Hotel 339
Rudding Park House & Hotel 195
Seckford Hall 367
Shrigley Hall Hotel...................239
The Springs Hotel 346
Stoke Park 200
Ston Easton Park 86
Tylney Hall 76
Welcombe Hotel 323

SCOTLAND

Ballathie House Hotel 457
Cally Palace Hotel 437
Dalmunzie House......................440
Gleddoch House 439
Letham Grange Resort 413
The Roxburghe Hotel...............449

IRELAND

Adare Manor 474
Ashford Castle 478
Dromoland Castle......................496
Kildare Hotel & Country Club ..484
Nuremore Hotel........................476
Parknasilla Hotel 497
Renvyle House Hotel 479

CHANNEL ISLANDS

St Pierre Park Hotel..................502

Hotels with shooting

Shooting on site, to which guests have access, can be arranged

ENGLAND

Bishopstrow House 349
The Boar's Head Hotel..............192
Carden Park 139
Chilston Park 243
Cliveden 240
Crathorne Hall Hotel 154
The Devonshire Arms Hotel......102
Ettington Park 321
Hambleton Hall 272
Hartwell House 71
Hazlewood Castle Hotel 199

Hotels with shooting continued

Headlam Hall 156
Hellaby Hall Hotel 304
Hunstrete House 82
Langar Hall 271
Linden Hall Hotel 265
Mere Court Hotel 219
Mill House Hotel 216
The Moat House 49
Nailcote Hall 153
Nunsmere Hall 142
Parkhill Country House Hotel ...238
Pengethley Manor 287
The Priest House On the River..163
Redworth Hall Hotel 267
Rookery Hall 261
Rudding Park House & Hotel ...195
Shrigley Hall Hotel..................239
Simonstone Hall 198
Ston Easton Park 86
Tillmouth Park 94
Tylney Hall 76
Welcombe Hotel 323
Wood Hall 351
Wood Norton Hall 171

WALES

Allt-Yr-Ynys Hotel 379
Lake Vyrnwy Hotel....................396
Llangoed Hall 387
Llansantffraed Court Hotel 380
Palé Hall 384

SCOTLAND

Cromlix House............................452
Dalmunzie House........................440
Gleddoch House 439
Kinnaird....................................424
Pittodrie House 446
The Roxburghe Hotel................449

IRELAND

Adare Manor 474
Humewood Castle 494
Longueville House 495
Sheen Falls Lodge 490

Hotels with fishing

Guests may obtain rights to fishing within the hotel grounds

ENGLAND

42 The Calls 224
The Arundell Arms 231
Beechfield House 220
Billesley Manor 320
Bishopstrow House 349
The Boar's Head Hotel 192
Callow Hall..................................66
Chevin Lodge Hotel 273
Chilston Park............................243
Coombe Abbey 152
Crathorne Hall Hotel 154
The Devonshire Arms Hotel......102
Ettington Park 321
The Gibbon Bridge Hotel 283
Hackness Grange 300

Hambleton Hall........................272
Hartwell House 71
Headlam Hall..........................156
Holne Chase Hotel......................68
Hunstrete House 82
Lakeside Hotel On Lake
    Windermere 357
Langar Hall 271
Langdale Chase..........................358
Langdale Hotel & Country Club .57
Linthwaite House Hotel 359
Lords Of The Manor Hotel 318
Lovelady Shield Hotel 53
Madeley Court 331
The Manor House Hotel 131
Mill House Hotel 216
Nanny Brow Hotel 58
New Hall....................................98
Nunsmere Hall........................142
Parkhill Country House Hotel ...238
Pengethley Manor 287
Pennyhill Park Hotel..................73
PowderMills Hotel 88
The Priest House On the River..163
The Priory 348
Quorn Country Hotel................232
Rampsbeck Hotel......................221
Rookery Hall............................261
Rowton Castle 309
Rudding Park House & Hotel 195
Sharrow Bay Hotel 222
Shrigley Hall Hotel Golf &
    Country Club 239
Simonstone Hall 198
Stapleford Park, An Outpost
    of The Carnegie Club............255
Ston Easton Park 86
Storrs Hall................................361
The Swan Diplomat 324
The Swan Hotel At Bibury 95
Welcombe Hotel 323
Whatley Manor 246
Wood Hall 351
Wood Norton Hall 171

WALES

Allt-Yr-Ynys Hotel 379
Bodidris Hall............................397
Gliffaes Country House Hotel....393
The Lake Country House 400
Lake Vyrnwy Hotel....................396
Llangoed Hall 387

SCOTLAND

Ballathie House Hotel 457
Cromlix House............................452
Dalmunzie House........................440
Dryburgh Abbey Hotel 463
Inver Lodge Hotel......................453
Kinloch House Hotel................421
Kinnaird....................................424
The Roxburghe Hotel................449

IRELAND

Adare Manor 474
Ashford Castle 478
Dromoland Castle......................496
Humewood Castle 494
Kildare Hotel & Country Club ..484
Longueville House 495
Nuremore Hotel........................476
Renvyle House Hotel 479
Sheen Falls Lodge 490

Hotels with health/fitness facilities

At the following hotels there are health/fitness facilities available

LONDON

The Ascott Mayfair 14
Brown's Hotel 19
Chequers of Kensington 23
Claridge's 24
Harrington Hall 30
The Hempel................................31
The Leonard 33
London Bridge Hotel 35
The Milestone Hotel 36
Number Eleven
    Cadogan Gardens 38
The Royal Horseguards................42
Swan Hellenic Minerva..............45

ENGLAND

Albrighton Hall Hotel................307
Alexander House 179
Appleby Manor Hotel 62
Ashdown Park Hotel 177
The Balmer Lawn 117
Billesley Manor 320
Bishopstrow House 349
Broomhill Lodge 290
Budock Vean Hotel 174
The Burlington Hotel..................96
Buxted Park Hotel 127
Carden Park 139
Careys Manor Hotel 118
Charingworth Manor..................146
The Cheltenham Park Hotel......135
The Chester Grosvenor..............140
Chevin Lodge Hotel 273
Cliveden 240
The Colonnade Town House 26
Combe Grove Manor 80
Dale Hill 337
The Devonshire Arms Hotel......102
The Dormy..................................103
Dormy House 115
Down Hall Hotel 100
Eastwell Manor 69
Ettington Park 321
Five Lakes Hotel 151
Foxhills 274
The Gibbon Bridge Hotel 283
The Glebe At Barford 350
The Grand Hotel 167
Grayshott Hall 185
Hanbury Manor 347
Hartwell House 71
Hellaby Hall Hotel 304
Hintlesham Hall 210
Hoar Cross Hall 230
Holbeck Ghyll Hotel 56
Ilsington Country Hotel 209
Kenwick Park Hotel 233
Kettering Park Hotel 214
Langdale Hotel & Country Club .57
Linden Hall Hotel 265
Lucknam Park 83
The Lygon Arms........................116
Mickleover Court 162
Monkey Island Hotel................110
Mount Royale Hotel 375
Nailcote Hall 153
Nutfield Priory 284
Oatlands Park Hotel 352
The Olde Barn Hotel................253
The Osborne Hotel....................338
Oulton Hall 226
The Palace Hotel......................339

The Palace Hotel 129
Park Farm Hotel & Leisure........268
Pendley Manor Hotel 340
Penmere Manor 176
Pennyhill Park Hotel..................73
Pontlands Park Country Hotel ...134
Redworth Hall Hotel 267
Rhinefield House Hotel 120
The Richmond Gate Hotel 285
Rowhill Grange 157
Rowton Hall Hotel 143
Royal Berkshire..........................65
Seckford Hall 367
Shrigley Hall Hotel..................239
Sketchley Grange Hotel 227
Sopwell House Hotel 292
South Lodge Hotel 204
The Spa Hotel 342
The Spread Eagle Hotel............258
Stapleford Park, An Outpost
    of The Carnegie Club............255
Swallow Belstead Brook Hotel ...212
The Swallow Hotel......................99
Swallow Sprowston Manor Hotel .270
The Swan Diplomat 324
The Tides Reach Hotel 298
Tylney Hall................................76
The Vineyard At Stockcross 264
Welcombe Hotel 323
Willerby Manor Hotel 207
Wood Hall 351
Wood Norton Hall 171
Woolacombe Bay Hotel 370
The Wordsworth Hotel 184

WALES

Bodysgallen Hall........................398
The Court Hotel & Restaurant..402
The Cwrt Bleddyn Hotel............406
Llyndir Hall Hotel 407
Miskin Manor 389
St. David's Park Hotel 390

SCOTLAND

Ardoe House Hotel....................410
Cally Palace Hotel 437
Culloden House Hotel................444
Forest Hills................................412
Houstoun House 471
Kinloch House Hotel..................421
Macdonald Crutherland Hotel...426
Mansion House Hotel................435
Marine Highland Hotel..............469
The Scotsman 434
Swallow Kingsmills Hotel..........445

IRELAND

Adare Manor 474
Aghadoe Heights Hotel..............491
Ashford Castle 478
Connemara Coast Hotel............487
Hayfield Manor Hotel 480
Kelly's Resort Hotel..................499
Kildare Hotel & Country Club ..484
The Lodge & Spa
    at Inchydoney Island 477
The Merrion Hotel 485
Nuremore Hotel........................476
Parknasilla Hotel 497
Sheen Falls Lodge 490

CHANNEL ISLANDS

The Atlantic Hotel....................503
Hotel L'Horizon 505
St Pierre Park Hotel..................502

Hotels with childcare facilities

Comprehensive childcare facilities are available, namely crèche, babysitting & organised activities for children.

LONDON

The Ascott Mayfair 14
Claridge's 24
Hendon Hall 32
The Leonard 33
The Royal Horseguards...................42
Twenty Nevern Square.....................43

ENGLAND

Albrighton Hall Hotel...................307
Alexander House 179
Appleby Manor Hotel 62
Ashdown Park Hotel 177
The Balmer Lawn 117
Billesley Manor..........................320
Bishopstrow House 349
Broomhill Lodge 290
Budock Vean Hotel 174
The Burlington Hotel.....................96
Buxted Park Hotel 127
Carden Park 139
Careys Manor Hotel 118
Charingworth Manor.......................146
The Cheltenham Park Hotel......135
The Chester Grosvenor 140
Chevin Lodge Hotel 273
Cliveden 240
The Colonnade Town House 26
Combe Grove Manor 80
Dale Hill 337
The Devonshire Arms Hotel......102
The Dormy................................103
Dormy House 115
Down Hall Hotel 100
Eastwell Manor 69
Ettington Park 321
Five Lakes Hotel 151
Foxhills 274
The Gibbon Bridge Hotel 283
The Glebe At Barford 350
The Grand Hotel 167
Grayshott Hall...........................185
Hanbury Manor 347
Hartwell House 71
Hellaby Hall Hotel 304
Hintlesham Hall 210
Hoar Cross Hall 230
Holbeck Ghyll Hotel......................56
Ilsington Country Hotel 209
Kenwick Park Hotel 233
Kettering Park Hotel 214
Langdale Hotel & Country Club .57
Linden Hall Hotel 265
Luckman Park.............................83
The Lygon Arms..........................116
Mickleover Court 162
Monkey Island Hotel.....................110
Mount Royale Hotel 375
Nailcote Hall............................153
Nutfield Priory 284
Oatlands Park Hotel 352
The Olde Barn Hotel......................253
The Osborne Hotel........................338
Oulton Hall 226
The Palace Hotel.........................339
The Palace Hotel.........................129
Park Farm Hotel & Leisure......268
Pendley Manor Hotel 340
Penmere Manor 176
Pennyhill Park Hotel.....................73
Pontlands Park Country Hotel...134

Redworth Hall Hotel 267
Rhinefield House Hotel.............120
The Richmond Gate Hotel 285
Rowhill Grange 157
Rowton Hall Hotel 143
Royal Berkshire 65
Seckford Hall............................367
Shrigley Hall Hotel......................239
Sketchley Grange Hotel 227
Sopwell House Hotel 292
South Lodge Hotel 204
The Spa Hotel 342
The Spread Eagle Hotel.............258
Stapleford Park, An Outpost
   of The Carnegie Club 255
Swallow Belstead Brook Hotel ...212
The Swallow Hotel 99
Swallow Sprowston Manor Hotel .270
The Swan Diplomat 324
The Tides Reach Hotel 298
Tylney Hall 76
The Vineyard At Stockcross 264
Welcombe Hotel 323
Willerby Manor Hotel 207
Wood Hall 351
Wood Norton Hall 171
Woolacombe Bay Hotel 370
The Wordsworth Hotel 184

WALES

Bodysgallen Hall 398
The Court Hotel & Restaurant ..402
The Cwrt Bleddyn Hotel...........406
Llyndir Hall Hotel 407
Miskin Manor 389
St. David's Park Hotel 390

SCOTLAND

Ardoe House Hotelt 410
Cally Palace Hotel......................437
Culloden House Hotel...............444
Forest Hills 412
Houstoun House 471
Kinloch House Hotel.....................421
Macdonald Crutherland Hotel...426
Mansion House Hotel.....................435
Marine Highland Hotel 469
The Scotsman............................434
Swallow Kingsmills Hotel...........445
Adare Manor 474
Aghadoe Heights Hotel...............491
Ashford Castle 478
Connemara Coast Hotel............487
Hayfield Manor Hotel 480
Kelly's Resort Hotel 499
Kildare Hotel & Country Club ..484
The Lodge & Spa at Inchydoney
Island..................................477
The Merrion Hotel 485
Nuremore Hotel & Country Club....476
Parknasilla Hotel 497
Sheen Falls Lodge 490
The Atlantic Hotel..................503
Hotel L'Horizon 505
St Pierre Park Hotel...................502

Hotels with conference facilities

These hotels can accommodate theatre-style conferences for 250 delegates or more.

LONDON

The Dorchester 23
Harrington Hall 26
Park Consul Hotel 34

ENGLAND

Albrighton Hall Hotel...............287
Belton Woods 165
The Burlington Hotel...................82
Carden Park 119
The Chase Hotel 270
The Dormy...............................88
Down Hall Country House Hotel 86
Five Lakes Hotel 130
The Grand Hotel 148
The Haycock 263
Linden Hall Hotel 246
Mollington Banastre...................122
Oulton Hall 206
The Palace Hotel 317
The Palace Hotel 110
Phyllis Court Club 184
Redworth Hall Hotel 249
Rudding Park House & Hotel 177
Shrigley Hall Hotel.....................219
Slaley Hall Hotel 247
Sopwell House Hotel 276
The Spa Hotel 320
Swallow Royal Hotel 96
Willerby Manor Hotel 190
Woodlands Park Hotel 129
Woolacombe Bay Hotel 349

WALES

Bryn Howel Hotel & Restaurant..382
St. David's Park Hotel 370
St. David's Spa 369

SCOTLAND

Airth Castle Hotel.....................415
Ardoe House Hotel......................392
Houstoun House 451
The Norton House Hotel 411
Prestonfield House 412
Thainstone House Hotel 393

IRELAND

Adare Manor 454
Connemara Coast Hotel...............468
Culloden Hotel 456
Dromoland Castle 479
Dunloe Castle 473
Galgorm Manor 455
Nuremore Hotel 458
Portmarnock Hotel 467
Slieve Donard Hotel...................478

Pride of Britain members

Amberley Castle 55
Bindon Hotel 327
Calcot Manor...........................332
Combe House at Gittisham........172
Congham Hall 217
Cromlix House 452
Eastwell Manor 69
The Elms 48
Esseborne Manor 60
The French Horn 311
Grafton Manor Hotel 121
The Greenway 136
Hazlewood Castle Hotel 199
Hotel Maes-Y-Neuadd...................395
The Lake Country House 400
Lewtrenchard Manor 228
Maison Talbooth 160
Michaels Nook..........................183
Netherfield Place Hotel.............87
Nunsmere Hall 142
Ockenden Manor 155
The Old Vicarage Hotel 366

Plumber Manor 325
Prestonfield House 433
Tyddyn Llan Hotel 391
The Well House 294
Whitechapel Manor 312

Relais & Châteaux members

Arisaig House...........................419
Ashford Castle 478
Dromoland Castle 496
Farlam Hall Hotel 108
Gidleigh Park 133
Hambleton Hall 272
Hartwell House 71
Kildare Hotel & Country Club ..484
Kinnaird 424
Le Manoir aux Quat' Saisons 276
Longueville Manor 506
Mallory Court 223
Marlfield House 488
Middlethorpe Hall 373
The Park Hotel Kenmare 489
Sheen Falls Lodge 490
Ston Easton Park 86
Summer Lodge 169
Washbourne Court Hotel 234

Small Luxury Hotels of the World members

Adare Manor 474
Amberley Castle 55
The Angel Posting House 186
Ashdown Park Hotel..................177
The Atlantic Hotel 503
Auchterarder House 415
The Bath Priory Hotel and
Restaurant..............................79
Bishopstrow House 349
The Chester Grosvenor..............140
Danesfield House 252
The Devonshire Arms Hotel...102
Hayfield Manor Hotel 480
The Hibernian 483
Hintlesham Hall 210
Holbeck Ghyll Hotel....................56
Homewood Park 81
Kinloch House Hotel....................421
Langshott Manor 180
Llangoed Hall 387
Loch Torridon Hotel 468
Lords Of The Manor Hotel 318
The McCausland Hotel.................475
New Hall 98
The Park Hotel Kenmare 489
Tylney Hall............................76
The Vineyard at Stockcross 264
Welcombe Hotel 323

Johansens Preferred Partners

Barrels & Bottles 11
Classic Malts..........................408
Dorlux.................................46
Ercol Ltd ....IBC
Hildon Ltd 7, 9, 530
Honda (UK) 472
Marsh UK Ltd...........................522
Moët Hennessy.........................IFC
Pacific Direct 376

Hildon Ltd., Broughton, Hampshire SO20 8DG, ☎ 01794 - 301 747

ORDER FORM

Call our 24hr credit card hotline FREEPHONE 0800 269 397.

Simply indicate which title(s) you require by putting the quantity in the boxes provided. Choose your preferred method of payment and mail to Johansens, FREEPOST (CB 264), 43 Millharbour, London E14 9BR, England (no stamp needed). Your FREE gifts will automatically be dispatched with your order. Fax orders welcome on 0171 537 3594

CHOOSE FROM 7 SPECIAL GUIDE COLLECTIONS – SAVE UP TO £56

TITLE	Normal Price	PRICE	SAVE	QTY	TOTAL
OFFER ONE					
3 Johansens Guides A+B+C	£42.85	£36.00	£6.85		
OFFER TWO					
4 Johansens Guides A+B+C+G	£58.80	£46.00	£12.80		
OFFER THREE					
5 Johansens Guides A+B+C+G+K PLUS Southern Africa Guide **FREE**	£71.75	£56.00	£15.75		
OFFER FOUR - The Executive Collection					
Business Meeting Venues Guide & CD-ROM M+R	£40.00	£30.00	£10.00		
OFFER FIVE - The Holiday Pack					
3 Johansens Guides D+E+F	£18.93	£9.99	£8.94		
OFFER SIX - The Digital Collection					
3 Johansens CD-ROMs N+O+P PLUS Southern Africa CD-ROM Q **FREE**	£69.85	£59.85	£10.00		
OFFER SEVEN - The Chairman's Collection					
Business Meeting Venues Guide & CD-ROMs M+R **PLUS** 5 Johansens Boxed Guides A+B+C+G+K, **PLUS** 3 CD-ROMs N+O+P **PLUS** Southern Africa Guide/CD ROM Q **FREE**, **PLUS** Mystery Gift **FREE**	£200.53	£149.00	£56.53		
Privilege Card PLUS The Millennium Guide		**FREE**			
1 Presentation box for offers 1, 2 and 3		£5.00	£20.00		
			TOTAL 1		

JOHANSENS PRINTED GUIDES 2000				
CODE	TITLE	PRICE	QTY	TOTAL
A	Recommended Hotels – Great Britain & Ireland 2000	£19.95		
B	Recommended Country Houses & Small Hotels – Great Britain & Ireland 2000	£11.95		
C	Recommended Traditional Inns, Hotels & Restaurants – Great Britain 2000	£10.95		
NEW D	Recommended Holiday Cottages – Great Britain & Ireland 2000	£4.99		
E	Historic Houses, Castles & Gardens 2000	£4.99		
F	Museums & Galleries 2000	£8.95		
G	Recommended Hotels – Europe & The Mediterranean 2000	£15.95		
NEW H	Recommended Hotels – Europe & The Mediterranean 2000 (French Language)	£15.95		
NEW J	Recommended Hotels – Europe & The Mediterranean 2000 (German Language)	£15.95		
K	Recommended Hotels & Inns – North America, Bermuda & The Caribbean 2000	£12.95		
NEW L	Recommended Hotels & Game Lodges – Southern Africa, Mauritius & The Seychelles 2000	£9.95		
M	Recommended Business Meeting Venues 2000	£20.00		

JOHANSENS CD ROMs DIGITAL COLLECTION 2000				
N	The Guide 2000 – Great Britain & Ireland	£29.95		
O	The Guide 2000 – Europe & The Mediterranean (English, French, German Language)	£22.95		
P	The Guide 2000 – North America, Bermuda & The Caribbean	£16.95		
NEW Q	The Guide 2000 – Southern Africa, Mauritius & The Seychelles	£16.95		
R	Business Meeting Venues 2000	£20.00		
S	Privilege Card 2000 (Free with your order. Additional Cards £20 each)	£20.00		

Postage & Packing (UK) £4.50 or £2.50 for single order and CD-ROMs
Outside UK add £5 or £3 for single orders and CD-ROMs

TOTAL 2

GRAND TOTAL 1+2+P&P

Name (Mr/Mrs/Miss)

Address

Postcode

Card No.

Exp Date

Signature

I have chosen my Johansens Guides/CD-ROMs and

☐ I enclose a cheque for £ _____ payable to Johansens

☐ I enclose my order on company letterheading, please invoice (UK only)

☐ Please debit my credit/charge card account (please tick).

☐ MasterCard ☐ Diners ☐ Amex

☐ Visa ☐ Switch (Issue Number)

A14

GUEST SURVEY REPORT

Your own Johansens 'inspection' gives reliability to our guides and assists in the selection of Award Nominations

Name of Hotel: _____

Location of Hotel: _____

Page No: _____

Date of visit: _____

Name of guest _____

Address of guest: _____

_____ Postcode _____

Please tick one box in each category below:	Excellent	Good	Disappointing	Poor
Bedrooms				
Public Rooms				
Restaurant/Cuisine				
Service				
Welcome/Friendliness				
Value For Money				

Occasionally we may allow other reputable organisations to write with offers which may be of interest.
If you prefer not to hear from them, tick this box ☐

To: Johansens, FREEPOST (CB264), 43 Millharbour, London E14 9BR

ORDER FORM

Call our 24hr credit card hotline FREEPHONE 0800 269 397.

Simply indicate which title(s) you require by putting the quantity in the boxes provided. Choose your preferred method of payment and mail to Johansens, FREEPOST (CB 264), 43 Millharbour, London E14 9BR, England (no stamp needed). Your FREE gifts will automatically be dispatched with your order. Fax orders welcome on 0171 537 3594

CHOOSE FROM 7 SPECIAL GUIDE COLLECTIONS – SAVE UP TO £56

TITLE	Normal Price	PRICE	SAVE	QTY	TOTAL
OFFER ONE					
3 Johansens Guides A+B+C	£42.85	£36.00	£6.85		
OFFER TWO					
4 Johansens Guides A+B+C+G	£58.80	£46.00	£12.80		
OFFER THREE					
5 Johansens Guides A+B+C+G+K PLUS Southern Africa Guide **FREE**	£71.75	£56.00	£15.75		
OFFER FOUR - The Executive Collection					
Business Meeting Venues Guide & CD-ROM M+R	£40.00	£30.00	£10.00		
OFFER FIVE - The Holiday Pack					
3 Johansens Guides D+E+F	£18.93	£9.99	£8.94		
OFFER SIX - The Digital Collection					
3 Johansens CD-ROMs N+O+P PLUS Southern Africa CD-ROM Q **FREE**	£69.85	£59.85	£10.00		
OFFER SEVEN - The Chairman's Collection					
Business Meeting Venues Guide & CD-ROMs M+R PLUS 5 Johansens Boxed Guides A+B+C+G+K, PLUS 3 CD-ROMs N+O+P PLUS Southern Africa Guide/CD ROM Q **FREE**, PLUS Mystery Gift **FREE**	£200.53	£149.00	£56.53		
Privilege Card PLUS The Millennium Guide		**FREE**			
1 Presentation box for offers 1, 2 and 3		£5.00	£20.00		
			TOTAL 1		

JOHANSENS PRINTED GUIDES 2000

CODE	TITLE	PRICE	QTY	TOTAL
A	Recommended Hotels – Great Britain & Ireland 2000	£19.95		
B	Recommended Country Houses & Small Hotels – Great Britain & Ireland 2000	£11.95		
C	Recommended Traditional Inns, Hotels & Restaurants – Great Britain 2000	£10.95		
NEW D	Recommended Holiday Cottages – Great Britain & Ireland 2000	£4.99		
E	Historic Houses, Castles & Gardens 2000	£4.99		
F	Museums & Galleries 2000	£8.95		
G	Recommended Hotels – Europe & The Mediterranean 2000	£15.95		
NEW H	Recommended Hotels – Europe & The Mediterranean 2000 (French Language)	£15.95		
NEW J	Recommended Hotels – Europe & The Mediterranean 2000 (German Language)	£15.95		
K	Recommended Hotels & Inns – North America, Bermuda & The Caribbean 2000	£12.95		
NEW L	Recommended Hotels & Game Lodges – Southern Africa, Mauritius & The Seychelles 2000	£9.95		
M	Recommended Business Meeting Venues 2000	£20.00		

JOHANSENS CD ROMs DIGITAL COLLECTION 2000

CODE	TITLE	PRICE	QTY	TOTAL
N	The Guide 2000 – Great Britain & Ireland	£29.95		
O	The Guide 2000 – Europe & The Mediterranean (English, French, German Language)	£22.95		
P	The Guide 2000 – North America, Bermuda & The Caribbean	£16.95		
NEW Q	The Guide 2000 – Southern Africa, Mauritius & The Seychelles	£16.95		
R	Business Meeting Venues 2000	£20.00		
S	Privilege Card 2000 (Free with your order. Additional Cards £20 each)	£20.00		

Postage & Packing (UK) £4.50 or £2.50 for single order and CD-ROMs
Outside UK add £5 or £3 for single orders and CD-ROMs

TOTAL 2

GRAND TOTAL 1+2+P&P

Name	(Mr/Mrs/Miss)
Address	
	Postcode
Card No.	Exp Date
Signature	

I have chosen my Johansens Guides/CD-ROMs and

☐ **I enclose a cheque for £** _____ payable to Johansens

☐ **I enclose my order on company letterheading, please invoice (UK only)**

☐ **Please debit my credit/charge card account (please tick).**

☐ **MasterCard** ☐ **Diners** ☐ **Amex**

☐ **Visa** ☐ **Switch** (Issue Number) _____

A14

GUEST SURVEY REPORT

Your own Johansens 'inspection' gives reliability to our guides and assists in the selection of Award Nominations

Name of Hotel: _____

Location of Hotel: _____

Page No: _____

Date of visit: _____

Name of guest _____

Address of guest: _____

_____ Postcode _____

Please tick one box in each category below:	Excellent	Good	Disappointing	Poor
Bedrooms				
Public Rooms				
Restaurant/Cuisine				
Service				
Welcome/Friendliness				
Value For Money				

Occasionally we may allow other reputable organisations to write with offers which may be of interest. If you prefer not to hear from them, tick this box ☐

To: Johansens, FREEPOST (CB264), 43 Millharbour, London E14 9BR

ORDER FORM

Call our 24hr credit card hotline FREEPHONE 0800 269 397.

Simply indicate which title(s) you require by putting the quantity in the boxes provided. Choose your preferred method of payment and mail to Johansens, FREEPOST (CB 264), 43 Millharbour, London E14 9BR, England (no stamp needed). Your FREE gifts will automatically be dispatched with your order. Fax orders welcome on 0171 537 3594

CHOOSE FROM 7 SPECIAL GUIDE COLLECTIONS – SAVE UP TO £56

TITLE	*Normal Price*	PRICE	SAVE	QTY	TOTAL
OFFER ONE					
3 Johansens Guides A+B+C	*£42.85*	£36.00	£6.85		
OFFER TWO					
4 Johansens Guides A+B+C+G	*£58.80*	£46.00	£12.80		
OFFER THREE					
5 Johansens Guides A+B+C+G+K PLUS Southern Africa Guide **FREE**	*£71.75*	£56.00	£15.75		
OFFER FOUR - The Executive Collection					
Business Meeting Venues Guide & CD-ROM M+R	*£40.00*	£30.00	£10.00		
OFFER FIVE - The Holiday Pack					
3 Johansens Guides D+E+F	*£18.93*	£9.99	£8.94		
OFFER SIX - The Digital Collection					
3 Johansens CD-ROMs N+O+P PLUS Southern Africa CD-ROM Q **FREE**	*£69.85*	£59.85	£10.00		
OFFER SEVEN - The Chairman's Collection					
Business Meeting Venues Guide & CD-ROMs M+R **PLUS** 5 Johansens Boxed Guides A+B+C+G+K, **PLUS** 3 CD-ROMs N+O+P **PLUS** Southern Africa Guide/CD ROM Q **FREE**, **PLUS** Mystery Gift **FREE**	*£200.53*	£149.00	£56.53		
Privilege Card PLUS The Millennium Guide		**FREE**			
1 Presentation box for offers 1, 2 and 3		£5.00	£20.00		

TOTAL 1

JOHANSENS PRINTED GUIDES 2000

CODE	TITLE	PRICE	QTY	TOTAL
A	Recommended Hotels – Great Britain & Ireland 2000	£19.95		
B	Recommended Country Houses & Small Hotels – Great Britain & Ireland 2000	£11.95		
C	Recommended Traditional Inns, Hotels & Restaurants – Great Britain 2000	£10.95		
NEW D	Recommended Holiday Cottages – Great Britain & Ireland 2000	£4.99		
E	Historic Houses, Castles & Gardens 2000	£4.99		
F	Museums & Galleries 2000	£8.95		
G	Recommended Hotels – Europe & The Mediterranean 2000	£15.95		
NEW H	Recommended Hotels – Europe & The Mediterranean 2000 *(French Language)*	£15.95		
NEW J	Recommended Hotels – Europe & The Mediterranean 2000 *(German Language)*	£15.95		
K	Recommended Hotels & Inns – North America, Bermuda & The Caribbean 2000	£12.95		
NEW L	Recommended Hotels & Game Lodges – Southern Africa, Mauritius & The Seychelles 2000	£9.95		
M	Recommended Business Meeting Venues 2000	£20.00		

JOHANSENS CD ROMs DIGITAL COLLECTION 2000

CODE	TITLE	PRICE	QTY	TOTAL
N	The Guide 2000 – Great Britain & Ireland	£29.95		
O	The Guide 2000 – Europe & The Mediterranean *(English, French, German Language)*	£22.95		
P	The Guide 2000 – North America, Bermuda & The Caribbean	£16.95		
NEW Q	The Guide 2000 – Southern Africa, Mauritius & The Seychelles	£16.95		
R	Business Meeting Venues 2000	£20.00		
S	Privilege Card 2000 *(Free with your order. Additional Cards £20 each)*	£20.00		

Postage & Packing (UK) £4.50 or £2.50 for single order and CD-ROMs
Outside UK add £5 or £3 for single orders and CD-ROMs

TOTAL 2

GRAND TOTAL 1+2+P&P

Name (Mr/Mrs/Miss)

Address

Postcode

Card No.

Exp Date

Signature

I have chosen my Johansens Guides/CD-ROMs and

☐ I enclose a cheque for £ _____ payable to Johansens

☐ I enclose my order on company letterheading, please invoice (UK only)

☐ Please debit my credit/charge card account (please tick).

☐ MasterCard ☐ Diners ☐ Amex

☐ Visa ☐ Switch (Issue Number) _____

A14

GUEST SURVEY REPORT

Your own Johansens 'inspection' gives reliability to our guides and assists in the selection of Award Nominations

Name of Hotel: _____

Location of Hotel: _____

Page No: _____

Date of visit: _____

Name of guest _____

Address of guest: _____

_____ Postcode _____

Please tick one box in each category below:	Excellent	Good	Disappointing	Poor
Bedrooms				
Public Rooms				
Restaurant/Cuisine				
Service				
Welcome/Friendliness				
Value For Money				

Occasionally we may allow other reputable organisations to write with offers which may be of interest. If you prefer not to hear from them, tick this box ☐

To: Johansens, FREEPOST (CB264), 43 Millharbour, London E14 9BR

ORDER FORM

Call our 24hr credit card hotline FREEPHONE 0800 269 397.

Simply indicate which title(s) you require by putting the quantity in the boxes provided. Choose your preferred method of payment and mail to Johansens, FREEPOST (CB 264), 43 Millharbour, London E14 9BR, England (no stamp needed). Your FREE gifts will automatically be dispatched with your order. Fax orders welcome on 0171 537 3594

CHOOSE FROM 7 SPECIAL GUIDE COLLECTIONS – SAVE UP TO £56

TITLE	Normal Price	PRICE	SAVE	QTY	TOTAL
OFFER ONE – The Basic Collection					
3 Johansens Guides A+B+C	£42.85	£36.00	£6.85		
OFFER TWO – The Extended Collection					
4 Johansens Guides A+B+C+G	£58.80	£46.00	£12.80		
OFFER THREE – The Full Selection					
5 Johansens Guides A+B+C+G+K PLUS Southern Africa Guide **FREE**	£71.75	£56.00	£15.75		
OFFER FOUR - The Executive Collection					
Business Meeting Venues Guide & CD-ROM M+R	£40.00	£30.00	£10.00		
OFFER FIVE - The Holiday Pack					
3 Johansens Guides D+E+F	£18.93	£9.99	£8.94		
OFFER SIX - The Digital Collection					
3 Johansens CD-ROMs N+O+P PLUS Southern Africa CD-ROM Q **FREE**	£69.85	£59.85	£10.00		
OFFER SEVEN - The Chairman's Collection					
Business Meeting Venues Guide & CD-ROMs M+R PLUS 5 Johansens Boxed Guides A+B+C+G+K, PLUS D+E+F, PLUS 3 CD-ROMs N+O+P PLUS Southern Africa Guide/CD ROM Q **FREE**, PLUS Mystery Gift **FREE**	£205.53	£149.00	£56.53		
Privilege Card PLUS The Millennium Guide		**FREE**			
1 Presentation box for offers 1, 2 and 3		£5.00	£20.00		
				TOTAL 1	

JOHANSENS PRINTED GUIDES 2000

CODE	TITLE	PRICE	QTY	TOTAL
A	Recommended Hotels – Great Britain & Ireland 2000	£19.95		
B	Recommended Country Houses & Small Hotels – Great Britain & Ireland 2000	£11.95		
C	Recommended Traditional Inns, Hotels & Restaurants – Great Britain 2000	£10.95		
NEW D	Recommended Holiday Cottages – Great Britain & Ireland 2000	£4.99		
E	Historic Houses, Castles & Gardens 2000	£4.99		
F	Museums & Galleries 2000	£8.95		
G	Recommended Hotels – Europe & The Mediterranean 2000	£15.95		
NEW H	Recommended Hotels – Europe & The Mediterranean 2000 (French Language)	£15.95		
NEW J	Recommended Hotels – Europe & The Mediterranean 2000 (German Language)	£15.95		
K	Recommended Hotels & Inns – North America, Bermuda & The Caribbean 2000	£12.95		
NEW L	Recommended Hotels & Game Lodges – Southern Africa, Mauritius & The Seychelles 2000	£9.95		
M	Recommended Business Meeting Venues 2000	£20.00		

JOHANSENS CD ROMs DIGITAL COLLECTION 2000

CODE	TITLE	PRICE	QTY	TOTAL
N	The Guide 2000 – Great Britain & Ireland	£29.95		
O	The Guide 2000 – Europe & The Mediterranean (English, French, German Language)	£22.95		
P	The Guide 2000 – North America, Bermuda & The Caribbean	£16.95		
NEW Q	The Guide 2000 – Southern Africa, Mauritius & The Seychelles	£16.95		
R	Business Meeting Venues 2000	£20.00		
S	Privilege Card 2000 (Free with your order. Additional Cards £20 each)	£20.00		

Postage & Packing (UK) £4.50 or £2.50 for single order and CD-ROMs

Outside UK add £5 or £3 for single orders and CD-ROMs

TOTAL 2

GRAND TOTAL 1+2+P&P

Name (Mr/Mrs/Miss)

Address

Postcode

Card No.

Exp Date

Signature

I have chosen my Johansens Guides/CD-ROMs and

☐ I enclose a cheque for £ _____ payable to Johansens

☐ I enclose my order on company letterheading, please invoice (UK only)

☐ Please debit my credit/charge card account (please tick).

☐ MasterCard ☐ Diners ☐ Amex

☐ Visa ☐ Switch (Issue Number) _____

A14

NO STAMP NEEDED

Johansens
FREEPOST (CB264)
43 Millharbour
London
E14 9BR